- ASSOCIATION OF UNDERWATER EXPLORERS -

ENCYCLOPEDIA OF FLORIDA SHIPWRECKS
VOLUME I: ATLANTIC COAST

Michael C. Barnette

- ASSOCIATION OF UNDERWATER EXPLORERS -

ENCYCLOPEDIA OF FLORIDA SHIPWRECKS
VOLUME I: ATLANTIC COAST

DISCLAIMER

Scuba diving can be very demanding and potentially dangerous, and may involve serious injury or death. Several of the shipwrecks described within this book are located in depths exceeding recreational diving limits, as designated by scuba-industry training agencies. This book in no way substitutes proper training and experience; the materials contained within are for informational purposes only.

The Association of Underwater Explorers (A.U.E.), founded in 1996, is a coalition of divers dedicated to the research, exploration, documentation, and preservation of the underwater environment. For more information on A.U.E., please visit our website at: http://uwex.us

Copyright © 2010 by Michael C. Barnette

All rights reserved. No part of this book may be reproduced in any form or by any means, electronic or mechanical, including photocopying, scanning, recording, or by any other information storage and retrieval system, without expressed written permission from the author.

ISBN 978-0-9743036-1-1

PREFACE

Volume I of the *Encyclopedia of Florida Shipwrecks* focuses on the Atlantic coast of Florida, from roughly the Georgia-Florida border, south to the border shared by Miami-Dade and Monroe Counties off the southern end of Elliott Key. I have been careful to focus on only those shipwreck events that occurred within this area. Early Florida shipwreck events, however, were frequently documented with only vague reference to the place of loss. For example, the "Gulph of Florida" was an ambiguous geographical reference used in the eighteenth century, which could include the area in the Florida Straits between the Florida Keys and Cuba northward to the Florida peninsula and the Bahamas Islands. Likewise, while Cape Florida was generally a well-recognized and specific geographic reference point, particularly after the construction of the first lighthouse there on the tip of Key Biscayne in 1825, earlier records sometimes used a very liberal application to what was considered Cape Florida, as demonstrated by an 1822 article, which stated, "U.S. schooner *Shark*, Lieut. Perry, lately visited the island called Key West, on Cape Florida…." It should be noted that I have avoided including vessels that were reportedly lost on the "Florida Reef," which generally is what we now generally consider to be the Florida Keys, unless other information clarified the place of loss; those entries will be included in Volume II.

While this work attempts to be the most accurate and comprehensive shipwreck inventory for Florida, it quite likely contains some inadvertent mistakes. Experience has taught me that the historical record can present numerous contradictions and outright errors, which, invariably and unfortunately, are passed on as facts. Diligent research can sometimes reveal these errors. In some cases, the information was simply wrong or transcribed incorrectly — geographical locations are confused and vessel names are contorted. In other situations, a specific shipwreck event did not result in the ultimate loss of a particular vessel, as many imperiled vessels were salvaged and put back in service. In some cases, archival newspaper articles do not reveal these facts for several months — or in extreme cases, over a year — after the initial shipwreck event. Therefore, these historical errors can very easily result in would-be explorers spending time, money, and energy in a futile wild-goose chase for a phantom shipwreck. As the adage goes, a little bit of knowledge can be a dangerous thing.

For example, the 209-foot long barkentine *Amazon* was reported burned at latitude 27° 25' north and longitude 79° 30' west (i.e., off Fort Pierce) on July 4, 1925. The hulk of the *Amazon*, however, did not ultimately sink off Florida, but drifted well north, eventually beaching in North Carolina, approximately thirteen miles from the Cape Fear River entrance. In another instance, the German bark *Lina* grounded on the Fernandina Bar in April 1898. She did not come to grief there, but was towed off the bar by the tug *Three Friends*. The tug continued on to Fernandina to take on a cargo of coal, and while she was away, the captain and crew of the *Lina* abandoned the sailing vessel, believing she would sink. The *Three Friends* eventually returned to the drifting and abandoned bark, and towed her to Jacksonville as a prize. Likewise, the 148-foot long sidewheel steamer *David Clark*, built in 1875 at Jacksonville, was not a complete loss following a widely documented fire at Fernandina in October 1889. Instead, she was repaired and worked off Florida for nearly five more years before being broken up in 1893. The 90-foot long tug *Transfer No. 8*, built in 1891 by Samuel L. Moore and Sons at Elizabethport, New Jersey for the New York, New Haven, and Hartford Railroad Company, foundered on the St. Johns River near Jacksonville on December 15, 1950; however, she was raised, repaired, renamed *William E. Coppedge*, and remained in documentation until 1954. In some cases, the basic facts are correct, but the location may be erroneous. The 96-foot long schooner *Walter* was reported by some sources to have been involved in a collision with the *Eleanor Bolling* (later the *Vamar*, which, coincidentally, was lost off the Gulf Coast of Florida in 1942) on October 21, 1932 off Fort Pierce. Scrutinizing this incident closely reveals the *Walter* was only damaged, and

the collision occurred in the Chesapeake Bay, far from Florida.

Newspapers frequently published inaccurate information, either getting the vessel name wrong or indicating a vessel would be a total loss when, in fact, it was later successfully salvaged. For example, *The Edinburgh Advertiser* reported the *Lady Provost*, Captain Clary, struck on the Amelia Island Bar on June 9, 1811, "and it was feared would be wrecked." Yet the *Lloyd's List* later reported she "got off with little damage." On November 20, 1874, *The New York Times* reported the grounding of the schooner *Carrie Walker* on the St. Johns Bar, indicating the vessel would "probably be a total loss." In actuality, the 100-foot long schooner was repaired in January 1875 and put back in service for almost 21 more years before being lost off Cape Cod in December 1896.

Several sources state the steamer *Northwestern* stranded at Matanzas Inlet, Florida, on March 22, 1920, resulting in one fatality. The *Northwestern*, official number 110486, was built by William R. Radcliffe at Cleveland, Ohio, in 1881 as the *Rufus P. Ranney*. The steel-hulled Great Lakes freighter was 247.5 feet in length, 36.3 feet in beam, and displaced 1,392 tons gross. In 1916, the vessel was sold, rebuilt for ocean service, and renamed *Northwestern*. Following the rebuild, the steamer registered a displacement of 1,645 tons gross. The *Northwestern* did indeed wreck at Matanzas Inlet in 1920, however, the loss occurred at Matanzas Inlet, Cuba, during a voyage from Charleston, South Carolina, to Havana with a cargo of coal.

Similarly, Steven D. Singer's book, *Shipwrecks of Florida*, includes the schooner *Red Wing* (from Bruce D. Berman's *Encyclopedia of American Shipwrecks*) as a Florida shipwreck. While the *Red Wing* was definitely lost near Indian River Inlet on the evening of October 22, 1891, the wrecking of the 28-ton fishing schooner actually occurred three and a half miles south of Indian River Inlet, Delaware, and not at the identically named location in Florida.

Yet another source of information that needs to be considered with a skeptical eye is the government's Automated Wreck and Obstruction Information System (A.W.O.I.S.). Aside from many position entries in the A.W.O.I.S. database that are extremely inaccurate, in some instances vessels are included that never sank in the first place. A good example is that of the British freighter *Elizabeth Massey*, which is cited as being lost on February 19, 1942, near Cape Canaveral. The confusion likely stems from the vessel's involvement with the tanker *Pan Massachusetts*, which was torpedoed and sunk on the same date. The *Massey* was steaming behind the tanker and witnessed the attack, eventually coming to the rescue of the *Pan Massachusetts's* survivors. The freighter continued into Jacksonville and ultimately survived World War II, but was later scrapped in 1964.

Researching Florida shipwreck events that have occurred earlier than the nineteenth century is particularly problematic. During this period, Florida had only a few established European outposts along hundreds of miles of isolated and poorly-charted coastline controlled by hostile natives. Shipping losses could easily go unreported due to the misfortune of wrecking along the coast where Ais or Calusa tribesmen quickly dispatched any trespassing Europeans who happened to wash up on the beach. In the absence of survivors, there typically was no documentation of a wreck's location. While there are documented shipping losses off the Florida Atlantic coast dating to the mid-sixteenth century, details were generally very vague and sometimes contradictory. Even with seemingly detailed information from survivors, the historical record from this period is fraught with errors and discrepancies. Take, for instance, the 1715 Spanish fleet disaster, which resulted in at least six vessels wrecked between Sebastian and Fort Pierce Inlets. While the event was extensively documented, and numerous artifacts have been recovered from known wreck sites, it is important to note that not one shipwreck has been positively identified. The wrecks included in this work and their corresponding coordinates merely represent the current hypothesis that is generally accepted by historians, archaeologists, and salvors.

A potentially useful example is *La Magdalena*. Upon his departure to Spain with the *Tierra Firme flota* in April 1563, Pedro Menéndez de Avilés, Captain-General of the Fleet of the Indies, assigned his son Juan Menéndez to command the *Nueva España* fleet once it had assembled and was ready for the voyage. On August 11, 1563, *La Magdalena* departed Havana along with 12 other ships of the *Nueva España flota* bound for Spain. The available information is confusing, as some sources state the fleet was struck by a hurricane around September 10, after clearing the Florida Straits and near Bermuda; reportedly, between three and five vessels were lost in the storm. Robert F. Marx, in his 1979 book *Spanish Treasure in Florida Waters, A Billion Dollar Graveyard*, states *La Magdalena*, Captain Cristobal Rodríguez, wrecked on a shoal off Cape Canaveral, and only 16 of the 300 on board reportedly survived the sinking. Yet, evidence suggests salvor Teddy Tucker may have discovered the remains of Juan Menéndez's *capitana* off the Bermuda coast. Additionally, other sources state *La Magdalena*, Captain Cristobal Rodríguez Garrucho, may have wrecked near Monte Cristi on the north coast of the Dominican Republic in 1563. The discovery, coupled with the historical timing of events (i.e., 25-30 days after departure would likely position the fleet well north of Cape Canaveral) and a contradictory shipwreck position, casts doubt on the veracity of *La Magdalena's* wrecking off Canaveral.

Yet another example with a different spin is the vessel *Santa Maria del Camino*. According to Marx (1987), the 350-ton *nao Santa Maria Del Camino*, Captain Diego Díaz (other sources cite Alonso Bolanos as master), was part of Captain-General Bartolemé Carrano's *Tierra Firme flota* when she was lost in 1554 on the coast of Florida (cited in other sources as occurring at approximate latitude 26° 30' north). Reportedly, subsequent salvage efforts by the Spaniards recovered the vessel's cargo. It should be noted that other 1554 fleet vessels documented in Marx (1979) as being lost on the Florida coast at approximate latitude 26° 30' north were actually lost off Padre Island, Texas. Known vessels wrecked off Padre Island include the *Santa María de Yciar*, *San Esteban* (cited incorrectly as *San Esteva*), and the *Espírutu Santo*. This error likely occurred because the cited landmark of *Rio Palmas* was apparently associated with Florida, and not the Rio Grande River as it frequently was by the Spanish. This error was compounded by the fact that the cited latitude could easily correspond to both the Florida and Texas coast.

I have definitely chased my share of ghost ships because of erroneous information. Perhaps one of the most frustrating was the steamer *Mississippi*. Built in Scotland in 1862, the 800-ton *Mississippi* was initially employed as a blockade runner named the *Memphis*. Her career as a blockade runner was short-lived though, as she was captured by the U.S.S. *Magnolia* in July 1862. She was sold to the U.S. Navy and converted into a cruiser, equipped with seven guns. As the U.S.S. *Memphis*, she served with the blockade fleet off Charleston, South Carolina, where she battled Confederate ironclads and helped capture three blockade runners. Two years after the end of hostilities, she was sold to W.F. Weld and Company of Boston, and entered commercial service as the *Mississippi*. Therefore, the dramatic loss of this historical vessel during a hurricane in August 1871 off Hillsboro Inlet definitely piqued my interest. However, not even a trace of wreckage matching the *Mississippi's* description could be found in the vicinity of Hillsboro Inlet. Returning to the archives, my persistence paid off when I learned that salvors, after a month of steady effort, managed to refloat the grounded *Mississippi*, which was then fully repaired and put back in service in July 1872; she operated until ultimately being lost to fire at Seattle, Washington, in May 1883.

The original puzzle was complicated even further by the introduction of a second reported wrecking of a steamer named *Mississippi*, this time in April 1874 on Brewster Reef, 15 miles south of Miami. Was this the same vessel reported as a "total loss" in 1871? Again, my time was better spent in the archives than on the water looking

for a wreck that simply didn't exist. I learned that this was a completely different vessel than the one involved in the 1871 event. This *Mississippi* was a 1,371-ton English steamer built in 1871. Following the wrecking on Brewster's Reef, random newspaper articles in May and June of 1874 all detailed that the steamer was likely to become a total loss. However, I pressed on, finally discovering the *Mississippi* was refloated by the Baker Wrecking Company after three months of work and safely arrived (under her own steam) at Key West on July 25, 1874. Therefore, neither *Mississippi* met her ultimate fate off the Florida coast, though many books document otherwise.

I would be remiss if I neglected to point out that I have also donated my share of errors to the collective pool of shipwreck research material. In my 2003 book, *Shipwrecks of the Sunshine State*, I included a short narrative on a vessel named the *Rockledge*, formerly the *General Worth*. In that book, I noted the *Rockledge's* rumored use as a floating brothel and casino on the Miami River, and the vessel was later reportedly "towed out past Key Biscayne and sunk on November 14, 1913. Her final resting spot is unknown." I later came upon a June 22, 1903 *Florida Times-Union* article that documented Captain Vaile had been selling the ship's furnishings with the anticipated breaking-up of the steamer *Rockledge*. Unable to find additional archival information supporting the 1913 scuttling of the steamer off Miami, I faced the realization that my original version was likely incorrect. Therefore, the *Rockledge* has been removed from this publication. While the point may now seem tortured, researchers must always remain skeptical and take nothing for granted (including the information included within these pages). It is imperative to try to confirm any information originating from a single source. Doing so can ultimately save you time, money, and frustration.

Divers exploring and attempting to identify particular wrecks should be aware of the applicable laws and regulations that may apply to their activities. On April 28, 1988, the Abandoned Shipwreck Act became law. The purpose of the Abandoned Shipwreck Act is to give title to certain abandoned shipwrecks that are located in state waters to the respective states, and to clarify that the states have management authority over those abandoned shipwrecks. In the absence of a research permit issued to a scientific or academic institution or a performance-based contract reached between the state and a Florida corporation (e.g., a treasure salvage entity), artifact collection within state waters, which extend three miles seaward on the Atlantic coast of Florida, is prohibited. Specifically, Title XVIII, Chapter 267 of the Florida Statutes states:

> (1)(a) Any person who by means other than excavation either conducts archaeological field investigations on, or removes or attempts to remove, or defaces, destroys, or otherwise alters any archaeological site or specimen located upon, any land owned or controlled by the state or within the boundaries of a designated state archaeological landmark or landmark zone, except in the course of activities pursued under the authority of a permit or under procedures relating to accredited institutions granted by the division, commits a misdemeanor of the first degree, punishable as provided in s. 775.082 or s. 775.083, and, in addition, shall forfeit to the state all specimens, objects, and materials collected, together with all photographs and records relating to such material.

Recovery of artifacts from waters in Biscayne National Park is also strictly prohibited.

This book is the result of over 10 years of continuous work researching and documenting Florida shipwecks. I hope within these pages you will find both education and entertainment. And, perhaps, motivation to further explore Florida's fascinating maritime history.

Yacht sunk at Miami during the 1926 hurricane (Florida State Archives).

ACKNOWLEDGEMENTS

Eve Anderson and the Thomaston Historical Society of Thomaston, Maine; Anthony Andreoni; Brian Armstrong; Heather Armstrong; Tracy Baetz and the Brick Store Museum; Erin Michelle Bailey; Kenneth Banks and the Broward County Artificial Reef Program; John Bax; Chas Betts; Jelle Bijlsma; Dave Boone; Jason Burns and Southeastern Archaeological Research, Incorporated; Joe Citelli; John Clarkson; Captain Wayne Conn; Bill Cook and the Bangor Public Library; Richard Cox; Hans-Wilhelm Delfs; Russ Derrick; George Detrio; T. Diedrich; Kerry Dillon; Wim den Dulk; Kelly East; Brian Fisher; Taffi Fisher-Abt; David Gallicham; Alan Geddes; Tom Gidus; Steve Gillespie; Robert W. Graham and the Historical Collections of the Great Lakes, Bowling Green State University; Mike Gray; Jayson Gulliford; Halcyon Dive Systems; Al Hart; Jan Harteveld; Christopher Havern; Matthew W. Hoelscher; Keith Holland; William T. Hultgren; George Irvine and Gavin Scooters, Incorporated; Claudia Jew and the Mariners' Museum; Richie Kohler; Alice L. Luckhardt; Marine Archaeological Research and Conservation, Incorporated; Jeff Milbrath; Keith Mille; the late Mark Mondano; Ben Moskoff; Mike Muscato and the Muscato Skunk Works; Steve Muslin; the late Bill Newman; Joe Nolin; John Noyes; Odyssey Marine Exploration; Dr. Michael Ott; Gene Page; Yvon Perchoc; Janet J. Phipps and the Palm Beach County Artificial Reef Program; William Rivers; Taryn Rodriguez-Boette and the Beaches Area Historical Society; Hans Rosenkranz; Derek Sands; William A. Schell; Peter Schliefke; Eugene Shinn; Jim Sinclair; Steve Singer; Dick Sloan; Roger Smith; Joseph Stegner; Jody Svendsen; Sara Thanner and the Miami-Dade County Department of Environmental Resources Management; William Thiesen; Jeff Turner; Neal Adam Watson and the Florida State Archives; the late Robert "Frogfoot" Weller; and Jeff Wilson.

- For Melanie -

A.W. THOMPSON

Launched by the West Bay Shipbuilding Company at West Bay City, Michigan in 1901, the *A.W. Thompson*, official number 107635, was a three-masted, steel-hulled barge 300 feet in length, 41.5 feet in breadth, and 2,279 tons gross burden. The Gulf Barge and Towing Company's barge *A.W. Thompson* sank on October 31, 1928, claiming the lives of Captain C.S. Bolt and crew member C. Howard. The *A.W. Thompson* was being towed from Mobile, Alabama, to Wilmington, North Carolina, with a cargo of phosphate rock by the tug *Ontario*. However, the *Ontario* ran low on fuel, and was forced to leave the barge to run in to port to replenish its supplies. The four survivors stated the barge foundered in rough seas soon after the tug's departure, forcing them to abandon ship in a small lifeboat. With no food or water, they drifted aimlessly in the small boat for almost a week until their rescue by a fishing smack 20 miles off Fernandina on November 6. Newspaper accounts cited several conflicting locations to where the barge foundered, including 100 miles southeast of Charleston, South Carolina, and 60 miles southeast of Brunswick, Georgia. As the survivors were picked up off Fernandina, it is likely the *A.W. Thompson* was lost somewhere near the Florida-Georgia border. In fact, there is an unidentified wreck in approximately 150 feet of water northeast of Mayport that may be the final resting spot of the *A.W. Thompson*.

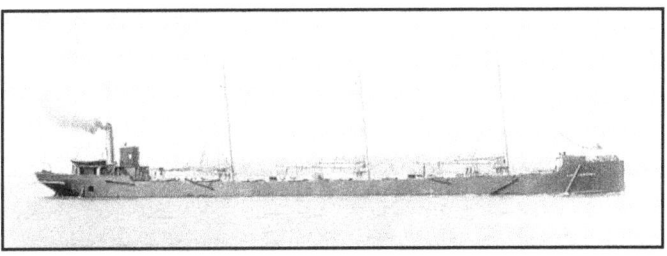

Barge *A.W. Thompson* (Historical Collections of the Great Lakes, Bowling Green State University).

ABACO SANDS

The *Abaco Sands* was a Dutch freighter originally launched on February 28, 1950, as the *Emke*. She was 137 feet long, 20 feet wide, and 240 tons displacement. In 1955 her name was changed to *Fendo*, and in 1980 she was finally renamed *Abaco Sands*.

The November 4, 1983, issue of *The Ledger* detailed the loss of the *Abaco Sands*:

> A 127-foot Bahamian freighter, the *Abaco Sands*, sank in 850 feet of water today about five miles east-northeast of the Lake Worth Inlet, the U.S. Coast Guard said. All six people aboard were rescued. The vessel, carrying a cargo of lumber, had five Bahamians and one Honduran aboard when it sank of causes unknown to the Coast Guard, said Joe Gibson, a spokesman at district headquarters in Miami. He said the six people were in the water when a Coast Guard rescue boat reached them after getting word about 11 a.m. that the ship was sinking. A U.S. Coast Guard rescue team plucked all six crew members from six-foot seas Thursday morning after a Bahamian freighter tipped over and sank off the Lake Worth Inlet. "There wasn't much to it," Coast Guard Petty Officer Greg Blakeslee said of the mid-morning rescue. He said one of the crew members of the 127-foot *Abaco Sands* radioed for help at 10:31 a.m., saying the ship was capsizing and all aboard were going to jump.

ABBIE S. OAKS

The schooner *Abbie S. Oaks* was built in 1845 at Seaville, Maine, as the *Arzoo*. A small schooner, she was 66 feet long, 19 feet wide, and displaced a mere 74 tons. Documentation indicates she was rebuilt in October 1868. At the time of her loss, she was owned by Oates and Doane and mastered by H.S. Rideout.

The *Abbie S. Oaks* was wrecked on the Florida coast one mile north of St. Augustine during a gale around September 20, 1878. Following her wrecking, the *Alton Telegraph* noted in its September 26, 1878, issue, "Her name might now be changed to 'Abbie Soaks'."

It should be noted that there were two spelling conventions for this vessel: *Abbie S. Oakes* in the *Record of American and Foreign Shipping*, and *Abbie S. Oaks* in *Lloyd's Register of American and Foreign Shipping*.

ABBY

The British Evening-Post, October 12, 1790, documented the wrecking of the *Abby*: "The *Abby*, of Whitehaven for Dublin, Captain Braithwaite, ran ashore with her hold full of water on August 17, 1790, near the *Thetis*, approximately three leagues from Cape Florida."

ADA BAILEY

The *Ada Bailey* was a schooner built in November 1884 at the Bath, Maine yard of A. Sewall and Company. She was 161 feet long, 33.2 feet wide, and displaced 496 tons. According to the *Florida Times-Union*, November 24, 1894, "Crew of the schooner *Ada Bailey*, of Philadelphia, which sank off New River Inlet (Fort Lauderdale) November 15, 1894, while carrying phosphate from Tampa to Philadelphia, were brought into Jacksonville by Captain Fozzard on the schooner *Biscayne*. The *Ada Bailey* grounded on Bahama Banks and began to leak badly. Captain headed for Florida mainland, but the schooner sank 20 miles offshore."

ADA J. SIMONTON

The schooner *Ada J. Simonton*, of Rockland, Maine, from Pensacola to Boston with a cargo of lumber, went ashore at Matanzas (also reported as near Mosquito Inlet) in the same hurricane that claimed the *City of Vera Cruz* in late August 1880. All the crew and one passenger were saved. The wrecked vessel was later sold at auction where she lay for $150. The *Ada J. Simonton*, official number 105190, was built in November 1872 at Camden, Maine. The schooner registered a length of 127.7 feet, a beam of 30 feet, and a displacement of 295 tons.

ADAMELIA

In 1960, the 110-foot long freighter *Adamelia* ran aground and sunk approximately 2.5 nautical miles east of Cape Florida Light, south of Miami. The vessel's owner later reported the vessel was demolished as a menace to navigation, allowing 17 feet of water clearance. The remains of the Adamelia can be found in 25 feet of water and are largely comprised of scattered hull plates and other associated debris.

ADA TOWER

On October 10, 1929, the four-masted schooner *Ada Tower* was reported aground east of Jacksonville on Atlantic Beach with a bad list and the crew of eight men unable to leave. The vessel was blown ashore while returning to Jacksonville in ballast from Port Tainamo, Cuba, under the command of her owner, Captain Hatfield. The October 11, 1929, issue of *The New York Times* stated, "With her four masts awry and her hull believed broken, the British schooner *Ada Tower*, 528 tons, lay aground in approximately three feet of water on the shore south of here today. The eight man crew remained on board." The *Ada Tower* was built in 1916 at Port Greville, Nova Scotia, and registered a length of 175.5 feet and a beam of 36.4 feet.

ADELINE

The small screw-steamer *Adeline*, official number 161939, was built in 1903 at New York. She was documented as 70 tons gross displacement, 110 feet in length, and 14 feet in breadth. She was reported to have burned at Fort Pierce on May 12, 1924.

ADMIRAL SAULTZEMAN

Hunt's The Merchants' Magazine and Commercial Review, Volume 40, recorded the basic details of the *Admiral Saultzeman's* wrecking: "March 16, 1858, Bremen ship *Admiral Saultzeman*, Van Eyck, from Rotterdam for Havana; totally lost on Hillsboro Bar; crew rescued by steamer *Daniel Webster*; materials saved by the Key West wreckers; value $50,000; expenses, $250; salvage $466.50; auction sales, $1,187.53."

ADONIS

The Evening Independent, October 22, 1920, included a piece on the loss of the schooner *Adonis*: "British three-masted schooner *Adonis*, bound from Jacksonville to Sagua la Grande, Cuba, drifted ashore opposite Jensen, without sign of human life aboard. The vessel's crew had been saved by the steamer *Crane Creek*. The crew deserted the ship when she sprang a leak 25 miles northeast of there, and were picked up by the passing steamer near Jupiter lighthouse. Waterlogged and sails fully set and lifeboats intact, the *Adonis* washed ashore opposite Jensen and was fast battered to pieces by heavy seas. The *Adonis* was carrying a cargo of yellow pine lumber when she was disabled in the gale."

AFRICAN

According to *The Lady's Miscellany and Weekly Visitor*, Volume 12 (1811), the Spanish brig *African*, Don Francisco Garcia, master, while en route from Havana for New York, went ashore at approximate latitude 27° 23' north on October 25, 1810. The vessel, cargo, and one man were lost in the incident. It was reported the *African* wrecked in the same general area as the Spanish ship *Union*, the ship *Caroline*, and the schooner *Triton*. The reported location would place the wrecks of these vessels in between Fort Pierce and St. Lucie Inlets.

AGENORA

The Sailor's Magazine and Naval Journal, Volume 10, reported the February 7, 1838, loss of the schooner *Agenora*, of and from Saco, Maine, seven miles to the southward of St. Augustine.

AGNES

The 583-ton steamer *Agnes*, built in 1865 at Philadelphia, departed New York on March 30, 1878, bound for Key West. On April 3, the *Agnes* was blown ashore by a gale and grounded on North Beach near Mosquito Inlet, adjacent to the wreck of the steamer *Narragansett*, which met her fate 30 years earlier (some reports claim that the *Agnes* actually smashed into the wreck of the *Narragansett*). Similar to the grounding of the *Narragansett*, no lives were lost in this later wrecking event. The wrecks of the *Agnes* and *Narragansett* were later demolished with dynamite, though remaining portions of the wrecks apparently lingered for years just off the beach.

Sinking of the *Agro Trader* (Broward County Artificial Reef Program).

AGRO TRADER

In 1965 the Spanish shipbuilding group AESA launched the 482-ton refrigerated freighter *Sierra Espuña* from its yard at Sestao, Spain. Built for the Madrid-based shipping company *Maritima del Norte S.A.*, the new reefer was 179.7 feet in length and 31.2 feet in breadth. The freighter was later sold to a Costa Rican company in 1977, whereupon she was renamed *Orosi*. In 1986, the vessel was acquired by the Honduran firm *Agro Trader S. de R.L.*, which renamed her *Agro Trader*. On September 29, 1986, the *Argo Trader* sustained major damage following a fire that broke out in the crew's quarters while the ship was berthed on the Miami River undergoing repairs. The Broward County Artificial Reef Program later purchased the vessel and renamed it the "Bud Krohn Reef" in memory of an avid fisherman and former captain of the *Jungle Queen* tour boat in Fort Lauderdale. In early December 1989, the vessel was scuttled in 440 feet of water to serve as a deep-water reef.

AJAX (1836)

The 627-ton ship *Ajax*, built in 1826 at Kensington, Pennsylvania, was 132.8 feet long and 32 feet wide. On November 14, 1836, the *Ajax* ran aground on the reef off Elliott Key that now bears its name. According to the *Niles' Weekly Register*, December 10, 1836, "The ship *Ajax*, Captain Hiern, from New York, for Mobile, was driven ashore on the 14th of November, near Tiger Creek, Carysfort Reef. The ship is a total loss – part of her cargo had been saved, in a damaged state. The A. had on board one hundred and twenty passengers. We are happy to state, that not a single life was lost."

Additional information on the loss of the *Ajax* was included in the admiralty records related to the vessel's salvage. In *Housman v. Ship Ajax* (Florida Supreme Court file number 0865), the following occurred:

> About 3 o'clock on the afternoon of Monday, November 14, 1836, Richard Roberts, master of the schooner *Splendid*, discovered a ship ashore on the eastern part of Carysfort Reef. On boarding her an hour later, he found that she was the *Ajax*, Captain Charles A. Heim [sic; the proper spelling of the captain was Charles A. Heirn], from New York to Mobile with an assorted cargo. Captain Heim at first refused assistance, but about 7 o'clock he called for help. Roberts brought the *Splendid* alongside and transshipped cargo until midnight. The violence of the wind and waves, which parted the schooner's "fasts and chains," then made him haul off, but he anchored and promised to remain to relieve the passengers and crew, if need be. In about half an hour his anchor broke, and he stood off and on in the Gulf, having first sent a boat to the master, telling him to raise a light if he needed help.
>
> The *Splendid* got back to the *Ajax* about 8 o'clock Tuesday morning, when W. H. Bethel arrived with the sloop *Sudlow*. The latter, at Captain Heim's request, at once took off the 40 cabin passengers and their baggage, the sloop's cabin and deck being reserved for their accommodation. "The wind and sea becoming severe, the sloop parted her fasts and chains, split two of her timbers and injured her bend and bow." As it was too dangerous to stay alongside, the *Sudlow* moved off and transshipped cargo by boat. Her underdeck was loaded by 6 o'clock in the evening. The *Sudlow's* crew then helped load the *Splendid*, hoisting goods from the *Ajax's* hold, as the ship had bilged during the morning. At midnight the *Sudlow* left for Key West.
>
> During the afternoon, the schooners *Caroline* and *Fair American* and the sloop *Thistle* had arrived. Their masters, John Wood, Latham Brightman, and Daniel Post, had consorted "ton for ton and man for man" to save goods from the *Ajax*. Their combined crews, 24 men, worked all night and "broke out of the lower hold by diving, damaged goods sufficient to load the *Thistle* by 8 o'clock the next morning." When the *Thistle* dropped off from the wreck, "she struck on the stock of an anchor carried out from the (Ajax)…beat a hole in her bottom, sunk and was totally lost with nearly all her lading, the weather preventing the other vessels rendering any effectual assistance, and even compelling them to seek shelter in Caesar's Creek."

At the time of her wrecking, few other reefs along the Florida reef tract had been given specific names. Therefore, well-known landmarks such as Carysfort Reef and Cape Florida were used liberally. In the above account, this author believes the cited Tiger Creek actually refers to Caesar's Creek on the southern end of Elliott Key, and the eastern part of Carysfort Reef was actually present-day Ajax Reef. While there are numerous unidentified wreck sites on Ajax Reef, according to Gene Shinn, there is a pile of scrap iron towards the middle of Ajax Reef that many divers in the 1950s referred to as the *Ajax*.

AJAX (1886)

On January 28, 1886, the *Halifax Herald* reported that "out of eight or ten schooners employed in the lighthouse (Ponce de Leon Inlet Light Station) work, five have been wrecked, viz: *Godfrey*, *Augusta Wilson*, *Ajax*, *Freewind*, and the *Johnson*; the *Mary Brown*, now lying at the lighthouse dock, is crippled. We have been assured that nearly all of them received the injuries resulting in wrecks on the inlet bar or in the river. Six men have also been drowned."

ALABAMA

The sloops (also described as wrecking smacks) *Alabama*, *Dread*, and *Caution* of Mystic, Connecticut, bound to Key West, were driven ashore and lost in a gale on September 7, 1838, approximately 12 miles north of Cape Florida. Only one man, Joseph Noble, survived the wrecking and subsequent slaughter at the hands of hostile Seminole Indians by joining the crew of the French brig *Courier* (*Courier de Tampico* or *Courier de Vera Cruz*), which was lost in the same vicinity. In addition to the crews of the *Alabama*, *Dread*, and *Caution*, most of the *Alna's* crew, wrecked in the vicinity, was also massacred. At the time, local tribes spared European sailors and only killed Americans wrecked on the Florida shore.

ALADDIN LAMP WRECK

Meylach (1971) stated the "Aladdin Lamp Wreck" was approximately 500 feet northeast of another wreck he called the "Keel Showing Wreck." This latter wreck is believed to be a documented site also known as the "Schooner Ballast Wreck." The "Aladdin Lamp Wreck" site is represented by a debris trail leading from deeper water up onto the shallowest portion of the reef, and was documented to possess egg-rock ballast, copper sheathing, and iron deadeyes along the path. A recovered pewter object resembling Aladdin's lamp gave this wreck its name. The position included in this work is based on Meylach's reported ranges of the wreck itself, as well as its relative position to the known location of the "Schooner Ballast Wreck."

ALBATROSS

Official records of the U.S. Life-Saving Service report that on September 16, 1888, "A chest of drawers drifted ashore near the Fort Lauderdale House of Refuge (Seventh District), eastern coast of Florida, during the night of the 15th, and was found the next morning by the keeper and taken to the station. It evidently came from the cabin of the Dutch brig *Albatross*, as it contained the official papers and journal of that vessel and a number of letters addressed to her commander." While it's unclear exactly where the vessel sunk, it's quite possible she was lost somewhere off the Florida coast. The brig *Albatross* was built in July 1868 at Hoogezand, Netherlands, by J.A. Hooites. She registered a length of 102 feet, a beam of 22.3 feet, and a displacement of 181 tons gross.

ALBINA

The American bark *Albina* was built in 1862 at Westbrook, Maine, by Thomas Dunham's Nephew and Company. She was 155 feet long, 32.9 feet wide, and displaced 801 tons. According to *The New York Times* of October 7, 1881, "The bark *Albina*, bound from Navassa for Baltimore, loaded with guano in bulk, stranded a mile east of Amelia Island lighthouse on the evening of October 6. She sailed from Navassa on September 12; on third day out sprung a leak; encountered a heavy gale on October 5; was making for a port of refuge drawing 23 feet of water; anchored last night, but was unable to hold her position. The vessel and cargo are a total loss. The crew was saved."

Additional information supplied by Captain Madison, reported in *The New York Times* on October 8, 1881, stated the *Albina* wrecked on the south breakers off Amelia Island. "Pumps clogged due to the nature of the cargo. At 3:00 p.m. Thursday she was beating off the bar, signaled for a pilot, but got none. At 7:10 p.m. came to anchor in 7 fathoms with 10 feet of water in her hold and heavy NE wind drifted her onto south breakers. It was evident she would be total wreck so crew soon took to boats. They were picked up by the pilot boat *Jenny Lind* and carried to Fernandina. The *Albina* was 800 tons register and owned in New York."

ALBINIA

A May 21, 1763, letter from New York reported the ship *Albinia*, Captain Gilbert, en route from Jamaica to London, was cast away on the coast of Florida[1]. A sloop from Havana rescued the captain and crew, who managed to safely get ashore, though they reportedly could not save anything from their wrecked ship.

ALBION (1787)

An October 20, 1787, dispatch from the *Royal Jamaica Gazette* included in the January 5, 1788, edition of the *London Chronicle* stated, "By advices from New Providence we learn, that the ship *Alfred*, Stupart, and *Albion*, Whitehead, both from this island (Jamaica), bound to London, were wrecked on the Florida shore about the middle of August last in a very hard gale of wind, but that no lives were lost."

ALBION (1790)

The brig *Albion*, Captain Birkett, was reported in October 1790 as being cast on the Florida shore during the same storm that wrecked the *Apollo*, *Thetis*, and *William and Elizabeth*[2]. It is unclear if she was later refloated or became a total loss.

ALECIA

On May 25, 1926, the *Alecia* reportedly burned at Turkey Point, inshore of Elliott Key in Biscayne Bay. The yacht *Alecia*, official number 220662, was built in 1911 at Toms River, New Jersey, and was 56.7 feet long, 13.5 feet wide, and 32 tons gross burden.

ALERT

The schooner *Alert* was built at Boston in 1888, and documented a length of 92.5 feet, a beam of 23.1 feet, and displaced 99 tons gross. According to the November 26, 1914, issue of *The Tampa Morning Tribune*, "The American fishing schooner *Alert*, under command of Captain Mallach, and carrying a crew of 10, bound from Gloucester, Mass., to St. Andrews Bay, Fla., loaded with ice to engage in the fishing business was driven ashore in high seas and heavy winds at Nassau Inlet on the night of November 23, 1914, coming to rest on her side. The captain and several of his crew walked down the beach to Mayport to report the wreck. The *Alert* was washed ashore close to where the schooner *Gracie D. Buchanan* was wrecked in 1910."

ALEXANDER

According to the *Lloyd's Evening Post*, October 28, 1763, the *Alexander*, Captain Johnson, from Jamaica for London, was lost to the westward of Cape Florida.

ALEXANDER JONES

The 134-ton, iron-hulled tug *Alexander Jones*, official number 105692, was built in 1877 at Baltimore, Maryland, and was 106 feet long and 23 feet wide. During her career, she was briefly employed as a filibuster, running arms to Cuba in 1897. In April, she was stopped by the cruiser *Vesuvius* and escorted into Fernandina to be turned over to the Collector of Customs. The event didn't thwart the tug's activities, however, as it was reported she successfully conducted an arms run the following month.

The *Alexander Jones* foundered at sea on October 14, 1910, during a hurricane that swept the coast. At the time of her loss, the tug was en route from her home port of Wilmington, North Carolina, to Knights Key to assist with work on the Overseas Railroad. Fortunately, Captain Sanders and his crew of seven men were saved by a passing steamer. Reportedly, the *Alexander Jones* sunk south of Miami off Fowey Rocks Light.

ALEXANDER NICKELS

Built in 1863 at Cherryfield, Maine, the *Alexander Nickels* was a 110-foot long, 26.75-foot wide, 271-ton hermaphrodite brig, whose hull was covered in protective metal sheathing in October 1866. On September 7, 1878, the *Alexander Nickels*, commanded by Captain Peterson, was en route from Cienfuegos, Cuba, to Boston, Massachusetts, when she stranded and went to pieces off Fort Lauderdale, approximately one and a half miles south of the New River; of the nine men on board, four were lost.

ALEXANDRA MCALLISTER

The *Alexander McAllister*, official number 256333, was a 95.2-foot long tug originally built as the *Socony 10* in 1948 at Port Arthur, Texas, by the Gulfport Shipbuilding Corporation. The 149-ton tug was later sold in 1960 and renamed the *Mobil 10*, before finally becoming the *Alexandra McAllister* in 1991. After her useful career ended, she was donated to the Volusia County Artificial Reef Program and sunk in 80 feet of water approximately 11 nautical miles off Ponce Inlet on July 29, 1995. The *McAllister* was deployed along with the tug *Thomas H.* and freighter *Rio Yuna*, which all rest just south of the U.S.S. *Mindanao*.

ALEXANDRO

A November 28, 1832, dispatch from New York, published on December 21 in *The Times*, stated the *Alexandro*, from Havana to Malagra, was lost near Cape Florida on October 8, 1832. Her crew and part of the cargo was saved, and carried into Key West.

ALFRED

An October 20, 1787, dispatch from the *Royal Jamaica Gazette* included in the January 5, 1788, edition of the *London Chronicle* stated, "By advices from New Providence we learn, that the ship *Alfred*, Stupart, and *Albion*, Whitehead, both from this island (Jamaica), bound to London, were wrecked on the Florida shore about the middle of August last in a very hard gale of wind, but that no lives were lost."

ALICE C. PRICE

The sidewheel steamer *Alice C. Price* was built in 1853 at New York, and was 151 feet long and displaced 238 tons. In 1861 she was reportedly lengthened, after which her registered dimensions were 169 feet in length, 26.6 feet in beam, and 320 tons gross burden. During the Civil War, she was chartered as a transport and operated in North Carolina and Florida. In mid-July 1864, the Union Army launched a series of raids against Confederate outposts along Trout Creek and the Nassau River, which resulted in the capture of the Holmes' sawmill on the Nassau River. Soldiers dismantled the machinery and loaded it aboard

Illustration of the sidewheel steamer *Alice C. Price* (Alfred H. Robson Collection).

the *Alice C. Price* to be carried to Empire Mills near Jacksonville, where it was planned to be reassembled and put in operation. On July 19, as the steamer was heading up river, she struck a torpedo (mine) about eight miles south of Jacksonville and quickly sank. No lives were lost in the event, and correspondence from August 1870 indicates the steamer was salvaged, likely by the firm of Johnson and Higgins, as it was noted that the *Alice C. Price's* machinery was taken out and nothing but valueless hull was left.

ALICE HOLBROOK

Built in 1890 at Camden, Maine, by H.M. Bean, the *Alice Holbrook* was a four-masted schooner 170.2 feet in length, 35.9 feet in breadth, which registered 772 tons. While en route on a voyage from Baltimore to Cuba, the *Holbrook* grounded eight miles north of Life Saving Station No. 4 at Fort Lauderdale on April 18, 1913. While some reports state the *Holbrook* wrecked on a reef, according to *The Evening Standard*, April 18, 1913, "The revenue cutter *Yamacraw* received a distress call from the schooner *Alice Holbrook*, pounding on sunken wreckage in Hillsboro Inlet, Florida." Fortunately, Captain Ellie and his crew were rescued; however, the schooner was destroyed in a storm a week after the grounding.

ALICE TEBB

Somewhere off the coast near the Florida/Georgia border lie the remains of the *Alice Tebb*. A brief radio report transmitted by their rescuers on September 28, 1940, summarized the fate of the freighter: "Wreck broken in half. All abandoned ship and are safe aboard the S.S. *Samuel Q. Brown*[3]."

The 2,426-ton freighter was originally built for the U.S. government towards the end of World War I by Grant Smith Porter of Aberdeen, Washington, as the *Abydos*. The vessel documented a length of 268 feet and a beam of 46 feet. Launched in May 1919, she was sold to A. Schubach and her name changed to the *Forest King*. She sailed under charter to the Alaska Pacific Salmon Company, mainly carrying lumber and other commodities between California, Washington, and Alaska. In 1937, her name was changed to the *Alice Tebb* upon her sale to the Southland Steamship Company. At the time of her loss, she was owned by the M.A. Wyman Lumber Company of Seattle.

On August 24, the *Alice Tebb* departed St. Helens, Oregon, en route to Baltimore to pick up a cargo of defense materials destined for the Panama Canal Zone. Steaming off the Florida coast on September 25, the wooden hull of the freighter failed after being buffeted by rough weather, and she began taking on water. Considering the *Alice Tebb* had been sitting idle at a Seattle harbor for three and a half years before being put back into service in March 1940, it is not surprising the seams of the aged wooden hull gave way. Once it was clear the freighter was sinking, Captain Alex Zugehoer ordered a distress message transmitted, which stated: "S.S. *Alice Tebb* in distress 31 north, 71 west. Seams opened up. Need assistance." This position, approximately 600 miles east of the Georgia coast, was obviously erroneous. Near daybreak, her navigator was able to take new bearings and found the *Alice Tebb's* distance from shore was only 70 miles. In subsequent radio messages, the freighter explained that observations had been impossible for two days and that they had given an approximate position based on their last "sun shooting."

Fortunately for the doomed vessel, the tanker *Samuel Q. Brown* arrived on the scene about two hours after receiving the *Alice Tebb's* corrected position on the morning of September 28. Arriving alongside the wallowing freighter, Captain John P. O'Brien put over the tanker's lifeboats to assist in transferring the *Tebb's* crew. At 11:30 a.m. the tanker reported she had taken aboard Captain Zugehoer and all members of the *Tebb's* crew, including a seaman who had a broken leg. While Captain O'Brien reported he would attempt to take the crippled vessel under tow, the *Alice Tebb* was eventually abandoned to sink to the bottom of the Atlantic Ocean.

The exact sinking position of the wooden-hulled freighter is shrouded in confusion. The final corrected position given in radio messages was latitude 31° 45' north and longitude 78° 55' west, approximately 100 miles southeast of Savannah, Georgia. Another report, however, cited her position as latitude 31° north and longitude 79° 30' west, while a third report stated she foundered at latitude 31° 35' north and longitude 78° 42' west. Hopefully, future exploration will document the final resting spot of the *Alice Tebb*.

ALICIA

The wreckers of the Florida Keys and their competitors from the Bahamas, collectively known as the Black Fleet, flourished in the nineteenth century as shipping increased through the Florida Straits. While the swift Florida Current moved shipping northward, the unforgiving coral reefs of the Florida Keys that bordered the northern and western corridors of this route claimed many victims. Occasionally, vessels would hug these reefs as they traveled south, in order to evade the strong northward push of the Florida Current. Rapidly changing weather, inaccurate charts, inexperienced captains, and swift currents led many ships to run aground on the shallow coral reefs, eventually to break apart and be lost.

Built at a Glasgow, Scotland shipyard in October 1883, the *Alicia* was 345.5 feet in length, 37.7 feet in beam, and displaced 2,795 tons. She was a solid iron-hulled, three-masted steamer outfitted with two decks, and powered by a 291 nominal horsepower two-cylinder engine manufactured by the London and Glasgow Company, Limited. Owned by *Linea de Vapores Serra* and ported in Bilboa, Spain, the steamer departed Liverpool in early April 1905, bound for Havana with her cargo holds full of fine silks, linens, silverware, household furniture, machetes, paint, pianos, wine, English ale, and liquor. On April 20, the *Alicia* slammed onto Ajax Reef and parted her seams. The Key West wrecking schooner *Mount Olive* was the first to arrive on the scene, eventually to be joined by over 70 other wreckers, including the tug *Three Friends*.

Salvage of the *Alicia* (© The Mariners' Museum, Newport News, Virginia).

Captain "Hog" Johnson was the master wrecker. During the salvage, Vincent Gilpin described the scene:

> Within a few hours the fleet surrounded her, a motley flock of sail craft, many quite small. We chanced to be lying nearby, and spent the day with them, on the shining green water that rolled lazily over the Reef from the purple Gulf Stream. The ship lay on the edge of the coral, with no sign of injury save a slight heel, but she was bilged and water-logged. On deck two crews of fifty each manned great tackles, their faces alight with joy, their mellow voices ringing out, adrip with glory, as the grand old chanties rolled across the waves, timing their pull on the cargo-nets. How their eyes gleamed as each load swung out on deck, and followed every item on its way to the schooners alongside! How they laughed and joked in the intervals! How the joy of life fairly lighted up the scene! It was the fun of wrecking at its best![4]

However, the salvage of the *Alicia* did not entirely proceed as agreeably as Gilpin's account. When the Black Fleet of the Bahamas arrived on the scene to find the valuable salvage job already being conducted by those from Key West, a dispute began. The dispute quickly led to a skirmish, during which several salvors were injured and a Bahamian launch was damaged. Knowing that the Black Fleet could quickly send for reinforcements to push the Key West wreckers off the *Alicia's* deck, Captain Johnson offered a quick compromise. He offered to split the salvage of the steamer equally and proceeded to paint a red line down the center of the *Alicia's* deck. By the time the insurance underwriter arrived on the scene, along with a British gunboat, the salvors were working peacefully side by side.

Captain Johnson coordinated the continued salvage of the dry cargo and then supervised as divers entered the flooded cargo holds to haul out the remaining material. Due to the invading seawater, cargo would inevitably foul and create a hazardous, sometimes toxic, working environment. The mixture of chemicals such as dyes, oil, paints, and drugs, as well as rotting material such as fish and rice, would seriously impair a diver's health. Mary Conrad, a witness to the grounding and subsequent salvage wrote, "The oddest thing about the salvage came from the soap suds. There were many cases of washing powder on the ship and the water became so soapy the men would not go into the hold[5]." Frequently, divers were temporarily blinded after working in fouled cargo holds.

Hopes of refloating the stricken *Alicia* were abandoned on July 25, and the wreck was sold to the highest bidder for scrap in September. Work continued until December, whereupon salvors used explosives to tear the hull apart to recover the machinery. The iron hull of the *Alicia* eventually settled in 20 feet of water in what is now Biscayne National Park.

The hull and superstructure have collapsed over the years, but the wreck remains contiguous, though heavily incorporated into the thriving marine ecosystem. Today, the remaining wreckage consists of the hull and keel of the ship. Conspicuously absent are the engine, her two double-ended boilers, and other machinery. The *Alicia* is still an impressive spectacle, alive with fish and other sea life seeking refuge under the sections of hull plate. The shallow depth allows the wreck to be explored by snorkelers, and it is a great site for novice divers. It also makes a relaxing shallow dive for more experienced divers who have made deeper dives earlier in the day. Due to its shallow depth, the wreck can be subjected to surge, as well as slight tidal current.

Scattered hull plates and bulkheads dominate the wreck site of the *Alicia*.

ALLIGATOR

The river steamer *Alligator* was built in 1888 at Norwalk off the St. Johns River. Initially, she was a screw steamer 57 feet long and 18 foot wide. In 1889, she was lengthened to 71 feet and converted to an inboard paddlewheel assembly to help her push through shallow and narrow portions of Florida's rivers for the Lucas Line. Between 1891 and 1895, Clarence B. Moore chartered the *Alligator* for use as a research vessel, in order to pursue his archaeological pursuits. In 1905, after a brief period of no activity, the *Alligator* was reactivated for use on the Ocklawaha River. Unfortunately, her return to service was short-lived, as she struck a snag and sunk in 1906. The steamer was eventually raised and repaired for continued use in northern Florida.

Scuttling charges send the *Almirante* to the bottom (George Detrio).

Steamer *Alligator* on the Ocklawaha River, July 26, 1901 (Alfred H. Robson Collection).

The ultimate fate of the *Alligator* was documented in the 1910 *Annual Report of the Supervising Inspector-General, U.S. Steamboat-Inspection Service to the Secretary of Commerce and Labor* thusly, "November 5, 1909: At midnight freight steamer *Alligator*, not in commission, was totally destroyed by fire in Crescent Lake, Fla. Loss, $4,000. No lives were lost." While not positively identified, the wreck of the *Alligator* is believed to rest in the shallow water of Grimsley Cove on the eastern shore of Crescent Lake.

ALMA H.

The *Alma H.* was a small steamer of 37 tons built in 1908. Her December 9, 1908, loss was detailed in the 1910 *Annual Report of the Supervising Inspector-General, U.S. Steamboat-Inspection Service to the Secretary of Commerce and Labor*, "Motor passenger steamer *Alma H.* was totally destroyed by fire at St. Augustine, Fla. Cause, supposed incendiary. Estimated value of vessel, $3,228. Amount of insurance on vessel, $1,400. Vessel will not be rebuilt. Had been out of commission."

ALMIRANTE

One of the older artificial reefs off Miami, the *Almirante* was originally launched by Cochrane and Sons, Limited, in Selby, United Kingdom, as the H.M.S. *Gillstone* (T355) on July 19, 1943. Commissioned into the Royal Navy on November 19, 1943, the *Gillstone* was an Isles Class trawler, 185 feet in length, 29 feet in breadth, displacing 545 tons. In 1947, her named was changed to *Argo* upon her sale to a Norwegian company. In 1952, she was converted to a refrigerated cargo ship. The vessel would change names numerous times in subsequent years: *Freedom First* in 1961; *Glenrock* in 1964; *Sea Enterprise* in 1969; and, finally, *Almirante* when purchased by Miami Maritime, Incorporated in 1970. After only a few years, however, her owners abandoned her on the Miami River. After numerous unsuccessful attempts to have Miami Maritime move their neglected vessel, the city of Miami had the upper decks of the *Almirante's* superstructure removed, and they then towed the derelict offshore and sunk it as an artificial reef on April 13, 1975.

The *Almirante* slips beneath the surface (George Detrio).

Also known as the "Banana Boat," the wreck of the *Almirante* sits mostly upright in 125 feet of water off Elliott Key. Her stern is twisted to port and portions have partially collapsed amidships due to the influence of Hurricane Andrew, which passed over the site in August 1992. Having been underwater for over 30 years, the remains of the *Almirante* are blanketed by abundant gorgonian growth, and other associated marine life is generally quite robust.

ALNA

The following wrecking event demonstrates the care one must taken when disseminating archival information. When researching this shipwreck, I learned this vessel was initially identified in newspaper articles on October 16, 1838, as the American brig *Alderly*. Numerous subsequent articles then documented the vessel as the brig *Olney*. In addition, significant contradictions in survivors' accounts appeared in various articles. Regardless of the name variation and contradictions, the unfortunate fate of this Portland, Maine brig and her crew is illustrative of the fates of many castaways on the desolate Florida coast from the early seventeenth century through the mid-nineteenth century. Captain Thomas and the *Alna* departed St. Jago de Cuba on August 19, 1838, bound for Boston. After a stop at Matanzas, Cuba, she sailed north with a light breeze. By September 5, the weather had changed dramatically, and soon blew a violent gale. On September 7, the brig was about 15 miles off the coast of Florida, but drifting rapidly on a lee shore. With seas making a clear breach over her and sweeping decks fore and aft, it was soon apparent that it would be impossible to prevent the total loss of the *Alna*. With the vessel's fate sealed, Captain Thomas decided to run the brig up on shore in the daytime, in order to better the chances of saving the lives on board. The *Alna* soon struck bottom, about 20 miles (also reported as 25 miles) north of Cape Florida, and the heavy waves soon carried her high on the beach so that the crew could easily jump from her to shore.

The crew remained near their stranded ship in hopes of encountering another vessel sailing along the coast to be rescued. Unfortunately, the Seminole Indians found them first. On the morning of September 9, seaman Stephen Cammett was startled by a musket report. To his horror, he saw mate Andrew Plummer drop to the sand, shot dead by a group of advancing Indians. Cammett was also shot, struck in his hand and leg. Fortunately, he was able to retreat into the cover of nearby palmetto scrub. Crewman Eleazer Wyer also managed to crawl to safety. From their hiding places, they witnessed the summary execution of the remaining crew. A third crewman, George Johnson, was eventually rescued by the wrecking schooner *America*. His harrowing and detailed story, which originally appeared in the *New Orleans Bee*, was also published in *The Adams Sentinel* on November 5, 1838:

> Among the vessels lost on the Florida reef, during the memorable gale of the 7th and 9th of September last, our readers may remember the brig *Olney*, Capt. Thomas. This vessel, which had left St. Jago de Cuba a few days previous, with a cargo composed of a million of cigars, a quantity of tobacco, and a large number of cedar logs, was wrecked on Friday, the 7th of September, about 20 miles to the north of Cape Florida. She had attempted to anchor, but the tempest was so violent that both our anchors snapped like pack thread, and she was driven high and dry on the Florida shore. The persons on board, comprising the crew of seven men, and a single passenger, remained in the brig in the continual expectation that the wreckers in the neighborhood would come to their relief. Two days after the *Olney* had gone ashore, while the captain and crew were at breakfast, the report of rifles was heard. On ascending the deck, what were the surprise and horror of these poor fellows, at beholding the brig in possession of some twenty ferocious and well armed Indians, who menaced them with immediate death in case of the slightest resistance. The crew were totally unarmed, and implicit obedience to the merciless savages constituted their sole chance of ultimate safety.
> They were ordered by signs to remove the cigars from the hold, and throw them on the beach. About one hundred half boxes had been removed, when Captain Thomas, a bold and irritable man, refused unconditionally to throw away any more of his cargo. One of the savages, enraged at his disobedience, knocked him down with the butt end of his rifle. This was the signal of attack, a volley of bullets was immediately discharged at the unfortunate commander, and having been pierced by two rifle balls, he was hurled, yet breathing, on the beach. One of the wretches, perceiving that he still lived, seized the hatch bar and plunged it in his breast, extinguishing every remnant of life. The crew were then commanded to go ashore. Scarcely had they touched the land, when a second discharge of rifles were made, by which five were killed. Of the remaining two, one who had escaped unwounded, fled so fast that the Indians were unable to overtake him. The other, Johnson by name, sprung towards some low bushes which grew at a short distance, and having heard that green branches were considered by the savages as a token of peace, fortunately bethought himself of making an effort to have his life spared. He plucked one of the bushes from the ground, fell on his knees, and held it up with signs of supplication. The savages understood the appeal and he was for a moment safe.
> They gave him an axe, and pointing to a smack which was lying at some distance

on the shore, bottom upwards, he was commanded to cut a hole into it. He obeyed, and the Indians took a quantity of beef out of it, which they made him carry to their encampment, which was some miles from the spot. Having arrived there, it appeared that the savages had only postponed the death of the poor fellow, for several of them leveled their rifles at him, and were about to fire, when a squaw rushed out of a wigwam, placed herself before him, and interceded so powerfully for his life that the Indians left him unharmed, and entered their tents.

As soon as Johnson found himself unobserved, he started with all the speed which the love of life could infuse in his frame, and soon reached the brig. He ascended her sides, and stowed himself among a number of cedar blocks which were on the deck. He lay there for 24 hours, trembling with apprehension, and expecting momentarily the return of the Indians, when, most happily, two wreckers came in sight; the crew jumped on board the *Olney*, and were felicitating themselves on the excellent prize they had obtained, when the Indians were once more seen approaching. Johnson immediately appeared from his hiding place, and called on them to save themselves. They all jumped on the shore from the bows of the brig, which lay about 2 feet from the water. Johnson followed, and such was the desperate resolution produced by the dread of death, that though he knew nothing of swimming, he boldly struck out into the deep water, reached the wreckers' boats, and was taken up, conveyed on board the *America*, from thence was carried to Key West, afterwards to Havana, in the U.S. schooner *Wave*, and was eventually conveyed to New Orleans. The other individual who saved himself by running, was likewise taken up by the *America*, and is now in Mobile.

We have this simple but thrilling narrative from the lips of George Johnson himself, and have little doubt of its entire accuracy. We have given it almost in the language employed by him. As is not uncommon, he is indebted for his life to the interposition of a woman.

Cammett and Wyer struggled separately northward. Traveling through marshes and along the beach, they both were miraculously rescued by the wrecking schooner *Mount Vernon* north of Lake Worth, and eventually transferred to the U.S. Revenue Schooner *Madison*. After rendering medical aid to the haggard men, they were returned to New England. They credited the care given by the wreckers thusly:

> It is our humane and highly pleasing duty to say of Captain George Alden and his crew, of the wrecking sloop *Mount Vernon*, that our treatment was in the highest degree, hospitable, over-generous – dressing our wounds, nursing us with parental kindness, giving us clothing, regretting, when we left, that they had no money to give us, and all of us feeding as if attached with the strongest ties of friendship.... To correct wrong impressions and wicked prejudices that exist against the wreckers on the coast of Florida, we feel bound by everything sacred to state, that, instead of being 'plunderers and pirates,' as they are often represented, it is the height of their ambition to save lives and property[6].

The beached wreck of the *Alna* was eventually burned by a detachment from the U.S.S. *Wave*.

ALONZO

According to *The Sailor's Magazine and Naval Journal*, Volume 10, the schooner *Alonzo*, on her outward passage from Baltimore for the St. Johns River, was wrecked on the bar of the latter port, November 3, 1837. Fortunately, the captain and crew were rescued and safely returned to Baltimore.

ALPHA

The *Alpha*, originally named the *Bahamian Alpha*, was an 85-foot long steel hulled schooner built in 1918. Stripped of her upper decks, she was sunk as an artificial reef on March 25, 1989, and she now rests in 80 feet of water off Fort Lauderdale. The *Alpha* is part of a small cluster of other vessels sunk as artificial reefs, which can be visited on the same dive, including the *Qualmann Tugs* (two 32-foot long tugs donated by Ray Qualmann Marine Construction) and the *Jay Dorman* (ex-*Panda*). In the winter, large aggregations of gag grouper can be found in this area.

The scuttling of the *Alpha* on March 25, 1989 (Broward County Artificial Reef Program).

ALTOMARY

The 24-ton gas yacht *Altomary*, official number 211656, was built in 1913 at Jacksonville, Florida. Documentation states she was 50.1 feet long and 16.2 feet wide. During the 1926 hurricane at Miami, the *Altomary* reportedly collided with a barge and sank in Biscayne Bay on the evening of September 18.

ALVARADO

The bark *Alvarado* was built in 1845 at Thomaston, Maine. The 299-ton vessel was 106 feet long and 25 feet wide. On August 25, 1861, *The New York Times* published a July 21, 1861, statement from one of the officers of the bark *Alvarado* on their capture by the privateer *Jefferson Davis*, as well as eventual loss of the ship, which originally appeared in *The Boston Transcript*:

> At 6:00 a.m. a sail came in sight, steering towards the bark. At 7:00 a.m. she crossed our bows and stood on the same way with us, and hoisted the English flag, and in a few minutes she fired a shot across our bows, and hauled down the English flag and ran up the Confederate flag. The mainsail of the bark was hauled up, and the vessel luffed in the wind. The pirate then lowered her boat, with twelve men well armed, and came alongside, and on board, saying the bark was a prize. On being asked by what authority, the captain of the boat's crew answered, "By the authority of that big gun and Jefferson Davis," and remarking that war was declared between the North and South, demanded my papers. It was of no use to resist, and so the ship's papers and manifest of the cargo were given him. The commander of the boat's company (Mr. Pestell, the First Lieutenant of the *Jefferson Davis*) sent the papers on board the pirate for the captain's inspection. We waited about two hours for his decision as to what he would do with the vessel and cargo. He finally sent a boat to the bark, with a prize captain and crew, eight in all. The officers and crew of the bark were ordered to put their things into the boat, ready to go on board the brig. In the meantime, the steward of the brig overhauled our stores, and some of his companions got up beef, pork, flour, etc. The pirates took about everything in the way of provisions, leaving one barrel of beef and two-thirds of a barrel of flour, and an inconsiderable quantity of small stores. After they had abstracted what they pleased, they left the bark, leaving the captain and wife and the cook on board. The prize captain then bore away to the westward, bound for St. Marys, coast of Florida. Nothing special occurred during the passage. Everything went on pleasantly until the morning of the 5th of August.
>
> At daylight they espied a sail to leeward, distant about ten miles. Capt. Hays then made all sail, and stood in, expecting to see the land soon. At 7:00 a.m. the land appeared in sight. The vessel continued to gain on us quite fast. At 11:00 a.m. the bark was run ashore abreast of Amelia Island. The man-of-war — which the vessel in pursuit of us turned out to be (U.S.S. *Jamestown*) — was then distant four or five miles. Capt. Hays asked the captain of the bark if he wished to go ashore with the pirates in the boat. He replied in the negative. The prize crew all took leave of the bark immediately. As soon as they left, the captain hoisted the Stars and Stripes, Union down, and did all in his power to lay the sails aback, but the wind blowing almost directly on shore, did not succeed.
>
> In the meantime the man-of-war had beat up to within about three miles of the bark. We then discovered a boat coming from the shore toward us. They came alongside, and two of the men jumped on board, saying, "We want you to go on shore." We asked them if we could take our private property with us. They answered, "No," but ordered us into the boat. They would not give us time to make preparations to get the captain's wife over the side into the boat, but put a rope round her waist and lowered her down. They hauled down the Union flag, and then pulled for the shore. When we landed, we were immediately surrounded by three or four hundred men, all armed, among whom were some of the most influential citizens of Fernandina. One of them was Senator Yulee, who begged the captain's wife to go to his house, which she did, and was treated with great consideration by Mrs. Yulee. The captain was kept under the guard of a file of soldiers. Subsequently the prize captain volunteered to go and bring our things on shore. By the time his crew had got half way to the bark, they saw boats coming from the man-of-war, which had beaten up within two miles of the bark, and anchored. They returned to the shore without accomplishing their purpose.
>
> The people now obtained two cannon from the fort, and as the boats from the vessel neared the bark, a constant firing

was kept up, but none of the balls hit the mark for which they were designed. The Union seamen and marines went on board the bark, and hoisted the Stars and Stripes. They then fired the vessel and abandoned her. In half an hour the vessel was enveloped in flames and shortly afterwards the main and mizzen masts fell over the side...the vessel continued burning all night, and the next morning the prize captain and crew went off to her and scuttled her, the vessel having burnt down below her between decks.

ALYCE B.

The 27-ton vessel *Alyce B.*, built in 1917, burned near Fowey Rocks Light on April 12, 1939.

AMANDA WINANTS

The steamer *Amanda Winants* was built in 1863 and quickly was enrolled to serve as a transport and wrecking tug during the Civil War. Following the end of hostilities, the *Winants* continued her work as a wrecking steamer, employed by Merritt and later the Coast Wrecking Company. Stationed at Key West, she assisted and salvaged numerous distressed vessels before finally disappearing in a storm off the Florida coast in October 1874, claiming 15 lives. On December 3, 1874, the *Boston Globe* reported a boat containing life-preservers marked "Winants," a broken compass, and some articles of clothing were picked up near Nassau Inlet. A later report stated a surf boat belonging to the *Amanda Winants* was found off Charleston, South Carolina. The final resting spot of the *Amanda Winants* has yet to be identified, but based on the available evidence, she likely foundered somewhere off Florida north of St. Augustine.

AMARYLLIS

For almost three years, the freighter *Amaryllis* slowly rusted apart while beached on Singer Island, approximately four miles north of Palm Beach. En route from Manchester, England, to Baton Rouge, Louisiana, the Greek-owned freighter ran aground on September 8, 1965, due to storm-churned seas created by Hurricane Betsy. For four months, a fleet of tugs unsuccessfully worked to pull the ship off the beach. Once the expense of saving the ship exceeded its value, Lloyd's of London paid off the insurance claim and the freighter was abandoned where she rested. In December 1965, Samuel McIntosh of Miami paid $25,000 for the beached ship. He, too, gave up efforts to refloat the ship and abandoned the project.

Over the next 32 months, the *Amaryllis* remained on the beach. As both an eyesore and an environmental threat, politicians and local business owners demanded the hulk be removed. In late January 1967, the security guard hired to watch the wreck at night, Clifford S. Valentine, 52, was arrested on charges of contributing to the delinquency of juveniles. He was accused of allowing local teenagers to use the abandoned freighter for late night parties. Approximately two weeks later, a suspicious fire broke out on the evening of February 12, 1967. The fire apparently began in the number two hold and burned for over a day. Finally, the U.S. Army Corps of Engineers proceeded to cut the *Amaryllis*'s superstructure away from her hull in order to lighten the ship. They then successfully managed to pull the remaining hulk off the beach in late August 1968. She

Starboard side view of the freighter *Amaryllis*, May 1960 (William A. Schell).

Amaryllis aground off Palm Beach in late 1965 (Florida State Archives).

was towed offshore, whereupon her seacocks were opened and she was allowed to sink stern-first in 90 feet of water.

The *Amaryllis* was originally built as the *Cromwell Park* by the Burrard Dry Dock Company, Limited, of Vancouver for the Canadian government in February 1945. The freighter was 442 feet in length, 57 feet in beam, and displaced 7,147 tons. In 1946, she was sold to the Canadian Transport Company and renamed the *Harmac Vancouver*. The vessel was sold yet again in 1948 to the Amaryllis Steamship Company, Limited, of Piraeus, Greece, and renamed the *Amaryllis*.

Due to the extensive scrapping prior to her sinking, the wreck of the *Amaryllis* now resembles a 400-foot long canoe as she sits on the bottom. With her bow pointing southward, the *Amaryllis* comprises a portion of an artificial reef site off Palm Beach known as "The Corridor," which also includes the yacht *Mizpah*, the patrol craft U.S.S. *PC-1174* (U.S.S. *Fredonia*), an 80-foot long barge, and piles of concrete pilings, all of which are linked by lines of limestone boulders. As the *Amaryllis* lies just north of the Palm Beach Inlet, it is best to dive it during flood tide, as an outgoing tide will pull murky water from the inlet directly over this area.

The wreck of the *Amaryllis*.

AMAZONE

The small Dutch freighter *Amazone*, 255 feet in length and 37 feet in beam, was constructed in 1922 at Zaltbommel, Holland, by the G. Meijer shipyard. Owned by the Royal Netherlands Steamship Corporation, she was overseas at the time Germany occupied Holland in World War II, and, thus, remained in service carrying cargo along the eastern seaboard of the United States and throughout the Caribbean. Due to the outbreak of hostilities, she was re-painted, equipped with float-free rafts, and outfitted with a 3.7-inch stern gun for defense.

Captained by Johannes Peter Giltay, the petite *Amazone* found herself leaving the placid waters of the Caribbean in April 1942. Bound for New York, she had picked up her cargo at Curacao and Haiti, loading her holds full of coffee, sisal, cocoa, dried orange peel (a famous product of Curacao), oil burners, and mail.

A month earlier, *Kapitänleutnant* Peter Erich Cremer of the German U-boat, *U-333*, departed the protective bunkers of La Rochelle, France, destined for the eastern seaboard of the United States. *Paukenschlag* (Operation Drumbeat) was meeting with great success off the unprepared ports and shipping lanes of the United States. Unfortunately, the trip across the Atlantic proved to be almost fatal for Cremer's small Type VII U-boat. An attack by a British aircraft and the ramming by the British freighter *Prestige* left the *U-333* crippled: both periscopes were destroyed, two torpedo tubes were useless from damage to the outer doors, and the conning tower was mangled, which produced a constant leak when the U-boat was submerged. However, the crew worked hard to repair the vessel, and the *U-333* successfully reached Florida just south of Cape Canaveral in May 1942.

May 5 found the *Amazone* steaming blacked-out along the Florida coast at nine knots, eventually passing the Jupiter Inlet light. Unbeknownst to the lookouts on the *Amazone*, the *U-333* had just made her American debut with an attack on the southbound tanker *Java Arrow* shortly before midnight. While a torpedo found her target, the *Java Arrow* remained afloat.

At approximately 3:40 a.m. on May 6, a single torpedo caught the *Amazone* off guard, striking below the waterline on the port side. The second torpedo of the initial salvo, fortunately, missed its target. But the inflicted damage was enough to cripple the Dutch freighter. Captain Giltay noted that the "engines were crippled and, immediately, flames leaped as high as the masts[7]." Preparations were quickly made to abandon ship as the *Amazone* took on an almost immediate list. The fire spread across the ship so rapidly that those trapped below decks, including the gun crew, had no chance to escape. Due to the growing flames, crewmembers on deck could not even reach the lifeboats, but they managed to throw life rafts over the side, which they boarded after jumping from their sinking ship. Those who successfully evacuated the sinking vessel soon found themselves floating past the patrol craft *PC-484*, which was in the vicinity. The survivors also spotted the *U-333*, which had surfaced to observe the sinking. The confusion created during the attack on the *Amazone* and the subsequent search for survivors allowed the *U-333* to slip off into the dark, eventually sinking the unescorted tanker *Halsey* a few hours later. The *PC-484* had spotted the survivors of the *Amazone* and returned to pick them up at 6:00 a.m. after securing the area. Twenty men survived the incident, while 14 perished in the attack and sinking.

Freighter *Amazone* in her war colors, 1942 (Mark Mondano Collection).

The wreck of the *Amazone*, the twelfth victim in nine days, had now become a navigational hazard, and it was both wire-dragged and leveled with explosives by the U.S. Coast Guard in 1943 and 1944. She was also the subject of several salvage attempts after the war. Today, the remains of the Dutch freighter lie on a sandy bottom in approximately 90 feet of water. The bow is easily identifiable, rising 15 feet off the bottom, with the anchors still resting tight in the hawse pipes. Aft of the bow, the wreck breaks down low to the sand. Amidships, the boilers can be found half buried in debris and sediment. The engine is located just aft of the boilers, lying on its side. From this point, divers can follow shaft alley to the extreme stern, which rests upended and stripped of her screw. A few random hull plates can be found off the portside in the sand, but the majority of *Amazone's* remains are isolated to the contiguous wreck site. Marine life consists of abundant snapper and sheepshead, with the occasional and wary grouper. Stingrays are often found in the sand or orbiting the wreck, escorted by large cobia. While small and of low relief, the wreck of the *Amazone* is an entertaining dive.

Boilers on the wreck of the *Amazone*.

AMBROSINE

The British bark *Ambrosine* was built in 1853 at Granton, England, and was 129.5 feet long, 29 feet wide, and displaced 434 tons. On September 26, 1866, en route from Cardiff, Wales, for Vera Cruz, the *Ambrosine* foundered off the coast of Florida. The captain, second mate, and three of the crew were saved after 36 hours on a raft. The 10 remaining crew were reported lost.

AMELIA

The 42-foot long steamer *Amelia* reportedly foundered on October 2, 1898, at Fernandina, during an intense hurricane that swept up the Atlantic coast.

AMERICA (1846)

The 255-ton brig *America*, of Boston, from Kingston, Jamaica, bound for New York with an assorted cargo went ashore "about 16 miles north of Cape Canaveral, near the mouth of the Indian River" on September 27, 1846, during a nor'easter[8]. Upon her grounding, the vessel broke in two, the cabin separating from the hull, washing away both boats. The passengers and crew, consisting of Captain Childs, eight men, former Consul to Martinique Mr. Flouroy and his wife, all survived by swimming ashore. The *America* was reportedly built in early 1845.

AMERICA (1885)

Built in April 1863 by S. Gildersleeve Company of Portland, Connecticut, the wooden-hulled screw steamer *America* was 166 feet in length and 31.8 feet in breadth. While she previously sailed for the Baltimore and Savannah Steamship Company, at the time of her loss, the 781-ton second-rate steamer was owned by W.R. Wilson.

In January 1885, the *America* departed New York, bound for Cuba with a cargo of general freight. Commanded by Captain F.C. Miller, she arrived safely to unload her freight and replace it with a cargo of sugar. On February 7, she departed for Boston. Traveling north, the

Painting of the steamer *America* (Mark Mondano Collection).

steamer encountered a winter gale off the Florida coast three days into her return trip. A leak was sprung and the steam pumps were manned, while the *America* kept on her course. Later in the day, still in the clutches of the storm, Captain Miller discovered that the leak was rapidly gaining on him. Early on the morning of February 11, he turned toward the coast, hoping to beach his vessel. However, rising water soon extinguished the boiler fires and left the vessel powerless and adrift. Fortunately for the crew of the *America*, the prevailing winds pushed the steamer towards shore. The *America's* decks were almost at the water's edge when the ship grounded on a sandbar just offshore of the beach.

With the vessel's decks awash and in an unstable sinking condition, the breaking waves steadily pushed the vessel over on her side and proceeded to rip her apart. The crew barely had time to retreat from the vessel, but they managed to work through the breaking surf and safely land on the beach. Soon after they had landed, the *America* began to go to pieces.

But their predicament was far from over. One of the crew summed up their situation: "Our troubles began in earnest after we landed. We had a worse time on land than we did on the sea[9]." At the time, the stretch of Florida beach where the crew found themselves was desolate with no settlements in the vicinity. Once the weather improved, they rowed back to sea and worked southward to Jupiter Inlet. Rowing inland, they worked 80 miles down the St. Johns River to Sanford, whereupon Captain Miller abandoned his crew. Captain Miller testified that they came ashore eight miles from Gilbert's Bar House of Refuge, hit shore without sleep for 40 hours, turned the lifeboats over and slept beneath them in wet clothes with the sand flies. Keeper Brown found them and provided food and shelter. Miller sold all salvaged material at a beach auction for $125 to Captain Thomas E. Richards[10]. The crew managed to beg their way to Jacksonville and eventually secured passage to Savannah. The mayor of Savannah paid for the men's trip to New York on the steamship *City of Augusta*, during which the crew shared stories of their adventure with survivors of the Italian bark *Vulpini*, who were shipwrecked off Sapelo Island, Georgia, in the same storm. *The New York Times*, March 3, 1885, reported the lost steamship *America* was valued at about $40,000, and there was little, if any, insurance on her.

AMERICAN COIN

According to *The Sailor's Magazine and Naval Journal*, Volume 25, the schooner *American Coin*, from Savannah to St. Augustine, was lost off the (St. Augustine) bar on the afternoon of January 29, 1853. She struck between the outer breakers and the swash channel, about two in the afternoon. The captain and all hands got ashore safely in a lifeboat.

AMERICAN EAGLE

The 38-ton shrimp trawler *American Eagle* was built in 1953. As reported in the *Galveston Daily News*, December 8, 1954, Captain Amuel Carujo and a seaman known only as "Clyde" were rescued by the U.S. Coast Guard when their foundering shrimper drifted ashore at Marineland, south of St. Augustine, on December 6. The *American Eagle* was lost in the same storm as the shrimper *Wanderer*.

AMIABLE ANTOINETTE

The Edinburgh Advertiser, February 18, 1817, detailed the loss of the *Amiable Antoinette*, from Charleston, on December 26, 1816, near St. Augustine; the crew and cargo were saved. This vessel may possibly be *L'Amiable Antoinetta*, which is listed in *Lloyd's Register of Shipping* for 1815 as a 60-ton single-deck French schooner of Havre, owned by its master, Captain Bozan.

AMIABLE GERTRUDE

The Spanish brig *Amiable Gertrude*, Captain Juan Ballabi, with a cargo of cocoa, which sailed from Havana on November 9, 1834, bound to Coronna and St. Andero, struck a reef near Caesar's Creek on November 12. Every effort to save the vessel was made until November 15, when she bilged. All hands were saved. A portion of the cargo was also saved, but much damaged, as well as the ship's rigging and other related gear[11].

AMOS BIRDSALL

As reported in *The Sailor's Magazine and Naval Journal*, Volume 19, the schooner *Amos Birdsall*, of New York, from Philadelphia for Brazos, Santiago, went ashore four miles south of Mosquito Inlet on January 28, 1847.

ANCIENT MARINER

The *Ancient Mariner* was sunk as an artificial reef on June 9, 1991. Formerly the U.S.C.G.C. *Nemesis* (WPC-111), the vessel had a distinguished 30-year career before her disposal in 68 feet off Deerfield Beach. Built by the Marietta Manufacturing Company at Point Pleasant, West Virginia, she was launched on July 7, 1934. The cutter was 165 feet in length, 25 feet in breadth, displaced 337 tons, and was capable of a 16-knot top speed. Stationed at St. Petersburg, she was commissioned on October 10, 1934.

With the outbreak of World War II, the *Nemesis* was deployed to defend the Gulf Sea Frontier. On May 21, 1942, she rescued 28 survivors from the sunken tanker *Faja de Oro*, and on June 7 she picked up 27 survivors from the torpedoed freighter *Suwied*. Between January 24 and

August 17, 1942, the *Nemesis* engaged in six separate depth charge attacks against enemy U-boats in the Atlantic and Gulf of Mexico. The *Nemesis* finished out the war conducting escort duty between Key West and New York. Following World War II, she patrolled between Florida and Cuba enforcing U.S. law, conducting search and rescue operations, and aiding Cuban refugees struggling to reach freedom on American soil. She remained in active service until November 1964, whereupon she was decommissioned and sold to Auto Marine Engineering, Incorporated of Miami.

Ancient Mariner as U.S.C.G.C. *Nemesis* (U.S. Coast Guard).

The ship was eventually converted into a floating restaurant in Fort Lauderdale's New River District, and opened as Livingston's Landing in 1979. The restaurant could not stay afloat financially, however, and was sold. Prior to reopening as the Ancient Mariner in 1981, she sunk at her dock. She was re-floated and finally reopened later that year, but an outbreak of hepatitis A that infected 97 diners in 1986 closed the Ancient Mariner's doors permanently; widely reported in newspapers, it was the largest food-borne hepatitis outbreak in Florida history. In subsequent years, new investors tried to operate the restaurant under a variety of names such as Anchorage Seafood, Chapman's River Raw Bar, and Cutters; however, all inevitably failed. Abandoned, the former cutter was acquired by the Broward County Artificial Reef Program.

Now a popular dive site, the wreck is an easy dive with

Sinking of the *Ancient Mariner* (Broward County Artificial Reef Program).

other wrecks in the near vicinity. The *Ancient Mariner* points to the southeast, and divers swimming off the bow will find the tug *Berry Patch*, as well as the remains of the *Chuck-A-Luck II* (formerly the *River Queen*) and the *C-Note*.

Inside the wreck of the *Ancient Mariner*.

ANDE

On November 24, 1996, an explosive ordinance team placed 24 six-pound plastic explosive charges within the hull of the *Ina Carrier*. An additional 16 cans of gasoline each were distributed along the bow, deck, and wheelhouse of the freighter to produce a pyrotechnic display for the media and boaters surrounding the anchored ship. Seconds after the detonation, the stern steadily settled under the water's surface until the entire vessel proceeded to take a dramatic starboard roll, spilling the cargo covers from their deck holds. Fortunately, the *Ina Carrier*, renamed the *Ande* in recognition of the reef's sponsor, Ande Monofilament Line, eventually righted herself as she came to rest on the bottom in 190 feet of water.

Ande as the *Jed Carrier* (Florida Fish and Wildlife Conservation Commission Artificial Reef Program).

The *Ande* was originally built in 1967 as the *Takasago Maru No. 5* in the Japanese shipyard of *Uwajima Zosensho*. The freighter was 293-foot long, 43 foot wide, and displaced 2,051 tons. During her career, she changed names several times: *Carib Carrier* in 1970 following her purchase by the Caribbean Cement Company, *New Providence* in 1972, and *Jed Carrier* in 1988. Jamaican-flagged, the *Jed Carrier* was employed by Lewis Shipping hauling lumber to various Caribbean ports. According to court records, the *Jed Carrier* eventually became involved in several court cases with insurance and lumber companies. Just prior to being sold to Palm Beach County for $145,000 in 1995, the freighter's name was changed one last time to *Ina Carrier*.

The *Ande* originally came to rest completely upright and intact just north of Lake Worth Inlet off Singer Island, her bow facing east. Following the passing of several hurricanes in 2004-2005, the *Ande* was ripped in half. While the forward section still sits upright, the stern lists almost 90 degrees on her port side. Due to the wreck's orientation — perpendicular to the normal northward-moving current — it is fairly easy for divers to intersect the *Ande* by descending just to the south of the wreck and drifting into the hull. Resting on a clean sand bottom, visibility typically exceeds 80 feet.

ANDRO

Like many vessels utilized by the artificial reef programs around the state of Florida, the sinking of the *Andro* was the result of a narcotics seizure. On March 13, 1985, the U.S.C.G.C. *Ute* (WATF-76) conducted an inspection on the *Andro* after coming across the Bahamian-registered vessel in the Yucatan Straits, 40 miles southwest of Cuba. The U.S. Coast Guard ultimately found 15 tons of marijuana on the *Andro*, arrested her seven-member crew, and escorted the vessel to Miami. The *Andro* was later purchased by the Miami-Dade Department of Environmental Resources and sunk off Haulover Inlet on December 17, 1985.

The drug-smuggling *Andro* was originally built as the yacht *Pawnee II*. Laid down as hull number 293 for Harry P. Bingham, the *Pawnee II* was launched on October 11, 1925, by the Newport News Shipbuilding and Drydock Company. Eventually completed on January 15, 1926, the 455-ton *Pawnee II* was 160 feet in overall length, 151 feet along her waterline, and 26.6 feet in breadth. She was powered by two Winton diesel engines developing a total of 900 horsepower, yielding a cruising speed of 13 knots. Five staterooms and four bathrooms for guests were located on the berth deck, while the dining saloon, living room, galley, and pantry were found on the main deck.

An amateur marine biologist, Mr. Bingham originally explored the waters of the Caribbean in 1925 aboard his first yacht *Pawnee I*, where he collected fish and other marine life. In 1926, he conducted his second expedition to the Pacific coast of Central America and the Gulf of California on the newly-built *Pawnee II*. Mr. Bingham had specially designed the *Pawnee II* to facilitate deep-sea trawling and research; a taxidermist's room and laboratory were located on the main deck. The third and final expedition took the *Pawnee II* to the Bahamas and Bermuda in 1927. His private specimen collection became so large that he ultimately hired a curator to help manage it. Later that year, Bingham started his own journal, the *Bulletin of the Bingham Oceanographic Collection*, which featured information gleaned from his research. In 1930, Bingham gave his collection to his alma mater, Yale University, which established the Bingham Oceanographic Foundation. At the time, his collection consisted of over 3,000 specimens, 200 of which were previously unknown.

Likewise, Mr. Bingham also parted with his beloved *Pawnee II* in 1930, whereupon it was renamed *Hardi Biaou* by the new owners. In 1938, the yacht was sold to the Virginia Pilots Association, converted into a pilot vessel, and renamed *Virginia*. The latter portions of her career are not well known, aside from the fact that her name was eventually changed to *Andro*, and in the early 1980s she operated as a freighter in the Bahamas.

The once proud yacht now sits in 103 feet of water with her bow on her starboard side. Portions of the wreck rise almost 40 feet off the bottom. Amidships, the *Andro's* funnel is resting practically upside down after it became dislodged from the hull. One of the vessel's large engines can be found adjacent to the funnel. The *Andro's* stern is listing to port with both screws still visible, though mangled. While she is largely remembered as a former drug-runner, it is fitting that the *Andro*, a vessel originally employed to further marine science, is now permanently serving as an artificial reef.

The *Andro* being prepared for sinking as an artificial reef (Miami-Dade County Department of Environmental Resources Management).

ANGLIN PIER WRECK

Immediately to the north of the Anglin Pier at Lauderdale-By-The-Sea are the remains of an unidentified shipwreck buried under the beach near the surf line. Based on the available information, including the presence of lead anti-fouling coating on the hull dating to after 1825, and the use of wire nails manufactured after 1890, the standing assumption is the wreck occurred sometime around the 1890 through 1910 timeframe. The lack of rigging may indicate the vessel was utilized as a barge when it ultimately came to grief.

ANN

In mid-July 1819, the British brig *Ann*, from Matanzas bound to Falmouth, England, was in distress off the Florida coast. Hoping for assistance, she instead encountered a gang of men from the smack *Lawrence* and another sloop, who boarded the *Ann* and proceeded to run her ashore. Six of the brig's crew joined the pirates, while the other four, including Captain Sunley, were murdered and thrown overboard. According to *The Edinburgh Advertiser*, June 16, 1820, Captain Sunley and the other victims "had ceased all resistance, and had surrendered all they possessed, but were stabbed in the act of supplicating for their lives." Several of the men who committed the crimes were captured in Charleston, South Carolina, where they were convicted of piracy and murder, and sentenced to execution.

ANNA (1810)

According to the *Bell's Weekly Messenger* of January 20, 1811, "The *Anna*, Hooper, from the Havannah [sic] to Baltimore, was totally lost 26th October on the Florida shore. Crew saved."

ANNA (1986)

The history of the *Anna*, a 225-foot long freighter sunk as an artificial reef off Jacksonville, is not entirely clear. Her original name has proven elusive, though some sources say the vessel was built at Leith, Scotland, in 1932, while still others suggest she may have been a Dutch freighter. While her past is still a mystery, the path to her sinking is relatively well known. The *Anna* was reportedly seized in 1981 following the discovery of narcotics hidden on board the vessel. While ownership of the vessel was being determined following the pending trial, the *Anna* was interned at Green Cove Springs, upriver from Jacksonville. Here she languished for five years before the Jacksonville Offshore Sportfishing Club and the Greater Jacksonville Kingfish Tournament Committee eventually purchased the former drug runner. After cleaning and additional preparation, the *Anna* was towed offshore and sunk as an artificial reef on July 16, 1986. She now rests on her side in approximately 110 feet of water.

ANNA A. TYNG

In a report dated April 1858 in *The Sailor's Magazine and Naval Journal*, Volume 30, the brig *Anna A. Tyng*, from Maine to St. Johns, Florida, stranded on St. Johns Beach.

ANNA BELL HYER

The 151-ton schooner *Anna Bell Hyer*, official number 105141, was built in June 1872 at Milford, Delaware, and registered a length of 90 feet and a breadth of 28.5 feet. On October 5, 1879, Captain J.J. Betts and the *Hyer* were close to concluding a trip from Alexandria to Jacksonville when the schooner wrecked on the St. Johns Bar. The vessel proved to be a total loss.

ANNA F.

The schooner *Anna F.*, official number 107624, was built in 1901 at Mobile, Alabama, and was 47.2 feet long, 12.5 feet wide, and 21 gross tons. The small schooner reportedly foundered off Fort Lauderdale on February 24, 1907.

ANNIE B.

Built in 1900, the 12-ton vessel *Annie B.*, official number 107540, burned November 28, 1914, at the mouth of Thomas Creek, on the St. Johns River.

ANNIE C.

The *Annie C.*, official number 204400, was a small, 9-ton steamer built in 1907, which stranded at Kissimmee on September 15, 1908.

ANNIE WOOD

According to an April 23, 1955, article by historians John Wilson Somerville and Ella Teague de Berard in *The Palm Beach Post*, the steamer *Annie Wood* burned at Hogan's Creek near Jacksonville in 1889.

ANTELOPE

As documented in *The Sailor's Magazine and Naval Journal*, Volume 13, the schooner *Antelope*, from Palatka, capsized in a squall in April 1841 about 10 miles to the northward of the St. Augustine Bar. While the crew was saved, the vessel proved a total loss.

ANTILLES STAR

The *Antilles Star* was a 165-foot long, 670-ton Dutch factory trawler sunk approximately 17 miles northeast of Ponce de Leon Inlet. Towards the end of her career, the 40-year old vessel had been intended to serve as a Caribbean freighter, but those plans were eventually abandoned, as was the *Antilles Star*. The trawler was eventually picked up by Associated Marine Salvage, Incorporated of Miami. Following cleaning and preparation as an artificial reef, the trawler was sold to the Volusia County Artificial Reef Program for $44,370. On the morning of June 29, 2004, the *Antilles Star* was slowly flooded, a process that took approximately 20 minutes. On its final descent, the bow rolled to port and crashed into the bottom in 84 feet of water. Following the 2004 hurricane season, however, the former trawler was found to be resting almost upright.

ANTONIO

On the afternoon of June 5, 1961, the 77-foot yacht *Antonio* departed Palm Beach headed across the Gulf Stream for Nassau, Bahamas. Shortly after clearing the inlet, fire broke out on the 68-ton vessel, which was built in 1932. While the six passengers escaped unharmed and were later rescued, the $270,000 yacht burned to the waterline and sank 15 miles off Palm Beach County[12].

APOLLO

On October 25, 1790, *The Times* reported the *Apollo*, Captain Cragg (also cited as Captain Craig), of Workington, was totally lost on Cape Florida, with nothing saved but the rum, cotton, and wood. Information was relayed from Captain Thomas Rennie of the *Edmund and George*, which also went ashore on Cape Florida but was later successfully worked off with no damage.

ARAUCANA

According to Marx (1979), the 10-gun Spanish ship *Araucana*, Captain Benito de la Rigada, sailing from Cuba to Spain, wrecked off Elliott Key on October 26, 1811, during a hurricane. A falling mast pierced the hull, forcing the crew to abandon ship in lifeboats as their ship sank in about 75 feet of water. The crew came ashore on Elliott Key and were picked up by a passing vessel and carried back to Cuba. The *Araucana* is also cited as a Spanish six-gun schooner. I have been unable to uncover any additional information on this vessel or its wrecking.

ARAWAK

The *Arawak*, a 115-foot, 201-ton wooden steamer built in 1938, was destroyed by flames that started in the galley only a few hours after it departed Jacksonville for Nassau, Bahamas, on September 23, 1941. Captain Roland Roberts said the flames, fanned by a high wind, spread with almost incredible swiftness. The captain, his crew of eight, and five passengers aboard abandoned ship about 15 miles offshore about an hour after the fire started. Captain Roberts described the events: "We had two boats, but the flames were so high we couldn't launch one of them, so all of us piled into a lifeboat built to accommodate 12. We hoisted sail, started using our oars and sent up flares to show where we were[13]." A Coast Guard surfboat met the *Arawak's* lifeboat approximately four miles off the coast and towed it to safety.

Apparently, the traumatic events did not phase at least one of the survivors, three-year old Allison Carroll. As the child stepped ashore, she laughed, pointed toward the rolling Atlantic and said: "Ocean."

"I should think you'd have had enough ocean by now," her mother replied[14].

Allison's sister abandoned ship with her favorite book, which she was reading when the fire broke out. "I finished it before it got dark, and it was good," she said[15].

The British steamer burned to its waterline before sinking late at night, which was observed by a large crowd of curious onlookers drawn to the beach to watch the fire. The *Arawak*, named for a tribe of sea-faring Indians from the Virgin Islands, came to rest in approximately 60 feet of water southeast of St. Augustine. As most of the vessel burned, and the wreck is heavily sanded in, the small site can be hard to find. The oil-fired engine is the largest feature on the wreck. Aft of the engine, a pile of quarried limestone rests amidships, while the shaft can be followed back to the small screw. Brass valves and electrical fixtures can be found around the engine, and one can observe large timbers just under the sand's surface. Coincidentally, the wreck of the *Arawak* lies is in close proximity to a permitted artificial reef site.

ARCADIA

The 188-foot long yacht *Arcadia*, owned by Mrs. Huntington Hardwick of Boston, sank in 20 feet of water off the county causeway at Miami during a storm on November 4, 1935[16]. The 274-foot long yacht *Charlena*, owned by Charles McCann of the F.W. Woolworth Company, also broke loose in the storm and jammed against the *Arcadia*, further damaging the sunken yacht, but the *Charlena* reportedly stayed afloat. After the incident, the *Arcadia* was raised and repaired, and later sold to Great Britain in 1940. The yacht was pressed into service with the Royal Canadian Navy, whereupon she was renamed H.M.C.S. *Elk*. The patrol yacht survived war and was sold to Saint John Marine Transports Limited, which renamed her *Grand Manan III*. The *ex-Arcadia* served as a Canadian ferry until 1965 and was ultimately scrapped at Baltimore, Maryland in 1969.

ARGOSY

On May 27, 1958, the 40-foot long yacht *Argosy* burned to its waterline and sank approximately three miles off Miami's Government Cut. Captain Ray Hatfield scrambled to a skiff tied off to the stern of the yacht and safely escaped the burning vessel.

ARIDA

The *Arida* was originally built for the military as a Landing Craft Infantry (Large), or LCI(L), which were designed to deliver soldiers quickly during an amphibious assault. These vessels had an empty displacement of 234 tons, a loaded displacement of 389 tons, were 158.5 feet in length, 23 feet in beam, and had a loaded draft of less than 6 feet. The two sets of quad diesel engines could carry a fully-loaded LCI(L) at 16 knots. A total of 923 LCI(L)s were built by 10 different shipyards from 1942 to 1944. After their combat usefulness was over, many were sold to foreign navies or private entities, or eventually scrapped.

The exact service history of the *Arida* is unknown, though she likely served as a small cargo vessel for a number of years prior to her deployment as an artificial reef in August of 1982. She now sits in 88 feet of water off Miami. Like many other shipwrecks in the area, the *Arida* was pummeled by Hurricane Andrew in 1992. The main

Arida going under (Miami-Dade County Department of Environmental Resources Management).

section of the almost upside-down wreck has collapsed in on itself. The wreck still attracts abundant marine life, as schools of tomtates, snapper, and goatfish flourish around the *Arida*.

ARIZONA SWORD

On January 15, 1946, the *Arizona Pine* was launched at the Portland, Oregon shipyard of Albina. The 3,133-ton freighter was 309 feet in length between parallels, and 48.8 feet in beam. In 1947, the vessel was renamed the *Arizona Sword*. On May 5, 1954, the freighter was involved in a collision with the collier *Berwindvale* in the Cape Cod Canal resulting in the sinking of the *Arizona Sword*. According to the incident report, the *Arizona Sword* lost control due to current sheer, turning broadside into the bow of the larger *Berwindvale*. The *Arizona Sword* was struck on her starboard side; she was abandoned as she listed to port and ultimately settled to the bottom.

The owners and the insurance companies carrying the insurance on the vessel and cargo abandoned the motorship and cargo as a total loss. Subsequently, the U.S. Army Corps of Engineers determined the sunken wreck constituted a menace to navigation, and it then became their duty to remove the abandoned freighter. On June 13, 1951, the Corps of Engineers invited bids on a contract for dismantling and removal of the wreck. George M. Bryne, having been the successful bidder on July 6, 1951, entered into a contract with the Corps of Engineers (acting as an agency of the United States Government) to remove the wreck from the canal for a sum of $227,000.

The salvaged *Arizona Sword* was eventually sold to Blue Stack Towing Company of Tampa and put in service as a seagoing barge in 1954. On January 13, 1961, the seagoing barge *Arizona Sword*, while in tow of the tug *Sally R*, sank off the coast of Florida approximately 10 miles off Palm Beach. She went down with her captain and six crewmen, as well as a cargo of bulk sulfur. The cook, George W. Richardson of Tampa, was the only known survivor, and escaped by crawling out a porthole. Richardson said 15-foot waves broke up the barge within minutes after a cable parted. He didn't even have time to grab a life jacket before abandoning the vessel.

ARMSMEAR

The sternwheel steamer *Armsmear*, official number 1877, was built at Hartford, Connecticut, in 1870. The 131-ton vessel was 76 feet long and 23 feet wide. Initially, the *Armsmear* ran as a ferry between Jacksonville and South Jacksonville, and then was bought in 1881 by A.M. Lyon's Jacksonville, St. Augustine, and Halifax River Railway. Ultimately, the *Armsmear* reportedly caught fire and burned at Palatka on December 14, 1887.

ARRATOON APCAR

Most shipwreck events are documented in some fashion or another. Whether detailed in newspapers, insurance reports, court inquiries, or other archival information, usually one can trace the history of a vessel to its ultimate fate. However, sometimes the passing of time fade the details of a particular casualty. Still other times, fate may lend a hand in hiding a shipwreck. Such is the case of the *Arratoon Apcar*.

The Florida coast south of Miami is punctuated with a plethora of reefs that come within just a few feet of the surface. Many of these have been named after the ships they claimed. Carysfort, Alligator, and Looe reefs all bear the names of unfortunate vessels that came to grief on their jagged coral. Fowey Rocks is yet another reef that earned its name after the sinking of the H.M.S. *Fowey*, detailed elsewhere in this work. Numerous other ships were lost on these treacherous reefs. Because of these maritime losses, lighthouses were constructed along the Florida reef line to warn potential future victims. Fowey Rocks Light was designed after the U.S. Lighthouse Board, originally established by Congress as the U.S. Lighthouse Establishment on August 7, 1789, received numerous complaints maintaining that the Cape Florida lighthouse on Key Biscayne was inadequate, due to its distance from the reef line. A plan to build a lighthouse directly on Fowey Rocks was approved in 1875. The beacon selected to grace the structure was a Henry-LePaute, first-order, revolving Fresnel lens that could be seen up to 17 miles seaward. The northernmost lighthouse, Fowey Rocks Light was the fifth of six screwpile lighthouses to be raised along the Florida reef line from 1852 to 1880.

The base pilings and wrought iron foundation of the tower were secured to the reef by the firm of Paulding and Kemble of Cold Spring, New York in 1877. Pusey, Jones and Company of Wilmington, Delaware, were contracted to finish the cast iron light tower and keeper's house. Hampered by bad weather and the lack of adequate supply vessels, work proceeded for over a year. As the nearest land was four miles away on Soldier Key, and there was a general lack of supply vessels, the work crews improvised and dwelled in tents erected on an 80-square-foot platform raised over the reef. On February 17, 1878, with work crews focused on finishing the keeper's house, the British steamship *Arratoon Apcar* crashed onto Fowey Rocks mere yards away from the improvised offshore camp.

The *Arratoon Apcar*, official number 43924, was launched on June 27, 1861, by the shipbuilders James Henderson and Son of Renfrew, Scotland. While various sources cite different vessel attributes, Lloyd's Survey Report IRN2512, dated August 18, 1861, states that the iron-hulled screw steamer was initially 261.7 feet in length, 35.2 feet in beam, 25 feet in depth of hold, and displaced 1,480 tons. She was powered by a 250-horsepower compound engine. The *Arratoon Apcar* was named after the founder of her original owners, Apcar and Company. The Apcar family was of Armenian descent, and established a furniture business in Bombay, India, in the early 1800s. The family migrated to the *Arratoon Apcar's* eventual home port of Calcutta in 1845 to become general merchants and ship owners. In late 1872, due to the delivery of a much larger vessel also christened *Arratoon Apcar*, the smaller steamer was sold to H.F. Swan of North Jesmond, Newcastle upon Tyne, and registered in London. Apcar and Company eventually abandoned the shipping business and sold their vessels to the British India Steam Navigation Company in 1912.

On January 20, 1878, Captain Pottinger and the *Arratoon Apcar* departed Liverpool, bound for Havana. At 7:40 p.m. on Sunday, February 17, the steamer ran aground on Fowey Rocks. The workers living on the platform adjacent to Fowey Rocks Light were shocked to observe the lights of the steamship turn and head straight for them. Fortunately, just before the ship collided into the camp, the shallow reef grounded her to a traumatic halt. Apparently, Captain Pottinger believed his position to be farther to the south as he turned his ship to the southwest in order to stay close to the western taper of the Florida Keys. However, he turned too early and collided with Fowey Rocks. The need for the lighthouse on Fowey Rocks was firmly validated by this dramatic wrecking event.

The winter weather rapidly dispatched the ship. Strong winds and heavy swells lifted the ship and slammed it back down on the reef. The *Arratoon Apcar* quickly bilged and settled further onto Fowey Rocks. The wreck of the *Arratoon Apcar* was yet another reminder of the inherent dangers to maritime commerce traveling along the Florida coast. As the disintegrating hulk was pummeled by the surf, numerous passing ships made note of her fate. The captain of the American steamer *Clyde* observed the wreck on February 21, as he too headed for Havana – the *Apcar's* intended destination. "We passed yesterday a steamer, English built, of about 1,200 to 1,500 tons ashore at Fowey rocks, Florida: her stack and mainmast went overboard as we were passing, no one on board: could not make out her name; evidently laden with coal[17]."

The fate of the *Arratoon Apcar* was reported in the *New York Maritime Register* on March 6, 1878: "The water was kept down til Wednesday, six a.m., when she filled rapidly, in a heavy sea, S.S.E., driving the steamer up on the reef, when the crew took to the boats and gained shore. The boat is rapidly going to pieces, the port side being all carried away. The cargo, consisting of 2,000 tons coal and general cargo, is a total loss." The steamer *Tappahannock* picked up Captain Pottinger and his crew of 24, and eventually landed them at New Orleans on March 12. The *Arratoon Apcar* quickly disappeared underneath the water's surface.

The wreck of the *Arratoon Apcar* has largely been forgotten due to its replacement by a fictitious wreck. Ralph Middleton Munroe moved to Florida in 1885 after becoming enchanted with the state during two earlier visits. His journal chronicled the early development of South Florida and, due to his employment with the Coast Wrecking Company, which would eventually become the Merritt and Chapman Company, he documented several shipwreck events. One such wreck, passed on to him by an acquaintance, was the wreck of the *Arakanapka*. Munroe details the construction of the lighthouse on Fowey Rocks, whereupon he mentions that the steamer *Arakanapka* almost collided with the structure before crashing and sinking on the reef. Yet, upon researching the background of this casualty in the *Lloyd's Register*, I found no data on a vessel named *Arakanapka*. Furthermore, there is no information whatsoever of any vessel named *Arakanapka* with the sole exception of its appearance in Munroe's journal. Unfortunately, due to Ralph Munroe's impeccable credibility, this shipwreck tale has been continuously and erroneously passed on, and appears in numerous other books.

Trying to determine the actual identity of the mystery wreck lying on Fowey Rocks was a bit frustrating. After following the *Arakanapka* trail to its end, I was told the remains of the steamer might belong to the *Mississippi*. The British steamer *Mississippi* did indeed run amiss of Fowey Rocks – on April 20, 1874, en route from New York to New Orleans with a general cargo, Captain Wrake crashed the *Mississippi* headlong into the reef at Fowey Rocks. After spending three months on the reef, however, the *Mississippi* was refloated and made her way to New Orleans. Furthermore, it should be noted this event occurred over three years before construction of Fowey Rocks Light began.

Portions of the shattered hull of the steamer *Arratoon Apcar*.

After successfully confirming the identity of the wreck on Fowey Rocks as that of the *Arratoon Apcar*, I wondered how Munroe mistakenly believed it to be the *Arakanapka*. As he was not in Florida at the time of the wrecking event, it is apparent that it was a simple phonetic mistake. As details of the incident passed from person to person, the name eventually evolved into the *Arakanapka* when documented by Commodore Munroe. This shipwreck testifies to the need for diligence when researching wrecking events; never take anything for granted.

The wreck of the *Arratoon Apcar* is one of three sites that lie in close proximity to Fowey Rocks Light. In fact, one of the wrecks can be found almost in the shadow of the light tower. The most likely site of the former British steamer is spread out and resting on a sloping reef in 10 to 25 feet of water. Similar to the wreck sites of the *Alicia* and *Lugano* that are found nearby, the site is dominated by her lower hull and iron members. No evidence of her engine or other machinery exists on the wreck. Sea fans and fire coral have encrusted the wreckage, while sergeant majors and other tropical fish patrol the remains. The *Apcar* is a wonderful wreck and makes for an easy dive for visitors of Biscayne National Park. Due to its shallow depth, the site can frequently experience a strong surge.

ARROW
Operating for the Pioneer Line, the steamer *Arrow* reportedly sank at South Jacksonville[18].

ARTIBONITE
The New York Times, April 2, 1990, reported a 118-foot long wooden-hulled Haitian freighter sank near Key Biscayne early Saturday, and four crew members spent six hours in a life boat before they were rescued. The hull of the freighter *Artibonite* split, and she sank 12 miles southeast of Fowey Rocks near the southern end of Key Biscayne.

ASHLEY
According to the *Dublin Newsletter* of February 8, 1736, the *Ashley*, Captain Jenkins, bound from Jamaica for London, was lost off of Cape Florida with her entire cargo, but the master and crew were saved.

ASK ME
The 29-ton vessel *Ask Me*, built in 1959, reportedly foundered off Fort Lauderdale on August 17, 1969[19].

ATHENE
The 82-ton trawler *Athene* reportedly sank on May 31, 1943 at approximate latitude 25° 35′ north, longitude 80° 05′ west (approximately one nautical mile southeast of Fowey Rocks Light).

ATHLETE
The loss of the steamer *Athlete* on February 12, 1886, was detailed in *The New York Times*, February 14, 1886: "The steamer *Athlete*, Capt. Parsons, burned at the wharf at New Smyrna early Friday morning. The vessel is a total loss, and half of the cargo was burned. Capt. Parsons had a narrow escape from suffocation. The loss is $20,000, and the insurance $10,000." Built in 1878 at St. Marys, Georgia, the sidewheel steamer *Athlete*, official number 106790, was 126 feet in length, 19.9 feet in breadth, and displaced 178 tons gross.

ATLAS
August 1816 newspaper reports documented Captain N. Thomson of the British ship *Atlas*, lost on the Florida reef near Cape Florida on June 5, arrived at Port Glasgow aboard the *Ariel*, along with the captain of the *Martha Brae*, also wrecked near Cape Florida. The crew and a portion of her cargo were saved. Information from *Lloyd's Register* indicates there were two ships named *Atlas*, both 360 tons burden constructed of a single deck with beams and sheathed in copper, sailing from Greenock to Caribbean ports with Thomson or Thompson as master; one was built in 1802 and the other in 1810.

AUGUSTA WILSON
On January 28, 1886, the *Halifax Herald* reported that "out of eight or ten schooners employed in the lighthouse (Ponce de Leon Inlet Light Station) work, five have been wrecked, viz: *Godfrey*, *Augusta Wilson*, *Ajax*, *Freewind*, and the *Johnson*; the *Mary Brown*, now lying at the lighthouse dock, is crippled. We have been assured that nearly all of them received the injuries resulting in wrecks on the inlet bar or in the river. Six men have also been drowned."

AUTO WRECK
Located just offshore of a narrow, isolated stretch of beach on Hutchinson Island, the oddly named "Auto Wreck" was discovered by the Real Eight Company around 1965. The site yielded numerous artifacts during its initial salvage, including white and black marble tiles, terra cotta tiles, ship's rigging, and a sword in a scabbard, however, the mystery wreck has eluded identification.

AVIS
The yacht *Avis* sunk at the foot of 10th Street during the September 1926 Great Miami Hurricane[20]. It is unclear if the yacht was ultimately refloated and repaired or scrapped.

BABY DARLING

On the morning of December 2, 1960, Captain Jack T. Warren departed Daytona Beach aboard his 38-foot shrimp trawler *Baby Darling*. Amidst a roaring nor'easter, Warren tried to turn around near Ponce de Leon Inlet when the wind and heavy seas cast the trawler over a sandbar onto her side. Fortunately, the U.S. Coast Guard pulled Captain Warren and a crewman off the vessel just as the *Baby Darling* broke apart and disappeared under the breaking waves.

BABY RUTH

The yacht *Baby Ruth*, which was reportedly seized (likely for rum running) and tied up at Miami, was ultimately wrecked near the docks of the Peninsular and Oriental Steam Navigation Company at the foot of Northeast Sixth Street in the wake of the September 1926 Great Miami Hurricane[21].

BALLARD PINES WRECK

The unidentified "Ballard Pines Wreck" is also known as the "Bent Anchor Wreck" or the "Brass Telescope Wreck," the latter name originating from the recovery of a brass spyglass found by Carl Lazzeri working under contract for the Mel Fisher Center, Incorporated. Other recovered artifacts, including black glass and case gin bottles and stoneware pottery, indicate this wreck may have been one of several vessels lost in a hurricane in 1810. Like other wreck sites off Sebastian southward to Fort Pierce, the "Ballard Pines Wreck" has no central core per se, and wreckage and artifacts are scattered over a large area just offshore and south of Floridana Beach.

BARBARA ANN

Early on the morning of March 2, 1990, the shrimp trawler *Barbara Ann* sank after a collision with the 700-foot long tanker *Canopus*. The 77-foot long *Barbara Ann* was approximately 23 miles off Melbourne at the time of the incident, and subsequently sank two hours after the incident. The trawler's two crew members were safely picked up by another fishing vessel after they fired flares in the early morning darkness. Now a popular fishing site for anglers out of Port Canaveral and Sebastian, the wreck of the *Barbara Ann* rests over on her port side in 135 feet of water. The wreck of the former dragger, oriented with its bow pointed northward, is mostly intact and rises approximately 20 feet off the bottom.

BAREFOOT MAILMAN WRECK

In 1959, several divers recovered nine or ten cannon, buttons, cannon balls, and other artifacts from an unknown shipwreck off Pompano Beach they subsequently named the "Old Silver Wreck." During the construction of a condominium in 1965, several individuals employed a bulldozer to haul large sections of the wreck up on shore in search of more artifacts. What was once a fairly intact nearshore wreck with significant sections of hull planking and ballast in 10 to 20 feet of water was haphazardly dragged and scattered along the beach. Subsequent in-water salvage work conducted in 1967 resulted in the recovery of additional artifacts, including 57 brass sheathing tacks stamped with the British Broad Arrow, an English Admiralty anchor marked with the British Broad Arrow, and several brass regimental buttons embossed with the words "Republique Francaise." In later years the site became known as the "Barefoot Mailman Wreck" due to its proximity to the Barefoot Mailman Hotel.

While not confirmed, there is speculation this site may be the remains of the H.M.S. *Amaranthe*, which was lost in late October 1799. As the H.M.S. *Amaranthe* was formerly the French brig-sloop *L'Amaranthe*, the presence of both British and French artifacts may lend credence to this theory, though archival information indicates the vessel may have wrecked farther north. Another thought is the "Barefoot Mailman Wreck" may be the remains of *L'Athenaise*. Like H.M.S. *Amaranthe*, *L'Athenaise* was formerly a French vessel captured by the British Royal Navy. Yet, *L'Athenaise* was later employed as a cartel ship, which by law were not allowed to be armed. Therefore, the recovery of numerous cannon from this site casts doubt on this theory. While the dragging of the wreck in 1965 seriously impacted the integrity of the site, supposedly over half of the wreck sill remains in shallow water southeast of the Barefoot Mailman Hotel, though is likely buried under several feet of sand.

BEAR WRECK

The "Bear Wreck" is an unidentified wreck in approximately 105 feet of water offshore of St. Augustine. While numerous boilers are present on the site, all of which have settled deep in the sand, no engine is immediately apparent. Perhaps it has fallen over and is buried, or perhaps the wreck is the final resting spot of a steamer barge. If an engine can be found at the site, one potential suspect may be the freighter *Cotopaxi*, lost in late 1925 and discussed later in this work. Regardless, the site consists largely of pancaked hull plates resulting from the vessel resting on her port side. The wreck hosts abundant marine life, including numerous invasive lionfish.

Diver swimming over the wheelhouse of the trawler *Barbara Ann*.

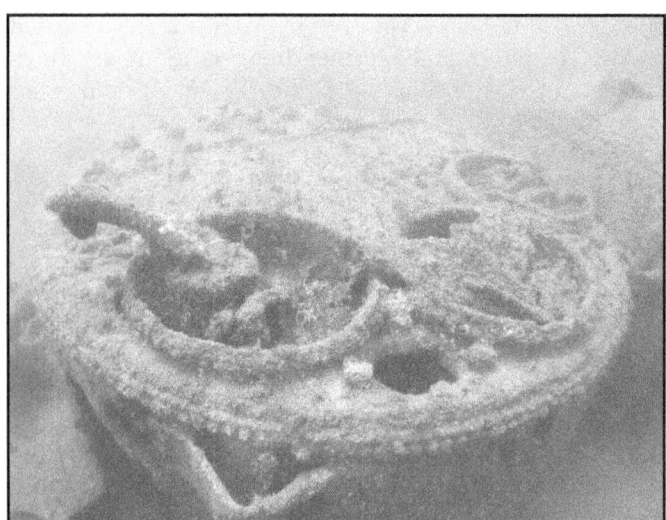
Upended boiler on the "Bear Wreck."

Portions of the "Bear Wreck's" bow with chain locker.

BELIEZE

According to the *London Chronicle* of January 16, 1777, the vessel *Belieze*, Captain Gelles, bound from Honduras to London, was lost on the coast of Florida on October 12, 1776.

BELLE OF TEXAS

During the summer of 1878, the steamer *Belle of Texas*, en route from New Orleans to run on the St. Johns River, went ashore in a gale two miles south of "Brown's Trail" opposite Hawks' Park (near New Smyrna). The wreck was stripped and the material was sold at auction in New Smyrna. "The wooden portion of the boat was purchased and brought to the mainland by Hart and Mendell, and considerable [sic] of the painted finishing is still in their lumber yards. In this way nearly every house on the coast comes to be partly made or finished off with wrecked lumber or parts of wrecks[22]."

The ship's bell was reportedly bought for $10 for use in the new Union church at New Smyrna. A February 1918 *New Smyrna News* article stated that a "pedestal of cement is to be erected at the corner of Faulkner and Washington streets, on which is to be placed the old bell which was taken from the wrecked steamer *Belle of Texas* some 40 years ago, and which was the first bell used to call the people to worship in this town."

BELLONA

The 16-gun privateer brigantine *Bellona*, Captain Harrison, from North Carolina, threw out most of her ballast while being pursued in December 1780 off St. Augustine. She eventually bilged on the south end of Anastasia Island after drifting onto the beach. One of her men drowned, and the others were taken prisoner at St. Augustine[23]. Additional information in the London Chronicle of February 17, 1781, stated Captain Murray of the 60th Regiment stationed at St. Augustine "saved the greatest part of her cannon, stores, etc."

BELZONA ONE

The 85-foot long tug *Belzona One* was sunk as an artificial reef in 70 feet of water on May 30, 1990. She was originally named *Mitza*, but over the course of her career she was known as *James G*, *Alco Caribe*, and *Holley*. After she was heavily damaged by a fire, she was eventually purchased by Belzona America, Incorporated, who then donated her to Miami-Dade County for use as an artificial reef. In 1992, Hurricane Andrew sheered off her upper deck, which is now lying in the sand next to the hull. The *Belzona One* rests off Key Biscayne in close proximity to two other tugs, the *Belzona Two* and *Belzona Three*, as well as the *Belcher Barge*.

Tug *Belzona One* (Miami-Dade County Department of Environmental Resources Management).

BELZONA TWO

The tug *Belzona Two*, official number 213149, was originally built as the *Henry E. Gillen* in 1915 at Ashtabula, Ohio, by the Great Lakes Engineering Works. The tug, equipped with a 400-horsepower steam engine, was 75 feet long, 20 feet wide, and displaced 96 tons. In 1917, she was inspected by the U.S. Navy and assigned identification ID-1789 for potential use as a patrol craft in World War I, but was never enrolled. During her long career, she changed

Belzona Two as the *Henry E. Gillen* (Historical Collections of the Great Lakes, Bowling Green State University).

hands and names several times: renamed *Lasalle* in 1922; the *John J. Roche* in 1940; in 1959 she became the *Barney Nelson*; the *Gayle K* in 1965, whereupon she was repowered with a 500-horsepower diesel engine; and in 1971, when acquired by Crocker Engineering, she was named the *Raven*. Ownership of the tug changed a few times in the 1970s, until she was dropped from documentation on December 14, 1979, and was laid up. On January 12, 1982, she was sold to Russell and Sandra Barnes of Miami, who redocumented the vessel two years later. The tug's service during this period is not accurately known, but supposedly she was involved in the Mariel Boat Lift from Cuba. Eventually, the old tugboat was sold into Honduran registry on August 6, 1990, and renamed the *Miramar Express*. Ultimately, Belzona America, Incorporated sponsored her as an artificial reef and she was sunk on February 4, 1991. She lies in 70 feet of water, approximately 150 feet west-northwest of *Belzona Three*.

Typically, there are rebar stakes in the sand guiding divers between the various wrecks in this area, which is known as the "Belzona Wreck Trek." While the tug is largely intact, Hurricane Andrew peeled open the amidships area. The 195-foot long upside down *Belcher Barge* can be found approximately 300 feet to the north-northwest, and from there divers can swim approximately 200 feet to the east to visit the *Hav Parker III* and *Schurger's Barge*.

BELZONA THREE

The last of three tugs donated by Belzona America, Incorporated, the 105-foot long *Belzona Three* was built in 1953 as the *Carinthia* for the LaFournier Towing Company. The tug worked for over 45 years until her engine gave out and she was deemed too expensive to refurbish. Byrd Diving and Salvage Company of Miami prepared the tug for use as an artificial reef. The vessel was renamed *Belzona Three*, and she was sunk on June 25, 1991. Approximately 100 feet due west of *Belzona One* and 150 feet east-southeast of *Belzona Two*, the *Belzona Three* is the largest and most intact of the three tugs.

BERNICE

The gas-powered freight vessel *Bernice* reportedly wrecked at Canal Point, on the eastern shore of Lake Okeechobee, during a storm in 1928. The 18-ton *Bernice*, official number 217648, built at Fort Lauderdale in 1918, was 63.5 feet long and 15.3 feet wide.

BEROSA

In an April 25, 1863, letter, Colonel Higginson of the First South Carolina Infantry revealed the fate of the Confederate steamer *Berosa* to Brigadier-General Saxton, U.S. Army. Colonel Higginson stated:

> My expedition up the St. Marys River last January was undertaken partly at the suggestion of Commander Hughes, U.S. Navy, of the gunboat *Mohawk*, to obtain information in regard to this very steamer. I ascertained that she was lying farther up the river than I could penetrate, waiting for new boilers, but that she was so old and worn out as to be utterly unserviceable.... She sailed from St. Marys on April 8, sprung a leak Thursday night, and after an unsuccessful attempt to save her by pumping and bailing, was abandoned by her crew Friday morning in the Gulf Stream; latitude 29° 50', longitude 79° 50'.

Additional information from another U.S. Army regiment to Admiral Dupont contradicted the above information, indicating the "vessel subsequently ran the blockade and foundered near shore, the crew barely escaping with their lives." The wreck of the *Berosa* has yet to be identified by divers.

Tug *Berry Patch* (Broward County Artificial Reef Program).

BERRY PATCH (1987)

The *Berry Patch* is a 65-foot tug sunk as an artificial reef off Hillsboro Inlet on August 15, 1987. She was originally built as the *A.L. Spencer* in 1940. The *Berry Patch* now lies in 70 feet of water with a slight list to port, and is in close proximity to several other artificial reefs: the *Ancient Mariner* is approximately 150 feet to the northwest, the 40-foot long workboat *C-Note* is approximately 100 feet to the

The wreck of the tug *Berry Patch*.

north, and the 50-foot long houseboat *Chuck-A-Luck II* is approximately 150 feet to the southwest. However, both the *C-Note* and the *Chuck-A-Luck II* are largely flattened and only consist of very low lying debris that may be hard to locate by divers in less than optimal visibility.

BERRY PATCH (1988)

Sharing the same name as the tug *Berry Patch* off Hillsboro Inlet, a 120-foot long freighter also called *Berry Patch* was sunk on October 1, 1988, off Pacific Reef south of Miami. The *Berry Patch*, reportedly the former coastal freighter *St. Joseph* built at Newcastle in 1944, was scuttled in 150 feet of water on the same day as the vessel *Hugo's April Fool*, which was sunk approximately 600 feet to the south. Additionally, the larger *Doc DeMilly* can be found resting between these two wrecks.

The small freighter *Berry Patch* is towed out to be sunk by U.S. Air Force f-4D fighters off Pacific Light (Miami-Dade County Department of Environmental Resources Management).

BERTHA RITTER

Built in 1899 at Jacksonville, the steamer tug *Bertha Ritter*, official number 3816, was 49.5 feet long, 13 feet wide, and displaced 27 tons gross. On February 25, 1911, the *Bertha Ritter* was consumed by fire off Black Point on the St. Johns River, which claimed one life.

BESSIE B.

The sharpie schooner *Bessie B.* was blown ashore the night of February 23, 1892, in a gale near Lake Worth Inlet; the vessel and cargo were reported to be a total loss[24]. The 13-ton schooner, approximately 50 feet in length, was owned by the Brelsford Brothers, and employed to transport cargo from Jacksonville for their general store at Lake Worth.

BETEK AR PEN

The *Betek Ar Pen* is reportedly the remains of a 70-foot long former dive boat that was scuttled as an artificial reef on June 6, 1997. She now rests in 110 feet of water, rising 15 feet off the bottom, and is immediately west of the 120-foot long freighter *St. Henry's Express*.

The derelict vesel *Betek Ar Pen* resting in front of the *Merci Rabbi* on the Miami River (Miami-Dade County Department of Environmental Resources Management).

BETSEY (1752)

On May 14, 1750, the *London Daily Advertiser* reported, "The *Live Oak*, Badger, arriv'd last Thursday at Bristol from South Carolina, and brings advice that the *Betsey*, Slater, was lost coming through the Gulph on the coast of Florida. She was coming from Jamaica, bound to Bristol; all the crew got into the boat and fortunately met with a sloop bound to Providence, which took them all up, and carried them save to that island. There were also (unreadable) other ships lost, but of what nation is not known."

BETSEY (1787)

The sloop *Betsey*, Captain Grant, en route from Nassau, Bahamas to Florida, was reportedly lost on the Mosquito Bar (Ponce de Leon Inlet) on October 25, 1787; of the 16 souls onboard, only 4 escaped with their lives[25].

BETSEY (1812)

The British ship *Betsey*, Captain Telley, sailing from St. Vincent, was reported as wrecked and a total loss at Amelia Island in 1812[26]. This vessel is most likely the 59-ton Newfoundland brig *Besty*, Captain S. Selly, built in 1804.

BETTY'S HOPE

On December 12, 1737, the *Betty's Hope*, Captain Souers, bound from Jamaica to London, was lost near Cape Florida; the master and most of the crew got to South Carolina[27].

BEVERLY M.

The *Beverly M.* was a derelict 85-foot long tugboat abandoned in the mud of Taylor Creek off the Indian River, which was later sunk as an artificial reef 10 miles offshore Fort Pierce on June 4, 1987. She was supposedly scuttled in 60 feet of water; however, the LORAN coordinates associated with the wreck place it in much deeper water. Therefore, either the cited depth is incorrect or the coordinates for the wreck are inaccurate.

BIG LADY

On May 11, 1960, the 67-foot shrimp trawler *Big Lady* foundered off Nassau Sound, towards the southern end of Amelia Island. The 99-ton *Big Lady* was built as hull number 193 by the Diesel Engine Sales Company (DESCO Marine, Incorporated) at their St. Augustine shipyard.

BIG AL

The *Big Al* is a 69-foot long, 19-foot wide tug built in 1954, which was sunk as an artificial reef on February 24, 2010. The tug had undergone repairs at American Custom Yachts in Stuart, but the owner was unable to pay the subsequent bill. The yard foreclosed on the owners after the tug sat idle for a year, and then donated the vessel to the Martin County Anglers Club. The *Big Al*, dedicated as *Glasrud Reef* in appreciation of developer Tom Glasrud's financial assistance on the project, now rests upright in approximately 190 feet of water nine nautical miles off St. Lucie Inlet.

BIJOU

On November 2, 1891, the American sloop yacht *Bijou* capsized in Biscayne Bay, "throwing her two occupants overboard. They clung to the overturned boat until it reached shore, whence they were taken by keeper to station and cared for[28]."

BILL BOYD

The 424-ton freighter *Bill Boyd* was originally christened the *Heino* on March 8, 1964, at Neuenfelde, Germany. The freighter sailed under several names during the course of her life: *Maude Wonsild* for Wonsild and Son of København, Denmark; *Maude Isa* for J.F. Staal of Allerød, Denmark; *Hehmberto*; *Marilyn*; and finally *Nata* for Arc Navigation. The freighter was ultimately renamed the *Bill Boyd* after a well-known fisherman and owner of Boyds's Bait and Tackle Shop in Fort Lauderdale prior to its sinking. Deployed as an artificial reef on July 18, 1986, the 211-foot long freighter now rests silently on the bottom in 280 feet of water.

Bill Boyd as *Maude Isa* (David Gallicham).

Dramatic sinking of the *Bill Boyd* (Broward County Artificial Reef Program).

Divers can find an old pickup truck in the forward cargo hold, its hood missing and engine exposed. Additionally, several shipping containers can be found in the forward and aft holds. The wreck is similar to several other coastal freighters utilized by various artificial reef programs off Florida. While invertebrate and gorgonian growth is not as luxurious as that found on shallower wrecks, amberjack, grouper, and snapper are commonly encountered around the *Bill Boyd*.

BILL NYE

The American schooner *Bill Nye* was constructed in April 1893 at the Madison, Maryland, shipyard of J.W. Brooks and Son. The schooner registered 80 tons gross, and was 82 feet in length, 24.3 feet in breadth, and 6.6 feet in depth of hold. The *Bill Nye* reportedly stranded at Fernandina on August 7, 1933.

BIRD ISLAND WRECK

Just to the north of Bird Island, at the entrance to Nassau Inlet, rests the lower hull of a large unidentified sailing vessel. Based on the estimated size of the site, potential identities for the "Bird Island Wreck" include the schooners *Gracie D. Buchanan*; *Jessie A. Bishop*, and *Theoline*, which were all just less than 200 feet in length.

BISCAYNE (1897A)

The initial report of the wrecking of the schooner *Biscayne* was reported in the *Florida Times-Union* on February 4, 1897: "The schooner *Biscayne* is a wreck on Sebastian beach with three of the five crew members drowned. It was lost while carrying hay and general merchandise from Jacksonville to Bay [sic]."

Additional details appeared in *The Marble Rock Weekly* on February 11, 1897, which stated, "Capt. Harry (also reported as Henry) Fozzard, of the wrecked schooner *Biscayne*, and Dan Deitz, the mate, arrived in Jacksonville Wednesday night. The schooner foundered ten miles off Jupiter Inlet last Saturday night (January 30, 1897) and Charles Hinson, of New York, Archie Lindsay, of Florida, and Roger Harris, of Key West, were drowned in attempting to leave the vessel."

BISCAYNE (1897B)

Coincidentally to the wrecking of the aforementioned schooner *Biscayne*, which came to grief in late January 1897, later that year there was a reported loss of a dredge vessel of the same name, which had been working on the Intracoastal Waterway in South Florida. An October 1897 newspaper account stated, "E.B. King, telegraph operator at Jupiter, wires Broward's *Three Friends* is anchored a mile north of the inlet and her tow, the dredge *Biscayne*, is ashore on rocky coast and breaking up. The life-saving crew took the men off the dredge. The tug *Three Friends* brought the dredge up from the New River (Fort Lauderdale). Weather grew worse and worse. Dredge anchored but the cables parted."

BISCAYNE (1974)

The 120-foot long freighter *Biscayne* was stripped and intentionally sunk in 60 feet of water as an artificial reef in December 1974 near Key Biscayne. Just to the east of the *Biscayne* is the wreck of the 100-foot long freighter *Miracle Express*. The *Miracle Express* was sunk several hundred yards offshore of the *Biscayne*, but Hurricane Andrew moved her into the side of the *Biscayne*, ripping the *Biscayne's* stern section loose, and significantly impacting the structural integrity of the *Miracle Express*. Due to her shallow depth and the fact that she has been underwater for 30 years, the *Biscayne* has been completely covered by corals, sponges, and other invertebrate growth.

BLACK GOLD

Black Gold was a yacht reportedly seized (likely for rum running) and tied up at Miami, which was later wrecked near the docks of the Peninsular and Oriental Steam Navigation Company at the foot of Northeast Sixth Street in the wake of the September 1926 Great Miami Hurricane[29].

BLOCKADE RUNNER WRECK

This wreck, believed to be a schooner, was reportedly named after a gold watch with inscribed information on the inside cover that apparently dated the wreck to the Civil War era[30]. The "Blockade Runner Wreck" consists of two main piles resting in an almost north-south orientation. Broken bottles and dishes have been found here. Based on Meylach's map, the wreck should rest just inshore of Ajax Reef in 15 feet of water.

BLOOMER

The New York Daily Times reported the fate of the schooner *Bloomer* on December 23, 1853, documenting, "The schooner *Bloomer*, of Frankfort, Maine, bound with a cargo of lumber from Mayport Mills, Florida, to Martinique, sprung a leak on December 11, 1853, and was beached the following day, 25 miles south of St. Johns Bar. The captain and crew were saved, but the vessel and cargo were a total loss." Other reports had the *Bloomer* wrecking on December 10, 1853, and only 12 miles below the St. Johns Bar.

BLUE CHINA WRECK

Approximately 1,200 feet beneath the Atlantic Ocean's Gulf Stream current off the Florida/Georgia coast, the wreck site known as the "Blue China Wreck" was first investigated by Odyssey Marine Exploration in early 2003, based on information supplied by a trawl fisherman who had recovered various artifacts in his net. At that time, the site consisted of a large, low-lying mound some 100 feet long by 30 feet wide, with a relief of approximately 15 feet at the center. A large quantity of extant hull structure was noted beneath the sand bottom, indicating a wooden-planked and -framed vessel. The fact that there was no visible evidence of machinery suggested a sailing ship. The long axis of the site runs roughly north-south, with two encrusted anchors at the south end. No wood was present beneath the anchors. Many encrusted masses of iron were scattered about the site, but the mound itself consisted primarily of a large quantity of porcelain and bottles. The site consisted of a debris field containing an estimated 2,500 items spread over cross timbers from a lower deck, which protruded from the bottom sediments. A considerable number of items from the cargo appeared

Ginger jar and leather shoe recovered from the "Blue China Wreck."

Examples of blue flow ware from the "Blue China Wreck."

Listing bow section of the *Blue Fire* resting on the bottom.

to have survived intact, including stacks of porcelain and pottery and dark colored glass bottles. More specifically, the stacked cargo included blue flow ware "chargers," or, large rectangular platters, large shallow serving bowls of similar design, and smaller plates or bowls of the same type. Also observed were heavy, dark green glass bottles, similar to those known to have been used for alcoholic beverages, scattered "ginger jars," also bearing the "blue flow" design, flat-sided clear drinking glasses, stoneware pottery that may have been ship's stores rather than cargo, large pitchers with sharp pouring spouts with banded patterns of decoration, and possible elements of ship's tackle. Based on their initial observations, Odyssey concluded the wreck site likely represented the lower portions of a medium-sized nineteenth century wooden merchant vessel, possibly a coastal trader.

A return to the wreck in 2005 found trawlers had significantly impacted the site, and there appeared to be little left that was undisturbed. The remaining ship's structure had been largely flattened, with only a few relatively deep crevices in the hull preserving some remnants of stratigraphy below the disturbance of trawl activity. The cargo also appeared to be even more dispersed, with more of the artifacts chipped or broken. If nothing else, this site demonstrates yet another destructive influence on submerged shipwrecks aside from storms, currents, and teredo worms.

BLUE FIRE

In late June 1980, the 183-foot long freighter *Blue Fire* traveled to Cuba as part of a "Freedom Flotilla" during the Mariel Boat Lift, and was expected to leave the Communist island with up to 5,000 refugees thought to be headed for Florida. However, the freighter was intercepted by the U.S. Coast Guard on July 5, 1980, approximately 37 miles south of Cuba as it steamed for the Cayman Islands after departing from Mariel Harbor. Mysteriously, when it appeared at Miami on July 9 under Coast Guard escort, the vessel held no exiles and was occupied only by its seven crewmen. Seized by the U.S. government, the *Blue Fire* was eventually transferred for use as an artificial reef.

The wreck of the freighter *Blue Fire* is testament to the power of an intense hurricane. Less than 10 years after its deployment as an artificial reef near Fowey Rocks in January 1983, Hurricane Andrew smashed into the hull of the freighter. The wreck was significantly impacted: the aft bridge superstructure was ripped from the lower hull and stern; amidships, the cargo hold reveals a prominent bend, as the storm swell attempted to fold the vessel in half; and the bow is kicked hard over to starboard. The *Blue Fire* rests in 120 feet of water in close proximity to some interesting coral reef habitat, which attracts thick schools of tropical fish species.

Diver over the *Blue Fire*.

BOBBY'S BOYS

The loss of the shrimp trawler *Bobby's Boys* was reported in the *Daytona Beach News-Journal*, July 30, 1996:

> A rock shrimp boat from Port Canaveral caught fire and exploded about 40 miles northeast of Ponce de Leon Inlet on Sunday as its crew watched from a nearby rescue boat. Coast Guard Senior Chief Ken Parks said Monday other boats had

picked up the wooden shrimper's four crew members, and none were injured. He said the Coast Guard's 41-foot vessel, based at the Ponce de Leon Inlet station here, headed for the disabled shrimper about 11 a.m. and poured water on the blazing 71-foot *Bobby's Boys*. Parks said his guardsmen seemed to be extinguishing the fire when "something on the interior of the boat blew up and shot flames about 25 feet in the air. That re-ignited the fire." Parks said the explosion may have been caused by the boat's propane tanks. The *Bobby's Boys* was still afloat and burning about 5:45 p.m. when the Coast Guard decided further firefighting efforts were futile and returned to the station with the shrimper's crew.... A Coast Guard helicopter dispatched Monday from Savannah spotted only an oil slick, debris and a life raft at the approximate location of the shrimper, Parks said.

The final resting spot of the *Bobby's Boys* has not been positively identified, though likely consists of the charred lower hull of the trawler, along with some associated machinery.

BONNE ADELLE

The demise of the *Bonne Adelle* was reported in *The Edinburgh Advertiser* on April 27, 1819: "The *Bonne Adelle*, from Havannah [sic], was wrecked on the Florida Coast 5th February. Crew saved."

BONNIE BIRD

According to *The Monthly Nautical Magazine and Quarterly Review* (Volume 2, Number 5, August 1855), the six-month old brig *Bonnie Bird* was abandoned June 3, 1855, approximately 12 miles northeast of St. Johns, Florida.

BORNEO

The Sailor's Magazine and Naval Journal, Volume 25, reported the brig *Borneo*, Captain Hodgdon, bound for Jacksonville, went ashore on the St. Johns Bar sometime before October 5, 1852, and became a total loss.

BOSTON EXPRESS

The passenger and RO-RO ("Roll On – Roll Off") cargo vessel *Boston Express* (IMO number 6520478) was built 1965, and was 196 feet in length and displaced 1,099 gross tons. On September 15, 2003, the *Boston Express* was towed approximately 22 miles offshore of Miami by Resolve Marine Group and scuttled in 2,200 feet of water. The vessel had been abandoned on the Miami River for over six years by its owners, who had ignored repeated demands by the U.S. Coast Guard to remove the potential navigational risk and environmental threat.

BOTTLE WRECK

Over time, this unidentified wreck has disintegrated to the point that no readily apparent remains of a vessel can be found at this site aside from a scattering of ballast rocks. The name of the wreck originates from the number of bottles recovered from the area in the 1950s, many of which were seltzer water "bullet bottles," named because of the rounded bottom that resembles a bullet. The bottles were embossed with the following in raised print: "MEDICATED AERATED WATERS, CANTRELL COCHRANE, BELFAST & DUBLIN." In addition, Gene Shinn recovered a single 400-pound cannon from the site in August 1957. The wreck reportedly can be found just inshore a rocky outcrop on Brewster Reef. Similar to other wrecks included in Meylach (1971), the cited coordinates in this book are based on estimated positions originating from the Meylach's ranges and maps, and may be slightly inaccurate. Patience, perseverance, and a keen eye will likely be required to find some of these old wrecks resting in Biscayne National Park.

BOW WOW

On November 25, 1934, the *Sarasota Herald* reported the shrimp boat *Bow Wow* was found wrecked and overturned near Ponce de Leon Inlet on November 24. The two fishermen aboard the shrimper were believed drowned.

BOXCAR WRECK

The unidentified "Boxcar Wreck" can be found inshore of Long Reef in about 15 feet of water. Typical of many wrecks in Biscayne National Park, it is distinguished by a sand "halo" directly around the wreck, which is then surrounded by dense seagrass. Wooden timbers appear as a dark rectangular mass in the center of the sandy pocket, which gives the site its name[31]. The timbers of the former vessel were secured with large bronze rods, most of which were salvaged in the 1950s for scrap.

BRANDY WINE

The *Brandy Wine* is one of four vessels sunk as artificial reefs in an area off Key Biscayne known as U.S. Customs Reef. The vessel was reportedly built in 1949, and was 135 feet in length, 22 feet in beam, and displaced 161 gross tons. The *Brandy Wine*, along with the *Miguana*, *Etoile De Mer*, and the

Brandy Wine (Matthew W. Hoelscher).

Tacoma, were seized by the U.S. Customs Service due to their use in smuggling drugs into Florida via the Miami River. On February 12, 2001, Customs inspectors discovered a false compartment under a waste oil tank in the forward cargo hold of the *Brandy Wine*.

The *Brandy Wine* was sent to the bottom following the detonation of scuttling charges on July 13, 2001. She now rests upright and intact in 145 feet of water. The small wheelhouse and superstructure grace the bow of the vessel. Swimming west off the stern of the *Brandy Wine*, divers will encounter the 101-foot long *Miguana*.

BRECONSHIRE

The wreck of the *Breconshire* lay just offshore Vero Beach, discernible by the presence of a large boiler that extends above the surface of the water, which marks her final resting place. The wreck of the *Breconshire* was notable because of the total lack of drama or tragedy associated with the event. Constructed in November 1883 as a three-masted, iron-hulled steamer at the shipyard of Sunderland Shipbuilding Company, Limited, of Sunderland, England, she initially sailed under the name *Numida* for the shipping firm of Porteus and Senior. She was capable of carrying a great deal of cargo for her time, boasting a length of 299.7 feet, a beam of 37.2 feet, and displacing 2,544 tons. Graced with two decks, she was powered by a 250 horsepower compound engine produced by Blair and Company, Limited, of Stockton, England. In 1887, her name was changed to *Breconshire* upon being sold to Jenkins and Company. On October 5, 1893, the *Breconshire* became the sole boat of the newly formed firm of Breconshire Steamship, Limited, though she was managed by the firm of Thompson, Elliot, and Company. The freighter's normal trade routes carried her from England to various ports in the Mediterranean, far from her current resting spot off Florida.

In February 1894, Captain Robert Taylor and the *Breconshire* departed England for ports in Italy and Sicily. After transferring cargo, the freighter left the Mediterranean for New York. While at New York, Captain Taylor learned that he was to proceed to Tampa. As the captain was not familiar with the eastern seaboard of the United States, he obtained charts for his upcoming cruise. Leaving New York harbor on April 25, the southbound *Breconshire* headed in ballast towards the warmer waters of Florida. Unfortunately, Captain Taylor found out en route that the charts he received were incomplete, and he now totally lacked any documentation on the area just south of Cape Canaveral. Passing the light of Cape Canaveral on the evening of April 29, the vessel changed to a southwesterly course in order to parallel the retreating coastline. Captain Taylor retired for the night with orders to be awakened at 1:00 a.m. in order to make a change in their course. The moonless night made it difficult for the lookouts to observe any hazards. It was noted, however, that just before midnight a dark area was visible to starboard, though this was dismissed as the wind working the surface of the water. At 1:00 a.m., the second officer ordered for the captain to be raised as he requested, and

Image of the steamer *Glamorganshire* – sistership of the *Breconshire* (Mark Mondano Collection).

while the captain acknowledged the message, he failed to come to the bridge. Shortly thereafter, the second officer sighted land that he estimated to be five to six miles off the starboard rail. Unfortunately, he decided not to summon the captain nor did he take soundings to learn the depth of water in which the vessel was traveling. At approximately 2:00 a.m., Captain Taylor appeared on the bridge to feel the ship grind to a halt beneath him. The *Breconshire* had run hard aground, and all attempts to move her off failed.

Early in the morning on April 30, the keeper of the Bethel Creek Life-Saving Station, along with local residents that heard the steam whistle of the *Breconshire* sound, learned of the stranded vessel. Upon daybreak, the crew of the steamer launched lifeboats and began to work the anchor cables in order to try to pull the vessel off the reef. It became apparent later that afternoon that all efforts were in frustration; the steamer was taking on water. The order to abandon ship was given calmly by Captain Taylor. The rest of the week was spent securing the ship's stores and personal effects of the crew. The crew removed the ship's compasses, dismantled the ship's rigging, and finally salvaged all items of value by May 3, 1894. With the wreck firmly embedded and with no hopes of being refloated, the ship was condemned on May 4. The next week witnessed the local residents proceed to scrounge through the wreck and recovering any remaining items they deemed valuable. On May 10, 1894, the wreck of the *Breconshire* was sold at auction for $301. The *Breconshire* was subjected to further salvage when professional wreckers from Key West and Jacksonville visited the site later that month.

Resting in approximately 20 feet of water amongst the hard bottom area where the vessel ran aground, the wreck site, also known as the "Boiler Wreck," provides an easy site to investigate the remains of a nineteenth century steamship. Due to its proximity to shore, the site is best dove during periods of calm weather. Moving south from the boiler, a diver will encounter the sanded-in remains of the ship's hull and framework. The amidships mast and some rigging can be observed about 40 feet south of the boiler. About 100 feet from the boiler, with the mast at about the midpoint, the bow can be found rising close to the surface. Winches and associated machinery are still present in this area, as well as a spare anchor that is still secure on the deck. A second anchor can be found just offshore of this section of the wreck. The engine and stern wreckage can be found to the north of the boilers, though the propeller is absent. As the wreck resides in shallow water, bathed by high nutrients and sunlight, the *Breconshire* has become thickly overgrown with encrustation. Corals and other invertebrates are found on every available portion of the wreckage. Abundant marine life and the seasonal appearance of lobster make this an appealing dive, in addition to the historical attraction that the wreck provides.

BREWSTER

On the evening of March 16, 1848, the 696-ton ship *Brewster*, carrying a cargo of cotton, lard, pork, and hemp, came to grief on the Florida Reef near Fowey Rocks. Admiralty Records at Key West from April 1848 (*John Curry at al. vs. the Cargo and Materials Saved From Ship Brewster*) provide the basic details on the loss of the vessel from Captain Thatcher thusly, "…on a voyage from New Orleans for Boston, as a consequence of hazy weather which obscured the land and a strong and unknown westwardly current in the Gulf, the existence of which is unknown to mariners generally struck on a reef to the northward of Carysfort Reef called the Fowey Rocks at the time specified in said libel and almost immediately bilged." While the wreck of the *Brewster* has not been positively located, it is quite possible that it resides on Brewster Reef, which is located to the immediate south of Fowey Rocks and was likely named following the loss of this vessel. Interestingly, Martin Meylach documented a wreck named the "Bottle Wreck" on Brewster Reef, which might be worth investigating.

BRICK WRECK

Resting very close to the north Fort Pierce Inlet jetty is an unidentified wreck named after the abundance of bricks found at the site. According to Tom Gore, the vessel was carrying English immigrants at the time of its loss sometime in the nineteenth century, but I have been unable to find information indicating how he came to that conclusion. No other information is available on the shipwreck, but the site definitely begs for additional investigation.

BRICKYARD WRECK

The "Brickyard Wreck," named after the site's proximity to Brickyard Landing on the St. Marys River, is an unidentified steamer wreck estimated to be 80-90 feet in length discovered by divers Howard Tower, Paul Hart, and Jim Lee in August 1984. The screw-powered, copper-sheathed vessel appears to have burned, which may have led to its sinking. This is further supported by the presence of extensive cultural material when first discovered, which included numerous pieces of china and a silver-plated spoon, indicating the vessel was not merely stripped and abandoned. One artifact was enscribed "Brown Brothers, Chicago," and the latest patent date found on material from the wreck was March 27, 1855. The wreck is located close to shore in 10-15 feet of water on the Florida side of the St. Marys River and approximately 13 miles upstream from where I-95 crosses the Florida-Georgia border.

BRITANNIA

According to Mowat (1964), the sloop *Britannia* was blown up on the St. Marys River in August 1776 by American forces. While I found reference to a sloop *Britannia*, Captain J. Yeomans, in Philadelphia during 1775, I have been unable to find any information regarding its reported loss on the St. Marys River in 1776.

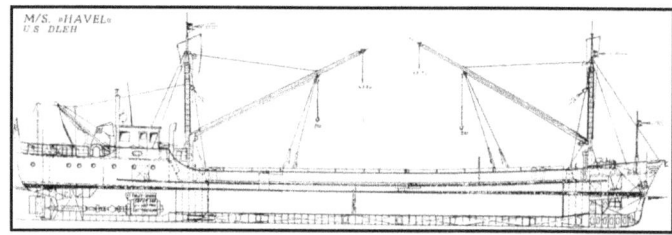

General arrangement plans of the coastal freighter *Budweiser Bar* built as the *Havel* (Mike Gray).

BUDWEISER BAR

The *Budweiser Bar* was named after the company that donated funding to help prepare the coastal freighter *Olive M.* for use as an artificial reef. Originally built in 1968 as the *Havel* by German shipbuilder *Deutsche Industriewerke A.G.*, she was 168.9 feet long, 27.9 feet wide, and displaced 384 tons gross. In 1977, the vessel was sold to the Bahamian company Miami Caicos Shipping, Limited, and renamed the *Olive M.* She was eventually appropriated by the Palm Beach County Artificial Reef Program, who razed the superstructure prior to scuttling the vessel on July 16, 1987. The wreck of the *Budweiser Bar* rests in close proximity to both the *Captain Tony* and the *Castor*. Departing from the stern of the *Budweiser Bar*, divers swimming approximately 600 feet to the northwest along a concrete rubble trail will encounter the *Captain Tony*; swimming approximately 500 feet to the east-northeast, divers will find the *Castor*. Scattered remains of the 70-foot salvage boat *Swordfish* can also be found off the bow of the *Budweiser Bar* wreck.

BULK TRADER

The *Bulk Trader* was a 180-foot long offshore supply vessel originally built in 1970 as the *Eastern Worker* at the Houston shipyard of Mangone Shipbuilding. The 337-ton work vessel was originally destined for the Gulf of Mexico oil fields, but eventually was employed as a coastal freighter throughout the Caribbean. During her three-

Diver over the *Budweiser Bar* wreck.

decade career, she changed names several times: *Harold Tide* in 1974, *Balboa* and then *Atlas VI* in 1985, *Maya Trader* in 1989, and finally, *Bulk Trader* in 1992. On October 4, 2002, the *Bulk Trader* was scuttled in 320 feet of water off Fort Lauderdale to serve as an artificial reef. Due to her depth, few divers have visited her. The wreck provides 40 feet of relief and likely supports numerous deepwater species like snowy and warsaw grouper.

BURROUGHS

The *Burroughs* was a British merchant vessel that departed Port Royal, Jamaica, on August 23, 1696, in a convoy of 12 vessels led by the British frigate H.M.S. *Hampshire* bound for London; also in the convoy was the barkentine *Reformation* and *Nantwich*, included later in this work. On September 23, after being separated from the other ships in the convoy during a gale, the *Burroughs* lost her masts and was wrecked between Cape Canaveral and Jupiter Inlet. It should be noted in Jonathan Dickinson's chronicle of the event, he mentioned passing the wreck of the *Nantwich*, as well as joining the survivor's of the *Nantwich* in present-day Vero Beach, but he did not mention spotting wreckage or survivors of the *Burroughs*.

CABANO

According to *The Miami News* of March 18, 1965, the 400-foot long freighter *Cabano* sank 18 miles off Miami en route to the Dominican Republic. Captain Hernando Golindo reported the vessel lost power and began taking on water at 2:00 a.m. and sank around 4:00 a.m. The six-man crew was rescued by the 38-foot long fishing vessel *Lady Poe* off Pompano Beach five hours after abandoning ship. The *Cabano*, owned by United States Panamanian Maritime Corporation was loaded with refrigerators, commercial equipment, and other general cargo.

CADILLAC

According to Davis (1925), the tug *Cadillac* sank at Palatka. Exact details of the vessel's service and demise are unknown.

CAICOS EXPRESS

The *Caicos Express* was launched as the *Waalborg* from the Makkum, Netherlands shipyard of C. Amels and Zoon on July 12, 1956. The Dutch coaster was 188.4 feet long, 29 feet wide, and 499 tons gross. After 18 years with her original owners, *E. Wagenborg's Scheepvaart & Expeditiebedrijf N.V.*, the *Waalborg* was sold on March 11, 1974, to Greek owners Palships Limited and renamed *Paleoupolis*. In 1981, she was sold to Cox Shipping Line, Limited in the Turks and Caicos Islands, renamed *Caicos Express*, and was promptly employed on a route between the islands and Miami. In addition to hauling cargo, the vessel appeared in four episodes of the television drama "Miami Vice." Broward County and the Pompano Beach Fishing Rodeo eventually purchased and prepared the freighter for sinking as an artificial reef, which occurred three miles south of Hillsboro Inlet on November 12, 1985. The *Caicos Express* settled on the bottom in approximately 240 feet of water two minutes after scuttling charges were detonated.

With a stern wheelhouse and engine room, as well as large forward cargo holds, the wreck of the *Caicos Express* is basically a clone of numerous other freighters sunk as artificial reefs off South Florida. Several large spools of thick cable scattered about the deck of the holds appear to be the only cargo. The following year, Broward County also sunk 160 pari-mutuel betting machines approximately 200 feet away from the wreck.

CAIRN

According to *The Times* of April 16, 1860, the *Cairn*, from Minatitlán, Mexico, sank on March 15, 1860, off Cape Canaveral; all hands saved. This vessel is possibly the 228-ton, iron-hulled schooner *Cairn*, built in 1858.

CALICO

The *Calico* was a former U.S. Navy, wooden-hulled minesweeper with a documented length of 124.8 feet and displacement of 234 tons. After she outlived her military usefulness, she was sold to private interests and converted into a trawler to pursue calico scallops off Cape Canaveral, eventually sinking on December 29, 1974, at approximate latitude 28° 18.5' north and longitude 80° 20' west. It is likely the final resting spot of the *Calico* is known locally as the *Calico Jack*, which is a wreck in 65 feet of water in fairly close proximity of the *Calico's* reported sinking location.

CALLIOPE

On March 23, 1926, the *Oakland Tribune* published details on the wrecking of the sloop yacht *Calliope*:

> The sloop rigged yacht *Calliope*, a 55-foot boat owned by W.E.D. Stokes Jr., son of the New York hotel magnate, was beached on Merritt Island, four miles north of Cape Canaveral, Fla., on the morning of March 15 after a three-day battle with the sea, coast guardsmen announced here last night. Stokes and his crew of two men were landed safely. The party was brought here and young Stokes left for Washington immediately, guardsmen declared. The yacht, abandoned where it beached, has not been moved. The landing followed a fight of three days and nights against an Atlantic gale, part of the time without sail or rudder. The following is a detailed sketch of the boat's fatal trip, as related by guardsmen:
>
> The *Calliope*, with Stokes and two other men aboard, started north from Miami, late in the afternoon of March 11, and the same night was struck by a terrific gale. The foresail was carried away and the sheet blocks were wrecked with great seas breaking over the boat. On the twelfth, the sails were repaired and the journey resumed with the motor running. The position of the boat at that time was estimated at 160 miles off the shore. A steamer hailed the small craft during the

Caicos Express just prior to her scuttling (Broward County Artificial Reef Program).

afternoon and after several attempts succeeded in passing a line around the foremast of the *Calliope*. The wind increased to gale proportions and the seas became monstrous. The steamer made an attempt to anchor and then the tow line broke. The *Calliope* lay to all night with a heavy sea breaking over her. The pumps were worked continuously, the water coming up to a level with the salon floor every two hours. The *Calliope* worked closer to the shore on the next day. On the morning of the fourteenth land was sighted and an effort made to reach Cape Canaveral. Off Mosquito Inlet the *Calliope* signaled for help but received no response. The sea was breaking high over the bar and the schooner was unable to enter the eight foot channel. The boat anchored a mile or so off shore and four miles north of the cape on the fourteenth. Practically out of gas with the motor beginning to 'cough,' not daring to risk the shoals to the south at night, two anchors were dropped, one with all the rope available, and the other with all the chain. The next morning the improvised sails were torn beyond repair and the motor refused to run. After a great deal of effort the last anchor was raised and the boat drifted towards the shore. The vessel refused to answer the helm and could not be brought to the winds. The rudder was gone. The boat touched shore and an hour later was buffeted into a complete wreck.

CAMUSI

The iron-hulled sternwheel steamer *Camusi*, official number 126805, was built in 1891 at Wilmington, North Carolina. She registered a length of 94 feet, a beam of 22.3 feet, and a displacement of 130 tons gross. According to the *1895 Annual Report of the Supervising Inspector-General, U.S. Steamboat-Inspection Service to the Secretary of Commerce and Labor*, on January 28 (also reported as January 26[32]), 1894, the steamer *Camusi* burned at her wharf at Palatka due to a fire of unknown origin. The vessel, valued at $5,000, proved to be a total loss.

CANADIAN WRECK

The "Canadian Wreck" was inadvertently discovered during the placement of an outfall pipe on the immediate south side of Hillsboro Inlet. During excavation of the outfall pipe trench, wood timbers with bronze fasteners were dug up and exposed. Apparently, the head of the bronze spikes were shaped like an arrowhead. Additional anecdotal information indicates a ballast pile was also known to exist in this area during the 1960s, but may now be buried under the beach.

CANNON PILE WRECK

The "Cannon Pile Wreck" is a site found approximately four and a half miles south of Sebastian Inlet that may represent one of the lost 1715 fleet vessels, a section from another wreck such as the "Anchor Wreck" just to the north, or perhaps a shipwreck totally unrelated to the 1715 disaster. The site rests in 12 to 18 feet of water 300 feet off the beach, just beyond the first reef line. Salvors have found over 12 cannon at the site, as well as ballast, eighteenth century era hand grenades, bar shot, and axe heads. Due to the recovery of material different than that typically found on the nearby 1715 shipwrecks, including several small iron cannon with dolphin-style lift rings, the latter scenario may be the best fit for this site. One potential theory is that the "Cannon Pile Wreck" is a salvage vessel of English origin lost in the 1730s or 1740s. The "Cast Iron Ballast Wreck" can be found approximately 500 feet offshore of the "Cannon Pile Wreck."

CAPE CHARLES

The shrimp trawler *Cape Charles*, built in 1945 at Fernandina, was 53.2 feet long, 16.1 feet wide, and displaced 33 tons. On November 26, 1962, the *Cape Charles* stranded on the beach a few miles above Cape Canaveral's north gate (approximate latitude 28° 36.1' north) during a strong nor'easter[33]. She began taking on water 24 hours earlier as the storm's constant pounding started ripping boards loose from the hull.

CAPTAIN BARTLETT

The *Captain Bartlett* was a 194-ton, 100-foot long, 33-foot wide dredge built in 1925 that burned at Miami on January 21, 1930.

Trawler *Captain A.B.* aground on Ponte Vedra Beach, December 2005 (U.S. Coast Guard).

CAPTAIN DAN

One of the more popular dive sites off Broward County, the *Captain Dan* rests upright and intact in 110 feet of water. The superstructure allows ample exploration potential, while a large hatch on the forward deck beckons divers towards the interior. Since her deployment, abundant gorgonian colonies and other encrusting

Captain Dan as the U.S.C.G.C. *Hollyhock* (U.S. Coast Guard).

organisms have colonized the wreck. The large vessel has significant relief, with the bridge towering off the bottom 40 feet. Named after Captain Dan Garnsey upon its reefing, the *Captain Dan* originally served as the U.S. Coast Guard buoy tender *Hollyhock*.

The U.S. Lighthouse Service designed the Hollyhock Class coastwise tender in 1934. Destined for construction and repair work, tending aids to navigation, and supplying remote light stations, the vessels measured 175 feet in length, 32 feet in breadth, and displaced 885 tons. The first ship of the class, *Hollyhock*, was launched in the midst of a strong blizzard on March 25, 1937, at the Defoe Boat and Motor Works, in Bay City, Michigan. The *Hollyhock* commenced duty based out of her first homeport in Milwaukee, Wisconsin. In 1939, the U.S. Coast Guard absorbed the U.S. Lighthouse Service. The *Hollyhock*, now designated WAGL-220, continued to serve in the Great Lakes region, finally transferring to her last station at Miami in 1962. The *Hollyhock* spent the next two decades serving along the South Florida coast, as well as at U.S. facilities in the Bahamas and Cuba. During her long career, she received commendations for her service in World War II and Korea, as well as service ribbons for her participation in the Mariel Boat Lift. A 1980 evaluation of the *Hollyhock*, however, reported the vessel was in poor condition and needed extensive maintenance to extend her service life. Due to budget cuts within the agency, the tender *Hollyhock* was ultimately slated for decommissioning. After one last cruise to repair aids to navigation, the *Hollyhock* was tied up for the last time on March 14, 1982. Over the next two weeks, gear and stores were removed from the vessel in preparation for her inevitable fate. At 11:00 a.m. on March 31, 1982, the *Hollyhock* was decommissioned. The vessel was slated for sale at public auction on November 1, though Department of State cables reported Jamaica was interested in acquiring the vessel. A request to delay the auction was made; however, the planned transaction eventually fell through. The former buoy tender was sold to a missionary and renamed the *Good News Missionship*. Due to mechanical problems, the *Good News Missionship* became stranded and slowly sunk in the Miami River. Abandoned, the Pompano Beach Fishing Rodeo purchased the vessel for use as an artificial reef. The former U.S. Coast Guard buoy tender *Hollyhock* was deployed to her final duty station off Pompano Beach on February 20, 1990.

CAPTAIN EARL

The 40-foot long shrimp boat *Captain Earl* disappeared off New Smyrna in February 1949. Planes and boats covered a 40-mile stretch from Ponce Inlet north to Matanzas Inlet looking for the overdue fishing vessel, however, no trace of the vessel or its two-man crew was found.

CAPTAIN FURNIE

The 51-ton fishing vessel *Captain Furnie*, built in 1979, foundered off Vero Beach on April 29, 1980[34].

CAPTAIN GREGORY

On July 16, 2001, the 89-foot long shrimp trawler *Captain Gregory* caught fire one mile offshore, approximately two miles south of the Mayport jetties. The wood and fiberglass shrimper was returning to port when a fire in the lower decks produced copious amounts of white smoke, but no visible flames. Efforts to extinguish the smoldering fire were unsuccessful and the boat was anchored prior to the crew abandoning ship. A rigid inflatable boat from the U.S.S. *Underwood* (FFG-36), which was nearby, rescued two of the three crew members, while the third

Looking aft towards the stern superstructure of the *Captain Dan*.

was taken off by the shrimper *Kevin and Chad*. The anchored *Captain Gregory* burned throughout the night, becoming a total loss.

CAPTAIN HARRY

While this Miami reef site potentially may sound like an interesting wreck, especially considering her former name was reportedly the *Lady Philomise*, the *Captain Harry* is actually a 90-foot long deck barge resting in 120 feet of water adjacent to some natural hard bottom habitat off Miami.

CAPTAIN STEVEN

The *Captain Steven* was a 70-foot long scallop boat that capsized 20 miles northeast of Port Canaveral on the night of April 17, 1985, drowning two crewmen. The crew of the dragger was hauling in their nets just after 10:00 p.m. when a large swell caused the boat to capsize. A second scallop boat, the *Judge*, was nearby when the *Captain Steven* capsized. Its crew rescued the skipper, Horace Goethe, and called the Coast Guard at Port Canaveral at 10:14 p.m. to report that the *Captain Steven* had overturned. The *Captain Steven* drifted north until finally grounding on a sandbar within 50 yards of the beach, approximately 6 miles north of Ponce Inlet[35].

CAPTAIN TAP

On March 7, 1959, the 41-ton trawler *Captain Tap* foundered off Cape Canaveral.

CAPTAIN TERRY

According to the *Ocala Star Banner* of February 6, 1988, "The two-man crew of a foundering shrimp boat abandoned the vessel off Crescent Beach Friday (February 5, 1988) after the boat began taking on water in rough waves, the Coast Guard reported. The crew of the *Captain Terry* abandoned the boat and was returning to St. Augustine aboard a SeaTow vessel. Coast Guard Petty Officer Jim Harmon said the boat couldn't be saved."

CAPTAIN TOM S. BACKMAN

The 68-foot long shrimper *Captain Tom S. Backman* ran aground off St. Augustine and was quickly destroyed by 12-foot waves on February 5, 1987. The trawler grounded after the skipper reportedly "lost control[36]." The captain and single crew member jumped overboard and safely swam ashore.

CAPTAIN TONY

The artificial reef *Captain Tony* began its life as the freighter *Spree* at the *Deutsche-Industrie Werke AG* in Berlin-Spandau, Germany. Launched on August 6, 1961, the *Spree*, official number 5337070, was a 445-ton general cargo freighter 174.8 feet in length and 30.8 feet in breadth. Over the years, the freighter hauled her cargo under many different names: in 1974 she was the *Timber Queen*; in 1975 she was renamed *Harcourt*; later the *Barcourt* in 1979; *Kimble*

Captain Tony as the *Kimble*, 1981.

in 1981; and shortly thereafter the *Sabine* in 1982; in 1988 she was known as the *Paul-Marie*; and then in 1990 she was christened the *Beck's* after her shipping company, which employed her on a regular run between Miami and Haiti for Best Beverage, Incorporated; then the *Christ Capable* in 1994; until finally in 1995 she was sold to the Honduran Company Venante B Shipping, whereupon she was simply called the *Venante B*. In short order, the German freighter was seized in 1995 for trafficking cocaine and subsequently sold at auction. Due to the untimely death of the new owner, the vessel was repossessed and sold to Palm Beach County for use as an artificial reef. Named in memory of Captain Tony Townsend, a local charter dive boat captain, the *Captain Tony* was sunk on October 22, 1996, off Boynton Beach, and now rests in 85 feet of water approximately 600 feet to the northwest of the *Budweiser Bar* wreck.

CAPTAIN'S TJK

A 65-foot long shrimp trawler, the *Captain's TJK* (also reported as *Captain's JTK*) was engulfed in flames on March 19, 1984, about 10 miles off Fort Pierce. The two crew members of the vessel were rescued without serious injuries, though the vessel was a total loss[37].

CAROLINE (1810)

According to *The Lady's Miscellany and Weekly Visitor*, Volume 12 (1811), the ship *Caroline*, Captain Curtis, which was of and from New Orleans and bound for Liverpool with a cargo of cotton, went ashore at approximate latitude 27° 23' north on October 25, 1810. The vessel and cargo were totally lost, and one of the crew died of fatigue three days after the incident. It was reported the *Caroline* wrecked in the same general area as the Spanish brig *African*, the Spanish ship *Union*, and the schooner *Triton*. The reported location would place the wrecks of these vessels in between Fort Pierce and St. Lucie Inlets.

CAROLINE (1838)

Documented in *The Hagerstown Mail* on October 19, 1838, "The schooner *Caroline*, of Key West lying at anchor, at Caesar's Creek, during the September 7 (1838) gale drove from her moorings out on the reef, struck and sunk. Master and crew all lost."

CAROLINE (1939)

In the 1921 edition of *Merchant Vessels of the United States*, the gas screw fishing vessel *Caroline*, registering 67 tons gross displacement, 71.3 feet in length, 18.2 feet in beam, and built in 1918 at St. Marys, Georgia, was reported to have foundered in Cumberland Sound on August 11, 1939.

CAROLINE EDDY

The 317-ton brigantine *Caroline Eddy* was built in Brewer, Maine, in 1862 for Eddy, Murphy, and Company. Eventually sold to A.P. Veazie of Bangor, Maine, the brig was 110.7 feet in length and 27.6 feet in beam. On August 27, 1880, Captain George A. Warren departed Fernandina for New York with stacks of lumber lashed to the deck. The following day, the *Eddy* ran headlong into a hurricane, which required the full skill of Captain Warren and his crew just to keep the brig afloat. Shortly after midnight, a tremendous sea struck the vessel forward, and, sweeping aft, washed away a hatch and yawl boat. Captain Warren was knocked down at the helm and stunned, and when he came to, he saw none of the crew around him. As he was about to dive overboard in despair, one of the sailors called out to him from the rigging where the others had taken refuge. In short order the pumps were choked, the brig filled rapidly, and the *Caroline Eddy* capsized. The men clung to the chain plates, which alone prevented them from being washed away and drowned. The hurricane had peaked and the huge seas swept over the waterlogged wreck. Finally, the deck load became loose and washed away. With it went the foremast, which caused the brig to slowly right herself. Some of the crew lashed themselves to the lee side of the mainmast, while others took to the remaining rigging for safety. For two days the wreck drifted at the mercy of the sea. All the provisions and water were washed away with the lumber, and the crew suffered from pangs of hunger and thirst. On the morning of August 31, the waterlogged brig struck bottom approximately two miles off the beach from Matanzas. The crew constructed a small raft and safely worked their way to shore. The wreck of the *Caroline Eddy* was sold where it lay for $100, while its cargo brought $425.

CASA BLANCA

Before serving as a bulk freighter, the *Casa Blanca* was built and employed in World War II as a tank landing ship (LST). The LST was designed to support amphibious assaults by carrying vehicles, cargo, and troops onto advanced beach heads. Originally designed by the Bureau of Ships in January 1942, the keel of the first LST was laid down on June 10, 1942. By the end of the war, 1,051 LSTs would be built. The LST specifications cited an unloaded displacement of 1,780 tons and a fully loaded displacement of 3,880 tons; a length of 327.75 feet; a beam of 50 feet; armament including one 3-inch gun, six 40 mm guns, six 20 mm guns, two .50 caliber machine guns, and four .30 caliber machine guns; and a 12-knot top speed produced by two General Motors diesel engines. Aside from its normal complement, the LST could accommodate approximately 140 troops, two to six 36-foot long landing craft, or a fully-equipped 191-foot long tank landing craft, which could be launched from the LST.

LST-475 was laid down on July 10, 1942, at the Vancouver, Washington, shipyard of Kaiser, Incorporated. She was launched on November 16, 1942, and commissioned into the U.S. Navy on March 20, 1943. Assigned to the Pacific Theater, *LST-475* participated in numerous amphibious operations in New Guinea and Leyte, as well as post-war occupational duties. During her short but busy military service, she earned six battle stars.

Converted freighter *Casa Blanca* at Boston, June 1957 (William A. Schell).

Following World War II, *LST-475* was decommissioned on April 24, 1946, and struck from the Naval Register on June 5 of the same year. On October 31, 1946, she was sold to the Suwannee Fruit and Steamship Company of Jacksonville, and renamed *Casa Blanca*. As a commercial vessel, she was utilized as a general cargo freighter for 25 years. The *Casa Blanca* was eventually scrapped and sunk off Jacksonville as an artificial reef in 1972. Initially, however, the converted freighter refused to sink. While the stern dropped beneath the surface, trapped air kept the hull buoyant. During the night, the *Casa Blanca* drifted and finally sank several miles from the planned position. The wreck's actual location was not learned for some time, and even then the coordinates were somewhat guarded.

The wreck of the *Casa Blanca* now rests in 105 feet of water approximately 30 nautical miles from the Mayport jetties. Over the years, the former LST has been reduced to a debris pile approximately 350 feet long, 80 feet wide, and 20 feet high. Heavily encrusted by corals and sponges, the wreckage provides abundant habitat for massive schools of shimmering baitfish, as well as grouper, snapper, and a variety of tropical species. During the winter, sand tiger sharks are commonly observed on the *Casa Blanca*, and it should be noted that sightings of great white sharks are also occasionally reported on the wreck. Due to its distance from the mouth of the St. Johns River, visibility consistently reaches 70-80 feet in the summer.

CASEY AND CANDICE

At 5:00 p.m. on October 20, 2000, a crewman on the 83-foot long shrimp boat *Casey and Candice*, out of Brunswick, Georgia, noticed the vessel was quickly taking on water and sent out a distress signal to the U.S. Coast Guard. Fortunately, the Coast Guard safely rescued the three crewmen before the vessel eventually capsized and sunk in 60 feet of water one mile offshore, approximately two miles south of Ponce Inlet.

CASHIER

As reported March 1838 in *The Sailor's Magazine and Naval Journal*, Volume 10, the brig *Cashier* was totally lost on the St. Johns Bar.

CAST IRON BALLAST WRECK

The "Cast Iron Ballast Wreck," located approximately four and a half miles south of Sebastian Inlet and just offshore of the "Cannon Pile Wreck," appears to be a late nineteenth to early twentieth century shipwreck. Named after the abundance of cast iron ballast bars found at the site, numerous railroad car wheels and parts can also be found in the area. Additionally, there is mention of salvage divers recovering several Colt pistols in 1992.

CASTOR

Designed as a shelter-deck coaster, the *Castor* was built as the *Dynacontainer IV*, but launched as the *Dorothee Bos* in 1970 at the Martenshoek, Netherlands shipyard of

Castor as the *Tropic* at Santa Lucia, West Indies, 1987 (Yvon Perchoc).

Bodewes Scheepswerven B.V. Over the next three decades, her name would change 14 times before ultimately being renamed *Castor* in 1998. She was 250 feet in overall length, 39 feet wide, and displaced 499 tons. On May 31, 1999, the *Castor* was stopped north of Venezuela by the H.M.S. *Marlborough*, which was carrying U.S. Coast Guard law enforcement officers. The boarding party found 8,687 pounds of cocaine in one of the Panamanian freighter's shipping containers, which, at the time, was the twelfth largest seizure on record. After being escorted to Miami, the *Castor* was eventually abandoned by its owner and

Stern superstructure of the *Castor*.

became a derelict. The freighter was then acquired by Palm Beach County for use as an artificial reef, and subsequently scuttled south of Boynton Inlet on December 14, 2001.

The wreck of the *Castor* now rests upright in 110 feet of water with its bow oriented to the south. She rests approximately 700 feet to the northeast of the *Budweiser Bar* wreck. Divers will encounter the *Castor's* main deck at 90 feet, which has already been transformed into a vibrant tapestry of color by encrusting marine life. Portions of her starboard hull and wheelhouse have collapsed, most likely due to the unusual hurricane season of 2004.

CATHARINE OSMOND

According to the *Bell's Weekly Messenger* of December 15, 1816, "The *Rebecca*, from Cadiz and Havannah to Savannah; and the *Catharine Osmond*, Vicary, from Havannah to Salem, are wrecked at Florida. Part of their cargoes saved, and carried to Nassau."

CATHERINE G.

The St. Johns River tug *Catherine G.* sank above Palatka; date unknown[38].

CATHERINE THOMAS

The 71-ton American schooner *Catherine Thomas*, built in 1848 at Fairhaven, Connecticut, Captain W.T. Barlow, stranded on the Mosquito Bar in March 1876, becoming a total loss.

CAUTION

The sloops (also described as wrecking smacks) *Alabama*, *Dread*, and *Caution* of Mystic, Connecticut, bound to Key West, were driven ashore and lost in a gale on September 7, 1838, approximately 12 miles north of Cape Florida. Only one man, Joseph Noble, survived the wrecking and subsequent slaughter at the hands of hostile Seminole Indians by joining the crew of the French brig *Courier* (*Courier de Tampico* or *Courier de Vera Cruz*), which was lost in the same vicinity. In addition to the crews of the *Alabama*, *Dread*, and *Caution*, most of the *Alna's* crew, wrecked in the vicinity, was also massacred. At the time, local tribes spared European sailors and only killed Americans wrecked on the Florida shore.

CELEBRATION II

While it is widely known that prowling German U-boats sunk numerous vessels off the Florida coast in World War II, the sinking of a 63-foot long charter boat off Palm Beach by a British submarine would likely be met with raised eyebrows. But on May 6, 1986, that's exactly what happened when the H.M.S. *Conqueror* sunk the yacht *Celebration II* nine miles off South Florida. The *Celebration II* had set out from Flagler Marina in West Palm Beach for West End in the Bahamas at 5:00 a.m. on May 6 for the start of a 10-day cruise, but shortly after heading offshore it began taking on water. Six passengers and a dog abandoned ship at 6:30 a.m. as the vessel foundered, and were soon picked up by the U.S. Coast Guard. But the *Celebration II* refused to sink, presenting a menace to navigation. The British submarine, on maneuvers in the area, blew the half-sunk charter boat out of the water after getting the owner's consent. As noted in the *Philadelphia Inquirer* on May 7, 1986, "'They sort of volunteered. They said, *We'll sink it for you*,' said Coast Guard petty officer Jesse Schmucker."

CERES

The fate of the brig *Ceres* was detailed in an October 14, 1824, dispatch from New York published in *The Edinburgh Advertiser* on November 12, 1824:

> By the schooner *Mars*, from Falmouth, (Jamaica), we learn, that, on the 23d ult., in lat. 30 10, long. 81 15, she fell in with the wreck of the British brig *Ceres*, Captain William Bird, from Honduras, bound to London. The *Ceres* had been knocked down on her beam-ends in the gale of the 14th; both masts and bowsprit went by the board, and she was made a complete wreck. The captain, chief officer James Bruce, second officer, carpenter, seven seamen, and a boy, were washed overboard. James Mitchell, of East Stonehouse, Devonshire, and Christian Anderson, of Norway, were taken from the wreck. They were almost dead, having been eight days on the wreck, with nothing to eat but raw salt pork, and nothing to drink except a little rain water that was collected in a piece of canvass [*sic*]. The two seamen have since recovered, and arrived in the *Mars*. The *Ceres* was loaded with mahogany and logwood. The same night (23d) the wreck drove ashore twelve miles south of St. Johns River, East Florida.

CHARLEE GIRL

The *Charlee Girl* was a 69-foot long trawler built in 1981. On the evening of May 15, 2010, the fishing vessel began taking on water off Port Canaveral. The crew abandoned the anchored vessel as water crept over the stern and it appeared the trawler was sinking. The *Charlee Girl* remained partially afloat for several days, however, eventually disappearing sometime after May 18. The reported sinking location of the *Charlee Girl* was latitude 28° 27.683' north, longitude 80° 23.671' west.

CHARLES CROOKER

On November 7, 1859, Captain Murray of the *Charles Crooker* found himself and his ship on the beach approximately 40 miles north of Cape Florida (also cited as 25 miles north of Cape Florida). She was en route from New Orleans to Liverpool with a cargo of 3,100 bales of cotton and 50 hogsheads of tobacco valued at over $180,000 when her trip was interrupted. Most of the cargo was saved, but the *Crooker* was left in the surf. The 960-ton ship was built at Bath, Maine, in 1849. Thirteen wrecking vessels carrying 123 men worked 25 days to salvage 1,730 bales of dry cotton and 804 bales of wet cotton. They also managed to strip the ship's rigging and recovered other materials before abandoning the wreck.

CHARLES DAVIS

The loss of the schooner *Charles Davis* was recorded in *The New York Times* on September 26 and 27, 1897, stating it "wrecked off the St. Johns Bar in late September 1897. She departed her home port of Philadelphia on September 16 for Jacksonville and is believed to have sunk following a gale that swept through the area on the evening of September 20. She was spotted sunk 30 miles due east (of Jacksonville) off the St. Johns Bar with her mast sticking up out of the water. All on board are thought to have been lost."

CHARLEY'S CRAB

In the early part of March 1993, Charles Muer and his wife were entertaining another couple in the Bahamas on their sailboat *Charley's Crab*. Named after Muer's popular South Florida seafood restaurant, *Charley's Crab* was a Freedom 40 ketch. With word of an impending storm, Muer planned on sailing back to Jupiter ahead of the gale. At approximately 2:45 p.m. on March 12, 1993, *Charley's Crab* was sighted and photographed by a U.S. Coast Guard patrol aircraft. The aerial photograph shows that *Charley's Crab* was flying its spinnaker at the time and heading slightly west of north approximately 90 miles from Jupiter. Unfortunately, later that evening the "No Name Storm" rapidly swept across the Florida peninsula, bringing 70-knot winds and 30-foot seas. Reportedly, Muer placed two calls from a cell phone carried on the *Charley's Crab* to Palm Beach County's emergency center at 4:25 and 4:27 a.m., respectively, but dispatchers only heard static on the line before being quickly disconnected. The *Charley's Crab* disappeared in the raging maelstrom and no trace has ever been found of the vessel. Based on the reported estimated speed and position of the sailboat by the Coast Guard aircraft, it is likely the *Charley's Crab* foundered off Florida just short of its intended destination.

CHARMING NELLY

A November 12, 1763, dispatch from Charleston, South Carolina printed in the *St. James's Chronicle* on January 12, 1764, revealed, "The schooner *Charming Nelly*, of and for this port, from St. Augustine, James Brown, master, was about a fortnight since, lost near the Matanzas, on the coast of Florida. Two French sloops in the Spanish transport service, from Havannah for St. Augustine, were lost about the same time, one at the Matanzas, the other at St. Augustine." Other sources refer to this vessel as the schooner *Charming Sally*.

CHATHAM (1852)

Early information in *The New York Times* published on September 20, 1852, stated, "Mail schooner *Chatham*, which left Charleston 8th, with the mail for Key West and Havana, was wrecked on the 12th September, twenty one miles south of St. Augustine, during a severe gale. No lives were lost and the mail was saved." A subsequent report published in the *Savannah Republican* on September 22, 1852, provided additional details on the wrecking, and a revised location:

> Capt Middleton and crew, late of the schooner *Chatham*, arrived at Charleston on Monday, in the schooner *Florida*, Capt. Willey from St. Augustine, and from the former the *Courier*, learns that on Saturday the 11th inst. about noon, the *Chatham* experienced a heavy gale from the south-east, and about two o'clock on Sunday morning, the wind having shifted to the east, and blowing right on shore, the sea at the time being very heavy, it was determined to run the vessel up on the beach, which was accomplished the same morning at about half past six o'clock, at a spot about fifteen miles south of St. Augustine.

CHATHAM (1910)

Constructed of iron in September 1884 at a Philadelphia shipyard, the steamer *Chatham* boasted a length of 265.4 feet, a beam of 40 feet, and a displacement

Steamship *Chatham* aground on the St. Johns River jetty (© The Mariners' Museum, Newport News, Virginia).

of 2,729 tons. On the morning of January 14, 1910, the Merchants and Miners Company steamer was finishing up her trip from her home port of Baltimore to Jacksonville when she soundly struck the north jetty at the entrance of the St. Johns River. In an instant she became a hopeless wreck. The collision resulted in a massive hole in the *Chatham's* hull, and 14 feet of water flooded the ship's hold. At the time of the wrecking, the Clyde Line steamer *Mohawk* was close behind the *Chatham*. Upon seeing the *Chatham* drive up on the rocks, the *Mohawk* immediately dispatched lifeboats to render assistance, eventually taking off 76 passengers and safely landing them in Jacksonville. The steamer was loaded with a cargo of flour, shoes, and general merchandise. While most of the cargo was beyond saving, apparently the water only soaked a half inch into the flour sacks, so quite a bit of this commodity was retained by locals.

The *Chatham* eventually slipped off the jetty and sunk by the bow, her aft section protruding from the water to mark her grave. Details on the wreck's subsequent removal were included in the *Annual Report of the Chief of Engineers, United States Army, to the Secretary of War for the Year 1911*:

> At a contract price of $29,500, work to remove the wreck began January 28, 1911, and was completed on June 24, 1911. Two charges of dynamite of 5 tons each were placed around and in the wreck and exploded. The first charge extended one half the length of the ship from the bow. The second charge extended from the stern over the portion not broken by the first explosion. Such pieces were then picked up as could be handled by the derrick barge in use and pieces of such weight as could not be handled were reblasted and broken until they could be. In all this work there was 32,660 pounds (16.33 tons) of dynamite used.

The report indicated prior to salvage, the bow of the vessel was in 36 to 40 feet of water, while the stern rested on the slope of the jetty. While salvaged heavily, portions of the *Chatham* still remain in shallow water on the north side of the Mayport jetties.

CHICHEMO

The 39-ton wooden-hulled fishing vessel *Chichemo* was built in 1953 at St. Augustine. On April 28, 1962, she reportedly burned 14 miles south of Jacksonville Beach.

CHIMAERA

According to Singer (1998), the 44-ton *Chimaera* collided with a floating object and presumably sunk 12 miles off Fowey Rocks Light on April 8, 1959.

CHIMALUS

The yacht *Chimalus*, owned by a Mr. White, was reported to be high and dry on Municipal Dock Four after being blown ashore on September 18, 1926, during the Great Miami Hurricane. The ultimate fate of this vessel is unknown.

CHLORINE BARGE

The wreck known as the *Chlorine Barge*, resting in approximately 100 feet of water 30 nautical miles east of Flagler Beach, is the former tank barge *TMI-11*, which was lost on March 11, 1996. The 330.9-foot long barge *TMI-11*, official number D271207, was built in 1956 by the Levingston Shipbuilding Company at Orange, Texas, for Transerve Marine. The 4,146-gross-ton barge was loaded with 1.9 million gallons of fifty percent dilute caustic soda solution when she sank. When the sunken barge was initially surveyed, it was discovered the vessel had severe structural damage in the stern and deck structure, and that all tanks had some degree of breaching, which allowed the caustic solution to freely leak into the Atlantic Ocean. In April, salvage teams worked to discharge as much of the hazardous cargo as possible in hopes of mitigating harm to the local ecosystem. Additionally, holes were cut in the barge's hull to allow further natural flushing, though restrictions were apparently installed to prevent diver access into the barge. Work was concluded in late July, by which time pH readings of the water around the wreck were at ambient levels. The *Chlorine Barge* has since been transformed into a thriving artificial reef, and is now a popular fishing and diving destination.

CHRISTMAS TREE

On January 9, 1985, a massive explosion ripped through the 83-foot long yacht *Christmas Tree* at its Watson Island Marina berth in Miami. No lives were lost, as the event was staged for an episode of the television show *Miami Vice*. The once elegant wooden-hulled yacht, originally built in 1926, was formerly owned by movie actress Bette Davis, who entertained many of her famous friends onboard the vessel in the 1930s. In recent years the *Christmas Tree* had fallen into disrepair, and was abandoned at its berth on Biscayne Bay. Producers of the television show purchased the leaky derelict for $500.

CINDY LEE

According to Singer (1998), the 30-ton vessel *Cindy Lee*, which was built in 1951, foundered off Jupiter on February 16, 1974.

CINNABAR

The *Cinnabar* was a palatial cruiser yacht owned by Mr. Phil Pomeroy, which was blown ashore at Municipal Dock Four at Miami on September 18, 1926, during the Great Miami Hurricane. Unlike many of the hurricane's other victims, however, the *Cinnabar* was quickly repaired and refloated. Tragically, less than a year later, the *Cinnabar* exploded and sank off Savannah Light on June 6, 1927, claiming the lives of Mr. Pomeroy and four others. The sole survivor was picked up by the tug *Peerless* north of St. Johns Bar after drifting on wreckage for four days without food or water.

The tanker *Cities Service Empire* at sea shortly before her sinking (Mark Mondano Collection).

CITIES SERVICE EMPIRE

The 465-foot long tanker was built as the *Ampetco* in 1918 at Sparrows Point, Maryland, by the Bethlehem Steel Shipbuilding Company. While originally destined for the U.S. Shipping Board, Emergency Fleet Corporation, with the conclusion of World War I, the *Ampetco* was sold to the distinguished Standard Oil Company in 1920. Originally established by John D. Rockefeller, Sr. in 1870, the Standard Oil Company grew to become the largest oil interest in the United States, controlling over 95 percent of the oil refining capacity by the close of the nineteenth century. This growth did not go unnoticed: the creation of the Standard Oil Trust in 1882 led to the passing of the Sherman Antitrust Act of 1890. This act, designed to prevent monopolies, was primarily aimed at the Standard Oil Trust. In 1911, after a series of lawsuits, the Standard Oil Trust was found to be in violation of the Sherman Antitrust Act by the U.S Supreme Court. The conglomerate was forced to dismantle its 34 affiliates, which included two of the larger companies, Standard Oil Company (New Jersey) and Standard Oil Company (New York), commonly referred to as Jersey Standard and Socony, respectively. Over time, the breakup of the Standard Oil monopoly would result in the creation of Exxon (Jersey Standard), Esso, Chevron, American, and Mobil (Socony). It is interesting to note that 88 years after one of the first big antitrust cases dissolved Standard Oil, Exxon and Mobil were scrutinized under the antitrust microscope when they announced plans for a merger in 1998. When finalized in 1999, the Exxon-Mobil merger represented the creation of the largest private oil and gas company in the world, as well as the biggest global corporation by revenue. The more things change, the more they stay the same.

Meanwhile, another conglomerate across the Atlantic also found itself in turmoil during the early twentieth century. In 1891, the Dutch and Belgian-American Petroleum Companies joined their shipping activities to become the American Petroleum Company of Rotterdam, Holland. At the outset of World War I, the company had nine ships in its fleet. Although the American Petroleum Company ships steamed under the neutral Dutch flag, five of them were lost due to belligerent action during the war. In an attempt to rebuild, the company was divided in 1920 to form the *Dutch Petroleum Industrie Maatschappij N.V.* and the Belgian-American Petroleum Company S.A. of Antwerp, Belgium. Following the split, the Dutch faction took possession of the remaining four ships, while the Belgian-American Petroleum Company was left without any vessels whatsoever. To remedy the situation, the company successfully acquired the *Ampetco* from Jersey Standard in 1922. After six years of service, the Belgian-American Petroleum Company sold the 8,103-ton tanker to the Cities Service Transportation Company of New York in 1928, whereupon she was renamed the *Cities Service Empire*.

At the outbreak of hostilities, and as the U-boat threat grew in late 1941, the *Empire* was outfitted with a five-inch deck gun that was mounted onto a round deck structure on the extreme stern of the tanker. With Captain William F. Jerman at the helm, the *Empire* steamed from Port Arthur, Texas, to Philadelphia with a full load of petroleum products in mid-February 1942. Onboard were a crew of 40 and an additional complement of nine Naval Armed Guards. The Armed Guard Service was a branch of the U.S. Navy that was given the responsibility of defending the U.S. merchant fleet. The November 17, 1941 repeal of Section Six of the Neutrality Act, which prevented arming of merchant ships, triggered a large-scale and

Image believed to document U.S Navy on scene following the sinking of the *Cities Service Empire* (Mark Mondano Collection).

fast-paced project of training personnel and acquiring weaponry. Three Armed Guard schools were responsible for training men to proficiently shoot ships and aircraft, as well as learn basic navigational and fire fighting skills. Out of 144,970 men that served on over 5,000 United States owned or flagged ships, the Naval Armed Guard suffered 1,810 fatalities.

On the morning of February 22, daylight found the tanker approaching Cape Canaveral. At the same time, *Kapitänleutnant* Ulrich Heyse of the *U-128* was sitting quietly on the seabed. Heyse had recently arrived to Florida and had sunk the tanker *Pan Massachusetts* just two days earlier; the *Pan Massachusetts* was the first merchant vessel sunk off Florida during World War II. Upon hearing the approaching target, the *U-128* quickly surfaced and attempted to plot a firing solution.

Amberjack swim over the stern deck gun of the *Cities Service Empire*.

Hastily, three torpedoes were fired at the approaching tanker from over a 3,000 feet distance, which all missed, passing off the bow and stern. Heyse recalculated the trajectory of the fully laden tanker and fired a fourth torpedo, which also went wide. By this time, the tanker had passed the U-boat and continued north, apparently unaware of the impending danger. The *U-128* pursued and fired two more torpedoes from a range of almost two miles. Approximately four minutes later, the two torpedoes connected with the starboard side of the tanker, instantly igniting a massive blaze that ran the length of the doomed vessel. Captain Jerman gave the order to abandon ship as the raging inferno that used to be the *Cities Service Empire* began to break up. Lifeboats on the starboard side of the ship were burned before the crew could launch them, as the deck of the tanker was awash in flames. Fortunately, several of the crewmembers were able to launch a life raft off the portside, whereupon 23 survivors climbed into the tiny raft. Describing their flight from the burning ship, oiler Frank Heap stated, "One of the fellows had a broken arm. We were all wet and the sea was beginning to burn around us where the oil had leaked. We waited for one guy who was swimming toward us and then tried to get away as fast as we could[39]."

The U.S.S. *Biddle (DD-151)* was in close proximity to the attack and quickly steamed to the scene of the disaster. Meanwhile, eight men trapped near the bow of the burning tanker found themselves clinging to a painter's staging. Unfortunately, two of them lost their strength and dropped into the flaming sea just as the U.S.S. *Biddle* arrived. With the destroyer now on scene, a launch was deployed in an effort to rescue the men from the sinking tanker. Herbert Goeler was one of the young Navy men onboard the rescue boat that tried in vain to reach the crippled *Empire*. In a conversation with this author, Goeler related how the intense flames kept them at bay, and they were forced to helplessly watch the tanker begin to sink quickly by the bow. Many of the crewmembers who had sought refuge from the fire on the painter's stage were now forced to jump for their lives. The stern of the *Cities Service Empire* then raised clear of the surface and followed the bow towards the bottom. Fifteen perished in the attack, including the 28-year old Captain Jerman, who was crushed by a lifeboat as he attempted to save one of his crewmen.

The wreck of the *Cities Service Empire* runs from southwest to the northeast, just askew of the generally north-northeast Gulf Stream, and sits bolt upright on a sandy bottom in approximately 240 feet of water. The stern deck gun still points astern, adorned by a large thicket of white *Oculina* coral that has enveloped the breach of the gun. All structure above the main deck has been flattened; only the random vertical bulkhead support remains. Due to her current disposition, it is probable that the wreck was depth charged several times after her sinking, as every fixture and vertical structure appears to have been vibrated loose. Portholes and other brass artifacts lie loose amongst the stern area. Approximately 80 feet forward of the stern, one can witness the impact area from one of the torpedoes. It appears as if someone took a bite out of the starboard side of the wreck as an entire tank section has been removed and flattened down to the sand. The sheer drop-off extends around the perimeter of the tank and into the centerline of the ship. One can proceed forward, following the remains of the catwalk that ran along the center of the ship. Debris familiar on a tanker, such as large brass valves, is strewn everywhere.

The entire forward superstructure and bridge had been lowered to the main deck level in a large debris area that extends the full width of the ship, further supporting evidence that the wreck was depth-charged. On my first visit to the wreck, I quickly spotted the ship's starboard telegraph amongst the debris, as well as the ship's helm, the binnacle with the compass bowl and cover lying next

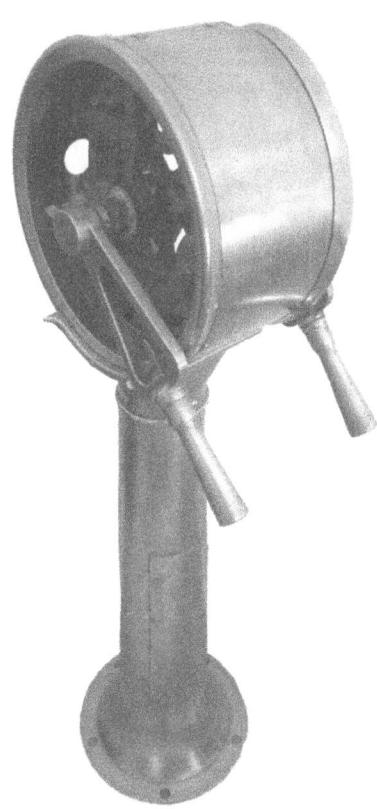

Restored bridge telegraph recovered from the wreck of the *Cities Service Empire*.

to it, and the portside telegraph. Brass lanterns were also found on the outside perimeter of the bridge area. Portholes can be seen throughout the wreck. The bell of the *Cities Service Empire* was found sitting loose on the bow and was recovered on June 10, 2001. Due to the wreck's disposition and relation to the current, a diver can view a good portion of the wreck while being swept along by the northward-moving Gulf Stream. Once off to the side of the wreck a bit, a diver can see the extent of the damage resulting from the torpedo attack. Forward of the torpedo hole, the portside hull has slowly peeled back and fallen to the sand. Aft of this hole, the hull plates are folded upward and outward, due to the force of the explosion. The skeletal framework of the ship is greatly exposed due to these missing hull plates.

Due to the strong surface current that is found over the wreck, the most prudent method for visiting the *Empire* is to drift into the wreck from the south. As one approaches the site, the remains of a large, square "float-free" raft will be observed in the sand just off the stern. The scene of the stern coming into view is incredible. With good visibility, divers can see the large screw and rudder just above the sand, while looking upwards, the barrel of the deck gun pointing off the stern is visible. Underneath the gun placement, the brass hubs of the auxiliary steering station still remain. Artifacts are abundant throughout this area, as portholes, auxiliary telegraphs, compasses, and china have been found amongst the shell hash that covers the lower decks. The engine is almost completely exposed, due to the wreck's ongoing collapse. The wreck of the *Cities Service Empire* is definitely an extraordinary dive, but one whose time is running out due to the forces of Mother Nature.

Helm recovered from the *Cities Service Empire*.

CITY OF AUSTIN

The 1,295-ton *City of Austin* was launched from Mystic, Connecticut, in August 1871. She was a schooner-rigged screw steamer constructed of oak, chestnut, and yellow pine, and boasted a length of 224 feet and a beam of 36.9 feet. At the time of her loss, she was owned by C.H. Mallory and Company.

On the evening of April 24, 1881, the *City of Austin* was on the final stretch of her run from the Bahamas back to Fernandina with a general cargo of hogsheads, sugar, and fruit. Captain Edgar O. Stevens had just turned over the ship to a pilot picked up from shore, and they were within three miles of their destination when the ship struck a shoal (Pelican Shoals) just offshore. The vessel became hopelessly grounded, so the captain proceeded to evacuate the ship. All passengers safely boarded lifeboats and were landed ashore. The steamer was reported to go to pieces shortly thereafter.

The ultimate fate of the wreck was recorded in the *Annual Report of the Chief of Engineers, United States Army, to the Secretary of War for the Year 1905*, "The removal of the wrecks of the *City of Austin*, *Franconia*, and *Puntalunos* [sic] in Cumberland Sound, Georgia and Florida, was completed. This work was done under emergency contract of August 8, 1903, at a total cost of $7,213.85."

CITY OF BRUNSWICK

The paddlewheel steamer *City of Brunswick*, official number 24194, was originally built in 1850 at New York as the *Thomas Collyer*. She registered an overall length of 123.8 feet, a beam of 22.7, and a displacement of 194 tons gross. On September 11, 1897, the *City of Brunswick* caught fire at a wharf in Mayport. The flaming steamer was cut loose to sink near St. Johns Bluff at Sisters Creek, where she burned to the water's edge.

CITY OF GEORGETOWN

On the morning of February 11, 1886, the 78-ton Spring Garden Line steamer *City of Georgetown* collided with the *City of Monticello* (*ex-City of Norfolk*) on the St. Johns River near Palatka. The ultimate fate of this vessel is unclear.

CITY OF SANFORD

Fire has long been a menace to shipping. The burning of the 115.4-foot long sternwheel steamer *City of Sanford* is just another example of the significance of this threat. Early on the morning of April 24, 1882, the *City of Sanford* was making its way down the St. Johns River from Sanford to Jacksonville when a fire broke out. The captain immediately rushed up to the pilothouse, turned the steamer for the riverbank, and grounded her in three feet of water within thirty feet of shore. Fire quickly consumed the steamer as passengers scattered about the top deck in various stages of apparel. A survivor related the tragic events as flames swept through the steamer:

> A group of five was on the rear deck, when the captain urged them to leap overboard into the water. Miss Ireland fell overboard, and the stern wheel caught her dress and was about dragging her under its paddles when the captain sprang overboard and extracted her. Mr. Ireland, who jumped after her was caught in the wheel and was also rescued by Captain Roberts. Mrs. Ireland and her little daughter and Mrs. Keep and her son were left on the decks. The ladies were about to jump overboard when the two children, seized with panic, ran back into the blazing saloon, and mother's love, stronger than fear of death, urged the two ladies after them. The four disappeared in the fiery furnace, and were burned to a crisp. Their remains were found afterward under their respective staterooms. They were but charred and blackened trunks, grasping the almost unrecognizable bodies of their children[40].

The steamer *George Bird*, which was also making its way to Jacksonville and was a few miles downriver, turned around upon seeing the massive glow growing off their stern. Approaching as close as they could without risking the safety of their own vessel, the *George Bird* picked up the survivors from around the burning pyre. At least nine passengers perished in the fire. The *City of Sanford* eventually burned to the water's edge at Point La Vista, becoming a total loss.

CITY OF VERA CRUZ

The *City of Vera Cruz* was a wooden-hulled, brigantine-rigged steamship built in Long Island, New York, by the John English shipyard in 1874. Built for Alexandre and Sons for the New York to Havana route, the passenger/freighter was 296 feet long, 37 feet in beam, and 26 feet in depth. She had three decks, while her hull was constructed of white oak, chestnut, and hackmatack timbers. Her hull was reinforced with iron strips, four inches wide and five-eighths of an inch thick, which were doubled and diagonally laid. Power was supplied by two compound cylinder engines that drove a single screw 15.5 feet in diameter. The vessel had accommodations for 100 passengers, fine furnishings, and electric bells for communication between different parts of the ship. The *City of Vera Cruz* was valued at approximately $200,000. Departing from New York on August 25, 1880, the *City of Vera Cruz* headed to Havana carrying 28 passengers, 49 crewmembers, and a wide variety of freight. Captain Edward Van Sice, a competent seaman with 20 years of experience, guided the vessel along the North River and out into the Atlantic. Nestled in the cargo holds were 1,000 barrels of potatoes, 800 barrels of lard, 500 barrels of fish, a streetcar bound for Mexico, candles, two teams of valuable horses, sewing machines, glassware, wine, beer, pistols, clocks, and a billiard table; the combined cargo was valued at $150,000. In addition, the mail ship carried 11 bags of letters and 11 bags of newspapers bound for Havana, as well as one dispatch bag from the State Department to the United States Consul at Vera Cruz.

Some reports indicate that the ship was loaded improperly, as survivors stated that the ship had a decided list soon after leaving port. For several days the ship traveled through rough seas, brisk wind, overcast skies, and driving rain. At 1:00 p.m. Saturday, August 28, Captain Van Sice was overheard remarking to the first officer, Mr. Harris, "I have just noticed that the barometer is falling rapidly. We are going to have a hurricane[41]." With this insight, Captain Van Sice ordered the streetcar and numerous barrels on deck to be thrown overboard. Thirty miles off the Florida coast near St. Augustine, the *City of Vera Cruz* ran headlong into the storm at 1:35 p.m.

Mr. A.K. Owen detailed the first moments of the hurricane, stating, "The real blast of the cyclone struck us on the port bow at about twenty-five minutes to two p.m. Saturday and listed the ship almost on her beam ends. From this time it became next to impossible to walk about without clinging to chairs, tables and other stationary of the cabin, and as all movable objects in the saloon were quickly thrown from port to starboard walking was exceedingly dangerous[42]." At 2:00 p.m. a heavy sea crashed into the ship, flooding the engine room and extinguishing the boiler fires.

Mr. Owen related how the skylights were washed away that evening and waves crashed into the saloon. Amidst their dire straits, the passengers kept calm: "By midnight the passengers were generally sitting upon or lying on the floor of the saloon conversing with and assisting each other, yet good cheer was the rule, and many

Painting depicting the *City of Vera Cruz* at sea (Mark Mondano Collection).

were the exchanges of wit and humor between them all[43]." He continued to describe the passengers' demeanor, saying "There was no such thing as excitement on board – even the children were quiet and reasonable[44]."

The final moments of the ship occurred early on the morning of Sunday, August 29. At 4:12 a.m., a massive sea "broke into the engine room and through the saloon, making a crash like a battery of artillery and striking terror for an instant into every one, dashing saloon passengers, tables, doors and the loose furniture together and into water knee deep[45]." It was also reported that Captain Van Sice was washed overboard when this sea smashed into the port side of the upper decks. Mr. Owen alluded to the possibility that Van Sice actually jumped ship, rather than being washed overboard. His opinion of the captain and crew contrasted sharply with previous newspaper accounts of the disaster that boasted of their courageous performance. Mr. Owen continued with his damning assessment of Captain Van Sice, revealing that he "…never came near the passengers during the storm, nor did he send to inquire into their condition, and it may be sincerely hoped that no other passengers may be left to so thoughtless and indifferent a man[46]."

As control of the vessel was lost and the situation worsened, preparations to abandon ship were made at daybreak. Tragically, the lifeboats were smashed against the hull of the ship as they were being lowered, crushing some of the passengers and crew in the melee and throwing the remainder to their death. The first officer, Mr. Frank M. Harris, as well as the second mate and several other crewmembers were killed as they attempted to launch a lifeboat from the starboard side. It was also reported that an ox, which had been washed overboard moments before, gored another lifeboat with its horns, rendering it useless. While the rest of the passengers and crew stared horrified at those who were consumed by the violent seas, the *City of Vera Cruz* settled lower into the water and finally gave up to the pounding Atlantic. At 6:00 a.m., she broke in two and quickly sunk to the bottom in a matter of minutes. The hurricane-ravaged sea was immediately littered with wreckage, personal belongings, luggage, and cargo. Mr. Owen described the scene:

> To say there were ten million pieces of wrecked stores all clashing together five minutes after the ship went to pieces would be a gross exaggeration, but even with such a statement no idea could be conceived as to the state of the case. Men, women, children, horses, cats and rats mixed in and went in, through and over this mass. The waves were fifty feet high, not in swells and ridges, but in peaks like sugar loaves. Four peaks beating like surf tore into each other. When we went up on one it was not to go down on the other side, but to be turned over at the top and sent rolling through the air to the opposite one, and so back and forth. This lasted about two to three hours, after which the waves took a more natural character and came in swelling ridges, and we whirled down and over them to the opposite side[47].

Those fortunate enough to survive the initial sinking now had to avoid being killed by the debris that was thrown around the surface. One survivor witnessed other survivors being smashed by timbers and other large pieces of debris. The majority of those who perished were said to have drowned within the first 10 minutes of the ship's sinking.

The main portion of wreckage from the *City of Vera Cruz* washed ashore approximately 12 miles from St. Augustine. Furniture, dry goods, copious amounts of mail postmarked "New York, August 25, via steamer City of Vera Cruz," wine, passengers' trunks, and bodies began washing ashore on Monday, August 30. Rumors of looting bodies and personal belongings circulated amongst the local citizens. Many bodies were searched for any form of identification and then promptly buried where they washed ashore due to their advanced state of decomposition. Included in the dead was General Alfred T.A. Torbet. General Torbet, a graduate of West Point, had a long and distinguished career in the U.S. Army during the American Civil War, and after the war served as Consul General at both Havana and Paris. Miraculously, of the 77 on board, 11 survivors made it safely to the beach after spending over 24 hours in the water.

The powerful hurricane that led to the sinking of the *City of Vera Cruz* was also responsible for the destruction

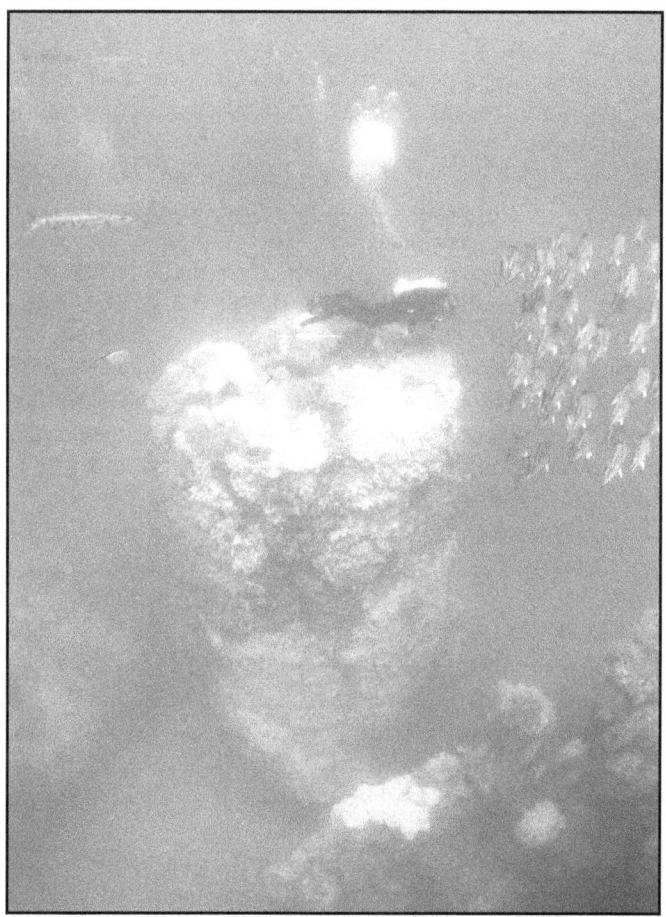

Diver swimming over one of the *City of Vera Cruz's* boilers.

of numerous other vessels. The *Caroline Eddy* was washed on the beach and wrecked; she was sold where she lay for $110. The schooner *Ada J. Simonton* went ashore at Matanzas with her cargo of lumber and was eventually sold at auction for $150. The schooner *Rosa Eppinger*, en route from Cedar Key, Florida for New York with a cargo of pine lumber, wrecked 16 miles north of Cape Canaveral with the loss of two lives. The bark *New Republic* was lost 11 miles from Mosquito Inlet. The brig *Long Reach*, bound from Apalachicola to Philadelphia with a cargo of lumber, went ashore 16 miles south of Mosquito Inlet, resulting in four deaths. An unknown copper-bottomed brig capsized and was found floating amidst the wreckage of the *City of Vera Cruz*. Over 100 miles of Florida's coast was strewn with wreckage and bodies originating from over 10 shipwrecks.

After the sinking, Captain Van Sice and the crew of the *City of Vera Cruz* were blamed for the loss by the Atlantic Mutual Marine Insurance Company, one of the insurance carriers for Alexandre and Sons. An insurance representative noted that the captain should have been wary of the falling barometer and could have avoided the storm stating, "He had plenty of warning[48]." Yet, many letters of support poured in for Captain Van Sice. One letter that defended the captain's honor stated that those "who had traveled with him during the past twenty years bear witness that there does not exist a better, more courageous or intelligent a commander of a steamer[49]." Still another maintained that they could "positively assert that never was there a better captain nor a kinder, braver man[50]." Given the large number of sinkings attributed to this one storm, it would appear that Captain Van Sice did everything in his power to save his ship, contrary to the claims made by the Atlantic Mutual Marine Insurance Company.

The wreck of the *City of Vera Cruz* was found in 1980 by a local shrimper, though others may have known about its location as early as 1978. The ship is in two main sections, both lying close to each other in about 78 feet of water. The engine and boilers provide the greatest relief on the site, rising 30 feet off the bottom. Valves and steam piping can be found in this area. The shaft, heavily adorned by colorful sponges, heads aft and terminates abruptly. Forward of the boilers, the wreck is dominated by low sections of wreckage, including random timbers and bronze spikes. Divers have recovered jewelry, bottles, china, assorted cargo, and personal effects. Presently, the wreck is largely buried under several feet of sand.

CLARA B.

On October 12, 1925, the pleasure boat *Clara B.*, owned by Captain Ed Arnold of Malabar, and under charter to the Melbourne Farms Development Company, capsized when attempting to turn around just outside Sebastian Inlet. The *Mexia Daily News*, October 12, 1925, presented the grim details:

> Eleven dead, at least two missing and 10 injured is the toll this morning announced by weary rescuers who spent the night searching for bodies and rescuing the injured from the *Clara* [sic], which turned over in the sea 22 miles south of here. It is said that there were 23 aboard the excursion boat, most of them from Wichita, Kansas. The boat capsized when it turned suddenly when the captain started to take it from Sebastian Inlet into the ocean and noticed a high sea running. The injured spent the night in an improvised hospital in a hardware store, the rescued and injured being beaten against the rocks along the shore. Eight bodies were taken from the water. Two persons died after they had been carried ashore. One of the latter was Mrs. Locke Davison, vice president of the Melbourne Farms Development Company. Davison had swam ashore and had hurried through the surf to where the little knot of survivors and rescuers had gathered. He eagerly scanned the faces of the group and then went to where the dead had been deposited. Without speaking a word to anyone, he dove back into the water and swam toward the wrecked boat. A short time later he was seen bearing the unconscious body of his wife toward the beach. A score of bathers struck out and brought the couple to shore. But efforts to resuscitate Mrs. Davison failed. Her husband is in a critical condition. The disaster taxed the medical resources of this small city. Physicians and nurses from several nearby cities were summoned and they worked throughout the night as rescue boats played about Sebastian Light in search of the missing. George Arnold, 12-year old son of Captain Edward Arnold of the yacht *Clara*, was one of the heroes of the disaster. He was standing near his father in the wheel house when the boat capsized. He was thrown clear and swam ashore where he commandeered a row boat and with two men returned to the scene of the disaster. Crouched in the bow, George directed his companions, whose combined efforts at the oars were needed to keep the craft afloat. He pulled three persons to safety. The dead were placed in a grocery store until relatives could be notified. Lack of hospital quarters forced the injured into private homes.

CLAUDINA

The vessel *Claudina* (also cited as *Glaudina*), Captain Valliant, bound from London to Pensacola, was reported as totally lost on the coast of Florida in the *Lloyd's List* of December 23, 1777.

CLEOPATRA

According to *The Sailor's Magazine and Naval Journal*, Volume 27, the "Brig *Cleopatra* of New York went ashore near St. Marys, Georgia, about September 29, 1854, after losing chains and anchors. She was from Charleston, in ballast, bound to Doboy Island."

CLUB ROYALE

The *Club Royale* was launched as the 1,528-ton ferry *Baltic Jet* at the Bremen, Germany yard of Heremann Roland on April 18, 1985. She was 234.5 feet long overall and 37.7 feet wide, powered by two 18-cylinder diesel engines. In November 1988, she was refitted as a cruise ship at Bremerhaven, and eventually sold to International Shipping Partners of Miami, who renamed her *Europe Jet*. Ultimately, the ship was chartered to operate as a casino ship off Palm Beach and renamed the *Club Royale* after the gambling company of the same name.

The 1995 hurricane season started early, with one of the earliest storm formations on record. The fifth storm began forming near the Bahamas, quickly strengthening into Hurricane Erin on July 31. Due to the storm's proximity, Captain Lars Engebretsen and a skeleton crew evacuated the port of Palm Beach on the evening of July 31, 1995, and headed north to get out of the storm's predicted path. However, the hurricane also took a turn to the north the following day, and its influence impacted the *Club Royale*. At approximately 5:30 a.m. on August 2, the cruise ship began to list. Eight crewmen abandoned ship, however, the captain, engineer, and cook stayed behind. The U.S. Coast Guard first picked up the distress signal from the ship's emergency beacon at 8:00 a.m. approximately 84 nautical miles northeast of Cape Canaveral. When two rescue helicopters arrived on scene around 1:00 p.m., they found no sign of the *Club Royale*. They did, however, spot the eight crew members who were hanging onto two rafts they had been in for nearly eight hours, riding huge swells. Two Coast Guard rescue swimmers struggled in 25- to 30-foot waves to help crew members into the rescue baskets, one at a time. Reportedly, the seas were so rough that one experienced Coast Guardsman became seasick, throwing up between rescues. They reached seven of the eight crew members that way; the merchant vessel *Jarvis Avouts* rescued the eighth man. The body of the engineer was eventually recovered from a life raft off the coast of Georgia on August 4.

COAL WRECK

Towards the south end of Amelia Island, the salvage group Amelia Research and Recovery Company discovered the remains of an unidentified wreck in approximately 10 feet of water they named the "Coal Wreck." While inspecting several magnetic anomalies, they uncovered portions of a ship's rigging, a mast stay, fasteners, and a copper fixture, as well as a significant amount of coal. As the wreck obviously did not fit the parameters of their targeted search effort, further investigation was not pursued. Even though the preliminary work conducted by Amelia Research and Recovery Company did not uncover the hull or other significant vessel architecture that could aid in a potential identification, the abundance of coal points towards the four-masted auxiliary schooner *Marie Gilbert* as a potential suspect vessel. The *Marie Gilbert* grounded on the Nassau Bar with a cargo of coal in 1907.

COLONIST

The sternwheel steamer *Colonist*, built at Kissimmee by Frank King and Paul Gibson, was 45 feet long, 13.7 feet wide, and 16.7 tons burden[51]. Named after an English colony at Narcoosee, she operated between there and Kissimmee until a railroad line connected the two points. Following numerous breakdowns, the steamer was beached next to the *Spray* at Kissimmee, where they both later burned in 1893.

COMET

The ferryboat *Comet*, operating for the Palatka-Crescent City Line, sank at Crescent City at some unknown date[52].

COMMODORE

On December 31, 1896, the tug *Commodore* departed Jacksonville on yet another filibustering run to Cuba. Captained by Edward Murphy, the sea-going tug *Commodore* was a veteran of several runs to Cuba. Built in 1882 at a Philadelphia, Pennsylvania shipyard and home ported in Greenport, New York, the wooden-hulled vessel was 122 feet in length, 21 feet in breadth, displaced 178.3 tons, and with her single engine could travel at a respectable 12 knots. Onboard as a recent addition to the crew was the young novelist Stephen Crane, lauded author of *The Red Badge of Courage*. Crane joined the crew of the *Commodore* as an opportunity to cover the war in Cuba. Unfortunately, Crane would not successfully reach Cuba

The wreck of the *C-Note* off Fort Lauderdale.

Image of the tug *Commodore* (Ponce de Leon Inlet Lighthouse Preservation Association).

on this trip. Instead, he would be presented with another story of struggle, the sinking of the tug *Commodore*, which he would later vividly capture in the short story, "The Open Boat. A Tale Intended to be After the Fact. Being the Experience of Four Men Sunk from the Steamer Commodore." Originally published in *Scribner's Magazine* in June 1897, "The Open Boat" is based on the real-life events that followed the sinking of the *Commodore* on January 2, 1897, as Crane and three other survivors drifted in a ten-foot dinghy for over 24 hours.

Filibustering, or the covert transport (i.e., smuggling) of guns, munitions, and supplies, had become a popular and profitable exercise in the waning years of the nineteenth century. The war in Cuba had been raging on and off for nearly 30 years, and many Americans supported the freedom fighters in their efforts to overthrow the Spanish rule of the island. The 1873 capture of the steamer *Virginius* and the subsequent execution of many of her crew, led to strict regulations against filibustering. With American policy prohibiting filibustering, captains had to be aware not only of Spanish naval vessels, but U.S. warships and revenue cutters enforcing the smuggling prohibition. Earlier in 1896, the *Commodore* was challenged by a U.S. revenue cutter and had to outrun the vessel to avoid capture. Other vessels were not as lucky. On November 7, 1896, the tug *Three Friends* successfully evaded capture from Spanish warships but was escorted back to Jacksonville by the cruiser U.S.S. *Newark*. The *Three Friends* incident resulted in a well-publicized Federal court decision that eventually "legalized" filibustering, much to the chagrin of the Spanish government (details on the *Three Friends* Federal court case can be found under its entry later in this work).

Resting at her berth on the St. Johns River on New Year's Eve Day, the *Commodore* was fully loaded with 15 tons of arms and ammunition, including 300 machetes, 40 bundles of Remington rolling-block rifles, 203,000 rifle cartridges, over 1,000 pounds of dynamite, and 14 cases of drugs and clothing. While it was now legal to carry arms to Cuba, the departure of the *Commodore* was still delayed at the Jacksonville Customs House. While officials were perturbed with the intent of the cargo, they nonetheless eventually cleared the tug for her voyage. The *Commodore* threw her lines in the early evening and slowly steamed along the St. Johns River, which was blanketed with a thick fog. Only two miles from their starting point, the tug abruptly ran aground on a mud flat. Stephen Crane's adventure got off to a slow start.

At 2:30 a.m., the U.S. Revenue Cutter *George S. Boutwell* threw a line to the tug and successfully pulled her off, allowing her to continue her voyage. Progress was halted when the *Commodore* again ran afoul of the notorious mud flats of the St. Johns, however, the tug managed to work herself off and continue her journey in short order. At 2:00 p.m. on January 1, 1897, the *Commodore* crossed the bar to the inlet, only to meet the heavy rollers of the wintry Atlantic. Helmsman Tom Smith pointed the bow of the *Commodore* southward as she slowly plunged through the pounding waves along the Florida coast. Late at night, Stephen Crane could not sleep due to the rough conditions. He made his way to the bridge and struck up a conversation with Smith in order to pass the time. Captain Murphy arrived on the bridge a short while later, only to inform Crane that the vessel was taking on water and that the pumps were apparently choked and couldn't keep up with the rising water. A bucket brigade was formed to rid the holds of water, while the engineer stoked the boiler with everything he could in order to run the tug into Mosquito Inlet (Ponce de Leon Inlet), 18 miles away.

Despite their attempts, the water gained on the men and eventually smothered the boiler fires. Still 15 miles from Mosquito Inlet and now without power, Captain Murphy was forced to drop anchor in order to keep the bow pointed into the seas to avoid being capsized. The crew managed to launch three lifeboats amidst the chaos of the heaving seas. Captain Murphy was the last man to leave the ship and boarded the third lifeboat, along with Stephen Crane, oiler William Higgins, and cook Charles Montgomery. Murphy decided to stay on scene to determine the fate of his vessel. In the pearly gray light of dawn, with the *Commodore* still fighting to stay afloat, Murphy noticed the appearance of the crew from the first mate's lifeboat on the stern on the tug. In the rough seas, the lifeboat had capsized and forced its crew to swim back to the *Commodore* in an attempt to fashion rafts for their second escape attempt. Unfortunately, their efforts were in vain as the tug quickly pitched over and sank beneath the surface.

At 10:00 a.m. on January 2, after successfully reaching the beach, the crew of the first lifeboat arrived at the Mosquito Inlet Lighthouse. Lighthouse keeper Thomas O'Hagan cared for the men and arranged for their transport back to Jacksonville. Unfortunately, the crew neglected to inform O'Hagan of the other survivors still working to reach the safety of the beach.

Meanwhile, Captain Murphy attempted to guide his lifeboat to Mosquito Inlet, but the weather and ocean conspired against him, carrying them to the north. Later that day, they eventually spied land and contemplated rowing through the massive surf. After agreeing that there were no other options available, the crew made a run for the beach. Just as they reached the boiling breakers and realized their fate would be sealed should they continue further, the crew of the lifeboat urgently reversed course and rowed back towards the open ocean to spend the night. By dawn, and with their strength fading, the crew realized that they must try for the beach once again. They methodically rowed toward the backs of the rumbling surf, working to keep the bow pointed forward. Crane related the succession of events:

> The third wave moved forward, huge, furious, implacable. It fairly swallowed the dinghy, and almost simultaneously the men tumbled into the sea. A piece of life-belt had lain in the bottom of the boat, and as the correspondent went overboard he held this to his chest with his left hand. The January water was icy, and he reflected immediately that it was colder than he had expected to find it off the coast of Florida. This appeared to his dazed mind as a fact important enough to be noted at the time. The coldness of the water was sad; it was tragic. This fact was somehow mixed and confused with his opinion of his own situation that it seemed almost a proper reason for tears. The water was cold[53].

Crane struggled to shore while Captain Murphy remained clinging to the keel of the capsized lifeboat. The survivors were exhausted due to the effort exerted in the frigid and storm-churned water. Miraculously, John Kitchell, a resident of nearby Daytona Beach, stripped off his clothes and ran into the surf to rescue the men in distress. Kitchell successfully rescued three of the crew, including Crane and Captain Murphy. Unfortunately, William Higgins perished during the episode.

Supported by American arms and munitions, the Cuban rebels successfully engaged the Spanish for another year until, in 1898, the *U.S.S Maine* exploded in Havana Harbor. That event quickly led to the Spanish-American War and, eventually, Cuban independence. The remains of the *Commodore* rested quietly on the bottom of the Atlantic until the 1960s, when local diver Don Serbousek located an unidentified wreck in 80 feet of water. It was not until 1986 when Elizabeth Friedman compared the manifest with the unique cargo found at the wreck site, that the identity of the wreck was determined to be that of the tugboat *Commodore*. Today, little remains of the filibustering tug. Also known as the "Twelve Mile Wreck," she is mostly sanded in with her engine dominating the site. Her shaft is exposed and can be followed aft to her partially buried single screw. It appears that her boiler exploded, most likely due to contact with the cold seawater, as large sections of boiler plating are scattered about the seabed. Ammunition and other portions of her cargo can be found along the bottom, which consists of sand and shell hash.

View of the gunboat *Commodore Barney* during the Civil War (National Archives).

COMMODORE BARNEY

The sidewheel steamer *Commodore Barney*, named after one of the Continental and U.S. Navy's first heroes, Commodore Joshua Barney, was originally built as the double-ended Williamsburg ferry *Ethan Allen* in 1859 at the Brooklyn, New York shipyard of Perrine, Patterson, and Stack. The *Ethan Allen*, official number 4900, was 143.6 feet long, 33.9 feet wide, displaced 538 tons gross, and was powered by a single cylinder walking-beam engine. On October 2, 1861, the vessel was bought by the U.S. Navy and commissioned as the U.S.S. *Commodore Barney* on October 11. Armed with four guns, she was dispatched to the North Atlantic Blockading Squadron, which found her cruising the Mid-Atlantic coast, as well as participating in numerous expeditions such as the seizure of Roanoke Island and New Bern, North Carolina. In August 1863, *Barney* was working up the James River, Virginia, when a torpedo (mine) exploded under her bow, resulting in the drowning of two men and causing significant damage to the vessel. After two more years of service in Virginia and North Carolina, U.S.S. *Commodore Barney* was sold at the Washington Navy Yard on July 20, 1865. In January 1866, the steamer was redocumented as the *Commodore Barney* and reentered service with Williamsburg Ferries in New York. In 1885, the vessel was sold to Florida interests. In early May 1901, the *Commodore Barney* helped evacuate close to 1,000 people from Jacksonville during a massive fire that eventually decimated the city. The ultimate loss of the steamer *Commodore Barney* occurred on September 22, 1901, when she sunk in the St. Johns River at the foot of Newnan Street near Jacksonville. She apparently remained there for several months, before being "raised, towed over to the railroad bridge, where her remains now lie[54]."

It is worth noting that the *Annual Report of the Chief of Engineers, United States Army, to the Secretary of War for the Year 1905*, included the following information, "On March 27, 1905, an allotment of $4,300 was made from the indefinite appropriation made by Section 20 of the River and Harbor Act of March 3, 1899, for removal of wrecks of the schooner *Ridgewood* and the steam ferryboat *Commodore Barney* from the St. Johns River, the former near McGuire's Mill and the latter at Jacksonville."

COMPTON'S WRECK

"Compton's Wreck," located in 25 feet of water approximately 2,000 feet off Vilano Beach, is likely the remains of a relatively modern 65-foot long wooden-hulled sailing vessel.

The tug *C-One* resting dockside (Miami-Dade County Department of Environmental Resources Management).

C-ONE

The *C-One* was a 110-foot long tug purchased by the Miami-Dade Department of Environmental Resources Management for use as an artificial reef. The aged tug was stripped of her engine and fittings in late 1990 and then towed from Jacksonville to Miami by the tug *Captain Donald* in preparation of her scuttling. On November 3, 1990, while approximately five miles southeast of Fort Pierce Inlet, the 60-foot long *Captain Donald* began taking on water, which flooded into her engine room. The three crewmembers were forced to abandon ship as the *Captain Donald* quickly sank underneath them, but all were quickly rescued without injury. The still-floating *C-One* was eventually towed to Miami following the dramatic and ironic event.

The *C-One* was finally dispatched on November 8, 1990. She was sunk in 68 feet of water off Haulover Inlet in the vicinity of several other artificial reefs. The *C-One* is straddled by the tug *Lady Carmen*, resting just to the west, and the 38-foot long tug *White Coast*, found just to the east. The two sections of the 155-foot long freighter *Conception* are found less than 200 feet to the north of the *C-One*. In addition, a 90-foot long barge and numerous concrete modules lie a short distance to the southeast.

The freighter *Conception* aground off Miami Beach, 1991 (Jayson Gulliford).

CONCEPTION

The *Conception* started her life in 1952 as the coastal freighter *Marie Christine*. The Dutch coaster was 164 feet in length, 26 feet in breadth, and displaced 390 tons gross. The petite vessel changed names numerous times: in 1966 she was renamed *Coria*; in 1976 she was sold to a Panamanian company and renamed *Paulrich Trader*; she was briefly renamed *Coria* again in 1982; in 1983 her name was changed to *M-Notte*; after being sold to a Honduran owner in 1987, she was known as *Lady Barbara*; and finally, she was renamed *Conception* or *La Concepcion* in 1989.

For over two months in early 1991, the Honduran freighter *Conception* was a fixture on trendy South Beach. The vessel, stacked high with trucks, bicycles, rice, beans, and other cargo, was en route to Haiti when it experienced engine problems, forcing it to drop anchor off Miami. The crew had been working to repair the freighter for almost two weeks when strong winds and high seas battered the crippled ship on February 3. The anchor of the *Conception* eventually gave way, and the freighter was thrown up on the beach.

Underwater image of the *C-One*.

Exploring the wreck of the *Conception*.

The ship was not refloated until March 31, and during the interim, the vessel was subject to lawsuits, looters, and graffiti. The *Conception* was subsequently towed up the Miami River to be cleaned, however, the owners of the ship eventually abandoned the freighter due to the massive salvage bill. Miami-Dade County bought the forfeited vessel for $40,000 to be scuttled as an artificial reef.

The *Conception* was sunk in 65 feet of water on June 7, 1991, approximately two miles off Haulover Inlet. The year after its scuttling, Hurricane Andrew ripped the ship into two pieces, which are now separated by a short distance. The fairly intact stern section is found the furthest north, while the collapsed midsection and bow rest to the southeast. The wreck of the *Conception*, or *La Concepcion*, is part of a reef cluster known as the "Miami Wreck Trek," and is in close proximity to the tugs *C-One*, *Lady Carmen*, and *White Coast*, as well as a barge and numerous concrete modules. On a day with good visibility, divers can easily visit all the wrecks on a single dive.

CONCRETE BARGE

Approximately one-half nautical mile off Elliott Key in 11 feet of water rests a large pile of solidified concrete in the shape of barrels, the wooden staves of the barrel long since rotted away. Looking closely in and around the perimeter of the pile, divers can observe the large wooden timbers of the vessel that carried this cargo. Though the site is called the *Concrete Barge*, it is unclear what kind of vessel she actually was when afloat. The pile of concrete rises to within 6 feet of the surface and is surrounded by dense seagrass habitat around its perimeter.

CONISCLIFFE

Built in 1891 at Bucksport, Maine, the three-masted schooner *Coniscliffe*, official number 136255, documented a displacement of 444 tons gross and 342 tons net, a length of 149.5 feet, a breadth of 33.1 feet, and a depth of hold of 12.3 feet. On April 8, 1921, en route from her home port of Mobile, Alabama, to Arecibo, Puerto Rico, the *Coniscliffe* caught fire approximately 50 miles off the east coast of Florida (also cited as latitude 27° 21' north, longitude 79° 31' west). The captain and crew evacuated the burning vessel and were later rescued by the British steamer *Parthenia*.

CONMAR

In September 1944, the 231-ton cargo vessel *Conmar* was reported sunk as a marine casualty at approximate latitude 26° north and longitude 80° west. Little else is known about this vessel or the circumstances of its sinking.

COPENHAGEN

The *Copenhagen* was a schooner-rigged, single-screw steamer built in Sunderland, England by J. Priestman and Company and launched on February 22, 1898. Owned by the Glasgow Shipowners Company, Limited, she was 325 feet in length, 47 feet in breadth, and rated at 3,297 tons. She had a double bottom hull and was powered by three triple expansion steam engines. Captained by William Jones, the *Copenhagen* was used to haul miscellaneous cargo across the Atlantic.

On May 20, 1900, the *Copenhagen* departed Philadelphia, bound for Havana with 4,940 tons of coal. Unfortunately for the *Copenhagen* and her crew of 26, this would be her last cruise. On the morning of May 26, she suddenly crashed into the reef, three-quarters of a mile offshore of Pompano Beach. Captain Jones attempted to work the ship off the reef, but to no avail. Her condition was reported in a May 28 telegraph: "*Copenhagen* stranded three miles south of Hillsboro Inlet, Florida, and remains, peak and forward ballast tank full, six feet in forehold, gaining on pumps six inches per hour; resting hard forward; other holds dry[55]." While she rested hard aground, initial reports indicated the ship should easily be saved.

A June 6 telegram detailed the involvement of local wreckers: "Has sunk in 24 feet of water, all holds filled; salvors abandoned job, and left with all crew except mate and engineers; National Board agent at ship; captain negotiating Merritt, New York; salvors report ship's bottom gone[56]." Several days later, the Merritt and Chapman Wrecking Company tugs *Merritt* and *Chapman* arrived on the scene to help off-load the cargo and lighten the ship. With Commodore Ralph M. Munroe as wreck master, the salvage tugs employed their huge centrifugal pumps to remove the coal and water from the holds of the stranded steamer. The salvors camped out on the stranded steamer during the grueling project, and Commodore Munroe eventually migrated to the roof of the *Copenhagen's* pilothouse, where he was able to find comfortable sleeping conditions in the stifling summer heat.

While the salvage effort incurred substantial complications, the Salvage Association special officer was still optimistic, as conveyed in a June 10 telegraph. "Surveyed vessel. Broadside sea, three-quarters mile from shore, full water, port rail just submerged high water. Diver reports extensive damage forward collision bulkhead, other damage amidships. Unable to ascertain extent; no apparent damage to stern or decks. Unable arrange here. Merritt's representative instructed return New York and report. My opinion can save if act promptly[57]." Work by Merritt continued for about a month. However, a massive fire in Hoboken, New Jersey, on June 30 resulted in the extensive damage and sinkings of several large steamships that commanded the attention of the Merritt and Chapman Wrecking Company. The salvage tugs were directed by the insurance underwriters, Lloyd's, to immediately abandon work on the *Copenhagen* and proceed to New York. Even though another salvage company arrived on the scene, work to save the vessel was slow and inefficient. A final telegraph describes the frustrating turn of events: "Salvors abandoned; nine pumps couldn't control flooding; settling heavy; boilers engines lifted; bottom gone full length; jettisoned thousands tons coal; hopeless[58]." The *Copenhagen* was abandoned as a total loss on July 17 and eventually broke apart on the reef. The vessel was valued at $250,000 and her cargo at $12,500. Captain Jones was deemed responsible for the sinking due to "improper navigation."

The *Copenhagen* can be found off the second reef line, just south of Hillsboro Inlet, in 20 to 35 feet of water. Much of her structure remained visible for several decades after the sinking, and her submerged hulk was used for target practice by aircraft during World War II. While her engine and boilers have been salvaged, a lone donkey boiler, used to power some of the auxiliary machinery, can be found amidships. Much of her framing and ribs can be observed, now heavily encrusted and incorporated into the reef ecosystem. The vessel is oriented with the stern to the north; the actual bow is located approximately 0.4 nautical miles south-southeast from the main portion of the wreck. One possible explanation for this separation is an abandoned salvage attempt during or post-World War II, when recovering scrap metal from local wrecks was a profitable venture for locals. The steamer *Copenhagen* became the fifth Florida Underwater Archaeological Preserve in June 1994, and was listed on the National Register of Historic Places on May 31, 2001.

COQUIMBO

The bark *Coquimbo*, originally the *Cochrina*, was built at Glasgow, Scotland, in 1876. She was 203.8 feet long and 33.7 feet wide. On February 2, 1909, the *Florida Times-Union* reported "The Spanish bark *Coquimbo*, carrying lumber and steel, hit a reef a half-mile below the Boynton Hotel and became a total loss."

COREY N CHRIS

Resting just offshore of Hillsboro Inlet lies one of the most visually spectacular artificial reefs in Florida. Commonly referred to as the "R.B.J.," this site actually consists of two shipwrecks: the *Corey N Chris* and the *Ronald B. Johnson*. The fact that there are two shipwrecks at one reef site is nothing special. The fact that the *Ronald B. Johnson* rests directly on top of the *Corey N Chris*, however, makes the site quite unique. The site could not have been planned better. Yet, it is interesting to note that the final orientation of the two wrecks occurred simply as a result of dumb luck.

The *Corey N Chris* was named after the two sons of Carlos Sanchez, a Boca Raton man who won a contest to name the new artificial reef. The *Corey N Chris* was originally the 130-foot long dredge *BC-246*, and was owned by the U.S. Army. Built in 1942 by the Nashville Bridge Company, the *BC-246* eventually was sold and renamed as the *Trident*. At the end of her useful career, the rusting dredge was acquired for $30,000 and sunk on May 18, 1986, through the efforts of the Pompano Beach Fishing Rodeo, Incorporated and Broward County. The vessel was originally intended to be placed in 200 feet of water, but she ultimately came to rest on the seabed at a depth of approximately 260 feet. Oriented with her bow pointing towards shore, there is a slight slope associated with the site; the depth around her stern approaches 270 feet, while the sand off her bow is 255 feet in depth.

Corey N Chris slipping under the surface (Broward County Artificial Reef Program).

The *Ronald B. Johnson* was a 226-foot long freighter formerly known as the *Otto*. The general cargo freighter was constructed at Deest, Netherlands, in 1955 for the Otto Shipping Company, Limited. The vessel was destined for use as an artificial reef after she had run aground in Kingston, Jamaica and was abandoned by her owners. Resolve Marine Group patched and refloated the vessel, which was subsequently towed to Florida. The U.S. Fish and Wildlife Service provided funds to help clean the vessel in preparation for use as an artificial reef. A young girl named the freighter after her uncle Ronald B. Johnson, a serviceman who died in Vietnam, following a raffle conducted by Broward County. During a joint operation with the U.S. Navy Explosive Ordnance Disposal team from Jacksonville, Resolve Marine Group sank the *Ronald B. Johnson* with C-4 explosives on May 15, 1988 – almost two years to the day after the sinking of the *Corey N Chris*. Amazingly, the hull of the *Ronald B. Johnson* came to rest directly across the deck of the dredge *Corey N Chris*. While the *Corey N Chris* is oriented along the east-west axis, the *Ronald B. Johnson* runs north-south over the perpendicular hull of the older dredge.

Two ships, their sinking separated by approximately two years, now rest in one discrete area off South Florida. Initially, the hull of the *Ronald B. Johnson* was fully supported by the hull of the *Corey N Chris*. While the bow

Scuttling of the *Ronald B. Johnson* (Broward County Artificial Reef Program).

Stern superstructure of the *Ronald B. Johnson*.

of the large freighter rested on the sandy seabed, the stern of the *Ronald B. Johnson* arced up and was suspended in the water column at an approximate 45-degree angle, rising to within 120 feet of the surface. Time and the forces of nature worked to weaken the integrity of the *Johnson*, and the influence of Hurricane Andrew in 1992 delivered the final blow, as the keel of the freighter collapsed fore and aft of its bisection with the *Corey N Chris*.

With a maximum depth averaging approximately 260 feet, the "R.B.J." is definitely a technical dive. Frequently, strong currents sweep over the site, and divers have also experienced cold-water upwellings that drop the bottom temperature below 50°F. When conditions are nice, the "R.B.J." can be an awe-inspiring dive. On a dive in January 2004, I had the pleasure of exploring the wreck site in brilliant blue, 74°F water, with perhaps 100 feet of visibility and a negligible current. The grapnel hook was secured into the forward kingposts of the *Ronald B. Johnson*. Commonly, the hook will encounter this portion of the wreck, as it is at the southernmost extremity of the "R.B.J." wreck site. Scootering down the line, I settled onto the stern superstructure to begin capturing the surreal scene with my camera. My buddies and I explored the cargo holds of the Johnson, noting the breaches in the hull from the scuttling charges that sent the freighter to the bottom. I worked to document the wreck site in all its glory, gratified to be experiencing such a wonderful dive in the middle of winter. Dropping down off the hull and onto the sandy seabed, I watched one of my buddies scooter under the hull of the *Ronald B. Johnson*, where it was still supported by the dredge *Corey N Chris*; it is not too often that a diver can swim entirely under a massive shipwreck.

The stern of the dredge rests at the eastern-most point of the site, which is in slightly deeper water than the inshore side of its conjoined neighbor, the *Ronald B. Johnson*. Both wrecks were enveloped by monofilament line from unlucky fishermen, while a few anchors were also spotted amongst the artificial reef site. On this particular day, there was an odd absence of marine life. Typically, it is not uncommon to observe grouper, amberjack, and other large denizens of the deep on the

"R.B.J." This day, only a few large mutton snapper made their presence known to my fellow divers as we traversed the wrecks.

After scootering around both wrecks, generally having an insane amount of fun, we made our departure plans as our bottom time approached 30 minutes. While my buddy released the line from the kingpost of the Johnson, we slowly ascended and drifted northward. My last glimpse of the ghostly stern of the *Ronald B. Johnson* was just as I ascended past 150 feet. Carried slowly to the north by the gentle current, I completed my decompression with the other divers, content in the fact that our time was well spent.

CORINNE

The 1895 *Annual Report of the Supervising Inspector-General, U.S. Steamboat-Inspection Service to the Secretary of Commerce and Labor*, listed the December 8, 1894, demise of the steamer *Corinne*, which burned at her wharf at St. Marys due to a fire of unknown origin. The vessel, valued at $2,000, was a total loss.

CORKY C.

On February 14, 1956, the 28-ton *Corky C.* burned off Fisher Island at the entrance of Government Cut at Miami.

CORKY M.

The *Corky M.* was a 41-foot long sailboat formerly known as the *Sea Bear*. The vessel was renamed in memory of diver George M. Micco and scuttled as an artificial reef on April 8, 1997. The *Corky M.* now rests in 65 feet of water in close proximity to the *Bruce Mueller*, which was a 45-foot long Chris Craft yacht built in 1955 and sunk as a reef in February 1996.

CORNWALL

On November 30, 1873, the British bark *Cornwall*, en route from Belize to London, ran aground on Ajax Reef. Much of her cargo of mahogany logwood was salvaged by Key West wreckers. The *Cornwall*, built in September 1863 at Bathurst, England, as the *Credenda*, was 136 feet in length, 30.58 feet in breadth, and displaced 389 tons. At the time of her loss, she was mastered by J. Coghlan and owned by Anderson and Company.

CORONA

The *Corona* was a sternwheel steamer, 57 feet long and 10.6 feet wide, built by Captain Ed Hall at Alva in 1908 using the engine from the steamer *Leonora*. Originally destined for the mail run on the Caloosahatchee, the steamer was later sold to Captain Menge sometime after World War I. The *Corona* reportedly wrecked at Canal Point on the eastern shore of Lake Okeechobee in 1928.

CORSAIR

As reported in the *St. Petersburg Times*, October 31, 1941, "Three members of the shrimp boat *Corsair* were rescued from a heavy sea half a mile off Ponce de Leon

Inlet yesterday after the trawler capsized and broke up while being towed across a bar by a Coast Guard surf boat."

COSME CALZADA

The *Cosme Calzada* was a 1,405-ton wooden sailing ship built in 1869 by Curtis Smith and Company of Boston, Massachusetts. She was 200 feet in length, 38.5 feet in beam, and depth of hold was 24 feet. She had traded hands and changed names several times during her life, including *Sarah Hignett, Henriette, Perla de Sitges,* and *Rosa Alefret.* Juan C. Calzada of Barcelona, Spain, owned the ship at the time of her loss.

At noon on October 17, 1904, the *Calzada* ran ashore three miles north of the Gilbert's Bar Life-Saving Station in a gale and terrible rainstorm. She was traveling in ballast from Gloucester, Massachusetts, to Brunswick, Georgia, though it is unclear why she missed her destination and continued sailing so far south. In the midst of the storm, one of the crew tied a line to his body and swam through the powerful breakers to shore. Aside from one man who became entangled in rigging and drowned, the entire crew safely made it to the beach.

The tired men stumbled down the beach to the cabin of Harvey Baker, who took them in, fed them, and kept them overnight. The following day, Mr. Baker brought them to the Gilbert's Bar Station and House of Refuge. The keeper, Mr. William E. Rea, informed the Spanish ambassador of the disaster. It is interesting to note that in the shipwreck report filed by Mr. Rea, the name of the ship is *Cosme Calzado*, though insurance records cite the last name (as well as the owner) as *Calzada*.

The wreck is located 900 feet off the beach in approximately 12 feet of water off Hutchinson Island. The wreck is dominated by the ballast pile, which is strewn for 120 feet along a bearing of 350°. The bow is found at the south end of the site, where an anchor, windlass, and capstans are scattered around the perimeter. Timbers with brass spikes can also be found amongst the wreck, though most are buried under the ballast. The wreck of the *Cosme Calzada* is easily accessible, though due to its shallow depth and close proximity to the beach, good conditions are dependent on prevailing wind and weather.

COTOPAXI

The steam freighter *Cotopaxi* disappeared off Florida during a storm in early December 1925. The 2,351 ton *Cotopaxi*, 252.9 feet in length between parallels and 43.6 feet in breadth, was built for the U.S. Shipping Board by Great Lakes Engineering Works at Ecorse, Michigan, in late 1918. The standard "Laker," built en masse for the war effort, was powered with a triple-expansion engine that produced a speed of 9.5 knots. Due to the end of the war in Europe, the freighter was eventually sold to the Clinchfield Coal and Navigation Company. The *Cotopaxi* departed Charleston, South Carolina, on November 29, 1925, bound for Havana with a cargo of coal. She ran head-long into a tropical storm that swept up the Atlantic coast, and on November 30, distress signals picked up at Jacksonville indicated the ship was leaking. After an exhaustive search from Norfolk to Cuba by Coast Guard vessels, no trace of the ship or her 33 men was ever found. In 1928, a lawsuit was heard by federal court on the loss of the *Cotopaxi*. The relatives of those lost filed a suit for damages totaling about $1 million. They claimed the vessel was unseaworthy following a grounding event off Argentina in 1919. Whether that damage facilitated the demise of the *Cotopaxi* will never be known for certain. The wreck of the *Cotopaxi* has yet to be located. One potential site worth investigating is the "Bear Wreck" off St. Augustine, which rests along the route the *Cotopaxi* would have taken to Cuba and possesses some of the features one would expect of a World War I "Laker."

COURIER DE TAMPICO

Available information on this particular wreck is contradictory, specifically the actual name of the vessel, date of loss, and ultimate fate. Admiralty records of the U.S. District Court for the Southern District of Florida document the wrecking of a brig named *Courier de Tampico* on August 30, 1838, at French Shoals (possibly French Reef). The same records also document the loss of a brig named *Courier de Vera Cruz*. *The Sailor's Magazine and Naval Journal*, Volume 11, documented the "French brig *Courier de Tampico*, from Havana for Bordeaux, was driven ashore near Cape Florida light, and with her cargo is a total loss. Only seven out of sixteen persons on board were saved." On October 16, 1838, *The Republican Compiler*, published the following expanded account:

> As reported in the *Key West Floridian* on September 15, in the gale on September 7, the French brig *Courier de Vera Cruz*, from Havana for Bordeaux, was driven ashore

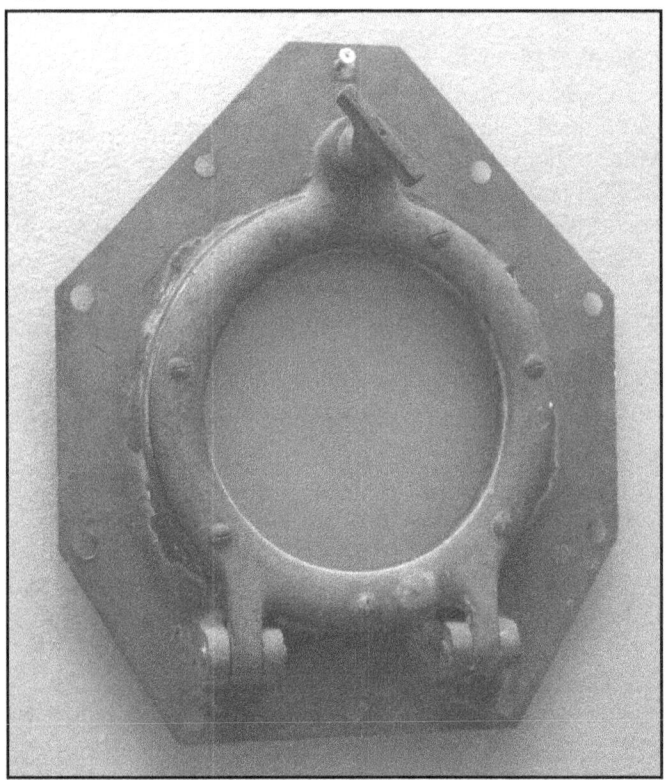

Porthole recovered from the *Cosme Calzada* in the 1970s.

about twelve miles north of Cape Florida Light, and only seven out of sixteen souls saved; brig and cargo lost. The survivors rescued from the devouring ocean were soon visited by a large party of armed Indians, who spared their lives because they were Frenchmen, saying that they only killed Americans. The captain and the six other survivors were taken from the beach after the gale was over by a smack bound to Key West.

A similar piece that appeared in the *Milwaukee Sentinel* on November 6, 1838, identified the captain of the *Courier de Vera Cruz* as Jules Julian, and further stated the vessel, which was from Havana bound for Bordeaux with a cargo of sugar and cigars, was totally lost about 12 miles north of Cape Florida. To cloud the issue even more, *The American Almanac and Repository of Useful Knowledge For the Year 1840; Statement of Salvages at Key West, Florida, for the Year 1838*, stated the "French brig *Courier de Tampico*, vessel and cargo saved, gross sum, $3,000."

Based on the above evidence, it would appear a French brig was definitely wrecked during a hurricane in 1838. The available information, including the survivor reports from other vessels wrecked in the storm, leads this author to believe the vessel in question was lost on September 7 north of Cape Florida, and not in late August on "French Shoals." Most accounts of the wrecking indicate the brig was totally lost; therefore, the statement of salvage perhaps only indicated a partial salvage of cargo, versus the rescue of the entire vessel off the beach. Conversely, the record could be totally inaccurate. Finally, while it is unclear if the vessel's true name was *Courier de Tampico* or *Courier de Vera Cruz* (both large port cities on Mexico's Caribbean coast), it is obvious that the newspaper accounts and other records are discussing only one vessel, regardless of the discrepancies in vessel name.

COYLET

The *Coylet* was a dry cargo freighter laid down by J. Laing and Sons, Limited, of Sunderland, England, in 1917 as the *War Rambler*. Completed in March 1918, the *War Rambler* was 400 feet in length, 52.4 feet in breadth, and displaced 5,495 tons. In 1919, she was sold to the Hindustan Steamship Company and renamed the *Waziristan*, and then a year later sold to Coylet Steamship Company. Renamed the *Coylet*, her new owners converted the single-deck freighter into an oil tanker consisting of five main cargo tanks: three forward of the machinery space and two aft.

On February 8, 1922, fire broke out aboard the *Coylet* off Key West, whereupon the vessel was promptly abandoned. The vessel continued to burn as it drifted north with the Gulf Stream. On February 14, the U.S.C.G.C. *Tallapoosa* came across the burning derelict off Cape Canaveral. As the abandoned tanker presented a menace to navigation, the *Tallapoosa* destroyed the *Coylet* by gunfire. The position of the incident was recorded as latitude 28° 51' north and longitude 79° 37' west, which is approximately 53 nm northeast of Cape Canaveral.

CRAZY JIM

The U.S. Coast Guard reported the 39-foot long, wooden-hulled vessel *Crazy Jim* sank in over 800 feet of water approximately four miles off Hollywood in 1976.

CRICKET

The loss of the steamer *Cricket* was detailed in *The New York Times* on June 26, 1869:

> The steamer *Cricket*, Capt. A.E. Lozier, from Key West, which port she left on the 10th inst. for New York, got short of fuel at the southward of Cape Canaveral, and arrived at St. Augustine Bar at 4 P.M. on the night of the 15th inst., with the last stick of wood in the furnace. They were obliged to burn bacon for fuel. The wind was blowing N.N.E. – no pilot in sight. They steered first for the outer channel buoy, and then made direct for the inner one, and brought up on the bar. Her keel broke and the sea made a clear breach over her; making her a total wreck. The Captain and crew abandoned her at 7 o'clock P.M., and arrived in the city. By great exertions they succeeded in saving some of their private effects, in a damaged condition. The steamer was owned by the Captain and valued at $10,000; no insurance…. The wreck lies between the outer and inner channel buoys, where the channel formerly was.

In 1995, a survey conducted by the St. Augustine Lighthouse Archaeological Maritime Program identified an approximate 120-foot long wreck site (SJ03310), which was primarily composed of an exposed riveted iron boiler, single-cylinder inverted steam engine, propeller shaft, four-bladed propeller, and buried wooden hull structure resting in 20 feet of water. Archaeologists studied the wreck site over the next few years and determined the wreck's keel may be fractured, which might be expected from the stranding of a steamer in shallow water. While not positively identified, it is possible this site off St.

Coylet burning at sea, February 14, 1922 (U.S. Coast Guard).

Augustine Inlet may represent the final resting spot of the steamer *Cricket*.

CROWN (1738)

According to the *Daily Post* of January 23, 1739, the British ship *Crown*, Captain Henry Jeffery, wrecked near Cape Florida. While all the reports of the *Crown's* loss reference Cape Florida, one article mentioned the vessel wrecked at approximate latitude 24° 50' north, which would place her off Lower Matecumbe Key.

CROWN (1857)

The 1,259-ton ship *Crown* was built at Quebec, Canada, in 1851, and its captain and owner was cited as T. Carrey. In January 1857, the *Crown* was en route from New Orleans to her homeport of Liverpool with a cargo of cotton, corn, and wheat, when the ship ran afoul of Ajax Reef. According to *The Sailor's Magazine and Naval Journal*, Volume 29, on "January 19, 1857, British ship *Crown*, ashore near Cape Florida, bilged. Value $250,000." Additional information was included in *Hunt's The Merchants' Magazine and Commercial Review*, Volume 38, which stated, "British ship *Crown*, Carey [*sic*], New Orleans for Liverpool, ashore off Caesar's Creek, total loss, value $250,000, expenses $9,500, sales $28,773, salvage $23,050."

CRUIZER PRIVATEER

An extract from a December 15, 1746, letter from Charleston, South Carolina, which appeared in the *London Evening Post* of February 10, 1747, revealed, "The *Cruizer Privateer*, of Philadelphia, lately taken by the *xebeques* [a type of Spanish ship], and afterwards fitted out from the Havannah, with another snow, was drove ashore at Cape Florida, and beat to pieces." All articles referred to the vessel as "*Cruizer Privateer*," but it is unclear if this is the true name of the vessel, or if the reports were merely referring to a type of vessel (i.e., a privateer).

CRUZ DEL SUR

The wreck of the *Cruz del Sur* is one of the more impressive deep artificial reefs off South Florida. The freighter was built by the German shipbuilder Lindenau in their Kiel shipyard, and launched as the *Tronstad* on July 7, 1956. The 1,995-ton vessel was 258 feet in overall length and 41 feet in breadth. Over the years, the freighter changed names several times, first to *Eva* in 1962, then to *Caribbean Tamanaco* in 1969, and finally to *Cruz del Sur* in 1977. Like many other freighters sunk as artificial reefs, the *Cruz del Sur* was seized by the U.S. Coast Guard for smuggling drugs on March 3, 1985, when a boarding party from the U.S.C.G.C. *Mesquite* found three pounds of marijuana hidden onboard. The forfeited vessel was purchased by Miami-Dade and Broward Counties, and sunk with explosives in 240 feet of water on December 16, 1986.

As the sinking of the *Cruz del Sur* was a joint project between Miami-Dade and Broward Counties, the former freighter was deployed basically on the border of the two

The freighter *Cruz del Sur* is towed offshore to be deployed as an artificial reef (Broward County Artificial Reef Program).

counties and less than one mile south of the Tenneco Towers site. The *Cruz* sits upright and intact, with her forward kingposts reaching to within 140 feet of the surface. Due to her location approximately seven miles south of Port Everglades, visibility is generally excellent over the wreck. While the cargo holds are largely bare, aside from some scattered hatch covers resting under a layer of fine silt, the decks of the wreck are adorned by a colorful layer of invertebrate growth, which hosts swarms of small tropical fish.

CUMBERLAND

The U.S. Army Corps of Engineers' hydraulic dredge *Cumberland* was built in 1902 at Belfast, Maine, at a cost of $158,450. The 1,870-ton vessel was 200 feet long, 40.67 feet wide, 23.5 feet in depth, and was fitted with two 18-inch centrifugal pumps. Her final sea trial occurred on December 11, 1902, where she met the specified speed and volume intake requirements of 10 knots and 18 tons per minute, respectively. When she was hauled out for repairs in May 1903, her wooden hull received a full coat of copper to inhibit marine fouling and, specifically, damage from wood-boring teredo worms. The *Cumberland* was originally built for use in connection with planned improvements of Fernandina Harbor, where she worked for her first two years. The dredge vessel also worked extensively in Savannah Harbor, Georgia, where she was eventually transferred in 1920.

On June 23, 1931, the *Cumberland* was en route from Savannah, her home port, to Mobile, Alabama, to be

Dredge *Cumberland* (U.S. Army Corps of Engineers).

drydocked for overhaul and repair. Unfortunately, the vessel strayed too close to shore and grounded just offshore Fort Lauderdale, reportedly on a pile of cement that was jettisoned by the *Frances Hyde* when she ran aground in the same area in 1913. Numerous vessels worked to refloat the *Cumberland*, but after two days it was apparent the fate of the dredge was sealed. The captain and crew abandoned ship on June 25 as the position of the vessel was becoming dangerous, and due to the flood of water, which was more than the pumps could handle. Over the following months, the *Cumberland* was stripped of her fittings by both legitimate salvors and covert looters, and then steadily beat down by the Atlantic Ocean.

The wreck of the *Cumberland* is not well known to local divers. Due to its location close to shore and the fact that it has been underwater for well over seven decades, little is left of the former hopper dredge. While not confirmed, the position derived from the reported coordinates cited above is in close proximity to the historical wrecking site. The *Cumberland* rests in approximately 10 feet of water off Lauderdale-By-The-Sea. The site was positively identified by John Noyes, who recovered a bronze plaque embossed with the vessel's name.

Bronze plaque recovered from the wreck of the dredge *Cumberland* (John Noyes).

CUSHNOC

The brig *Cushnoc*, sailing from Cardenas for New York with a cargo of sugar, sprung a leak on June 2, 1853, and was run ashore near Cape Florida. The vessel was determined to be a total loss. Apparently, this was not the first time she wrecked on the coast of Florida, as indicated by correspondence from Key West published in *The New York Times* on May 10, 1852: "The brig *Cushnoc*, wrecked on this coast some years since, and now owned by Messrs. Ladd and Standard, of your city, in the New York and St. Mark's line of packets, put into this port a few days since leaking. It was the intention of her consignee, Hiram Benner, Esq., to have discharged the cargo, and have hove the vessel out; upon second consideration her top works were merely caulked and she sailed for St. Marks on the 27th ultimo."

CYNOSURE

The brig *Cynosure* became the victim of fire during a voyage from Rockland, Maine, to New Orleans, Louisiana, on May 25, 1857. The fire consumed the vessel, burning it to the water's edge at Elliott Key south of Miami. According to *Hunt's The Merchants' Magazine and Commercial Review*, Volume 38, the brig was valued at $30,000 and mastered by Captain Anderson.

CYRUS BUTLER

According to *The Sailor's Magazine and Naval Journal*, Volume 10, the "Bark *Cyrus Butler*, from New Orleans for Liverpool, went ashore in the severe gale of August 1, 1837, and bilged, at Hillsboro Inlet. The crew arrived at Key West in an open boat, having been at sea 11 days."

D & D II

According to the November 30, 1960, *Ocala Star-Banner*, the Texas shrimp boat *D & D II* was abandoned off Flagler Beach. The shrimper apparently was damaged by high winds and shipped water the night before. It was taken in tow by another shrimp boat, the *Tommy T*, on the morning of November 30; however, it was abandoned when the two vessels were about two miles offshore and later foundered. The 46-ton *D & D II* was reportedly built in 1945.

DAISY FARLIN

The schooner *Daisy Farlin* was built in August 1891 at the Bath, Maine, shipyard of Kelley, Spear, and Company. The sailing vessel registered a length of 151.6 feet, a breadth of 34.2 feet, and a displacement of 467 tons gross. In early 1898, the Benner Line schooner carried guns and cannon valued at over $2,000,000 to Key West and the Dry Tortugas in preparation of the Spanish American War. In total, the *Daisy Farlin* carried four ten-inch guns, measuring 30.5 feet long and weighing 67,000 pounds each; two eight-inch guns, 26.5 feet long and weighing 32,000 pounds each; and two twelve-inch mortar carriages, weighing 76,000 pounds each.

In October 1910, the *Daisy Farlin* was towed into Newport, Rhode Island, by the tug *Tormentor* in a heavily-damaged state due to an intense gale. Most of her rigging was lost and her deck house was smashed. In November 1915, the schooner returned to the Kelly, Spear, and Company yard to undergo repairs and an overhaul. A brief notice published in the *Galveston County Daily News* on November 21, 1919, stated the "steamship *Gulfmaid* reported by radio today that she had the crew of the schooner *Daisy Farlin*, off Brunswick. One of the crew was reported in need of surgical attention. The *Farlin* left Port Arthur Texas for Tunis on October 18." Additional information indicates the *Daisy Farlin* was lost or abandoned approximately 70 miles east-northeast of the St. Johns Bar.

DALLAS NEAL

The *Dallas Neal* was a wooden-hulled shrimp trawler built in 1952 by the Diesel Engine Sales Company (DESCO Marine, Incorporated) at their St. Augustine shipyard as hull number 318. The 67-foot long shrimper reportedly foundered approximately five miles east of Melbourne on October 19, 1974.

DAMOCLES

As related in a story by Roman philosopher Cicero, Damocles was a member of court to Dionysius II of Syracuse. Constantly flattering to Dionysius, the tyrant offered to switch places with Damocles for a day. Accepting the offer, Damocles was waited on like a king, but during an extravagant meal he noticed a sharpened sword hanging by a single thread directly above his head. Immediately, he lost all desire to be king. The "Sword of Damocles" is a tale used to demonstrate the imminent peril faced by those in positions of power.

The 148-foot long steamer *Damocles* was built in 1927 and used for passenger cruises across the English Channel. On March 18, 1982, the then Cayman-island flagged *Damocles* was seized by the U.S.C.G.C. *Courageous* after an at-sea inspection found a hidden cargo of 28-tons of marijuana worth $17 million on board the ship. Towed into Port Canaveral, the vessel sat idle while officials attempted to determine ownership of the ship. During her four-year internment, the *Damocles* took on water and eventually listed sharply against a bulkhead and sunk. Declared a derelict, she was towed offshore on May 19, 1987, to be used as an artificial reef. At just after 4:00 p.m., a single scuttling charge blew a four-foot hole in her hull and she plunged stern first to the bottom in under 10 minutes. The *Damocles* is largely intact and is a popular site with divers and fishermen. Numerous concrete culverts can be found in the sand surrounding the wreck.

DANIEL WEBSTER

The *Daniel Webster* was a sidewheel steamer built in 1851 at New York. The 850-ton ship was 225 feet long and 30 feet wide, and was powered by a walking beam engine with a stroke of 56 inches, 11 feet. In a detailed account published in *The New York Times* on October 8, 1866, Captain Bolger described the loss of his vessel due to a hurricane:

> Left New York September 27, bound to Mobile, with 44 passengers. October 1 – Wind northeast; moderate sea; everything going well until dark, when a heavy cross-sea set in from the eastward; wind increasing to a hurricane. At 10 P.M. it burst upon us with terrific violence. Found ourselves off Cape Canaveral, in 13 ½ fathoms of water. Hauled to the wind and stood to the eastward. October 2 – Wind still unabated, with a tremendous cross sea; 6 P.M., shipped a heavy sea, which carried away the forecastle hatch-house, and swept the forward decks, also causing ship to leak badly; set the pumps working; 7 P.M., engineer reported the water to be still increasing, vessel laboring heavy; 10 P.M., water put out the fires, all hands, including passengers, bailing; we then prepared the boats with necessary stores, etc., satisfied that no human power could save the ship. Midnight, began shipping heavy seas, ship rolling fearfully, expecting her to founder momentarily. October 3 – Gale still continuing, but with less violence, with an awful sea; all hopes of saving the ship gone, as she was sinking rapidly. 4 A.M. – Began launching the boats; launched the starboard boat, which was immediately stove and lost; at daylight found we must abandon the ship, and began launching the boats, when providentially the steamer *George*

Cromwell hove in sight and immediately bore down for us, and soon succeeded in transforming our passengers and crew to her deck in safety. The last boat had hardly succeeded in leaving the wreck when the vessel sunk, going down stern first.

The wreck of the *Daniel Webster* likely rests off the central east coast of Florida. Cape Canaveral was the last landmark reported, approximately 36 hours before her loss, though it is unclear how far offshore she stood, and if the hurricane pushed the steamer towards the north or south of the Cape.

The coaster *Dantor* sailing as the *Ameland*.

DANTOR

The *Dantor* was originally built in the Netherlands as the *Ameland* in 1974. Completed in December 1974, the 826-ton cargo ship was 203.7 feet long and 29.8 feet wide. In 1988 her name was changed to *Afhanelijk* and in 1998 she was sold to Haitian owners and renamed *Dantor*. The *Dantor* was seized on January 31, 2001, by the U.S. Customs Service after agents followed a rental truck that had been loaded with 880 pounds of cocaine from the freighter. Following the forfeiture of the vessel as an asset held by drug smugglers, the *Dantor* was prepared for use as an artificial reef and sunk on May 2, 2002, off Hollywood. The freighter now rests upright and intact in 128 feet of water.

A school of Atlantic spadefish cruise over the bow of the *Dantor* (Matthew W. Hoelscher).

DAVID KEMPS

The ferry *David Kemps*, official number 157288, was built in 1891 at New Berlin, Florida. The 57-ton screw steamer, 87.5 feet long and 20.9 feet wide, was employed by the Jacksonville-Mayport-Fort George Island Line. On June 18, 1897, the *David Kemps* was lost to fire at Black Creek, just off the St. Johns River.

DAVID NICKELS

The *David Nickels*, official number 6110, was built in 1845 as a bark at Searsport, Maine. In 1870, the vessel was converted to a schooner, whereupon she registered a length of 94.6 feet, a beam of 24 feet, and a displacement of 205 tons. The *David Nickels*, Captain Wyman, encountered a hurricane in mid-October 1876 during a voyage from Philadelphia for Mobile. The *Boston Daily Globe*, November 11, 1876, detailed the fate of the schooner:

> On the morning of the 19th ult. she anchored off Florida Reef, which was ten miles distant. As the storm abated the sea rose to a tremendous height, and she rolled both her masts away. In going over the side they ripped the deck up, the water rushed below and filled her. To save their lives the crew took to the boat, but in the act of leaving one man fell overboard and was drowned. The boat was headed for the shore, which was covered with surf as far as the eye could reach and it was with great difficulty she could be kept from swamping. While trying to land she was capsized twice, and all hands would have perished in the surf but for the timely aid of a boat from Cape Florida lighthouse, which succeeded in saving them. They were taken to the lighthouse and kindly treated.... The vessel sank shortly after she was abandoned and became a total loss. The crew saved nothing, but the clothes they wore, and they were almost torn off them on the surf.

Based on the above account, it would appear the *David Nickels* was lost off Key Biscayne. Other sources specifically indicate she wrecked at Fowey Rocks.

DAVID T.

Originally built as a landing craft, the 200-foot long converted freighter *David T.* was sunk as an artificial reef off Fort Pierce on October 9, 1982. The wreck rests in 80 feet of water.

DAVIS-HOLDEN WRECK

The "Davis-Holden Wreck" is a site located approximately 1,000 feet offshore and a half mile south of Fort Pierce Inlet. First documented in 1965, divers found ballast rock, metal fastenings, and other assorted artifacts from an early nineteenth century shipwreck. In subsequent years, salvors have recovered three iron howitzer guns, ironstone china, crockery, anchors, buttons, and parts of a ship's bell. It is believed the wreck was lost in the 1830-1840 timeframe and may have been involved with the Second Seminole War.

DAYLIGHT

The *Daylight*, official number 6819, was a 70.7-foot long, 16.4-foot wide sidewheel steamer built in 1873 at Palatka, which burned on the Indian River in the mid-1870s.

DEAL

Shortly before dawn on June 3, 1925, crews from the attending tugs *Mohave* and *Nemo* rescued Captain Percy Jackson and 13 men from the dredge vessel *Deal* before it foundered in heavy seas 15 miles north of Jupiter Light. The *Deal*, owned by the Waldeck-Deal Dredging Company, was being towed from Fort Pierce to Fort Lauderdale when it encountered a wild nor'easter, which produced 30-foot seas and overtook the dredge's pumps. Minutes after the last man was hauled onboard the *Mohave* at 2:30 a.m., the *Deal* heeled over and vanished in 110 feet (also cited as nine fathoms) of water, her lights still blazing as she dived under the waves. The *Deal*, 100 feet in length and 50 feet in beam, was valued at $70,000. According to an article in *The Miami News* on June 3, 1925, no attempt would be made to raise the sunken vessel.

The scrapped hulk of the *Deep Freeze* just prior to her deployment as an artificial reef (George Detrio).

DEEP FREEZE

The *Deep Freeze* was originally launched at the Neuenfelde, Germany shipyard of shipbuilder *J.J Sietas Schiffswerft* on December 15, 1958, as the *Marie Horn*. Commonly known as a "reefer," the *Marie Horn* was 231.6 feet long, 33.5 feet wide, and displaced 1,138 tons gross. In 1969, she was sold to Trans Caribbean Lines of Miami, registered in Liberia, and renamed the *Deep Freeze*. On January 9, 1972, the *Deep Freeze* was rocked by an explosion and then swept by an ensuing fire while moored at Puerto Limon, Costa Rica. The gutted freighter was eventually towed to Miami, where she was stripped of her superstructure and later scuttled as an artificial reef on October 1, 1976. The wreck of the *Deep Freeze* rests in 135 feet of water with the top of her hull rising to within 110 feet of the surface. While relatively intact, the freighter's stern was twisted from the remainder of the hull by Hurricane Andrew in 1992. There are several other wrecks in close proximity to the *Deep Freeze*, including the *St. Henry's Express* and the *Pimelious*. Coincidentally, the *Deep Freeze* now rests approximately 12 miles north of the *Ultra Freeze*, another reefer built by *J.J. Sietas* at the same shipyard.

DEEP TUG

Officially known as Stan's Reef #1, the "Deep Tug" was originally built as *LT-529* for the U.S. Army in June 1944 by Levingston Shipbuilding at Orange, Texas. The large tug was 143 feet in length, 33 feet in width, and displaced 505 tons. After a long career with the U.S. Army, mostly serving in the Pacific, *LT-529* was sold in 1981. On July 18, 1985, the dormant tug, then owned by West Indies Transport Equipment Company (W.I.T. Equipment), broke loose from its mooring on the Indian River during a storm and came perilously close to smashing into a bridge before the U.S. Coast Guard was able to get control of the vessel. Following the incident, W.I.T. Equipment donated the tug to the Fort Pierce Fishing Club, which paid $15,000 to get the vessel ready to be towed and sunk. On October 5, 1985, two valves in the tug were opened, which allowed the tug to flood and eventually sink in approximately 200 feet of water. The former *LT-529* can now be found just offshore the U.S.S. *Muliphen*.

Construction of the tug *LT-529* (National Archives).

DEEPWATER II

The 44-ton shrimp trawler *Deepwater II*, 59 feet long and 18 feet wide, was reportedly lost on January 24, 1960, at approximate latitude 30° 31' north and longitude 80° 28' west. Four months later, the shrimper *Majo* trawled up a lift raft in their nets approximately 15 miles north of Mayport, which was identified as coming from the *Deepwater II*.

DEFIANCE

On June 22, 1973, the 97-foot long yacht *Defiance* mysteriously burned before sinking roughly 13 nautical miles east of Port Canaveral in 70 feet of water. While three crew members safely escaped the inferno, the disaster unfortunately claimed one life. In the days following the sinking, newspaper articles stated the vessel was owned by Pied Piper Yacht Charters, which purportedly was a shell company for Roy M. Cohn. Mostly remembered as an aide to Senator Joseph McCarthy, Cohn was a prominent figure during the probes of alleged Communist subversion in American government and society. At the time of the *Defiance's* loss, Cohn was under constant oversight from the Internal Revenue Service for delinquent income taxes, and it was speculated that Cohn had ordered the vessel scuttled to collect on a $200,000 insurance policy. Today, the wreck of the *Defiance* is occasionally visited by spearfishermen and anglers. The hull of the former yacht is broken down and low to the shell-strewn bottom, though the bow, resting on its starboard side, rises approximately eight feet off the bottom and presents the highest relief.

DEFIANT

The ocean-going tug *Defiant* was sunk as an artificial reef on November 11, 1996. The stout tug, approximately 150 feet in length and 34 feet in beam, now rests in 133 feet of water 33 nautical miles east of Ponce Inlet. While they may be hard to locate, it should be noted that scattered randomly near the *Defiant* are 26 U.S. Navy A-6 Intruder aircraft that were also sunk by Volusia County.

DELAWARE

The loss of the steamer *Delaware* was reported on June 15, 1865, in *The New York Times*, which stated, "Last week while crossing St. Johns Bar, on the Florida coast, she ran aground and could not be worked off. She had on board the Seventh United States Regulars and a large number of women and children, all bound to Jacksonville. No lives were lost. The machinery and furniture will be saved, but the vessel itself, it is reported, will prove a total loss."

Additional information documented, "The *Delaware* was lost while in the transport service on May 24, 1865, just inside St. Johns Bar, on the coast of Florida, during a heavy gale. Her hog frames being badly broken and the hull seriously strained, so she became almost a total loss. Most of the machinery and furniture was saved. She was purchased by the War Department, April 13, 1863, for $100,000, and the remains of the hull sold, in June 1866, for $105. She was on a trip from Hilton Head at the time of her loss[59]."

The schooner *Deliverance* stranded on Ponte Vedra Beach (Beaches Area Historical Society).

DELIVERANCE

The British two-masted auxiliary motor schooner *Deliverance* became stranded south of Ponte Vedra Beach on December 13, 1947. The 120-foot long vessel was en route from Bermuda for Jacksonville with a cargo of 40 tons of scrap iron when she grounded in eight feet of water. The 10-man crew jumped overboard and safely swam to shore. Over the next few days, waves poured into the 51-year old wooden-hulled vessel as it settled deeper into the sand. It is unclear if the schooner was eventually pulled off the beach, was partially salvaged, or simply disintegrated in the winter surf. An article published two days after the grounding, however, stated personal effects as well as the vessel's instruments were removed from the helpless *Deliverance*.

DEL NORTE

On October 17, 1847, the schooner *Del Norte*, plying between Key West and Jacksonville, was totally lost and abandoned near the St. Augustine Bar[60].

DELPHINE

The 35-ton vessel *Delphine*, owned by Captain Into, sank at Pier Four on September 18, 1926, during the Great Miami Hurricane. It is unclear if the *Delphine* was raised and repaired, or written off as a total loss following the storm.

DELTA

The American schooner *Delta* departed Moss Point, Mississippi, on September 1, 1926, only to encounter a massive hurricane on September 18 off South Florida, which totally wrecked the vessel at Delray Beach. Captain George C. Sherman drowned while trying to reach the beach after the initial stranding of the schooner. The *Delta*, official number 212810, was a 317-ton schooner 118.3 feet in length and 30.5 feet in width, which was built in September 1892 at Cheverie, Nova Scotia, by Roderick Rose.

D.E.M.A. TRADER

The *D.E.M.A. Trader* was a 333-ton general cargo ship built in 1957 that was last known as the Belizean-flagged *G.G.D. Trader*. The approximately 165-foot long freighter was seized by the U.S. Customs Service for smuggling narcotics. In conjunction with the 2003 Dive Equipment and Marketing Association (D.E.M.A.) annual convention that was held in Miami, the *G.D.D. Trader* was renamed the *D.E.M.A. Trader* and sunk as an artificial reef on October 28, 2003, off Key Biscayne. The wreck of the *D.E.M.A. Trader* rests upright and intact in approximately 80 feet of water just to the north of the tug *Rio Miami* and to the west of the *Sarah Jane* artificial reef site. Large openings were cut in the sides of the superstructure to allow safe penetration into the former galley and cabin areas. Tons of concrete culvert pipes and junction boxes were also loaded into the ship's cargo hold to produce additional complex habitat for marine life.

DENNIS

Sunk on July 28, 1992, as part of the John Maydak Memorial Reef along with the 50-foot long tug *Nancy*, the

Dennis was a 70-foot long, 18-foot wide tug owned by A.M.E. Ships Equipment. The *Dennis* now rests in 65 feet of water off Miami, while the *Nancy* can be found a short distance away to the northwest.

The tug *Dennis* just prior to her sinking (Miami-Dade County Department of Environmental Resources Management).

DESTINO A

The brig *Destino A* was originally built in September 1871 at Fiume, Austria, as the *Domenico*. The 430-ton vessel was 120.3 feet long and 27.5 feet wide. On March 10, 1879, the *Destino A*, en route from St. Marys, Georgia, for Spain with a cargo of lumber, stranded on the north breakers of Pelican Shoal at the mouth of the St. Marys River, and was deemed a total loss.

DEWITT CLINTON

DeWitt Clinton was an early American politician who served in the United States Senate and was the sixth Governor of New York. During his tenure as governor, he was largely responsible for the construction of the Erie Canal. This accomplishment, as well as his contributions during his earlier work with the Erie Canal Commission, helps explain the naming of the dredge *DeWitt Clinton*. The Bethlehem Steel Company of Sparrows Point, Maryland, delivered the *Clinton* to the Ellicott Machine Corporation on October 31, 1910. The 603-ton dredge was 148 feet long. After a long career working along the Atlantic Coast, the neglected *DeWitt Clinton* sank in the Cooper River near Charleston, South Carolina, on November 14, 1994, and subsequently leaked a significant amount of diesel fuel into the river. After salvage operations to prevent the further release of fuel, the dredge was raised, cleaned, and towed to Florida by Associated Marine Salvage, Incorporated of Miami. On May 12, 1995, the *Clinton* was deployed as an artificial reef by the Broward County Bomb Squad.

The former dredge *Clinton* being towed offshore to be sunk as an artificial reef (Broward County Artificial Reef Program).

The dredge *DeWitt Clinton* now rests in 170 feet of water less than two miles off Hillsboro Inlet. The wreck has a double hull design, similar to a catamaran, but with squared-off ends possessing two big rings near the top and bottom that could host anchor pilings when in service. The interior of each hull pontoon has long, silty corridors that require care when exploring. The wheelhouse is large and has some interesting growth on it, making for an entertaining swim-through.

DIAMONDFIELD

The 374-ton schooner *Diamondfield*, official number 200095, built in 1903, foundered in September 1917 off Tillman (Brevard County), resulting in the loss of seven lives.

DIANA

The *Lloyd's List* of December 10, 1774, reported that vessel *Diana*, Captain Buckley, bound from Jamaica to Rhode Island, had wrecked on Cape Florida. The crew was saved but the ship and cargo were lost.

DICKEY BOY

The *Dickey Boy* is a sunken trawler resting in approximately 90 feet of water off Cape Canaveral. Little is left of the wreck today, as salvors used explosives to recover the vessel's machinery and bronze propeller.

DIDO

The 256-ton hermaphrodite brig *Dido* was built in 1851, and registered a length of 90.8 feet and a width of 24.3 feet. *The New York Times* reported the loss of the *Dido* on January 20, 1859, due to her grounding on the New Smyrna Bar. The January 9 dispatch also included that "Captain Edwards, with his crew, attempted to cross the bar, his

Dredge *DeWitt Clinton* (U.S. Army Corps of Engineers).

boat was upset in the breakers, and he was drowned." While not specifically detailed, it is believed the wrecking of the *Dido* occurred on January 1, 1859.

DIE VERNON

Volume 10 of *The Sailor's Magazine and Naval Journal* documented the loss of the schooner *Die Vernon*, of New York, on the Indian River, January 11, 1838. While the vessel was lost, the crew was saved.

DIXIE CRYSTAL

On September 21, 1945, the 123-ton vessel *Dixie Crystal*, built in 1895, stranded at Vilano Beach near St. Augustine[61]. Her ultimate fate is unknown.

DOC DEMILLY

The popular wreck of the *Doc DeMilly* was originally completed as the refrigerated freighter *Domburgh* in August 1949 at the *Werf de Noord N.V.* (North Shipyard) of Alblasserdam, Netherlands. At her launching, the 1,117-ton *Domburgh* was 253.5 feet long and 40 feet wide. In 1962 (also cited as 1968) her mid-ship superstructure was removed and her hull was lengthened to 280.8 feet. In 1975, the *Domburgh* was sold and renamed *Forwarder*, and renamed yet again in 1982 to *Nuevo Rio*. By early 1985, the freighter had outlived its usefulness and was subsequently sold by its owners, North River Terminals, Incorporated, to Fish and Game Unlimited for $15,000 for use as an artificial reef. The *Nuevo Rio* was renamed the *Doc DeMilly* after beloved Homestead veterinarian John DeMilly Jr., who was senselessly robbed and murdered in October 1985 just hours before his 73rd birthday.

Doc DeMilly as the Domburgh, 1949.

On March 6, 1986, the freighter *Doc DeMilly* was sent to the bottom a half-mile east of Pacific Reef. The anchored vessel was subjected to numerous concrete-filled bombs dropped by U.S. Air Force F-4D Phantoms from the 93rd Tactical Fighter Squadron of Homestead Air Force Base, as well as 200 pounds of explosives rigged by the Dade County Metro Bomb Squad. As the explosive charges were detonated, the Air Force fighters dropped their cargo, with over two-thirds of the practice bombs missing their mark. The smoking *Doc* eventually sank stern first, her bow rising high out of the water before slipping under the waves. The freighter came to rest upright and intact in 145 feet of water.

Exploring the bow of the Doc DeMilly.

While one of the best dives off Miami-Dade County, unfortunately the *Doc DeMilly* is inconveniently sited midway between Miami and Key Largo. While a long boat ride is required to visit this wreck, it's definitely worth the price of admission. Similar to many other wrecks off Miami-Dade County, the *Doc DeMilly* was also impacted by Hurricane Andrew, which twisted and snapped the wreck into two pieces. While the bow section is still upright, intact, and pointing southward, the stern is angled away to the east and listing dramatically to port. The wreck presents significant vertical relief, allowing divers numerous places to escape the swift northward currents that are encountered frequently on the *Doc*. While the wreck itself is impressive, the abundant marine life is perhaps the marquee attraction. It is not uncommon to observe several dozen goliath grouper on the wreck, and schools of graceful spotted eagle rays frequently make an appearance over the freighter. Just to the south of the *Doc DeMilly* lies the *Hugo's April Fool*, formerly the 115-foot long freighter *Danbo*, and to the north rests the *Berry Patch*, which used to be the 155-foot long freighter *Saint Joseph*.

Diver investigating one of the many practice bombs found in the sand off the stern of the Doc DeMilly.

In between these sites, an observant diver may come across one of the many large, concrete practice bombs that were dropped on the *Doc DeMilly*.

DOLPHIN (1747)

On January 14, 1748, the *London Intelligencer* reported, "There is advice that the *Dolphin*, Stephens, from Carolina to Antigua, was lost on the coast of Florida, on the 5th of October (1747); and 25 other vessels."

DOLPHIN (1748)

According to the *General Evening Post* of October 15, 1748, "The *Dolphin*, Capt. Bagott, for North Carolina, is lost near Cape Florida. She had been taken, and met with accident as the Spaniards were going with her for the Havanna [sic]."

DOLPHIN (1836)

The *Dolphin* was a copper-fastened two-masted steam schooner that utilized both sails and side-paddle wheels, which was built in 1835 by New York shipbuilders Bishop and Simonson. Her low-pressure engine and heavy-copper boiler was built by James Allaire of New York[62]. The *Dolphin* was 115.5 feet long, 16 feet wide, and displaced 133 tons gross. A December 1836 report, published in the *Charleston Mercury*, described the loss of the *Dolphin*:

> On Saturday last, 19th inst., about 4 o'clock in the afternoon, the Steam Packet *Dolphin*, Capt. Rudolph, off St. Johns Bar, stopped to take a Pilot on board, and in the act of starting the engine the boiler burst, and unfortunately killed fifteen persons. The *Santee* was lying at anchor inside the bar, and saw the explosion take place, whereupon she raised steam and proceeded for the wreck. When within about a half mile of the wreck met a pilot boat off (the) Bar, having on board, Col. Brown, lady, three children and servant, Mrs. Gibbs and son, and Capt. Rudolph; at the same time picked up one of the *Dolphin's* boats, with three men belonging to her and one of the St. Johns Pilots. On the arrival of the *Santee* at the wreck, she took off Dr. Martin, U.S.A., and Messrs. Waldron and Donaldson. The small boat of the *Santee* was then sent to a man who had drifted about a mile on a piece of timber, from the wreck, and while getting him on board the boat, another person was discovered about 150 yards from them, with his head just above water, who proved to be Colonel Dell of Jacksonville, slightly wounded, much exhausted, and succeeded in saving him. It getting dark, the *Santee* returned inside the bar with (the survivors)…the *Dolphin* sunk in four fathoms of water.

The wrecking of the *Dolphin* claimed 15 lives. On March 23, 1837, the *Jacksonville Courier* reported a grisly discovery, stating, "On March 5 inst. the bodies of two men, the pilot, Captain Kemory, and Lieutenant MacKay, were found on the beach, three or four miles south of the St. Johns Bar. MacKay's gold watch was still in his pocket. It was believed that a strong wind blew over part of the *Dolphin's* wreckage which dislodged the two bodies. Lieutenant MacKay was buried at St. Augustine with military honors."

DONAL G. MCALLISTER

The tug *Donal G. McAllister*, official number 249150, was built in 1946 at the Port Arthur, Texas, shipyard of Gulfport Boiler and Welding Works, Incorporated. The *McAllister* was 95.2 feet long, 24.1 feet wide, and 136 gross tons. After a long career working in New York Harbor, the aged tugboat was sunk as artificial reef on June 23, 1998. She now rests in 75 feet of water just south of Port Everglades.

The last minutes of the *Donal G. McAllister* afloat (Broward County Artificial Reef Program).

DONALD RAY

The *Donald Ray* was a 55-foot shrimper built in 1950. On March 7, 1957, the trawler departed Mayport for the fishing grounds east-southeast of Jacksonville. That evening, the weather intensified and building waves buffeted the wooden hull of the shrimp boat. When another fishing vessel finally raised the *Donald Ray* on the radio, she reported she was in a sinking condition and needed immediate assistance. At the time, Captain John Gordon Gavagan stated the engines of the *Donald Ray* were still operating, but the pumps had failed, which forced the crew to bail with buckets to stem the flooding water. On the morning of March 8, numerous U.S. Coast Guard and Navy vessels, as well as a helicopter and an amphibious aircraft, rushed to the scene to assist the stricken *Donald Ray*. The amphibious aircraft *Dumbo I* finally located the shrimp trawler at 4:18 p.m. on March 8 approximately 30 miles south-southeast of the St. Johns River Bar and "18 miles off the coastline on a line due east of Fleming Island." The aircrew also reported the vessel afloat but dead in the water. Unfortunately, due to a miscommunication between the various rescue entities, poor weather conditions, and other vessels in need of assistance, daylight faded before a rescue vessel could reach the *Donald Ray*, and the shrimp trawler disappeared during the night of March 8. During the last contact with the doomed shrimper, Captain Gavagan reported the vessel was in 16 fathoms of water.

DORIS

The *Doris* was built in March 1887 at Dundee, Scotland. The bark was 248.6 feet long, 35.4 feet in beam, and displaced 1,353 tons. According to a February 8, 1902, article in the *Florida Times-Union*, the four-masted bark *Doris* wrecked at Boynton on January 10 and was a total loss.

DOROTHY

According to an article that appeared on October 31, 1928, in the *Key West Citizen*, "Captain Hoke D. Brown, 28, was seriously burned when the fuel tender *Dorothy* exploded this morning at Miami Beach docks after taking 700 gallons of gasoline aboard. The explosion occurred when Brown attempted to start the boat's engine. Blazing fiercely, the *Dorothy* drifted into the open bay a total loss."

DOVE

The November 18, 1773, loss of the slaver *Dove* was documented on March 10, 1774, in the *Virginia Gazette*, which stated, "December 28. On the 18th ultimo, in the night, the schooner *Dove*, from Africa for St. Augustine, was entirely lost on the coast of East Florida, about a league to the south of Smyrna. The master, two seamen, and about 80 slaves (out of 100 on board) were drowned; the rest swam ashore." The schooner *Dove* immediately went to pieces.

DOVER

Somewhere on the south side of the St. Johns River jetty, the wreckage of the steamer *Dover* remains buried under the sand. According to the *Annual Report of the Chief of Engineers, United States Army, to the Secretary of War for the Year 1913*:

> On February 12, 1913, the sum of $5,000 was allotted for the removal of the steamer *Dover*, which went ashore south of and near to the south jetty at the mouth of the St. Johns River, Fla., on the night of October 2, 1912, while attempting to enter the mouth of the river. After going ashore the vessel was carried nearly 3,000 feet southward by wave action until it rested partly on the south jetty and appeared to be in danger of being carried over the jetty and into the channel. The *Dover* was an iron ship built in 1873; was 165 feet long, 25 feet broad, and 12 feet deep, and of 397 tons net register. She carried only a small miscellaneous cargo. Work began on April 16, 1913, and was completed May 13, 1913. The wreck was first burned and then broken up with dynamite. The pieces were disposed of in a deep pocket on the south side of the south jetty and have now been almost completely covered over with sand. The total cost for removing this wreck was $2,750.83.

DRAGON

According to *The Edinburgh Advertiser*, March 28, 1809, "The *Dragon*, Ayres, from Hayes and Barbadoes [sic] to Liverpool, is totally lost off Florida."

DREAD

The sloops (also described as wrecking smacks) *Alabama*, *Dread*, and *Caution* of Mystic, Connecticut, bound to Key West, were driven ashore and lost in a gale on September 7, 1838, approximately 12 miles north of Cape Florida. Only one man, Joseph Noble, survived the wrecking and subsequent slaughter at the hands of hostile Seminole Indians by joining the crew of the French brig *Courier* (*Courier de Tampico* or *Courier de Vera Cruz*), which was lost in the same vicinity. In addition to the crews of the *Alabama*, *Dread*, and *Caution*, most of the *Alna's* crew, wrecked in the vicinity, was also massacred. At the time, local tribes spared European sailors and only killed Americans wrecked on the Florida shore.

This derelict hulk of a former drift boat was scuttled off Miami in the 1980s (Miami-Dade County Department of Environmental Resources Management).

DRIFTWOOD

On January 14, 1949, Captain John Pellett and five passengers departed Dania on the 39-foot long cabin cruiser *Driftwood* for a planned fishing excursion to Bimini, Bahamas. The group apparently never made it across the Gulf Stream, and disappeared somewhere off the Florida coast. A January 22 radio conversation between two unidentified shrimp boats indicated the cruiser was spotted with engine problems somewhere between Fort Pierce and Daytona Beach. After extensive aerial and surface vessel searches, no trace of the missing *Driftwood* or its passengers was ever found.

DUE BILL

According to *The Edinburgh Advertiser* of August 16, 1816, the schooners *Due Bill* and *Waterwich* (also appeared as *Water Witch*), both of Savannah, wrecked near St. Augustine in the beginning of June during a storm.

DUNHAM WHEELER

The five-masted schooner, *Dunham Wheeler*, was built in 1917 at the Percy and Small shipyard in Bath, Maine. Owned by the Pendleton Brothers, the elegant sailing vessel was 255 feet in length, 44 feet in beam, and displaced 1,926 tons. On October 23, 1930, the vessel departed Venezuela with a cargo of goat manure. As she sailed northward along the Florida peninsula, she encountered a strong gale just south of Cape Canaveral on the evening of November 7. The schooner was buffeted by a strong wind that ripped six sails from her masts. The high seas prevented new canvas from being raised, so Captain John A. McIver opted to drop anchor and ride out the storm. Due to the constant pounding of the waves, the vessel began to leak at a rate that surpassed the capability of the schooner's pumps. With the hull breaking apart, Captain McIver fired distress flares at approximately 2:00 a.m. on November 8. The Merchants and Miners Transportation Company steamer *Upshur*, also disabled from the storm and riding at anchor nearby, spotted the flares. Unable to assist, the *Upshur* radioed a general distress message that brought the United Fruit Lines steamer *Aztec* to the scene of the foundering schooner. Deploying oil to smooth the seas, the *Aztec* launched a lifeboat and rescued the crew of 10 from the *Dunham Wheeler*. Two hours later, the five-masted schooner slipped bow first beneath the waves. After the incident, Captain McIver, a veteran of 50 years at sea, alluded to the panicked crew. "There was no mutiny. I know how to handle my men. I've got something in there to take care of them with," to which he opened a bag and brandished a marlin spike. He continued, "But some of them were scared, all right[63]."

Known locally as the "Liberty Wreck," the *Dunham Wheeler* has been largely sanded in. Her remains, resting in 70 feet of water, consist of a large windlass, scattered rigging, chain, traces of decking, and a large anchor. While the majority of the hull is entombed in sand, the site should be monitored after strong winter storms or fall hurricanes that may excavate the wreck, providing a brief glimpse of this magnificent sailing ship.

The five-masted schooner *Dunham Wheeler* in drydock (© The Mariners' Museum, Newport News, Virginia).

E.S. RUDDEROW

The schooner *E.S. Rudderow*, 87 tons, of Charleston, South Carolina, for Indian River with government stores, was wrecked at the latter place on December 14, 1857. While the vessel and cargo a total loss, the captain and crew were saved[64]. *The Sailor's Magazine and Naval Journal*, Volume 30, cited a Captain Chadwick as the *Rudderow's* master, and the vessel was valued at $3,000. While several sources cited the schooner was lost at Indian River, it is possible she wrecked more specifically at Indian River Inlet.

EARL GALLEY

On July 21, 1739, *The Englishman's Journal* reported, "A private letter from Carolina advises that the *Earl Galley*, Capt. Robert Codd, belonging to Bristol, bound for the Isle of Wight from the Bay of Honduras, was in her passage stranded the 27th of April, about twenty leagues to the northward of Cape Florida. The captain and fourteen of the crew took to the long boat, in which they arriv'd the 19th of May at Charles Town (Charleston, South Carolina)."

EAST FLORIDA MERCHANT

According to the March 10, 1774, issue of the *Virginia Gazette*, on December 2, 1773, "the brig *East Florida Merchant*, Captain Losthouse, from London for St. Augustine, with a valuable cargo on board, after waiting a fortnight at anchor, attempted to get over the bar, but it falling a dead calm, she struck, and after lying ten days, went to pieces; about two thirds of her cargo, greatly damaged, was got on shore." An earlier article also cited the vessel as a brigantine.

The sinking of the *Eben-Ezer II* off Dania Beach (Broward County Artificial Reef Program).

EBEN-EZER II

The 85-foot long Haitian island freighter *Eben-Ezer II*, built in 1960, appeared to make more illicit cargo runs than legitimate ones towards the end of her career. On May 19, 1997, she became disabled and was towed into the Miami anchorage area. The U.S. Coast Guard conducted a boarding and found 14 Haitian citizens aboard, only 6 of which were documented as crew members. The U.S. Immigration and Naturalization Service identified those who were not documented and deported them on May 20.

On November 1, 2001, U.S. Customs Service discovered 12.8 pounds of cocaine smuggled in the helm stand of the rusty freighter after it moored in the Miami River following a trip in ballast from Port-au-Paix, Haiti. Due to the narcotics found on board, the vessel was seized by the U.S. government. The Broward County Artificial Reef Program paid $10,000 for the ship, which then cleaned and striped the *Eben-Ezer II*. On May 14, 2002, the ship was scuttled in 70 feet of water south of Port Everglades.

ECHO (1844A)

As documented in *The Sailor's Magazine and Naval Journal*, Volume 17 (1844), "Schooner *Echo*, Hastings, from Savannah, for Turks Island, in ballast, was wrecked night 17th June on Mosquito Bar, Florida. Vessel total loss."

ECHO (1844B)

A December 21, 1844, dispatch from St. Augustine stated the schooner *Echo*, Captain Snow, with a cargo of live oak bound for Norfolk, was lost on the bar off New Smyrna on December 14, 1844. The schooner was departing and within 100 yards of the bar when one of the blocks on the lee fore brace parted, allowing the topsail to fly into the wind, which set her on the south breakers. While the crew was saved, the vessel and cargo were a total loss[65].

The Florida Master Site File includes information on a wreck site believed to be the schooner *Echo*. The entry does not include details on the particular vessel, however, nor does it explain why the site (VO00180), which is located under the pool of a condominium along the Intracoastal Waterway approximately nine miles north of Ponce de Leon Inlet (i.e., the cited wrecking location for both entries), was believed to be a schooner named *Echo*.

ECHO (1858)

The New York Times reported the March 7, 1858, wrecking of the brig *Echo* on the north shoal of the St. Johns Bar on March 15 during a voyage from New York to Jacksonville. It is possible that this loss occurred to a 143-ton vessel of the same name, 71.8 feet long and 21 feet wide, which was built in 1838 at the Bay of Fundy.

EDITHANNA

The March 16, 1911, loss of the 20-ton yacht *Edithanna*, built in 1904, was reported on March 30 in the *New Jersey Courier*:

> Capt. Joel Van Sant and his mate, Morgan Morris, two mariners, both of this place, were compelled to abandon the yacht *Edithanna* at sea off Jupiter Inlet, Florida, recently and were picked up by the French cruiser *Gloire*, which landed them at Annapolis, MD. They had been cruising in Florida waters and visited Havana, Cuba, whence they sailed for Tuckerton on March 13. They ran into a storm that was too much for their craft and were

69

blown off shore, and would probably have gone down with their schooner had not the French cruiser come along. The *Edithanna* was owned by Thomas Henderson of Philadelphia and had a crew of four men.

Other reports indicated she was abandoned (or sunk) approximately 20 miles northeast of Jupiter.

EDITH DAWSON

In late November 1932, the *Edith Dawson*, a three-masted wooden schooner of Lunenberg, Nova Scotia, was bound for Nova Scotia from Turks Island, Bahamas, with a cargo of salt when she encountered an intense four-day Atlantic gale. An article in the *Galveston Daily News*, published December 6, detailed the final events of the *Dawson*:

> Last Wednesday morning at 4:15 o'clock, distress signals from the *Edith Dawson* were observed off the port bow of the tanker *Sylvan Arrow* and the course was changed toward them. "On coming close," the captain said, "we made out a three-masted schooner with her sails torn to ribbons by the winds, and apparently beyond control. The schooner hailed us and requested the crew to be taken off, as the vessel was sinking."
>
> It developed that the seams had opened during the pounding of the waves that the little vessel had withstood for hours and the swells were breaking over the decks. The seepage and the water shipped had soaked the salt cargo, which by the time the *Sylvan Arrow* hove to was changed into a sort of mush in the hull of the schooner, defying the attempts of the pumps and helping the seas to put a finish to the job of sinking the vessel. All pumps were put into operation, according to Capt. Stephen White of the *Edith Dawson*, but the slush in the holds was so thick that the pump engines labored under the load and one by one were completely and hopelessly disabled. His crew of six young Canadians, he said, had stuck to their duties without a whimper, and worked without relief throughout the raw gale and the whipping seas long after hope of saving the vessel had gone. The *Sylvan Arrow* sent word to the sinking schooner that "We will stand by and take your crew off at daylight." As a high sea was still running at daylight the crew of the *Sylvan Arrow* poured fuel oil by the barrels onto the waters, quieting them to a great extent.
>
> "Owing to the sea and heavy rolling of the schooner the crew from our boat was unable to get alongside the *Edith Dawson*. Taking up a position close on the lee quarter of the schooner they made communication by line, getting the seven Canadians into the lifeboat and eventually brought them back to the *Sylvan Arrow*, which had taken up a position to the leeward of the wreck. During the rescue proper, the small dog mascot aboard the *Edith Dawson* made an attempt to reach the lifeboat, jumping overboard, but fell prey to sharks."

The *Edith Dawson* was set afire by the fleeing crew in order to remove it as a potential menace to navigation. One newspaper report stated the *Sylvan Arrow* encountered the foundering schooner 150 miles east of Fernandina.

EDITH L. ALLEN

The *Edith L. Allen* was built in 1890 at Richmond, Maine, by shipbuilders T.J. Southard. She was 185 feet long, 39.1 feet wide, and displaced 969 tons gross. The four-masted schooner had a streak of poor luck and was almost wrecked on numerous instances. On February 4, 1902, the schooner came ashore and stranded at Atlantic City, New Jersey, but fortunately was pulled off before becoming a total wreck. The following year, the *Edith L. Allen*, Captain Paul LeBlanc, stranded on a shoal in the Bahamas on November 5, 1904, during a journey from Norfolk, Virginia, to Charlotte Harbor. Fortunately, wreckers were able to lighten the vessel and pull her off her potential sandy tomb. On the night of December 17, 1904, during fair weather, Captain LeBlanc and the *Allen* struck a submerged wreck near Cape Hatteras and only managed to stay afloat because of her cargo of lumber. Continuing her apparent cursed service record, the *Edith L. Allen* was involved in a collision with the Gloucester schooner *Norumbega* off Delaware in April 1906, which sent the fishing schooner to the bottom while the *Allen* limped into Baltimore, Maryland. Finally, later that same year, the *Edith L. Allen* was lost while en route from Baltimore, Maryland, to Port Arthur, Texas, with a cargo of steel rails. Reports document she foundered approximately 25 nautical miles off Fort Lauderdale (latitude 26° 10' north and longitude 79° 38' west) on June 17, 1906; her crew was rescued by the schooner *Jacob S. Winslow*, and landed in New York.

EDWARD

The yacht *Edward* was wrecked and piled up on the docks of the Peninsular and Oriental Steam Navigation Company in the wake of the September 1926 Great Miami Hurricane[66].

EIDSVAG

Like many other vessels sunk as artificial reefs off Florida, the *Eidsvag* was confiscated after law enforcement officers found smuggled narcotics onboard. She was purchased by the Palm Beach County Artificial Reef

Committee for $9,500 at a Miami auction, and subsequently sunk with 110 pounds of explosives detonated by the Palm Beach County Sheriff's Department Bomb Squad on December 16, 1985. The freighter, controversially renamed the U.S.S. *Owens* after the county commissioner, Jerry Owens, came to rest in 110 feet of water and now provides habitat for numerous resident goliath grouper.

In December 1941, the *Eidsvag* was completed as the *Empire Sound* for the British Ministry of War by Richards Ironworks Limited of Lowestoft, England. She was 137 feet long, 24.6 feet wide, and displaced 315 tons. In 1943, she was transferred to the government of the Netherlands, and renamed the *Zuiderhaven*. Following the end of World War II, she was sold to the French company *Enterprise Generale de Transport Maritimes* and renamed the *Tamise II*. In later years, she changed hands and names numerous times: in 1950 she was sold to another French interest, *S.A de Ciments de Dannes*, and renamed *Cimcour II*; a Norwegian company bought the vessel in 1953, which named it *Sjaholm*; in 1965 she was known as the *Pokal*; she became the *Bjerkosund* in 1968 while sailing for Peddership-Pedersen and Sonner; finally, in 1972, she was renamed the *Eidsvag*. In 1985, she was sold to the Honduran shipping company Nick Ocean International, where she apparently was recruited as a drug runner.

EIGHT CANNON WRECK

The "Eight Cannon Wreck" has not been confirmed, but the Florida Master Site File indicates as many as eight cannon were recovered from a site approximately one-half mile north of Port Everglades Inlet during the 1960s and 1970s. Apparently, concrete blocks were deposited at the site to aid in relocation efforts.

ELAINE

The motor vessel *Elaine* burned seven miles south of Jupiter on the morning of April 10, 1923, claiming the life of Captain William Fontein. The engineer of the *Elaine* was rescued by the steamer *Trivia*[67].

EL AVISO CONSULADO

Part of the 1733 fleet that met with disaster in the Florida Keys, *El Aviso Consulado* (an advice or dispatch boat) found itself north of Key Largo along with the scout ship *Nuestra Señora del Populo* (*El Pinque*) during the July hurricane. After *El Pinque* wrecked on the reef with her poop deck awash, Captain Don Pedro Arrambide of the damaged *El Aviso* approached to rescue the crew and passengers and carried them to the nearest land. Archival information indicates *El Aviso* was later abandoned, as a letter to the Consulado of Cadiz stated both *El Pinque* and *El Aviso* were found grounded with no one onboard. The letter cited the location of both as *Cabeza de los Martires*, 12 leagues north of the *Capitana*, which was wrecked off Tavernier. On July 17, survivors of *El Pinque* and *El Aviso* were picked up by the vessel *San Joseph* (*El Africa*), which safely returned to Cadiz, Spain, to bring news of the disaster. Reports from mid-August stated *El Aviso* was still afloat, and potentially later repaired and put back in service. Therefore, it is unclear if this documented site is *El Aviso*, another dispatch boat lost in the 1733 hurricane, or a wreck entirely unrelated to the 1733 fleet.

Craig Hamilton located a wreck around 1950 that he believed to be *El Aviso Consulado*. Lying in 10 feet of water on the face of the north end of a patch reef south of Pacific Reef, Hamilton found a quantity of ballast leading off into deeper water. In this area he also found cannon balls, bar shot, broken pottery and china, brass buttons and buckles, and other shipwreck material. Approximately 600 feet south of the reef, he located five nine-pounder cannon, which he felt were the right type and size to have originated from an *aviso*.

EL CIERVO

El Ciervo, Spanish for "The Stag," was a captured French frigate that was one of six vessels comprising Captain-General Don Antonio de Echeverz y Zubiza's *Los Galeones* (known as the *Tierra Firme* fleet prior to 1648), which departed Havana harbor on July 24, 1715, along with five other ships of the *Nueva España* fleet and a single French merchant vessel, the *Grifon*. *El Ciervo*, carrying a cargo of Brazilwood and tobacco, disappeared in the early morning hours of July 31, 1715, during a massive storm that devastated the combined fleet. It is believed the former French frigate sank in deep water off Florida, possibly north of Cape Canaveral, though her final resting spot has yet to be discovered.

EL ESPIRITU SANTO EL MAYOR

El Espiritu Santo el Mayor was a 480-ton Spanish galleon that sunk during a hurricane in 1626, somewhere between St. Lucie Inlet and Cape Canaveral; the sinking claimed over 200 lives. While not conclusively proven, treasure hunters have worked a site approximately 14 miles off the coast they believe may be the wreck of *El Espiritu Santo el Mayor*. This claim may be supported by the rumor of several bronze cannon supposedly recovered by trawlers working the area several decades ago. Another vessel sailing with the fleet was the *Santísima Trinidad*, which also sank off Florida in the same general area, but has not been positively identified.

ELIM

The *Elim* was a Norwegian bark built in July 1876 at Arendal. She was 125.6 feet long, 29.8 feet wide, and displaced 469 tons. During the September 1878 hurricane, the *Elim*, with a cargo of mahogany, stranded three miles north of Mosquito Inlet. Hawks (1887) said she went ashore a little above Green Mound. The vessel and cargo was sold at auction. The purchasers hauled the logs up on the ridge with a stationary engine and took them across to the river on a tramway, where they were loaded and sent north. The *Elim* proved to be a total loss. The hurricane also stranded the *Dora Ellen*, Captain William Johnson, north of Mosquito Inlet, in close proximity to the *Elim*. Unlike the Norwegian bark, however, the *Dora Ellen* was successfully worked into deeper water and eventually saved.

ELIZA

Information received from Nassau on October 7, 1818, which was printed on January 6, 1819, in *The Times*, reported the loss of the brig *Eliza*, as well as the potential murder of its captain. The dispatch stated:

> By late arrivals from the coast of Florida, information has been received here, that a brig named the *Eliza*, of Halifax, had been found on the shore there, no person being on board, and having several appearances of blood on the deck. Not far from the brig were seen several persons in a tent, who, on the approach of a boat from one of the wreckers, made off in a boat which they had with them, leaving their bedding, etc. in the tent. There is reason to suspect this vessel is the *Eliza*, of Halifax, Murphy master, which sailed from Kingston, Jamaica on the 11th ult. (September 11) for Halifax, and that the crew had destroyed the master of her, and made off with some money supposed to have been on board; the brig had no cargo when found.

Other sources document the place of loss as "Carysford Reef," so the *Eliza* may more accurately be a Florida Keys shipwreck.

ELIZA MALLORY

On the morning of November 4, 1859, the ship *Eliza Mallory*, Captain Gwyne (also reported as Captain Burritt), was blown ashore on the Florida coast. The ship was laden with 4,923 bales of cotton bound from New Orleans for the Pacific coast port of San Blas, Mexico. According to Admiralty records of the U.S. District Court for the Southern District of Florida, "The ship lay within thirty feet of the beach, about 65 miles to the northward of Cape Florida, full of water, heading north east and her stern toward the beach with about 10 or 11 feet water under her forward." Other reports cited the wrecking location as 60 miles north of Cape Florida, as well as "on Jupiter Inlet." Over the span of several trips, the wrecking schooner *Champion* recovered 1,706 bales of cotton from the ship and off the beach, while other wreckers contributed in the rescue of several hundred more bales, as well as a portion of the ship's provisions, her canvas, rigging, and other materials. The 647-ton *Eliza Mallory* was built in 1851 at Mystic, Connecticut, and was 130 feet long and 33.5 feet wide.

ELIZABETH

The wrecking of the Bull Line freighter *Elizabeth* is yet another example where diligence is required in following news and other correspondence well after the original incident to determine the ultimate fate of a vessel. Numerous newspapers documented that the 324-foot long steamer was driven aground only a half-mile off Miami Beach during a hurricane on November 4, 1935. The *Charleston Gazette* reported on November 6, "Through a driving rain last night the vessel, its radio apparently rendered useless, used rockets and flares to signal distress. Once she flashed 'We need help at once. We have seven feet of water in the hold.' The cutter *Saranac*, however, radioed the *Elizabeth* seemed in no immediate danger and was resting easily.'" While there was mention of potential salvage operations of the 2,482-ton *Elizabeth* in the wake of the grounding, definitive information on the fate of the freighter appeared on May 14, 1936, when it was reported the *Elizabeth* was scuttled off Miami Beach in 600 feet of water.

The freighter *Elizabeth* dockside at Miami, 1925 (Florida State Archives).

ELIZABETH ELLEN

The *Elizabeth Ellen*, 132.3 feet long, 31.4 feet wide, 580 tons, was built in 1845 at Haddam, Connecticut. On November 18, 1859, the ship departed New Orleans, Louisiana, bound for Bremen, Germany, laden with a cargo of 1,507 bales of cotton, 65 hogsheads and 34 bales of tobacco, and a barrel each of rice and hominy. Captain Archibald Staigg reported "boisterous" weather throughout the entire trip. On December 3, amidst heavy rain squalls, the ship struck on the rocks north of Cape Florida. While the crew attempted to put out anchors and chain to work the vessel off, the captain described the next moments: "a heavy sea setting in, the ship was thrown on her beam ends with great violence, carrying away the fore topmast, main topmast and mizzen top mast, with rigging and sails attached and two boats and the hawsers and lines that lay coiled on the house. The ship working and pounding heavily, we cut away the lower mast to ease her."

The ship lay 200-300 yards off the beach. On December 5, they "landed some provisions, stores, and sails and constructed a tent to live in, not considering it safe to remain on board of the ship as she was momentarily in danger of breaking up." That evening, the wrecking smack *Beckwith* showed up and offered her assistance. The ship lay broadside to the beach in eight feet of water, with her bow facing north; she was found bilged with seven and a half feet of water in her hold. The *Beckwith* cited the *Elizabeth Ellen's* position as 45 miles north of Cape Florida, though other wrecking vessels reported her laying 20 miles southward of the bark *Mary Coe* and 8 miles southward of *Eliza Mallory*, which would place her approximately 57 miles north of Cape Florida.

ELIZABETH FREEMAN

The four-masted schooner *Elizabeth Freeman*, official number 226542, was launched from the yard of the Atlantic Coast Company at Thomaston, Maine, on August 14, 1920. The schooner, 1,665 tons gross, 1,540 tons net, was 232 feet long and 41.5 feet wide. The christening of the vessel was performed with roses by Miss Elizabeth Freeman of Wollaston, Massachusetts, for whom the vessel was named.

On October 22, 1927, the crew of the *Elizabeth Freeman* was rescued by the British steamer *Sythian*, 15 miles north of the St. Johns Bar, when fire of an undetermined origin suddenly enveloped and destroyed the four-masted schooner. The *Freeman* was bound from Jacksonville to Boston with a cargo of 1,250,000 feet of creosote ties. The fire was discovered a little more than an hour and a half after the vessel had left its tug tow at the mouth of the St. Johns River. Of the incident, Captain M.C. Decker said, "It seemed as if the ship became afire all at once. It was not twenty minutes after the blaze was detected that the sails were flaming and the fire was sweeping the boat from forward to stern." Dense smoke hindered efforts made to fight the flames, he said. The *Sythian* was passing southward in ballast from Europe and picked up the seamen who had put out in a lifeboat. On October 24, reports stated the U.S. Coast Guard was watching over the still-burning *Elizabeth Freeman*, now only four miles off the mouth of the St. Johns River. While the vessel was declared a total loss, it is unclear if the vessel was allowed to sink offshore, or if the charred hulk was towed in after the fire was extinguished.

ELIZABETH PERRY

The wooden-hulled shrimp trawler *Elizabeth Perry* was built in 1949 by DESCO Marine, Incorporated of St. Augustine, and was 67 feet long and displaced 99 tons gross. The shrimper reportedly foundered a half mile off St. Augustine Inlet on December 14, 1958.

ELLA

An April 1858 report in *The Sailor's Magazine and Naval Journal*, Volume 30, stated, "Schooner *Ella*, from Charleston to St. Augustine, wrecked on St. Augustine Bar; valued $6,000."

ELVIRA GASPAR

The 185-ton schooner-rigged diesel dragger *Elvira Gaspar*, 87.8 feet in length and 21.5 feet in beam, was built in 1929 at Essex, Massachusetts. Most of her career was spent operating out of Gloucester with the Portuguese fishing fleet. On June 10, 1942, the dragger was acquired by the U.S. Navy and converted for patrol service at South Boston, Massachusetts. The former fishing vessel, armed with three 20 mm gun mounts, was commissioned as U.S.S. *YP-429* on July 27, 1942. While operating off the Florida coast, the improvised patrol vessel was damaged in a collision on January 8, 1943, but was not sunk (as cited in some sources). On May 1, 1943, the disabled vessel was

Elvira Gaspar as *YP-429* (National Archives).

towed to Morehead City, North Carolina. Apparently, the damage was deemed too significant to warrant repairs, as the *YP-429* was decommissioned on May 27, 1943. On November 24, 1944, the *Elvira Gaspar* was reported lost at approximate latitude 28° 27' north and longitude 80° 32' west. This is possibly an inaccurate incident report, which was not uncommon during World War II, similar to the erroneous sinking report of the *Elizabeth Massey*. Therefore, it is possible the *Elvira Gaspar* was not actually lost off Florida.

EMELINE

The Sailor's Magazine and Naval Journal, Volume 10, documented that the "Schooner *Emeline*, from St. Augustine for Indian River, went ashore on Indian River Bar, 29th Jan. (1838) – vessel and cargo totally lost."

ÉMERILLION

The 29-gun vice-flagship *Émérillion*, Captain Nicolas d'Ornano, was part of Jean Ribault's fleet that returned to Fort Caroline near present-day Jacksonville on August 28, 1565. On September 12, after an earlier skirmish with a Spanish armada, Ribault's fleet pursued the warships and prepared to overtake them near St. Augustine when an intense hurricane struck Florida. The storm pushed Ribault's fleet out to sea, allowing the Spaniards to escape. The *Émérillion* eventually wrecked north of Mosquito Inlet (Ponce Inlet) within two miles of fellow French vessels, auxiliary *Épaule de Mouton* and transport *Truite*, and north (some sources cite 15 miles north) of Ribault's flagship *Trinité*, which grounded north of Cape Canaveral.

EMILY B.

Built in 1887 at Jacksonville, the 43-ton schooner *Emily B.*, official number 135948, was 90 foot long and 18 feet wide. The details of the *Emily B.*'s sinking were reported in *The Indianapolis Star* on January 8, 1912: "After battling all night with the waves the crew of the schooner *Emily B.*, bound from Jacksonville to Palm Beach, was rescued early today in Mosquito Inlet. The schooner, in attempting to run the inlet last night, struck a bar and broke in two. Members of the crew were compelled to jump overboard and cling to bits of wreckage throughout the night, until they were picked up by rowboats today."

EMILY SEARS

The *Emily Sears*, official number 203728, was a 44-ton fishing vessel 63.6 feet long, 18.1 feet wide, built in 1906 at Gloucester, Massachusetts. The *Sears* foundered off St. Lucie Inlet on September 7, 1934.

EMMA

According to Singer (1998) the composite-built *Emma*, a 43-ton vessel built in 1940, foundered three miles south of Fort Pierce on September 26, 1947.

EMMA KNOWLTON

The schooner *Emma Knowlton* was built in May 1891 at Rockport, Maine, and was 142 feet long, 33 feet in beam, and registered 353 tons displacement. The *San Antonio Light and Gazette*, April 1, 1911, reported on the *Knowlton's* peril: "The tug *Three Friends*, from Knights Key to St. Johns Bar spoke to the schooner *William R. Winslow*, thirty miles southeast of Cape Canaveral yesterday and received notification that the captain and crew of the schooner *Emma Knowlton*, which was abandoned at sea ninety miles south east of St. Johns Bar in a sinking condition, were aboard. The crew of the *Knowlton* was rescued from an open boat at sea. The derelict reported by steamers 140 miles due east of the bar riding on its beam ends is evidently this abandoned schooner." Another newspaper account stated the schooner was sighted by the Norwegian steamer *Bratland* on March 27, abandoned and making north with the sea off St. Augustine. The final resting spot of the *Emma Knowlton* has yet to be identified.

EMMA M. ROBINSON

The *Emma M. Robinson* was a small schooner, 76.5 feet long and 23.6 feet wide built in 1881 at Milford, Delaware, which stranded six miles below Fort Pierce (also reported as two and a half miles north of the Gilbert's Bar Life-Saving Station) on May 16, 1920, during a storm. She had departed Jacksonville on May 12 with Captain W.H. Moore at the helm, en route for Central America with her partner ship *Thomas B. Cator*. No lives were lost, but the *Robinson* soon went to pieces after her grounding. The *Cator* was also wrecked in the storm.

EMMA WHITE

The *Emma White*, a small steamer originally owned by Hubbard Hart, ran between Palatka and Silver Springs. Later, she was bought by Captain Gray. During the Civil War, she was sunk in the channel at the southern end of Lake George (also reported sunk in the St. Johns River near the bar) in an attempt to block access to Union forces.

EMPECINADA

The *Empecinada*, a Spanish vessel of six guns, Captain Juan Villacencio, en route from Cuba for Spain, wrecked on Amelia Island Bar during a winter gale on January 8, 1815, while trying to enter the port. The vessel quickly went to pieces, though the crew and cargo were saved.

ENDURANCE

The New York Times, January 31, 1926, reported, "News that the tug *Endurance* of New York, which left on Dec. 30 to tow a dredge to Tampa, had sunk in a storm off the Florida coast was conveyed yesterday in a telegram sent by Captain and owner Harry Tellessen. Both the dredge and tug were lost, but entire crew saved." The steamer *America* reported the tug was wrecked six miles off West Palm Beach and that the vessel was left with all lights showing. Therefore, it is unclear where the tug eventually foundered, as she may have drifted a significant distance north in the Gulf Stream.

ENGLISH CHINA WRECK

I was taken to this mysterious site just off Elliott Key in 2002 by the late Brenda Lazendorf of the National Park Service while returning from the wreck of the *Mandalay*. She shared that the site may represent the final resting spot of the *Hubbard*, a merchant vessel that apparently wrecked in the vicinity in 1772. Surrounded by seagrass, the site is dominated by an abundance of broken white glazed china shards that litter the bottom, 15 feet below the surface. Curiously, there are no obvious signs of wreckage here, and it's hardly a site worth visiting for the average diver. Regardless, I have included it in this work in hopes one day additional archival information will surface, and we will finally learn the history of this unidentified site.

ENTERPRISE (1854)

The Sailor's Magazine and Naval Journal, Volume 26, indicated the schooner (also cited as brig) *Enterprise*, from Boston for Jacksonville, capsized 12 miles east-northeast of the St. Johns Bar on January 27, 1854. Reportedly, the *Enterprise* went entirely over, with her bottom up. Captain Gordon and crew were taken off by the brig *Mantanzas*, from Havana, and carried into Jacksonville the next day.

ENTERPRISE (1871)

As documented in *The New York Herald* on December 22, 1871, the schooner *Enterprise*, Captain Allen, en route from Jacksonville for New Smyrna with groceries and lumber, wrecked inside the bar at Mosquito Inlet on December 5. While the crew was saved, nearly all the cargo was lost.

ÉPAULE DE MOUTON

The French auxiliary *Épaule de Mouton* (Shoulder of Mutton), Captain Machonville, was part of Jean Ribault's fleet that returned to Fort Caroline near present-day Jacksonville on August 28, 1565. On September 12, after an earlier skirmish with a Spanish armada, Ribault's fleet pursued the warships and prepared to overtake them near St. Augustine when an intense hurricane struck Florida. The storm pushed Ribault's fleet out to sea, allowing the Spaniards to escape. The *Épaule de Mouton* eventually wrecked north of Mosquito Inlet (Ponce Inlet) within 2 miles of fellow French vessels, the transport *Truite* and vice-flagship *Émérillion*, and north (some sources cite 15 miles north) of Ribault's flagship *Trinité*, which grounded north of Cape Canaveral.

ERICA OF EXUMA

On January 1, 1977, the U.S. Coast Guard sank the foundering *Erica of Exuma* at approximate latitude 27° north and longitude 79° 53' west due to damage sustained in heavy weather. The *Erica of Exuma* was an improvised roll-on, roll-off cargo vessel, which was originally a 114-foot long landing craft converted at a Netherlands shipyard and delivered to Palm Beach via freighter in December 1966.

The barkentine-rigged screw steamer *Erl King*.

ERL KING

The Erl King, also known as the *Erlkonig* in German or the *Ellerkonge* in Scandinavian, was a mythical elf character who caused mischief for children. The vessel *Erl King*, official number 52820, was an iron auxiliary steamer or screw brig, 305.6 feet in length and 34.1 feet in breadth, built by A. and J. Inglis Shipbuilders and Engineers of Glasgow, Scotland, in September 1865. The steamer displaced 2,178 tons, was barkentine rigged with a full poop deck, and had accommodations for approximately 50 first-class passengers. Barkentines were similar to barks in that they both possessed three masts. Barkentines, however, were square-rigged only on the fore mast, while barks had both the fore and main mast sails square rigged. She was owned by Robertson and Company of London, but sailed under charter for several companies, including the Temperley and Donaldson Lines. She was skippered by Captain John Pinel during her first few years of service while participating in the Australian and China trade in the Pacific.

On January 18, 1881, the *Erl King* ran aground on Tennessee Reef, but she was successfully pulled off, repaired, and put back in service. She was lost almost 11 years later on December 16, 1891, when Captain Crocker ran the steamer aground on Long Reef during a voyage from Swansea, England to New Orleans, Louisiana. First news of the grounding came from correspondence from the British steamer *Feliciana*, which passed the *Erl King* apparently "afloat with two anchors out." On December 21 the owners of the vessel in London received the following disheartening telegram from an insurance representative in Key West: "*Erl King*: Wreckers saving cargo; ship dangerous position; think certain total loss; came myself from her yesterday; engine-room full of water; tide ebbing flowing in compartments; doing all possible for you[68]." The fate of the vessel was sealed. By January 5, 1892, surveyors recommended the immediate sale of the wreck by auction. Only 200 tons of cargo was recovered, though some of her machinery and fittings were salvaged before she was totally abandoned. Furthermore, it was reported that large portions of her hull were salvaged for scrap during World War II.

Found in 18 feet of water, visiting divers can see the outline of the collapsed hull framed by metal hull plates and other assorted wreckage. The remains of her cargo, concrete stored in wooden barrels, have now solidified and can be observed scattered amongst the wreckage.

ESCORT (1839)

Reported on January 1839 in *The Sailor's Magazine and Naval Journal*, Volume 11, the schooner *Escort*, from New York, for St. Johns, having sprung a leak during the passage, was run ashore three miles south of Matanzas Inlet. The vessel proved to be a total loss.

ESCORT (1894+)

Built at Jacksonville in 1879, the steamer *Escort*, official number 135384, was 52.7 feet long, 9.7 feet wide, and displaced 11.6 tons gross. According to Davis (1925) the *Escort*, which operated on the TV for the Palatka-Crescent City Line, burned near Palatka. While no date is provided, the *Escort* disappears from documentation sometime between 1895 and 1897.

ESCORT (1926)

Owned by Phoenix Utility Company, the tug *Escort* was blown ashore on Biscayne Boulevard during the September 1926 Great Miami Hurricane[69]. The ultimate fate of the *Escort* is unknown.

Sinking of the *Esjoo* (Miami-Dade County Department of Environmental Resources Management).

ESJOO

The *Esjoo* was a 70-foot long vessel deployed as an artificial reef on June 1, 1987. Records indicate that the recorded depth was 51 feet and the intended site was the Anchorage Reef near the *Patricia* tug.

ESMERALDA

In 1994, an unidentified wreck resting in 200 feet of water off Miami was accidentally discovered. Following a dive to the wreck of the ferry *Mystic Isle*, local divers Tony Martinez, Jack Javech, and Jim Vahey fouled their anchor and drifted off the artificial reef. The northward moving Gulf Stream serendipitously carried their grapnel hook directly into a second wreck, of which they were unaware. Descending the line to free their anchor, the divers observed a virgin wreck resting in the sand. Artifacts were very conspicuous, possibly indicating that the vessel sank unexpectedly and was not a planned artificial reef. The team documented the site and proceeded to recover several artifacts in attempts to identify the wreck. Several Ashcroft gauges were recovered, as well as the bronze engine manufacturer's plaque. After countless dives over numerous years, no artifacts were found that positively identified the wreck.

Similar to the initial discovery of the wreck, the determination of her true identity was just as much a matter of happenstance. During my research on another vessel, I came across documentation for a yacht called the *Esmeralda*, which sank at Miami during a hurricane in 1926. The original explorers were aware of the existence of the *Esmeralda*, but ran into dead-ends when trying to connect her with their unidentified wreck. A nagging suspicion prompted me to follow up on the *Esmeralda*.

The *Esmeralda*, official number 96368, was originally built in 1897 as the *Hiawatha* at the Morris Heights, New York shipyard of the Charles L. Seabury Company. The 219-ton, steel-hulled yacht was 147.1 feet in length, 21.1 feet in beam, and was powered by a 1,000 horsepower engine produced by the Gas Engine and Power Company. For the first portion of her life, the *Hiawatha* was ported in Cincinnati, Ohio, though she was later moved to Detroit, Michigan. The *Hiawatha* was the personal yacht of millionaire Julius Fleischmann. Julius was the son of Charles Fleischmann, founder of Fleischmann and Company, the yeast firm that would quickly expand to become an industry giant under Julius's tenure. Julius Fleischmann would also serve as the mayor of Cincinnati for two terms beginning in 1900; at 28 years of age, he was the youngest mayor to serve the city to date. The *Hiawatha*, which was acknowledged to be one of the fastest and most attractive yachts plying the waters along the East Coast, frequently traveled to Fleischmann's summer retreat of Wickford, Rhode Island. After almost three decades of dependable service, the yacht was sold in 1924 to Thomas J. Peters, whereupon she was renamed the *Esmeralda* and moved to Miami.

The *Esmeralda* sank off the Municipal Dock during the Great Miami Hurricane on September 18, 1926. Striking in the early morning, the Category 4 hurricane claimed many vessels. The schooner *Delta*, bound from Gulfport, Mississippi, to Nassau, Bahamas, ran headlong into the storm; the massive seas and 140 mile-an-hour winds smashed the ship to pieces, sending her to the bottom off Lake Worth. The steamer *St. Lucie* was sunk off Elliott Key. Dozens of ships and barges, such as the schooners *Kessie Price* and *Rose Mahoney*, were cast ashore on Biscayne Boulevard by the massive storm surge. When the storm climaxed over Miami harbor, numerous terrified individuals leapt from their sinking vessels. Arriving on the scene, Police Officer P.M. Hannan was credited with saving 23 people as he risked his life by continuously swimming a line out to the crippled yachts and a sinking dredge. Of the six passengers onboard the *Esmeralda*, one individual perished when the yacht sank at her mooring. Over 300 people in South Florida died in the fast-moving hurricane.

The *Esmeralda* and several other large wrecks lay in Miami Harbor for over a year. Efforts to raise the yacht were complicated when the derrick barge used in the salvage sank twice. Finally, the submerged hulk was raised from the bottom in December 1927. The *Esmeralda* was then unceremoniously towed to sea and disposed of on December 27. There she remained until the trio of curious divers discovered the final resting spot of what they eventually dubbed the "Mystery Wreck." With the construction information in hand, we were able to confirm the identity of the "Mystery Wreck" as that of the *Esmeralda*. The bronze engine manufacturer's plaque documents her place and date of origin as Morris Heights, New York, 1898. Furthermore, measurements of the wreck's length and beam also corroborate the dimensions of the *Esmeralda*. Sometimes luck and chance play as vital a role as diligent research when trying to identify a wreck. As it turns out, commercial fishermen were long aware of the wreck of the *Esmeralda*, which was

The yacht *Esmeralda* as the *Hiawatha* (Historical Collections of the Great Lakes, Bowling Green State University).

locally known as the "Piney Jack Hole Wreck."

The long, graceful lines of what is obviously a yacht are still apparent, even after numerous decades under water. While the steel hull is largely intact, the wooden decking and bulkheads have long since been consumed by the voracious appetite of teredo worms. Portions of the upper deck and hull have delaminated from the main hull and remain off the starboard side of the wreck. It appears she collided with the seabed bow first, as the stem and raked bow have fractured off the rest of the hull and rest at an awkward angle. The remainder of the wreck is upright but listing to port. Numerous artifacts remain on the wreck, including several portholes and light fixtures. There are three or four large tubs with matching sinks resting in the stern of the ship. The bronze screw still rests at the terminus of the shaft, and is crafted with a very interesting swept taper. The funnel appears to have collapsed and rests in the sand along the portside of the wreck. She was powered by a triple expansion engine, which still can be found nestled within the machinery spaces towards the stern. Undoubtedly, more artifacts remain within the wreck; however, the majority of her hull is buried by a considerable amount of sediment. Numerous large grouper and hogfish frequent the wreck, and an occasional sailfish may be spotted by an observant diver during decompression, particularly in the spring.

ESPARTA

Upon their introduction to the United States in 1870, bananas quickly became a popular food item, with over 16 million bunches consumed annually at the close of the nineteenth century. Established on March 30, 1899, the United Fruit Company audaciously took control of the profitable banana trade. While the fledgling company became the leader in this trade, their financial stability was tenuous at best. The company depended on a large fleet of decrepit and slow freighters to deliver a product that had a limited lifespan. Delays in the delivery of fruit, especially in ships with no refrigeration or adequate ventilation, allowed the bananas to quickly ripen and led to a dramatic reduction in profit. In order to remedy this situation, the United Fruit Company contracted with the Belfast, Ireland shipyard of Workman, Clark and Company to produce three refrigerated freighters that would help save the company from financial ruin. The contract to build the three ships was signed on November 12, 1903. Named after ports in Central America, the *Esparta*, *San José*, and *Limon* would become the technological pioneers in the "Great White Fleet" of the United Fruit Company. Workman, Clark and Company's hull number 211 would become the *Esparta*.

The *Esparta*, official number 212606, was delivered on October 27, 1904. The coal-fired, single-screw vessel was 330.6 feet in length, 44.5 feet in breadth, displaced 3,365 tons, and could travel fully loaded at just over 12 knots. With her four decks, the freighter also had accommodations for 18 passengers. Due to the refrigerated holds and greater speed, the *Esparta* could deliver up to 45,000 stems of bananas before the fruit had ripened, elevating profits. The hulls of the three freighters were painted stark white to help reflect the tropical sun, while the funnels were emblazoned with a white diamond on a red band. Promptly after being put into service, the *Esparta's* career was tarnished after she collided with the lighthouse tender *Magnolia* on the Mississippi River. While the accident resulted in no casualties, the event was well-publicized, as President Theodore Roosevelt was a passenger aboard the *Esparta*. After this early embarrassment, the freighter would soon redeem itself after setting the single largest cargo record by transporting 56,000 stems of bananas from Costa Rica to New Orleans in 1906. In 1922, the heavily used freighter was converted to an oil-burning vessel and also received upgraded refrigeration equipment. As the years wore on, the aging vessel began to show signs of wear. From June through November 1938, she was laid up in New York and received some much needed attention. She would meet her fate off Jacksonville less than four years later.

Early on the morning of April 9, 1942, the 3,365-ton *Esparta* was steaming off Jacksonville, en route to New

The United Fruit Company freighter *Esparta* (William T. Hultgren).

York from Honduras with a cargo of bananas, coffee, and general merchandise. Just offshore, *Kapitänleutnant* Reinhard Hardegen, aboard the Type IXB U-boat *U-123*, observed the unarmed freighter heading north. Just after 1:00 a.m., Hardegen placed a single torpedo into the starboard hull of the *Esparta*, aft of amidships and adjacent to the number four hold. The vessel quickly took on a starboard list as water rushed into the aft cargo holds. Ten minutes after the attack, with the vessel a total loss, the crew abandoned ship. One crewmember lost his life in the attack.

While technically a Georgia wreck, due to her proximity to the Florida border, the *Esparta* is frequently visited from boats originating from Amelia Island and Mayport. After her sinking, the wreck was subjected to razing in order to eliminate her as a hazard to navigation. Regardless of the demolition work, portions of the freighter still stand high off the bottom, rising to within 40 feet of the surface. She now rests on her starboard side in approximately 60 feet of water and is generally considered a very easy dive. Sections of the wreck are heavily sanded in, thus navigation around the large, scattered site might be challenging for novice divers in low visibility conditions.

Reinhard Hardegen, who succeeded in sinking the first vessel in U.S. waters of World War II when he attacked the tanker *Norness* on January 12, 1942, would also have a considerable impact on Florida during the war. Hardegen would become one of the most successful U-boat commanders, sinking 23 ships rated at over 119,000 tons. Perhaps his most notable achievement was that he was one of a minority within the *Unterseebootwaffe* to survive the war. The *U-123* was scuttled at Lorient, France in 1944; however, she was raised and put into service by the French as the *Blaison* until her final decommissioning in 1959. Like Hardegen, the United Fruit Company also survived the war, and expanded to eventually become known as the Chiquita banana company.

ESPERANCIA

In the early 1980s, South Florida was the desired destination for thousands of immigrants from various Caribbean countries. The first wave came during the Mariel Boat Lift, as Cuban exiles headed north for the Florida Keys. Then came a flotilla of barely-floating vessels filled with desperate Haitians seeking to escape a politically repressed island nation ruled by Jean-Claude "Baby Doc" Duvalier. Tragically, many would never survive the journey. The loss of the wooden-hulled freighter *Esperancia* in the surf off Highland Beach in southern Palm Beach County demonstrated that sometimes death comes only feet from the desired American Dream. The *Esperancia*, reportedly between 50 to 70 feet in length, split apart off Highland Beach, spilling its human cargo into 15-foot seas on March 28, 1982. Days after the sinking, 21 bodies were found washed up on the beach amidst debris from the vessel; only six people escaped the sinking of the *Esperancia*. The tragedy of the *Esperancia* came only five months after another Haitian freighter, *La Nativité*, sank in the waters off Broward County, littering Hillsboro Beach with the broken bodies of 33 refugees.

Esso Bonaire III (Florida Fish and Wildlife Conservation Commission Artificial Reef Program).

ESSO BONAIRE III

The tanker *Esso Bonaire III* was originally built in 1939 as the *Poling Bros. No. 17* for Chester A. Poling, Incorporated. Built by John H. Mathis and Company at Camden, New Jersey, the 402-ton bulk-oil carrier was only 146.3 feet in length and 27.2 feet in breadth, with a 4,450 barrel capacity. In 1979, the vessel was sold and renamed twice – first as *Tanker Iso No.1*, and then later to *Ilso No. 1*. In 1984 she was sold and given a more conventional name, the *Emperador I*; in 1985 she operated as the *Nicodemus III*; and then finally, she was sold and rechristened the *Esso Bonaire III* in 1989.

On March 19, 1989, a U.S. Coast Guard boarding team discovered a cargo of 50,000 pounds of marijuana hidden in the hull of the Honduran-flagged *Esso Bonaire III* after it was intercepted approximately 50 miles east of the Abaco Islands in the Bahamas. The forfeited drug smuggler was purchased later that year by Palm Beach County and prepared as an artificial reef. The vessel was stripped down and cleaned, and holes were cut in the hull to facilitate the scuttling. After being towed out on site and partially flooded on July 23, 1989, the *Esso Bonaire III* refused to sink. Eventually, the contractor hired to tow the vessel out to the deployment site, Resolve Marine, employed their tug *Resolve Eagle* to ram the *Esso Bonaire III* to help send it to the bottom. The wreck of the *Esso Bonaire III* rests in approximately 90 feet of water off Jupiter and typically hosts significant numbers of adult goliath grouper, which provides an excellent photographic opportunity.

ETHEL (1890)

The petite schooner *Ethel*, built in 1868 at Canning, Nova Scotia, was 77 feet long, 26.2 feet wide, and displaced 78 tons. On April 12, 1890, Captain Lyman of the schooner *Bessie B.* arrived at Jacksonville with news of the schooner *Ethel*'s sinking. He described his approach to the scene:

> We left Lake Worth Wednesday morning and reached Cape Canaveral about noon Thursday. As we were passing the bay which makes in between Cape Canaveral

and False Cape I saw some floating wreckage on the starboard side and headed for it. We found a piece of a vessel's rail about twenty feet long and a big piece of planking from the bridge. There was nothing to identify the vessel, and on shore we could see lumber and barrels washed up, and so ran as near as we could and sent a boat ashore. The first thing I found was a cabin transom covered in canvas on which was painted in black letters 'Ethel.' Scattered along for a considerable distance were barrels and boxes, which were gathered together. We found five cases of bacon, several cases of pork branded with John G. Christopher's name, and eight barrels of flour. There were also some more pieces of wreck and another section of rail which had been pieced with new wood. The name 'Ethel' was on another fragment which I picked up[70].

Based on his observations, Captain Lyman offered a probable scenario onto the loss of the schooner *Ethel*:

It is pretty certain that she struck on the shoals to the north of Cape Canaveral on Bull, Ohio, or the Hetzel Shoals. I think she hit the Hetzels, which are to the northwest of the Cape, and with the prevailing northeast wind the wreckage would have drifted in about the direction where we found it. We crossed the track of the wreck several times, as was shown by the lumber scattered about. I feel certain that all on board were lost, unless possibly they may have been rescued by some passing vessel, although the course is considerably west of the track for Nassau steamers[71].

As fate would have it, the crew was rescued by a passing vessel, the British schooner *Pajaro*. Captain William D. Garvin and six other individuals abandoned the *Ethel* in a sinking condition off Cape Canaveral on April 5, 1890, after the schooner sprang a leak during heavy weather. They were eventually brought to Nassau where they informed the American consulate of the episode.

ETHEL (1895)

According to the 1896 *Annual Report of the Supervising Inspector-General, U.S. Steamboat-Inspection Service to the Secretary of Commerce and Labor*, on March 27, 1895, the steam launch *Ethel* was wrecked while crossing Lake Worth Bar. While there was no loss of life, the vessel proved to be a total loss; she was valued at $500.

ETHEL (1918)

The freighter *Ethel*, official number 216102, 176.3 feet in length, 36.1 feet in breadth, was built in 1918 at Portland, Oregon. She was powered with a 400-horsepower gas engine and registered a displacement of 718 tons gross, 555 tons net. On October 23, 1918, the *Ethel* reportedly foundered off St. Augustine.

ETOILE DE MER

French for "Star Fish," the *Etoile De Mer* was an 80-foot long former fishing vessel that was converted and used as an inter-island freighter in her later years. On January 18, 2001, the *Etoile De Mer* was seized after the U.S. Customs Service received an anonymous tip of suspicious activity on the ship, which was moored in the Miami River. As part of "Operation Riverwalk," agents inspected the freighter and found 186 pounds of cocaine, worth $1.5 million wholesale, in two duffel bags hidden in a false wall between the cargo hold and the engine room. The vessel was seized by the U.S. government and eventually sunk along with two other Miami River narcotic-smuggling ships, the *Brandy Wine* and the *Miguana*, on July 13, 2001. The *Etoile De Mer* now rests in 135 feet of water off Key Biscayne at U.S. Customs Reef, and is a short swim to the west of the *Miguana*; swimming east off the bow of the *Etoile De Mer* will take you to the bow of the *Miguana*. The *Tacoma* can be found by swimming approximately 500 feet to the northwest.

EULALIA

The 231-ton passenger steamer *Eulalia*, official number 136556, built in 1896, burned on Lake Beresford on April 25, 1910.

EUNICE M.

On March 17, 1938, the 49-ton vessel *Eunice M.*, built in 1906, caught fire, burned, and sank approximately eight miles off St. Lucie Inlet while en route from Fort Pierce to the Bahamas.

EUPHEMIA

The ferryboat *Euphemia*, which operated for the Jacksonville-Green Cove Springs Line, "stranded on shores of Dunn's Lake, where her hull was in evidence many years[72]." While it is unclear exactly when or where the steamer came to grief, it is worth noting that Dunn's Lake is now known as Crescent Lake.

EUREKA II

On December 14, 1930, the 10-ton excursion vessel *Eureka II*, 64.6 feet in length and 20.6 feet in breadth, which was built in 1921 at Coconut Grove, exploded and sank in 10 feet of water off Bug Light, 15 miles south of Miami. The vessel, owned by Captain Clarence Styles of Miami, was built on two pontoons with a well in the center into which a glass viewing port could be lowered. The *Eureka II* was approximately two miles off Bug Light returning to Miami from a trip to the shallow coral reefs south of the city when an engineer discovered smoke pouring from the engine room. A moment later came a cry for fire extinguishers. Before the startled passengers realized their plight, flames licked rapidly into the paneling of the boat. A violent explosion soon followed. Panic-stricken passengers rushed from one end of the craft to the other looking for lifeboats, but apparently the *Eureka II* carried none. As the fire steadily consumed the vessel, life preservers were torn from their hangings and hastily donned, as passengers jumped from the two decks of the burning *Eureka II*. Arthur S. Deen was one of the passengers rescued: "Smoke began coming from the engine room as we sailed along," he said. "Then there was an explosion followed immediately by two more. Flames began to leap out of the engine room. The craft began to go to pieces it looked like. It rocked and seemed like it was sinking. Some of the passengers were blown into the water by the explosion, but when the boat started to sink the rest of us jumped in[73]."

Fred G. Norman, New York City police sergeant: "The whole crew seemed to be crazy. As I got to the door, flames began to lick up around the paneling. People began to rush madly toward the front and back of the boat, fore and aft, screaming fire. Panic reigned. No one gave orders or tried to organize the situation[74]."

Four bodies were recovered by rescue boats and five others were unaccounted for and believed drowned. It is unclear if the charred remains of the *Eureka II* were raised for the subsequent investigation by the U.S. Steamboat Inspection Service (even though the *Eureka II* was gas propelled), or if the hull and engine of the excursion vessel were left to disintegrate on the bottom.

EVADNE

The *Evadne* was a three-masted lumber schooner built by C.H. McLennan at River John, Nova Scotia, in 1900. She was 129.2 feet long, 34 feet wide, and displaced 405 tons. In 1917, the *Evadne* was abandoned in the Florida Straits while carrying a cargo of lumber, and eventually washed up at Caesar's Creek, south of Miami. According to Bessie Wilson DuBois (1975), a large portion of the schooner also came ashore south of Jupiter Inlet. She related how Harry DuBois, a former member of the local life-saving crew, came upon the wreck south of the inlet approximately 100 yards from shore:

> As they came nearer, they saw it was the bottom of a ship about 150 feet long. All that remained of the upper part of the craft was the captain's cabin on the after part.... The captain's cabin had evidently been hastily abandoned, for all his personal effects remained, including his razor.... He also salvaged the ship's bell from the roof of the cabin. The compass could be seen, set in gimbals, by the ship's wheel.... He managed to find the sextant, taffrail log, and sounding lead, also the ship's log, the captain's raincoat, a big straw hat, and a pair of antiquated handcuffs.... A day or so later the wreck washed up on the beach, and Harry and his son were able to salvage rope and plumbing fixtures.

EVANGELINE

According to the 1904 *Annual Report of the Commissioner of Navigation to the Secretary of Commerce and Labor*, the *Evangeline* was a small 21-ton steamer built in 1889 that reportedly caught fire and burned on Horseshoe Lake on February 15, 1904.

EVEN TIDE

The American bark *Even Tide*, Captain J.C. Parks, en route from Florida to New York with 190,000 feet of lumber, struck on the Pelican Shoal on January 9, 1867[75]. Every effort was made to get her off, but all efforts were in vain. The captain and crew abandoned the *Even Tide* on January 13, and soon thereafter the bark went to pieces. The *Even Tide* was built in 1854 at Prospect, Maine, and was 118 feet in length, 28 feet in breadth, and displaced 348 tons gross, 285 tons net.

EVERGLADE

The steamboat *Everglade* was owned by Frederick DeBary and operated as a ferry for the DeBary Line, which was established in 1876. The steamer *Everglade* was built for the consolidated DeBary-Baya Merchants Line in 1884, and documented a length of 134 feet, a beam of 37.3 feet, and a displacement of 413 tons gross. Her ultimate demise is nebulous: according to Davis (1925), the *Everglade* burned at Jacksonville, while another source states she was dismantled at Jacksonville in 1897 (possibly after burning), and yet a third potential fate suggests she was abandoned in March 1900.

EXPORT

On September 4, 1838, the brig *Export*, Captain C.M. Morrill, of Kennebunk, Maine, sailed from Mantanzas, Cuba, with a cargo of sugar and coffee, bound for Boston. On September 6, she experienced a severe gale, which quickly intensified into a hurricane. While trying to ride out the storm, the *Export* struck on Ledbury Reef on September 7. With high seas breaking over the brig, the crew got out the long boat and made for shore. According to *The American Almanac and Repository of Useful Knowledge for the Year 1840*, the *Export* was totally lost, though half of the cargo was saved, resulting in an award of $1,990.72 to the local wreckers.

F.A. KILBURN

Named after the president of the Watsonville Oil Company, the *F.A. Kilburn* was a 728-ton wooden-hulled steamer, 201.2 feet in length and 29.8 feet in breadth, built in 1904 at Fairhaven, California, by the H.D. Bendixsen Shipbuilding Company. The *Kilburn* was powered with a single triple-expansion engine, and possessed two decks and two masts; information indicates she may have been schooner-rigged for auxiliary sail. In her early years she sailed for the North Pacific Steamship Company between Portland, Oregon and California ports. In 1918, she was sold to the Mexican Fruit and Steamship Company and made her way to the Atlantic coast. On June 11, 1918, the *F.A. Kilburn* caught fire off American Shoal Light. Captain Wailard and all the crew, numbering 31, were saved. *The Galveston Daily News*, June 26, 1918, reported a June 18 dispatch that a large derelict steamer thought to be the *Kilburn* was sighted bottom up three miles off Palm Beach. It is unclear where the steamer ultimately sunk to the bottom, but it's highly probable she is resting somewhere off the Florida coast.

The steamer *F.A. Kilburn* underway off California (Humboldt State University Library).

F.C. BENNETT

The yacht *F.C. Bennett* (also reported as the *F.A. Bennett*) wrecked at the shore end of the Baltimore and Carolina Line docks during the September 1926 Great Miami Hurricane[76].

FAIR WEATHER

As reported in *The Edinburgh Advertiser* on December 24, 1811, "The *Fair Weather*, from Amelia Island to England, is lost on Amelia Island Bar."

FALCON

On April 22, 1564, René Goulaine de Laudonnière departed Havre, France, with 300 Huguenot settlers aboard a fleet of three vessels, including the 80-ton *Falcon*. In late June they arrived in North Florida, where they established a triangular compound near the mouth of the St. Johns River, called Fort Caroline in honor of Charles IX. There Laudonnière and the settlers endured a harsh 14 months of disease, mutiny, and starvation, which finally ended on September 20, 1565, with the capture of Fort Caroline by a Spanish force led by Pedro Menéndez de Avilés. Laudonnière and other survivors fled back to France aboard the *Perle* and *Levière* after reportedly scuttling the *Falcon* and bark *Tiger*.

FAME

According to Marx (1987), the American vessel *Fame*, Captain Bennett, wrecked on the Florida coast in 1810 en route from New Orleans to Liverpool. I have been unable to uncover any additional information on this vessel or its wrecking.

FANNIE DUGAN

The sidewheel river steamboat *Fannie Dugan*, official number 120012, built in 1872 at Portsmouth, Ohio, was 165.4 feet long, 28.4 feet wide, and 260 tons gross. Owned by Captain Robert Bagby, she steamed between Huntington, West Virginia, and Cincinnati, Ohio. The *Fannie Dugan* possessed thirty staterooms that surrounded a central, 120-foot long salon; each stateroom had one door opening in to the grand saloon and one opening out to the promenade deck. Due to the need for river steamers in Florida, the *Dugan* was transferred from her Ohio River route to the St. Johns River in 1882. Following an overhaul that switched out her boilers and paddlewheels, the *Dugan* went into service to replace the *Frederick DeBary*, which was lost by fire in 1883; the DeBary-Baya Line later purchased her in 1884. Her Florida service, however, was short-lived. After only two years on the St. Johns, several sources state the *Fannie Dugan* was abandoned on the north bank of DeBary Creek near the entrance to Lake Monroe, and while partially salvaged in 1886, as well as in the 1960s, portions of the wreck can apparently still be found along the shoreline. Another source states she was merely broken up at Jacksonville in 1886.

FANNIE KIMMEY

As reported in *The New York Times* on February 7, 1898, "The schooner *Fannie Kinney* [sic], Captain Fisher, which sailed from Philadelphia January 28 with a cargo of coal bound for this port, foundered about five miles north of the mouth of the St. Johns River early this morning. No lives were lost, but the vessel is probably a total wreck." The *Fannie Kimmey*, official number 120388, was built in November 1879 at Milton, Delaware, by J.L. Black and Brothers. She registered a length of 129 feet, a beam of 32.8 feet, and a displacement of 384 tons gross.

FANNIE S

The small, 7-ton gas vessel *Fannie S*, official number 205938, built in 1908, caught fire and burned on October 30, 1914, on the St. Sebastian River.

FANNY

As documented in the *Lloyd's List* on March 24, 1782, the British vessel *Fanny*, Captain Farquar, bound from Jamaica to Liverpool, went ashore to the northward of

Cape Florida and bilged on March 7, 1782. The crew was taken off the wreck by a Providence privateer and it was hoped part of her cargo would be saved.

FANNY FERN

The 17-ton sidewheel steamer *Fanny Fern*, official number 9692, was built in 1868 at Jacksonville, and served as a ferryboat between that city and the villages of Riverside, Reed's Landing, South Shore, and Alexandria, on the opposite shore of the St. Johns River. On January 22, 1873, an explosion shattered the small steamer near Jacksonville, claiming three lives.

FANNY SPRAGUE

Constructed in 1872 at South Boston, Massachusetts, the fishing steamer *Fanny Sprague*, official number 120030, was 105 feet long, 16.6 feet wide, and displaced 89 tons gross. Based out of Boothbay, Maine, the *Fanny Sprague* was heavily involved in the whaling industry in the 1880s, as well as other important North Atlantic fisheries of the day such as mackerel. She later migrated south to participate in the menhaden fishery, whereupon she stranded and was lost at Fort George Inlet near Fernandina on April 30, 1917.

FATHOM II

The *Fathom II* was a converted 136-foot long mine sweeper, originally built in 1943 by the Greenport Basin and Construction Company of New York. At the time of her loss she was owned by Fathom Expeditions, and had been redocumented as a research vessel for planned use as a salvage and treasure-hunting platform. On the morning of October 16, 1972, approximately one mile east of the St. Johns River mouth, the *Fathom II* was involved in a collision with the 579-foot long tanker *Gavrion*. As a result of the collision, the 278-ton, wooden-hulled *Fathom II* was cut in half and sunk in 38 feet of water. All seven crewmen aboard the *Fathom II* safely escaped the sinking ship. Following litigation, the wreckage of the *Fathom II* was eventually removed from the shipping channel where it sunk.

FAVORITE

The excursion sailing vessel *Favorite* reportedly went to pieces and sunk behind one of Biscayne Bay's spoil islands during the September 1926 Great Miami Hurricane; as of 1934, the wreck still remained completely sunk in the mud where she sank[77].

FEARLESS

The steamer *Fearless*, built in 1897 at Palatka, was 50 feet in length and 15.3 feet in breadth. On June 11, 1906, the steamer, captained by W.S. Cone, sunk on the St. Johns River at Colee due to unknown causes. As damage to the vessel was very slight, the vessel was immediately raised. The following year, the *Fearless* would not be so lucky. According to the *Annual Report of the Supervising Inspector-General, U.S. Steamboat-Inspection Service to the Secretary of Commerce and Labor*, 1908, "April 29, 1907: Steamer *Fearless*, while lying at Colee dock April 29 between 12 midnight and 1 a.m., was discovered on fire in forward hold. Fire extinguishers and other means of extinguishing fire were used, but steamer burned to water's edge. No lives lost."

FELISA

On August 30, 1880, the steamer *New York*, struggling through hard southeast gales, sighted a dismasted vessel off her bow. The crippled ship proved to be the Spanish bark *Felisa*, en route from New Orleans to her home port of Barcelona. A lifeboat was lowered to take off the 13-man crew, several of whom were seriously injured. The *Felisa*, Captain G. Anye, departed New Orleans on August 13 with a cargo of 47,320 staves, and experienced heavy gales for three days beginning August 27. On August 28, the *Felisa*, "in latitude 28° north, longitude 80° 12' west, Jupiter bearing south by east 63 miles, and Cape Canaveral northwest half west, and 34 miles distant, was compelled to cut away the spars in order to keep the vessel from foundering[78]."

The New York Times published a September 11, 1880, article stating, "an incoming vessel reports that the abandoned bark *Falecia* [sic] was seen a few days ago lying in 15 fathoms of water 18 miles southeast by east of Cape Canaveral. Both anchors were out, and the fore and main masts were gone. The wreck was lying in the track of vessels bound around Cape Canaveral." The tragic loss of the steamer *City of Vera Cruz* during the same storm soon dominated the news, and the fate of the *Felisa* ultimately went unreported; however, as the vessel disappears from the vessel registers after 1880, it is likely she foundered, was scuttled as a hazard to navigation, or was towed in and condemned. The 305-ton bark *Felisa* was built in August 1865 at Sestria Pon'te, and registered a length of 122.1 feet and a beam of 28.7 feet.

FERZIEHM

The *New Smyrna Daily News*, December 2, 1925, reported "The two-masted British schooner *Ferziehm* was blown ashore north of Daytona Monday night (November 30) and six men of the crew were drowned when the schooner foundered in the shallow water. Three members of the crew swam ashore, helped by the strong onshore wind. The vessel is said to have been loaded with liquor and the captain and all members of the crew were West Indian negroes." Additional information documented the wrecking of the rum runner, reportedly carrying 2,000 cases of liquor from the Bahamas, as three miles south of Flagler Beach. It should be noted that the spelling of the vessel's name varies considerably in various sources, including *Ferziehin*, *Ferziehn*, and *Ferziebin*.

FIDES

The screw freighter *Fides*, official number 221192, was built in 1921 at Jacksonville. The 61-ton vessel was 57.4 feet long and 18.2 feet wide. On March 21, 1924, the *Fides* burned at Jupiter, becoming a total loss.

FIVE BROTHERS

On January 30, 1914, the *New Smyrna Daily News* reported on the disposal of an abandoned barque. The information stated, "During the previous Democratic administration, that of Grover Cleveland, the barque *Five Brothers*, a derelict drawing 25 feet of water, with decks awash, passed over the bar and was towed back to the ocean." While the article implies the *Five Brothers* was towed offshore to be sunk, it is unclear what ultimately happened to the barque.

FLEETWOOD III

The 55-ton yacht *Fleetwood III* was owned by Florida businessman Commodore J. Perry Stoltz, known for building the Miami Beach Fleetwood Hotel in 1924. The yacht was one of over 60 vessels sunk in September 1926 during the Great Miami Hurricane. The wrecked *Fleetwood III* was eventually raised, towed up the Miami River, and abandoned near 27th Avenue[79].

FLORDI GUADIANA

According to the October 13, 1813, issue of *The Edinburgh Advertiser*, "At Amelia Island, there is but one vessel afloat. The Portuguese ship *Flordi Guadiana* (late *Alexander Hamilton*) is ashore and bilged." Other reports stated she was carrying a cargo of cotton, and she was driven ashore and bilged on Cumberland Island on September 17, 1813.

FLORIDA (1825)

According to *The Edinburgh Advertiser*, June 3, 1825:
The *Florida*, White, from St. Augustine to the Havannah [sic], was struck by a heavy sea on the 3d March, two days after she sailed, and swamped. All the passengers who were below decks, to the number of twenty-four, were instantly drowned. The crew, and several passengers, in all sixteen persons, who were on deck, remained for several days thereon, when ten out of the sixteen took to the long boat, and gained the land in the neighbourhood of St. Augustine three days after. The *Florida* was met three days after the long boat left her without any person on board.

The ultimate fate of the *Florida* is unclear; she may have been towed in, or perhaps she was burned and/or scuttled to remove her as a menace to navigation.

FLORIDA (1857)

The wrecking of the *Florida* was succinctly reported in *The Sailor's Magazine and Naval Journal*, Volume 29, which detailed, "January 27, 1857, pilot boat *Florida*, Captain Frow, burned and sunk near Cape Florida; 196 tons; value $17,000." The actual loss of the 90-foot schooner *Florida* in 1857 was a bit ironic. Built in Key West, the *Florida* was used in the salvage of shipwrecks that came to grief on the Florida reef tract. While transshipping the cotton cargo from the British ship *Crown*, which ran aground on Ajax Reef on January 19, 1857, the tables were quickly turned on the *Florida*, and she became a total loss. As darkness fell during the salvage operation, the 132-ton wrecking schooner *Florida* began striking bottom. The captain directed another wrecking vessel to come alongside to take on some of the cotton stowed on the deck of the *Florida* before repositioning the schooner. During this process, a crewman knocked over a lantern that was on deck of the *Florida*, which caught the bales of cotton on fire. The flames quickly engulfed the *Florida*, which was pinned between the two ships. In an attempt to save the other two vessels, the *Florida* was cast adrift and allowed to burn to the waterline and sink just offshore.

FLORIDA (1904)

On April 2, 1904, the U.S. Army Corps of Engineers' dredge *Florida* was launched at Jacksonville to replace the obsolete *Suwannee*, which had been in operation since 1888. Built by the Merrill-Stevens Engineering Company, the new sternwheel steamer dredge was 131 feet in length, 28 feet in beam, and registered a displacement of 175 tons. In 1908, she underwent an overhaul, during which she was lengthened to 152 feet and widened to 29.9 feet. With her 12-inch centrifugal pump, the *Florida* was initiated by clearing the channel at the Volusia Bar, after which she saw constant work for 13 years throughout Northeast and Central Florida. According to the July 5, 1918, *St. Augustine Evening Record*, the *Florida* was pummeled by a fierce gale that ultimately sent her to the bottom on July 3 off Crescent Beach. The sinking claimed the lives of the dredge *Florida's* designer, U.S. Army Corps of Engineers' Chief Engineer for the Florida District, General John Warren Sackett, and two crew members. For a period after the sinking, portions of the wreck were exposed above the surface and visible from shore. Ironically, in January 1920, the hydrographic survey vessel *Isis* ran afoul of the wreck while charting its remains, and sank just off the beach about a mile away from the *Florida*.

Today, the wreck of the *Florida* rests in approximately 50 feet of water just over a mile offshore Crescent Beach. The former dredge is relatively intact, resting roughly north-south, and its remains are enveloped in a blanket of corals and invertebrates. Some portions of the wreck are broken down and unrecognizable, though other sections, such as the stern paddlewheel assembly at the stern, and the A-frame and dredge arm at the bow, are easily identified. While the *Florida* is a relatively shallow site, divers should be aware that visibility is typically low due to its proximity to shore, and occasional significant surge can make navigation around the encrusted wreckage potentially hazardous.

FLORIDA LEAGUE OF ANGLERS MINESWEEPER

The *Florida League of Anglers Minesweeper*, or *F.L.A. Minesweeper*, was sunk as an artificial reef off Broward County on July 8, 1986. Though cited as a Bluebird Class minesweeper, it appears she was actually a YMS-1 Class, YMS-135 Subclass Auxiliary Motor Minesweeper. All of

The rusting *F.L.A. Minesweeper* just prior to her scuttling in deep water (Broward County Artificial Reef Program).

the 481 wooden-hulled YMS-1 Class Minesweepers built during World War II were 136 feet long, 24.5 feet wide, displaced 270 tons, and were originally powered with two 800-horsepower General Motors 8-268A diesel engines. The specific identity and associated history of this vessel is unknown, but it's likely she saw some action during World War II. The *F.L.A. Minesweeper* now rests in 390 feet of water northeast of the *Rebel*.

FLY

The 27-ton British sloop *Fly*, Captain James Walker, was documented to have operated in the slave trade between Africa and the West Indies. A small vessel, the *Fly* typically carried less than 50 head on its journey across the Atlantic. For example, in August 1787, the *Fly* departed its home port of Bristol for Sierra Leone, on the west coast of Africa. There, Captain Walker intended to load on 35 captives for his voyage to Tortola. In August 1789, Captain Walker was on a return trip to the West Coast of Africa from Jamaica when the *Fly* wrecked at Cape Florida on the evening of August 14. While no lives were lost, the vessel was eventually abandoned and set on fire. It is also worth noting that the December 25, 1789, *Lloyd's List* documented the vessel *Fly* as lost on the "Martyrs," which is typically considered to be the Lower Florida Keys.

FLYING CLOUD

Built in 1911, the 28-ton *Flying Cloud* reportedly foundered on Lake Worth in July 1969[80].

FORMENTO

As documented in *The Sailor's Magazine and Naval Journal*, Volume 20, "The Spanish brig *Formento*, from Havana bound to Vigero, Gallacia, struck the reef seven miles north of New River Bar, March 8, 1848, and capsized and sunk in a gale." The *Formento* was laden with a cargo of sugar and liquor, and combined with the value of the vessel, the wrecking represented a loss of $40,000. The remains of the brig *Formento* should rest somewhere near Pompano Beach.

FORTITUDE

On April 15, 1784, the *Whitehall Evening Post* reported that, "Advice is received that the ship *Fortitude*, Cap. Jones, bound from Jamaica for Bristol, was lately lost on the coast of Florida, and most of the crew perished."

FORTUNA II

The 38-ton shrimper *Fortuna II* was built in 1907 for the Versaggi family. The loss of the 65-foot long shrimp boat was recorded in the February 2, 1938, issue of the *St. Augustine Record*:

> Unable to cross the dangerous bar off of Anastasia Island because of a mountainous sea, the *Fortuna II*, one of the largest of the local shrimp boats, sprung a leak and was beached by its crew south of Ponte Vedra late yesterday afternoon. The 65-foot fishing yawl, owned by Versaggi and Sons of this city, was trying to fight its way through a driving wind and high sea to the Fernandina port when it began to sink and the crew had to beach the craft and swim for their lives. The shrimper, valued at around $8,000, was being pounded by a heavy sea today, and it is feared that it will be totally wrecked. Two other shrimp boats, one belonging to Versaggi and Sons and one owned by the Salvador interests here, were also caught in the stormy weather that is now engulfing the coast and have been riding at anchor off of Anastasia Island since yesterday morning, shrimp dealers stated. Unable to cross the bar, the boats are in danger of sinking and the lives of the

crews are imperiled. The *Fortuna II* tried to reach port yesterday morning but the crew found it impossible to cross the local bar because of a high, rolling sea.

Reportedly, the *Fortuna II* eventually broke up soon after the grounding, and proved to be a total loss. Recently, archaeologists from the St. Augustine Lighthouse Archaeological Maritime Program discovered a wreck in the vicinity of Ponte Vedra Beach they believe may represent the remains of the shrimp trawler *Fortuna II*.

FORTUNE (1772)

The snow *Fortune*, Captain Robert Richardson, bound from Jamaica to London with a cargo of rum, sugar, and cotton, was lost on November 18, 1772, along the Florida coast. Details included from a March 30, 1773, article in the *General Evening Post*, stated, "…in Lat. 23° 43' north, sprung a leak, which they finding impossible to stop, they on the 18th, having four feet of water in the hold, attempted to reach the Florida shore, in order to save their lives; but in Lat 28°, struck upon a breaker, where the vessel and cargo are lost; the crew, except a man and a boy, are saved." The wreck of the *Fortune* should rest close to the beach in the vicinity of Melbourne.

FORTUNE (1782)

On March 10, 1783, *Parker's General Advertiser and Morning Intelligencer* reported, "They write from Barbadoes, that the *Fortune*, Capt. Roach, from that port for London, was lately lost on the coast of Florida, and all the crew perished." Based on the typical delay of reporting shipwreck events during this period, the *Fortune* likely was lost in late 1782.

FOR YOUR EYES ONLY

On the morning of November 23, 1987, the 105-foot long yacht *For Your Eyes Only* began taking on water just east of Hillsboro Inlet. Pumps were unable to keep up with the flooding water, and the yacht, valued at $3.2 million, soon sank in 41 feet of water. The 11 passengers and crew safely evacuated the sinking vessel. Owner Alex Woskob contracted Titan Salvage to raise the sunken yacht, which was successfully accomplished on November 31.

FOXFIRE

The "Foxfire," resting in approximately 80 feet of water north of Cape Canaveral, consists of the wreckage from an aircraft powered by a single, nine-cylinder radial engine. The site is small, as the majority of the aircraft is buried under the sand; however, the upside-down engine is exposed with one bent blade of the propeller protruding from the bottom. It is believed the wreck is a General Motors Wildcat, BuNo 46833, which was piloted by Merle E. Mattair on September 28, 1944, when he was forced to ditch east-northeast of Chester Shoal near Cape Canaveral during gunnery practice. Fortunately, Mr. Mattair survived the crash, as well as World War II.

FRANCES

The 60-foot long yacht *Frances*, official number 1141226, was originally built in 1892 at Solomons, Maryland as the *Lula and Sadie*. The 20-ton vessel stranded at Miami on January 2, 1915.

FRANCIS (1843)

A January 1843 report in *The Sailor's Magazine and Naval Journal*, Volume 15, documented, "Schooner *Francis*, of Key West, was wrecked at the mouth of Indian River. Crew supposed to have been murdered by the Indians, from their having been seen near the spot, and from the appearance of the wreck."

FRANCIS (1921)

On December 10, 1921, the U.S. Coast Guard Cutter *Yamacraw* found the derelict schooner *Francis* at latitude 28° 44' north and longitude 79° 43' west (approximately 45 nautical miles east of Cape Canaveral). The *Yamacraw* pumped out the abandoned schooner and took her in tow, presumably back to Jacksonville. After towing the *Francis* a distance of 102 miles the schooner took on water during a gale and sunk. The *Yamacraw* reported a depth of 8 fathoms over the wreck.

FRANCIS (1962)

The shrimp boat *Francis*, with a crew of three, was reported missing off St. Augustine on April 2, 1962. Almost five months after its disappearance, two divers found the wreck of the *Francis* resting in 75 feet of water 15 miles east of St. Augustine. The divers reported the rigging was intact and there was no sign of collision.

FRANCIS V. SYLVIA

The schooner *Francis V. Sylvia*, official number 201610, was built in 1904 at Essex, Massachusetts, and was 85 feet in length, 21.7 feet in beam, and 95 tons gross burden. The *Sylvia* reportedly foundered on November 16, 1943, at approximate latitude 25° 22' north, longitude 80° 08' west, which is just east of Pacific Reef.

FRANCONIA

It is said that those who choose to ignore history are destined to repeat it. Such is true of Captain O'Brien and the steamer *Franconia* on July 28, 1890, when they carelessly strayed onto a shoal at the entrance to the harbor of Fernandina. After grounding on the shoal, the same shoal that devoured the steamer *City of Austin*, the steamer caught fire and burned to its waterline.

At the time of her loss, the steamer *Franconia* was an old ship and not in good condition. She was built at Kennebunk, Maine, in 1863, and saw service as a Union gunboat during the Civil War. She was 179 feet long, had a 30 foot beam, and displaced 675 tons. She was traveling in ballast, as she was chartered to carry 900 tons of phosphate from the Dennellen Company in Fernandina to Baltimore. According to a newspaper report of the incident, "The *Franconia* was spoken by the pilot boat *Agnes*

Bell about 5 o'clock Monday afternoon three miles east of the bar, but the Captain refused a pilot, feeling confident that he could make the port safely, depending on the chart. She fetched up on the same quicksand shoal where the *City of Austin* was wrecked some years ago. It is the general opinion that had not the fire occurred she would have been a loss anyhow, as she was badly grounded, and the high water failed to float her, but buried her bottom deeper in the shifting sands[81]."

Captain O'Brien of the *Franconia* related the fate of his vessel:

> We left New York July 23, and had a rough passage, with head winds all the way. Arrived off Fernandina Bar at 5 P.M. on the 28th, and was spoken by pilots, but did not take any, thinking it unnecessary, as I had a good chart, etc. I was about abreast of the *City of Austin* wreck when the vessel became unmanageable. A strong southwest wind was blowing at the time and the vessel was drawing seven feet forward and fourteen aft. I stopped the engines and backed, and just as the vessel touched bottom let go the anchor. The anchor chains parted and the vessel drifted upon the shoal, where she pounded some. At 11 P.M. she began making water. I worked the steam pumps and kept the water down until 1 A.M. today, when one of the pumps gave out and the water gained until there was six feet in the hold[82].

Apparently, while the crew was topside manning the pumps during the night, an oil lamp was left burning below decks. The constant pounding on the shoal must have overturned it, as fire broke out on the *Franconia* in the early morning hours of July 29. Captain O'Brien continued, stating, "About daylight fire was discovered aft in the room where the sailors and firemen slept. It spread very rapidly, and finding it impossible to stop the fire, I lowered the boats and all hands, sixteen in number, got in and pulled away from the blazing vessel. The lifeboat from the tug *Wade Hampton* took several persons from our overloaded boats and we boarded the tug and came to town. The crew managed to save most of their personal effects. The vessel had no insurance, either marine or fire[83]."

Unfortunately for divers, the U.S. Army Corps of Engineers removed the wreck of the *Franconia*. The project was documented in the *Annual Report of the Chief of Engineers, United States Army, to the Secretary of War for the Year 1905*, which stated, "The removal of the wrecks of the *City of Austin*, *Franconia*, and *Puntalunos* [sic] in Cumberland Sound, Georgia and Florida, was completed. This work was done under emergency contract of August 8, 1903, at a total cost of $7,213.85."

FRANK

On November 12, 1851, *The New York Times* printed, "The steamer *Magnolia*, arrived here (Savannah) today (November 10) from Florida, reports that the brig *Frank*, of Boston, went ashore on Amelia beach, on the 8th, she parted both her chains, and it is thought will prove a total loss. She had no cargo."

FRANK E. STONE

The 1877 wrecking of the schooner *Frank E. Stone* was recollected by the *Daytona Beach Observer* on August 29, 1936:

> Captain Charles Fozzard, early pioneer of the Halifax River area, was the hero of the wreck of the schooner *Frank E. Stone*. On June 28, 1877, the ship ran into a severe storm and Fozzard attempted to bring it across the ill-fated bar of the inlet (Ponce Inlet). The schooner lacked enough ballast, however, and the wind blew her over into the tumultuous waters of the inlet and her sails dragged in the rough waves. Passengers and crew clung to the keel, and a valiant effort was made to cut loose a tender being towed astern, but without success. Fozzard swam ashore, where he procured a boat with which he rescued all his crew and passengers, except three who had lost their grip on the keel and had drowned.

FRANKLIN

According to *The Sailor's Magazine and Naval Journal*, Volume 10, the schooner *Franklin*, of and from Philadelphia, for Mobile, together with cargo was lost on the Florida coast in September 1838; passengers and crew saved.

FRANKLIN BAKER 2ND

Singer (1998) states the 100-ton trawler *Franklin Baker 2nd* sank on November 13, 1943, at latitude 26° 09' north and longitude 79° 52' west.

FRED W. HOYT

The 59-ton schooner *Fred W. Hoyt*, built in 1881 and named after Frederick Willis Hoyt, a well-known merchant in Fernandina Beach, burned at Amelia Beach on December 18, 1883, at 2:00 a.m., at the mouth of the Amelia River. The source of ignition was believed to have been the cook's stove.

FREEDOM EXPRESS

The *Freedom Express* (IMO number 5079018) was originally launched on February 19, 1958, as the 1,631-ton freighter *Container Enterprise*. In 1988, the 262-foot long vessel operated as the *Isacar I*; sold in 1991, she was renamed *Sea Container*; acquired by yet another firm in 1998, she sailed as *Isamar*; and finally, in 2000, she was sold to the Panamanian firm Carib Workboat and renamed *Freedom Express*. In June 2003, the container ship suffered damage to her hull in the Miami Anchorage Channel. Vessel registration was later withdrawn from the Republic of Panama due to safety deficiencies, and the ship was abandoned at Miami. On June 13, 2003, the *Freedom Express* was towed approximately 27 miles offshore Miami by the tug *Doyle* and scuttled in 2,270 feet of water.

Freedom Express towed offshore for disposal (Titan Salvage).

FREE SPIRIT ENTERPRISE

In 1981 the 43-foot long vessel *Free Spirit Enterprise* reportedly burned and sank at latitude 28° 39.7' north and longitude 80° 23.3' west.

FREEWIND

On January 28, 1886, the *Halifax Herald* reported that "out of eight or ten schooners employed in the lighthouse (Ponce de Leon Inlet Light Station) work, five have been wrecked, viz: *Godfrey*, *Augusta Wilson*, *Ajax*, *Freewind*, and the *Johnson*; the *Mary Brown*, now lying at the lighthouse dock, is crippled. We have been assured that nearly all of them received the injuries resulting in wrecks on the inlet bar or in the river. Six men have also been drowned."

FREIGHT CONSOLIDATOR

Built in 1945, the *Freight Consolidator* was one of 254 LSMs (landing ship, medium) launched by Brown Shipbuilding Company of Houston, Texas during World War II. After the war, she was converted into a freighter and was eventually purchased by the Miami Terminal Transport Company. She registered a length of 213.5 feet, a beam of 38 feet, and a displacement of 960 tons. On the morning of May 18, 1970, the vessel was en route from Miami to Tampa for an overhaul, when crewmembers stated vibrations shook the propeller loose and it gashed a hole in the hull, though it's likely she struck a submerged object. The *Freight Consolidator* flooded and sank approximately 20 miles southeast of Miami at 4:45 a.m. The vessel's skeleton crew was rescued two hours later by a passing tanker.

FROLIC (1816)

The American vessel *Frolic*, Captain Kennedy, sailing from Havana to Charleston, stranded on Anastasia Island near St. Augustine in 1816[84]. The cargo and crew were saved.

FROLIC (1910)

As reported in *The New York Times* on October 20, 1910, "During a storm at St. Augustine on October 18, 1910, the sloop *Frolic* was dashed to pieces against the seawall and a power launch was sunk in the bay."

FUGGEDABOUDIT WRECK

The "Fuggedaboudit Wreck" was first visited by A.U.E. divers in 2001. Resting in 290 feet of water off Sebastian, the wreck appears to be a large freighter that was most likely a World War II casualty. The bow is pointed northward, and she sits bolt upright on a sand and mud bottom. Amidships, the superstructure is dramatically deteriorated, while areas forward are absent of decking and hull plates, which reveal the skeleton of the freighter. A deck gun is present on the stern, though the platform has torn loose from the ship and the gun now points straight down at the sand. A curious phenomenon is conspicuous in the forward and aft cargo holds: apparently the ship burned furiously after her initial attack, as the remains of what appears to be her cargo of metal ore, which looks to have melted but is now solidified, is found level with the cargo hold coaming. No analysis has yet been performed to determine the nature of the unknown metal. Reviewing wartime casualty lists, it is noted that the freighter *Ohioan*, carrying a cargo of manganese ore, was torpedoed in deep water off Boynton Beach. Records indicate, however, the *Ohioan* sank quickly and was apparently unarmed. Another potential suspect may be the *Umtata*, which was also carrying ore. The *Umtata* was attacked off Miami, though no definitive record details her actual sinking after the attending tow vessel abandoned the disabled freighter.

Of particular interest is the outrageous abundance of stark-white *Oculina varicosa* coral colonies that cover large portions of the wreck. Deep-water fish species such as warsaw grouper, snowy grouper, and speckled hind are found in abundance here. Due to the depth and location, a dive to this wreck can be demanding. Strong currents, cold bottom temperatures, and poor visibility can be expected. It is hoped that future dives will result in the recovery of an identifying artifact.

G.B. FRATE

The details of the sinking of the *G.B. Frate* were published in the *St. Petersburg Times* on December 4, 1961:

> All five crewmen of a small cargo ship were rescued unhurt from offshore Florida water yesterday, six hours after their Bahamas-bound ship sank. Peter Degregory, 35, West End, Grand Bahamas, said the large bow landing gate suddenly fell open and the ship began flooding. The vessel, the *G.B. Frate*, was a 56-foot converted landing craft. "We got the gate closed, but water pressure had shifted the gasket and we couldn't stop the water. But we were holding our own until an auxiliary pump quit and the engine room flooded" Degregory said. It had left Lake Worth Inlet south of Palm Beach a few hours before the Coast Guard picked up distress signals saying the vessel was sinking. The five crewmen were found in a dinghy about 15 miles off shore and were picked up by a Coast Guard helicopter. The *Frate* was hauling concrete blocks, sheet metal, and an automobile on its regular run from Palm Beach to West End.

The coaster *Geja* as the *Aktjo*.

GEJA

Gebrüder Niestern completed the coastal freighter *Aktjo* at their Delfzijl, Netherlands shipyard in 1937. The new freighter was 122.2 feet long and 21.5 feet wide, and was originally owned by Feike Middendorp. In October 1944, the vessel was renamed *Eindhoven*, but reverted back to her original name the following year. On January 25, 1957, the coaster was sold and renamed *Geja*; at the time of her loss she was owned by St. George Shipping Company of Nassau. At 3:30 a.m. on December 6, 1975, the *Geja* was swamped by a giant wave eight miles off Key Biscayne (approximate latitude 25° 42.217' north, longitude 80° 00.650' west), which shifted her cargo of lumber, food, fertilizer, and large appliances; the freighter sank five minutes later. Captain Donald Albury, six crew members, and the captain's wife were rescued from a lifeboat after drifting for almost five hours by the fishing vessel *Restless Five*, which was led to the lifeboat by flares dropped by a helicopter operated by a Miami radio station scouting the offshore fishing grounds, which spotted the lifeboat approximately one mile offshore Miami.

GENERAL BURNSIDE

On February 27, 1864, *The New York Times* printed details on the loss of the U.S. transport *General Burnside*, which "grounded on St. Johns Bar and became a total wreck. All crew saved." A March 3 dispatch published in *The New York Times* on April 13, 1864, added that a "fearful gale" struck the region on the evening of February 18, and that the following day, "Off St. Johns Bar, and well in on the coast, the propeller *Burnside*, Capt. Wilcox, was seen going to pieces, but Capt. Faircloth could not render the least assistance." It should be noted that the *General Burnside* associated with this event was documented as a screw steamer, and is different than the sidewheel steamer U.S.S. *General Burnside*.

GENERAL JACKSON

As published in *The Times* on December 6, 1821, "The American sloop *General Jackson* is wrecked on the coast of Florida. Crew arrived at Havannah [*sic*] 5 October."

GENERAL WHITNEY

Named after the General James S. Whitney, the father of Henry Melville Whitney, who was the president of the West End Street Railway of Boston and an executive in the Metropolitan Steamship Company, the steamer *General Whitney* was built at a Wilmington, Delaware shipyard in 1873. Fabricated out of iron, she was a 1,846 gross ton screw steamer that primarily carried freight between Boston and Jacksonville for the Metropolitan Line. At the time of her loss, however, she was chartered to the Morgan Line to haul cargo between Florida ports and New Orleans. On April 17, 1899, she steamed from New Orleans carrying hides, copper, canned fruit, vegetables, cotton, and other general merchandise. At the helm was Captain J.W. Hawthorne, an experienced mariner who had sailed for the Metropolitan Line for many years. On the evening of April 21, the *Whitney* approached Cape Canaveral and the final stretch of her journey. She encountered heavy seas earlier that evening, but it was nothing Captain Hawthorne had not experienced before. Yet, the aged steamer finally yielded to the incessant pounding, and one of her bulkheads sprung a leak. All hands were ordered to the pumps, but the holds soon began to fill with water. Despite their best efforts, the crewmen of the steamer were fighting a losing battle. With the vessel settling fast and sure to founder, crew and officers abandoned ship in two lifeboats approximately 50 miles offshore around midnight.

The two groups of survivors were quickly separated in the darkness, surrounded by the breaking seas of the Atlantic. Captain Hawthorne was with a group of 15 crewmembers, and First Officer Mattison commanded the other lifeboat with 14 men. Using a compass, Mattison

General Whitney (© The Mariners' Museum, Newport News, Virginia).

directed the lifeboat through the heaving waves towards shore. Due to a strong wind, the men were unable to make much headway. They spent all night and the following day working toward the safety of land. After spending over 36 hours in the exposed boat, without freshwater but yet drenched by waves that spilled on top of them, the desperate men finally sighted land. As they approached the beach off St. Augustine, they fabricated a flag and successfully got the attention of someone on shore. Captain Allen of the yacht *Baldwin* immediately went to their assistance and affected a rescue. Tragically, the fate of Captain Hawthorne and his lifeboat was not as bright. While he successfully guided his command to shore the day after the sinking, the lifeboat capsized in heavy surf during his attempt to land at the Mosquito Lagoon House of Refuge at present-day New Smyrna Beach. Twelve men, including Captain Hawthorne, were drowned.

The 1899 *Annual Report of the Supervising Inspector-General, U.S. Steamboat-Inspection Service to the Secretary of Commerce and Labor* stated the steamer foundered at latitude 28° 40' north, longitude 79° 39' west. The remains of the *General Whitney* have yet to be identified, however, it is possible the steamer rests in deep water to the north of Cape Canaveral at a site known locally as the "Snowy Grouper Wreck." Hopefully future exploratory dives will discover this lost shipwreck.

GENE'S CANNON WRECK

On November 3, 1957, Gene Shinn and Craig Hamilton recovered two carronade-type cannon from an unidentified wreck resting in 18-20 feet of water on the front of Elkhorn Reef off Elliott Key. Mendel Peterson determined the armament was cast by the Baldwin Company of England in 1811. Both guns were stamped with the British crown and rated for 12-pound shot. Also found scattered amongst the ballast and rigging were two cutlass blades, as well as lead numbers, which were thought to have been secured to the hull to indicate the vessel's depth of keel. Some have speculated this wreck is the same as a site known as the "Yellow Brick Road."

While this latter site is directly inshore of the "Pillar Dollar Wreck" (*Victoriosa*), which Shinn mentioned as a point of reference, it is also a significant distance south of Elkhorn Reef. As Shinn related the reef adjacent to the cannon site was basically awash at low tide, this author believes "Gene's Cannon Wreck" is a completely different site and unrelated to the wreck of the "Yellow Brick Road."

GENESEE

The luxury yacht *Genesee* grounded on a sandbar just offshore Vero Beach while on a trip from Boston to Miami on November 3, 1925. The steel-hulled, schooner-rigged yacht was 119 feet in length, 27.7 feet in beam, and displaced 212 tons. She was built in 1900 at the Crescent Shipyard of builders Cary, Smith, and Barbey in Elizabeth, New Jersey. The *Genesee* was said to be one of the prettiest yachts afloat at the time, which is probably not an understatement given her original owner was noted multi-millionaire William K. Vanderbilt, Jr. The yacht was later owned by G. Sibley Watson, the capitalist and sportsman of Geneesee Valley, New York, who then sold it to wealthy Washington, D.C., politician Sylvanus Stokes, Jr.

Stokes was aboard the *Genesee* on a cruise south to Miami when a gale pushed the yacht onto a sandbar approximately three miles south of Vero Beach. Initially, the grounding did not appear too severe, as she was still over one mile offshore. The tide and heavy seas pounded the helpless yacht for over 24 hours, however, moving it to within 50 feet of the beach. Her fate sealed, the U.S. Coast Guard focused on rescuing the crew. On the morning of November 4, over 100 men showed up to help lay a cable so the crew could reach shore safely. By 5:30 p.m., the ship had been successfully evacuated. With the *Genesee* abandoned, the yacht was left to the mercy of the sea. Over the next several days, the upper decks were torn to pieces by the unrelenting surf. Reportedly, in the 1930s there was a salvage attempt to recover the $10,000 worth of lead ballast aboard the wrecked yacht. Over the years, the wrecking of the *Genesee* has faded from memory. Portions of the once elegant yacht have been found intermingled with the "Sandy Point Wreck" north of Fort Pierce Inlet.

GENEVA

On June 13, 1926, the brigantine *Geneva*, Captain V.H. Bowden, caught fire approximately 25 miles southeast of Fowey Rocks. The crew fled the burning ship and was rescued by the tanker *Gulf State*. The following day, the vessel, keel-up, was reported as a menace to navigation as it continued to burn while slowly drifting north, 50 miles north of Miami at approximate latitude 26° 28' north, longitude 79° 44' west. The *Geneva*, official number 86230, was built in 1892 by Mathew Turner at Benicia, California, and was 150 feet long, 36.3 feet wide, and 495 tons burden.

GEORGE (1778)

The loss of the armed schooner *George* was reported in an August 20, 1778, letter from East Florida Governor Patrick Tonyn to Lord George Germain, Secretary of State for America, stating, "I am sorry to inform your Lordship, that the *Otter* Sloop of War, and the *George* armed schooner armed for the service of this Province were lately lost off Cape Canaveral, in a violent storm the crews only saved. They sailed from this port (St. Augustine) in pursuit of a rebel privateer which carried off thirty negroes from the Smyrnea [sic] settlement[85]." The loss of the H.M.S. *Otter* is reported in other sources as August 24-25, 1778, so one must question the cited date of the letter to Lord Germain, or the reported wrecking date of the *George* and *Otter*.

GEORGE (1810)

Reports from Charleston dated October 13, 1810, included in *The Lady's Miscellany and Weekly Visitor*, Volume 12, stated, "The brig *George*, Decone, of New York, for Liverpool, was lost in the same gale near St. Augustine, and one of the seaman, named James Woods, was drowned; the remainder of the crew were saved." According to the *Bell's Weekly Messenger* of December 23, 1810, however, "The *Hanover*, Baxter, and the *George*, Decone, from Liverpool to Amelia Island, were lost near Amelia Island about the 20th October." While the date slightly preceded that cited for the wrecking of the *African*, *Caroline*, *Triton*, and *Union*, the same storm likely claimed all of these vessels.

GEORGE AND MARY

An October 1837 report included in *The Sailor's Magazine and Naval Journal*, Volume 10, stated, "Schooner *George and Mary*, from Charleston for Jacksonville, went ashore eight miles N. of St. Augustine, and bilged; vessel and cargo lost; crew and passengers saved."

GEORGE C. COLLINS

The schooner-rigged white oak and chestnut hull of the *George C. Collins*, 150 feet in length, 28 feet in breadth, displacing 236 tons, was built by George Goodspeed of New York. The machinery, a vertical direct engine with a 36-inch diameter of cylinder and a single tubular boiler, which turned an 8.3-foot diameter iron screw, was supplied by Woodruff and Beach. While owned by the New York and Hartford Steamboat Company after completion, she initially ran as a government transport during the Civil War. On March 27, 1865, en route from Hilton Head, South Carolina, the *Collins* reportedly stranded on the St. Johns River.

GEORGE HARRIS

On September 23, 1879, *The New York Times* reported, "the schooner *George Harris*, of Boston, bound for Pensacola for lumber, sprang a leak off Cape Canaveral on Tuesday last [September 16], and, after 12 hours at the pumps, with six feet of water in the hold, she was beached. All hands were saved. The captain and crew arrived here [Jacksonville] today on the steamer *Weikieva* [sic], from the upper St. Johns River." The wrecking actually occurred to the brig *George Harris*, which was built in December 1852 at Prospect, Maine. The 221-ton brig, owned by Ansley and Company of Boston, was 107 feet in length and 25.2 feet in breadth.

GEORGEA

The steamer *Georgea* was originally owned by Captain H.T. Baya and operated as a ferry for his Baya Line. Following the merger with the DeBary Line, the *Georgea* was released to the Jacksonville-Crescent City Line. The *Georgea* reportedly burned on St. Johns River, though the specifics of her demise are unknown[86].

GEORGE'S WRECK

"George's Wreck" is dominated by a significant number of large timbers suggesting a fairly articulated wreck flattened out and inundated with sediment. The wreck is reportedly located inshore of Ledbury Reef in 25 feet of water, surrounded by seagrass bottom. "George's Wreck" is another site included in Meylach (1971), and the range bearings are taken over long distances. Therefore, relocating this wreck may take some patience.

GEORGES VALENTINE

The wreck of the Italian bark *Georges Valentine* in 1904 was but one of many maritime disasters that illustrated the indispensable services of the U.S. Life-Saving Service. Prior to 1871, the U.S. Life-Saving Service was impeded by stations that were too far apart and that lacked sufficient numbers of attendants. By 1878, however, when it became a stand-alone entity, there were stations approximately every five miles stretching from Cape Cod to Cape Hatteras. The remainder of the east coast had stations where needed, generally confined to isolated dangerous points. The lifesavers patrolled the beach day and night, warning vessels off the coast, and responded to shipwrecks and other emergencies whenever they occurred. In many instances, they rowed offshore to disabled vessels to render assistance, re-rigging them and guiding them to places of safety. The summary for 1904 amply validated the U.S. Life-Saving Service's $1.8 million budget: 785 disasters involving 5,044 individuals, with only 37 lives lost.

Locals inspect the demolished remains of the bark *Georges Valentine*; note the cargo of timber at left (Florida State Archives).

Furthermore, the Service saved $8,175,210 worth of property from the $10,585,350 value of the vessels and cargo involved.

Originally built as the bark *Cape Clear* by Bowdler, Chaffer, and Company at Liverpool in March 1869, the *Georges Valentine* was 189.7 feet in length, 31.2 feet in breadth, and displaced 882 tons. The ill-fated *Valentine* was cast ashore in the dark of night during a brutal October storm. The bark struck the rocks just south of the Gilbert's Bar House of Refuge with such force that her three steel masts collapsed almost simultaneously, killing a member of the crew. The breaking surf proceeded to rapidly dispatch the stranded *Georges Valentine*, tearing off portions of the wreck with each crashing wave. The 11 remaining crewmembers were soon forced to abandon what little was left of their ship before they, too, were swept away and dashed upon the rocks. Struggling for shore, only seven men successfully emerged from the breakers, more dead than alive.

The first survivor to reach shore was Victor R. Erickson. Exhausted, he nonetheless started along the beach in search of assistance. Coming upon one of his fellow crew trapped underneath some wreckage, he freed the man and carried him along in his quest for help. They soon found the Gilbert's Bar Station at approximately 9:00 p.m., and alerted the sole caretaker of the disaster. Stabilizing the men and putting them to bed to rest, the lone lifesaver then struck out for the scene of the shipwreck. In the midst of the storm, he successfully rescued the five remaining survivors, valiantly working until dawn. The storm continued to rage for two days, resulting in the complete annihilation of the *Georges Valentine*. Had the House of Refuge not existed, the seven survivors would have likely perished, even after reaching the beach.

While the *Georges Valentine* was dashed to pieces by the 1904 storm, sections of her hull and masts were eventually interned just offshore Hutchinson Island. Over the past century, she slowly settled and was encrusted with a thin growth of corals, sponges, and other invertebrates. Unfortunately, the remarkable 2004 hurricane season resulted in some exposed portions of the wreck being buried by sand. Large portions of the hull consisting of iron beams, wooden timbers, and portions of the masts are still exposed, and numerous encrusted artifacts including portholes, deadeyes, and other brass objects can be observed scattered around the site by astute divers.

GEORGIE

The *Georgie*, official number 83203, was a brig built in October 1881 at Walton, Nova Scotia, by William Vaughn. Owned by J.F. Whitney and Company and mastered by Captain Le Blanc, the British sailing vessel was 107 feet long, 29 feet wide, and displaced 229 tons. The brig *Georgie* reportedly went ashore approximately two miles north of Hillsboro Inlet during a storm on October 10, 1894 (also reported lost in September 1894), and was a total loss. In the 1960s, a lifeguard found and recovered a large anchor from inside the first reef line just south of the Deerfield Beach Pier, which is thought to have been from the wreck of the *Georgie*. Unfortunately, the remainder of the wreck is buried under excess sand deposited in the area during beach nourishment activities.

GERTRUDE

The 12-ton gas vessel *Gertrude*, official number 206325, built in 1905, reportedly burned on the Nassau River on February 11, 1915.

GHOST

Sometime in 1981, the 68-foot long fishing vessel *Ghost* was reported to have sunk at latitude 29° 04.8' north and longitude 80° 53' west, which is approximately two nautical miles east of Ponce de Leon Inlet.

GHOST TUG

The "Ghost Tug" is a tug boat approximately 50 feet in length, which rests in 38 feet of water just over four nautical miles north of Boca Inlet. The circumstances on how the tug ended up on the bottom, as well as her real name, are a mystery. Regardless, the wreck makes for an enjoyable and easy dive for beginners, and the typically abundant marine life offers a wonderful photographic opportunity.

GIL BLAS

The 130-ton schooner *Gil Blas*, named after the main character in a book of the same name written between 1700 and 1730 by Alain-Rene LeSage, was built in 1831 at the harbor of Shoreham, England. In September 1835, she sailed from Havana for Spain with a load of cigars and cane sugar. Unfortunately, she encountered a strong hurricane that carried her aground just off the beach approximately nine miles north of the New River, near present-day Fort Lauderdale. William Cooley, along with other area settlers, initiated salvage on the wrecked ship. While they were working on the vessel, Seminole Indians raided the Cooley settlement, slaughtering Cooley's wife and three children. Those working on the ship fled for their lives, taking shelter at the Cape Florida lighthouse. William Cooley returned the next day to bury his family

Small gun recovered from a wreck thought to be the *Gil Blas* (Fort Lauderdale Historical Society).

before he, too, abandoned the area for Indian Key. The incident spawned the Second Seminole War and inhibited any further settlement of what would become Broward County for almost 50 years.

The U.S. Army, fearful that the armament and cargo of the *Gil Blas*, which included six tons of lead, would fall into Indian hands, dispatched a vessel to the scene in order to salvage the wreck. In a letter to Lieutenant Thomas J. Lieb, Commander M.P. Mix of the U.S.S. *Concord* wrote, "It is reported that Indian Key is in great danger, and the object of sending you there is its protection. When you arrive you can leave the Marines under Sergeant Wright and proceed to the wreck of the *Gil Blas* on shore near New River, and ascertain if the lead on board is in such a situation as that the hostile Indians can get to it; and if so, do your utmost with the assistance of Capt. Armstrong to place it out of their power[87]."

On July 24, 1836, Lieb reached the wreck of the *Gil Blas* on the U.S. transport schooner *Motto* and reported, "... anchored off the brig *Gil Blas*, went into her and examined her hold, by diving, but could not find or see any lead in her. Capt. Armstrong and myself thought it best to set fire to her, which we did that she might become sanded[88]." While the lead was not recovered, cannons and ammunition were recovered and were employed in the defense of Indian Key.

The *Gil Blas*, burned to the waterline, eventually was forgotten and sanded over just offshore of what is today Fort Lauderdale. Recent efforts by the Broward Marine Archaeological Council have focused on identifying the final resting spot of the vessel. Conducting remote sensing surveys, they initially believed they found the wreck in 1985, only to discover another missing vessel. A second wreck, believed to be the *Thales*, was found 300 feet offshore and under nine feet of sand, approximately one mile north of Hillsboro Inlet. Little is known about the *Thales*, which ran aground near Hillsboro Inlet on January 11, 1859. To the south, they found a wreck site they believe to be the *Gil Blas*. Approximately 300 feet off the beach and largely covered by sand, scattered wreckage was revealed. While claims of its discovery were issued, positive identification has yet to be made.

GILBERT SEA

The coastal freighter *Gilbert Sea* (IMO number 6610546) was built in 1966 as the *Geulborg* by *Scheepswerf Gebroeders Sander* at Delfzijl, Netherlands. Originally employed by *E. Wagenborg's Scheepvaart & Expeditiebedrijf N.V.*, the coaster was 175.8 feet long, 28.7 feet wide, and displaced 529 tons. In 1977, the freighter was sold to Taylor Corporation, Limited of Nassau, Bahamas, and renamed *Miranda*. She was later sold to a Honduran company, reflagged, and renamed *Paradie Express* in 1996, and then *El Compa* in 1999. Later that same year, she was renamed *Gilbert Sea*. In 2001, the *Gilbert Sea* changed her flag state to Bolivia and registered with *Registro Internacional Boliviano de Buques*.

On June 4, 2001, while searching the *Gilbert Sea* during "Operation Riverwalk," the U.S. Customs Service and Coast Guard seized 74 pounds of cocaine worth $630,000

Gilbert Sea as the *Geulborg* (Jelle Bijlsma).

wholesale. Inspectors initially found two pounds of cocaine inside paint cans on the forward deck, while further inspection of the ship revealed additional cocaine in various locations, including in a 55-gallon oil drum that had a false bottom. The vessel was forfeited, sold to Palm Beach County for use as an artificial reef, and summarily sunk in 90 feet of water on March 17, 2002.

A view of the *Gilbert Sea's* disarticulated stern and demolished wheelhouse.

Part of the Governor's River Walk Reef, the *Gilbert Sea* is the furthest north of four wrecks; all four vessels (*Sha Sha Boekanier*, *St. Jacques*, *Thozina*, and *Gilbert Sea*) were confiscated for smuggling narcotics and are of similar design. While the *Thozina* rests further to the east than the other three ships, the *Gilbert Sea* rests generally inline with the *Sha Sha Boekanier* and *St. Jacques*, and 800 tons of deployed concrete bridge material connect the wrecks of the *St. Jacques* and *Gilbert Sea*. Since their deployment, all four freighters have been significantly impacted by hurricanes, which have flattened their cargo holds and torn each of their hulls in half. The bow of the *Gilbert Sea* is resting hard over on its starboard side, while the stern is listing to port. The wheelhouse has collapsed from the superstructure, revealing the remains of the wooden deck. Nevertheless, the wrecks of the Governor's River Walk Reef still offer a fantastic diving experience, and the twisted hulks perhaps offer a more interesting underwater scene than if the freighters were still upright and intact.

Due to the proximity of the Gulf Stream to the coast of Florida in this area, current is often significant. Due to all the vertical relief offered from the wrecks and additional concrete material, however, divers can easily hide in the lee of structure and leap-frog from wreck to wreck. Typically, visibility is phenomenal, and it's not uncommon to observe massive goliath grouper, sea turtles, roving sting rays, and sharks while drifting along the Governor's River Walk Reef.

GINGER

The 48-foot sport fisherman *Ginger* was launched in May 1955 at Miami, and was equipped with comfortable accommodations for 10 persons and the most modern navigational equipment. The vessel was destined to work as a charter vessel during the tourist season, and then permitted to operate as a commercial fishing vessel in the off-season. It was during one of her commercial trips off Daytona Beach that the *Ginger* sank in the early morning hours of November 20, 1955, after being swamped by a sudden squall line. All four persons aboard, wearing life jackets, were rescued from the water by the nearby fishing vessel *Mako*. Exhausted and half drowned, the four men watched from the *Mako* as the *Ginger* went under stern first at 2:00 a.m. One of the rescued crewmembers described the final events in the *Daytona Beach Morning Journal* of November 21, 1955, stating "First the stern light went out. Then the bow light, high in the air, slid into the water." The wreck of the *Ginger* rests approximately 32 nautical miles offshore of Ponce de Leon Inlet in 120 feet of water. The former sportfisherman is significantly broken down and consists largely of the engine block and associated debris.

GIOVANNI

The November 9, 1884, loss of the bark *Giovanni*, Captain Matindis, was recorded in the *Annual Report of the Operations of the United States Life-Saving Service for the Fiscal Year Ending June 30, 1885*, which documented:

> The British bark *Giovanni*, of Malta, with a crew of eight men, bound from Black River, Jamaica, to Trieste, Austria, stranded at noon about seven and a quarter miles north of the Orange Grove House of Refuge (Seventh District), coast of Florida. She had sprung a leak in a gale of wind, and, the pumps failing to free her, the captain ran her ashore to save the lives of himself and crew. The vessel was soon discovered by the keeper of the house of refuge, who repaired to the spot without delay, and, finding she could not be saved, conducted the crew to the station in his boat. He fed and sheltered them for seventeen days, or until he was enabled, on November 26, to put them on board a passing steamer, the *Eureka*, on her way to New Orleans from New York. The bark and cargo were a total loss.

GLAD TIDINGS

The *Glad Tidings*, official number 85837, was originally crafted as a barkentine when built in April 1884 by G.W. Cottrall at Bath, Maine. At launching, she was 159 feet long, 33.1 feet wide, and displaced 654 tons gross. Later converted into a schooner, the *Glad Tidings*, en route from Baltimore, Maryland, to Mayport with a cargo of coal, was lost off Fernandina on October 17, 1907. Reports stated, "Capt. Nickles and six men of the schooner *Glad Tidings* were picked up off the Fernandina Bar this morning by the pilot boat *Francis Elizabeth*. The *Glad Tidings* struck on the bar last night. The pumps were worked, but the water in the hold gained, rapidly forcing those aboard to take to the lifeboat. The schooner sank soon after they left it. The lifeboat withstood rough weather until the pilot boat appeared[89]."

GLADIATOR

On the evening of October 1, 1898, a severe hurricane struck Fernandina. The damage was considerable in the wake of the storm, and "the tug *Gladiator* sunk, and is a complete wreck[90]."

GLADYS

The steam yacht *Gladys*, from Jacksonville to Cuba, was wrecked at Lake Worth Inlet on the night of April 30, 1892; there were no lives lost[91]. The *Gladys* was launched in 1890 by William R. Osborn of Peekskill, New York, and was 62 feet long, 11 feet wide, and displaced 11 tons.

GLANDENA

The *General Evening Post* of December 23, 1777, reported, "The *Glandena*, Valliant, from London to Pensacola, with dispatches, is totally lost in a hard gale of wind on the coast of Florida."

GLOBE

The 23-ton gas vessel *Globe*, built in 1928, foundered at Jacksonville on July 10, 1928[92].

GODFREY

On January 28, 1886, the *Halifax Herald* reported that "out of eight or ten schooners employed in the lighthouse (Ponce de Leon Inlet Light Station) work, five have been wrecked, viz: *Godfrey*, *Augusta Wilson*, *Ajax*, *Freewind*, and the *Johnson*; the *Mary Brown*, now lying at the lighthouse dock, is crippled. We have been assured that nearly all of them received the injuries resulting in wrecks on the inlet bar or in the river. Six men have also been drowned."

GOLDEN LION

Twenty-nine cast members of a theatrical group and three crewmen safely escaped the 85-foot long yacht *Golden Lion* as it sank just offshore Miami's Government Cut on March 21, 1976. The *Golden Lion*, which was en route to the Bahamas, struck a submerged log, which ripped a hole in its bow and sent the yacht to the bottom in 35 minutes.

Newspaper reports indicated the owners were making preparations to raise the sunken vessel.

GRACE

According to Singer (1998), the 24-ton vessel *Grace*, which was built in 1924, stranded on the St. Sebastian River near St. Augustine in January 1962.

GRACE DEERING

The *Grace Deering*, official number 85483, was launched as a bark in May 1877 at Cape Elizabeth, Maine. Built by J.F. Randall, the vessel was 151.8 feet long, 33.1 feet wide, and displaced 784 tons gross. The *Deering* was eventually converted into a barge, and redocumented as an unrigged vessel displacing 627 tons gross. On November 1, 1906, the *Grace Deering* foundered off Miami. Fortunately, her crew of six survived the episode.

GRACIE D. BUCHANAN

On February 11, 1910, the four-masted schooner *Gracie D. Buchanan* reportedly wrecked near Jacksonville, with one report stating the specific location as Nassau Inlet. The schooner, official number 85995, was 194 feet long, 40 feet wide, and displaced 1,141 tons gross. She was launched in May 1888 at Bath, Maine, by the New England Shipbuilding Company.

GRACIE J.

On December 28, 1910, the 12-ton gas steamer *Gracie J.*, official number 205428, built in 1908, burned on the St. Johns River.

GRADCO PIONEER

The *Gradco Pioneer* was originally built at Bay City, Michigan, in 1944 as the *Charlie Bambsu*, official number 251751. The diesel motor vessel was 80 feet long, 15.5 feet in beam, and displaced 70 tons gross. In 1948, she was renamed *Gradco Pioneer* and served as a fisheries research vessel soon thereafter. Towards the end of her career, she was employed as an inter-island freighter that made runs through the Caribbean and U.S. Virgin Islands. On June 20, 1965, the *Gradco Pioneer* reportedly caught fire and burned approximately one mile north of the sea buoy off Miami.

GRANADA

Singer (1998) states the 45-ton *Granada*, built in 1947, was lost during a storm at Fort George Inlet, three quarters of a mile north of the St. Johns River jetties. The *Granada* was most likely a shrimp trawler.

GRAND TURK

An August 26, 1839, dispatch printed on September 17 in *The Times*, stated the vessel *Grand Turk*, en route from St. Ubes to New Orleans, ran on shore on "Foy's Rock near Florida" (Fowey Rocks) on July 5, 1839. The crew and materials were saved, and the wreck was later sold where she lay.

GROUPER

The 32-foot pleasure boat *Grouper* was blown onto the north jetty at Fort Pierce during a violent nor'easter and pounded to pieces on October 21, 1952. The two passengers safely swam ashore.

GULFAMERICA

On a pleasant April evening along the Jacksonville beachfront, men and women casually strolled amidst the numerous bars and restaurants open for business, while cars slowly cruised along the strip. Periodically, screams from those riding the nearby roller coaster would pierce the still night air. *Kapitänleutnant* Reinhard Hardegen, of the German U-boat *U-123*, also enjoyed the evening festivities as he watched the brilliant lights just offshore. The United States still believed itself far-removed from the hostilities that raged in Europe. Throughout 1942, *Kapitänleutnant* Hardegen and his colleagues of the German *Kriegsmarine* would easily change that perception.

Several days earlier in Port Arthur, Texas, the Gulf Oil Corporation tanker *Gulfamerica* was finishing onloading her cargo of 90,000 barrels of fuel oil in preparation for her maiden voyage to New York. Recently delivered from the Sparrows Point shipyard of the Bethlehem Shipbuilding Corporation Limited, the tanker displaced 8,081 tons, boasted a length of 445 feet, and had a 64-foot beam. The vessel was also outfitted with one four-inch gun, as well as two 50-caliber Browning Mark II machine guns in bridge nests manned by seven Naval Armed Guards.

The evening of April 10, 1942, found the *Gulfamerica* blacked out, radio silent, and traveling north at a swift 14 knots close to the Florida shore. Unfortunately for Captain Oscar Anderson and a crew of 47, the silhouette of the large tanker was easily spotted by the *U-123*. Hardegen followed the ship for over an hour until he gained optimal firing position just offshore of his target, approximately four miles off Jacksonville Beach. The U-boat commander did not want to miss this valuable target, having only two remaining torpedoes from a very successful hunt off Florida. At 10:20 p.m. (also recorded as 8:22 p.m.), Hardegen fired one of his last torpedoes at the *Gulfamerica*. The torpedo approached from an angle of 35 degrees from the stern and scored a direct hit on her starboard side in the number seven tank. While Anderson reported a second torpedo striking the engine room shortly after the first, the explosion was most likely the result of her boilers rupturing.

The peaceful night erupted into a cataclysm of fire. As the shocked crowd on the beach watched in disbelief, the shadow of the attacking U-boat moved into position to finish off the crippled tanker. Reinhard Hardegen slowly moved the *U-123* between the burning tanker and the beach, in order to prevent the chance of any accidental shelling on the beach crowd. In doing this, Hardegen placed the safety of his vessel and crew in jeopardy. While the U-boat motored into position, Captain Anderson immediately gave the order to abandon ship as he simultaneously threw a weighted bag with confidential papers overboard. As the survivors fled the inferno, the *U-123* proceeded to fire several rounds into the *Gulfamerica* with its deck gun, while red tracer fire from the submarine's machine guns raced overhead in an attempt to knock out the radio antenna.

In short order, rescue vessels from Mayport sped to the scene of the disaster and managed to pick up 29 survivors; 19 of the crew and Naval Armed Guards perished in the attack. Assigned to one of the rescue vessels, a 50-foot long shrimper, was Bob Barker of Holly Hill. He related that when he arrived at the wreck, the tanker was rolled partly over on her starboard side. The bridge was awash, but the bow remained out of the water, so Barker boarded the tanker and salvaged the *Gulfamerica's* bell, keeping it as a souvenir.

Aircraft from the nearby Naval Air Station also arrived and dropped flares in order to locate the attacking U-boat. Several hours later, the fleeing U-boat was forced to submerge after being spotted by a search plane just off St. Augustine. The destroyer U.S.S. *Dahlgren* found itself in the near vicinity of the U-boat and dropped six depth charges, seriously damaging the *U-123* as she sat on the bottom in 72 feet of water. The attack disabled the port engine, knocked out most of the batteries, and bent the shafts and screws of the submarine. At this point, Reinhard Hardegen was about to set scuttling charges and abandon ship, however, at the last moment he changed his mind. Copious amounts of air were released from the helpless *U-123*, revealing her location. Yet, the *Dahlgren* did not follow up on her initial attack, much to the confusion and delight of Hardegen. At approximately 4:00 a.m. on April 11, after harmlessly passing directly overhead the *U-123* several times as she sat on the bottom, the *Dahlgren* departed the scene. Several hours later the resilient Hardegen surfaced to find no sign of surface ships, and anti-submarine aircraft were four to five miles distant. *Kapitänleutnant* Hardegen managed to slip off into deeper waters and spent the next few days tending to his crippled vessel. Even with the extensive damage, the crew managed to repair the *U-123* to the point where she was again a threat. The *U-123* would culminate her voyage by sinking the *Leslie* and, shortly thereafter, the *Korsholm*, before heading back to her base at Kiel, Germany.

Aerial photograph of the crippled *Gulfamerica* (© The Mariners' Museum, Newport News, Virginia).

After burning for several days, the wreck of the *Gulfamerica* finally rolled completely over on her starboard side and sunk in 60 feet of water on April 16, 1942. The *Gulfamerica* was demolished as a navigational hazard, which reduced it to a tangled mass of debris, hull plate, and piping that covers a large area of sea bottom. Furthermore, the tanker was one of several wrecks offered at auction for salvage rights in 1957. Earl W. Helmers of Chicago purchased the *Gulfamerica*, as well as the freighter *Lillian Luckenbach* off Virginia Beach and the freighter *Caxaca* in the Gulf of Mexico, for the sum of $1,280. It is unclear if the wreck was actually salvaged. Regardless, the flattened remains of the tanker, popular with local fishermen, are often totally enshrouded with schools of glimmering baitfish.

GULFLAND

The German *Kriegsmarine* was not the only menace to shipping during World War II, as the wreck of the tanker *Gulfland* can attest. Prudence dictated that vessels travel blacked out at night in order to avoid running into prowling U-boats. While the lack of navigational lighting

The tanker *Gulfland* at sea (William T. Hultgren).

The abandoned tanker *Gulfland* in flames and drifting (National Archives).

may have mitigated the chance of running afoul of a U-boat, it obviously increased the chance of merchant vessels running into one another. On the night of October 20, 1943, the northbound *Gulfland* collided with the southbound tanker *Gulfbelle*, both of which were owned by Gulf Oil Company of New York. The resulting collision ignited a massive fire that covered both vessels from stem to stern, killing 88 men, and eventually sending the *Gulfland* to the bottom.

The *Gulfland* was built in 1918 by the New York Shipbuilding Corporation at Camden, New Jersey. The new tanker was 391 feet long with a 51-foot beam. Just prior to the collision, she was heading to Jacksonville, Florida, fully loaded with aviation fuel from the port of Beaumont, Texas. The southbound *Gulfbelle* was traveling in ballast from New York to Houston, Texas.

Late at night and just short of their planned destination, two members of the Naval Armed Guard who were assigned to the *Gulfland* witnessed the sudden appearance of the *Gulfbelle*, which proceeded to strike the port bow of the *Gulfland*. The initial collision spread highly flammable fuel over the two vessels that promptly exploded, consuming the two vessels in an intense inferno. The two guards, Joseph O'Brien and Walter Atkinson, immediately leapt over the side of their now burning ship and swam for their lives. Joseph O'Brien described the tragic incident:

> I was on watch about 10:50 p.m. as we rode northward along the Gulf Stream. Suddenly I spotted another ship bearing down from the north. It appeared to be about 75 yards away. It looked as if it was going to pass us, but as the ship approached I saw it was going to be close. I turned and started for the telephone to report it to the bridge, shouting as I ran to Walter Atkinson, another member of the gun crew. Before I got to the telephone, there was a crash. A terrific explosion followed and I was blown about ten feet across the deck. Regaining my feet, I raced through the flames and jumped overboard off the stern. I guess I was the first one off the ship. I swam as fast as I could for awhile until I thought I was safe. Then I stopped to look back. Waves of flame were coming toward me on the water and they almost caught me. Burning gasoline covered a wide area. I could hear a lot of screaming and yelling from the direction of both ships and I knew a lot of boys were trapped. It was awful[93]!

Only two others survived from the *Gulfland*. The *Gulfbelle* did not fare any better; 51 out of a crew of 72 perished in the fire. Christopher P. Finley, 28, of Miami, third assistant engineer aboard the *Gulfbelle*, was at his post at the time of the crash. "I knew something terrible had happened," he declared, "but every hand in the engine room stayed at his post, and that saved a lot of lives. Two explosions followed immediately. I cut off the engines and rushed

The *Gulfland*, grounded on the wreck of the *Republic*, continues to burn (Florida State Archives).

Salvage of the sunken *Gulfland* (Florida State Archives).

The *Guy Harvey* sailing as the *Voorwaarts*, 1957 (John Clarkson).

topside. Forward and amidships were a holocaust. The forward magazines and gun turrets were exploding. I knew the aft magazines would go any minute. I jumped into the sea off the fantail[94]."

The *Gulfland* drifted off, eventually grounding on the remains of the *Republic*, which had been torpedoed and sunk on February 21, 1942. The pyre on the wrecked tanker continued for an amazing 53 days before she was finally sunk by the U.S. Navy. After the less intense fire on the *Gulfbelle* subsided, she was salvaged. Towed into Port Everglades to be repaired, she eventually returned to service as the Panamanian-flagged *Poucou*. In September 1944, a naval diver, Captain Richard Brown, successfully refloated the hulk of the *Gulfland*. However, before he could tow the wreck into port, a storm battered the once strong tanker, shearing off a portion of the bow, which returned to the bottom of the Atlantic. The bulk of the tanker remained afloat throughout the storm, and was later towed into port to be scrapped. The remaining bow section rises 15 feet off the bottom in approximately 30 feet of water just north of Jupiter Inlet. The small section of wreckage did yield a badly corroded bow lantern, which is now on display at the House of Refuge Museum in Stuart.

GULFSPRITE

In 1916, the *Gulfsprite*, official number 213870, was launched at South Jacksonville. The small screw freighter was only 60.8 feet long, 16.4 feet wide, and displaced 47 tons gross. At the time of her loss, she was apparently utilized as a barge. On January 5, 1926, an explosion rocked the Gulf Refining Company's barge *Gulfsprite* while it was at Miami, resulting in the death of three crew members.

GUY HARVEY

Named after marine artist Guy Harvey who helped fund and promote this artificial reef project, the *Guy Harvey* was originally spawned as the coastal freighter *Voorwaarts* at the Dutch shipyard of H.W. Bodewes, Martenshoek, in 1957. The Dutch coaster was 197.6 feet in length, 30.6 feet in breadth, with a gross displacement of 499 tons. Like many other coasters, the vessel was extensively used by a variety of owners. In 1978 the freighter was sold to Denmark and renamed the *Fredrika*; two years later she was renamed *Emma*; then she was reflagged by first British then Honduran owners in 1984 and 1985, respectively; in 1989 her name was changed to *Vincentian* before quickly changing ownership to Anguilla that same year, and renamed *Emma A*; the freighter was reflagged under Guyanna and renamed *Endezo* in 1992; then, finally sailing under a Honduran flag as the *Lady Kimberly* in 1997. Unfortunately, due to fatigue and neglect, the vessel had outlived her usefulness, and she was abandoned at Port-au-Prince, Haiti, later that year. The Pompano Beach Fishing Rodeo appropriated the vessel for use as an artificial reef and towed the crippled freighter back to Fort Lauderdale. Guy Harvey laid his artistic touch to the gutted vessel, painting billfish and sharks on its wheelhouse and hull. On May 10, 1997, the former *Lady Kimberly* was laid to rest in 145 feet of water. She now rests upright and intact, and encrusting organisms have long since covered over Harvey's paintings.

Deployment of the *Guy Harvey* (Broward County Artificial Reef Program).

GYPSY GIRL

On July 17, 1950, the 52-ton shrimp boat *Gypsy Girl*, built in 1945, caught fire and burned two and a half miles north of the north jetty leading into Fernandina Harbor and Cumberland Sound.

H.B. PLANT

Not all Florida shipwreck events have occurred off the Atlantic and Gulf coasts. Throughout the 1800s and into the early 1900s, prior to the expansion of the railroads, river steamers were vital to commerce and transportation to towns within the state's interior. Vessels succumbed to snags in the river, storms, and fire. The loss of the steamer *H.B. Plant* demonstrated the constant danger of fire aboard ship. The *H.B. Plant*, official number 96681, was an iron-hulled sidewheel steamer built in 1880 at Wilmington, Delaware. She was 137 feet long, 26.5 feet wide, and displaced 287 tons gross.

The steamer *H.B. Plant* shortly after completion at Wilmington, Delaware (Alfred H. Robson Collection).

The People's Line steamer *H.B. Plant* burned to the water's edge in Lake Beresford, a large lake off the St. Johns River north of Orlando, on the morning of April 29, 1890. The fire was first discovered at 3:45 a.m., caused by a lamp explosion while a watchman tried to refill the lamp while it was still burning. A large oil can was overturned and streams of oil flowed over the deck, which instantly ignited the blaze. A hose was directed on the fire in short order, but it was a futile action, as the fire had already enveloped the forward portion of the steamer. Cries of 'fire' rang throughout the ship, and passengers in their nightclothes quickly started flocking the upper rear deck in search of safety. Load after load of passengers were rowed to shore, approximately a half mile away. Those left on the ship intently watched the small lifeboat, awaiting their chance to escape the inferno. Canoes from nearby Beresford Landing joined the effort. Panic ensued when the situation became dire, but Captain Hall kept the deckhands back with a revolver while the women and children got into the boats. In the end, all but three lives were saved. The steamer, valued at $50,000, was totally destroyed.

The wreck of the steamer *H.B. Plant*, lost while plying the highway of her era, ironically lies in close proximity to a modern highway. On a daily basis, thousands of commuters traveling on Interstate I-4 pass within one mile of the nineteenth century steamer as they drive over Lake Beresford. Little of the wreck likely remains due to the fire and potential salvage after the sinking.

H.G. BERRY

The wrecking of the brig *H.G. Berry* was published in *The New York Herald* on August 28, 1871, which stated she "went ashore fifty yards from the wreck of the *S. & W. Welsh* (15 miles south of Cape Canaveral). She is a total wreck. She had a cargo of sugar and molasses." The *Berry* was built in 1855 at Boothbay, Maine, by W. and J. Seavy. The 297-ton brig was 106 feet long and 28.5 feet wide.

H.M.S. AMARANTHE

The H.M.S. *Amaranthe* was originally the 150-ton, 12-gun (also listed as 18-gun) French brig-sloop *L'Amaranthe*, built in 1793 at Le Havre, which was later captured by Captain Strachen of the H.M.S. *Diamond* on December 31, 1796, off Alderney in the Channel Islands. She was 85 feet in length and 28 feet in breadth, and was later armed with 14 cannon (twelve 24-pounder carronades and two light long guns) while sailing under the British flag. Under the command of Captain George H. Blake, the H.M.S. *Amaranthe* patrolled in the Caribbean until her wrecking on October 25 or 27, 1799, on the Florida coast. One report states she was wrecked 22 leagues south of Cape Canaveral, which would place her just north of Fort Pierce Inlet. In the days following the wrecking, 24 of the 86 crew members died of starvation before rescue.

H.M.S. BERMUDA

The H.M.S. *Bermuda* was a 14-gun sloop built in 1795. The *Bermuda*, Captain Thomas Morton, reportedly foundered around August 27, 1796, in the "Gulph of Florida." There is no record of any court martial associated with the vessel's loss, indicating there were likely no survivors.

H.M.S. FOWEY

The 709-ton H.M.S. *Fowey*, a fifth-rate British warship, was launched in 1744 at Hull, England. Heavily armed with 44 six-, nine-, and twelve-pound cannon spread on two decks, she was a formidable addition to the Royal Navy fleet. After a brief stint in European waters, Captain Francis William Drake sailed the *Fowey* across the Atlantic to patrol along North America and in the Caribbean. In early June 1748, the man-of-war captured a Spanish merchant vessel, the *St. Judea*, in the Florida Straits. While escorting the *St. Judea* and two British merchant ships to Virginia, the H.M.S. *Fowey* ran aground on a reef off Elliott Key at 2:30 a.m. on June 27. In an attempt to raise the forward portion of the vessel clear of the reef, Captain Drake ordered the forecastle guns (two six-pounders) disabled and thrown overboard and other cannon moved aft. Finally, the *Fowey* broke free of the reef in the early afternoon. The collision with the reef, however, breached the hull of the ship, resulting in a steady flood of water. On June 28, after reviewing his perilous situation, Captain Drake opted to run his command back up on the reef in an attempt to prevent her sinking. Unfortunately, the ship rode up and over the reef, shearing off her rudder and enlarging the gash in her hull. As the *Fowey* drifted south, it was apparent to all that the fate of the ship was sealed. Captain Drake dropped anchor and prepared for the inevitable. After the remaining cannon were spiked and most of the muskets thrown overboard, the crew transferred to the British merchant ship *Jane*, while the sea cock was opened to scuttle the *Fowey*. Captain Drake and his crew, along with the Spanish prisoners, crowded aboard the British merchant ships and sailed for Charleston, South Carolina, arriving on September 3, 1748. Captain Drake, a descendant of Sir Francis Drake, faced a court martial over the loss of the *Fowey*, though he was eventually acquitted of any wrongdoing. Captain Drake would go on to become Governor of Newfoundland from 1750 to 1752 before he finally passed away in 1789. While the H.M.S. *Fowey* was abandoned, the memory of the vessel's fate was bestowed to the reef that led to her sinking, now known as Fowey Rocks.

The rediscovery of the wreck in 1978 by Gerald Klein initiated a legal firestorm. Klein initially believed the then unknown wreck to be that of one of the 1733 *flota* wrecks and requested title in Admiralty Court. Klein had visited the wreck several times, and recovered numerous artifacts that were found lying on the surface or by gently fanning the sand. Because the wreck resided within Biscayne National Park, the National Park Service (N.P.S.) opposed the salvage of the site, resulting in the intervention by the Department of Justice on behalf of the United States government. While the N.P.S. knew of an unknown wreck resting somewhere in Legare Anchorage as early as 1970, they knew nothing more than it was rumored to be an eighteenth century vessel. It was not until 1981 that the wreck was tentatively identified as the H.M.S. *Fowey* by Florida State University graduate student Richard Johnson[95].

A heated and highly publicized dispute ensued within the confines of the United States District Court. The eventual landmark decision in 1983 in favor of the United States government stated that the H.M.S. *Fowey* was a cultural resource site, and not a shipwreck in regard to Admiralty salvage. The judge noted that in terms of the salvage requirement of "marine peril," the site had apparently been safely buried and relatively stable, and no peril appeared to exist until the salvor began work on the site. While custodianship of the wreck was granted to the United States government for the "public benefit[96]," public access to the wreck is currently prohibited.

In retrospect, it is interesting to note that while the United States government claimed ownership of the vessel in the lawsuit, which they misidentified as a "wooden British merchant vessel[97]," the government of the United Kingdom maintained that they retain sovereign rights and continued ownership of their shipwrecked warships. These "sovereign immunity" provisions, which are reciprocated by most nations, are based on Articles 95 and 96 of the United Nations Convention on the Law of the Sea (1982), and established principles of international maritime law. Curiously, the N.P.S. nomination of the H.M.S. *Fowey* to the National Register of Historic Places referenced the fact that under customary international law, access by any United States National to a foreign shipwreck entitled to sovereign immunity is prohibited. Permission to access the wreck site is required from the respective sovereign and that, then, it is only to individuals named by the sovereign for specific purposes. Even should one obtain permission to visit the H.M.S. *Fowey* from the United Kingdom Ministry of Defense, the rightful owner of the wreck, access would still be prohibited by the Draconian measures implemented by the N.P.S. Further, one wonders if this visitation policy will be extended to other foreign warship wrecks in Florida waters, such as those of the 1622, 1715, and 1733 *flotas*.

In the years since the wreck was first identified, the H.M.S. *Fowey* has been extensively studied. Archaeologists were also given a rare privilege of studying the wreck following Hurricane Andrew in 1992. The archaeological survey found a substantial portion of the 126-foot vessel exposed in 28 feet of water, a side effect of the massive hurricane. Artifacts identified at the site reveal the wreck's identity as a Royal Navy warship. Iron ballast and cannon, swords still in their scabbards, as well as copper gunpowder barrel hoops marked with the British Broad Arrow that denote ownership under the crown, were found amongst the scattered wreckage. English-manufactured pewter, glass, and ceramic tableware were also documented. After their research was complete, the N.P.S. backfilled the site with sediment to cover and protect the exposed wreckage.

H.M.S. OTTER

Built at Depford, England, in 1767, the H.M.S. *Otter* was a 305-ton sloop-of-war, armed with 14 guns, mostly six-pounders. A sloop-of-war was constructed specifically as a warship, having heavier timbering and scantling, as well as raised bulwarks to protect gun crews, and could be rigged as a brig, schooner, or ship. Crewed by approximately 100 sailors, she was 95 feet long and 27 feet wide. During the American Revolution, the *Otter* was assigned to the North American Station. After arriving in Boston, she was sent to Virginia to prevent the vital colony's loss to rebelling colonists. Specifically, the *Otter* played a notable role in the Raid of Hampton, the Battle of Great Bridge, and in numerous raids on the shore line of Norfolk in late 1775 into early 1776. Later, the *Otter* was dispatched to Florida under the command of Lieutenant George Wright. In August 1778, she was at St. Augustine when she weighed anchor along with the armed schooner *George* to pursue a reported privateer in the area. Hepper (1994) included a report that stated as "she searched along the coast of Florida, the weather deteriorated and by 24 August, she was in a tropical storm, with hurricane force winds. She decided to run before the wind towards the land and at about six o'clock in the morning sighted land near Cape Canaveral. An hour later, she struck the ground very hard and immediately started beating violently. This, combined with the surf constantly breaking over her, led to the sloop breaking up. All the crew managed to struggle ashore, without loss." The exact wrecking spot of the H.M.S. *Otter* has yet to be identified.

H.M.S. WOLF

Reportedly lost somewhere off the east coast of Florida on March 2, 1741, the H.M.S. *Wolf*, built at Deptford,

England, in 1731, was a 244-ton, two-masted sloop-of-war 87 feet in length armed with 14 guns.

H.M.S. ZENOBIA

According to Clowes (1900), the H.M.S. *Zenobia* was a 10-gun schooner that wrecked off Florida near Hobe Sound in 1806. The replacement *Zenobia* was ordered on October 1, 1806, so it obviously wrecked sometime before this date.

HALCYON

On February 22, 2009, the sleek, 56-foot long Sunseeker yacht *Halcyon* was cruising approximately two miles off Elliott Key when a fire broke out in the engine room. Shortly before 10:30 a.m., smoke was observed coming from the engine as the owner noticed the boat running slower than normal. When the door to the engine room was opened, the true extent of the fire was discovered. After attempts to extinguish the fire failed, the four passengers abandoned ship. The *Halcyon* continued to burn before ultimately sinking in 35 feet of water off Key Biscayne. Sea Tow later raised the burned hulk of the *Halcyon* and towed it into Miami.

HALF MOON

The shipyard of *Krupp Germania-Werft* of Kiel, Germany built the *Half Moon*, originally named the *Germania*, in 1908. The 154-foot long hull of the two-masted schooner yacht was constructed of chrome-nickel steel that displaced 366 tons. With 15,000 square feet of sail, she was a fast vessel designed by the well-known German yacht architect Dr. Max Oertz. Upon completion, the *Germania* was presented as a wedding gift from Bertha Krupp to her husband, Count Gustav Krupp von Bohlen und Halbach. During her racing career, the *Germania* participated in numerous regattas and won the distinguished German Emperor's Cup. In 1914, the *Germania* and her sister ship, *Meteor*, were in England preparing for the Cowes Regatta. With war on the horizon, a destroyer was dispatched to escort the vessels back to Germany. The *Meteor* was taken in tow and the *Germania* was ordered to set sail immediately, though they had no idea that war had been declared. As a result, upon stopping at Southampton for water on the morning of August 4, 1914, the yacht was detained by the British Officers of Customs. The captain and crew of the *Germania* would become some of the first German prisoners of World War I. As a prize of war, the yacht sat idle for three years until she was sold at auction for £10,000. The vessel was renamed *Exen* and was sailed across the Atlantic to New York. The owner of the *Exen* eventually declared bankruptcy and the yacht was again put on auction. On July 14, 1921, former Assistant Secretary of the Navy, Gordon Woodbury, purchased the yacht for $10,000, whereupon he renamed her *Half Moon*, after explorer Henry Hudson's ship.

Gordon Woodbury took great strides to repair and refurbish the neglected yacht throughout the remainder of 1921. With plans to sail the South Seas, he departed New

White grunt schooling over a shipwreck (Matthew W. Hoelscher).

York and sailed southward in January 1922. Woodbury encountered an intense nor'easter off the Eastern Shore of Virginia, however, that almost sank the *Half Moon*. According to a January 31, 1922, article in *The New York Times*, "the mainsail, compass, jibboom, a dinghy, and a lifeboat were swept away within a few seconds of each other. An enormous sea struck the little craft some hours later, carrying Mr. Woodbury and the entire crew overboard. By clinging to the rail the sidelashes and the rudder, every one of the crew with the exception of John Stolsvig, quartermaster, finally managed to crawl aboard." Fortunately, the vessel was kept afloat and she was towed into Hampton Roads for repairs. Woodbury reconsidered his sailing plans and sold the *Half Moon* for $10,000. The lead keel of the yacht was salvaged but the *Half Moon* itself survived the scrap yard. In 1926, the *Half Moon* was in Miami when a massive hurricane pummeled South Florida. The former racing yacht was just one of many vessels that sunk at its moorings in the Miami River. She was eventually raised in 1928, and converted for use as a fishing barge and casino off Key Biscayne by Captain Ernest D. Smiley. The *Half Moon* would come to rest in her current position at the entrance of Bear Cut during a storm in 1930. Breaking free from her moorings, she drifted until grounding on a shallow shoal where she bilged and sunk. Over the years, the sleek yacht continued to break up and slowly settled into the sand of the shoal.

The wreck of the *Half Moon* originally came to the attention of local maritime historian Terry Helmers. He noted a wreck on the charts and was easily able to locate the submerged remains of a sanded-in vessel in the middle of Bear Cut off Virginia Key. After notifying various underwater archaeologists of the site, he initiated a diligent archival search to identify the unknown vessel. He initially thought the wreck was that of the *Haroldine*, a 205-foot long four-masted ship that grounded in 1906. The *Haroldine* was en route to the Florida Keys with a load of aggregate for use in Flagler's Overseas Railroad when she came to grief off Bear Cut. She eventually went to pieces after a gale swept through the area. Upon further research it was apparent that the ship on which Terry Helmers was diving was not the *Haroldine*. The *Haroldine* was a wooden-hulled schooner, while the mystery wreck was much smaller and was constructed of metal. Eventually, documentation indicated that the wreck was that of the *Half Moon*. The final resting spot of the *Haroldine* has yet to be identified.

The *Half Moon* can be found resting near Marker Number Two, and is usually easily visible from the surface. The depth over the wreck varies with the tide, but averages 4 feet over the wreck and 10 feet over the sand bottom. She rests listing to port with her bow pointing to the southeast. The shallow water allows unlimited time to explore the remains of the wreck and its associated marine life. Soft corals and sponges cover much of the wreck. Her bow and stern are still very much intact, while the starboard side appears to have suffered damage amidships, possibly from another vessel that may have run aground on the wreck. Many of her features, such as the steering station near the stern, can still be identified on the wreck. Portholes and other artifacts can be spotted throughout the Underwater Archaeological Preserve, which was established in 2001. Due to her location near Bear Cut, it is best to dive the wreck near the slack of an incoming tide in order to experience optimal visibility. Obviously, it is not prudent to dive this shallow wreck during periods of rough weather.

HALLANDALE BEACH WRECK

An unidentified wreck was located in shallow water approximately 200 feet off Hallandale Beach just south of Fort Lauderdale. During an excavation in 1960, six iron cannon were recovered, as well as a swivel gun, canister shot, musket balls, an anchor, and miscellaneous other artifacts. The cannon were determined to be of English origin; one cannon was decorated with a crown and the initials "GR," which stands for George Rex, which commonly appeared on English cannon upon the crowning of King George I in 1714; the British Broad Arrow stamped on top of the breech and on the casacabel; the

Cannon recovered from the "Hallandale Beach Wreck" (Broward County Historical Commission).

numerals "7-1-7" forward of the touch hole; the numeral "2" at the side of crest; and the letter "G" (George) at the end of the trunion. Based on the information gleaned from the cannon, the wreck is believed to be an English ship possibly lost during the War of Jenkins Ear around 1740. While pure speculation in the absence of definitive information, it should be noted the 14-gun sloop-of-war H.M.S *Wolf* was lost somewhere on the Florida east coast on March 2, 1741.

HALLIE K.

The schooner *Hallie K.* was built in 1891 at Solomons, Maryland, and was 53 feet long and 15.6 feet wide. According to the *Syracuse Herald*, December 16, 1935, "The motor of the *Hallie K.*, a motor schooner, broke down and the vessel sprang a leak, 30 miles northeast of Jupiter Light. Captain Victor G. Malone and his crew manned the pumps all night on their storm tossed ship." The crew of the vessel, which was used in the lobster fishery, was rescued by the steamer *Siboney* before the 20-ton *Hallie K.* ultimately foundered off the Florida coast on December 14.

HALL OF FAME WRECK

The "Hall of Fame Wreck" is an unidentified, partially buried shipwreck resting in only three feet of water in the surf zone directly adjacent to the Swimming Hall of Fame in Fort Lauderdale.

HALSEY

The *Halsey*, built in 1920, was one of the numerous tankers produced by the Alameda, California shipyard of Bethlehem Shipbuilding Corporation Limited. Launched into service for the Malston Company of Delaware, she was 435 feet in overall length with a 56-foot beam. Typical of many tankers, she had a stern deckhouse while her bridge superstructure was just forward of amidships. On May 6, 1942, the *Halsey* was headed to New York with a full load of fuel oil, gasoline, and naptha taken on at Corpus Christi, Texas. Just before dawn, as the ship moved north along the coast of Florida on calm seas, a torpedo from the *U-333* struck her port side, splitting her open amidships. Miraculously, the tanker's highly volatile cargo did not ignite. The engine of the *Halsey* was quickly brought to a stop while the flammable vapors of her cargo slowly enveloped the stricken vessel. Just after 5:00 a.m., the crew worked to escape the sinking *Halsey* in two lifeboats. Surviving the initial explosion, the survivors now found themselves fighting for consciousness amidst the poisonous naptha fumes that leaked from the slowly settling vessel. At 5:40 a.m., a second tanker came on scene and offered assistance to the two drifting lifeboats. The crew of the *Halsey* declined the offer, wisely fearing the still lurking U-boat. Fortunately for the tanker, Captain Peter Cremer of the *U-333* was confronted with a malfunctioning torpedo that armed itself while still in the tube. The torpedo that was destined for this new target had to be manually ejected before it detonated within the U-boat. This distraction provided enough time for the tanker to place a safe distance between itself and the marauding *U-333*. Returning to his initial target, Captain Cremer placed another torpedo into the side of the *Halsey* just after dawn that ignited a raging inferno around the stricken vessel.

The tanker *Halsey* headed to sea (Mark Mondano Collection).

The tanker soon slipped under the surface while her escaping cargo continued to fuel the fire that burned along the surface of the Atlantic.

The wreck sits in 80 feet of water and is broken into three large pieces. The bow sits upright with her anchors tight in the hawse pipe. The interior of the bow and the forward tanks have collapsed, now filled with swarming snook and other marine life. Swimming aft, large sections of wreckage provide interesting swim-throughs. The inverted amidships section is found at a traumatic fracture point. Entry into the interior of the amidships section can easily be made in this area, or other access points near the seabed. Off to starboard rest a few condensers buried in the sand. The keel of the hull gradually slopes down and disappears into the bottom. The large and mostly intact stern section can be found in perfect alignment with the keel, though it is separated by perhaps 60 feet of empty sand. The upright stern is separated at one of the aft tank bulkheads, rising vertically 30 feet from the sea bottom. Several ladders descend into the intact tanks, with sand having replaced its former cargo of petroleum products. Dropping off the rounded fantail, divers can sink down into a washout to inspect the large rudder of the former tanker. The tanker has been transformed into a thriving marine community, and is a popular destination for area fishermen. Abundant numbers of snook, permit, cobia, snapper, sheepshead, and grouper can be found swimming amongst the high-relief habitat that the *Halsey* now provides. Goliath grouper, formerly known as jewfish, can also be found hiding in the various tanker holds of the vessel. Turtles and eagle rays also make frequent visits to the wreck. Divers should also take note of the various patches of debris found off the main wreck site. These areas also hold significant quantities of fish, as well as succulent spiny lobster. On a day with no current and good visibility, the wreck of the *Halsey* is not to be missed.

HANNAH
The diary of British loyalist Josiah Smith reported the British ship *Hannah*, Captain Humphries, sailed from St. Augustine on December 28, 1780, for St. Johns to take on naval stores for London[98]. Unfortunately, the pilot grounded her on the bar at the river's mouth and she was totally lost.

HANOVER
According to the *Bell's Weekly Messenger* of December 23, 1810, "The *Hanover*, Baxter, and the *George*, Decone, from Liverpool to Amelia Island, were lost near Amelia Island about the 20th October."

HAPPY DELIVERY
According to the *Middlesex Journal* of July 17, 1770, "The *Happy Delivery*, Carter, from Halifax to Pensacola, has been lost in a hard gale of wind on the coast of Florida, and only three of the crew saved."

HAPPY RETURN
On October 18, 1766, the *Gazetteer and New Daily Advertiser* reported, "The *Happy Return*, Denwiddie, from Virginia to Pensacola, has been wrecked on the Florida shore."

HAROLDINE
The four-masted schooner *Haroldine*, official number 95802, was launched on March 29, 1884, at North Weymouth, Massachusetts, by N. Porter Keen. The 1,225-ton schooner documented a length of 209 feet and a

***Halsey* shortly after being torpedoed (Mark Mondano Collection).**

breadth of 40.5 feet. On January 2, 1898, she was lost on a reef off Cape Florida, reportedly near Bear Cut. A January 5, 1898, article in *The Evening Democrat* stated "The tug *A.F. Dewey* has just returned from the schooner *Haroldine*, wrecked on Cape Florida reef, and confirms the report that the schooner and cargo will be a total loss." Ralph Munroe later bought the wreck of the *Haroldine* at auction for $7.50 with plans to salvage the schooner. A winter gale soon broke the vessel up, however, and all that was recovered was her figurehead and bronze capstan cover.

The schooner *Haroldine*, grounded and bilged (Historical Museum of Southern Florida).

HAROLD J. MCCARTY

The schooner *Harold J. McCarty*, official number 96248, built in 1893 at Bath, Maine, registered a displacement of 312 tons gross, 297 tons net, a length of 133.1 feet, and beam of 31.8 feet. The *McCarty* stranded on Lake Worth Beach on March 25, 1911, resulting in one fatality.

HARRIET A. WEED

During the Civil War, numerous advances in weaponry made their appearance. One such weapon was the underwater mine, at the time called a torpedo. Confederate forces used these infernal devices with great success throughout the South. The danger of mines in the St. Johns River was not a secret. Union forces knew that Confederate soldiers were watching for an opportunity to sink mines in the river, as a number of deserters had come across the lines with explicit information on mining activities. The river was dragged periodically to remove these invisible threats. Unfortunately, these preventative measures did not help the tug *Harriet A. Weed*. In fact, the *Weed* became the third vessel in less than two weeks to be destroyed by mines in a small stretch of the river near Jacksonville.

The *Harriet A. Weed* departed Jacksonville for the Atlantic with the survey schooner *Caswell* in tow on the morning of May 9, 1864. The tug was a relatively new vessel, and had served as a pilot boat off St. Johns Bar prior to the Civil War. Due to hostilities in the region, however, she was armed with two guns and employed as a picket boat, as well as serving as a transport. The tug and her tow were following the steamer *Boston*, which also had a schooner in tow. When opposite the mouth of Cedar Creek, a point approximately halfway to the mouth of the river, the *Harriet A. Weed* ran upon two mines. They exploded simultaneously, resulting in the complete annihilation of the tug. Captain J.R. Swift was thrown into the air a distance of 20 feet as the smoking remains of the tug disappeared under the surface of the river. The sinking took the lives of five men and injured the remaining 36 crew and soldiers who were onboard. Later that day, the U.S.S. *Vixen* was inspecting the hulk of the *Harriet A. Weed* when they noticed ripples just under the surface. They subsequently dragged the river and pulled up six other keg-style mines.

The wreck of the *Harriet A. Weed* has not been positively located. It is unclear if portions of the vessel still remain on the bottom of the river, or if it was completely removed after the Civil War. Correspondence from August 1870 indicates the *Weed* was subjected to salvage, as it was noted the wreck was "Raised and machinery taken out," though the hull was documented as being of no value.

HARRINGTON

On August 6, 1747, the *London Evening Post* reported the following:

> We have advice from Jamaica, that the *Harrington*, Capt. James, from that island, fell in with a Spanish man of war, of 70 guns, and 500 men, 10 leagues windward of the Havanna; and after a running fight of 14 hours, the *Harrington* struck; the enemy fir'd 200 shot; they plunder'd the Captain of all, except his sword. There were on board the Spaniard several Irishmen; the captain also being Irish, told Capt. James he deserv'd to be hang'd for fighting against a King's ship. They were carried to the Havanna; from thence the Captain was sent in a flag of truce for South Carolina, and a few leagues from the shore of Florida the vessel founder'd; those on board took to their boat, and got safe to Florida, and are since got to their desir'd ports in America.

From the article, it is unclear if the *Harrington* was lost off Cuba or if it was dispatched to South Carolina (as a prize) to ultimately founder off Florida; it's entirely possible the wreck cited in the article occurred to an entirely different vessel.

HARRIOT

The brigantine *Harriot*, Captain Powell, was lost in 1751 "to the leeward of Cape Florida" during a voyage from Honduras; the captain, part of the crew, and cargo, were saved by a ship bound for St. Augustine[99].

HARRY LEE

While operating as a passenger steamer for the Palatka-Crescent City Line on the St. Johns River, the *Harry Lee* sank near Palatka at some unknown date[100].

HARRY T. HAYWARD

At 11:00 a.m. on August 20, 1902, the four-masted schooner *Harry T. Hayward* slid down the ways into the Georges River at the Washburn Brothers shipyard in Thomaston, Maine. The new 1,100-ton vessel was built for the general merchandise trade and was 190 feet in length, 40 feet in beam, and 19 feet in depth. The *Hayward* later spent some time at a Bath, Maine shipyard in the spring and summer of 1906 to repair damages sustained from a collision with the German steamer *San Miguel* earlier in the year. On October 18, 1910, Captain Nash was guiding the schooner *Harry T. Hayward* from Boston to the Florida Keys with a cargo of gravel intended for the Florida East Coast Overseas Railway when they wrecked on the reefs a half-mile off False Boca Raton at 4:00 a.m. Three of the crew were drowned while trying to launch a boat, which compelled the remainder of the officers and crew to remain on the wreck. There they clung to the rigging for 12 hours before being saved. The wreck of the *Hayward* has yet to be identified, but unless salvaged, the site should be marked by a fairly large mass of coral-encrusted gravel.

HATTIE

The sidewheel steamer *Hattie*, official number 11796, was built in 1860 at Jacksonville by Captain Jacob Brock for his steamboat line running between Lake Monroe and Jacksonville. Documentation following a rebuild in 1867 indicated she was 131 feet long, 25.3 feet wide, 217 gross tons, with two decks and a rounded stern. On April 12, 1864, Union naval forces captured the steamboat while hidden at Deep Creek on the St. Johns River. Jacob Brock eventually reacquired his steamer following the war, later selling it to Joseph R. Page of Jacksonville in 1877. Reportedly, the *Hattie* stranded on July 9, 1880, while on a run between Jacksonville and Kings Ferry, Georgia. The vessel was salvaged before being abandoned.

HATTIE ROSS

The schooner *Hattie Ross*, official number 11708, was built in 1858 at Falmouth, Maine. She was 95.2 feet long, 26.5 feet wide, and displaced 183 tons. During the September 1878 hurricane, the *Hattie Ross* was driven ashore 12 miles south of Cape Canaveral (also cited as stranding north of Cape Canaveral) and became a total loss; one life lost[101].

HAYNE

On March 15, 1845, the brig *Hayne* wrecked approximately five miles south-southeast of Cape Florida while en route from Charleston to Havana with a cargo of rice. According to salvage records, wrecker Solomon Howes was awarded $1,000 for his efforts. The *Hayne* was possibly refloated, as a brig *Hayne* was in service in November 1846.

HAZARD

The vessel *Hazard*, Captain New, bound from Honduras to London, was reported in the December 10, 1789, issue of *The Times* as totally lost near Cape Florida. Her crew was saved.

HEATHER BARKER

Reportedly built in 1874, the *Heather Barker* was a 74-ton schooner, Captain Moore, which sank on October 15, 1882, off Black Point on the St. Johns River, en route from Jacksonville for Fruit Cove with a cargo of lumber[102]. However, I have been unable to find any additional information on this vessel or its reported loss, and it should be noted there are several peculiar similarities to Singer's reported loss of the schooner *Jarlington*.

HEAVY MOON

On May 2, 1947, the 100-foot long Honduran freighter *Heavy Moon* sprung a leak as she approached her destination of Miami with a cargo of bananas. After U.S. Coast Guard efforts to dewater the sinking vessel failed, the *Heavy Moon* was towed to a sandbar off Fisher Island on the south side of Government Cut and beached. Captain Andros Diaz and seven crewmen were taken off the crippled vessel, which subsequently capsized. On May 5, the wrecked banana boat was refloated by the tide and drifted into Biscayne Bay. A tug eventually chased down the derelict and beached her again on a nearby sandbar 100 yards from her original beaching site. It is unclear if the *Heavy Moon* was eventually raised and salvaged, or towed offshore and scuttled.

HELEN C.

The 28-ton *Helen C.*, built in 1937, burned off Cocoa Beach on September 15, 1952[103].

HELEN T.

On December 27, 1917, the 436-ton barge *Helen T.* stranded off Jupiter Light[104].

HELMA

According to Singer (1998) the 172-ton *Helma*, built in 1925, was wrecked on the Miami River during Hurricane Donna on September 10, 1960.

HENRY BARGER

As reported in *The Sailor's Magazine and Naval Journal*, Volume 13, "Schooner *Henry Barger*, of New York, from Baltimore for Pilatka [sic], Flor., was totally lost 19th Oct. (1840) on St. Johns Bar."

HENRY NIN

Singer (1998) states the 98-ton Jacksonville vessel *Henry Nin*, built in 1871, burned at Palatka on December 14, 1887. I have been unable to find any additional information on a vessel by this name or on the reported incident.

HERALD

The British brig *Herald*, Captain Hancock, ran ashore at Elliott Key, near Cape Florida, on December 31, 1842 (also reported as December 6, 1842). She was en route from Vera Cruz, Mexico, bound to Swansea, England[105]. Admiralty reports on file in Key West state she wrecked on Ledbury Reef and was carrying a cargo of copper.

HERCULES

The steamer *Hercules* was built in 1905 at Tomkins Cove, New York. The freighter, official number 201785, displaced 163 tons gross and 111 tons net, and was 93 feet long and 24.8 feet wide. The *Hercules* reportedly foundered in deep water on June 9, 1923, at approximate latitude 30° 43' north and longitude 79° 35' west (roughly 95 nautical miles east of the St. Marys River mouth).

HERMITAGE

Carrying a cargo of sulfur, the American schooner-rigged barge *Hermitage* departed Galveston, Texas, on November 12, 1924, for a North Atlantic port. The *Hermitage* was in tow of the tug *Barryton*, along with the barge *Dykes*. On November 22, when east of St. Augustine, the *Hermitage* unexpectedly foundered. It is believed the cargo of the barge shifted, possibly due to a leak that allowed one side to take on an uneven load. Fortunately, the entire crew of the barge was taken off by the *Barryton*. The sinking location was reported at approximate latitude 30° 06' north and longitude 79° 43' west (approximately 94 miles east-northeast of St. Augustine). This position would place the *Hermitage* in deep water; however, if the vessel floated for any duration before ultimately sinking, she could possibly rest in diveable depths. Coincidentally, there is a wreck in approximately 150 feet of water northeast of Mayport that is worthy of investigation. The unidentified wreck is a large vessel that appears to be a converted barge. Divers have also reported an odd residue within the wreck's interior that may be the remains of the *Hermitage's* sulfur cargo. Additional exploration is definitely warranted. The *Hermitage* was built in 1919 by the Union Shipbuilding Company of Baltimore, Maryland. She was originally a five-masted schooner, 306 feet in length and 50 feet in breadth that displaced 2,111 tons gross.

HESS MARINER

The *Hess Mariner* was launched on January 14, 1945, as the *Midway Hills*. Built by the Marinship Corporation at their Sausalito, California, shipyard for the U.S. War Shipping Administration, she documented a length of 523.5 feet and a breadth of 67.9 feet. In 1948, the Type T2-SE-A1 tanker was sold to the Cape Horn Steamship Corporation and renamed the *Chryss Jane*. She was renamed *Hess Mariner* in 1956 upon her sale to the Colonial Steamship Corporation, which leased the tanker to Hess, Incorporated. The Hess Tankship Company apparently later bought the vessel outright in 1961.

On the evening of October 1, 1961, while on a voyage between Houston, Texas, and Perth Amboy, New Jersey, an engine room explosion rocked the 10,564-ton tanker *Hess Mariner*. The explosion occurred when the main turbine generator disintegrated, which punched a hole in the main condenser and flooded the after spaces of the vessel. A skeleton crew of four men tried for six hours to save the tanker from sinking, but finally gave up and abandoned the ship before dawn on October 2. The four joined the 33 other crewmen who had abandoned the tanker to the nearby *Texaco Nevada* and *Esso Suez*, which arrived at the scene soon after the *Hess Mariner* sent an S.O.S. in the wake of the explosion. According to the U.S. Coast Guard, which had a cutter and aircraft in the area, the *Hess Mariner* disappeared at 9:26 a.m. Its stern had projected several hours from the Atlantic's surface, giving rise to some hope of salvage. The reported sinking site was at approximate latitude 31° 10' north and longitude 79° 09' west (approximately 125 nautical miles east-northeast of the St. Johns River mouth), which places the wreck in very deep water.

HESTER

The sloop *Hester*, Captain Timmons, sank at St. Marys during a hurricane that devastated the area on September 17, 1813[106].

HETTY

According to a report published in *The Edinburgh Advertiser* on June 27, 1809, "The *Hetty*, from Amelia Island to Liverpool, is on shore on the North Breaker, Amelia Island."

HIAWATHA (1919A)

An oddity to the narrow and winding rivers in Northeastern Florida was the inboard stern-wheeled steamboat. Representative of this type of vessel was the *Hiawatha*, official number 200721, which plied the Oklawaha River for the Hart Line. Built at Palatka in 1904 by Hubbard Hart, she was 89 feet long, 23.5 feet wide, and displaced 129 tons gross. The *Hiawatha* was eventually abandoned in 1919 at Hart's Point, East Palatka. The derelict was ultimately removed in the early 1980s.

The derelict *Hiawatha* in 1954 (Alfred H. Robson Collection).

HIAWATHA (1919B)

The 13-ton vessel *Hiawatha*, official number 208334, burned on July 13, 1919, at Courtney.

HILDA

The Norwegian bark *Hilda*, Captain Torjussen, from New Orleans bound to Bremen, Germany, went ashore six miles south of St. Augustine. One man drowned, and her cargo of tobacco and staves were a total loss[107]. The 491-ton bark was originally built as the *Thyra* in 1856 at Maine.

HIRAM AND WILLIAM

The August 16, 1816, issue of *The Edinburgh Advertiser* included the names of numerous vessels lost in a gale off Florida, one of which was the *Hiram and William*. The article stated, "The *Atlas* and *Martha* are the only Jamaica ships that have suffered in the gale in the Gulf of Florida. Numerous reports are today posted in Lloyd's books, of vessels lost during the storm. The following are their names: the *Cossack*, from Havannah [sic] to Hamburgh [sic]; the *Zanga and Fairley* of Nassau; the *General Pike* of Charlestown to Metanza; the *Merraganzet* [sic], from Havannah [sic] to Bristol; the *Hiram and William*, from Charleston to St. Marys." Based on its route, the *Hiram and William* possibly wrecked off the northeastern coast of Florida.

Diver explores the remains of a houseboat sunk as an artificial reef off Miami in the 1980s (Miami-Dade County Department of Environmental Resources Management).

HOPE (1791)

The ship *Hope*, Captain George Chapell, sailing from Jamaica to Charleston, South Carolina in ballast, was driven on shore in a violent gale of wind on the morning of January 10, 1791, approximately 40 leagues south of St. Augustine (likely near Cape Canaveral). The crew, with sails, rigging, and other materials, were saved by the sloop *Tamar*.

HOPE (1796)

On August 19, 1796, *The Edinburgh Advertiser* reported the brig *Hope*, Captain West, bound from Havana to America, as lost near Cape Florida.

HOPE FOR PEACE

The *Bell's Weekly Messenger* of March 25, 1821, reported "The *Hope for Peace*, Baker, from New Orleans to Charleston, was upset and dismasted on 25th Jan. in the Gulf Stream, and totally lost on the 30th, on the coast of Florida. Crew saved."

HORATIO

According to *The Edinburgh Advertiser*, June 07, 1811, "The *Horatio*, Captain Turner, was totally wrecked at Amelia Island."

HOTLINE

On the afternoon of April 3, 1989, a fuel leak ignited a fire aboard the 40-foot long commercial fishing vessel *Hotline* approximately two miles offshore Ponce de Leon Inlet. Captain Paul Pickett and his crewman abandoned ship in a life raft and were picked up by the inbound fishing vessel *Super Critter II*. The U.S. Coast Guard extinguished the fire, but one side of the boat had burned away and collapsed, causing the vessel to founder and sink[108].

HOWLAND

According to Davis (1925), the St. Johns River tug *Howland* sank at South Jacksonville and was never raised.

HOWLET

The demise of the *Howlet* likely would have been a mystery if not for a highly amazing set of circumstances. Towards the end of 1748, General Winslow, a Boston merchant, dispatched his ship *Howlet* on a trading voyage to the Gulf of Mexico. On board was his former servant, who sailed as the *Howlet's* cook. After its departure, nothing more was heard of the *Howlet* and General Winslow eventually assumed the vessel was lost with all hands. Approximately 10 years later when boarding a vessel in England, Winslow was shocked to see his former servant, who shared details of the *Howlet's* wrecking upon their reunion. A May 22, 1760, article in the *London Chronicle*, revealed, "The *Howlet* was by stress of weather driven on shore near Cape Florida, where the crew were made prisoners by the Indians, who put them all to death, except himself, whom they saved on account of his colour, and sold him to a Spanish merchant of the Havannah." Several years later, the servant escaped his enslavement by swimming offshore to a ship he sighted from New England, on which he eventually became cook and traveled to England where he told his story to General Winslow.

HUDSON

The 124-ton tugboat *Hudson* was built in 1893 at Camden, New Jersey, and was 93.2 feet long and 20.5 feet wide. Six men were killed after the *Hudson*, which was towing the former U.S. Navy tug *Locust Point* from Charleston, South Carolina, to Mobile, Alabama, crashed into the jetty at the mouth of the St. Johns River on the evening of December 19, 1946. Only one crew member survived the accident. According to *The Bee*, December 23, 1946, "Luther Brown, Durham, N.C., deckhand who was rescued from the jetty rocks after leaping into heavy seas, told Coast Guard officers he believed Capt. Oscar L. Cudworth, also of Wanchese, had gone down with the ship. When the *Hudson* started sinking, Brown said the captain told the crew that each would be 'on his own.' Cudworth then re-entered his cabin and shut the door, the seaman reported. The survivor said he believed other crewmen had refused to leave the vessel in the belief they would be cut to pieces on the rocks." The *Hudson* was owned by the Wood Towing Company of Norfolk, Virginia.

HUGH DE PAYENS

Named after a French knight from the Champagne region of France who was the co-founder and first Grand Master of the Knights Templar, the three-masted schooner *Hugh de Payens* was launched in June 1910 at Rockland, Maine. The vessel, official number 207630, registered a length of 144 feet, a beam of 35.9 feet, and a depth of hold of 10.1 feet. In September 1919, en route from Mobile, Alabama to Ponce, Puerto Rico, the 416-ton schooner was caught in a massive hurricane while off the Dry Tortugas. The crew abandoned ship and was later rescued by a Cuban steamer. In the wake of the storm, the turtled *Hugh de Payens* was observed off Key West. The U.S.C.G.C. *Seminole* destroyed a projecting spar from the schooner *Hugh de Payens* on October 16, 1919, off Cardenas, Cuba. The schooner itself drifted along in the Gulf Stream and eventually was washed ashore three miles south of Pablo Beach (present-day Jacksonville Beach) with all her masts gone. Reportedly, the fishing schooner *Cora P. White* got a line to the schooner but was unable to pull her off the beach.

Following the passing of a tropical storm in 2001, the articulated lower hull of a schooner was exposed on Ponte Vedra Beach. Simply known as the "Ponte Vedra Wreck," the approximately 90-foot long site, which last appeared in the late 1950s, is believed by locals to be the final resting spot of the schooner *Hugh de Payens*.

The grounded hulk of the *Hugh de Payens* at Ponte Vedra Beach (Beaches Area Historical Society).

The *Hugo's April Fool* being prepared for its scuttling (Miami-Dade County Department of Environmental Resources Management).

HUGO'S APRIL FOOL

The wreck known as *Hugo's April Fool* was formerly the 252-ton freighter *Danbo* (IMO number 5225289), which was built in 1918. The 115-foot long freighter was scuttled as an artificial reef in October 1988, and now sits upright and generally intact in 145 feet of water, though sections of her superstructure have collapsed. The heavily-encrusted *Hugo's April Fool* rests approximately 250 feet south of the *Doc DeMilly*.

HUNTRESS

Built in 1906 at New York, the 76-ton yacht *Huntress*, official number 203683, was 78.9 feet long and 22 feet wide. On January 6, 1913, she burned at Cape Canaveral with the loss of three lives. At the time of her loss she was owned by Frederick W. Chesebrough.

HUPALONG

On January 23, 1928, approximately one mile out of Fort Lauderdale and directly offshore the local U.S. Coast Guard base), the 38-foot long yacht *Hupalong* exploded and burned. The two men abandoned the craft to a small launch they were towing. The burning *Hupalong* was eventually towed a short distance offshore where spectators on the beach watched it burn to the water's edge and sink[109].

HURON

In early June 1816, the ship *Huron*, Captain Snow, en route from Charleston, South Carolina to St. Marys, encountered a stiff northeast gale and "thick weather" approximately 12 miles southeast of the St. Simons Lighthouse[110]. The vessel eventually wrecked near St. Augustine sometime in the morning of June 8, 1816. An account from a passenger on the shipwrecked *Huron* reported that on June 8 they were taken to the Governor of Spanish Florida in St. Augustine from their landing point on Anastasia Island, 20 miles to the south.

HUSTLER

The facts surrounding the loss of the steamer *Hustler* were included in the 1897 *Annual Report of the Supervising Inspector-General, U.S. Steamboat-Inspection Service to the Secretary of Commerce and Labor*. It stated: "December 26, 1896: Steamer *Hustler*, while lying at Clark's Dock, Jacksonville, Fla., caught fire and was totally destroyed. Cause of fire unknown. Loss of property, $5,000. Insurance, $3,000. Loss of life, none."

Hydro Atlantic as the *Delaware* (U.S. Army Corps of Engineers).

HYDRO ATLANTIC

Built at Yard 51 of the Sparrows Point, Maryland, facility of the Maryland Steel Company in 1905, the *Hydro Atlantic*, official number 260377, started her career as the U.S. Army Corps of Engineers' hopper dredge *Delaware*. Her steel hull was originally 315 feet in overall length, 52 feet in beam (molded), 22.5 feet in depth, and displaced 4,050 tons. The two side drags of the *Delaware* could dredge to a maximum depth of 45 feet. A workhorse for the Corps, she worked constantly to keep shipping lanes clear from shoaling and safe for navigation. In 1922, the *Delaware* dredged 1,366 loads for the Philadelphia District, which removed a total of 2,378,593 cubic yards of material. The *Delaware* was sold in 1950 to Construction Aggregates Corporation and renamed *Sand Captain*. In 1961, following a rebuild, she was renamed *Ezra Sensibar*. The rebuild deepened her draft, increasing her hopper capacity from 3,076 cubic yards to approximately 5,000 cubic yards, and most likely rebuilt her superstructure, which was originally constructed of wood. The hopper dredge worked on the Chesapeake Bay Bridge Tunnel project, dredging sand to help construct the man-made islands for the tunnel. Work was postponed in late 1962, however, when an engine room fire required her to proceed to New York for repairs.

In 1968, the Hydromar Corporation of Delaware bought the aging ship and renamed her *Hydro Atlantic*. After several more years of active service dredging channels and inlets, she outlived her usefulness and was condemned to the salvage yard. As the *Hydro Atlantic* was being towed by the tug *Elizabeth II* to the scrap yard at Brownsville, Texas, her hull gave way and she sank in approximately 175 feet of water one mile east of the Boca Raton Inlet on December 7, 1987. Apparently, the towing operation neglected to maintain the four pumps that were needed to keep the leaky 82-year old vessel afloat, and she began to wallow behind the tug. By the time the situation was recognized, it was too late. The tug parted the tow lines and the dredger quickly settled beneath the surface.

Sitting bolt upright, the bow of the *Hydro Atlantic* points generally southward with her forward mast reaching to within 100 feet of the surface, while the deck is encountered at approximately 145 feet. The bridge and superstructure present several levels to explore, with the collapsed aft-facing bulkheads allowing easy entry into the interior. Railing still lines the perimeter of the vessel. Moving aft, a large access hold is bordered by winches and other machinery. A large crane can be found along either side of the ship, the operator's chair long since vacant.

Hopper dredge *Hydro Atlantic* at Kearny, New Jersey, August 1972 (William A. Schell).

Diver on the wreck of the *Hydro Atlantic*.

Swimming past the single stack, divers will encounter the engine room skylights, which present one of many points of entry into the interior of the ship. Dropping down past several catwalks and then moving forward, divers will be confronted with a large panel of gauges and controls that used to power the dredges on the ship. The boiler room can be found on the opposite side of this area. Heading towards the stern, there is an aft hold that allows abundant areas to explore. While divers have recovered numerous artifacts, there are still many brass fittings, gauges, and assorted material still remaining on the ship.

The wreck of the *Hydro Atlantic* is perhaps one of the most visually stunning wrecks in South Florida. The surfaces of the vessel have largely been incorporated by gorgonians, and areas appear very much like a pasture of purple sea fans that oscillate in the current. It is also interesting to note that exotic Indo-Pacific fish species, such as moorish idols and yellowbar angelfish, have been observed on this wreck. This is most likely due to the wreck's proximity to Boca Raton Inlet and the Intercoastal Waterway, where local aquarists may release their unwanted specimen fish. The moderate depth offers a wonderful wreck for initial technical training. Even veteran wreck divers will enjoy a dive on the *Hydro*. Divers should be aware that strong currents can be encountered here and the wreck is abundantly outfitted with monofilament line from fishermen.

A view of the *Hydro Atlantic's* coral-encrusted bridge.

ICAROS

The schooner *Icaros* was built in 1887 at Bremerhaven, Germany, and during her long career she sailed for German, Scandinavian, Greek, American, and Honduran owners. In December 1940 the *Icaros* began a residency at Miami as a pleasure yacht for its owner, C.E. Sorenson, vice president of the Ford Motor Company. On October 8, 1942, the schooner was acquired by the U.S. Navy as an auxiliary service craft and commissioned as *YAG-16*. However, the U.S. Navy soon found her unfit for service and abandoned her at Miami in January 1943, where she sat idle for several months before she traded hands yet again.

As reported on September 15, 1945 in the *Toronto Daily Star*, "Raging winds drove the two-masted, 80-ton Honduran schooner *Icaros* on to the North Miami Beach at noon. Seven men took to a lifeboat and reached land safely. Six were sheltered at the North Miami Beach police station and the other was removed to a hospital for treatment of injuries. The Coast Guard reported there was no hope of saving the ship." Another article reported crewman Cecil Wedeburn drowned when he swam back out to the wrecked schooner in an attempt to save his dog, which was left on the ship; ironically, the dog rode the ship all the way into the beach safely. The *Icaros* was cast up on the beach, where it remained for over two years. The schooner was successfully refloated on September 18, 1947, though the vessel was reportedly in sad shape and was likely scrapped.

IDA E. LATHAM

The 463-ton three-masted schooner *Ida E. Latham*, official number 100125, was built in August 1874 at Belfast, Maine, and was 137 feet long and 33 feet wide. In early 1888, newspaper accounts documented the *Latham* went ashore on Long Island, New York, and was abandoned by her captain and crew. She was eventually partially dismantled and pulled off the beach, and later sold at auction in Greenport, New York, for $6,400. The schooner was then overhauled, recommissioned, and put back in service. At 3:00 a.m. on January 14, 1889, the *Ida E. Latham*, Captain Albertsen, en route from New York to Fernandina with a cargo of salt, stranded north of the channel at the latter destination.

I. HOWLAND

On October 7, 1881, *The New York Times* reported the brig *I. Howland*, from Fernandina, with a cargo of lumber, went ashore on Bird's Island, near St. Augustine Light, during a storm the night of October 5. The following day she broke up and became a total loss. The *I. Howland* was 110.5 feet long, 28 feet wide, and displaced 233 tons. She was built in November 1868 at Waldoboro, Maine.

ILO

Built in May 1874 at Port Jefferson, Long Island, the *Ilo* was a 33-ton oak-hulled schooner 51 feet in length and 19.7 feet in breadth. On the morning of November 16, 1886, the *Ilo*, Captain Overton, was riding her anchor off Lake Worth, waiting for the weather to calm before entering the inlet to unload her cargo of lumber she carried from Jacksonville. At 7:00 a.m., her chain parted and she promptly grounded. While the *Ilo* proved to be a total loss, her cargo was salvaged.

IMAGINATION

On the morning of May 31, 2007, the 65-foot long motor yacht *Imagination* began taking on massive amounts of water while cruising offshore Miami, forcing the crew to broadcast an emergency mayday message. Within 15 minutes, vessels arrived on scene to rescue a family of six just before the yacht plunged to the bottom approximately 13 miles off Haulover Inlet.

IMOR

The *Imor* was an 84-foot long, 21.5-foot wide trawler built in 1958 at Gdansk, Poland. The fishing vessel was later converted to conduct oceanographic research for the Polish government. In August 1991, the stripped trawler was sunk as an artificial reef off Fort Lauderdale. The *Imor* now rests upright in approximately 170 feet of water, with her bow pointing south.

Deployment of the *Imor* as an artificial reef (Broward County Artificial Reef Program).

INCHULVA

The *Inchulva*, official number 99439, was built as the *Alberta* in September 1892 by W. Gray and Company, Limited of West Hartpool, England. The single-screw freighter was 386 feet in length, 48.6 foot in beam, and with her two iron decks she displaced 4,823 tons. The 381-horsepower triple expansion engine was produced by the Central Marine Engine Works of West Hartpool, England. Initially sailing for W. Tapscott and Company, the *Alberta* was sold in 1898 to the Inchulva Shipping Company, Limited, whereupon she was renamed the *Inchulva*. The vessel was managed by the firm of Hamilton, Frasier, and Company.

In September 1903, under the command of Captain G.W. Davis, the *Inchulva* headed to Newport News, Virginia, from Galveston, Texas, with a final destination of Hamburg, Germany. In her cargo holds she was carrying 234,000 bushels of wheat, 180 square bales of cotton, 963 sacks of brewer's grain, 72,600 feet of pine lumber, 150 bales of "ixtle," and 1,840 sacks of cottonseed meal. On the evening of September 11, the *Inchulva* ran into a violent storm that threatened to part the seams of the steamer. Captain Davis attempted to ride out the storm and dropped both anchors just offshore Delray. The *Inchulva* eventually lost the war of attrition, as both cables parted and she was pushed into shallow water where she became hopelessly grounded. The pounding waves caused her cargo to shift, which expedited her structural fatigue and eventual structural failure. She broke apart in heavy seas on the morning of September 12. Of the crew of 28, the sinking claimed nine lives. When the steamer commenced to break up, the chief engineer foolishly went to his cabin to retrieve $100. He was never seen again. Three others were washed overboard by heavy seas. The other five fatalities occurred during an attempt to reach the shore through the raging surf.

The salvage of the *Inchulva* proceeded shortly after her fate was sealed. The *Jacksonville Evening Metropolis* confirmed the accident on September 17, stating, "A dispatch from Miami says the auxiliary schooner *Klondike*, Cabal, master, laden with valuable fittings from the British steamer *Inchulva*, brings the first authentic reports from the several wrecks north of this point (Jupiter)." Unfortunately, the *Inchulva* broke in half on September 18, and only 178 bales of cotton were saved. Captain Davis, as well as his First and Second Officers, were brought before a Naval Court held at the British Vice Consulate at Jacksonville on September 19. As the captain and crew conducted themselves appropriately and made every effort to save the ship and crew, the court exonerated Captain Davis and his officers from all blame.

Known locally as the "Delray Wreck," the *Inchulva* rests in 20 feet approximately 500 feet offshore. The wreck has deteriorated over the years, both from salvage and from the forces of nature. Scattered wreckage, now heavily encrusted and supporting a thriving abundance of marine life, can be found settling in the sand just a short swim from the south end of the beach.

INDIAN RIVER

In 1861, a new sidewheel steamer was launched at the Glasgow, Scotland shipyard of Robert Napier for the blockade-running firm of Fraser, Trenholm, and Company. Christened *Neptune*, her quarter-inch-thick iron hull was 166.6 feet long and 27.4 feet wide, and displaced 294 tons. She was equipped with dual inclined engines with 42-inch diameter cylinders and 42-inch piston stroke, and two upright cylindrical boilers, which could produce a top speed of approximately 15 knots. During her first two years of operation, she successfully completed four runs between Cuba and Confederate ports. On June 14, 1863, the U.S.S. *Lackawanna* ran down and captured the *Neptune* off Mobile Bay. Following her capture, the U.S. Navy purchased the *Neptune* from the Prize Court for $40,000. Outfitted with two 24-pounders, she was renamed the U.S.S. *Clyde* on August 11, 1863. After her commissioning, she steamed to Key West for service with the East Gulf Blockading Squadron. After the end of hostilities, she arrived at the Philadelphia Navy Yard on August 10, 1865, and was decommissioned a week later. On October 25, 1865, she was sold at auction in New York to Colonel Henry T. Titus and Dr. John Westcott for $11,400.

Titus and Wescott purchased the *Clyde* for use in their venture to establish a fishing and mercantile business in Brevard County known as the New York and Indian River Fishing Company. They furnished their new steamer, which they renamed the *Indian River*, with ice bunkers and cooling compartments for 40 tons of seafood. Apparently, the work also entailed the lengthening the hull of the steamer to 200.5 feet. On December 2, 1865, the *Indian River* departed Jacksonville and headed south. The following day, while attempting to run into the Indian River Inlet, she struck on the bar and bilged. A portion of the cargo was taken off and wreckers from Key West were summoned to salvage the vessel[111]. Reportedly, the hull of the *Indian River* remained where she wrecked for many years. It is unclear if the vessel was later removed or if it simply deteriorated and was sanded over.

INDUSTRY (1764)

Less than a mile offshore of St. Augustine and lying in 18 feet of water, trace remains of a sailing vessel were found in 1995 during an extensive mapping of submerged cultural resources by Southern Oceans Archaeological Research, Incorporated. First dove in 1997, eight cannons, three anchors, two grindstones, shot for the cannons, and numerous other artifacts were found throughout the site. The cannons were found lying muzzle to cascable (head to foot), as if in a stowed position, in the lower hull. In 1998, the site was relocated and one seven-foot long cannon was recovered during the 1998 season. After cleaning, the cannon was identified as a six-pound gun marked with the British Broad Arrow, the crest of King George II. This artifact provided a valuable clue to the identity of the unknown ship, as the crest of King George II dated the wreck to between 1727 and 1760. Subsequent archival research indicated that the wreck might be that of the British sloop *Industry*, lost in 1764 while carrying cannons and supplies to the British garrison at St. Augustine.

The *Industry* set out from New York carrying subsistence money, six-pound guns, ammunition, and "artificers tools" as requested to supply several of the outposts and settlements being taken over from the Spanish after the ownership of East and West Florida was ceded to England by the Treaty of Paris of 1763. John Ogilvie was in charge of the Ninth Regiment at the British garrison in St. Augustine in 1764. Unfortunately for Ogilvie, on May 5, 1764, the *Industry* ran aground on a sandbar after Captain Daniel Lawrence failed to successfully navigate the constantly changing shoals on the approach to the St. Augustine Inlet. John Ogilvie described the wreck and his current situation to Commander Thomas Gage in a May 13, 1764, letter to the British North American Command in New York:

Sir,

I have the Hon'r of Your Excellency's

letter, I am extremely sorry to acquaint you that the *Industry* Transport, Commanded by Captain Lauranes [*sic*] was unfortunately cast away off the Bar of St. Augustine the 6th Inst. Sent all boats in this Post out to her Assistance ordered a Guard to take care of the wreck, fortunately sav'd six Boxes of Money some Flower [*sic*] and carpenter's tools. Shall send a Return of them to Col. Robertson in order to lay it before you. Now Sr. I ant [*sic*] by leave to observe that this Post must be ruined and undone if their [*sic*] is not some step taken to put a stop to the Villainous proceedings of Loseing [*sic*] Vessels on the Bar here which are insured above their value: I am told that Capt. Laurences's Vessel was insur'd, he never sent to acquaint me that he was off, by that means the Reg't was lost, not having Boats to bring him in. The Inhabitants of East Florida consist of a set of People who have absconded from other Colonies for Debts and other Causes, as the wreck was greatly scattered along the coast it was impossible for the Guard to extend itself so far, so that the inhabitants have taken a great many of the King's Arms, propose making a search in order to see if I can detect any of them. If I do I shall be glad to know from your Excellency whether or not my power extends so far as to make an example of some of them, which would be absolutely necessary for the good of this Colony, have sent express the sloop *Anne* to acquaint you of this disaster. A Mr. Furst informs me that the Creek Indians are very tardy in giving Satisfaction for the murder they have Committed in the back Settlement of a South Carolinian. In case an Indian War the small artillery are absolutely necessary for the defence [*sic*] of the advanced Posts, you may be assured I'll do everything in my power for securing these Posts in the best manner possible.

The vessel, hopelessly stranded on the shoal, succumbed to its own weight and settled deep into the sand, eventually breaking up and slipping beneath the surface. While much of its cargo may have been salvaged, numerous artifacts remain, including the numerous cannon that were trapped below decks as ballast.

Due to her age, the suspected *Industry* wreck attracted the attention of archaeologists who refer to the site as the "Tube Wreck." Unfortunately, it also attracted the attention of more nefarious characters who used the cover of darkness to pillage the wreck. Sometime in early 1999, thieves used their prop wash to excavate the wreck, creating a large crater and exposing numerous artifacts. They then proceeded to steal two 2,000-pound cannon from the wreck site. The theft, a violation of Florida's Historic Preservation Act, cast a bad light on both shipwreck divers and shipwreck salvors in general. Fortunately, archaeologists continue to document the wreck and recover certain artifacts. In 1999, a three-foot long swivel gun was recovered from the wreck in order to initiate conservation for eventual display at the St. Augustine Lighthouse and Museum.

INDUSTRY (1766)

The ship *Industry*, Captain Owens, reportedly wrecked off Cape Florida in November 1766 during a voyage from Jamaica; out of a crew of 43, only the captain, mate, and 10 hands survived the event and were picked up by the *Nancy* and returned to Jamaica[112].

INDUSTRY (1837)

On September 13, 1837, the wrecking sloop *Energy* observed the British schooner *Industry* stranded about 40 miles north of Cape Florida at approximate latitude 26° 13' north. She was bound from Montego Bay, Jamaica, to Canada laden with sugar when she went aground on September 12 and bilged. Additional reports from other wrecking vessels the following week stated the schooner was in an exposed situation with the sea breaking over her and the sea ebbing and flowing in her hold. According to *Hunt's The Merchants' Magazine and Commercial Review*, Volume 2, the *Industry* was under the command of Captain Dixon when she wrecked during a violent storm on her return trip to Quebec.

INGRID

The Norwegian bark *Ingrid*, Captain Olsen, sailed from Pensacola for Rio de Janeiro on March 18, 1895, with a cargo of lumber. The *Galveston Daily News* of April 8, 1895, reported the steamer *El Rio* sighted the *Ingrid* ashore a mile north of Fowey Rocks Light on April 5. The stranded bark had sails out and had appeared to have gone ashore just a short time before the observation, and the crew was engaged on throwing her cargo of lumber overboard in an attempt to lighten the vessel. On April 10, 1895, the crew of the wrecked *Ingrid* was brought into Key West onboard the schooner *Harris Brothers*[113].

INTREPID

Dispatches from Charleston, South Carolina, dated October 13, 1810, included in *The Lady's Miscellany and Weekly Visitor*, Volume 12 (1811), declared:

> The packet sloop *Intrepid*, Fowler, from St. Marys, of and bound for Savannah, with a number of passengers, encountered the same gale, and was driven ashore at St. Augustine Bar; the vessel and cargo entirely lost, as also we are sorry to say, several of the passengers; among those who perished were Mrs. Fowler, the wife

of captain F. with her three children; Miss Fisher of Savannah, sister to Mrs. Fowler, and Mrs. Batey, an elderly lady, and her female servant. Mrs. Beard, of St. Marys who was on board, was providentially saved by drifting on shore on a part of the quarter deck; as was also Captain Fowler and most of the crew. Our informant assures us that most, if not all of those who were drowned might have been saved, but for the inhuman and unpardonable indifference of the inhabitants, who would not render them any assistance.

While the date slightly preceded that cited for the wrecking of the *African*, *Caroline*, *Triton*, and *Union*, the same storm likely claimed all of these vessels.

IRON BALLAST WRECK

Just over one mile north of Sebastian Inlet in shallow water just beyond the surf zone, divers can find the remains of a wreck dominated by the presence of iron ballast bars scattered over the limestone bottom, hence the name of the site. Additional shipwreck material includes barrel hoops, cannon balls, and a large iron anchor with a steel stock. While the wreck has been investigated by archaeologists, the wreck's identity is still unknown. The site is also known as the "Spanish House Wreck," and is located at a popular surfing beach. In fact, surfers have actually reported striking wreckage, which rises dangerously close to the surface in the surf zone.

ISAAC COLLINS

On November 21, 1911, the schooner *Isaac Collins* reportedly stranded in Biscayne Bay. The *Collins*, official number 100443, was built in 1889 at Essex, Massachusetts, and was 89 feet long, 23.5 feet wide, and 98 tons burden.

ISABELLA

On August 27, 1751, the *London Evening Post* reported, "The *Isabella*, Capt. Powers, from the Bay of Honduras for New York, was lost in her passage to the leeward of Cape Florida, with her cargo. The captain and crew are since arriv'd at St. Augustine."

ISABELLA S.

Built in 1964 at the Florence, Italy shipyard of Cantieri di Pisa, the *Isabella S.* was a 58.8-foot long flybridge motor yacht. On March 26, 1990, the donated vessel was sunk in 394 feet of water within the Haulover Artificial Reef Site off Miami.

ISIS (1882)

The 73-ton iron-hulled sternwheel steamer *Isis*, official number 100017, was built in 1870 at Wilmington, Delaware. On November 6, 1882, the *Isis* sunk in Lake George. Details of the loss were reported in *The Freeborn County Standard* on November 16, 1882:

At Jacksonville, Florida, information has just been received of a steamboat disaster on the upper St. Johns River. The steamer *Isis*, of an independent line, running in opposition to the DeBary Line of steamers, while crossing Big Lake George during a heavy gale at 3 o'clock Monday morning foundered when midway across the lake. The chief pilot, fireman and a deck hand, names unknown, were drowned. The cook is also reported as drowned. The steamer *Rosa* rescued the remainder of the passengers and crew. The *Isis* was one of the largest freight boats on the St John's River. She was a stern wheel, iron hull steamer of ordinary size, owned by a joint stock company. She was valued at $12,000, and so far as learned was not insured. The particulars of the affair are meager.

ISIS (1920)

According to Lloyd's 1902 *Register of Yachts*, the twin-screw, steel-hulled *Isis* was built in 1902 at Newburgh, New York, by T.S. Marvel and Company. The 377-ton steamer yacht *Isis* was 200 feet in overall length (also cited as 180.4 feet in other sources) and 24.6 feet in breadth. Her twin triple-expansion engines, supplied by W.A. Fletcher and Company, drove two screws at a maximum speed of 17 knots. The elegant yacht, designed by J. Beaver Webb, was originally built for brothers William S. and John T. Spaulding at a cost of $225,000. In 1807, President Thomas Jefferson signed a bill mandating the "Survey of the Coast," which resulted in the formation of the U.S. Coast and Geodetic Survey, the oldest scientific agency in the federal government. The Survey developed seafloor charts, mapped the coastline, and calculated tides and other oceanographic functions. In April 1915, the Survey purchased the *Isis* from the Spauldings for approximately $60,000, and she was put into service that year to conduct coastal surveys. Due to the United States' entry in World War I, however, the U.S. Navy acquired the yacht in September 1917. Commissioned into the U.S. Navy as a patrol vessel, the U.S.S. *Isis* served as flagship for the commander of Squadron 2 Cruiser Force in New York. Upon the end of hostilities, the *Isis* was decommissioned

Survey steamer *Isis* (National Oceanic and Atmospheric Administration).

Bow view of the *Isis* (National Oceanic and Atmospheric Administration).

in early 1919 and returned to the U.S. Coast and Geodetic Survey. On February 28, 1920, the *Isis* was operating near St. Augustine taking soundings. One of her additional tasks was to map the wreck of the U.S. Army Corps of Engineers' dredge *Florida*, which was lost in July 1918. Unfortunately, the *Isis* strayed too close to the submerged hulk of the *Florida*, which opened up a hole in her hull. In an attempt to save his ship, Lieutenant Commander Luce opted to beach his vessel. With waves continually breaking over the hull, the yacht quickly became entombed in sand and was abandoned.

In early October, engineer A.B. Saliger utilized the wreck as an experiment to investigate options for salvaging sunken vessels. According to Mr. Saliger, "Any submerged vessel can be raised, but the question to be considered is whether the cost will be practical or not[114]." At the time, lying parallel to the beach, the *Isis* was buried in 10-15 feet of sand with only her masts showing above the water's surface. A series of electrically operated discs were to burrow under the vessel pulling chains behind them. The chains were connected to pontoons in order to then float the ship. Apparently, the salvage attempt was unsuccessful, and the once elegant steamer was left in the surf. Due to the wreck's location in the surf zone, the *Isis* is not a viable dive site.

ISLAND CITY

The wooden-hulled trawler *Island City* was built as hull number 176 by DESCO Marine, Incorporated at their St. Augustine shipyard in 1950. On December 24, 1971, the 67-foot long fishing vessel foundered north of Fowey Rocks Light. The *Island City* was also reported lost in Biscayne Bay, 20 miles south of Miami; crewman Juan Caruso drowned in the sinking.

ISLANDER

According to an April 23, 1955, article by historians John Wilson Somerville and Ella Teague de Berard in *The Palm Beach Post*, the sidewheel steamer tug *Islander* burned at Hogan's Creek near Jacksonville around 1889.

J. E. STEVENS

The steamer *J.E. Stevens* (also cited as the *James E. Stevens*) burned at her wharf at Mayport on July 26, 1894. The steamboat had operated for the Jacksonville-Green Cove Springs Line and was valued at $10,000, with only partial insurance. The cause of the fire was unknown.

J.H. LANE

The *J.H. Lane* was a 372-ton brig built in April 1869 by B.F. Carver at Searspoint, Maine. Owned by J.H. Lane, the brig was 134 feet long and 31 feet wide. In April 1886, the *Lane* wrecked off Jupiter in a gale while en route from Cuba for Philadelphia, Pennsylvania, with a cargo of molasses. The square-rigged vessel dropped its anchors offshore in an attempt to ride out the storm, but at 1:30 a.m., on April 19, the cables parted, and the brig was pushed ashore. By daylight, people on shore observed several men clinging desperately to the wreckage, while large waves crashed over the ship.

Illustration of the brig *J.H. Lane* (Mark Mondano Collection).

Captain Alonzo Shute managed to launch a small boat with the entire crew aboard; however, it was pushed under the stern of the wrecked *J.H. Lane* and capsized by a spilling wave. The crew held on to ropes and the side of the lifeboat as they slowly moved toward shore. A keeper from the Gilbert's Bar Life-Saving Station tied a rope around his waist and worked his way out to the exhausted men. One by one they were helped to shore, with the exception of the steward who disappeared in the surf. Throughout the remainder of the day, the brig was steadily broken up by the pounding surf. Approximately 400 casks of molasses were salvaged, but the wreck was a total loss.

J.W. PHILBRICK

The *J.W. Philbrick* reportedly burned February 14, 1873, at Jacksonville. Additional details on this vessel are unknown.

JACK PILAFIAN

The *Jack Pilafian* (commonly, and erroneously, called the *Jack Falafian*), named after a past president of the Tropical Anglers Club who passed away in December 1994, is an 80-foot long steel tugboat sunk as an artificial reef in 150 feet of water off Key Biscayne on April 3, 1998. The tug is upright and intact, and it's possible to navigate the interior from bow to stern. While small, the *Jack Pilafian* is an attractive wreck.

JACKIE B.

The 99-ton shrimp trawler *Jackie B.*, 67 feet in length, was launched in 1948 as hull number 98 at the St. Augustine shipyard of the Diesel Engine Sales Company. On November 8, 1960, the shrimper foundered approximately 20 miles off Mayport.

JACKIE FAYE

According to Singer (1998), the 20-ton steel-hulled vessel *Jackie Faye*, which was built in 1947, foundered two miles offshore the Florida coast, approximately five miles north of Melbourne, on April 5, 1952.

JACKSONVILLE DRY DOCK

The "Jacksonville Dry Dock" was built in 1944 by the Chicago Bridge and Iron Company of Seneca, Illinois, as the U.S. Navy yard floating dry dock *YFD-65*. The dry dock, later redesignated as medium auxiliary floating dry dock *AFDM-9*, was 622 feet in length, 124 feet in breadth, 57 feet in height, and had a displacement of 8,000 tons and a lifting capacity of 18,000 tons. Following the end of World War II, and with little need of the dry dock by the U.S. Navy, the structure was leased to a Jacksonville shipyard. The lease agreement required the return of the dry dock to Norfolk, Virginia, at the end of the lease period. Due to her age, *AFDM-9* would have required an extensive and expensive overhaul to make her seaworthy. On December 31, 1987, the dry dock was stricken from the Naval Register. Concurrently, the Jacksonville Offshore Sport Fishing Club worked to acquire the vessel for use as an artificial reef.

Photograph of a submarine in the dry dock *AFDM-10* (U.S. Navy).

On September 13, 1989, *AFDM-9* was escorted out of the St. Johns River by attending tugs, which proceeded to tow her 45 miles southeast of Jacksonville. This location placed the dry dock approximately equidistant between Jacksonville and St. Augustine. Once on site, the dry dock's seacocks were opened and the massive structure sunk 120 feet to the bottom of the Atlantic. Unfortunately, the influence of several hurricanes in following years collapsed the wing walls of the dry dock, and she now rises only 15 feet off the sea floor. While the dry dock may not be as visually impressive as she would be fully intact, the collapse actually increased the amount of benthic structure to serve as habitat for marine organisms. The wreck of *AFDM-9* is a popular diving and fishing destination. Due to its proximity to deeper water, it is not uncommon to encounter wahoo, kingfish, tuna, billfish, and other large pelagic species over the dry dock.

JACQUELINE A.

On August 10, 1986, the 60-year-old, 103-foot long wooden-hulled *Jacqueline A.* was dashed against the rocks of North Hutchinson Island, littering Vero Beach with teak, oak, and mahogany for almost two miles. The *Jacqueline A.* was en route from Port Canaveral to Miami, where its owner, Kelly Fairbanks, planned to restore it. Unfortunately, as Fairbanks and a mate worked below decks to unclog a bilge pump around 5:00 a.m., an inexperienced deckhand ran the ship aground. The stranded ship was promptly pounded to pieces. Newspaper accounts stated Fairbanks was planning to salvage the ship's two engines, generator, and some of the brass fittings.

JADE BEACH WRECK

The "Jade Beach Wreck" is an unidentified wreck located in shallow water off Pompano Beach just north of the *Copenhagen*. Bronze spikes, including one stamped "BIRMINGHAM," and copper-sheathed hull planking were uncovered, and an old *Skin Diver* magazine article reportedly cited this wreck as a British vessel lost around 1815, though the basis for that conclusion is unknown.

JALI

On July 21, 1985, the 76-foot long luxury yacht *Jali* departed Naples for Rhode Island. Just days before, the 123-ton yacht was donated to the University of Rhode Island by Dewey Gargiulo, owner of Naples Tomato Growers. In the early morning hours of July 23, a fire broke out on the yacht, forcing the crew of four to hastily abandon ship 15 miles off Miami. "If you can imagine – the boat burning behind you and the flames at your fanny – and jumping into the water in the dark and all," said Kenneth Munroe, trustee of the University of Rhode Island Foundation, the university's fund-raising arm[115]. Reports stated the fire appeared to originate in the stack area, where the exhaust is channeled from the engine room through the decks. The four men boarded a lift raft and fired a signal flare just after 3:00 a.m., to attract the attention of the sportfishing boat *El Tity*, which rescued the group. The *Jali* burned furiously and then sunk off Government Cut.

JAMES

The ship *James* wrecked approximately 50 miles north of Cape Florida on March 27, 1836, en route from Mobile, Alabama, for Cowes, England, with a cargo of 1,081 bales of cotton. The subsequent salvage of the ship *James* was detailed by Dodd (1944), which is paraphrased here:

> The schooner *Hester Ann*, John H. Geiger, master, and the schooner *Caroline*, John Wood, master, were in Key West when they heard of the wreck of the ship *James* north of Cape Florida in 1836. They sailed at once, but ran out into the Gulf to inform the schooner *Amelia*, James Andrews, master. The *Amelia*, in turn, informed the fourth member of the consortship, the schooner *Splendid*, Richard Roberts, master. When the four schooners arrived at the wreck, their combined crews cooperated in loading them, all four vessels staying on the scene until the last had a full load. In 16 hours the 38 members of the crews, assisted by eight men hired from the *James*' crew, broke out, transshipped, and restowed 519 bales of cotton. For their services the four wreckers were awarded $12,313.55, which was 40 percent on the cargo saved. The salvage was distributed under the standing rule in such cases, "ton for ton, and man for man according to tonnage." The *James* went ashore March 27, word of the wreck reached Key West April 3, libel proceedings were instituted April 19, and Oliver H. Jones, special agent for the underwriters, intervened in the suit on May 19, to prevent unnecessary sale of part of the cargo. Incidentally, while in Key West, Jones heard that there had been a collusive agreement between the master of the *James* and the masters of 4 of the 12 vessels that wrecked the ship. The four masters had agreed to pay $2,500 for the exclusive privilege of wrecking the *James*. The agent tracked one of them to his home on Long Island, and secured an affidavit which resulted in the forfeiture of the salvage awarded to the guilty wreckers.

JAMES BOATWRIGHT

The *James Boatwright* was a steamer built in 1835 at New York. In 1837, the steamer was in the employ of the U.S. government under charter at a rate of $4,000 per month. While in the government service, the *James Boatwright* was lost near Indian River Inlet (present day

Fort Pierce Inlet) on April 22, 1838. A claim was filed for her loss, "alleged to have sunk from injuries inflicted by worms in Florida waters," though contradictory statements indicate she sunk due to damage sustained while crossing the bar and to negligence. A report on her loss was included in the First Session of the 26th Congress, U.S. Senate, extracts of which follow:

> Departed Charleston, South Carolina, on January 14, 1838, under the command of Captain B.W. Donnell. Arrived at the mouth of the Indian River, near Fort Pierce. At the mouth of this river was a bar, which, according to the testimony of Captain Donnell, "was passable only at spring tides, or twice a month," and the service required of the *James Boatwright* was to tow vessels in and out of the inlet when there was sufficient depth of water over the bar to permit their passing it. The rest of the time she lay at anchor at the usual anchorage around at the mouth of the Indian River, when the worms are exceedingly destructive to wooden bottomed vessels. After being about two months at this place, Captain Donnell states, that he became anxious for the safety of the boat, on account of the worms, and requested of Lieutenant Hooker permission to return with her to Charleston to overhaul her and repair damages. But that, in answer to his representation of the condition of the boat, and his request to return to Charleston Lieutenant Hooker replied "that he was very willing to allow me (Captain Donnell) to go, but as there was no other steamboat, he could not spare mine until another came in to relieve me, as he could not do without one." This was about the 1st of April. Soon afterward, upon repeating the request, and expressing his increasing fears for the safety of the boat, Captain Donnell had permission to go to Charleston with some Indian prisoners, and Monday the 28d of April was the time appointed for his leaving the river on his return. On Sunday morning, the 22d of April, Captain Donnell towed a vessel over the bar, and, after casting her off discovered the buoy of an anchor which had been lost by some vessel. He stopped to take it up, which detained him a short time, and, in returning over the bar, the boat touched the bottom, although he states "the rub was not heavy enough to do any injury, nor did any manifest itself." He got back to anchor at seven o'clock in the morning, and during the day had the boat scraped. He further states that, about one o'clock on Monday morning, a leak was discovered, which increased rapidly, and nonwithstanding every effort to arrest it by the crew and fifty men sent from the fort, it continued to increase, and about twelve o'clock meridian, on Monday, she sunk. He also says he has "no doubt that she was lost by reason of the injury from worms[116]."

Lieutenant Hooker responded to Captain Donnell's account:

> The boat was ordered to leave Indian River for St. Augustine, Florida, 23d of April, where she was to report to the quartermaster. On Sunday, the 22d of April, she towed a vessel over the bar of the river safely, but, instead of returning immediately, as she should have done, and as she was ordered, she remained at sea fishing for anchors, for the personal profit, I have no doubt, of Captain Donnell, who was in command of her. While in this employment, the tide ebbed so much that the boat could not recross the bar without collision. She struck. My pilot, (Mr. Amow) who was on board the boat at the time of striking, assured me that the blow was a severe one, and that it unquestionably occasioned her loss, by wrenching a plank from her bottom. The opinion of my pilot is entitled to great weight, for he had been a number of years in the service and on that coast[117].

Other circumstances attending the loss of the *James Boatwright* seem to confirm both Lieutenant Hooker's and Mr. Amow's statements: "The boat was discovered to be in a sinking condition about 10 o'clock P.M., on the 22d April; and such was the rapidity with which the water entered her hold, that forty men, with pumps, buckets, and barrels, could not prevent her going to the bottom. Large fish were also seen in her hold, which we would scarcely expect to find had the leakage been caused by worms. The plank wrenched from the bottom of the boat must have been under her machinery, as the opening through which the water entered could not be found[118]."

While the *James Boatwright* settled on the bottom, the steamer's engine was soon saved from the wreck. The crippled hull of the *Boatwright* was apparently left to rot where she originally sank. It is unclear if the derelict hulk was later removed or if traces of the steamer *James Boatwright* may still remain hidden on the bottom near Fort Pierce. A suspect site for the *James Boatwright*, however, may be located adjacent to Mangrove Island, opposite of Cook Point along North Beach Causeway Drive in Fort Pierce. Reportedly, a wreck site (SL00023) was discovered when a dredge impacted wooden timbers and ballast while moving fill material for a bridge around 1967.

JAMES JUDGE

The four-masted schooner *James Judge*, built in 1890 at Wilmington, Delaware, by Jackson and Sharp Company, was 159 feet long, 36 feet wide, and displaced 680 tons. On October 16, 1904, the *James Judge* went ashore four miles south of Palm Beach during a storm while en route from Cardenas, Cuba, for Jacksonville. A total loss, the schooner was sold at a beach auction to Miami wreckers. A June 24, 1905, *Florida Times-Union* article mentioned the hulk of the *James Judge* would be floated and removed; at the time of the article it was buried in the sand where she was beached the year before. The *James Judge* was eventually abandoned, though locals utilized the hulk as a fishing pier for several years.

JANE

According to Volume 22 of *The Sailor's Magazine and Naval Journal*, the "British ship *Jane*, from Liverpool for Savannah, was cast away on Cumberland Island, November 1, 1849."

JANE M. HARWOOD

Built in 1864 at Bowdoinham, Maine, the 597-ton bark *Jane M. Harwood* (also cited as *J.M. Harwood* and *Jane M. Harward*) was 140 feet long and 30 feet wide. Homeported in Bath, Maine, the vessel was owned by John Harwood. Information in Admiralty Court records mention that on October 31, 1865, wrecker Richard Roberts boarded a vessel lying ashore about twelve and a half miles north of Cape Florida, and was informed she was the American bark *Jane M. Harward* [sic], bound from New Orleans for Havre with a cargo of cotton. She was stranded on the beach and dismasted with her bow pointing northwest.

JANE ROSS

The British barque *Jane Ross*, Captain Henry Middleton, was found on Hillsboro Reef on December 5, 1867, about 45 miles north of Cape Florida. The barque was bound from Cardenas, Cuba, to New York with a cargo of sugar, molasses, and asphalt, in hogsheads. Wreckers at once tried the pumps but after two hours it was learned that the barque's keel was lost. Soundings showed 11 feet of water forward and about 20 feet astern. The vessel's rigging and spars were cut away, and some of the cargo was saved, but due to the perishable state of some of the cargo (i.e., already wet), as well as toxic fumes in the holds, much of it was abandoned.

The *Jane Ross* was built in April 1861 at Pictou, Nova Scotia. The 250-ton vessel was 108.8 feet long and 24.3 feet wide. While Admiralty records indicate the *Jane Ross* was a total loss, for some reason the vessel reappears in documentation in 1871 after a three-year absence, finally disappearing from the books in 1873. It is worth noting that the last survey was conducted in New York in 1865, so it's possible an attempt to repair her was made at some point after her wrecking, or the vessel's later inclusion in the *Record of American and Foreign Shipping* was erroneous.

JANET

On March 26, 1895, the sloop *Janet*, of Fort Pierce, attempted to cross the bar at Jupiter Inlet in heavy surf conditions. The first sea that struck the sloop completely filled her, carried away her head gear, and washed away her cabin. The next one pushed her on top of her towed dinghy and smashed it. The *Janet* was eventually beached with the assistance of the local life-saving crew, who then hauled the vessel above the high tide line on skids and rollers. Unfortunately, the sloop was damaged beyond repair, so the owner sold the wrecked vessel for five dollars where she lay.

JARLINGTON

According to Singer (1998), on September 15, 1882, the 17-ton schooner *Jarlington*, Captain Moore, capsized on the St. Johns River off Fruit Cove while sailing from Jacksonville for Fruit Cove. See entry for schooner *Heather Barker*.

JAXSHIPCO NO. 4

The *Jaxshipco No. 4*, official number 167820, was a 75-ton steel barge built in 1920 at Jacksonville, which foundered off Miami on April 1, 1920.

JAY DORMAN

The schooner yacht known as the *Jay Dorman* was originally built as the *Panda* in 1938 by Camper and Nicholsons, a company established in 1863, but with shipbuilding roots extending back to 1782. Reportedly, the 130-foot long yacht was given to Vietnamese Emperor Bao Dai by the French government sometime after World War II in an attempt to appease the puppet leader. After a later career as a charter boat operating out of Antigua, the aging yacht was appropriated by the Broward County Artificial Reef Program and sunk in 80 feet of water on February 28, 1988. The reef was named after 23-year old Jay Dorman, who, in May 1987, was killed along with Randy Barber by a lightning strike after the pair sought shelter under a tree

Bow of the *Jay Dorman*.

The broken off stern section of the *Jay Dorman*.

during a storm on a Fort Lauderdale golf course. The *Jay Dorman* is part of a small cluster of other vessels sunk as artificial reefs, which can be visited on the same dive, including the *Qualmann Tugs* (two 32-foot long pusher tugs donated by Ray Qualmann Marine Construction) and the *Alpha*. Due to Hurricane Andrew, all of these wrecks have deteriorated considerably, but still offer a pleasant diving experience.

JAY SCUTTI

On December 29, 1960, the 140-ton tug *Arikok* was launched by Jonker and Stans from their shipyard at Hendrik-Ido-Ambacht, Netherlands. She was built for the Aruba Ports Authority to serve as a harbor tug at Oranjestad. Later, she was sold to the Meta Corporation of the Netherlands Antilles and Aruba. On November 18, 1984, the U.S.C.G.C. *Cherokee* seized the 95-foot long *Arikok* 30 miles north of Grand Bahama Bank with 15 tons of marijuana on board. The forfeited vessel was bought at public auction for $14,000 by Fort Lauderdale businessman Dale Scutti, who wished to sink the tug off his beachfront home to serve as an artificial reef in memory of his son, Jay Scutti, who was an avid diver. On September 19, 1986, after an initial failed attempt, the Broward County Sheriff Department's bomb squad successfully detonated 45 pounds of dynamite, which sent the rusting tugboat to the bottom, 70 feet under the surface. The *Jay Scutti*, its bow pointing northward and listing to port, now rests amidst a cluster of other wrecks that can be explored on the same dive. They include the remains of the 45-foot long sloop *Moonshot* (formerly the *Sanctuary*) and the 95-foot long sailboat *Pride* (also known as the *Harbour Towne*) just to the south of the *Jay Scutti*, and to the north divers will encounter the 40-foot long hull of the sailboat *B.H. Lake*, the 132-foot long offshore supply vessel *Ken Vitale* (formerly the *Tracy*), and the 90-foot long Belizean freighter *Merci Jesus*.

JEFFERSON

Volume 22 (1849) of *The Sailor's Magazine and Naval Journal* reports, "Brig *Jefferson*, hence for St. Marys, Georgia, was wrecked on Amelia Island, July 4."

JEFFERSON DAVIS

By the time the Confederate privateer *Jefferson Davis* came to grief on a sandbar off St. Augustine on August 18, 1861, she had become well known and feared by vessels conducting commerce with the Union. While she effectively operated as a privateer for only a short duration, the *Jefferson Davis* and Captain Louis M. Coxetter would not only successfully capture nine ships in seven weeks, but would also test the legal boundaries of naval warfare.

The 187-ton brig, armed with five antique British cannons, was described as having black mastheads and yards, and a black hull, as well as being very rusty. The *Jefferson Davis* originated as a much different vessel upon her completion as the *Putnam* in 1845. Built in a Baltimore, Maryland shipyard, the *Putnam* was framed out of oak as a single-deck, fully-rigged brig that was soon employed in the profitable slave trade under the name *Echo*. Captured off Cuba with 271 slaves on August 21, 1858, by Lt. John Newland Maffitt of the U.S.S. *Dolphin*, the *Echo* was forfeited to the government of the United States. Auctioned under her original name *Putnam* in January 1859, she was bought by Captain J. Robert Hunter of Charleston, South Carolina. With the onset of the Civil War, Captain Hunter and the other shareholders applied for a letter of marque. The application also proposed a name change to *Rattlesnake*; however, on May 23 the State Department opted for the *Putnam* to be renamed as the *Jefferson Davis*, in honor of the President of the Confederate States of America. The brig was commissioned as a privateer on June 18, 1861, at Charleston.

A privateer is an armed merchant ship commissioned by a national government of a belligerent country (in this case, the Confederate States of America) to interdict and capture enemy merchant vessels on the high seas. The legal course normally followed by a government is to issue a "letter of marque" to the would-be privateer legitimizing what would normally be considered piracy. The motivation for the national government to follow this quasi-legal process was the ability to deploy a low-cost naval force quickly that would be capable of attacking and

Sinking of the tug *Jay Scutti* (Broward County Artificial Reef Program).

destroying the merchant fleet of an enemy. The Confederacy had no navy, few shipyards, no real skill in shipping or shipbuilding, and no industrial capacity to support the construction of a naval fleet. With no established naval tradition, the Confederacy looked for new and innovative means, such as the employment of privateers, to fight off the overwhelming Union Navy.

Privateering was an aspect of Confederate naval strategy where armed private vessels holding a government commission (i.e., letter of marque) were utilized to capture or destroy Union ships of commerce. One goal of the program was to help destroy the blockade by forcing the Union Navy to draw more and more ships off the blockade line to chase privateers. The reduction in the effectiveness of the blockade would, in turn, help insure that supply lines would stay open. The second goal of the letters of marque was a more traditional one – the procurement of supplies and war material. Although the process of developing a privateering fleet was commenced via presidential proclamation in April 1861, Confederacy President Davis wanted to insure that the rules of law were followed. Accordingly, he issued no letters of marque until the Confederate Congress passed proper legislation authorizing the action. *An Act Recognizing the Existence of War Between the United States and the Confederate States and Concerning Letters of Marque, Prizes, and Prize Goods* was passed by the Confederate Congress on May 6, 1861, and subsequently approved by President Davis.

On June 28, 1861, the *Jefferson Davis* left Charleston Harbor to the cheers of supporters and well-wishers. On July 1, the *Enchantress* departed Boston bound for Cuba with a mixed cargo. On July 6 the *Jefferson Davis* captured her as a prize of war. William W. Smith, a Savannah pilot, was put on board the *Enchantress* with a crew of four and ordered to take the vessel to a Confederate port. On July 22 off Hatteras, North Carolina, the *Enchantress* was recaptured by the U.S.S. *Albatross* and taken to the Navy Yard in Philadelphia. Here Smith and his crew were arrested by Deputy United States Marshall Thomas B. Patterson and taken to Moyamensing Prison on August 2. On October 22, 1861, in the United States Circuit Court in Pennsylvania, Smith was tried for piracy. During Smith's trial, his legal defense introduced the Constitution of the Confederate States of America, as well as the Confederate Act authorizing the President to issue letters of marque. Not convinced by the argument that William Smith was engaged in a legal act of war, the jury found Smith guilty on October 25 and condemned him to death.

Summarily, on November 9, Confederate Secretary of War J. P. Benjamin directed that the highest ranking Union prisoner of war confined in Richmond would be held for execution in the same manner as adopted by the United States for the execution of "prisoner of war" William Smith. An additional 13 Union prisoners of high rank were subsequently directed held as long as other Confederate sailors were slated for trial as pirates. Among this latter group was the grandson of Paul Revere, who had been captured at Bull Run. As a result, the presiding judge of the United States Court in Philadelphia overruled the verdict of the Smith trial, stating in part that Confederate sailors could not be treated any differently than Confederate soldiers. With that action he refused to try any more privacy cases. On February 15, 1862, Smith and all other prisoners were transferred to the custody of the United States Secretary of War as prisoners of war. Between this action and that of President Abraham Lincoln in the declaring of a blockade of the Southern ports, rather than simply declaring the ports closed, the United States was forced to grant to the Confederacy the rights of a belligerent despite its claim that the southern states were an organized mob and insurrectionists. As members of the armed forces of a belligerent, the crews of captured privateers were entitled to be treated as prisoners of war.

The *Jefferson Davis* arrived off St. Augustine on August 16 but had to wait offshore nearly two days due to rough weather. Upon her approach to St. Augustine Inlet, she grounded on one of the treacherous shoals. She attempted to work herself free, pitching over her armament in an attempt to lighten the vessel. Unfortunately, she was hard aground, and all attempts to free her were unsuccessful. The crew salvaged what they could before abandoning the privateer, rowing into St. Augustine with church bells ringing out a hero's welcome. Over the years, the *Jefferson Davis* has been slowly entombed in the same sand shoals that led to her demise. Her location is presently unknown, but undoubtedly she remains in shallow water just offshore St. Augustine Inlet.

JEMINS

According to the *Public Advertiser* of March 17, 1767, the *Jemins* (also cited as *Jemima*), Captain Hastings, en route from Rhode Island to Pensacola, wrecked on Cape Florida, resulting in the loss of both the vessel and cargo.

Archival image of the ship *Jennie Hight* (Bangor Public Library).

JENNIE HIGHT

The 1,116-ton ship *Jennie Hight* was launched on November 6, 1865, from John T. Tewksbury's shipyard in

Brewer, Maine, for Captain J.K. Nickerson. In January 1866, while on her maiden voyage from Bangor to New Orleans, the *Jennie Hight* was lost on the Florida coast. A newspaper advertisement offered her salvaged sails, standing and running rigging, hawsers, chains and anchors, blocks, capstans, and steering gear, which were listed as "just as good as new, having been in use only 18 days."

JENNIFER

The 60-foot long yacht *Jennifer*, owned by Kenneth Parker, chairman of Parker Pen Company, went down approximately 25 miles off Pompano Beach on April 22, 1957, after apparently striking a submerged object. The captain and two others onboard the yacht, which was en route to the Bahamas, were rescued by the freighter *Holstein*.

JENNY G.

On December 11, 1990, the dredge *Jenny G.* was sunk approximately three miles east of Jupiter Inlet to serve as an artificial reef. The dredge, 55 feet long and 45 feet wide, had been abandoned along the Indian River near Stuart. As the derelict was leaking oil and damaging sea grass habitat, the dredge was removed, cleaned, and sunk at a cost of $15,500. Concrete culverts were loaded into the vessel's hold to enhance the artificial habitat. The *Jenny G*, also known as the *Miss Jenny*, now rests upside down in approximately 90 feet of water roughly 250 feet southeast of the *Esso Bonaire III* and 200 feet north of the *Zion Train*.

JEREMIAH LEAMING

According to *The Sailor's Magazine and Naval Journal*, Volume 33, the *Jeremiah Leaming* was a "131-ton schooner of New York, reported burned at Jacksonville December 1860, valued at $7,000."

JESSIE A. BISHOP

Originally built for the Benedict-Manson Marine Company of New Haven, Connecticut, the *Jessie A. Bishop*, official number 205405, was launched at the Rockland, Maine, shipyard of the Cobb Butler Company on July 16, 1908. The 754-ton, four-masted schooner was 188.9 feet long and 38 feet wide, and mastered by Captain Caleb A. Haskell. On January 1, 1912, the *Jessie A. Bishop* stranded at Nassau Inlet, on the south end of Amelia Island.

JESSIE B. SMITH

The *Jessie B. Smith* was a schooner built in April 1865 at Hartford, Connecticut. The 322-ton vessel was 110 feet in length and 28 feet in beam. The schooner departed Jamaica on August 24, 1878, en route to New York with a cargo of logwood. When off the northeast coast of Florida, the *Jessie B. Smith* encountered a hurricane that eventually left her stranded on the beach near Mayport. On September 10, she was driven to the St. Johns Bar after enduring five days of heavy weather. When she approached the breakers, she let go both her anchors, but she was steadily driven ashore five miles south of the St. Johns Bar at daybreak on September 11[119].

JESULA II

Early on the morning of March 28, 1991, the 177-foot, 498-ton Honduran freighter *Jesula II* caught fire southeast of Elliott Key. The vessel had just departed Miami carrying a general cargo including rice, flour, sugar, clothing, bicycles, and several automobiles, and was bound for Gonaives, Haiti. After the U.S.C.G.C. *Chandeleur* fought the fire in vain for almost 12 hours, the smoldering vessel was eventually towed past the 100-fathom contour, where the U.S.C.G.C. *Dauntless* fired several shots into the charred hulk to scuttle it in 650 feet of water at reported latitude 27° 47.4' north and longitude 80° 03' west (also reported as latitude 27° 47.65' north and longitude 79° 01.63' west).

JESUS MARIA

According to Roger Smith (in Bass, 1996), the *Jesus Maria* was a Spanish vessel participating in the salvage of the ill-fated 1715 fleet on the Florida coast when it rolled over and sank in 1716. Based on the discovery of a bundle of five cannon lashed muzzle-to-breech, he speculates the final resting spot of the *Jesus Maria* may be located at a site known as the "Riomar Wreck." While this theory is worthy of further scrutiny, it should be noted that many believe the "Riomar Wreck" represents the grave of the *Nuestra Señora del Carmen y San Antonio*. I have been unable to find any additional the purported loss in 1716 of a vessel named *Jesus Maria*.

JIM ATRIA

Launched on February 22, 1961 at the Groningen, Netherlands, shipyard of builder *Noord Nederlandse*, the *Jim Atria* was originally known as the *Poinciana*. Owned by *Stoomboot Maatschappij Hillegersberg*, the 498-ton freighter was 226.6 feet in length, 33.7 feet in breadth, and was powered by an eight-cylinder *Stork Werkspoor* diesel engine. In 1966, ownership was changed to associate company *Stoomboot Maatschappij Oostzee-Willemstad*. Finally, in 1972, she was owned by the Poinciana Trading Company, Limited, of the Cayman Islands, which employed her on runs throughout the Caribbean. On September 21, 1982, the *Poinciana* was pulled away from her berth on the Miami River in preparation for her departure to Haiti and the Dominican Republic. Almost immediately, she took on a severe starboard list. After several hours, the *Poinciana* sunk to the mud bottom of the Miami River, coming to rest on a 69,000-volt power line that served the South Beach area of Miami Beach. Apparently, due to a mistake in converting kilograms to pounds, the freighter was overloaded with 300 tons of cargo, more than 160 tons beyond the vessel's rating of 139 tons. After four days of blocking the busy Miami River, the freighter was offloaded and successfully refloated. She was eventually abandoned at Miami by her owners as repair costs and legal fees mounted. She sat rusting at her berth for five years before being acquired by the Broward County Artificial Reef Program. Fort Lauderdale

Jim Atria as the freighter *Poinciana* (William A. Schell).

developer and avid diver Jim Atria donated $10,000 to help sink the freighter, which was later named after him in appreciation of his financial assistance. In late August 1987, the freighter was towed to Port Everglades for final preparations before finally being sunk as an artificial reef on September 23, 1987, almost on the exact five-year anniversary of her earlier sinking in the Miami River. The *Jim Atria* originally came to rest on her port side in just over 110 feet of water. Six years later, Hurricane Andrew's storm surge righted the vessel and moved it offshore, where she is now found in 135 feet of water. Heavily encrusted with a thick garb of gorgonians and orange cup coral, the *Jim Atria* is a fantastic dive and one of the larger intact recreational-depth wrecks off Fort Lauderdale.

Sinking of the *Jim Atria* (Broward County Artificial Reef Program).

JOAN AND URSULA

The 60-ton fishing vessel *Joan and Ursula*, built in 1937, was homeported in New Bedford, Massachusetts, and owned by brothers Ernest R. and Ernest M. Murley. The trawler had a long career fishing off New England, which included a few unfortunate incidents. On December 21, 1946, the *Joan and Ursula* went aground near Cuttyhunk, but was pulled free several days later without incident. The dragger was later involved in a collision with the fishing vessel *Pilgrim* approximately 25 miles southeast of Martha's Vineyard on August 17, 1966, which tore a hole in her hull near the waterline. While she weathered these ordeals, the *Joan and Ursula* ultimately foundered 10 miles south of St. Augustine on August 5, 1972.

JOHN HOWARD

A January 9 dispatch from New Smyrna published in *The New York Times* on January 20, 1859, stated, "The schr. *Jno. Howard* (or *Harwood*), of Harwich, Mass., from Boston for this port, struck on the bar, filled, and will be a total loss." A later statement that appeared in *The New York Times* on February 2, 1859, however, indicated the schooner *John Howard* was lost on the St. Johns Bar. This may possibly be the 274-ton clipper schooner *John Howard*, launched in 1855 at East Greenwich, Captain Baker.

JOHN H. TINGUE

The luxurious three-masted schooner *John H. Tingue*, official number 76525, was built at a cost of $36,000 in September 1884 at Fairhaven, Connecticut, by H.H. Hanscom. The 553-ton vessel was 151 feet long, 35 feet wide. On October 5, 1899, the *John H. Tingue* was en route from Philadelphia to Jacksonville with a cargo of 699 tons of coal when she encountered an intense storm that resulted in the schooner wrecking on the beach at Cumberland Island.

JOHN MCLEAN

The *John McLean*, a 133-ton sidewheel steamer, 122.7 feet long, 22.2 feet wide, was built in 1837 at Charleston, South Carolina. In November 1838, the *John McLean*, under charter of the U.S. Army, was carrying Captain Harvey

Brown and a detail of soldiers to an outpost at New Smyrna to bolster the military presence in the region during the Second Seminole War. On November 15, 1838, she became stranded on the bar at the entrance to Mosquito Inlet. Around sunset the tide and breakers pushed her ashore. The steamer was a total loss, along with the cargo of ammunition and muskets, although all on board made land safely. The *Santee* later rescued Captain A.S. Adams and the stranded crew and troops, and took them to St. Augustine, arriving there on November 18, 1838. Some of the machinery from the *John McLean* was also salvaged and brought to St. Augustine by the *Santee*.

JOHN R. WILDER

The small, 34-ton schooner *John R. Wilder*, built in 1854 at Savannah, Georgia, to serve as a local pilot boat, was 62 feet in length and 16 feet in breadth. During the Civil War, the *Wilder* was put to work running the blockade between Savannah and the Bahamas. Later, she was burned and scuttled at Savannah to prevent her capture by Union forces. In 1867, the schooner was raised, rebuilt, and relaunched by her original builder. On October 6, 1899, the *John R. Wilder* sank at Fernandina during a hurricane.

JOHN WAYNE

According to Singer (1998), the fishing vessel *John Wayne*, built in 1944, wrecked on the beach seven miles south of Ponte Vedra Beach on January 7, 1965. This is most likely the shrimp trawler *John Wayne*, which is also mentioned in the entry for the *Sea Farer*.

JOHN WESLEY

On November 3, 1865, salvor Joseph Lowe boarded the American bark *John Wesley*, which was filled with water and stranded on the beach 21 miles north of Cape Florida. She was bound from New Orleans to Liverpool with a cargo of 1,460 bales of cotton when she was run aground during a hurricane around October 23. The 521-ton *John Wesley* was built in 1852 at Searsport, Maine. Originally owned by R.P. Buck and Company, she was 128 feet in length, 30 feet in beam, and 15 feet in depth of hold.

Painting of the bark *John Wesley*.

JOLLY TAR

According to the December 10, 1796, issue of *The Star*, "The brig *Jolly Tar*, Captain Brayman, was stranded on or about the first of September, on the coast of Florida; she was bound from Jamaica for Norfolk, Virginia; her cargo, rigging, sails, and crew saved."

JOSEPH AND JANE

The *Joseph and Jane*, Captain Lane, from South Carolina for Antigua, was lost near Cape Florida in late 1747 or early 1748[120].

JOSEPH B. THOMAS

The four-masted schooner *Joseph B. Thomas*, official number 77447, was built in 1900 by Washburn Brothers at Thomaston, Maine. She was 220 feet long, 42.3 feet wide, and displaced 1,564 tons. On March 21, 1909, the four-master stranded "just below" Fowey Rocks Light en route from Baltimore, Maryland, to Key West with a cargo of 2,500 tons of gravel for the Overseas Railroad.

George Detrio believes a wreck off Brewster Reef locally called the "Chain Wreck" or "Bell Wreck" may be the remains of the *Joseph B. Thomas*. This wreck, named after the recovery of a large bronze bell in 1982, rests in approximately 60-70 feet of water to the south of Fowey Rocks Light. The site is dominated by two boilers, a large anchor, and copious amounts of gravel on the seabed.

Launching of the four-masted schooner *Joseph B. Thomas* (Thomaston Historical Society).

While the presence of two boilers is odd for a sailing vessel, the abundance of gravel can't be ignored. Gene Shinn also recalled a site he dived in the 1950s near Fowey Rocks that consisted of a large quantity of pea-sized rocks, which may be consistent with the cargo carried by the *Joseph B. Thomas*. It is unclear, however, if Shinn was diving the original grounding site in shallow water near Fowey Rocks, the actual "Bell Wreck" in deeper water, or an entirely different wreck altogether. Regardless, further investigation of the "Chain Wreck" or "Bell Wreck" site is definitely warranted.

JOSEPH CROWELL

Volume 14 of *The Sailor's Magazine and Naval Journal* printed that the "U.S. transport schooner *Joseph Crowell*, Goodwin, went ashore October 2 (1841), about 25 miles to the northward of Fort Pierce, Indian River. The vessel and cargo an entire loss." Other newspaper articles cited the vessel's name as *Jo. Croswell*.

JOSEPH MEIGS

The *Joseph Meigs* was originally a 338-ton whaling ship built in 1842 at Mattapoisett, Massachusetts. After several successful years hunting whales, she was destroyed by fire at Mattapoisett Harbor on June 27, 1846. With 1,000 barrels of whale oil on board, she burned throughout the night in a "brilliant spectacle." Charred to the water's edge, she was towed ashore where her upper works were rebuilt and she was relaunched in 1847. Her 1863 documentation cited a 103.5 foot length, a 27.8 foot beam, and a displacement of 354 gross tons.

According to Admiralty records, Beto Gonzales of the wrecking sloop *Julia Nathan* spotted the stranded *Joseph Meigs* at daylight on July 14, 1863; the *Meigs* had wrecked near Fowey Rocks at 3:30 a.m. that morning. At the time of the grounding, Captain Levi Baker was guiding the *Joseph Meigs* from Boston to New Orleans with a cargo of government stores consisting of hay, ice, lumber, rice, coffee, and sheet iron. On July 18, 1863, the gunboat *Sagamore* went to the assistance of the *Meigs*, ashore on the reef and a total wreck near "beacon letter P." Reportedly, she was situated in about 12 feet of water on the eastern side of the reef. Based on the $5,751.33 value of salvaged cargo and material, salvors were awarded $1,725.40 (30 percent).

JOSEPHINE

The schooner *Josephine* stranded at Mosquito Inlet on March 30, 1850, at the conclusion of her voyage from Charleston, South Carolina, to New Smyrna. An extract of a letter received from New Smyrna dated April 2, 1850, was published in the *Commercial Advertiser* on April 24, 1850, which documented the fate of the schooner:

> The *Josephine* is a perfect wreck, and what is worse, there can be no doubt that Mr. Thomas Hall and the sailors have perished. Their bodies have not been discovered but we are keeping a daily look out for them. The *Josephine* reached Mosquito Bar on Saturday, the 30th March in the afternoon at low water. She had sprung her main topmast, and her jib sail was badly torn and as it was blowing hard, Capt. Murray deemed it the safest course to try and get in, although the water was breaking everywhere. He ran in by the usual marks, and got over the outer and worst breakers without touching, but when within a short distance of the smooth water, the *Josephine* grounded hard and fast, about 4 o'clock P.M. Capt. Murray was washed overboard near dusk and seeing a hatch near he swam to it, and upon it, reached the shore, after being a long time in the water. He passed through the South breakers and landed on the South beach. Mr. Hall and the sailors declined attempting to land in the small boat, thinking it safer to hold on to the vessel. When Capt. Murray was washed off, the three were standing at the mainmast, but the Captain thinks they could not have remained on her much longer. Nearly the whole of the cargo is a total loss. The vessel drifted ashore, and lies bottom upward on the South beach.

JOSEPHINE H. II

On July 22, 1947, the yacht *Josephine H. II* burned on the Nassau River near Nassauville in Northeast Florida. The motor yacht *Josephine H. II*, official number 210215, was built in 1912 at Detroit, Michigan by the Bosserdet Yacht and Engine Company, and was 51.3 feet in length, 13 feet in beam, and 36 tons in displacement. In 1917, the yacht was commissioned into the U.S. Navy in July 1917 as U.S.S. *Josephine H. II* (SP-245), and patrolled along the Detroit River and Lake St. Clair. Following the war, she was returned to her owners for use as a private yacht.

JOYCE MOORE

On the afternoon of January 7, 1985, the trawler *Joyce Moore* capsized and sank while towing the disabled fishing vessel *Carib 6* back to Port Canaveral. The four men aboard the *Joyce Moore* were thrown into the water as their vessel rolled, but were rescued 30 minutes later by the U.S. Coast Guard. The wreck of the *Joyce Moore* rests in approximately 65 feet of water 15 miles southeast of Port Canaveral.

JULIAN

The *Julian*, bound from St. Ubes, Portugal, for Savannah, Georgia, was lost on the "island of St. Anastatia, Florida, 15th March (1817). Crew, passengers, and part of the cargo saved[121]." Marx (1987) cited this vessel as a ship, but it's possible this wreck could be the 224-ton copper-sheathed brig *Julian*, which was built in Philadelphia in

1809; the only *Julian* that appears in the *Lloyd's Register of British and Foreign Shipping* during this time period, she disappears from documentation after 1818. It is also worth noting that Marx (1987) makes mention of a ship named *Hambro*, Captain Patterson, sailing from St. Ubes, Portugal, to Savannah, Georgia, as wrecked around March 12, 1817, approximately 12 miles south of St. Augustine; he states the crew was saved, but the ship and cargo were lost. No vessel of that name, however, appears in the *Lloyd's Register* within five years of this event. It is possible *Hambro* is an erroneous entry, as *The Edinburgh Advertiser* of June 13, 1817, includes the same information as Marx but makes no mention of the vessel name. Specifically, it states, "The Hamburgh ship – , Patterson, from St. Ube's to Savannah, was wrecked off Florida, 18 miles south of St. Augustine, 12th March. Crew saved; cargo nearly total lost." Due to the similarities in route, wrecking date, and wrecking location, it is likely the unidentified vessel noted in the June 13 article is, in fact, the *Julian*, and there was no ship named *Hambro* lost near St. Augustine in 1817.

JULIET

The ship *Juliet* went ashore and bilged on November 7, 1859, near Cape Florida during the same storm that impacted the ships *Eliza Mallory*, *Charles Crooker*, *Jupiter* (refloated), and *Heidelberg* (refloated), brig *North*, and bark *Mary Coe*.

JUNO BEACH WRECK

The "Juno Beach Wreck" is an unknown shipwreck, possibly a sixteenth or seventeenth century Spanish vessel, located off Juno Beach, south of Jupiter Inlet. The site is also called the "Last Galleon" because it is believed to be the last shipwreck in Florida waters to be awarded an Admiralty lease before the passage of the Abandoned Shipwreck Act of 1988. Over the years, salvors have found a 12-foot anchor, a large amount of ballast, lead sheathing, ship's fittings, stone and iron cannonballs, musketballs, and pottery. Material has apparently been found scattered in an east-west pattern from 85 feet of water inshore to a depth of 25 feet.

JUPITER STAR

The 498-ton freighter known as the *Jupiter Star* was launched on May 19, 1956, as the *Ubbergen*. She was built by *B.V. v/h Scheepswerven Gebr. Van Diepen* at their Waterhuizen, Netherlands, shipyard for the vessel's first owner, the South Holland Shipping Company. The 498-ton general cargo freighter was 225.9 feet long and 33.5 feet wide. In 1961, the *Ubbergen* was converted into a livestock carrier for the purpose of ferrying horses. With a capacity of 202 horses, over the course of five years she carried more than 50,000 horses between Amsterdam and the Baltic Sea port of Klaipėda, Lithuania. In 1966, she was retrofitted back to her original configuration of a general cargo vessel. The freighter traded hands numerous times over the next three decades: in 1968 she was sold to Peter Schaa Sr., of Leer, Germany, who renamed her the *Hella Schaa*; in 1976

Jupiter Star as *Ubbergen*.

she was sold to a Cypriot company and renamed *Katerina El*; she was renamed *Kostas* in 1979 after being sold to a Greek firm; in 1983 she was sold to the Cassandra Shipping Company and renamed the *Nita II*; two years later she sailed as the *Pallini*; in 1990 she operated as the *Eleni M.* for Gaya Shipping, Incorporated; a year later she was known as the *Nitsa*; in 1993 she was sold to a Honduran company and renamed *Falcon*; in 1994 she traded hands yet again and was renamed *Christopher & Natalie*; and finally, in 1994, she was sold to the Belizean shipping company Rose Shipping Limited and renamed *Rosemarie*. It is unclear when the vessel became known as the *Jupiter Star*, as this name does not appear in the vessel's documentation history. Abandoned to rust on the Miami River, the vessel was later sold for use as an artificial reef.

The Atlantic Gamefish Foundation helped prepare the freighter, which was renamed the *Cleve Jones, Sr.* after the founder of the Jones Boat Yard, prior to its August 14, 2002, scuttling at the Pflueger Artificial Reef Site off Miami. The former *Ubbergen* now rests intact on its port side, in approximately 160 feet of water. It is possible for divers with the requisite training and experience to penetrate down the funnel into the engine room, where numerous gauge panels can be observed.

Sinking of the *Jupiter Star* (Miami-Dade County Department of Environmental Resources Management).

K-119

The loss of the airship *K-119* off the Florida-Georgia border on November 8, 1952, presents a unique Florida wreck. Built by the Goodyear Aircraft Corporation, the blimp had an envelope capacity of 425,000 cubic feet. The K-ship was heavily used by the U.S. Navy during World War II for antisubmarine patrol duties in the Atlantic and Pacific. The 40 foot-long aluminum-skinned control car carried the crew, armament, and two engines. It was also equipped with communication equipment and an ASG-type radar unit capable of detecting objects at a distance of 90 miles. Armament for the K-ship normally included four torpex-filled Mk. 47 (350-pound) bombs, a 50-caliber Browning aircraft machine gun mounted in the forward part of the control car, and additional Browning rifles that could be installed in the aft windows of the car. As the K-ship had a normal endurance of over 26 hours at cruising speed, and could also hover or make slow-speed searches at low altitude, the operation of these airships resulted in the detection of numerous enemy submarines, as well as locating and assisting in the rescue of many vessels, aircraft, and persons in distress.

Stationed at Naval Air Station Glynco near Brunswick, Georgia, the *K-119* was participating in anti-submarine maneuvers offshore the Florida-Georgia border when a freak accident caused the blimp to drop out of the sky. A Plexiglas window on the side of the control car suddenly popped out, hit the right propeller, and was then shot through the helium-filled bag. The *K-119's* crew turned for base, and attempted to lighten the craft by pitching equipment out the windows. While they managed to cover about 30 miles, the crippled airship nonetheless settled down onto the surface of the Atlantic Ocean. The crew managed to get only one of the two life rafts out of the airship, but within a few minutes, others were dropped from two sister blimps and planes in the umbrella of rescuers overhead. About an hour and a half after they hit the water, the submarine U.S.S. *Sea Dog* took them aboard. The sub tried to tow the disabled blimp but was unable to get a satisfactory hold, and was finally forced to sink it with machine gun fire to prevent it from becoming a menace to shipping.

This was not the only time a blimp crashed and sank off the Florida-Georgia border. On December 5, 1957, a ZP5K-Class Navy blimp experienced a complete engine failure and slowly began sinking towards the turbulent surface of the Atlantic Ocean 55 miles off the coast. The crew began radio messages shortly after the power failure, and began shooting flares after their radios went dead. The radio distress messages were picked up by the aircraft carrier U.S.S. *Essex*, which was operating in the area with the destroyer U.S.S. *Harold J. Ellison*. Both ships steamed toward the reported position, and eventually spotted flares as they neared the crippled airship. The *Ellison* put out small boats to pick up the crew as they escaped the blimp, which was being whipped by a 35-knot wind. One by one, the eight men on the settling blimp slithered down a rope into the small boats, each one getting out before the blimp finally touched down and sank.

The wreck sites of these blimps have yet to be documented by divers. As the airships lacked a rigid airframe, the sites would likely be dominated by the remains of the small control car and its two engines.

KEMAH

Built in 1907 at West Haven, Connecticut, the yacht *Kemah*, official number 204388, was 72 feet in length, 20 feet in beam, and 58 tons in burden. On September 18, 1926, the *Kemah* (incorrectly cited as the *Kenaha* in newspaper reports), owned by Mr. Waters, sunk at Pier Three during the Great Miami Hurricane. It is unknown if she was later raised and repaired, or ultimately written off as a total loss following the storm.

KEN M.

The *Ken M.* is a tug that was sunk in 1992 as an artificial reef off Fort Pierce Inlet. She now rests in approximately 130 feet of water just inshore the U.S.S. *Muliphen*. This vessel may possibly be the tug *Ken M.*, official number 0237353, built in Port Arthur, Texas, in 1938, which was 64.1 feet long and 17.9 feet wide.

KENNEDY

The sternwheel steamer *Kennedy*, built in 1901, was 122 feet in length and 140 tons burden. For most of its career, the steamer was employed by the Florida East Coast Railway and operated out of Boot Key Harbor near Marathon during the construction of the Key West Extension. Later owned by the Florida Navigation Company, the *Kennedy* was chartered to run on the Cape Fear River in North Carolina between Wilmington and Fayetteville. On February 24, 1914, the steamer caught fire and burned on the St. Johns River shortly after departing Jacksonville for North Carolina.

Schooner *Kessie C. Price* ashore at Bayfront Park following the 1926 Great Miami Hurricane (Florida State Archives).

KESTREL

The ship *Kestrel*, Captain Turner, went ashore at Cape Florida in August 1848 while on a voyage from New

Orleans to Liverpool and was subsequently condemned. The 810-ton *Kestrel* was built in 1845 at St. John, New Brunswick, Canada, and was owned by Gibbs and Company at the time of her loss.

KING FISH

On September 24, 2009, the 78-foot shrimper *King Fish* began taking on water approximately a half-mile south of the Mayport jetties. Reportedly, a towing block had broken loose and punctured a hole in the ship's wooden hull, which allowed the engine room to flood. The invading seawater also compromised the trawler's electrical system, and the *King Fish* soon lost power. The two fishermen were taken off the drifting *King Fish* around noon by a U.S. Coast Guard rescue boat, just before the vessel ran aground. While fuel and other hazardous materials were removed from the stranded vessel, heavy surf over the next several days inflicted heavy damage to the trawler, which ultimately proved to be a total loss.

The trawler *King Fish* grounded near Mayport (U.S. Coast Guard).

KINGFISHER

The 36-ton *Kingfisher*, built in 1909, reportedly foundered off West Palm Beach on December 18, 1927, with the loss of six lives.

KINSDALE

Marx (1979) states the British ship *Kinsdale*, Captain Dent, wrecked on a sandbar near Cape Florida during a storm on April 18, 1638, and was a total loss. I have been unable to uncover any additional information on this vessel or its wrecking.

KNOCKOUT

According to Singer (1998), the 32-ton fishing vessel *Knockout* foundered approximately 10 miles north of Port Everglades on January 27, 1963. Built in 1954, the *Knockout* was 46.3 feet long and 16.8 feet wide.

KONA

The gas screw yacht *Kona*, official number 206467, was built in 1909 at Baltimore, Maryland. She displaced 43 tons gross, and was 60 feet in length and 17.4 feet in beam. On October 29, 1921, the *St. Petersburg Times* printed news of the *Kona's* wrecking:

> Search continued today along the beach in the vicinity of the mouth of the St. Johns River at Mayport, and up the river itself, for bodies of members of the crew of the auxiliary yacht *Kona*, a 43-ton vessel which was wrecked on the jetties Tuesday (October 25) night or Wednesday (October 26) morning during the tropical storm. The body of a negro, with a life preserver attached to it bearing the name of 'Kona of Roslyn' found on the beach near Mayport yesterday was the first evidence that a wreck had occurred in this vicinity. The wreck of the *Kona* was found on the end of the south jetty. The report was current among marine men last night that a vessel with a cargo of liquor had been wrecked off Mayport and that quantities of bottled contraband had been thrown upon the beach. It was not established whether the reported cargo was aboard the *Kona*.

Reefing of the freighter *Korimu* (Palm Beach County Artificial Reef Program).

KORIMU

One of the more recent artificial reefs off South Florida, the 260-foot long *Korimu* was sunk in 230 feet of water off Palm Beach on March 16, 2007. The 698-ton freighter (IMO number 7022497) was originally built as the *Supremity* by shipbuilder *Nieuwe Noord-Nederlandse Scheepswerven* at their yard in Groningen, Netherlands. She was launched in June and finally completed in October 1970. In 1980, the vessel was sold and renamed the *Celtic Crusader*. In 1983, she was renamed *Korimu* after her purchase by Bernuth Marine Shipping, Incorporated, who subsequently employed the freighter to transport cargo between Caribbean and Central American ports. In 1995, vessel documentation states she displaced 1,918 gross tons, indicating the vessel may have undergone an overhaul at some point. The vessel eventually became a derelict along the Miami River, and was purchased for $75,000 to be utilized as an artificial reef. The West Palm Beach Fishing Club donated $10,000 towards the cost of the project, which allowed the club to rename the artificial reef site the "John Rybovich Endowment Reef" after a prominent Palm Beach boat builder. When I first explored the wreck of the *Korimu* shortly after its sinking, we found the freighter intact, upright, and resting with its bow pointing southward into a roaring current. Due to the intensity of the current, the majority of the dive was spent in the refuge of the cargo holds and stern superstructure. Regardless, due to its significant vertical relief, the wreck of the *Korimu* is enjoyable to explore.

KORSHOLM

The 336-foot long freighter *Korsholm*, named after a Swedish town, was built by the Aktieb shipyard of Gothenborg, Sweden, in 1925. Originally built for the Swedish American Line, she was eventually sold to the Swedish American Mexican Line in 1928. During her shipping career, the *Korsholm* participated in several maritime rescues, plucking seamen from the sinking schooners *General Byng* in 1928 and *Esther* in 1933. The freighter herself was involved in a few calamities. She caught fire and was severely damaged off Canada in 1931. Another incident found the *Korsholm* anchored off Dakar in 1940, amongst the Vichy French fleet. She was moored next to the French battleship *Richelieu*, the primary target of an Allied air raid late at night. During the attack, the Swedish freighter was heavily damaged and again caught fire. Towed out of harm's way, the fires were eventually brought under control, much to the relief of the *Korsholm's* crew. After this incident, the Allies took possession of the freighter, and she began operating under the British Ministry of Shipping.

On April 11, 1942, the *Korsholm* had finished loading her holds full with 4,593 tons of phosphate and moved out of the entrance of Tampa Bay en route for Liverpool, England, via Halifax, Nova Scotia. After two days, Captain Wickburg found himself steaming off Cape Canaveral early on the morning of April 12. Captain Wickburg prudently steamed along with the vessel blacked out and was working his way north close to shore in shallow water. Unfortunately, the *Korsholm's* course failed to deter the *U-123*, as the daring *Kapitänleutnant* Reinhard Hardegen boldly shadowed the freighter.

Thus far, Hardegen had conducted a successful cruise, sinking the *Muskogee*, *Empire Steel*, the Q-ship *Atik* (*Carolyn*), *Esparta*, and *Gulfamerica*. Just two hours earlier, the *U-123* sunk the tanker *Leslie* off Cape Canaveral. Now *Kapitänleutnant* Hardegen found himself with a heavily damaged vessel low on fuel, an exhausted crew, and no torpedoes. Hardegen was presented with yet another target when the lurking U-boat detected the northbound *Korsholm*, along with several other vessels. Working to gain position on the freighter, the *U-123* eventually maneuvered into an ambush off her starboard side and opened fire at 2:00 a.m. At long range, the initial salvo demolished the bridge. The gun crew of the *U-123* walked their shots along the starboard waterline, destroying the starboard lifeboat.

Upon the initial attack that left the bridge in ruins, the crew had prepared the port lifeboat in order to abandon ship. A pause in fire from the U-boat led several of the crew to believe that the attacker had fled, so many of the crew returned to their cabins to recover personal belongings and clothing. It is presumed that Captain Wickburg and others died when the *U-123* resumed its attack. After witnessing lifeboats drift off from the crippled freighter, Hardegen focused on finishing his work and added several more holes to the portside waterline. With the *Korsholm* now aflame and sinking, the *U-123* moved off as patrol craft approached the scene around 4:00 a.m. The attack claimed nine lives and sent the *Korsholm* to the bottom. *Kapitänleutnant* Hardegen eventually worked his way back to Kiel, but not without first sinking the steamer *Alcoa Guide* 300 miles east of Cape Hatteras,

Starboard profile shot of the freighter Korsholm (Mark Mondano Collection).

North Carolina, on April 17. During this second Drumbeat patrol, Hardegen sank 10 ships for a total of 57,170 tons. For the great success he experienced on this patrol, Hardegen received the Oak Leaves to his Knights Cross while still at sea.

Kapitänleutnant Reinhard Hardegen managed to survive the war as one of the most successful U-boat commanders. After the war, Hardegen spent more than a year in British captivity, eventually returning home in November 1946. He then managed to build a successful oil trading company and participated as a member of Parliament in his hometown of Bremen for over 30 years.

The wreck of the *Korsholm* now lies scattered approximately six miles offshore. In 1944, the wreck was wire-dragged and demolished as a navigational hazard. The site resembles a landscape of twisted metal and debris. The bronze propeller is easily visible on the wreck site, serving as a landmark for visiting divers. Due to its proximity to shore, visibility is usually around 10 feet, though it can exceed 50 feet on exceptionally calm days.

KOSSUTH

As reported in a December 1857 dispatch that appeared in Volume 30 of *The Sailor's Magazine and Naval Journal*, "British ship *Kossuth*, from New York to New Orleans, wrecked on the Florida coast. Value $50,000."

sailboat was built in 1978, was 42.8 feet long and 14.6 feet wide, carried the radio call sign WSX2742, and the vessel identification number 599589. While we were able to put a name on the wreck, we have yet to learn any details on the *Kringeline's* sinking.

After cleaning the starboard bow area, the name *Kringeline* appears, which identifies the wreck.

The wreck of the sailing vessel *Kringeline*.

KRINGELINE

In early 2007, I explored a mystery shipwreck in approximately 310 feet of water just outside Boca Inlet. A friend had recently acquired the numbers from a fisherman who was curious about the wreck's identity. Our first dive discovered the wreck to be that of a sailboat sitting intact and upright on a clean, sand bottom with its bow pointing toward shore. Searching through the wreck, we found the sails stowed and the cockpit chocked with eisenglass curtain, which may indicate the vessel was traveling during foul weather when lost. Early speculation was that the mystery sailboat might have been the *Charley's Crab*, lost during a storm in 1993. On a later dive, I managed to clean heavy encrustation off the bow, which revealed the name *Kringeline*. Subsequent research indicated the 23-ton

L. MCNEILL

Built in 1899 at Jacksonville, the *L. McNeill*, official number 141582, was a 145-ton sidewheel passenger steamer that was 93.3 feet long and 22.2 feet wide. On January 8, 1916, the steamer stranded at Mosquito Inlet. News of the vessel's wrecking was reported on February 4, 1916, in the *New Smyrna Daily News*:

> The 120-foot steamer *McNeil* [sic], owned and operated by the Howard Transportation Company, which has been hard and fast aground at Mosquito Inlet since January 14, has broken in two. Owing to the steady settling of her stern and the suction of the sand her timbers have at last parted, leaving her a helpless wreck. George F. Crouch, the company's local agent, announces her as a total loss. Her owners probably carry fire insurance but no marine insurance. She has already been stripped of all movable fittings and cargo, including a small number of orange crates which were taken out of her the day after she struck the bank. The only articles of value remaining are her boiler and engines. The company will remove them in a few days and leave the hull to go to pieces. The *McNeil* [sic] was built somewhere in Georgia a great many years ago and has ploughed through southern waters ever since. Her last route lay between Jacksonville and Fort Pierce. The steamer went on the bar on Saturday, January 8, when the tide was pretty well flooded. When she first struck there was fully a foot of water around her hull. Today sand measuring three feet in depth has buried her.

L-SILHOUETTE

On June 14, 2003, the freighter *L-Silhouette* (IMO number 7529457) departed Miami bound for Haiti with a cargo of rice, beans, plastic chairs, cooking oil, and other assorted goods, but engine problems experienced shortly after their departure forced the vessel to drop anchor off Hollywood to address the situation. Early on the morning of June 16, the *L-Silhouette* radioed the U.S. Coast Guard requesting assistance, as the freighter was apparently taking on water and in danger of sinking. After rescuing the eight Haitian crew members and one passenger, the U.S. Coast Guard enlisted salvage company Titan Maritime to haul the listing freighter five miles offshore to deep water to prevent the vessel from becoming a hazard to navigation and to minimize any environmental impact; the vessel was released approximately five miles offshore after excessive flooding, ultimately sinking in just over 600 feet of water.

The freighter *L-Silhouette*, 206.6 feet long, 34.8 feet wide, and 697 tons gross burden, was built in 1976 as the *Antxon Mari* for Spanish owner Antonio Vega de Seoane

L-Silhouette as the *Antxon Mari*, 1985 (Brian Fisher).

and later sailed as the *Nidia Leonor*. At the time of her loss, the *L-Silhouette* was owned by Shipping Transportation of Miami. It is interesting to point out the U.S. Coast Guard at Miami was apparently fairly familiar with the freighter, as they cited the vessel for spilling oil in the Miami River in March 2001 (as *Nidia Leonor*), and later detained her in January 2003 for several safety issues, notably including poor integrity of watertight doors throughout the ship.

LA BARBARA

The auxiliary schooner yacht *La Barbara* was launched at Morris Heights, New York, in May 1900. Built for William Marks of Philadelphia, the schooner measured 68 feet in length and 15.5 feet in breadth, and was outfitted with a 24-horsepower naphtha auxiliary engine. An initial report of the schooner's loss was reported in *The New York Times* on February 1, 1903, which related, "Telegrams which reached this city yesterday reported the loss of the auxiliary centerboard yacht *La Barbara* belonging to Dr. E.M. Culver of this city, twenty miles south of Jupiter Inlet, Fla., Thursday (January 29) night. Only the crew were on board, and all managed to escape and even saved some of the vessel's costliest fittings after she ran upon the beach."

Additional details appeared in the February 4, 1903, issue of the *Florida Times-Union*, which stated, "The two-masted schooner yacht *La Barbra* [sic] went ashore in dead calm conditions one mile north of Delray House of Refuge on January 28, 1903, and became a total loss."

LA ESCLAVITUD

The Spanish brigantine *La Esclavitud*, owned by Ciprián Martínez de Peón, left Havana on March 17, 1786, with a schooner commanded by Miguel Fornary, carrying funds ($40,000 in silver pesos) and provisions for troops at St. Augustine. On the afternoon of May 3, the watch tower on Anastasia Island observed two vessels approaching from the south as dark storm clouds loomed on the horizon. A storm soon hit, preventing the vessels from entering St. Augustine. Five days later, the schooner returned and reported she had lost sight of *La Esclavitud*, which was never heard from again.

LA NATIVITÉ

On the morning of October 26, 1981, residents of Hillsboro Beach discovered the broken bodies of numerous Haitian refuges that were cast ashore when their 30-foot sailboat *La Nativité* swamped and broke apart in the surf just 200 feet offshore. The tragic journey began on August 26, when 63 Haitians who had paid up to $2,000 for passage to the United States crammed on board *La Nativité* at Cap-Haïtien in northern Haiti. Shortly after setting off, the decrepit sailboat made landfall in eastern Cuba. The refugees stayed there for nearly a month while their vessel was repaired. *La Nativité* set off again, but quickly washed up on a tiny islet off the Cuban coast. The sailboat again returned to the mainland where, finally, on October 23, the hopeful Haitian refugees were towed offshore and into the Florida Straits. Several days later, buffeted by 30-knot winds and 5-foot seas, the sailboat spilled its human cargo into the Atlantic just offshore Broward County. Of the 63 passengers, 33 perished in the surf, including 2 pregnant women.

LADY BANNERMAN

The *Lady Bannerman* was a schooner built in the Bahamas in 1855. Rebuilt in 1872, the vessel was 79 feet in length, 23 feet in breadth, and displaced 78 tons. During her early career, the *Lady Bannerman* was employed as a wrecking schooner off the Bahamas. Later, she ran fruit from Port Antonio, Jamaica, to Jacksonville. On one of these voyages, Captain Curry and the *Lady Bannerman* encountered a brutal winter gale. On January 13, 1889, after losing her foremast, the schooner wrecked 15 miles north of Cape Canaveral, quickly becoming a total loss.

LADY BEATRICE

The 104-ton trawler *Lady Beatrice* began her life in 1979 as hull number 2193 at the St. Augustine shipyard of the Diesel Engine Sales Company. After constant work for almost two decades, the 73-foot long wooden-hulled shrimper capsized in heavy seas approximately one mile off Flagler Beach on December 12, 1997. Captain Terry Norton radioed a distress call at 1:30 a.m. after noticing the trawler was taking on water during rough weather. He also said he had a possible fire on board in the engine room. By the time the U.S. Coast Guard rescue boat arrived, the vessel had partially submerged and the lower decks were flooded. Captain Norton and two crew members were safely rescued. Interestingly, the Coast Guard was apparently very familiar with the *Lady Beatrice*, having assisted Captain Norton three times in the prior five months to the sinking, including pumping the trawler out twice. The following day, the submerged *Lady Beatrice* drifted from offshore Flagler Beach to just north of Ormond Beach. The hulk of the drifting shrimper actually resulted in locals calling the Coast Guard with reports of a whale shot by a harpoon[122]. Over the next few days, the trawler broke apart, and debris from the *Lady Beatrice* began washing up on Flagler Beach, including wooden hull planks, a television, the vessel's compass, and various bits of furniture.

LADY CARMEN

The *Lady Carmen* was formerly a 45-foot long tugboat that was sunk as an artificial reef in July 1999 off Miami. Encrusted with a thin veneer of marine life, the tug rests in 65 feet of water, listing slightly to starboard. In the immediate vicinity of the *Lady Carmen*, divers can also explore an 80-foot long barge to the south, the tugs *White Coast* and *C-One* to the east, and the 150-foot long freighter *Conception* to the northeast, all of which are within easy swimming distance from each other.

View of the tug *Lady Carmen*, which rests off Miami.

LADY CLARA

On December 28, 1910, the 13-ton gas steamer *Lady Clara*, official number 204472, built in 1907, burned at Grassy Point on the St. Johns River.

LADY FREI

The *Lady Frei* was a 102-foot long square-rigged brigantine schooner built in 1913 in Denmark. While her early history is rather murky, her final years are well-documented. In 1981, the vessel was repossessed from Richard Chesbrough by First Interstate Bank of San Francisco, who then donated it to the non-profit Dade Marine Institute in Miami to be used as a training vessel in the school's work with juvenile delinquents. By early 1984, the *Lady Frei* had fallen into disrepair and vandals had opened a hole in her hull. Beyond rescue, the brigantine – one of only 14 in the world left sailing – was towed offshore Miami and sunk as an artificial reef in December 1986. Resting in 60 feet of water, the wreck has disintegrated significantly since its scuttling, and the only thing recognizable at the site is the engine block from the small auxiliary motor.

LADY K

The 38-foot shrimp trawler *Lady K*, formerly the *Mr. Ed*, crashed into the north jetty of Ponce de Leon Inlet in the early morning hours of October 7, 1977. The U.S. Coast Guard had a boat from the local station on scene minutes after receiving the incident report. The two crewmen had abandoned ship and were safe on the jetty, while the fishing vessel was found banging against the jetty rocks due to the wave action. The Coast Guard attempted to take the boat in tow, but as they passed the east end of the north jetty, the *Lady K* capsized and sank within five minutes. On October 11, newspaper reports stated the captain was on scene with a salvage crew attempting to raise the sunken shrimper, which was valued at $21,000.

LADY M. JOHNSON

The 46-ton fishing vessel *Lady M. Johnson* foundered at the entrance of the St. Johns River along the north jetty between buoys 8 and 10 on March 18, 1970[123]. Due to the vessel's sinking location, she was undoubtedly removed as a hazard to navigation.

LADY OF THE LAKE

Volume 28 of *The Sailor's Magazine and Naval Journal* reported, "Brig *Lady of the Lake*, from Boston for Jacksonville, in a heavy gale of wind, parted both chains and went ashore about two miles south of St. Johns Bar, November 9, 1855. No lives were lost."

LADY NICOLE

The sinking of the 70-foot long trawler *Lady Nicole* 10 miles offshore Cape Canaveral was reported in the *Daytona Beach News-Journal* on December 18, 1999:

> The Coast Guard was notified that the 70-foot shrimp boat *Lady Nicole* was taking on water about 5 p.m. Thursday (December 16), said Ensign Mark Pesnell of U.S. Coast Guard Group Mayport in Jacksonville. The Coast Guard cutter *Drummond*, on space shuttle support duty off Cape Canaveral, was dispatched toward the last known position of the vessel. After the rescue it was learned the trawler was actually named the *Dallas Down the Hatch*, and had been ordered to stay in port following a U.S. Coast Guard safety inspection that cited the vessel for poor hull integrity and other safety violations. However, the captain changed the name of the vessel to *Lady Nicole* and slipped out of port.

LADY SARA II

The *Lady Sara II* was a 66.7-foot long shrimp trawler built in 1978. On January 30, 1997, the trawler was taken in tow approximately four miles south of St. Augustine Inlet by the trawler *Dorothy E.* after the *Lady Sara II* lost power and began taking on water. The *Dorothy E.* safely towed the crippled trawler farther offshore to prevent her from being cast up on the beach, but after a while the captain of the *Lady Sara II* insisted he be towed into St. Augustine. Unfortunately, due to the combination of rough sea conditions and an ebbing tide, several tow lines parted and the drifting *Lady Sara II* eventually ran aground on a sandbar approximately one mile south of the St. Augustine Inlet and quickly began breaking apart. Captain William Wilder radioed that he and crewman Rufus Greene couldn't remain on board, and both jumped into the water about 4:45 a.m. Tragically, both perished in the turbulent Atlantic.

LAERTES

The *Laertes*, named after the father of Odysseus in Homer's *Odyssey*, was laid down at the Taikoo Dockyard and Engine Company in Hong Kong to help meet the demand for merchant freighters that occurred upon the end of the First World War. At 424 feet in length and 52 feet in breadth, the *Laertes* possessed a single 413-horsepower triple expansion engine that turned a single screw, pushing the 5,868-ton vessel along at a maximum speed of almost 14 knots. While originally built for the Ocean Steamship Company, most of her career was served with the Blue Funnel line under the Dutch flag of *Nederlandsche Stoomvaart Maatschappy Oceaan*. When Holland fell to the Germans at the outset of World War II, the *Laertes* was seized while in a foreign port and eventually put into service for the U.S. Maritime Commission.

In April, the *Laertes* loaded her 5,230-ton cargo of war material destined for Bombay, India, to support the effort against the advancing Japanese military machine in Indochina. Included in the shipment were 3 airplanes, 17 medium tanks, and 20 trucks, all stowed tightly in her cargo holds and packed in shipping containers that were secured to the deck. Riding low in the water due to her hefty cargo, the *Laertes* departed New York Harbor and proceeded down the coast, stopping off at several secure harbors to avoid steaming at night in the now U-boat infested waters. By May, Captain C.J. van Heel had safely reached Florida. Approaching Cape Canaveral early on the morning of May 3, he initiated preparations to steam around the treacherous point of land. Meanwhile, *Kapitänleutnant* Heinrich Bleichrodt and the *U-109*, recent additions to the coast of Florida, were also running southbound, just north of the Cape. Bleichrodt would eventually become one of the most successful U-boat commanders of the war, responsible for the sinking of 27 vessels for a total of 158,957 tons. Like the other commanders of the Florida U-boats *U-123*, *U-333*, and *U-564*, Bleichrodt would also survive the war, passing away in 1977.

The *U-109* observed two targets moving in opposite directions and chose to continue on its general course, giving chase to the southbound vessel. The lighthouse at Cape Canaveral continued to operate during the war, and it now illuminated both the *Laertes* and the pursuing U-boat. In an attempt to avoid detection and the defensive fire from the stern deck gun of the *Laertes*, the *U-109* maneuvered to gain position on the freighter. Bleichrodt successfully moved past just offshore of the blacked out freighter. At approximately 5:00 a.m., a torpedo smashed into the port bow quarter of the Dutch ship. The *U-109* proceeded to fire two other torpedoes at the ship, however, only one reached its target.

Captain van Heel quickly transmitted a distress call

Port side profile view of the freighter *Laertes* underway (Mark Mondano Collection).

and gave the order to abandon ship. As the lifeboats were being lowered, a third torpedo was observed headed right for amidships. Those who were in the portside lifeboat watched in horror as the torpedo passed under their lifeboat and exploded against the hull adjacent to them; all 17 who were in the lifeboat were instantly killed. Two other lifeboats successfully made their escape while others were forced to jump ship. Four seamen remained on the bow of the stricken freighter, only swimming off after the sinking vessel settled onto the seabed 60 feet below; all told, 48 out of a crew of 66 survived the incident.

Lying approximately nine miles off the Cape Canaveral light, the wreck of the *Laertes* covers an expansive area. While the wreck was extensively blasted and wire-dragged, the current disposition of the wreck is still generally articulated. The wreck lies with its bow facing southwest. Due to the shallow depth, it would be thought that the cargo would have been salvaged, but the cargo of war material can be found throughout the site, including a solitary and remarkably intact M3A General Lee tank (though the top turret is missing). The eroded remains of several trucks can be observed as well, though they generally consist of only tires, radiators, and engine blocks. The forward and aft masts lie broken on either side of the wreck. The large boilers of the "Dutch Wreck" rise 15 feet off the bottom and provide a good landmark when investigating the wreck site. The starboard boiler remains in line with the vessel while the port boiler has been knocked askew. Aft of the boilers, the debris extends roughly 50 feet to either side. The stern is mangled with the portside quarter kicked far over on itself. The wreck has yet to produce many artifacts, possibly attributed to the lack of visitors and the fact that many sections of the wreck are sanded in. Visibility on the wreck of the *Laertes* fluctuates drastically due to its proximity to Cape Canaveral; visibility generally averages 20 feet. While the wreck may not be productive for artifacts, the extensive amount of debris provides rich habitat for marine wildlife. Snook, cobia, grouper, Goliath grouper, barracuda, and snapper swarm about the wreck, most notably around the large boilers. The wreck itself is not very colorful and is dominated by brownish hues, contrasted only by colorful tropical species that dart about the site.

LAKELAND

The *Lakeland* was originally laid down on December 9, 1944, at Brown Shipbuilding Company's Houston, Texas, shipyard as *LSM-373*. The LSM (Landing Ship, Medium) was 203.5 feet in length and 34.5 feet in beam, displaced 1,095 tons when fully loaded, and was powered with twin Fairbanks Morse direct-drive diesels. She had the capacity to carry five medium or three heavy tanks, six tracked landing vehicles, or nine DUKW amphibious trucks, as well as almost 50 troops. Launched less than three weeks later on December 30, *LSM-373* conducted her shakedown cruise in early 1945 before departing for the Pacific Theater on March 4, 1945. After passing through the Panama Canal, she reached Eniwetok Atoll in the Marshall Islands on May 4. During the final weeks of World War II, *LSM-373* participated in operations in the Marianas, Solomons, and Okinawa. After the Japanese surrender, the landing ship transported troops and supplies for occupation forces in Korea and China throughout 1945 and into early 1946. *LSM-373* eventually returned to the United States, and after

The landing ship U.S.S. *Lakeland* (Naval Historical Center).

decommissioning on October 14, 1946, she was placed in the Atlantic Reserve Fleet at Green Cove Springs. On February 28, 1958, *LSM-373* was recommissioned at the Charleston Naval Shipyard in South Carolina to serve as a logistic supply ship. On October 14, 1959, she was renamed U.S.S. *Lakeland*, however, she was decommissioned the following month and struck from the Naval Register in January 1960. The Portsmouth Salvage Company in Chesapeake, Virginia, purchased the surplus landing ship on October 6, 1960.

The *Lakeland* was converted for use as an inter-island freighter, and was employed for over two decades before finally being scuttled as an artificial reef off Miami on June 16, 1982. The *Lakeland* now rests almost completely upside down in 135 feet of water and is oriented with her bow pointing west. While the inverted hull does not present an appealing dive visually, there are numerous penetration points that allow access under and into the interior of the vessel. An extensive debris field can be found extending from the wreck; to the north, numerous cement mixer drums that were also deployed to serve as artificial reef material can be found scattered along the bottom. These were actually deployed a considerable distance from the *Lakeland*, but Hurricane Andrew tumbled them along the bottom towards the freighter.

LANDRAS

The loss of the bark *Landras* was reported on January 26, 1897, in the Iowa newspaper, *The Semi-Weekly Northern Vindicator*. It should be noted that I have been unable to find any documentation of a vessel named *Landras*. Therefore, it is possible that this event was a hoax fabricated by some bored individual, as these fictional "message in a bottle" stories are not uncommon. Regardless, due to the possibility that I simply missed the relevant archival information on the vessel, I am including the newspaper details below:

> A bottle was picked up seven miles below St. Augustine, Fla., which contained a message stating that the bark *Landras* foundered at sea January 15. The message, which was signed by Capt. Gonzales, was the log of the vessel from the time she left port until she foundered. According to the message, the *Landras* left Boston January 3, in command of Capt. Gonzales and manned by a crew of twelve men. January 12 the vessel sprang a leak. The pumps were manned and the men worked day and night, but at noon on January 15 it was apparent that the vessel was doomed. The captain and crew took to the boats and had hardly got clear of the vessel when she sank. The message concludes: "We have little food and water, and must perish unless soon picked up."

L'ATHENAISE

L'Athenaise was a 350-ton, copper-sheathed French naval vessel built in Normandy, France. In 1803, she was captured by H.M.S. *Leviathan* during the fall of present-day Haiti and taken to Port Royal, Jamaica, where she laid idle for over 14 month before her eventual employment as a cartel by the British Royal Navy. A cartel is a ship commissioned in time of war to exchange prisoners, or to carry communication between belligerents. Cartels were unarmed aside from a single signal gun, and could carry no cargo or war supplies. On October 2, 1804, *L'Athenaise*, along with 28 crew and guards, set sail from Port Royal carrying 182 French prisoners and 2 women bound for England. With illness spreading through the British crew and an incompetent captain at the helm, the fate of *L'Athenaise* was bleak when she encountered a gale off the Florida coast. The cartel eventually grounded on a reef in heavy seas, before ultimately being thrown ashore just south of Hillsboro Inlet on November 1. Lieutenant G.J. Honey's account of the wrecking was published in the *London Mercury*, which documented the wrecking event:

> The Master who had been sent in command of this ship had been a mate in a merchantman belonging to the agent victualler at Kingston, and, being found unfit for his station, was given charge of this unfortunate vessel in order to get rid of him. We found it necessary to keep him from liquor by every means in our power, but he escaped all our vigilance, and after cutting away the foresail, took the desperate resolution of getting drunk. Consequently, the ship was not wore, and, standing on, soon gained the eddy current, which runs to the southward along the coast of Florida. If common attention is paid, the change in colour in the water along this coast gives the seamen full time to avoid danger; however, in our case, the first thing seen was breakers about a mile away on the lee beam. The seaman who made the discovery instantly told the Master, whom he found quite drunk and half asleep on the poop, and after an altercation was knocked down. A sufficient noise was soon made on deck to alarm everyone, but the loss of the ship was inevitable. Directly I went on deck the anchor was cut away; but before she brought up, the ship struck on a coral reef with a tremendous crash. The scene that followed is indescribable; there were upward of two hundred men crouching on the deck, naked, and mostly praying and confessing their sins, whilst the sea broke over her mast heads, and to heighten the confusion, the mizzen mast fell across the deck, breaking one man's ankle, and

maiming several others. The sea soon threw the ship over the reef into deep water, and fortunately she remained afloat until she reached the beach. She was gradually sinking, and on striking the beach a few seas soon filled her.

L'Athenaise quickly settled into the sand in the surf zone, tantalizingly close to the sanctuary of the beach. Volunteers swam out a line to the beach from which a larger hawser was transferred to land, though two perished in the effort. Most of the crew and prisoners then pulled themselves through the pounding surf to shore using the hawser line. Captain James Cox and a few other crewmen opted to stay onboard and wallow in their inebriation. The following day, the seas relented and the captain and other stragglers made it to shore. Due to his irresponsible and incompetent behavior, many of the French prisoners rallied for Captain Cox's lynching, but the British crew favored his pardon. On November 4, most of the shipwrecked party marched north for St. Augustine. After over two weeks of toil along the Florida coast, a motley group of 131 souls trickled into the garrison at St. Augustine. While the French received favorable treatment from the sympathetic Spanish, the English were relegated to a "miserable dungeon without even straw to lie on." Lieutenant Honey finally reached Charleston, South Carolina, via an American schooner on December 5, 1804. The wrecking location of *L'Athenaise* was recorded by Lieutenant Honey as approximate latitude 26° 10' north.

LAVINIA

Designated official number 141500, the tug *Lavinia* was built in 1897 at Palatka, and was 58 feet in length, 13 feet in breadth, and displaced 29 tons gross. In October 1925, the tug burned on the St. Johns River at Green Cove Springs.

LEDBURY

A report from Philadelphia dated October 26 included in the November 16, 1769, issue of the *Virginia Gazette*, cited the following:

> Friday arrived here Captain McCulloch from Jamaica, who informs that on the 16th inst. he saw a snow ashore on Key Largo, about 25 leagues to the northward [sic] of Cape Florida, which on going ashore he found to be the snow *Ledbury*, Captain John Lorain, from Old Harbor, Jamaica, for Bristol, with a load of cigars, who on the 29th of September had a violent gale of wind, which obliged them to cut away her foremast, and the mainmast soon after went overboard, in which condition she drove high and dry ashore, when the people's lives are all saved, and about two thirds of her cargo, but the vessel lost.

The position of the *Ledbury's* wrecking was also documented as 15 leagues north of Cape Florida, north of Elliott Key near Cape Florida, Sands Key north of Elliott Key, and north of Caesar's Creek. The vessel was eventually burned after salvage. Ledbury Reef now bears the name of the wrecked snow.

LEJOK

The three-masted schooner *Lejok* was built at Milbridge, Maine, in 1901 and owned by Captain Charles L. Smith and others of Ellsworth, Maine. She was 134.6 feet long, 33 feet in beam, and 10 feet in depth, and she displaced 247 tons net and 311 tons gross. On March 22, 1906, the *Lejok* was involved in a collision 40 miles off New Jersey that punched a hole in her hull below her waterline. Captain Norwood and the crew of the *Lejok* abandoned ship, but the schooner remained afloat – likely assisted by her cargo of lumber – and was towed into port by the pilot boat *New York*. In March 1920, the *Lejok* was on another lumber run, this time between Jacksonville and Puerto Rico. After becoming waterlogged and in a sinking condition, the schooner was abandoned. On March 16, 1920, the *Galveston Daily News* printed the three-masted schooner *Lejok* was abandoned on March 4 at latitude 29° 12' north, longitude 79° 10' west (approximately 90 nautical miles east of Ponce de Leon Inlet); her crew was picked up by the steamer *Gutheil* on March 6 at latitude 29° 50' north, longitude 78° 14' west.

LENA M. CORBETT

Reportedly, the *Lena M. Corbett* was originally an Atlantic Fleet water barge during World War I. She eventually migrated to Miami in 1927, where she was employed in the lobster industry. She was also outfitted to bring fresh water to the Miami Aquarium. During a storm in late September 1928, the steel hull of the *Corbett* broke loose from her moorings and eventually sunk under the abutments of the Southwest Second Avenue Bridge[124]. It should be noted that I have been unable to find any information on a barge by this name, or additional information if the reported wreck was eventually removed; the 1934 news article indicated she remained under the bridge for the six years since her 1928 sinking.

Advertisement featuring the yacht *Leonie*.

LEONIE

Built in 1917 at Camden, New Jersey, by the John H. Mathis Yacht Company, the 164-ton yacht *Leonie*, official number 215231, was 100 feet in length and 20.7 feet in breadth, and was valued at $100,000. From 1926 to 1936, the *Leonie*, owned by copper magnate Murray Guggenheim, wintered in St. Petersburg. On January 1, 1943, the yacht was acquired by the U.S. Navy and redesignated as U.S.S. *Leonie* (YHB-19). After the war, she was turned back over to her owner. On September 1, 1961, the yacht *Leonie* burned while at Miami.

LEON RODDY

The *Leon Roddy* was a small push tug owned by Fort Myers Shell and Dredging Company that was apparently built in 1956 at Palatka. In 1973, the *Leon Roddy* was reportedly towed approximately eight nautical miles east of St. Augustine Inlet and sunk in 65 feet of water.

LESLIE

Kapitänleutnant Reinhard Hardegen and the Type IXB U-boat *U-123* quietly surfaced just offshore the coast of Florida on the afternoon of April 12, 1942. *Kapitänleutnant* Hardegen was on his second *Paukenschlag* (Drumbeat) cruise to the eastern seaboard of the United States, and the experienced commander had staked out the productive grounds near Cape Canaveral. The cape was a point of land that jutted far out into the Atlantic, and like Cape Hatteras, North Carolina, it funneled shipping traffic into an easily manageable hunting zone, while also providing deep water to provide an escape route. On his first cruise, Hardegen found an ill-prepared Allied coast, teeming with easy targets. Hardegen and the *U-123* sank nine ships for a total of 53,173 tons on their first Drumbeat cruise, to which *Grossadmiral* Karl Dönitz recognized with the following message, "To the drumbeater Hardegen. Bravo! You beat the drum well. BdU (*Befehlshaber der Unterseeboote*: Commander in Chief, U-boats)[125]."

The *Leslie* was launched in 1919 by the small shipyard of the McDougall Duluth Company in Duluth, Minnesota. Originally named the *Lake Flagstaff*, she was one of many vessels built around the Great Lakes in response to a large demand for shipping during World War I. The "Laker," as she and her brethren were called, was 255 feet long, had a beam of 44 feet, and displaced 2,609 tons. Propulsion was provided by a single triple expansion steam engine, capable of 1,500 horsepower, which turned a single steel screw. The *Lake Flagstaff* was sold to the Lykes Brothers Steamship Company and renamed the *Stella Lykes*. She then made her way to Worth Steamship Company, who chartered the vessel to W.R. Grace and Company. Renamed *Leslie*, she began to be outfitted to serve in wartime conditions. Gun tubs were placed on the stern and amidships in preparation for the addition of guns upon her return to New York from her first cargo run. Unfortunately, the *Leslie* never completed her first cruise.

Departing New York on March 4, 1942, with Captain Albert Ericksson at the helm, the *Leslie* proceeded south, stopping off at several ports upon the approach of darkness in order to rob the marauding U-boats the cover of night to attack potential targets. After successfully delivering her cargo of general goods and steel to ports in South America, she steamed to Antilla, Cuba, where she loaded 3,300 tons of bagged sugar in early April. After a quick stop in Havana, the *Leslie* departed for her return trip to New York on April 11. The *Leslie* was heading due north along the Florida coast when she was spotted late in the afternoon of April 12 by the surfaced *U-123*. With only one torpedo left in his arsenal, it took Hardegen seven hours to maneuver the *U-123* to within 1,800 feet of the small freighter, as he only had one engine functioning. Forty seconds after launch, the last torpedo ever fired by Hardegen connected with the *Leslie* in the number three hold, just aft of the amidships superstructure on her starboard side. The damage from the attack caused the freighter to take an immediate list to starboard and settle by the stern; within 15 minutes the *Leslie* was sitting on the bottom, with only her bow and top of the bridge above

The petite freighter *Leslie* as the *Stella Lykes* (William T. Hultgren).

water. Though the attack was efficient and the sinking swift, there were only three fatalities on the *Leslie*, possibly attributed to the tightly packed cargo of sugar that may have absorbed the shock of the explosion.

Today the *Leslie* rests in 85 feet to 100 feet of water off Cape Canaveral. As performed on other shipwrecks in the area, the *Leslie* was demolished as a hazard to navigation. The stern section of the wreck lies hard over on her port side, and the aft structure has collapsed from the main hull and lies next to the stern. The bow is inverted, but can be easily penetrated, while the amidships area and cargo holds are a bit more mangled, with portions strewn out into the sand. A large boiler that extends out of the wreckage is easily identifiable in this portion of the wreck. While a few portholes and the compass have been recovered, much more undoubtedly lies hidden in the sand. Visibility generally averages around 20 to 30 feet in this area, and the wreck provides a haven for both small tropical species and larger predatory fish.

LET HER B

The keel of the British brigantine *Let Her B*, official number 49111, was laid down for Captain James Hyland at Pictou, Nova Scotia on January 2, 1865. The last vessel built by noted shipbuilder James Rose, she was 85 feet in length, 26 feet in beam, and displaced 169 tons gross. On October 25, 1867, en route from St. Johns, New Brunswick, for Havana with a cargo of shooks (nails) with Captain Graham at the helm, the *Let Her B* struck on Pacific Reef and became a total loss.

LET'S GO

The 36-foot long charter boat *Let's Go* exploded and sank February 25, 1949, approximately three miles northeast of the St. Lucie Inlet; the four passengers safely jumped overboard and were picked up by a nearby vessel.

LEV LOU

The *Lev Lou* was an approximately 85-foot long converted crash boat, which sank during Hurricane Cleo on August 27, 1964. The *Lev Lou*, owned by Captain Bill Raymond, was anchored in the lee of Peanut Island when it broke loose, pounded against a dock, and ultimately sank at Riviera Beach.

LIBERTY

Bernard Romans, in his book *A Concise Natural History of East and West Florida*, published in 1775, details the loss of the schooner *Liberty* thusly, "In the year 1773, I came a passage from Mississippi, on board the schooner *Liberty*, commanded by Capt. John Hunt, we had the misfortune to be over-set at sea, and I conducted the wreck into this place (Rio d'ais, Indian River), when having lost out boats and caboose, with every other thing from off the deck, we nailed together three half hogsheads, in which a man and a boy went on shore, and brought us sand off, to make a kind of caboose."

LILLIAN L.

Built as the yacht *Onward* at Bascom, Ohio, in 1906, the 29-ton *Lillian L.*, official number 202815, was 63.5 feet long and 10.8 feet wide. On November 19, 1926, the yacht foundered at Palm Beach.

LILLIE

The 64-foot long passenger steamer *Lillie* was built in 1900 by Captain Clay Johnson, who ran the vessel between Kissimmee and Bassinger. Around 1926, the vessel was sold to E.P. Dann, who took the *Lillie* to Miami and had it rebuilt as a launch to be used on Biscayne Bay. It was eventually abandoned on the New River around 1933.

The paddlewheel steamer *Lillie* (Alfred H. Robson Collection).

LINDA

On May 14, 1977, the Panamanian-flagged freighter *Linda* departed Port Everglades for Venezuela, but engine trouble quickly delayed its voyage. After repairs, the freighter resumed its journey two days later, but soon faced another obstacle when the port side ballast tank experienced an uncontrolled flood three miles off Tavernier in the Florida Keys. While the *Linda* was initially anchored offshore to deal with the situation, the captain ultimately ordered his vessel grounded in 10 feet of water on Molasses Reef at 2:30 a.m. on May 17 to prevent its sinking. The vessel was eventually salvaged, pulled off the reef, and towed to Miami. Unfortunately, the *Linda* soon sank in the Miami River and was abandoned. The ship was raised on November 8, and later towed approximately 15 miles off Miami and scuttled by the U.S. Coast Guard on December 21, 1977.

The *Linda* was originally launched as the *Manicouagan* on April 21, 1955, at the Newport, Wales shipyard of Atlantic Shipbuilding Company, Limited for the Quebec and Ontario Transportation Company, Limited. The freighter was 258.8 feet long, 44 feet wide, and 2,313 tons gross burden. The vessel was soon renamed *Colonel Robert R. McCormick* where she operated on the Great Lakes. In 1967, she was sold to Shallow Draft Bulk Carriers, Limited and moved to the Caribbean, where she sailed as the *Montagu Bay*. The freighter was sold again in 1977 to the Panamanian shipping firm All-Trading Company, whereupon she was finally named *Linda*.

LINDA JO

Locally known as the "Military Wreck," this wreck rests in approximately 160 feet of water east of Sebastian Inlet. The former trawler is extremely broken down and low-lying, and largely consists of a windlass, outriggers, and random debris. This may possibly be the 67-foot long wooden-hulled trawler *Linda Jo*, built in 1972 by St. Augustine Trawlers, Incorporated. Registration for this vessel went inactive around 1993, which may be related to this vessel's potential loss.

LITTLE STEVIE

The 27-ton *Little Stevie*, which was built in 1943, foundered on November 29, 1949, at approximate latitude 29° 02' north and longitude 80° 25' west (i.e., approximately 26 nautical miles east of Ponce de Leon Inlet)[126].

LITTLE TALBOT ISLAND WRECK

In May 1987, a shipwreck was exposed at the foot of a sand dune in the tidal zone on Little Talbot Island, south of Nassau Inlet. A survey of the wreck revealed a portion of a heavily-framed vessel fastened with wooden treenails, copper bolts, and iron spikes, and also possessed several iron reinforcing frames. Analysis of these features indicates the vessel could likely date from anywhere between 1820 and 1920. In 2007, Tropical Storm Andrea impacted the wreck and carried it to the southern end of Little Talbot Island, which dislodged some of the wreck's timbers. Potential identities for the "Little Talbot Island Wreck" include the schooners *Alert*, *Gracie D. Buchanan*, *Jessie A. Bishop*, *Theoline*, and *Velasco*.

LIVELY

The ship *Lively* (or *Lovely*), bound from Hamburg, Germany, to Charleston, South Carolina, was originally reported to have wrecked in 1797 at latitude 31° 16' north and longitude 80° 30' west[127], but a later account stated the vessel drifted ashore near St. Augustine[128].

LIZZIE BAKER

The *Lizzie Baker*, official number 15550, was a sidewheel steamer built in 1864 by Lawler and Brainerd at East Albany, New York. The steamer displaced 506 tons gross, and was 170 feet in length and 29 feet in breadth. During her career, she operated for the Jacksonville-Charleston Line as well as the Jacksonville-Savannah Service. According to *The Consitution*, December 12, 1875, "*Lizzie Baker*, from Jacksonville for Savannah, was snagged on St. Johns Bar at four o'clock on December 10, 1875, and sunk in three minutes. A total loss. Crew and passengers saved." A portion of her cargo, consisting of cotton, cottonseed, and general merchandise, was salvaged. Other reports state her loss was due to striking the submerged wreck of the *Welaka*, which stranded on the St. Johns River Bar on December 13, 1857. It is unclear when or if the wreck of the *Lizzie Baker* was removed, but she was apparently still visible in 1879.

LIZZIE B. WILLEY

An April 6 dispatch included in *The Indianapolis Star* on April 7, 1915, carried information on the loss of the schooner *Lizzie B. Willey*. It stated, "The members of the crew of the three-masted schooner *Lizzie B. Willey* were rescued today off the Florida coast by the Southern Pacific steamship *Proteus*, according to wireless message received here. The schooner, which left Savannah March 31 for Pawtucket, was in a waterlogged condition, having sprung leaks in the gale of Saturday. The *Proteus* left New Orleans April 3 for New York. The *Lizzie B. Willey* carried a crew of seven. She was built in Thomaston, Me., in 1881 and has a gross tonnage of 573." The *Willey*, official number 140485, was 150.4 feet long and 34.1 feet wide; built by Dunn and Elliot.

LIZZIE E. DENNISON

The wrecking of the American schooner *Lizzie E. Dennison* is rather confusing due to numerous cited accounts of her loss. An article in the *New Smyrna News* printed on March 15, 1918, claims the vessel foundered 25 miles off Titusville on the morning of March 11. While making good headway, she sprung a leak during a gale and quickly went under. Captain Burt Killand and his crew of eight managed to clear the sinking ship on various bits of floating debris, and safely landed on the beach that evening. However, a March 15 piece in the *Indian River Chronicle* states the schooner was blown "on the rocks," and her crew came ashore on a piece of the cabin and in a skiff. A third contradictory report appeared in the 1919 edition of the *Annual List of Merchant Vessels of the United States*, which documented the *Lizzie E. Dennison* stranded on Hetzel Shoal on March 10. The *Lizzie E. Dennison* was a 452-ton schooner, 141.5 feet in length, 33 feet in beam, built in 1890 at East Deering, Maine. She sailed for Cuba March 9 with a cargo of lumber. Regardless of the actual cause for her loss, the wreck of the schooner *Lizzie E. Dennison* has yet to be identified.

LIZZIE HEYER

The *Lizzie Heyer*, official number 15936, was a schooner built in October 1873 at Thomaston, Maine, by Walker, Dunn, and Company. She was 137 feet in length, 31 feet in beam, and displaced 360 tons. In October 1898, the *Lizzie Heyer* wrecked off Fernandina. Another source reported the loss of the schooner farther north on Stafford Shoals off Cumberland Island.

LIZZIE L. SMITH

The *Lizzie L. Smith* wrecked near Mosquito Inlet (also reported as three miles south of the inlet) on October 11, 1878, while on a voyage from New York to Tampico, Mexico; while the vessel was a total loss, the crew was saved[129]. Built in October 1877 at Crisfield, Maryland, the *Lizzie L. Smith*, official number 140274, was a small vessel, displacing but 25 tons. Her master was listed as Captain G.P. Washington.

LOANDO

Built as the steam yacht *Promise* in 1877 at Greenpoint, New York, the *Loando*, official number 150120, had a waterline length of 88.4 feet, an overall length of 103 feet, a width of 16.9 feet, and a gross displacement of 42 tons. In July 1908, the yacht was sold at auction for $2,650. On May 20, 1915, the *Loando* foundered off the Florida coast. The crew of the yacht was safely assisted to shore the same day by Keeper Clinton P. Honeywell and his assistants of the Cape Canaveral Light Station.

LODONA

Hurricanes have taken a great toll on shipping off the Florida coast. Vessels large and small have been consumed by a hungry ocean, either slowly broken apart or suddenly pulled under. The steamer *Lodona* was yet another casualty to succumb to the Atlantic during hurricane season. A barkentine-rigged, iron-hulled steamer, the *Lodona* was built at Hull, England, in 1862. She was a fine vessel, 210 feet long, 27.5 feet wide, and displaced 750 tons. Owned by L.C. Pierson of London, England, she was initially employed as a blockade runner. In that capacity, however, she was a dismal failure, as she was captured on her very first run. Upon her arrival in port at Bermuda in early July, her suspicious intentions were noticed by the United States Consul. On July 2, he noted: "It seems from the statement of the master, that no bond was given and no oath was made to the manifest or crew list." He continued, stating: "She has a cargo principally of ardent spirits, some drugs, amongst which is a large quantity of quinine, clothing and other merchandise. The master has requested me to endorse his license, which I have refused to do, on the ground his cargo is principally contraband; and further, their associations are such here as to leave little doubt in my mind that their license was not obtained in good faith." Over the next week, the Consul kept a close eye on the *Lodona*, as well as other suspected blockade runners in port. On July 7, he noted that Captain Raphael Semmes was visiting the steamer quite often.

As the *Lodona* prepared to leave Bermuda, her captain attempted to refill her bunkers with coal. Unfortunately, the United States Consul refused to allow it. He documented his amusement at the charade: "Every scheme human ingenuity could invent has been resorted to induce me to let him have coal; he went so far as to offer me $1,000 if I would go to the other end of the island and remain two days, and leave my business in the hands of a merchant here." When the *Lodona* ultimately departed Bermuda, the U.S. Navy was expecting her arrival off the United States coast. She was captured by the U.S.S. *Unadilla* while trying to run the blockade off South Carolina on August 4, 1862. The war prize was taken to Philadelphia where she was eventually purchased from the court after judgment by the U.S. Navy. The U.S. Navy commissioned the vessel U.S.S. *Lodona* at the Philadelphia Navy Yard on January 5, 1863. Ironically, her initial assignment was with the South Atlantic Blockading Squadron off South Carolina. Stationed off Charleston and Bull's Bay, she captured the English brig *Minnie* as she attempted to run the blockade on April 20. During the summer, her 100-pound, 30-pound, and four 24-pound Parrott guns, as well as her nine-inch Dahlgren gun trained on Confederate fortifications surrounding Charleston Harbor. After an overhaul in Philadelphia throughout October, she steamed back south to resume her blockading duty. She quickly scored a prize on November 15, when she captured the schooner *Arctic*. The *Lodona* continued to serve off South Carolina until Lee's surrender and the end of hostilities. The U.S.S. *Lodona* headed back to the Philadelphia Navy Yard, whereupon she was decommissioned on May 11, 1865, and sold at public auction on June 20.

The *Lodona* was purchased by John Jewett and Sons C.H. Mallory and Company for service between New York and New Orleans. It was in this capacity when she was lost in August 1871. The *Lodona* had left her berth on August 12 with a full cargo of assorted merchandise, valued at more than $200,000. She was under the command of Captain H.R. Hovey, and carried 34 passengers and crew. On August 16, the *Lodona* encountered a heavy swell as she steamed southward along the Florida coast. With sound engines and stout hull, few worried about the degrading weather. By 3:00 a.m. on August 17, a hurricane enveloped the *Lodona*. As the crew worked to keep the boilers stoked, crashing seas steadily ran into the skylight. At 7:30 a.m., tragedy struck the English steamer. Louis Wolf, a mess boy on the *Lodona*, described the chain of events: "About half-past seven we struck a reef and she shifted over on her beam ends. The captain was in the pilot house at the time she shifted, and he fell out and stumbled while trying to catch hold of the main rigging. The sea broke over the ship and washed him off and carried away the pilot house. The captain was not seen any more. Some of the crew got into a boat and when about thirty yards off the ship the *Lodona* turned over and capsized[130]."

Those who survived the capsizing now found themselves amidst mountainous seas. At the time, Wolf stated the Florida coast was 10 miles distant. Some of the crew managed to stay afloat in their lifeboat, while several others, like Lewis Wolf, clung to the wreck as it was gradually pushed to shore. The *Lodona* eventually grounded in the breakers, approximately 1,000 feet offshore. Those who could swim set off for shore. Lewis Wolf and two other men remained on the wreck for two

Illustration of the steamer U.S.S. *Lodona* (Naval Historical Center).

days, but set out for shore on a raft when conditions calmed. At that time, they reunited with the chief engineer and other crew who swam for shore as soon as the *Lodona* grounded off the beach. They had walked south approximately six miles to Cape Canaveral Light where the keeper told them they needed to walk back north to the nearest Custom House station. The survivors struggled northward without food and with very little water. Along the way they passed numerous bloated bodies from the wreck; the storm claimed 21 lives from the *Lodona*. Several of the crew fell behind, exhausted from the ordeal. Eventually, approximately 14 miles south of Smyrna, Lewis Wolf met a man who agreed to provide them food and water. He eventually hailed a small boat from the beach, which took him to St. Augustine to report the news. While the *Lodona* was a first-rate steamer, those around the wharves in New York suspected how she met her demise. They surmised the steamer was swamped owing to a peculiar structure on her upper works. Instead of a clear deck over which the waves could sweep without obstruction, the owners added a large cabin 60 feet long soon after purchasing the steamer. As a high bulwark extended from the cabin to the bow, a wave crashing into the cabin would have no chance to escape, and would load down the ship and soon swamp her. If the water were caught forward by the bulwark, the result would be similar, as the scuppers would allow the escape of only a small fraction of a massive wave weighing several hundred tons. The grave of the *Lodona* has not been identified to date. The iron hull of the steamer likely rests just offshore the surf zone, however, since the wreck resides on Cape Canaveral, the security zone around the complex complicates exploration.

LOFTHUS

The *Lofthus*, originally named the *Cashmere*, was an iron bark that grounded off Boynton Beach following a storm on January 31, 1898. A bark was a class of vessel typified by three masts, of which the fore and main masts were square-rigged. Built in October 1868 by T.R. Oswald in Sunderland, England, she was 222.8 feet in length, 36.7 feet in beam, displaced 1,277 gross tons, and possessed two decks. She was originally employed by the Liverpool Shipping Company, Limited and managed by H. Fernie and Sons. Under her official number 58930, *Lloyd's Register of American and Foreign Shipping* noted that one of her two decks was replaced in 1890 and that she underwent repairs in 1893 due to previously incurred damages. With the advent of the compound steam engine, iron barks such as the *Lofthus* were relegated to carrying bulk cargo, the delivery of which was not particularly time-sensitive. Many of these vessels were appraised at no more than their value as scrap. As such, numerous Norwegian shipping firms readily purchased them towards the end of the nineteenth century. The *Lofthus* was eventually sold to *Barque Lofthus Actierederi*, and was home ported in Lillesand, along the southeast coast of Norway.

With Captain Fromberg at the helm, the *Lofthus* departed Pensacola on January 21, 1898, with a cargo of

View of the *Lofthus* stranded off Lantana (Marine Archaeological Research and Conservation).

pitch pine. She encountered a winter storm and was blown ashore 10 days later, coming to rest in close proximity to the *Oh Kim Soon* off Lantana. The *Lofthus* was pushed to within 200 feet of the beach before she sunk into the sand and ground to a halt. While her fate was sealed, the event itself was fortunately absent of any tragedy or loss of life. All 16 of her crew safely departed the ship and made their way to Jacksonville where the incident was reported. With her bow pointed to the north, the ship sat upright and absolutely still, with the exception of the rhythmic pounding of the rolling surf. Local residents turned out to inspect the grounded vessel. In fact, the Voss family was invited aboard to have dinner with Captain Fromberg and his family. The Vosses noted that the ship was splendidly appointed, with rich exotic woodwork throughout the cabin and ornate silverware gracing the table. The vessel was salvaged and stripped of her expensive fittings by mid-March, and the wreck with her cargo of 800,000 feet of lumber was auctioned off for $1,000. Apparently, not all the lumber could be reached easily, and there were reports in September 1898 of plans to use explosives to gain access into the holds. After the salvageable timber was recovered, the *Lofthus* was allowed to be slowly beaten beneath the waves.

The *Lofthus* now rests quietly in 20 feet of water, approximately 550 feet off the beach. Known locally as the "Bottle Wreck," the site is an easy dive that can be witness to splendid visibility due to the highly reflective, clean sand bottom. Isolated to the north is a skeletal section of bulkheads that used to frame the bow area, the remainder of which is largely buried. Swimming aft, portions of the deck framing can be found on the bottom, while an iron mast juts up from its sandy tomb. A 60-foot section of the amidships hull rises off the seabed, which provides good seasonal habitat for spiny lobsters. To the extreme south resides a cluster of wreckage from the stern, including an inverted section of deck framing and portions of the steering mechanism. In between these three major features are other random sections of hull plating and miscellaneous wreckage. Due to the wreck's proximity to shore, sand ripples propagating from the beach facilitate diver navigation.

The *Lollie Boy* at left, along with the steamers *Forester* and *Ocklawaha*, docked at Palatka (Alfred H. Robson).

LOLLIE BOY

The 86-ton inline sternwheel steamer *Lollie Boy* (also cited as *Lollyboy*) was built in 1873, and ran on the Ocklawaha River, as well as up the St. Johns River to Lake Harney, for H.T. Baya. On November 11, 1877, the *Lollie Boy* sank while heading from Silver Springs to Jacksonville with a general cargo.

LONG ISLAND EXPRESS

On the morning of October 3, 1986, the 157-foot long freighter *Long Island Express*, owned by Albury's Investment Holdings, Limited of Nassau, capsized approximately 15 miles offshore Lake Worth Inlet. According to Captain Hanson Henry, "We had two pumps running constantly, but we couldn't keep up with the water. Finally we got so low that water was splashing over the railings. We were throwing the cargo overboard but it didn't help[131]." The vessel was en route from Palm Beach to Andros, Bahamas, with a cargo of 12,000 concrete blocks, bags of cement, and sheet rock. Fortunately, the five-man crew was rescued by a U.S. Coast Guard cutter just minutes before the vessel rolled over and sank.

LONG REACH

The September 8, 1880, edition of *The New York Times* detailed the wrecking of the brig *Long Reach*, bound from Apalachicola for Philadelphia. The vessel stranded on Turtle Mound off Cape Canaveral in the same storm that claimed the steamer *City of Vera Cruz*, and eventually became a total loss. The *Long Reach*, official number 15318, was built in May 1868 at Bath, Maine. The 225-ton hermaphrodite brig was 113.9 feet long and 28.3 feet wide.

LOUISE

The steamer *Louise* operated on the St. Johns River as a ferry between Mayport and Jacksonville. On February 16, 1890, she was on a routine voyage up the river. Captain Charles Floyd and a crew of five men tended to their duties while seven passengers were lying asleep in the cabin. At approximately 1:30 a.m., the *Louise* suddenly crashed into an obstruction, later determined to be a sunken wreck. Taking on water, the ferry sank in two minutes. Captain Floyd gave the following account of the disaster:

> When the boat struck we rushed to the cabins and called to the passengers to make for the lifeboat. The water rushed in so fast that the boat could not be reached, and we finally got onto a liferaft and cut it loose. This was on the hurricane deck, to which we had retreated. There were ten persons on the raft, and myself and Eph Hood in the water. I threw my arm over a stick of wood, which aided me in keeping above the surface. Wesley Evans, a young colored passenger, went down with the boat and was drowned. We were not in the water very long, for the mate of the schooner *Jesse W. Starr* came to us and took us all in[132].

The *Louise* came to rest in 55 feet of water near Hunter's Mill. Nothing of the wreck was visible above the surface of the St. Johns River, save about five feet of her smokestack. According to Davis (1925), the steamer *Louise* was raised, however, it burned soon thereafter at Arlington, opposite of Jacksonville.

LOWRANCE

Since its intentional sinking as an artificial reef off Fort Lauderdale on March 31, 1984, the wreck of the *Lowrance* has become one of the most popular technical diving destinations in South Florida. At 420.5 feet in overall length and 55.1 feet in width, she is also one of the largest. Named after the manufacturer of recreational marine electronics that donated funds to help sink the vessel, the *Lowrance* sits in approximately 200 feet of water. The hull of the former freighter provides significant vertical relief, with the main deck found at a depth of 165 feet and the shallowest portion of the wreck rising to within approximately 150 feet of the surface.

The *Lowrance* as the *Ciudad de Cali*.

The *Lowrance* originally slid down the ways as the *Ciudad de Cali* (IMO number 5074381) on April 3, 1953. The 4,327-ton refrigerated freighter was built by Canadian Vickers, Limited at their Montreal shipyard for the Colombian shipping company *Flota Mercante Grancolombiana S.A.* In 1972, the freighter was sold and renamed *Rio Amazonas*. She traded hands yet again in

The *Lowrance* as the converted barge *Mazon* (Broward County Artificial Reef Program).

1980, and sailed under the name *Mazon*. In 1981, the freighter's mid-ship superstructure was razed and she was converted into a barge. The ambitious owner apparently intended to load the *Mazon* with scrap steel and tow the vessel to Japan to sell off the entire package. The project stalled, however, and the barge sat idle in Port Everglades before eventually being acquired by the Broward County Artificial Reef Program.

The *Lowrance* heads for the bottom (Broward County Artificial Reef Program).

Found approximately 2.5 nautical miles outside Hillsboro Inlet, the 420-foot long hull of the *Lowrance* rests perpendicular to the generally northward-moving Gulf Stream; even during periods of significant currents, divers usually have no problem hitting this massive target. It is also worth noting that the wreck of the *Renegade* is found approximately 700 feet due north of the *Lowrance*, should divers find themselves on the bottom and in between the two artificial reefs. The midship area is perhaps the most interesting, though the remaining upper decks have experienced significant collapse in recent years. For divers with the requisite training and experience, the wreck of the *Lowrance* offers a fantastic circuit through the engine room. Divers can enter through a hatch on the main deck of the vessel that leads down a hallway, eventually opening up above the engine room. Gorgonian-choked skylights above allow ambient light to trickle down onto the catwalks that line the perimeter of the room. Dropping down, divers can work their way around equipment,

Inside the engine room of the *Lowrance*.

eventually exiting through one of several large holes cut out during the vessel's preparation for sinking, or via a smaller hole produced by the explosive charges that sent the former freighter to the bottom.

LOYAL SCRANTON

The schooner *Loyal Scranton* was built in July 1854 at New York. She registered a length of 115 feet, a breadth of 30 feet, and a displacement of 380 tons net. Captain Amos N. Lowden was the master of the schooner at the time of her loss, which occurred on a voyage from New York for Mobile, Alabama. According to a statement of a survivor, "Was on the schooner, *Loyal Scranton*, which, with her captain, was lost on the Florida coast, the last of March (1868). Nine of the crew were saved from a raft, on which they floated for thirty hours, their only subsistence being a case of preserved peaches which floated within their reach from the wreck[133]."

L.T. KNIGHT

The schooner *L.T. Knight*, official number 15425, was built in 1853 at Frankfort, Maine, and was 106.3 feet long, 27.2 feet wide, and displaced 203 tons. On June 5, 1879, the schooner stranded at Little Tiger Island opposite of Fernandina with a cargo of lumber bound for Rio de Janeiro. While the *L.T. Knight* continues to be documented until 1885 (last recorded inspection in April 1879), she was reported as a total loss following the stranding.

LUBRAFOL

On May 9, 1942, the *U-564* was sitting just off the southeast coast of Florida monitoring the shipping lanes for potential targets. The commander of the submarine, *Kapitänleutnant* Reinhard Suhren, had taken the helm of the *U-564* in April 1941 and would eventually sink 19 ships for a total of 96,444 tons. Suhren, along with Peter-Erich Cremer (*U-333*) and Reinhard Hardegen (*U-123*), whose trio of U-boats would successfully hunt off the east coast of Florida, would all, fortunately, survive the war. One of Suhren's targets was the Panamanian tanker *Lubrafol*,

The tanker *Lubrafol* departing port (© National Maritime Museum, London).

which appeared on the southern horizon and grew in size as it approached the patient U-boat commander.

The *Lubrafol*, built in 1924 in Newcastle, England, for the Gulf Oil Company, steamed northward, en route to New York from Aruba, carrying 67,000 barrels of number two heating oil in its holds for the War Shipping Administration. On board was a complement of 44 men consisting of a merchant crew of 38 and a U.S. Naval Armed Guard contingent of six men. At 4:15 a.m., as Captain Van Schoenber and the *Lubrafol* passed approximately three miles off Pompano Beach and the Hillsboro Lighthouse, the telltale thud and subsequent explosion of a torpedo rocked the 7,138-ton tanker.

Two torpedoes hit on the starboard side in short succession. The first ignited the number five tank; the second tore into the number one tank a few moments later. The damage was severe, and soon the ship was engulfed in flames. The foremast toppled onto the bridge from the force of the explosion. No mayday could be given, as the radio antennae were destroyed. The captain ordered the engines stopped at once and turned the helm hard over as to bring the ship broadside to the prevailing wind. The order to abandon ship was given shortly thereafter as the survivors piled into the lifeboats and tried to evacuate from the sinking ship and the growing sea of fire. U.S. Coast Guard boats were at the scene at once and towed the lifeboats clear of the burning oil and to safety. The 31 survivors eventually were landed at Boynton Beach. Thirteen crewmembers were lost either from the initial attack or from jumping overboard into the flaming ocean. The burning tanker did not sink immediately, and the Gulf Stream current slowly carried the vessel northward along the coast. The tanker eventually plunged for the bottom just north of Cape Canaveral, approximately 150 nautical miles from the initial point of attack.

The wreck of the *Lubrafol* now rests in approximately 180 feet of water equidistant from Port Canaveral and Ponce Inlet. On a calm day, a continuous stream of oil leaking to the surface reveals the tanker's location. Oriented with her bow to the north, the wreck resides on a bare limestone bottom. Divers may note an odd five-foot deep trench along the western perimeter of the *Lubrafol's* hull. Apparently, the weight of the tanker has compressed the limestone seabed over the years, forming this interesting benthic anomaly. The most prominent features of the *Lubrafol* can be found on the eastern or offshore side of the wreck, where the debris field from the superstructure is spread across the seafloor. The wreck appears to have rolled as she slipped under the waves, as the forward half of the ship is almost completely turtled. There is significant damage to the bow, with the sides folded back from the stem. The forward gun tubs can be found inverted and adjacent to the hull, in close proximity to the forward mast. Swimming along the mast, divers may still view the crows nest and signal horn. The remains of the forward superstructure and bridge are not prominent on the wreck, aside from a row of portholes along a loose bulkhead. There is substantial access into the inverted hull, but divers should be cautious, as a significant quantity of jelled oil can still be found congealed in the forward tanker holds. The stern section is twisted and sheared off from the remainder of the hull, lying on its starboard side. The stern deck gun can be found resting in the sand, its barrel still pointing aft. A large amount of

Lubrafol in flames and drifting off the Florida coast (William T. Hultgren).

Andrew Donn inspects the remains of the crow's nest.

debris and bulkheads can be found just forward of the gun, where the stern deckhouse has fallen onto the seabed below. One of the boilers is visible spilling out of the hull at the point where the wreck is twisted forward of the stern. Flanges, piping, and valves can be found scattered amongst the wreckage, all common fittings for a tanker. Divers rounding the fantail of the wreck will encounter the large port side screw, which provides a very surreal and picturesque scene. The wreck is largely devoid of any marine growth, and the surfaces of the wreck are dominated by brown hues, punctuated only by random sprigs of stark-white *Oculina varicosa* coral. Due to its distance offshore, however, the wreck of the *Lubrafol* supports healthy fish populations. Large schools of amberjack swarm about the upper hull, while a copious amount of red snapper dart amongst the wreckage on the bottom. Gag, scamp, and warsaw grouper also dwell within the confines of the wreck. Several lionfish (*Pterois volitans*), an introduced species naturally endemic to the Indo-Pacific, can also be found in the debris field.

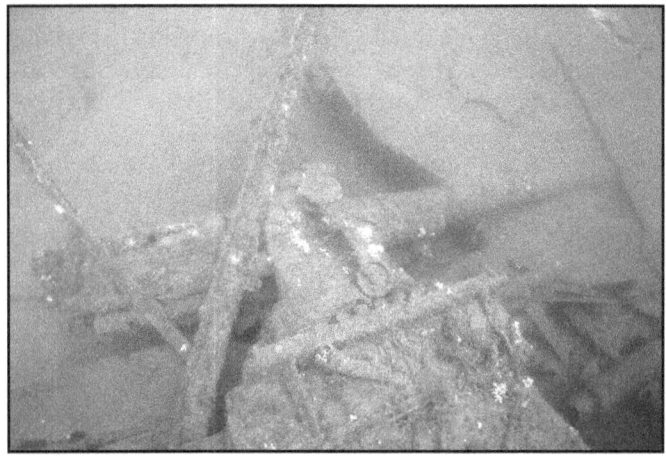

The *Lubrafol*'s stern deck gun resting on the seafloor.

Diving conditions on the *Lubrafol* can vary greatly due to its proximity to the Gulf Stream, as well as Cape Canaveral. Typically, current is not as severe as that experienced on offshore wrecks south of the Cape. Nonetheless, current exceeding three knots is not uncommon. Dynamic temperature conditions can also be experienced on the *Lubrafol*. Upwelling events can introduce frigid water on the bottom, with temperatures as low as 48°F. Fortunately, water exceeding 80°F near the surface in the summer allows divers to thaw out during decompression. While dive conditions are always an unknown on this wreck, a visit to the tanker *Lubrafol* is definitely worth the gamble.

LUCY

The *Galveston Daily News* printed the following on August 31, 1873: "Five sailors made their appearance in Petersburg, Virginia, on Thursday last, who stated that they were a part of the fifteen survivors of the crew of the steamship *Lucy*, which was burned at sea forty-five miles off Cape Canaveral, on the 15th instant. Their names are as follows: Charles Williams, George Johnson, J.E. Willis, George Fisher, and Thomas Richardson. Two of the party were suffering from terrible burns, which substantiates the truth of their story." This may possibly be the 314-ton steamer *Lucy*, built in 1863 at Liverpool, which was 212 feet long and 20.3 feet wide. This vessel, owned by Benner, Brown, and Pickney, and mastered by Captain Ellis, disappeared from documentation after 1874.

LUELLA

The *Luella* was a 131-ton schooner built in 1845 at Waldoboro, Maine. Rebuilt in 1865, vessel documentation indicates her displacement was reduced to 104 tons. In 1868, the *Luella* entered Mosquito Inlet and discharged her cargo, but as Captain James E. Burgess was sailing her back out to sea, she grounded and became a total wreck. According to Hawks (1887), "She was of over a hundred tons burden, and had discharged her cargo on the bank of the old mill site. The cargo consisted of the boilers and engine and all the machinery of the mill, brick for setting the boilers, and a stock of goods that cost over $4,000. In going to sea the captain undertook to cross the bar on a falling tide and with but little wind; a great many have made the same mistake. She touched on the south shore, and never got off. The sand filled in around her, and she stood high and dry for a long time, her tall masts answering as beacons and a warning to other sailors."

LUGANO

Lying quietly in 25 feet of water adjacent to the reef that sealed her fate, the remains of the *Lugano* are luxuriously enveloped in corals and sponges. In turn, the wreckage supports a colorful array of tropical species, small grouper, and schools of yellowtail, as well as numerous moray eels and lobster that can be found under the collapsed hull plates. The superstructure is absent on the site, though large portions of her skeletal hull and ribs remain. Over the years, various artifacts have been found scattered about the wreck, such as silverware, Royal Ironstone china, and numerous bottles. During her internment since she came to grief on Long Reef on the

The steamer *Lugano*, aground on the reef (© The Mariners' Museum, Newport News, Virginia).

afternoon of March 9, 1913, the *Lugano* has been transformed into an enjoyable dive site.

Originally built as the *Navarro* in December 1882 by the Barrow Shipbuilding Company, the single screw, iron-hulled steamer was 350.1 feet in length, 40.1 feet in beam, and displaced 3,770 tons. In 1897, D. Rollo and Sons of Liverpool overhauled the *Navarro*, whereupon her name was changed to *Lugano*. Employed by the Atlantic and Eastern Steamship Company, Limited, the British steamer was on a routine cruise from Liverpool to Havana with a cargo of rice, silks, wines, and general merchandise, as well as 116 passengers emigrating from Spain to Cuba. Unfortunately, Captain J. Penwell was unaware that he was dangerously off course, exacerbated by high winds and heavy seas, as he passed south of Miami. Suddenly, the bow of the *Lugano* ran hard onto the shallow coral of Long Reef. Hopelessly stuck, the captain ordered the flood valves to be opened in order to fill the ship and prevent further pounding from the unrelenting waves. A wireless distress call was also made that was received at Key West. The tug *Rescue* was dispatched and managed to safely transfer all the passengers.

Over the course of the next few weeks, foul weather continued to hamper the salvage of the *Lugano*, her holds filled with 15 feet of water. Over 75 wreckers worked the wreck and managed to recover a large portion of the cargo that was carried to Key West. After sitting on the abrasive reef for almost a month, the hull of the steamer began to give way. By April 4, the crew of the *Lugano* abandoned the wreck and headed to Key West. Salvors finally surrendered the vessel to the sea on April 15, and removed their pumps and equipment from the mammoth holds of the steamer. Further work on the wreck consisted of the removal of her rigging and the use of explosives to recover machinery.

While the *Lugano* gave herself to the sea, she did not want to go alone. On February 12, 1917, the fishing yacht *Ada M* struck the submerged hull of the *Lugano* and nearly sank. A few years later, the steamer *Calicorock* ran afoul of the wreck and heavily damaged her portside hull on November 30, 1919. Fortunately, the steamer was able to make port for repairs. Eventually, the wreck of the *Lugano* was marked on nautical charts as a hazard to navigation. During the 1950s, the wreck was heavily salvaged for scrap iron, which was sold to Japan for $65 per ton. Local salvors used dynamite to break apart sections of the *Lugano* (as well as the *Alicia* and others), which were then hauled off the bottom. Aside from the hull itself, copious amounts of ceramics and vintage clothes irons were also recovered from around the site. Today, the wreck largely is dominated by scattered sections of lower hull members heavily encrusted by gorgonians and fire coral.

LUMBER WRECK

In the 1980s, the entire wooden hull of a wreck known locally as the "Lumber Wreck" was exposed in 18 feet of water off Red Reef Park in Boca Raton. Heavy wooden timbers and portions of her hull, randomly injected with iron spikes and copper nails, were visible resting on the sand bottom, while schools of baitfish darted just above the wreckage. Due to the active beach nourishment program in South Florida, the entire wreck has since been covered up. The area warrants observation should a hurricane or strong winter storm uncover the vessel and allow a brief glimpse at this unidentified wreck.

LYNN

According to Singer (1998), the *Lynn* was a 441-ton barge built in 1914, which stranded at Lake Worth Inlet on February 16, 1926.

LYON

The schooner *Lyon* went ashore on the north breakers off St. Augustine in 1836; the crew was saved but the vessel was a total loss[134].

MACHOTE

The *Machote* was a 2,026-ton freighter 325 feet in length and 46.2 feet in beam. The vessel was built as the *Svolder* in 1941 by Nylands Verksted in Oslo, Norway. The freighter fortunately survived World War II while under German control and was later chartered to a South American company following hostilities. In 1955, the *Svolder* was sold to a German company and renamed *Henry Boge*. She traded hands and changed names three more times in her career: in 1959 she was renamed *Christina Bischoff*; in 1963 she sailed as *San Pedro*; and in 1966 she became *Machote*. Apparently, from this point on, the *Machote* largely sat idle at Tampa. This neglect doomed the vessel, as the ship steadily rusted in place. In early 1970, port officials grew concerned that the *Machote* and another freighter, the *Leeuwarden*, both owned by Caribbean Federation Lines, may sink at their berths and pollute local waters. Finally forced to take action, the Dutch company evaluated their options. Unfortunately, surveyors determined the extent of repairs to keep the rusting *Machote* afloat far exceeded her value. Therefore, her owners penned a deal to have both *Machote* and *Leeuwarden* broken up and sold for scrap at the Italian port of La Spezia. While the vessels were towed out of Tampa and into the Gulf of Mexico on October 20, the two derelict freighters collided. As a result of the collision, the *Machote* began leaking badly and soon was in danger of sinking. The U.S. Coast Guard denied the damaged vessel access back into Tampa Bay due to fears the vessel would founder in the channel and block shipping traffic. The owners hastily tried to find another breaking yard along the Gulf of Mexico in hopes of extracting some value out of the vessel in lieu of letting her sink. After several days without finding an alternative option, the owners pressed on with their original plan and directed the tug *Ciclone* to tow the freighters around Florida and into the Atlantic. As they approached South Florida on October 30, the convoy tried to enter Miami. At this point, the *Machote* was sinking at the bow and with a 25 degree list to port. Like Tampa, the vessels were refused entry until the *Machote* was pumped out and stabilized. Finally, on October 31, the *Machote* foundered under tow at latitude 26° 45′ north and longitude 79° 36′ west (i.e., approximately 23 nautical miles due east of West Palm Beach). The *Leeuwarden*, a former troop transport that participated in the Bay of Pigs invasion of Cuba, was successfully towed to Italy and scrapped.

MADAKET

The wreck off Ponce de Leon Inlet locally known as the "Mannacamp" is actually the hopper dredge *Madaket*. It rests in approximately 80 feet of water north of Cape Canaveral and hosts an abundance of marine life. The *Madaket* was 350 feet long, 52 feet wide, and had a capacity of 7,000 tons. Owned by Resolve Marine Group, she was equipped for their busy salvage operations. At the time of her loss, however, she was contracted to carry sand from Ocean Cay, Bahamas to Fort Pierce. In January 1986, she was caught in a strong winter storm and foundered after her accompanying tug lost power. Now a popular diving and fishing spot, the wreck offers signifcant relief and supports abundant marine life. A large crane can also be found strewn along on the bottom and extending away from the barge.

MADAWASKA

The schooner *Madawaska*, en route from Baltimore, Maryland for St. Augustine, ran aground on the bar while attempting to enter the harbor of St. Augustine on the morning of April 26, 1855[135]. News accounts concluded that she was full of water and would most likely go to pieces. The *Madawaska* was launched in June 1832 at Bath, Maine.

MAGGIE II

The 25-ton vessel *Maggie II* foundered four miles east of Port Everglades on November 11, 1956.

MAGGIE JONES

The schooner *Maggie Jones* was reportedly driven ashore on the evening of August 16, 1893, at Fernandina.

MAGGIE MAE

The 30-foot long fishing vessel *Maggie Mae* capsized and sank 25 miles off Port Canaveral on August 14, 1985. Reportedly, the *Maggie Mae* ran over a thick hawser line earlier that day, which caused the boat's engine to cut off. Captain Edward Smith jumped over to cut the line out and inspected the running gear, which appeared undamaged. However, just over an hour later the *Maggie Mae* began taking on a substantial amount of water, leading to her sinking. The captain and his one crewman managed to get off a distress call with the vessel's position before abandoning ship. After floating on debris for almost two hours, the fishing boat *Heavy Duty II* rescued the two men approximately eight miles from the reported sinking location.

The sunken remains of the steamer *Magic City* after being rammed by the *Parthian* (Florida State Archives).

MAGIC CITY

On February 17, 1910, *The New York Times* published details on the wrecking of the *Magic City*: "On February 16, the steamship *Parthian* rammed and sank the Cook Steamship Company's steamship *Magic City* at the mouth of the St. Johns River. The *Magic City* was loaded with merchandise for Miami, and was going out to sea near the jetties when the *Parthian* struck her. The wrecked vessel is now lying in twenty-four feet of water. Efforts will be made to raise her."

The wreck of the *Magic City* remained on the bottom of the St. Johns where she wrecked opposite present-day Mayport until she was ultimately removed as an obstruction by the U.S. Army Corps of Engineers the following year. The work was documented in the *Annual Report of the Chief of Engineers, United States Army, to the Secretary of War for the Year 1911*:

> Work began January 12, 1911, and was completed March 10, 1911. Dynamite was used to break the vessel into pieces which could be handled by the derrick barge in use. One thousand one hundred and fifty pounds of dynamite were used in this work. The wreck (formerly the lighthouse steamer *Laurel*) was a wooden hull, twin screw steamer, built for the United States Lighthouse Establishment in 1876 at Baltimore, Md. She was 134 feet long, 25 feet beam, and 10 feet depth of hold. The rated tonnage was 315 gross tons and 213 net tons. She was sunk in collision on February 16, 1910. Her bow was in 15 feet and her stern in 19 feet of water at mean low water. The vessel was loaded with miscellaneous cargo, most of which had been removed.

The *Laurel* was built for the Lighthouse Board by the Columbian Iron Works at a cost of $40,000. After over 30 years of service, a 1907 annual report on Lighthouse Board activities and assets included the following in regard to the *Laurel*: "She is so old and frail that she is beyond economical repair, and it is not unlikely that she will, on survey, be condemned, and that her sale will be ordered in the near future." True enough, on June 19, 1909, the *Laurel* was sold at auction for $1,050, whereupon she was renamed *Magic City* and put to work hauling passengers and freight along Florida's coast until her loss the following year.

MAGNOLIA (1882)

The 22-ton schooner *Magnolia*, built in 1878, wrecked on the Mosquito Inlet Bar on March 9, 1882, while en route from Jacksonville for Smyrna. Tragically, a few weeks after the loss, the *Magnolia's* master, Captain S. Artelle, perished during his journey home when the steamer *City of Sanford* burned a few miles upriver of Jacksonville on the morning of April 24, 1882.

MAGNOLIA (1928)

Built in 1918 at Jacksonville, the small screw steamer *Magnolia*, official number 215928, was 53.7 feet in length and 22 feet in beam, and displaced 47 tons gross. On October 24, 1928, the *Magnolia* burned at Jacksonville.

MAJO

Built in 1947, the *Majo* was a small shrimp trawler owned and operated by Captain Bill Wells. The *Majo* stranded near Ponte Vedra Beach on August 31, 1960.

MAJOR WILLIAM BARNETT

On August 3, 1859, while operating on the St. Johns River, the boiler of the sidewheel steamer *Major William Barnett* exploded, resulting in the deaths of the captain and three passengers. The explosion devastated the upper deck and severely damaged the vessel's machinery. The 240-ton steamer was built in 1851 at Camden, New Jersey. She was 119.5 feet long and 24.6 feet wide. The *Barnett* served as a ferry in Pennsylvania, North Carolina, and South Carolina, before heading to Florida to operate on a run between Jacksonville and Black Creek. Later, she ran between Fernandina and Enterprise.

MANDALAY

Aboard the steel schooner *Mandalay*, New Years Eve 1966 passed with the typical revelry associated with the dawn of a new year. Twenty three vacationers had been enjoying their 10-day "adventure at a leisurely pace," as advertised by the *Mandalay's* owners at Windjammer Cruises, Incorporated. However, for the passengers aboard, already uncomfortable from the heaving 10-foot seas, the New Year was about to take a frightful turn. Around 1:00 a.m., 26-year-old Norwegian Captain Asmund Gjevik turned in, believing he was in deep water as he neared Fowey Rocks Light. Unfortunately, Captain Asmund had, on this, his first trip at the helm of the

The *Mandalay* stranded on the reef (Historical Museum of Southern Florida).

Mandalay, miscalculated his distance from the light. The error carried them close to shallow water and the dangerous coral reefs found off Elliott Key. At 3:00 a.m. the *Mandalay* ran hard aground on Long Reef, throwing passengers from their berths. The heavy surf drove the vessel farther on the reef, sealing her fate. At 3:43 a.m., an S.O.S. was sent just before the vessel lost power. Fortunately, three helicopters safely recovered the 24 passengers and flew them to Homestead Air Force Base, while the 12 crewmembers were picked up by a Coast Guard patrol boat and taken to Miami.

After news of the grounding spread, looters converged on the site in heavy seas and stripped the schooner of her compass, sextant, and chronometers, as well as passengers' cameras, watches, and other personal effects. Only the approach of salvage tugs dispersed the scavengers. The tugs proceeded to work into the early evening and managed to turn the vessel seaward, however, heavy seas kept the decks awash and parted seams in her steel hull the following day. Pumps were unable to keep up with the flooding water, and the *Mandalay* eventually succumbed to the slow beating of the Atlantic. In the weeks following the grounding, Paul Tannehill furnished large portions of his home on Elliott Key with teak wood recovered from the wrecked schooner. Unfortunately, the Tannehill home was later destroyed by Hurricane Andrew in 1992.

The *Mandalay* was originally built as the *Hardi Biaou* in 1928 by the Neponset, Massachusetts's shipyard of George Lawley and Son Corporation. Her overall length was 112 feet with a 24-foot beam. The schooner was eventually renamed the *Valor* upon her sale in 1931. Upon her purchase in 1957 by Windjammer Cruises, Incorporated owner Mike Burke, she was renamed the *Mandalay* and outfitted to be the "red carpet ship of the Windjammer fleet[136]."

View of the skeletal bow section of the *Mandalay*.

The *Mandalay* now rests in 10 feet of water with a slight port list, a short distance from the wreck of the *Lugano*. Only the skeletal frame of the vessel remains. The engine and other machinery were quickly pulled from the wreck. In fact, the extraction of the engine was performed so rapidly that salvors didn't even bother properly severing fuel hoses and cables. Clamps can still be observed on hoses where the engine was literally ripped from the hull. Both masts were also recovered, leaving only the mast steps to be found fore and aft of the engine, and some scattered rigging leading off the starboard side of the wreck. A fuel tank is the largest object found on the wreck, reaching to within three feet of the surface; many times the tank is awash at low tide, facilitating site location. Near the bow, visitors can observe portions of the teak deck and brass fixtures. The rudder lies under the hull adjacent to the hub where the screw was salvaged, while bulkheads with portholes lie off the port side of the wreck. The wreck of the *Mandalay* has been covered by a wide range of coral species; gorgonians and stony coral heads can be found clinging to every available steel surface. Divers should take caution around the large fuel tank due to copious amounts of fire coral, especially as the wreck can be subjected to significant surge because of its shallow depth. Abundant schools of grunts swarm about the wreck, while solitary barracuda patrol the perimeter of the site. Parrotfish, nurse sharks, moray eels, surgeonfish, and numerous other reef inhabitants can be found in the various niches amongst the wreck. Because of the abundant marine life, shallow depth, and articulated wreckage of the *Mandalay*, this wreck is one of the best to be found in Biscayne National Park.

MANFRED

The 66-ton schooner *Manfred* was built in 1852 at Baltimore, Maryland. On November 23, 1860, *The New York Times* stated the *Manfred*, Captain Guion, was totally lost at New Smyrna on November 13. The schooner was valued at $1,200.

MAPLE LEAF

During archaeological investigations in 1989 and 1992, the sunken hull of the U.S. transport *Maple Leaf*, entombed in the muddy bottom of the St. Johns River, poured forth a remarkable variety of well-preserved artifacts. Swords with personal inscriptions, elaborately carved pipes, shaving mugs, a bayonet, shoes, pistol shot, conch shells, and musical instruments all provided valuable clues into the design and purpose of the *Maple Leaf*, but also insight into the personalities of some of its passengers. In some instances, entire lockers and boxes of material were found just as they had been packed over 120 years earlier. Archaeologists were astounded when even pieces of newspapers and portions of books emerged from the water completely legible. The intact lower hull of the vessel contained the greatest variety and quantity of cultural material from the Civil War known to exist. The vessel had lain dormant, buried in mud and under 24 feet of water, ever since striking a Confederate torpedo (mine) on April 1, 1864, and sinking 10 minutes later.

The sidewheel steamer *Maple Leaf* was built in Kingston, Ontario, by John Counter in 1851 for the Lake Ontario steamboat trade, carrying passengers, freight, and livestock. The wooden-hulled vessel was 173.2 feet in length, 24.6 feet in breadth, and displaced 600 tons. Two

Illustration of the sidewheel steamer *Maple Leaf* (Keith Holland).

cargo holds fore and aft of the central walking beam engine allowed for copious amounts of cargo. The main deck housed the galley and crew quarters, while the saloon and passengers' quarters, found just aft of the pilothouse, were located on the deck above. Above the saloon deck was the upper hurricane deck that stored three of the vessel's lifeboats. She operated on Lake Ontario until September 1, 1862, whereupon she was sold to J.H.B. Lang and Charles Spear of Boston, Massachusetts for $25,000. There was an immediate need for transport ships by the U.S. Army, and a charter contract for the *Maple Leaf* was signed the following day.

On March 26, 1864, Captain Henry W. Dale steamed the *Maple Leaf* south from Hilton Head, South Carolina, towards Jacksonville. After a layover in Fernandina due to foul weather, the side wheeler arrived at Jacksonville on March 30 at 5:00 p.m. The transport, under the direction of an experienced river pilot, then traveled to Palatka with a load of cavalry and soldiers. After discharging the cavalry, she was ordered back to Jacksonville. At approximately 4:00 a.m. on April 1, 1864, the service career of the *Maple Leaf* came to a dramatic end. Captain Dale, during the subsequent Army investigation in Jacksonville on April 2, gave the following account of the events:

> Nothing unusual occurred till 4 o'clock on the morning of April 1st. At that hour I was in bed and asleep but was awakened by a tremendous crash, and heavy report. The saloon was filled with a sickening stench, the timbers were breaking as there was a great tumult. I sprang out and in two minutes the water was over the floor of the saloon. The wheels turned perhaps five times after the crash. The steamer immediately sank, so as to leave about three feet of water in the saloon. It was about four fathoms water. There were on duty forward, the second officer and three men besides the pilot and quartermaster in the pilot house. All I can say of the course of the disaster is that it must have been a torpedo. I judge that it opened the vessel about thirty feet from the stem, right under her bottom. Everything gave way amidships in that portion of the boat. The floor settled immediately. I think it was a torpedo entirely submerged as it burst so far under. Had it been on the surface where it could have been seen it would probably have burst at the bows and perhaps done little damage. We immediately got out all the boats, as soon as possible. We had four boats on board, one was under the saloon deck on the guard and could not be got at, two were on the cranes, one on each quarter, and one on the hurricane deck. We took off all the crew and passengers numbering fifty eight persons and the mail. Two deck hands and two firemen went down with the boat being in the forecastle at the time.

The survivors took to the lifeboats and rowed to Jacksonville, 12 miles distant, arriving there at approximately 8:00 a.m. The gunboat U.S.S. *Norwich* was immediately dispatched to assess the condition of the wreck and pick up four Confederate prisoners who were left on the *Maple Leaf* following the evacuation. As the officers of the *Maple Leaf* boarded the vessel to inspect the damage and recover personal belongings, they found the deck and bow working loose in the water. Captain Dale considered the vessel and cargo a total loss. The wreck was abandoned and the *Norwich* returned to Jacksonville. News of the sinking reached the Confederates a short time after the incident. An expedition was immediately sent in order to investigate. On April 2, three Confederate soldiers boarded the vessel to inspect it. Realizing that they could not benefit from the submerged hull, they set fire to the ship, which burned the saloon deck to the water's edge.

In February 1882, and again later in January 1889, the *Maple Leaf* was cleared to allow 18 feet of clearance over the wreck. The wreck of the *Maple Leaf*, as well as the nearby wrecks of the 470-ton U.S.S. *General Hunter* and the smaller gunboat *Harriet A. Weed*, also sunk by Confederate mines several weeks later, resides in a prominent bend of the St. Johns River off Mandarin Point, approximately twelve miles south of downtown Jacksonville. However, the majority of the *General Hunter* was raised in October 1864 and sold at auction in December 1865.

The hull of the *Maple Leaf*, absent of her upper decks, lies near the east side of the navigation channel with the bow pointing to the east, perpendicular to stream flow. The wreck is almost completely buried under a thick layer of sediment, and very little of the *Maple Leaf* protrudes above the mud to reveal the site. Portions of her machinery can be found scattered amongst the wreck, mute testimony to the efficacy of the explosives used to clear the wreck as a navigational hazard. While not recommended as a dive site, the *Maple Leaf* definitely commands attention as a significant cultural resource repository.

MARANA

As much as divers love shipwrecks, it is highly doubtful any diver would want to actually be involved in one. Yet, that's exactly what happened on December 28, 1965, when a group of divers found themselves abandoning ship as their yacht *Marana* sank from underneath their feet while en route from Miami to the Bahamas for a dive trip. "Fourteen Bimini-bound skindivers, most from the Chicago area, took a premature swim yesterday when their 43-year-old, 75-foot houseboat sank in rough seas about 17 miles east of here[137]." After taking to liferafts, the group was picked up in the Florida Straits approximately an hour later by the tanker *Amoco Delaware*.

MARBERON

On November 10, 1959, *The Miami News* reported the shrimp boat *Marberon* crashed into a jetty and sunk at the Vilano Beach Inlet on the night of November 9. The two-man crew "escaped with minor injuries and a dunking in the chilly water," and were eventually picked up by a nearby boat.

MARCELLY

On February 15, 1831, the British brig *Marcelly*, of Greencock, Captain Monroe, grounded at Bear Cut Bar near Cape Florida. The vessel was en route from New Orleans for Glasgow with 991 bales of cotton. While the *Marcelly* proved a total loss, the cargo was landed on the beach and then carried to Key West by the wrecking schooner *William Ross*. The brig was later burned to recover her copper (presumably sheathing), and the following month, only her stem and stern remained above water to mark the wreck, which was approximately a half-mile from shore.

MARGARET ANN

A November 1842 report stated the schooner *Margaret Ann*, Captain Johnson, went ashore on St. Marys Bar during a voyage from Charleston, South Carolina for Jacksonville; supposed to be a total loss[138].

MARGARETHA

The 152-ton German brig *Margaretha* was built in 1863. The brig was bound for Hamburg when she encountered a gale on the night of August 25, 1871, during which her foremast and main topmast was carried away. A day or two later, the captain of the *Margaretha* spoke to a steamer while off Jupiter Inlet, and arranged for a tow to a safe anchorage for a sum of $4,000. The brig was towed northward to the point approximately 10 miles off the St. Johns Bar where the *Margaretha's* anchors were let go in 15 fathoms of water. Captain Floyd of the tug *R.L. Mabey* proceeded to the anchored vessel, which was flying a flag of distress. According to the September 6, 1871, edition of *The New York Herald*:

> The *R.L. Mabey* took her in tow as a salvor and brought the brig and all hands over the St. Johns Bar as far as the river buoy, where she ran aground (on August 31), and, as the sea was sweeping over the tugboat and running into the engine room, Captain Floyd thought best to cut the hawser in order to avoid injury to the tugboat. The brig was, therefore, left aground. Captain Floyd intended to get her off at high tide the next morning, but as the brig is built in the style of an old Dutch galleon and draws about 18 feet of water, it is considered very improbable if she can be moved. The vessel is owned by Carl Krogel, the master, and his father in law. The vessel had on board a cargo of 4,577 quintala of Campeche logwood, valued at $6,000.

After the wrecked *Margaretha* was salvaged of anything of value, the hulk was eventually abandoned. In September 1889, work to remove the wreck resulted in tragedy. *The New York Times* reported, "this morning while the crew of a lighter engaged in jetty work on St. Johns Bar who were engaged in blowing up the wreck of the brig *Margarette* [sic], which lay in the channel off Mayport, two men, R.T. Moore, son of Capt. A.C. Moore, and Grandison Powell, were soldering a 25 pound can of dynamite, it exploded and blew them to atoms."

MARGARET THOMAS

On September 10, 1904, the four-masted schooner *Margaret Thomas* was launched by the Washburn Brothers at Thomaston, Maine. Named after the daughter of Washington B. Thomas of Boston, the schooner registered a length of keel of 193.7 feet, beam of 40 feet, depth of hold of 19.5 feet, and a displacement of 1,400 gross tons. The three decks of the *Margaret Thomas* were framed of Virginia oak and planked with yellow pine. On February 29, 1924, the waterlogged schooner was abandoned by her crew off the coast of Florida; they were rescued by lifesavers from the Mosquito Lagoon station. The Coast Guard cutter *Yamacraw* was dispatched to search for the drifting schooner and tow her to port, but it's unclear if she found the abandoned vessel.

MARGUERITE

According to November 29, 1821, edition of *The Times*, "The *Marguerite*, from Havannah [sic] to Antwerp, was wrecked on the coast of Florida during a gale on the 14th of September; part of the cargo expected to be saved, she had been plundered of 80 bags of coffee the second night after sailing, by a schooner under the Independent flag." The *Marguerite* was lost in the same storm that claimed the *Cosmopolite*.

MARIA (1796)

According to the *London Daily Advertiser*, October 15, 1796, "The *Maria*, Gilchrist, a Transport, from Jamaica, is lost on Ludberry [sic] Reef, in the Gulf of Florida." While the date is unknown, the cited place of loss is likely present-day Ledbury Reef off Elliott Key.

MARIA (1811)

The Edinburgh Advertiser published the following on June 25, 1811: "A ship from Liverpool, commanded by

Forster, supposed to be the *Maria* of London is blown up at Amelia Island."

MARIA BECKFORD

The *Maria Beckford*, Captain Boyd was included in the September 9, 1772, edition of *Lloyd's List* as stranded near Cape Florida; she was reported as a total loss.

MARIA M. KLOTS

The schooner *Maria M. Klots*, bound from St. Augustine, in ballast, to Wilmington, North Carolina, was wrecked on the St. Augustine Bar on October 26, 1844[139].

MARIE

On April 27, 1911, the 13-ton gas steamer *Marie*, official number 92923, built in 1899, burned on the Indian River.

MARIE CONCETTI

The small shrimp boat *Marie Concetti* was returning from a fishing trip when a violent explosion ripped through the vessel four miles off Fernandina on July 11, 1927[140]. While injured in the blast, Sam K. Jones managed to swim to the northern jetty, where he was picked up by a passing yacht. The other crew member, Wilker Crews, was not a strong swimmer. Fortunately for Crews, the vessel's mascot, an English setter named Prince, amazingly swam to help the youth. Crews grasped Prince by the tail with both hands, and the dog towed him almost four and a half miles to the north jetty buoy, where a passing shrimp boat rescued the two. The *Marie Concetti* was a total loss.

MARIE GILBERT

On April 20, 1907, the four-masted auxiliary schooner *Marie Gilbert* went ashore north of Mayport on the Nassau Bar with a cargo of coal. Her crew of eight was landed safely. With seas breaking over the *Marie Gilbert*, tugs attempted to pull her off, but ultimately were unsuccessful. In February 1908, the wreck of the schooner was sold at auction for $485. The *Marie Gilbert* was launched on April 28, 1906, at Mystic, Connecticut, for the Gilbert Transportation Company. The 586-ton schooner was 166.6 long and 36.2 feet wide. In July 1906, a 150-horsepower gasoline engine was added to the four sticker.

MARIGALERA

The *Marigalera*, more commonly called the *Maria Galante*, was a *balandrita* (also referred to as a *fragatilla* and a *patache*), a small one-masted ship used to support the remainder of the fleet, purchased by Captain-General Don Juan Esteban de Ubilla in Havana prior to departing for Spain in July 1715. There is some speculation that this was formerly a British vessel captured by one of Captain-General Don Antonio de Echeverz y Zubiza's scout ships off Cuba around 1714, renamed *San Miguel de Excelsis*, and later sold to Ubilla, who renamed her after his flagship, *Nuestra Señora de La Regla*. Loaded with a cargo of tobacco, the *Marigalera* disappeared early on the morning of July 31, 1715. While not confirmed, there is some speculation that the *balandrita* now rests off Treasure Shores Beach Park. Also known as the "Cannon Wreck," the site is widely scattered in 15 feet of water 200 to 400 feet off the beach. Wreckage extends northward for approximately 1,000 feet, and may be mixed in with wreckage from another merchant ship that wrecked in 1890. Another theory suggests the site previously thought to be the *Nuestra Señora de Las Nieves* off Frederick Douglass Memorial Beach is, in fact, actually the *Marigalera*.

MARION (1950)

The 35-ton vessel *Marion*, built in 1946, beached one mile south of the south jetty at Fernandina Beach on June 15, 1950[141].

MARION (1998)

On April 3, 1998, the 80-foot long tug *Marion* was sunk in approximately 160 feet of water off Miami to serve as an artificial reef. The tug was not anchored during deployment, however, and the vessel was not relocated after its scuttling. The approximate position of her sinking was recorded as 25° 42.196' north, 80° 04.970' west.

MARIPOSA

H.B. Cromwell and Company, owners of the steamer *Mariposa*, stated she was a strong vessel, to the extent that nothing short of a hurricane could disable her. Unfortunately, the *Mariposa* encountered just such a hurricane in early October 1870 somewhere off the Florida coast. The only evidence of her tragic fate was random portions of the vessel that washed ashore north of Hillsboro Inlet. Captain Doane, of the wrecked bark *William Rathbone*, reported his men picked up a life jacket on October 15 marked "*Mariposa*; B.F. Towne, sailmaker, New York." Furthermore, he stated two of his men saw the stern of the *Mariposa* with her name painted on it near their beached ship on October 17. Another dispatch documented that a plank that Captain Doane himself picked up a plank having the words "*Mariposa* leaking" painted on it[142]. The *William Rathbone* reportedly went ashore approximately 11 miles north of Hillsboro Inlet on October 11.

The *Mariposa* was a 1,082-ton screw steamer built by W.H. Webb of New York in 1864. She was built after the style of a man-of-war, of solid live oak, with copper fastenings, and was fitted out in first class style. Captain Willetts and a crew of 35 men departed New Orleans for New York on October 5 with a cargo of 1,672 bales of cotton and a large quantity of hides and flour. Due to the yellow fever quarantine regulations, she carried no passengers on this trip. She likely had a typical cruise for several days until encountering the hurricane as it rolled through the Florida Straits.

Based on when and where the storm struck, as well as where the wreckage washed up, the *Mariposa* likely came to grief off the Florida Keys or Miami. A Key West paper reported the gale commenced on the afternoon of October 7, and continued unabated until October 11. Following the storm, the steamer *Mississippi* reported passing 11 wrecks between Jupiter and Bahia Honda, and wreckage consisting of general merchandise was strewn for over 50 miles north of Cape Florida. To date, the wreck of the *Mariposa* has not been located.

MARS

The British brig *Mars*, Captain Irvin, ran ashore on Fowey Rocks on February 25, 1851, en route from Cardenas, Cuba, for Halifax, Nova Scotia, with a cargo of molasses. While the vessel was a total loss, 166 hogsheads and tierces of molasses, rigging, chains, anchors, and other ship materials were saved; the wrecked hull was reportedly sold for $55,000 and the remaining cargo for $7[143].

MARSHA T.

The tug *Marsha T.* was sunk in 70 feet of water as an artificial reef in April 1998 just north of the Palm Beach County line along with the tugs *Sun Mariner* and *Sea Inspector*. This may possibly be the tug *Marsha T.*, official number 270697, built in 1944 at Ironton, Ohio, which was 44.2 feet in length, 13.7 feet in beam, and 34 gross tons in displacement. Other information indicates the *Marsha T.* was originally a landing craft (LCM-6) that was later converted to a tug.

MARTHA (1753)

According to the *London Evening Post* of July 19, 1753, the brigantine *Martha*, Captain Powers, was lost "to the leeward of Cape Florida" en route from the Bay of Honduras; the captain and part of his crew were saved.

MARTHA (1868)

Information on the loss of the *Martha* off Mosquito Inlet was provided by Hawks (1887), who stated, "About 1868 the sloop *Martha*, belonging to Capt. Frank Smith of Indian River, capsized in a gale off the inlet and floated ashore on the south beach. Two men were drowned, and their bodies came ashore north of the inlet. The cargo of salted mullet in barrels was partly saved."

MARTHA (1870)

In February 1870, the schooner *Martha* stranded eight miles north of Mosquito Inlet and was a total loss[144].

MARTHA BRAE

On August 13, 1816, *The Edinburgh Advertiser* published, "The brig *Martha Brae*, William Parish, master, from Jamaica to Whitehaven, was driven on shore on June 6, 1816, in the gale near Cape Florida, where she went to pieces in a few hours; a passenger and one of the boys drowned; cargo totally lost."

A later extract published in *The Edinburgh Advertiser* on August 30, 1816, provided additional details on the vessel's loss:

> The brig *Martha Brae*, of Whitehaven, William Parish, master, sailed from Jamaica on the 18th of May, bound to Whitehaven; and on the 6th inst. in a severe gale, was driven on shore near Indian River, on the coast of Florida, where she went to pieces in a few hours; part of the cargo consisting of rum, drifted on the beach. Mr. Bowman, a passenger, and one of the crew, were drowned. The master and the rest of the crew, having reached the shore, remained there in great distress for seven days, during which they had nothing to subsist on but a cask of water, which they providentially found on the beach, a keg of tamarinds, and a few cocoa-nuts [*sic*], when they fell in with some of the inhabitants of Key-Buskeen [*sic*], who took them to their settlement, and treated them with the greatest kindness and hospitality. Captain Parish and his surviving crew arrived here a few days ago, and take this opportunity of expressing their grateful thanks to the inhabitants of Key-Buskeen [*sic*] for their humanity.

At face value, the mention of Indian River would indicate the *Martha Brae* wrecked well north of Cape Florida. The documented assistance of local settlers from "Key-Buskeen," likely Key Biscayne, would indicate the *Martha Brae* was indeed lost near Cape Florida.

MARTHA T. THOMAS

The three-masted schooner *Martha T. Thomas* was built in June 1891 by Washburn Brothers at Thomaston, Maine. She was 174.3 feet in length, 37.2 feet in breadth, and displaced 790 tons gross. In June 1903, the schooner was rammed and nearly sunk by the battleship U.S.S. *Massachusetts* on a clear night off Boston, Massachusetts. The battleship struck the schooner on her starboard side, tearing off the main chain plates, carrying away rails, and damaging some hull planking that caused her to leak. Fortunately for the *Martha T. Thomas*, her cargo of pine lumber prevented her from going to the bottom. However, a cargo of lumber would not prevent her wrecking later that year during a voyage from Apalachicola to Baltimore, Maryland. On September 11, 1903, the *Martha T. Thomas* encountered a gale off the Florida coast, which split the schooner in half when she was beached approximately nine miles south (also reported as north) of Jupiter. Captain Watts and his crew survived the event.

MARY (1766)

A December 5 dispatch from Georgia that appeared in the January 24, 1767, edition of the *London Chronicle* relayed the following:

> ...the sloop *Mary*, James Sheffield, master, which sailed from Savannah for St. Augustine, with the Hon. William Grover, Esq., Chief Justice of East Florida, and

other passengers, was cast away on the coast of Florida, to the southward of the Matanzas. All the people on board, except two of Mr. Grover's servants, who were drowned, got on shore, where they remained until taken off by a Bahamian sloop, on board of which Mr. Grover died of a disease he had contracted from the fatigue and hardships he had undergone. The sloop is arrived with the others safe at St. Augustine.

MARY (1778)

The *Mary*, Captain Hoincastle, on a voyage from Jamaica to London, was lost off Cape Florida while attempting to evade two American privateers in December 1778[145].

MARY (1783)

On April 19, 1783, the *Mary*, Captain Stafford, bound from St. Augustine to London, was lost off the St. Augustine Bar[146].

MARY A. HOLT

During a voyage from Cedar Keys to New York in November 1878, the schooner *Mary A. Holt* was abandoned off Fernandina. This may possibly be the 193-ton schooner *Mary A. Holt*, official number 17631, built in November 1867 at Ellsworth, Maine; this vessel was 105 feet long and 28 feet wide.

MARY ANN

The 157-ton brig *Mary Ann*, built in 1851, was abandoned at sea on October 21, 1853, while sailing from Falmouth, Jamaica, for Jacksonville. The following is an extract from her log describing her loss:

> Blowing a fresh gale from the northward; at 3 P.M. (October 18) hove the brig's head to the eastward. Latitude at meridian 29° 17' N.; longitude 79° 50' W. At 8 P.M. 20th, while lying to, under balanced reefed mainsail, the wind suddenly hauled to the N.W.; took in the mainsail; and at 8 1/2 P.M.; while lying to under bare poles, with a heavy sea running, the wind suddenly blew with the violence of a hurricane. So sudden was the change, that all attempts to get the vessel off before the wind were useless. The vessel was hove down, the head-stays were immediately cut away; also the weather fore-rigging; but the vessel being nearly on her beam-ends, could not get rid of the foremast in time to prevent being thrown completely on her beam-ends. Three of the crew were washed overboard, but succeeded in regaining the vessel. The house, galley, and everything moveable were swept from the decks. Cut away the weather main rigging, and the foremast shortly after went above the circle rail; which was shortly after followed by the mainmast, about 20 feet above the saddle, tearing away the step, and ripping up the decks; when she partly righted; and after passing through the cabin into the hold, shifted the ballast, when she righted, with 3 feet water in the hold, which was pumped out. The crew, having all their effects swept away, the provisions completely spoiled, being well on the eastern edge of the stream, with no suitable spars for jury masts, deemed it imprudent to continue any longer by the vessel. At 3 P.M., having erected a signal-staff, hoisted the ensign union down, a hermaphrodite brig being in sight, passed within hauling distance, almost, but only condescended to notice us by a passing glance. She is probably commanded by a man utterly devoid of humanity; and I am sorry I did not ascertain the name of his vessel so that I might give his name publicity. The bark *Brazilliero*, of New York, being astern of the brig and seeing her pass without offering to render us any assistance, immediately bore down, and after a great deal of trouble, in consequence of the sea, took us all on board; and for the kind assistance received from Capt. Campbell, myself and crew tender him our most sincere thanks[147].

The cited position of the *Mary Ann* on October 18 was approximately 60 nautical miles east of Ponce de Leon Inlet. It is unclear, however, where the storm carried the vessel during the three days before she was abandoned, as well as where she may have ultimately sunk after potentially drifting for an additional unknown period.

MARY B.

The *Mary B.* was a small, 14-ton schooner built in 1885, which stranded on January 6, 1904, at Gilbert's Bar.

MARY BELLE

The *Mary Belle* (also cited as *Mary Bell*) was an approximately 11-ton sternwheel steamer, 47 feet long, 10 feet wide, owned by Major J.A. Allen, which was built around 1880. The small steamer carried parties on Lake Tohopekaliga, Kissimmee River, and Lake Okeechobee. The *Mary Belle* reportedly sunk on the Kissimmee River at Bassinger around 1884.

MARYBOB TWO

Four men perished when 18-foot seas capsized the 35-foot long charter boat *Marybob Two* as it tried to navigate into the St. Lucie Inlet on October 2, 1965. A lone survivor, obviously still in shock, was found wandering aimlessly along a nearby beach. The hulk of the *Marybob Two* was tumbled to pieces in the raging surf.

MARY C.

On April 11, 1913, the 14-ton gas vessel *Mary C.* burned at Mayport; the *Mary C.* was built in 1910.

MARY COE

The bark *Mary Coe* was built in the village of Noank, Connecticut, by the shipbuilding firm of Robert Palmer and Company in 1856. During a voyage from Mobile, Alabama, for Havre, France, with a cargo of 3,150 bales of cotton, Captain Avery encountered a late-season storm on November 4, 1859. The gale beached the 560-ton *Mary Coe* approximately 77 miles north of Cape Florida and 12 miles to the north of the wrecked *Eliza Mallory*. The wrecking schooner *Flying Arrow*, which was dispatched to work the *Mallory*, sighted the *Mary Coe* on November 21. With the fate of the bilged *Mary Coe* sealed, the *Flying Arrow* proceeded to salvage 366 bales of cotton, which were carried to Key West and sold at auction. The bark was then stripped of its rigging and any other useful materials, and abandoned on the beach.

MARY F. CARSON

Built in November 1872 at Milford, Delaware, the 277-ton schooner *Mary F. Carson* was 122.5 feet in length and 32.4 feet in breadth. On the afternoon of March 3, 1883, Captain Williams was on the verge of concluding his voyage from New York to offload his cargo of coal at Jacksonville. As he was attempting to cross the St. Johns Bar and head into the channel of the St. Johns River, the *Carson* stranded on the south breakers. The cargo was a total loss, but portions of the *Mary F. Carson* were saved.

MARY F. GODFREY

The schooner *Mary F. Godfrey* wrecked on the jetties near Pilot Town (Mayport) at the mouth of the St. Johns River on May 11, 1903[148]. The schooner was quickly pounded to pieces against the jetties as the captain and crew of seven narrowly escaped with their lives. The *Mary F. Godfrey*, official number 91518, was built in 1882 at Tuckahoe, New Jersey. She registered a length of 140.4 feet, a beam of 34.5 feet, and a displacement of 447 tons gross.

MARY AND JANE

According to the November 17, 1788, edition of *The Times*, the vessel *Mary and Jane*, Captain Pennymont, bound from Jamaica for Liverpool, was lost on the Florida shore; the crew was saved.

MARY KINGSLAND

On March 1, 1861, the yacht *Mary Kingsland* departed St. Augustine for Key West. "On the morning of March 5, about five o'clock, a heavy north-east gale broke upon the little craft, and, despite their best exertions, they found

Loss of the *Mary Kingsland* (Florida State Archives).

themselves doomed to be driven on the Florida coast. Yielding to the fury of the tempest, they headed for the beach, and, nerved to superhuman efforts, met the awful crash of the beach and surging billows; and, bruised and exhausted reached the inhospitable shore[149]." After three days of suffering on the desolate stretch of beach, two brothers set off for Jupiter Lighthouse, which was located 18 miles to the north. Unfortunately, their appeal for aid was rejected by the "inhuman lightkeeper," and the two were forced to return empty-handed to the make-shift camp. Finally, on March 16, the steamer *Catawba* sighted the wrecked yacht and survivors on the beach; during their time stranded on the beach, the survivors subsisted mainly on the tops of the palmetto trees that grew around them. After several trips through heavy surf in the steamer's longboat, all of the crew and passengers were rescued. The *Mary Kingsland* was valued at $4,000.

MARY LINDA

According to Singer (1998) the 35-ton *Mary Linda* collided with the range light one mile northeast of the Mayport jetties on November 4, 1946.

MARY STAR OF THE SEA

The 138-foot long Panamanian-flagged freighter *Mary Star of the Sea* sunk in rough seas while sitting in the Miami anchorage just over a mile offshore on October 21, 1990. At 8:45 p.m., the crew of the 265-ton freighter, built in 1955, made a distress call to the U.S. Coast Guard stating that they were taking on water. The five-man crew was eventually removed from the ship when they could not keep up with the incoming water, and the freighter settled on the bottom. She came to rest in 27 feet of water with only her mast protruding from the ocean's surface. Coincidentally, the sinking occurred just three days after the sinking of the freighter *Raychel* a short distance away in the shipping channel.

The State of Florida contracted to have the abandoned *Mary Star of the Sea*, affectionately named the "Mary Star of Debris," moved from its current site and deployed in another area to serve as a deep-water artificial reef. Divers from Resolve Marine Group cut up the vessel underwater using thermal cutting gear. The midsection of the freighter was sectioned up by the divers and then placed onboard a barge by crane prior to its deployment in deep water. The bow was removed from the remainder of the wreck, patched to hold air, and then floated free from the bottom to be towed to the new site. The heavy stern section, along with its engine and machinery, was rigged and lifted from the bottom by a crane, and then towed midwater to its final resting spot. All work was completed by December 22, 1990. The wreck of the *Mary Star of the Sea*, as well as that of the *Raychel*, illustrate that shipwrecks continue to occur off Florida. While there have been vast technological advancements in the past five decades, the sea still takes its toll.

The remains of the coastal freighter now rest in approximately 210 feet of water. A relatively short distance separates the sections, and technical divers can visit both sections on one dive if they have scooters or if aided by the prevailing current, as one section is found a short distance to the northeast from the southernmost section.

View of the tug *Mary St. Phillip* (Broward County Artificial Reef Program).

MARY ST. PHILLIP

The tug *Mary St. Phillip* and a 120-foot long barge comprise the *Mariner II* artificial reef site off Broward County, and are therefore known locally as the *Mariner II Tug* and *Mariner II Barge*. The two surplus vessels were acquired from Tampa for a total cost of $64,800, and towed to Fort Lauderdale for cleaning. The original barge actually sunk off the Florida Keys en route from Tampa; however, the contractor located a substitute barge to be used at the reef site. The *Mary St. Phillip* was originally built for the U.S. Army in December 1943 as the 249-ton large tug *Major Ocea L. Ferris* (LT-6) by the Jakobson Shipyard at Oyster Bay, New York. The *Ferris* was 115 feet in length and 28 feet in breadth. Unfortunately, the U.S. Army failed to keep accurate records of their vessels, so the service record of LT-6 is unclear. It's likely she participated in some capacity during World War II, as several of her sister ships, including LT-5, reportedly served in "Operation Mulberry," which was the construction of two artificial harbors during June 6-14, 1944, in conjunction with "Operation Overlord," better known as the D-Day invasion of Normandy, France. Regardless, she was later renamed the *Captain Eric J. Newman*, then *Falcon*, before finally operating as the *Mary St. Phillip*. The tug apparently had portions of its superstructure removed prior to sinking in 125 feet of water on May 1, 1993. The *Mariner II Tug* rests approximately 400 feet to the north of the *Rodeo 25*, and 800 feet south of the *Mariner II Barge*, which is just offshore of the freighter *Union Express*.

MARYLAND

The wreck of the *Maryland* appears to be the remains of a dredge vessel resting in 120 feet of water off Cape Canaveral. The vessel's potential identification originated from the recovery of a bell found by Allen Perkins in 1986, which was embossed with the name "MARYLAND." To date, no other identifying artifacts have been discovered from the wreck site, nor has any additional information been uncovered on the loss of the *Maryland*. It should be noted that a dredge named *Maryland*, which was owned by Captain John Emile, periodically operated in Florida in 1919 through 1926, when it worked to widen and deepen the Fort Pierce Inlet and associated channels. It is unclear if Emile's dredge *Maryland* is the same as the wreck resting off Canaveral.

Schooling fish over a windlass on the wreck of the *Maryland*.

The wreck appears very similar to a barge, but with a fair amount of machinery. While boilers can be found amidships, the vessel does not appear to have its own means of propulsion; instead, one can find a notched stern where an attending tug can nestle in to push the work platform to its required destination. The boom arms for the cutter head can be seen resting in the sand off the front of the wreck. The wreck of the *Maryland* is an excellent floundering spot at certain times of the year.

MASCOTTE

The tug *Mascotte*, owned by J.C. Lengle of Jacksonville, went ashore on Cumberland Island during a gale on March 29, 1893. Details of the wrecking appeared in *The New York*

Times on March 31, 1893:

> She was towing a schooner bound for Satilla River. The hawser parted and wound around the tug's propeller, rendering her helpless. The tug's sails were set, but were blown away. The anchor was dropped and the tug lay to for two hours, when the chain parted and the tug grounded. The cabin was washed away. The crew attempted to launch a lifeboat, which overturned. Then the crew attempted to swim ashore, and by the aid of life preservers landed, terribly exhausted. The steward was drowned. Capt. Potter is thought to be dying from exposure. The rest of the crew are in a critical condition.

MASSA E. GUECCO

The Italian bark *Massa E. Guecco* was lost six miles below Palm Beach, hitting a reef 300 yards offshore on January 15, 1905. At the time, the vessel was en route from Pensacola for Buenos Aires, Argentina, with a cargo of lumber. Fortunately, the captain and crew survived the stranding and reached the safety of the beach. Captain Pietro Musante later lamented, "I would rather be buried in these sands than to see my beautiful ship a complete wreck. My honor is gone. I have lost everything[150]." The beached vessel was eventually stripped of its rigging, and a large portion of the lumber was sold at auction. The hulk of the *Massa E. Guecco* was later abandoned, left to share the lonely stretch of beach with the wrecked schooner *James Judge*, which was located two miles to the north.

MATANZAS

The freight ferry *Matanzas*, official number 203346, was built in 1906 at Palatka for service in Northeast Florida. The screw steamer registered a length of 73.8 feet, a beam of 15.3 feet, and a displacement of 43 tons gross. On December 18, 1916, the *Matanzas* ironically stranded at Matanzas Inlet.

MATTIE RICHMOND

According to Singer (1998), the schooner *Mattie Richmond* stranded 20 miles south of Jupiter Inlet in February 1870. I have been unable to find any additional information on this vessel or wrecking event. It is possible the date or name of the vessel is erroneous, as the same original source utilized by Singer incorrectly documented two other losses attributed to this timeframe and location (brig *Moreno* and schooner *Minerva*).

MATTIE S.

On January 22, 1894, the sloop *Mattie S.* wrecked in the breakers south of the Gilbert's Bar Life-Saving Station while on a trip from Lake Worth for Titusville. The sloop's crew of two men was rescued by a nearby schooner. Later, the Life-Saving Station keeper arrived on the scene and helped the men strip the wreck before traveling back to the station with them, which was two and a half miles north, where he furnished them with food and clothing.

MAURICE R. SHAW, JR.

The *Maurice R. Shaw, Jr.* was originally built as the four-masted schooner *Charles M. Struven* by E. James Tull in 1917 at Pocomoke City, Maryland. The *Struven* registered a length of 171.2 feet, a beam of 37 feet, and a displacement of 632 tons. As sail was overshadowed by steam power, the *Struven* was later converted into a barge and renamed the *Maurice R. Shaw, Jr.* On November 4, 1942, the *Maurice R. Shaw, Jr.* foundered while under tow approximately four miles off Jupiter Light.

MAWAGRA II

On November 3, 1910, the 23-ton gas steamer *Mawagra II*, official number 203288, built in 1906, exploded and burned on the St. Johns River.

MAXINE D.

The *Maxine D.* was a 165-foot long offshore supply vessel built in 1970 by the Burton Shipyard at Port Arthur, Texas. After years of service in the oil fields, the 198-ton *Maxine D.* was sunk as an artificial reef in 80 feet of water off Volusia County. The vessel rests upright and intact in a roughly north-south orientation. The wreck of the *Antilles Star* can be found just to the south of the *Maxine D.*

Maxine D. (Volusia County Artificial Reef Program).

MAY BELLE

On March 7, 1915, E.O. Eshelby, millionaire manufacturer and publisher of the *Commercial Tribune*, and nine other passengers escaped the yacht *May Belle* after it struck a submerged wreck and sank in 18 feet of water near Fowey Rocks[151]. Eshelby's yacht *May Belle*, valued at $10,000, was 46 feet long, 11 feet wide, and was equipped with a 24-horsepower engine. Newspaper accounts state the yacht was almost completely wrecked "and may only be saved after considerable expense."

MAY LI

Eight people were rescued from the 50-foot long *May Li*, which sank one mile offshore St. Lucie Inlet on May 25, 1981. The vessel sank after a large wave caused the boat to pitch violently, knocking the anchor through the wooden hull of the *May Li*. The nearby vessel *Passing Gear* rescued the passengers off the sinking *May Li* and took them to shore.

MAYPORT

At 9:10 p.m. on December 22, 1898, the steamer *Mayport* was destroyed by fire of unknown origin while at her Mayport dock on the St. Johns River. The burning vessel was cut loose and drifted out to sea. The steamer was valued at $9,500[152].

Undated photograph of an unidentified vessel capsized in the St. Johns River at Mayport (Beaches Area Historical Society).

MECHANIC

The sidewheel steamer *Mechanic*, official number 17867, was built in Camden, New Jersey, in 1856. She registered a length of 124.6 feet, a beam of 28.3 feet, and a displacement of 288 tons gross. The ferry, operating for the Jacksonville, St. Augustine, and Halifax River Railway, reportedly was the finest looking craft of its kind in any waters south of New York City, capable of carrying eighteen hundred people. On August 15, 1891, the steamer *Mechanic* stranded on the St. Johns River near Jacksonville. According to Davis (1925), the *Mechanic* "eventually wore out in service and lies buried under the South Jacksonville waterfront."

MELBA

On December 22, 1914, the *Melba* burned at Trout Creek off the St. Johns River. The 27-ton *Melba*, official number 204912, was built in 1907.

MELDA

On November 30, 1939, the shrimp boat *Melda* was found cast up on the beach at Melbourne. Mysteriously, there was no trace of Captain Shannon Hardee or his crew of two men. Captain Hardee was last seen as another trawler passed the *Melda* in heavy seas off False Cape near Cape Canaveral on the evening of November 26, 1939. The events leading up to the wrecking of the *Melda*, as well as the disappearance of her crew, remain a mystery to this day.

MELROSE (1853)

A March 1854 report stated the schooner *Melrose*, from Florida for New York with a cargo of lumber, was recently "consumed by fire near Satilla, Florida[153]."

MELROSE (1904)

After gale force winds lashed the coast for three solid days in October 1904, Florida slowly dug itself out from the debris left in the storm's wake. Telegraph lines were down and railroad tracks were obstructed. As communication through the state was restored, news of the wrecking of numerous vessels along the coast trickled in. The four-masted schooner *James Judge* was aground four miles south of Palm Beach. The three-masted bark *Zion* wrecked five miles north of Fort Lauderdale. Most tragic was the loss of the *Melrose*, which resulted in seven deaths.

The *Melrose* was traveling from Jacksonville to Nassau, Bahamas. She was a 186-ton British schooner built in August 1893 at Harbor Island, Bahamas, by the shipbuilding firm of Albury and Company, and was 107.8 feet long and 27.2 feet wide. Just before sunset on October 15, a great wave swept over the schooner, capsizing it and throwing the passengers and crew into the sea. Mrs. Hallen, one of the passengers, was immediately lost, but Captain Kelly and the crew managed to grasp the side of the vessel. Two other passengers, Mr. and Mrs. Weller, were also thrown in the water, but clung to the rigging. When the ship rolled back upright, a mast fell and crushed Mrs. Weller, and her lifeless body washed back overboard. Mr. Weller suffered several broken bones but survived the catastrophe. The *Melrose* drifted along in the storm, but all the survivors were eventually cast off the waterlogged ship by massive waves that rolled across her decks. Eventually, the five survivors of the disaster washed ashore at Palm Beach[154]. The sinking position of the *Melrose* is currently unknown, but is likely in deep water off Palm Beach.

The coaster *Mercedes I* as the *Rita Voge* (Richard Cox).

MERCEDES I

The *Mercedes I* was built as the German coastal freighter *Jacob Rüsch* in March 1952 by Herbert Ranke's shipyard in Cranz-Neuenfelde (Hamburg). The 785-ton coaster was 190.2 feet long and 30.5 feet wide. As was common amongst the European coaster fleet, the *Jacob Rüsch* changed owners and names numerous times, though stayed largely in German hands: in 1963, the freighter was sold to Otto Nagel of Lübeck and renamed *Rosita Maria*; later, she sailed as *Rita Vöge* when sold to Heinz Georg Vöge of Hechthausen in 1968; finally, the vessel was sold in 1976 to a Panamanian interest and renamed *Mercedes I*. At the time of her loss, the *Mercedes I* was owned by Venezuelan shipping firm *Distribudora Navieras del Caribe S.R.L.*

High and dry on the beach (Broward County Artificial Reef Program).

On November 23, 1984, the *Mercedes I* broke from her mooring during a storm and grounded at high tide on the posh beachfront of Palm Beach. The freighter was carried inshore by 15-foot swells, crashing into the seawall of Mollie Wilmot's home, nearly going into her pool. The freighter's 12-man crew weathered the stranding and safely stepped from the ship to dry land. Following the crew's lead, the vessel's owner also abandoned the ship, leaving the State of Florida to deal with the derelict. In the weeks following the stranding, numerous unsuccessful attempts were made to pull the vessel off the beach. The abandoned *Mercedes I* became an annoying fixture as it remained on the beach adjacent to Rose Kennedy's winter

Scuttling of the *Mercedes I* (Broward County Artificial Reef Program).

Divers over the collapsed cargo hold of the *Mercedes I*.

compound. Finally, on March 6, 1985, at a total cost of $223,000, a salvage crew from Don Jon Marine Company, Incorporated managed to wrestle the *Mercedes I* off the beach during the month's strong lunar high tide. The freighter was towed to Port Everglades where she was stripped and cleaned for use as an artificial reef. On March 30, 1985, the former German coaster was sunk 100 feet to the bottom of the Atlantic Ocean off Fort Lauderdale. Over the years, numerous storms have significantly impacted the once-intact *Mercedes I*. Large sections have collapsed, while portions of the hull have been ripped loose and are now found scattered in the sand. Regardless, the wreck of the *Mercedes I* still offers an interesting dive, and the wreck cluster comprising the *Jay Scutti*, *Tracy*, and *Merci Jesus* can be found approximately 1,600 feet to the northwest.

Mercedes II as the *Syracuse Socony* (Historical Collections of the Great Lakes, Bowling Green State University).

MERCEDES II

In 1921, the harbor fuel tanker *Syracuse Socony* was launched at the Elizabethport, New Jersey yard of John W. Sullivan (Bethlehem Steel Company). The harbor tanker, originally built for the Standard Oil Company, was 188.4 feet long and 28.3 feet wide. The *Syracuse Socony* worked around New York in her early years, headed into the Great Lakes for a brief stint, and then returned to the East Coast. In 1945, the vessel was sold to R.T.C Number Fifty One Corporation and renamed *Franklin Reinauer*; as the *K.H. Dunbar* and then the *Du-Val*, she worked for the Dunbar Transfer Company; in 1954, the Erie Navigation Company purchased the tanker and renamed her *Cemico Erie*; she later operated as the *John F. McKay* when owned by the Independent Petroleum Transportation Service, Incorporated from 1958-1963; Gotham Tankers Corporation in 1963, and then the Heating Trade Specialties Corporation from 1963-1975, who converted her to a barge and renamed her *Draga de Arena* in 1965. Spanish for "Sand Barge," the *Draga de Arena* was sold to her last owner, Eastern Seaboard Pile Driving, in 1975. The barge eventually migrated south to Florida and later grounded on a sandbar in the Intracoastal Waterway near a Riviera Beach marina in February 1985, which presented a hazard to navigation. Locals named the derelict the *Mercedes II*, a reference to the freighter *Mercedes I* that remained grounded approximately five miles away in Palm Beach. Martin County eventually purchased the barge from owner Ronald Rickert for $10,000 to be sunk as an artificial reef. On May 19, 1985, the *Mercedes II* was scuttled approximately 6.5 nautical miles offshore Stuart. The former harbor tanker now rests in 85 feet of water and lies east-west. The wreck of the *David T.* can be found a half-mile inshore of the *Mercedes II*.

Profile view of the *Merci Jesus* (Broward County Artificial Reef Program).

MERCI JESUS

On April 28, 1998, the U.S. Customs Service seized over 900 pounds of cocaine worth an estimated $7.5 million from the 90-foot long coastal freighter *Merci Jesus*. The narcotics were concealed in a hidden compartment on the Belizean-flagged vessel. On August 11, 1998, the former drug runner was sunk in 70 feet of water off Fort Lauderdale. Today, the *Merci Jesus* rests with its bow facing south towards the *Tracy*, which can be found approximately 300 feet away.

MERCI RABBI

The 85-foot long *Merci Rabbi* is believed to formerly be the converted Haitian freighter *Tortue Express*. The *Tortue Express* was seized by the U.S. Coast Guard and the U.S. Customs Service on March 27, 1996, following a search that discovered 117 pounds of cocaine hidden onboard. It is unclear when the vessel was renamed *Merci Rabbi*, but she was ultimately sunk off Miami as an artificial reef in February 1997. County records indicate she is located in 120 feet of water, but only a barge exists at that site. Based on archival photos of the vessel prior to its sinking, the artificial reef cited as *Nick Comoglio* or *Nick C.* is actually the *Merci Rabbi*. Apparently, at some point after the deployment of the *Merci Rabbi*, the wreck of the former

Merci Rabbi (Miami-Dade County Department of Environmental Resources Management).

freighter was renamed after Nick Comoglio, a Miami-area diver who disappeared during a dive while training to break the deep air record (at that time 513 feet) on July 3, 1995. Nick failed to surface on the dive off Hillsboro Inlet after apparently signaling he reached a depth of 450 feet; his body was never found. The wreck of the *Merci Rabbi* (a.k.a., *Nick C.*) rests upright in 165 feet of water off Haulover Inlet.

MERMAID

In 1896, the independent St. Johns River steamer *Mermaid* had a bad streak of luck. On April 22, the *Mermaid* was turning around two lighters approximately nine miles from Jacksonville when a towline got caught amidships and she capsized[155]. The steamer was raised, $350 worth of damage was repaired, and she was put back in service, however, just over a month later on May 24, the *Mermaid* caught fire while docked at Palatka. This incident left the steamboat ferry a total loss. The cited value of the burned *Mermaid* was $4,000.

MERRIMACK

According to a September 3 dispatch included in the November 4, 1817, issue of *The Edinburgh Advertiser*, "The American brig *Merrimack*, from Havannah for New York, has been wrecked on the Floridas [sic]. The cargo is nearly all lost, and the crew are on their way to this port in one of the wreckers."

MERSEY

According to an article printed in *The New York Times* on November 4, 1865, the "British ship *Mercy* [sic], from Honduras went ashore 200 miles north of Key West. Four of the crew picked up in dying condition. Captain and crew taken to rafts and boats." The ship was laden with a cargo of mahogany when it wrecked during a gale on October 23; the four survivors were picked up October 26. The ship was lost in the same storm that claimed the schooner *Minnie* and barks *John Wesley*, *Caroline* (*Caroline Nesmith*), and *M.E. Smith*. The ship *Mersey* was launched as the *Nathaniel Thompson* on January 3, 1848, at Kennebunk, Maine, by J. and G.P Titcomb. The 546-ton ship was 142 feet long and 28 feet wide. At the time of her

Painting of the *Mersey* as the *Nathaniel Thompson* (Brick Store Museum, Kennebunk, Maine).

loss, the *Mersey* was owned by Montgomery, Fox, and Company, and homeported in Liverpool.

MESSENGER

The *Messenger* was one of 441 wooden-hulled subchasers built during World War I. Framed in white oak with yellow pine hull planking, the subchasers were 110 feet in length, 14.7 feet in width, and displaced 75 tons fully loaded. Following the war, the surplus Navy vessel was decommissioned and sold to Clark Dredging Company of Miami, who converted the former subchaser into a tug. On September 18, 1926, the *Messenger* sunk in her slip during the Great Miami Hurricane. She was eventually raised, repaired, and put back into service.

On November 8, 1930, the tug *Messenger* grounded approximately 600 feet south of Jupiter Lighthouse during an intense gale. According to the *Syracuse Herald*, November 9, 1930, "Life lines were brought into use tonight by the Jupiter Light House crew, near here, to remove Captain Charles Russel and six members of the crew of the tug *Messenger* after the tug drifted into the breakers at Jupiter Beach. The *Messenger's* steering gear was disabled and anchors failed to hold. The light house crew reported that the tug was in danger of pounding to pieces. The *Messenger* was en route from Miami to Fort Pierce to aid the grounded freighter *Lillian*, owned by the Baltimore and Carolina Line." Helplessly stranded, the *Messenger* was steadily broken apart by the pummeling of the surf. It's unclear if the *Messenger* was salvaged after her wrecking, but it's possible the former subchaser's triple six-cylinder engines, each weighing over 6,000 pounds, may still mark the ship's grave just off the beach and south of Jupiter Inlet.

METAMORA

The Florida-built sternwheel paddle steamer *Metamora* was first registered at Jacksonville in 1890, when she began operating for the Lucas New Line between Silver Springs and Palatka. The *Metamora* was 87 feet in length, 21.5 feet in beam, and only 3.4 feet in depth. With her inboard paddles, she was uniquely outfitted to operate on the narrow and winding Ocklawaha River, a tributary of the St. Johns in Northeast Florida. On March 19, 1903, the *Metamora* wrecked on the Ocklawaha River, which was documented in *The Atlanta Constitution* the following day:

> The steamer *Metamora*, of the Lucas line, running up the Acklawaha [sic] River, sunk this morning a little after 3 o'clock, four miles above the mouth of the river. As the passengers were all asleep and the steamer sunk without almost a moment's warning, it is almost a miracle that so few were drowned. Rufus King and Walter Watson, both colored residents of Palatka, were drowned. Manuel Myers, the well known pilot, who was at the wheel when the boat went down, was the first to discover that the boat was sinking. He immediately called Captain Mercier, who had just retired Engineer Fred Priest, who was on duty at the time, also noticed the peculiar lurching of the vessel and turned on the midship siphons, but finding no water, he started aft and discovered that the vessel was sinking stern first. Engineer Rosignol by this time was on deck and ordered all hands to the cabin top. In an instant the vessel made to port, striking the timber on the north bank of the river, and with a crash rebounded to the starboard and sank, submerging the second deck and filling the state rooms with water. With an ax Engineer Rosignol [sic] broke in the doors and windows, while other members of the crew under Captain Mercier carried out the half drowned passengers, some of whom had to be passed to the cabin roof over the outer rail. A boat was immediately sent to Welaka and within an hour row boats and launches were at the scene of the disaster. On these the terror-stricken women and

The steamer *Metamora* on the Ocklawaha River, 1893 (Alfred H. Robson Collection).

children were taken to Welaka, where they were clothed and fed. Little or no baggage belonging to the passengers has been recovered. Many escaped in their night clothing only. The boat lies at an angle of almost 45 degrees. It is thought she can be floated. It is not known with certainty what caused the boat to sink, but it is believed that her hull struck a sunken log, causing her to spring a leak. There were twenty passengers on board and all were saved. The two men who were drowned were of the crew.

Additional details were published in the March 21 edition of *The Atlanta Constitution*, which revealed, "The money and valuables of the passengers have been found and restored to their owners. This amounted to a considerable sum, one of the passengers, W. Hamilton, having lost $1,000 in money, and his mother lost all of her jewelry, including several diamond rings. Captain Lucas, owner of the steamer, says it will be raised at once and refitted."

As a result of the investigation into the sinking, the license of Chief Engineer Frederick Rossignol was suspended for one year, while the license of Assistant Engineer Frederick Priest was revoked. Salvors worked to eventually refloat the *Metamora*, though it's unclear if she was put back into service and details of her final disposition are unknown.

MIAMI LCI(L)

On October 16, 1969, the stripped-down hull of a former landing craft was scuttled off Miami in approximately 200 feet of water. During World War II, hundreds of these large infantry landing craft, or LCI(L), were produced. They were 158.5 feet long, 23.3 feet wide, and displaced 216 tons when empty. While the actual identity of this vessel is unclear, it is possible she was *LCI(L)-1088*, built in 1944 by Consolidated Steel Corporation, Limited, at Orange, Texas. During World War II, she participated in Pacific Theater operations as a ferry, as well as landings during the Battles of Mindanao and Tarakan. She was decommissioned on August 4, 1946, but was later recommissioned and redesignated as a large infantry landing ship, *LSI(L)-1088*, in February 1949. On March 7, 1952, she was converted, reclassified as a coastal minesweeper, and renamed U.S.S. *Sandpiper* (AMCU-38). In 1955, the craft was again reclassified, this time as a coastal mine hunter, MHC-38. On January 1, 1960, the U.S.S. *Sandpiper* was struck from the Naval Register and later transferred to the Miami Power Squadron in October.

MICHELLE

On November 6, 1972, the tug *Michelle* sank off Florida while towing the barge *BT-1793* south from Norfolk, Virginia. The sinking of the Miami-based tug claimed three lives, but fortunately three others were rescued by the U.S. Coast Guard; one man was found clinging to the barge during the night following the wreck, while a second man was found just before dawn amidst debris two miles east of Indiatlantic. The *Michelle* now rests in 50 feet of water approximately four and a half nautical miles off Melbourne.

MIGUANA

U.S. Customs Reef off Miami consists of three vessels – the *Brandy Wine*, *Etoile De Mer*, and *Miguana* – scuttled in close proximity to each other, all of which were seized by the U.S. Customs Service for attempting to smuggle narcotics into Florida via the Miami River. The *Tacoma* is also considered part of U.S. Customs Reef, but was sunk later and rests approximately 500 feet to the northwest of the previously-mentioned trio. On February 27, 2001, drug-sniffing dogs from a boarding team participating in "Operation Riverwalk" sensed cocaine near propane tanks towards the stern of the 101-foot long *Miguana*. A closer examination of the tanks revealed they were not properly installed and were unusually heavy. Further scrutiny found that the tanks contained 125 pounds of cocaine worth $1.1 million. On July 13, 2001, explosive scuttling charges sent the *Miguana*, a former garbage scow converted into a dry cargo freighter, 140 feet to the bottom of the Atlantic off Key Biscayne. The wreck of the *Miguana* now rests in between the larger *Brandy Wine*, which can be found by swimming east off the stern, and the *Etoile De Mer*, which lies west off the *Miguana's* bow. The wreck of the *Miguana* has easy access into its interior where divers can view the former garbage scow's engine.

MILLER BROTHERS

Built in 1952 at St. Augustine as hull number 309 by the Diesel Engine Sales Company (DESCO Marine, Incorporated), the *Miller Brothers* was a 67-foot long shrimp trawler. On November 22, 1963, the *Miller Brothers* foundered approximately seven miles south of New Smyrna Beach.

MILLER LITE

The wreck of the freighter now known as the *Miller Lite* was originally launched at Travemünde, Germany, by builder *Schlichting Werft* on September 28, 1957, as the *Mimi Horn*. The 741-ton refrigerated cargo ship, built for Heinrich C. Horn of Hamburg, Germany, was 172 feet in length and 28 feet in breadth. Reportedly, the vessel originally operated transporting frozen fish from Spanish fishing trawlers. The Hamburg South American Line eventually acquired the *Mimi Horn* in 1965, which then later sold it to a Panamanian company in 1968, whereupon it was renamed *Shirley B*. The reefer changed names several more times: in 1970 she operated as both the *Aquarius* and then *Hybur Transport*, and in 1983 she was renamed *Principe Maya*. The aged freighter was purchased for $30,000 in 1987 by Broward County and the Pompano Beach Fishing Rodeo for use as an artificial reef. The former German reefer was renamed *Miller Lite* in tribute to Fishing Rodeo sponsors Miller Brewing Co. and its local distributor, William Thies and Sons, and scuttled on May 17, 1987. Now covered by gorgonian growth, the wreck

View of amidships on the freighter *Miller Lite*.

sits upright in 165 feet of water, with its deck found at a depth of approximately 145 feet. While the front bulkheads of the wheelhouse have collapsed, the rest of the *Miller Lite* is intact. The engine room is fairly large and easy to navigate.

MILLIE

The 153-ton barge *Millie*, official number 51198, built in 1889 at Tomkins Cove, New York, foundered on September 18, 1926, during the Great Miami Hurricane.

MINERVA (1777)

The vessel *Minerva*, Captain Callahan, was reported lost at Florida in the April 19, 1777, issue of *Lloyd's List*.

MINERVA (1811)

According to the May 7, 1811, issue of *The Edinburgh Advertiser*, the British ship *Minerva*, Captain McNeily, was

The schooner *Minerva*, stranded June 1920 at Anastasia Island (Historical Collections of the Great Lakes, Bowling Green State University).

sailing from Londonderry to Amelia Island when she was lost on Amelia Island Bar on March 2. While the crew was saved, the ship was lost.

MINERVA (1870)

Schooner *Minerva*, from Havana for Bristol, Rhode Island, sprung a leak about 4 a.m., when 15 miles south of Jupiter Inlet. She was run ashore to prevent her sinking in deep water, and went to pieces three hours after striking. The crew consisted of seven men, one of whom, James Murphy, of Fall River, was drowned[156].

MINERVA (1920)

The three-masted schooner *Minerva*, official number 16628, was built by William A. Jones in 1863 at Lorain, Ohio. She registered a length of 126 feet, a beam of 25.9 feet, and a displacement of 292.9 tons gross. In 1885, she was remeasured in Chicago and documented a length of 125.4 feet, a breadth of 26.6 feet, and a displacement of 222 tons gross. In 1916, the *Minerva* moved out of the Great Lakes and her enrollment was transferred to Tampa. On June 25, 1920, the *Minerva* stranded on Anastasia Island.

MINNIE

The Mystic, Connecticut schooner *Minnie*, Captain Appleman, was lost off Jupiter Inlet on October 23, 1865, en route to Key West. The steamer *Fung Shuey* rescued Captain Appleman and four crew members who took to the schooner's life boat.

MINNIE LOUISE

The *Minnie Louise* was built in October 1883 at Sherbrooke, Nova Scotia, by Charles McIntosh. The British schooner was 101 feet long, 27.5 feet wide, and displaced 223 tons. On January 16, 1892, the schooner *Minnie Louise*, Captain Pettigrew, was reported as a total loss on the north breakers near Fernandina.

MIRACLE EXPRESS

The 100-foot long cargo ship *Miracle Express* was scuttled as an artificial reef in 65 feet of water in July 1987. One month earlier, the small inter-island freighter had been intercepted and seized by the U.S.C.G.C. *Cape Current* while trying to smuggle illegal aliens into Florida. On August 22, 1992, Hurricane Andrew pushed the *Miracle Express* onto the nearby wreck of the *Biscayne*, which resulted in the *Miracle Express* breaking apart into several large pieces. Today, there is little left of the *Miracle Express* aside from scattered debris adjacent to the *Biscayne*.

MIRAMAR

The disappearance of the yacht *Miramar* in December 1925 spawned a nagging mystery, as well as numerous lawsuits. The *Miramar* was launched on April 31, 1910, from the yard of her builders, the Gas Engine and Power Company and Charles L. Seabury and Company, Consolidated, of Morris Heights, New York. The sleek steel yacht was 115 feet long overall, 94 feet along the waterline, 17 feet in beam, displaced 230 tons, and was schooner-rigged, with two pole masts. When built, the vessel had the appearance of a modern steam yacht, although she was powered by two six-cylinder gasoline engines producing 100 horsepower each. The yacht was originally owned by the Eisenlohr Brothers of Philadelphia, but at the time of her loss, she was owned by hotel magnate E.M. Statler.

The *Miramar* departed Charleston, South Carolina, on November 30, bound for Palm Beach. She was joined by her accompanying 40-foot long fishing launch for the south-bound trip. Statler had leased the two boats for four months and was expecting their delivery by December 3. The two vessels were last seen between Savannah and Jacksonville by a U.S. Coast Guard cutter on November 30. The *Miramar* and the fishing launch were never heard from again. Thirteen crewmen disappeared with the ships. In the wake of the disappearance, several lawsuits were brought against Statler by the families of the crewmen, claiming he required the *Miramar* be delivered to Florida by traveling offshore versus the Intracoastal Waterway, which apparently was reckless and dangerous in their eyes. What fate befell the *Miramar* is still open to speculation. Perhaps one day divers will come across a lean, elegant steel hull resting quietly on the seafloor, and the mystery can finally be solved.

MISERY

On March 16, 1920, the 34-ton motor vessel *Misery*, official number 219391, stranded on the St. Johns River.

MISS CHARLESTON

The shrimp boat *Miss Charleston* reportedly sank south of St. Augustine on December 15, 1949; her three crewmen were rescued by the fishing vessel *Terry Boy*[157].

MISS CINDY II

Debris from the 66-foot long steel-hulled shrimp trawler *Miss Cindy II* began washing up on the beach at Amelia Island State Park on the evening of October 12, 2007. The day before, the dragger was approximately four miles off Cumberland Island when Captain Bobby Hall noticed the vessel was taking on water. The U.S. Coast Guard responded to the vessel's distress call and successfully rescued Hall. When the Coast Guard returned the next day, the *Miss Cindy II* was no longer afloat, having sunk sometime during the night.

MISS DANIA BEACH

The 126-foot long *Miss Dania Beach* was a former Canadian Navy anti-submarine patrol vessel, which was scuttled as an artificial reef on May 29, 2004. The 210-ton vessel was sunk during Dania Beach's centennial celebration, though the reef was later dedicated to the memory of Robert E. Derecktor, a well-known local shipbuilder, whose company Derecktor Shipyards donated the vessel. The *Miss Dania Beach* now rests in 70 feet of water in close proximity to the 55-foot long former LCM *Emmi Boggs*, the 40-foot long former yacht *Summerfield*, and the tug *Donal G. McAllister*.

Photograph of the *Miss Dania Beach* at Port Everglades.

MISS EILEEN

The 67-foot long wooden-hulled shrimp trawler *Miss Eileen* was built in 1958 as hull number 701 by the Diesel Engine Sales Company of St. Augustine. On February 10, 1977, the *Miss Eileen* foundered off Cape Canaveral.

MISS FERNANDINA

On April 15, 1999, the 85-foot long trawler *Miss Fernandina* departed Port Canaveral on a routine fishing trip. That evening, Captain Kenny Jones radioed a fellow shrimper to request assistance after entangling his nets in his running gear. The captain also reported the *Miss Fernandina* was experiencing electrical issues and was listing slightly. By the time the other vessel arrived at the last reported position of the *Miss Fernandina*, 65 miles east of Flagler Beach, there was no sign of the trawler. On April 16, the U.S. Coast Guard initiated an intensive search for the vessel, which was ultimately called off on April 21, a day after two bodies were observed floating face down in the water approximately 240 miles east-northeast of Jacksonville Beach; no trace of the *Miss Fernandina* was ever found.

MISS FLAGLER

The 48-foot long cabin cruiser *Miss Flagler*, valued at $60,000, was scuttled along with the body of Captain Joseph Serzan 40 to 50 miles offshore Daytona Beach on December 28, 1971. The 69-year old Captain Serzan, who passed away on December 14, had served the family of Florida railroad tycoon Henry M. Flagler for 40 years. Flagler's granddaughter, Mrs. Matthews, planned the sinking as a tribute to Serzan, who was considered a close family friend.

MISS GLENDA II

Five crew members of the motorized barge *Miss Glenda II* (also reported as the *Miss Glenda IX*) were rescued by a freighter on February 7, 1983, after the vessel foundered in heavy seas approximately 15 miles off Boca Raton. The 107-foot long *Miss Glenda II*, built in 1957, was en route

163

from Miami to the Bahamas with a cargo of cement and concrete blocks.

MISS HARRIET ANN

The *Miss Harriet Ann* was a 76-foot long shrimp trawler that had finished up a three-day fishing trip and was heading back to the dock at Mayport on July 16, 1996, when a crewman fell asleep at the helm, which resulted in the shrimper grounding on a sandbar 200 feet offshore just south of Ponte Vedra Beach. Approximately 400 gallons of diesel spilled into the ocean following the 5:00 a.m. stranding. Waves crashed over the entombed trawler, which opened up the seams in the hull, broke the keel, and steadily flooded the vessel. Over the course of 24 hours, the *Miss Harriet Ann* completely broke apart, spreading debris over a three-mile stretch of beach.

MISS ILSE

The 67-foot long wooden-hulled shrimp trawler *Miss Ilse* was built in 1950 as hull number 186 by the Diesel Engine Sales Company (DESCO Marine, Incorporated) at its St. Augustine shipyard. On November 22, 1957, the *Miss Ilse* stranded on Flagler Beach.

MISS JO

Built in 1950, the 44-ton *Miss Jo* reportedly burned on Lake Okeechobee near Moore Haven on April 3, 1952[158].

MISS KARLINE

The 85-foot long trawler *Miss Karline* was sunk in 55 feet of water as an artificial reef in May 1989. In August 1992, Hurricane Andrew ripped the vessel open, and the wreck now lists heavily to one side with only her bow and stern recognizable. The *Miss Karline* is part of the "Miami Wreck Trek," which also includes the 65-foot long tug *Patricia* resting a short distance away. The two wrecks, as well as a boulder pile and other artificial reef material, are all linked by rebar stakes, which, along with the shallow depth, makes the "Trek" a good site for novice divers.

Miss Karline (Miami-Dade County Department of Environmental Resources Management).

MISS LINDA

The 40-foot shrimper *Miss Linda* ran aground and disintegrated at Ponce de Leon Inlet on February 4, 1959. The shrimp boat became stranded as she tried to assist a sister vessel, the *Judith Fay*, which had run aground as it was entering the inlet. The fleet had departed New Smyrna Beach that morning, but high winds forced them to return to the dock. The *Miss Linda* was attempting to get close to the stranded *Judith Fay* to rig a tow line when she also became grounded. Three Coast Guard boats sent to the scene managed to refloat the *Judith Fay*, but could not help the Good Samaritan fishing vessel. The hull of the *Miss Linda* was soon breached, forcing the crew to abandon ship. As the *Judith Fay* and the Coast Guard boats returned to the docks with the rescued men, the *Miss Linda* was "beaten to slivers by the elements[159]." News articles mentioned this was the most recent loss of a shrimp boat at New Smyrna Beach since the wrecking of the *Mary L.* the previous January, which ran aground on the beach, broke up, and later sold as junk.

MISS LOURDIES

On June 6, 2009, the dry cargo freighter *Miss Lourdies* was scuttled as the "Miracle of Life" artificial reef site off Boca Raton. The vessel is upright and intact, with the top of the wheelhouse first encountered at a depth of 100 feet, the deck at 125 feet, and the sand at a depth 140 feet. The Haitian-flagged freighter was acquired for use as an artificial reef after U.S. Customs Service agents found a steel compartment hiding almost 340 pounds of cocaine during a June 26, 2008, inspection at the Port of Miami. The vessel was originally built in 1972 as the offshore supply vessel *Safe Tide* by Burton Shipyard, Incorporated at Port Arthur, Texas. She was 165 feet in length, 38.4 feet in breadth, and displaced 649 tons gross. She later sailed as the *Norpac III*, *Sea Bird*, and finally, *Miss Lourdies*.

MISS LIBBY

The 55-foot long shrimp trawler *Miss Libby*, built in 1958, stranded at Crescent Beach on the morning of December 16, 1972. Eight foot seas subsequently broke up the wooden trawler, littering the beach with debris for miles.

MISS LUCY

The *Miss Lucy*, official number 500886, was a 37.5-foot long, 16-foot wide, 26-ton pushboat built in 1965 at Berwick, Louisiana, which was sunk as an artificial reef in 225 feet of water off Miami in May 2001.

MISS LULA

The 51-foot long shrimp trawler *Miss Lula*, built in 1954, stranded at Ponte Vedra Beach on June 3, 1974.

MISS MARYLN LOUISE

The 74-foot long trawler *Miss Marlyn Louise* sank approximately nine miles off West Palm Beach on March 12, 2001, after taking on water from a leak. A U.S. Coast Guard HU-25 Falcon jet picked up the emergency beacon from the vessel around 5:00 a.m. that morning, and the four crew members were eventually rescued by the freighter *A.V. Canster*.

MISS SHIRLEY

On the morning of March 16, 1990, the 73-foot long shrimp boat *Miss Shirley* (also reported as *Miss Charlene*) caught fire three miles off Jupiter Inlet. The three crew members abandoned ship and were later pulled out of the water by a U.S. Coast Guard patrol boat. One report stated the Coast Guard battled the blaze for several hours before the shrimper ultimately sank around noon, while another report stated the wood-hulled vessel burned to the waterline with salvage crews planning to tow the wreck into port. This vessel is possibly the 83-ton trawler *Miss Shirley*, which was built in 1977 by the Diesel Engine Sales Company of St. Augustine.

MIZPAH

The yacht *Mizpah* was originally built as the *Savarona* by the Newport News Shipbuilding Company in 1926 at a cost of $1.3 million for James Elverson, Jr., owner of the daily newspaper *Philadelphia Inquirer*. The beautiful vessel was 185 feet in overall length, 27 feet in beam, and had a cruising range of 7,000 miles. The vessel's name originated from a reference in the Bible, Genesis 31:49, which states: "And Mizpah: for he said, the Lord watch between me and thee, when we are absent from one another."

Upon Elverson's death in 1929, Eugene F. McDonald, Jr., President of the Zenith Radio Corporation, bought the graceful yacht to serve as his home and floating laboratory in Chicago. Renamed the *Mizpah*, the 549-ton yacht was the largest pleasure boat on the Great Lakes at the time. In the 1930s, she took part in numerous adventures, including polar expeditions, a treasure hunt in Costa Rica, as well as a mysterious scientific cruise to the Galapagos Islands. In 1937, McDonald equipped the yacht's Marconi room with "the most powerful new radio marine telephone installation in existence, practically twice as powerful as those found on the large ocean liners[160]." The radiophone could perform both ship-to-ship and ship-to-shore calls in the same manner as a long distance land call. Eugene McDonald turned over the *Mizpah* to the U.S. Navy for war service in March 1942.

The patrol yacht U.S.S. *Mizpah* (Naval Historical Center).

The yacht was converted at Sturgeon Bay, Wisconsin, which included the addition of armament in anticipation of her duty as a patrol craft. She was commissioned into the U.S. Navy as the U.S.S. *Mizpah* (PY-29) on October 26, 1942. Following the end of World War II, she was sold to H.O. Merren and Company of Roatan, Honduras, and probably employed as a coastal freighter. The *Mizpah* eventually ended up in Tampa with a broken crankshaft and became a derelict, destined for the scrap yard. In 1967, Eugene Kinney, Eugene McDonald's nephew and current vice-president of Zenith, learned of the *Mizpah's* plight and purchased her. Due to the impracticality of repairing her though, Kinney donated her to the U.S. Army Corps of Engineers for use as an artificial reef associated with a marine science study. With her upper deck razed, she was scuttled off Palm Beach on April 8, 1968.

Divers over the top deck of the *Mizpah*.

The wreck sits upright in 90 feet of water with her bow pointing north, though portions of the hull have collapsed due to the impact of numerous hurricanes. Penetration into the hull is easy, though divers may have to share the interior with several large Goliath grouper that have taken up residence within the wreck. Visibility can be excellent since the wreck rests north of the inlet, though visibility can be greatly influenced by an outgoing tide, especially when outflow from Lake Okeechobee is significant. The wreck rests along an artificial reef corridor with the *PC-1174*, the *Amaryllis*, and a barge, all of which are connected by a trail of rock and concrete. With a gentle north current, divers can easily drift over all the wrecks on one dive.

MOANA II

According to a March 23, 1938, article in *The Miami News*, the 38-foot long twin cabin cruiser *Moana II* caught fire and was destroyed in Government Cut at Miami on March 22, 1938. The *Moana II* struck a submerged object offshore earlier in the day, and was being towed through the inlet by the *Fish Hawk* when a suspected battery short ignited a fire. The burning *Moana II* was abandoned and allowed to drift to the south side of the jetties and eventually sunk.

MOHAWK

The 10-ton vessel *Mohawk*, official number 208087, burned on July 12, 1919, at Courtney.

The Clyde Line steamer *Mohican* resting dockside (Mark Mondano Collection).

MOHICAN

Built in 1904 at Philadelphia, Pennsylvania, the Clyde Line freighter *Mohican* was 238 feet in length, 40 feet in breadth, displaced 2,255 tons, and carried a crew of 26. Just a few years after her construction, the steamer was involved in a heroic rescue at sea. On December 14, 1907, the *Mohican* rescued the crew of the 1,100-ton schooner *Augustus Welt*, which sprung a leak following a gale and foundered off Cape Lookout, North Carolina. The *Mohican* arrived just as the schooner settled and began sinking. While the crew of the *Mohican* was successful in saving others, their efforts would eventually be focused on their own ship and their own lives.

On May 10, 1925, the crew of the *Mohican* discovered a fire in the aft hold of the ship while en route from Jacksonville to Miami with a general cargo. The ship dropped anchor in Canaveral Bight to allow the entire crew to battle the blaze. The tanker *Tulsa* pulled alongside the *Mohican* to lend assistance. Meanwhile, a crowd grew on Cocoa Beach to catch a glimpse of the unfolding spectacle three miles out to sea. As darkness fell, the glow from the still-burning fire could be seen from shore. It eventually became apparent the fire was steadily spreading out of control, so the crew scuttled the *Mohican* to extinguish the flames and evacuated to the *Tulsa*. By morning, all that was visible from the beach was the funnel and masts of the freighter *Mohican*. Over the next several days, the cargo of the *Mohican* slowly began washing ashore. Building materials, such as heavy oak doors, window and door sashes, as well as lard and oil cans, tires, and a refrigerator, were salvaged by people living in the vicinity. It is interesting to note that fire was apparently a common occurrence on Clyde Line steamers, as the company lost six steamers in the span of six years due to blazes at sea.

Over the next several years, the wreck gradually came apart in pieces, with sections of the *Mohican* washing up on the beach. As her steel hull still presented a menace to navigation, the Salvage Section of the Bureau of Ships eventually demolished the hulk in 1944. While the sinking of the *Mohican* and its subsequent demolition were both well documented, the wreck has somehow escaped the attention of other researchers, as well as most divers.

The wreck rests in approximately 35 feet of water in two distinct sections. The demolition of the freighter was extremely effective, as the site is largely composed of flattened hull plates and twisted debris. A thin veneer of encrustation and sporadic gorgonians cover most every surface. Because the wreck lies in such close proximity to Port Canaveral and the shipping channel, visibility is typically poor. Furthermore, on my visits in 2005 and 2006, the entire wreck was covered by a thick layer of fine sediment, likely a result of the record number of hurricanes to impact Florida in 2004. Clouds of spadefish swirl around the wreck, and the abundant wreckage is likely utilized by grouper and snapper as well.

MOLLIE S. LOOK

Built in 1904 at Machias, Maine, by E.J. White, the three-masted schooner *Mollie S. Look* was 159 feet long, 36.2 feet wide, and was listed at 572 tons. On February 14, 1908, en route from Norfolk to Carrabelle with a cargo of coal, a storm drove the *Look* onto the beach approximately 1.5 miles north of the New River Inlet at Fort Lauderdale. While no lives were lost and portions of the ship's rigging were salvaged, the *Mollie S. Look* was beat to pieces by the winter storm.

MOLLY

In 1764 the sloop *Molly* wrecked on Cumberland Island while on a voyage from Kingston, Jamaica, to Savannah, Georgia. The captain and crew salvaged the vessel's sails, rigging, and a portion of the cargo. The remainder was picked over by locals from St. Marys and those living on Cumberland Island.

MONAHAN

The tug *Monahan* (commonly, but incorrectly, cited as *Monachan*) was sunk in 80 feet of water off Mayport in 1995 to serve as an artificial reef. She now rests upright and intact in 80 feet of water. The *Monahan*, official number 279546, was built in 1959 at Norfolk, Virginia, and was 56.9 feet long, 16.3 feet wide, and displaced 51 gross tons.

MONOMOY

The *Monomoy* was reportedly an 82-foot long yacht sunk off Fort Lauderdale as an artificial reef in 1970. The former yacht rests in 60 feet of water on the seaward edge of the third reef line, though it is significantly broken up and partially sanded over. This vessel could possibly be the former motor yacht *Monomoy*, which was operated by the War Department (U.S. Army Corps of Engineers) in the late 1930s.

MONTAGUE

The vessel *Montague*, Captain Pickle, bound from Jamaica to Liverpool, was lost near Cape Florida in July 1774. The crew and 30 hogsheads of sugar were saved, and carried to New Providence, Bahamas; Captain Pickle and the crew of the *Montague* continued on to Cowes, England, aboard the *Portland*.

MONTAGUE DOYLE

The brig *Montague Doyle*, from Wareham, Massachusetts, for Jacksonville, was wrecked around September 30, 1855, on the St. Johns Bar 16 miles from Jacksonville[161]. The vessel bilged and filled with water. The crew was saved after being on the wreck 20 hours without food or water, and then having to walk ten miles before finding any assistance.

MORENO

On November 4, 1870, *The New York Herald*, reported the "Brig *Moreno*, Philips, from Havana for Sydney, CB, was totally wrecked off Jupiter Inlet Oct. 8, at about 4 A.M. The crew consisted of eight men. The captain remained with the wreck while the second mate, James Horton, with the men, went up to Charleston. The hull of the vessel is good, but too high ashore to be got off. Sails and rigging saved."

MORGAN'S WRECK

Also called "Charlie's Wreck," this site is found northeast of Pacific Reef Light resting in 42 feet of water at its offshore side and 35 feet on its inshore perimeter. According to Meylach (1971), the wreck consists of a 60-foot long ballast pile rising 6 feet off the rocky seafloor. The site was reportedly salvaged heavily in the 1950s and '60s.

MORRIS RUSSEL

As reported in Volume 13 of *The Sailor's Magazine and Naval Journal*, the British brig *Morris Russel*, from Montego Bay, Jamaica, sprung a leak and was run ashore about 20 miles north of Mosquito Inlet on October 8, 1840. While the vessel proved to be a total loss, the crew was fortunately saved.

MUNTZ METAL WRECK

The "Muntz Metal Wreck" is an unknown shipwreck resting in approximately 40 feet of water 10 miles north of Cape Canaveral. Anchor chain, iron mast stepping, and hull sheeting known as Muntz metal were observed at the site. Muntz metal (alpha-beta brass) sheeting was an alloy patented in 1838 to replace copper as anti-fouling sheathing on vessel hulls. Therefore, it is likely this unknown shipwreck originally sailed in the mid- to late nineteenth century.

MUSCOGEE

The 117-ton paddlewheel steamer *Muscogee* was built in 1837 at Pittsburgh, Pennsylvania. According to *The Sailor's Magazine and Naval Journal*, Volume 10 (1838), "The steamboat *Muscogee* of Columbia (Ga.) was wrecked in a gale of wind, and went down about 30 miles to the northward of Cape Florida, on the 23d May. There were 22 persons on board, three of whom were washed from the deck by the sea. The rest took to the boats just as the steamer went down, and after being out four days, were picked up and landed at Key West."

MUTUAL SAFETY

The *Mutual Safety* was a sidewheel steamer built in 1842 at New York. She registered a length of 163.5 feet, a breadth of 26.7 feet, and a displacement of 420 tons gross. On October 11, 1846, the *Mutual Safety* wrecked during a storm on Fort George Island (also reported as stranded on the St. Johns River).

MY BOYS

On the morning of October 4, 1996, the 62-foot shrimp trawler *My Boys* became disabled approximately one mile off Flagler Beach when heavy seas allowed the trawl net to become fouled in the vessel's running gear. The trawler set her anchor, but the continuous pounding parted her lines and she went adrift. The shrimper washed up at Flagler Beach later that afternoon, and over the course of several days of foul weather, the *My Boys* was gradually beat to pieces.

MYSTERY J.

The British auxiliary schooner *Mystery J.* was one of the best known rum runners operating between Florida and the Bahamas. On September 18, 1926, the schooner sank in the south slip of the Peninsular and Oriental Steam Navigation Company docks at the foot of Sixth Street during the Great Miami Hurricane[162]. The schooner had previously been damaged during a July hurricane while at Nassau, Bahamas. The *Mystery J.* was eventually raised, repaired, and put back into service; however, she reportedly disappeared after departing Miami for Nassau on January 10, 1927, bound for Nassau. No trace of the schooner or its 18 passengers and 5 crewmen were found.

MYSTIC

The sidewheel steamer *Mystic*, official number 17717, was built in 1866 at New Bern, North Carolina. The 168-ton steamboat was 116.6 feet long and 21.3 feet wide. The *Mystic* was abandoned in 1887 at Grassy Point on the banks of the St. Johns River.

MYSTIC ISLE

The *Mystic Isle*, hull number 573A, was a car/passenger ferry built in 1942 by the Burger Boat Company of Manitowoc, Wisconsin. The first all-steel, all-welded passenger boat of its kind on the Great Lakes, she was built to replace the Erie Island Ferry Company's vessel *Erie Isle* on the run between Catawba Island, Put-In-Bay, and Middle Bass. The stout ship was 103 feet in length, 32 feet in breadth, and had room onboard for 335 passengers and 20 cars per trip. The *Mystic Isle* served in that capacity until she was sold in 1950 to the Fishers Island Ferry District of New York. In March 1978 she was traded to the Blount Marine Corporation of Warren, Rhode Island, as partial payment for a new ferry. The *Mystic Isle* arrived in Florida when Donald Marshall of Fort Lauderdale acquired her in July 1979. The aging ferry was almost immediately sold to Starboard Navigation Company of Panama, who converted her into a fishing vessel. On June 2, 1984, the U.S.C.G.C. *Diligence* seized the *Mystic Isle* about 100 miles northeast of Miami when she was found carrying a load of marijuana. Towed into Miami, she sat in the Miami River for almost two years before being sunk in 200 feet of water to serve as an artificial reef on May 30, 1986.

The wreck of the *Mystic Isle* sits upright and intact off Virginia Key. The small wreck is easy to penetrate through the large automobile opening in her hull just below the wheelhouse. Just off the stern and to the north of the wreck rests the yacht *Esmeralda*. It is possible for experienced divers to visit both wrecks on the same dive should they be using scooters or if a swift, north current is running.

Starboard bow view of the ferry *Mystic Isle* (Al Hart).

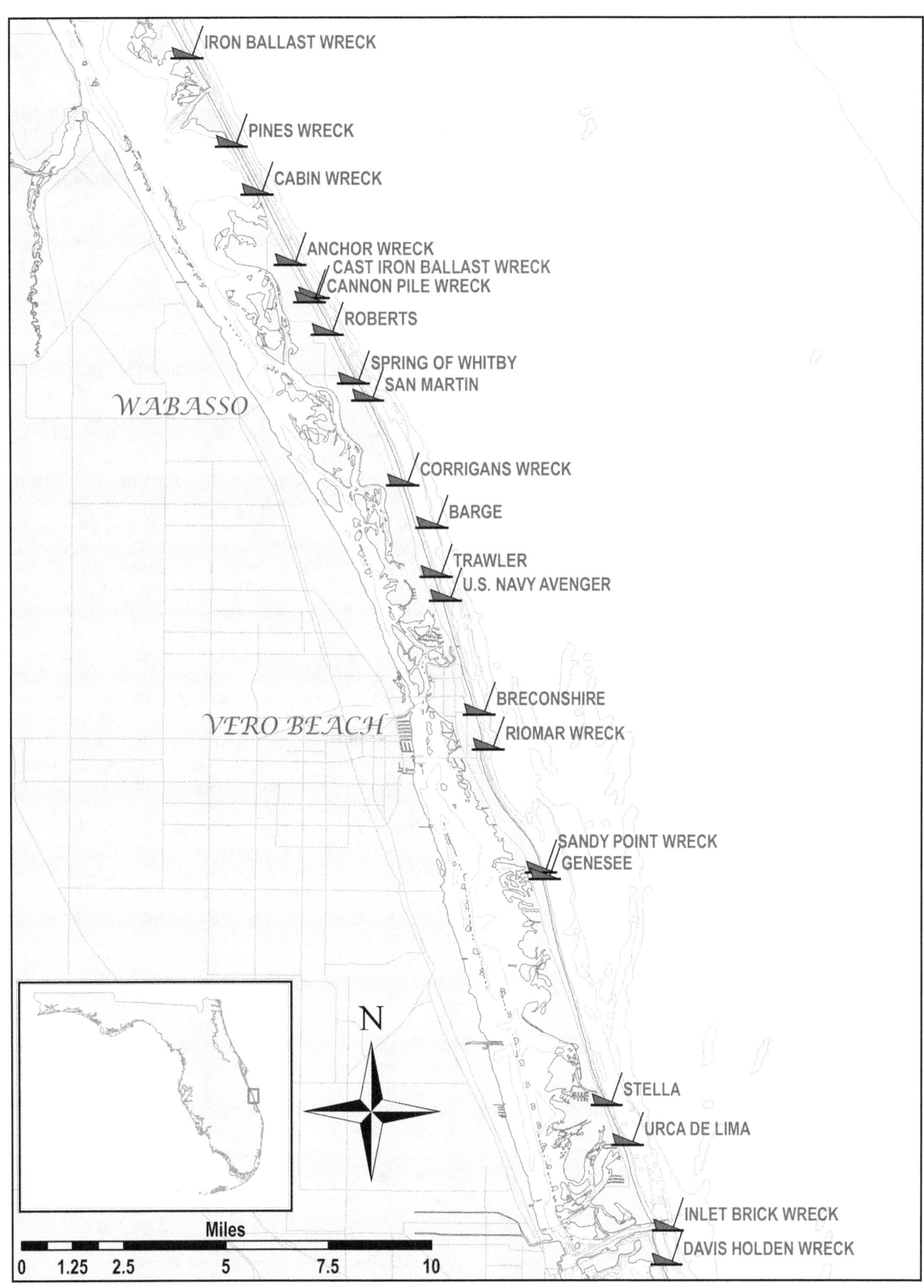

Map depicting the various nearshore shipwrecks between Fort Pierce and Sebastian Inlets.

169

NANCY LEE

Owned by the Biscayne Navigation Company, the *Nancy Lee* was an excursion steamer that was reported to be high and dry on Municipal Dock Four after being blown ashore on September 18, 1926, during the Great Miami Hurricane. The ultimate fate of this vessel is unknown.

NANCY MORAN

The tug *Nancy Moran*, only 21 days in service, was sunk in a collision with the U.S.S. *PC-451* approximately 12.5 miles offshore Hollywood on the morning of December 26, 1941. The *Nancy Moran* was built by Gulfport Shipbuilding Company at Port Arthur, Texas, and was on her delivery trip to New York at the time of her loss. The new tug was 105 feet long, 25 feet wide, displaced 212 tons gross, and was powered with a 1,200-horsepower diesel engine. Prior to leaving from New Orleans on December 23, she was given instructions from the U.S. Navy to run without lights to avoid potential detection by German U-boats. As the *Nancy Moran* steamed north, the *PC-451* was patrolling south with the destroyer U.S.S. *Biddle* (DD-151), but far offshore where typically only northbound traffic would travel; at 3:36 a.m., the *PC-451* reported Hillsboro Inlet Lighthouse on her starboard beam, 11 miles distant. At 4:45 a.m., the two vessels spotted each other in the dark. Both the *PC-451*, which was also running blacked out, and the *Nancy Moran* furiously attempted a turn to starboard to avoid a collision. Unfortunately, the effort was too late, as the bow of the *PC-451* struck the tug on the port side almost amidships. The damage doomed the *Nancy Moran*, which rapidly flooded and sank in deep water.

NANON

The *Nanon*, official number 130570, was a 45-foot long Burgess sloop launched at Boston, Massachusetts, on April 25, 1889. She registered a length of 50.3 feet, a beam of 16.5 feet, and a displacement of 26 tons; however, she was later converted to a gas yacht. On September 3, 1916, the *Nanon* stranded at Anastasia Island.

NANTWICH

The British bark *Nantwich*, Captain John Smith, wrecked south of Fort Pierce Inlet on September 24, 1696, while traveling with the bark *Reformation*, which was lost off Jupiter.

NARRAGANSETT

The coast of Florida from Cape Canaveral to St. Augustine has witnessed the grounding of countless vessels. Dangerous shoals near the approaches of Ponce de Leon Inlet and St. Augustine Inlet have trapped several vessels that strayed from the safe water of the main channel. Still others have been blown ashore during violent storms as they hugged the coast during their approach to Cape Canaveral. While vessels off southern Florida were able to drop anchor and hold their position due to the presence of hard bottom or coral reefs, the coastal areas north of Cape Canaveral are predominantly composed of homogenous sand. Vessels in peril of being blown ashore would drop their anchors only to find themselves slowly and helplessly worked inshore by massive swells and rolling surf. After grounding in shallow water or being cast upon the beach at low tide, many ships slowly deteriorated in the ensuing weeks by the constant beating of heavy surf, eventually becoming total losses.

The *Narragansett* was a 576-ton sidewheel steamer built in 1836 at the New York shipyard of William Brown for the Boston and New York Transportation Company. The steamer, at 212 feet in length and 27 feet in breadth, had a high length-to-beam ratio. There were accommodations for 300 passengers. She was powered by two low-pressure 145-horsepower engines that were apparently too powerful for the wooden-hulled vessel. While the hull was stiffened with diagonal iron strapping, she was laid up for repairs constantly due to the stress exerted by the engines.

The vessel arrived in Providence, Rhode Island, on October 13, 1836, where she hosted a trip down the Providence River for the Board of Directors of the Boston and New York Transportation Company. Unfortunately, as soon as the guests were seated for dinner, the steamer heeled over to one side, throwing people, china, glasses, and the elegant meal to the deck. The event did not bode well for the ship. In 1840, the Boston and New York Transportation Company merged with the New Jersey Steam Navigation Company. In 1846, the *Narragansett* was sold to a New Orleans company for employment in the Gulf of Mexico. While en route from New York to New Orleans, she was caught in a strong storm on October 28, 1847. Eventually, she was pushed up on the beach five miles north of Ponce de Leon Inlet at North Beach. While the event sealed the fate of the steamer, the entire complement of crew and passengers calmly departed the vessel the next morning.

The *Narragansett* was abandoned and slowly settled into the sand, however, a heavy gale in 1868 broke the ship into three large sections and proceeded to refloat two of them. The two sections of wreckage managed to drift south and washed into the Ponce de Leon Inlet, where they eventually grounded approximately a half-mile apart. The hull of the *Narragansett* was sheathed in copper with each panel weighing approximately 50 pounds. Locals eventually stripped these sections of the valuable copper, which was detailed by Hawks (1887): "During the bluest time of 1867 or 8, when the old mill was idle – there was nothing to do and almost nothing to eat – there came a gale that brought a piece of the old wreck ashore opposite where the wreck stood; two portions drifted in at the inlet, and one stranded on the sand-bar above Pacetti's, and the other below his house one-half mile or so. These were a real copper mine to us, for we got several hundred pounds of copper sheathing and bolts. The sheathing was in two layers, the sheets weighing 50 lbs. each." The wreck of the *Narragansett* was noted on a navigational chart for several years due to the exposed boiler and sternpost near the Halifax River channel at the inlet, but presently there are

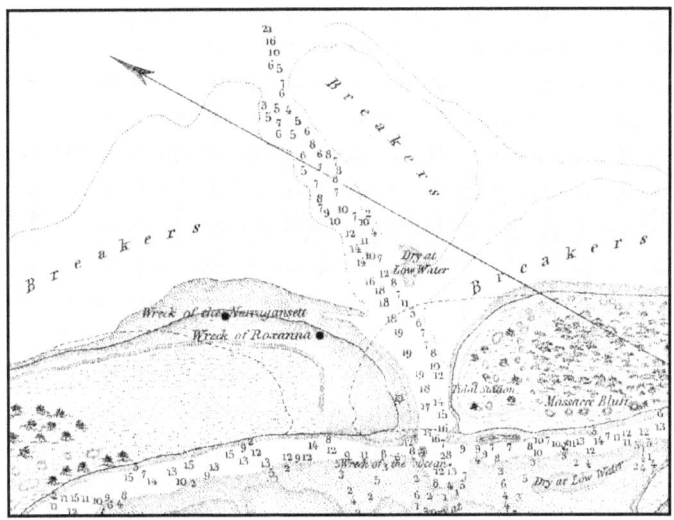

Historical map of Mosquito Inlet marking the wrecks of the *Narragansett* and *Roxanna* (Mark Mondano Collection).

no remains to be found of the steamer. Some more copper spikes and other miscellaneous fittings have been recovered over the years, but the vessel itself was efficiently dispatched by the Atlantic's relentless surf.

Florida Master Site File VO00179 documents a reported wreck site on the south interior side of Ponce de Leon Inlet that apparently was significantly impacted by dredge operations around 1971. Dredge activities cast iron ballast, copper and lead sheathing, pottery and glass shards, wood, and bronze fasteners onto the onshore spoil area, where they were picked over by local residents. Analysis of the material resulted in an estimated 1840 through 1860 timeframe. Therefore, this material could have been associated with the steamer *Narragansett* or some other shipwreck.

NARWAL

The *Narwal* was a coaster built at the Foxhol, Netherlands shipyard of *Vooruitgang Scheepswerf*. Launched on June 5, 1939, the 291-ton freighter was 136 feet in length and 24.9 feet in beam. In June 1967 the *Narwal* was sold to Swedish owners. Later, she operated for Seahorse Shipping Company, Limited, and was homeported at Kingstown, St. Vincent. The *Narwal* eventually outlived her usefulness, and was acquired for use as an artificial reef at a cost of $9,500 and scuttled in 115 feet of water off Miami on April 17, 1986. The coaster used to be an excellent dive site until Hurricane Andrew visited South Florida in August 1992. The massive hurricane obliterated the *Narwal*, breaking her into several large pieces. Over time, the wreck has further collapsed, and now largely consists of flattened hull plates in the sand.

NASSAUVIAN

In 1919, the three-masted schooner *J.W. Somerville*, official number 219057, which was 160.2 feet long, 35.2 feet wide, and 547 tons gross, was built at Pocomoke City, Maryland. The *Somerville*, en route from St. Andrews Bay to San Juan, Puerto Rico with a cargo of lumber, was caught in a hurricane in September 1921, with the loss of all hands. The drifting derelict, found dismasted and capsized 40 miles off the Dry Tortugas, was salvaged by the U.S. Coast Guard. Towed into Key West, the wreck was subsequently purchased by W.C.B. Albury, who converted the schooner into a motor freight vessel, and renamed her *Nassauvian*. On April 27, 1930, the *Nassauvian* reportedly burned at Jacksonville.

NATHAN CLEAVES

The fishing schooner *Nathan Cleaves*, official number 18679, was built in May 1871 at Essex, Massachusetts. The vessel registered a length of 79 feet, a breadth of 23 feet, and a displacement of 76 tons. The *Nathan Cleaves* arrived at Indian River on March 21, 1895, to establish a fishing business, but after her arrival, the master decided to sell her outfit, and all of the crew, except one man, left for home. The schooner remained idle until the owner arrived on March 24. On April 8, the schooner was attempting to leave the harbor at Indian River Inlet when she struck bottom and ultimately became a total loss.

Wreck of the *Nathan F. Cobb* on Ormond Beach (Florida State Archives).

NATHAN F. COBB

On December 5, 1896, the American schooner *Nathan F. Cobb*, of Rockland, Maine, wrecked one mile south of Ormond Beach. She was sailing for New York with a cargo of lumber when a storm stripped away her masts and cast the disabled vessel onto the beach. The *Nathan F. Cobb*, official number 130513, was built in November 1890 by Cobb, Butler, and Company in Bath, Maine. She was 167.2 feet long, 35.1 feet in beam, and 674 tons gross. The official

Image of the coaster *Narwal* (Jan Harteveld).

U.S. Life-Saving Service report details the events leading up to and following the *Cobb's* wrecking:

> Sprung a leak at sea and became waterlogged. Sails were blown away in gale and she was thrown on her beam ends. The masts and cabin were carried away and two men were washed overboard. When main and mizzen masts went, she righted and then drifted helplessly for three days. On the morning of the 5th she was driven on the beach near Ormond, in the midst of heavy breakers. Assistance was requested from Jupiter Inlet station. In the meantime, it was decided that at low water an attempt to reach the imperiled men would be made without waiting for the outfit from Jupiter Inlet Station, and Superintendent Shaw went to the town to procure the necessary lines. He had already sent his small surfboat to the beach, and while he was away six attempts were made by citizens to reach the wreck but failed on account of the heavy surf. Then another small boat, a metallic dinghy, was carried to the beach and two volunteers started out in it against the warnings of some of the bystanders. By dint of masterly surfmanship they succeeded in launching and pulling out to within a short distance of the wreck, but in trying to reach a line drifted down to them from it, the boat capsized, throwing them into the angry sea. By almost superhuman efforts one of them managed to swim ashore and was hauled through the surf half drowned; the other stayed by the boat, but after righting once, it capsized again with him and he sank from sight, beyond help. The superintendent had just returned to the beach with gear when this casualty occurred. The little surfboat was made ready for a final attempt to reach the shipwrecked men at low water. A line having been made fast in the stern, the superintendent and one volunteer, Captain Edward DeCoucy, removed their outer clothing and prepared for the encounter. At that moment a man was seen to leave the wreck with a line and start for shore. Instantly the surfboat was pushed out into the breakers and the two determined men began the struggle to meet the daring swimmer. By constant and intelligent action he was reached in the tumultuous sea and safely grasped the stern of the boat, making his line fast. The crowd on shore, seeing that the rescue was made, hauled the boat and all hands safely to the beach. Communication being now established, life-preservers were sent out to the wreck and the remaining five men were hauled ashore without mishap.

For days following the event, locals came out to inspect the stranded schooner. The beached hulk was stripped of anything of value, and then eventually left to be consumed by the sand and surf of Ormond Beach.

NATHAN HANAU

The 513-ton ship *Nathan Hanau* was built in 1848 at Kingston, Massachusetts, by shipbuilder Joseph Holmes. In early 1859, the *Nathan Hanau* departed Boston with a cargo of ice, furniture, and shoes, bound for her home port of New Orleans. On March 2, 1859, the vessel grounded on Brewster Reef (also reported near Cape Florida) and soon bilged. The vessel and cargo were worth a combined value of $30,000; wreckers were awarded $2,049 for saved cargo. It should be noted that the March 15, 1859, edition of *The New York Times* included a March 13 dispatch from New Orleans, which stated the ship *Nathan Hanan* [sic] arrived at New Orleans on March 12. Based on the available insurance records, however, it would appear this dispatch was incorrect.

NAVIGATOR

According to *The Sailor's Magazine and Naval Journal*, Volume 19, the schooner "*Navigator*, from St. Marks, about October 7 (1846), for New York, went ashore on the beach of Florida – a total loss." It is unclear exactly where the *Navigator* was lost; however, a hurricane in October 1846 affected shipping primarily throughout the Florida Keys. Regardless, due to the language used, it is possible the schooner went ashore somewhere north of Cape Florida.

NAYA

The 24-ton yacht *Naya*, official number 208735, was built in 1911 at Miami. She was 51.4 feet in length and 14.5 feet in breadth. On April 27, 1930, the *Naya* reportedly stranded at Cape Canaveral.

NELLIE F. BURGESS

Built in July 1867 at Belfast, Maine, the 141-ton schooner *Nellie F. Burgess*, official number 18492, was 92 feet long and 26 feet wide; her captain and owner was James E. Burgess. In November 1871, the *Burgess* stranded on Mosquito Inlet Bar during a gale and was reported as a total loss.

NELLIE N.

The shrimp trawler *Nellie N.* capsized and broke up in heavy seas off Ponce Inlet on October 29, 1963[163]. The sinking claimed one life.

NELLY

The American ship *Nelly* (also cited as *Netty*), Captain Smith, sailing from Philadelphia to St. Augustine, was lost on the St. Augustine Bar in 1766. Her crew and a portion of her cargo were saved.

NELSON

According to the *Bell's Weekly Messenger* of April 14, 1822, "The English brig *Nelson*, was wrecked on the Florida shore 31st Jan. Crew saved, and arrived at Eastport 24th Feb. in the *Beaver*, from Jamaica."

NEPENTHE

The 40-foot shrimp boat *Nepenthe* was sunk at Fernandina on November 27, 1932, during a strong nor'easter[164].

NEPTUNE (1802)

On August 28, 1802, *The Times* reported the loss of the *Neptune*, Captain Casbury, from New Orleans to Greenock, out 14 days, on the coast of Florida; the crew and part of the cargo saved.

NEPTUNE (1816)

Shipping intelligence from *Lloyd's List* dated January 31, which was included in the February 2, 1817, edition of *Bell's Weekly Messenger*, documented the vessel *Neptune*, Captain Conolly, stranded on the Amelia Bar and bilged during a voyage from Amelia Island to Jamaica.

NEPTUNE (1822)

The *Bell's Weekly Messenger* of July 21, 1822, reported, "The *Neptune*, Duncan, from Jamaica to Dublin, was seen on shore and bilged on the Floridas, by the *Ann*, Carden, arrived at Bristol from Jamaica." While Marx (1987) and others cite this vessel as a Florida shipwreck, subsequent newspaper reports indicate she was either misidentified or was refloated, repaired, and put back in service in short order. For instance, shipping intelligence dated September 26, which was included in the October 11, 1822 issue of *The Edinburgh Advertiser*, stated "*Neptune*, Duncan, Leith, Memel, ballast." Likewise, on November 19, 1822, *The Edinburgh Advertiser* noted the *Neptune*, Captain Duncan, departed Memel, Germany (now Klaipėda, Lithuania) on October 29 for Grangemouth, England, with a cargo of timber.

NERO

According to the *St. James's Evening Post* of July 4, 1747, "The *Nero*, Capt. Balion, from Plymouth for North Carolina, was taken by the Spaniards, sent for the Havanna, but lost near Cape Florida."

NERVINA

On February 22, 1948, the *Sarasota Herald Tribune* reported the 40- to 50-foot long fishing vessel *Nervina* burned to the gunwales and sank approximately five miles off Jacksonville Beach on February 21. The captain was believed to have perished in the incident.

NETTIE LANGDON

The *Nettie Langdon*, official number 18799, was a three-masted schooner built in 1874 at East Boston, Massachusetts. The single-deck vessel registered a length of 129 feet, a breadth of 30 feet, and a displacement of 393 tons gross. On August 27, 1881, the *Langdon* was caught in a hurricane off South Carolina, which capsized the schooner. Her masts, sails, and rigging were promptly cut away, which allowed the vessel to right itself. The *Langdon* was not out of trouble yet, though, as the disabled craft was then driven onto the shoals at Cape Romain the following day; two men perished in the wrecking. The schooner was eventually pulled off the shoals, repaired, and put back in service. In 1883, her registration was transferred to Jacksonville. Almost eight years after her earlier episode, the schooner *Nettie Langdon* again stranded on a shoal, this time at the mouth of the St. Johns River while being towed out to sea on September 6, 1889. However, it is possible that she didn't prove to be a total loss, as the *Nettie Langdon* was still listed in the 1894 registers.

NEVA

The 226-ton brig *Neva* was built in 1864 at East Machias, Maine, and was 103 feet long and 26.3 feet wide. At the time of her loss she was owned by Simpson and Clapp, and her master was Captain E.J. Talbot. On January 8, 1866, the *Neva* wrecked on the south breakers of the St. Johns Bar during a gale. Ten perished in the event, including the captain; only the second mate and two seamen were saved. In the wake of the storm, the *Neva* was cast up on the beach 12 miles south of the bar. Several days later, the bodies of those lost in the wreck washed up on the beach, and "and on examination, marks of violence were discovered, and no doubt remained that they had been murdered. The second mate has been arrested, and is under examination at Jacksonville[165]." An article in the February 12, 1866, edition of the *Petersburg Daily Index* included additional details on the grisly turn of events:

> About four weeks ago – on the 8th of January – the brig *Neva*, of East Machias, Maine, a fine vessel one year old, two hundred and thirty tons, went ashore on St John's Bar, Florida (at the mouth of the river, below Jacksonville), and the second mate and two seamen were the only persons who got ashore alive. They reported that the vessel had been lying at anchor outside the bar waiting for the sea to go down that they might cross, when a terrible gale on the 8th came on, and drove the vessel ashore and that Captain Talbot, Mr. John Stuart (mate), the pilot, passengers, and one or two seamen perished by drowning. But it now appears such was not the case – they were really murdered.
> The head of Captain Talbot was horribly crushed, in an entirely different manner from what would probably have occurred

by contact with any floating piece of wreck. The pilot's body was covered with stabs from some long, sharp instrument, and similar marks of atrocity were visible on the person of a lady passenger. A fearful cloud of mystery hangs over the matter.

While the *Neva* was reported to have eventually beached 12 miles south of St. Johns Bar, the *Annual Report of the Chief of Engineers, United States Army, to the Secretary of War for the Year 1888* indicates a different ultimate fate, stating:

At the side of Ward's Bank, in the jetty channel at the mouth of St. Johns River, Florida. This is reported to be the wreck of the German brig *Neva*, loaded with logwood, which was sunk in this position about 1857. She lies at the edge of the ship channel, imbedded in the sand in 6 feet of water. That portion of the wreck clear of the sand is 95 feet long and 23 feet wide. Work to remove the *Neva*, as well as the remains of the U.S.S. *Columbine*, was approved on April 23, 1888, but was postponed on May 2, due to approach of the hot and unhealthy season.

Finally, the *Annual Report of the Chief of Engineers, United States Army, to the Secretary of War for the Year 1890* detailed, "The remainder of the wreck, supposed to be that of the German brig *Neva*, was removed by the contractor from Ward's Bank at the mouth of the St. Johns River. About 36 cords of its cargo of logwood were recovered."

NEW BALION

On August 26, 1747, the *General Advertiser* published, "The *New Balion*, for North Carolina from Plymouth, was taken after two days sail by a Spanish privateer, and in her passage for the Havanna was lost near Cape Florida." This may be the unknown snow that reportedly wrecked with the *Cruizer Privateer* in late 1746.

NEW JERSEY

As reported in a March 1838 dispatch in *The Sailor's Magazine and Naval Journal*, Volume 10, the schooner *New Jersey*, from Philadelphia, was totally lost on the St. Johns Bar.

NEW REPUBLIC

The bark *New Republic* was reported lost 11 miles from Mosquito Inlet in the same storm that claimed the *City of Vera Cruz* in August 1880. The British bark *New Republic*, official number 59977, was built by McKay and Warner in October 1870 at Quebec, Canada. The 580-ton sailing vessel was 148 feet long and 31.6 feet wide.

NEW RIVER

On February 15, 1930, the rudder of the glass-bottomed excursion boat *New River* struck a sand bar in Bear Cut near Miami, which shattered the glass viewing port and flooded the vessel[166]. The 63 passengers onboard evacuated the vessel as it settled into the shallow waters of Bear Cut. Due to the location and shallow depth where the vessel sank, it was likely raised and repaired soon after the incident; the vessel's inclusion in this work is largely due to the uniqueness of the wrecking incident. The *New River*, official number 220051, was built in 1920 at Fort Lauderdale, and was 63.3 feet in length, 16.1 feet in beam, and 19 gross tons in displacement.

NEW YORK CENTRAL NO. 3

Newspaper reports documented the derelict tug *New York Central No. 3*, which had been abandoned for some time on the Miami River, was demolished as artificial reef on June 11, 1973. Unfortunately, the sinking created a significant oil slick when over 300 gallons of crude oil escaped from the wreck off Miami Beach. Records indicate a vessel known as the "Fire Boat" was scuttled in 222 feet of water off Miami to serve as an artificial reef in June 1973, which may be the derelict tug. Details of the tug's history are unknown, but this vessel may possibly be the tug *New York Central No. 3*, official number 214507, built in 1916 at Wilmington, Delaware for the New York Central Railroad Company. This tug was 104.3 feet long, 24.8 feet wide, and displaced 210 tons.

NICHOLAS ADOLPH

The *Nicholas Adolph* was a 321-ton, single-decked Finish ship built in 1805, Captain N. Hass. On January 22, 1815, the *Bell's Weekly Messenger* reported, "The *Nicholas Adolph*, Haas, was lost on Amelia Island Bar about the 10th November. Part of the cargo saved." While the 1815 edition of *Lloyd's Register* documents the ship departed Liverpool for America in the fall of 1814, apparently the *Nicholas Adolph* was not lost, as she appears in the *Lloyd's Register* for several years after the supposed 1814 event. She is later owned in Sweden, and her master is reported as J. Tysen in 1819. It is possible that she was pulled off the bar after the grounding and repaired, as post-1815 the *Nicholas Adolph* is documented as only 312 tons burden.

NICHOLAS AND SARAH

The *London Evening Post* of August 30, 1753, reported, "The *Nicholas and Sarah*, Capt. Luton, from Honduras, is lost near Cape Florida; the captain with part of the crew and cargo, were saved by a ship bound for St. Augustine."

NINA FAY

The 72-foot long shrimp trawler *Nina Fay*, built in 1952, stranded a couple hundred feet north of Marineland near St. Augustine on the morning of December 16, 1972. Eight-foot seas subsequently broke up the wooden trawler, littering the beach with debris for miles.

NOAH SMITH

The steel-hulled, stern ramp trawler *Noah Smith* almost met its fate on October 15, 1982, when it grounded on the

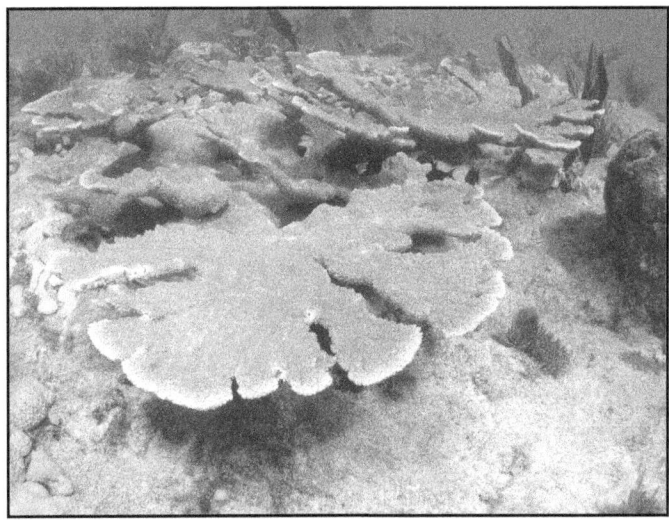

coral reefs off Looe Key, but it was eventually pulled off successfully. It is unclear when the *Noah Smith* actually sank, but she now rests in 110 feet of water almost equidistant between Port Canaveral and Sebastian. With its bow facing northward, the shrimper lists hard over to starboard. A significant breach in the deck forward of the wheelhouse allows easy access into the interior. Heavily encrusted in sponge and other invertebrate growth, the wreck is a thriving oasis for marine life. Typically surrounded by a cloud of baitfish, with roving barracuda and snook, the *Noah Smith* can be a productive site for flounder and gag grouper.

NOBLE BOUNTY

According to an October 27, 1787, dispatch from Jamaica published in the January 5, 1788, issue of the *London Chronicle*, "The *Noble Bounty*, Herbert, from this island for London, was lost on Cape Florida Reef; the crew saved by Capt. Black, of the *Friendship*."

NO NAME WRECK (BREVARD)

The "No Name Wreck" is an unidentified wreck in the surf zone off Eau Gallie Beach in Brevard County. Some of the ballast stones apparently are scattered along the shore, and additional wreckage, including several iron knees, are occasionally exposed at low tide. Based on the reported presence of the iron knees, it is suspected this vessel dates to the mid-nineteenth century.

NO NAME WRECK (ST. LUCIE)

Florida Master Site File SL00039 documents a reported wreck site in approximately 10-15 feet of water north of Fort Pierce Inlet and just south of the wreck of the *Stella*. The wreck is scattered over a fairly wide area, but apparently consists of two separate ballast piles. Material uncovered at the site in the 1970s included slate, a piece of marble, one small iron cannon, cannon balls, musket shot, and small fragments of sheet lead. The wreck is over a half-mile north of the *Urca de Lima*, so it's likely this is a completely separate site.

NORINA

The Austrian bark *Norina* was built in August 1868 at Trieste. The 579-ton vessel was 141 feet in length and 30 feet in beam. On March 31, 1879, the *Norina*, Captain Sutora, wrecked on the Florida coast. Details of the event were documented in the official U.S. Life-Saving Service report, which stated:

> The Austrian ship *Norina*, of Trieste, bound from New Orleans to Gibraltar, with a cargo of corn and lumber, sprung a leak off the coast of Florida, and in a few hours went ashore about ten miles north of Station No. 2, Seventh District, Florida. The crew, consisting of thirteen persons, landed in the ship's boat, but in so doing capsized and lost the water and provisions they had taken from the ship. Three of the number went in search of assistance and reached House of Refuge (Station) No. 2, Seventh District, about daylight on the 1st of April. The acting keeper, after giving the weary men breakfast, took his boat and returned with the sailors, taking bread and water along, and going up the Indian River until opposite the ship. Here they disembarked, and cut their way through a mango [sic] swamp to the sea-shore, where they found the captain and the remainder of the crew the vessel lying about a quarter of a mile from the land with bow to the shore, sails set, and the sea running so high as to preclude any possibility of reaching her. In this condition of things the keeper took the men to the station, where everything was done to make them comfortable until the next day, when the weather permitted a return to the vessel to save the crew's clothing and the few provisions that remained. This they did, and then returned to the station, where they remained five days, when they found opportunity to leave. The ship and cargo were a total loss.

NORNA

The fishing schooner *Norna* was built in 1893 at Eau Gallie and documented a length of 52 feet, a beam of 18 feet, and a displacement of 23 tons. In September 1900, the *Norna's* owner, Fred Fisher, employed the schooner as a mother vessel at the West Palm Beach wharf, where she received and packed the catch from a fleet of smaller fishing vessels. On October 28, 1906, the *Norna* foundered on Lake Worth.

NORTH

Built at Mystic, Connecticut, in 1855, the 297-ton brig *North* was 106 feet long and 26 feet wide. On November 4,

1859, the *North*, Captain Davidson, en route from Galveston, Texas, to New York with a cargo of 1,021 bales of cotton, went ashore 65 miles north of Cape Florida (also reported as "on Jupiter Inlet") along with the *Eliza Mallory*. Wreckers were unable to work the wreck until the beginning of December, which resulted in the salvage of only 150 bales of cotton and portions of the brig's rigging.

NORTH EASTER

Hull number 575 was launched from the St. Augustine shipyard of the Diesel Engine and Sales Company (DESCO Marine, Incorporated) as the shrimp trawler *North Easter* in 1956. A standard DESCO boat, the shrimper was 67 feet in length and displaced 99 tons. On April 22, 1980, the *North Easter* broke up in the surf south of Turtle Mound, though the three-man crew got off the vessel uninjured. As the vessel wrecked along the Canaveral National Seashore, salvage crews worked to remove the shrimper in the days following the event.

NORTH STAR

The 354-ton American ship *North Star*, Captain J. Galway, built in 1808, while on a voyage from Dublin, Ireland, to Amelia Island, wrecked at the latter location in May 1811.

Noula Express just prior to her sinking (Palm Beach County Artificial Reef Program).

NOULA EXPRESS

The *Noula Express* was built in 1939 as the *Danaland* by *Scheepswerf T. Van Duijvendijk* at Lekkerkerk, Netherlands. Originally owned by Svend Hansen of Kragesand, Denmark, the *Danaland* was 114 feet in length and displaced 148 tons gross. In 1941, the coaster was sold and renamed *Trean*. The vessel changed hands again in 1954, whereupon she sailed as *Kornmod*, which is Danish for "Harvester." In 1968, the vessel's history gets murky, however, at some point the freighter was rebuilt, which replaced her simple wooden stern deckhouse for a larger, raised steel structure. Eventually named *Noula Express*, the vessel was appropriated by the artificial reef programs of Palm Beach and Broward Counties after her seizure due to her role in narcotics trafficking. On July 12, 1988, the *Noula*

View of the stern superstructure of the *Noula* resting on her port side.

Express was scuttled off Boca Raton Inlet. The *Noula* now rests in 75 feet of water generally oriented north to south just offshore the wrecks of the *Sea Emperor* and *United Caribbean*. The stern rests on her port side while the remainder of the former coaster is twisted and mangled amidst some coral hardbottom habitat. Keen observers may also still see the pummeled remains of a 20-foot long submersible resting amongst the *Noula's* remains, which was found abandoned on a beach – likely from a covert drug smuggling attempt – in November 1988, salvaged by Kellerman Diving and Salvage Company, and sunk next to the *Noula* in late September 1989.

NUESTRA SEÑORA DE CONCEPCIÓN

The *Nuestra Señora de Concepción*, under the command of Don Manuel de Echeverz, son of Captain-General Don Antonio de Echeverz y Zubiza, disappeared with the loss of 135 men during the July 30-31, 1715, hurricane that devastated the combined Spanish treasure fleet. Her manifest stated she carried 3,000 pesos, 15 serons of cocoa, 1 chest vanilla, almost 16 tons of Brazilwood, 1,440 cured hides, and tobacco on her return journey to Spain. While there is speculation the *Concepción* was carried farther north by the hurricane and possibly wrecked near Cape Canaveral, the final resting spot of the vessel has yet to be positively identified.

NUESTRA SEÑORA DE LA POPA

In 1714, Captain-General Don Antonio de Echeverz y Zubiza's scout ships captured a small Dutch *galera* (galley) off the Colombian coast, which they called *La Holandesa* ("The Dutch Ship"). Echeverz later purchased the captured vessel for 2,000 pesos at auction at Porto Bello, Panama. Renamed *Nuestra Señora de la Popa*, Captain-General Echeverz employed the small vessel in his *Los Galeones* fleet, which sailed for Spain from Havana on July 24, 1715. During the hurricane on July 31, the upper decks of the *Nuestra Señora de la Popa* were carried intact over the reefs and deposited high and dry on the Florida coast at *Palmar de Ays*, sparing the life of Captain Sebastian Mendez and most if not all others onboard. Historical records indicate Captain-General Echeverz utilized the wrecked vessel as his quarters following the disaster while coordinating initial salvage efforts. Due to its exposed nature on the beach, the wreck of *Nuestra Señora de la Popa* was likely stripped of anything valuable before ultimately being burned to conceal the nearby wrecks of the Spanish fleet.

Illustration of a Spanish galleon (Florida State Archives).

NUESTRA SEÑORA DE LA REGLA, SAN DIMAS Y SAN FRANCISCO SAN XAVIER

The *capitana* of Captain-General Ubilla's ill-fated 1715 *Nueva España* fleet was *Nuestra Señora de La Regla, San Dimas y San Francisco San Xavier*, a galleon 150 feet in length, 471 tons in burden, and armed with 50 cannon. On March 28, 1715, almost as a harbinger of things to come, a storm struck Veracruz, Mexico, casting the *Regla* onto a nearby reef. With Spain in dreadful need of the treasure she was to supply, the *Regla* was quickly repaired and departed with the *Nueva España* fleet for Havana on May 11, 1715, to rendezvous with Captain-General Echeverz's *Los Galeones flota*. Upon her sailing from Havana for Spain on July 24 with the combined fleet, the manifest of the *Regla* included the following treasure: almost 2.6 million pesos in coins and bars; 23 chests of worked silver; 62 chests of gifts; 1 small chest of gold bars, doubloons, and pearls; 730 leather bags of cochineal; 241 leather bags and chests of indigo; 17 chests of vanilla beans; 6 chests of chocolate; 70 sheets of copper; 730 tanned leathers; 4 chests of Chinese porcelain; 11 tons of Brazilwood; 9 chests of pottery; and 14 jugs of balsam. On July 29, the first signs of an impending storm were obvious out of the southeast. Ubilla decided to try and run at full sail to the Bahama Bank in order to avoid getting trapped in the narrow Bahama Channel when the full force of the storm struck the fleet. The *flota*, however, had yet to clear the outermost islands of the Bahamas when the wind began to howl. Early on the morning of July 31, the passengers and crew realized the magnitude of the situation and turned to prayer. The massive waves and driving wind carried them to the northwest and toward the Florida coast. By the time they heard the rumbling surf over the reef, it was too late. The *Regla* struck the outer jagged reef with such force that the *capitana's* hull sheared. While the lower hull remained trapped against the third reef approximately 1,500 feet offshore, the upper decks apparently were stripped from the remainder of the ship and carried towards shore, which scattered cannon and debris over a large area. Most on the shattered *Nuestra Señora de La Regla, San Dimas y San Francisco San Xavier* lost their lives, including Captain-General Don Juan Esteban de Ubilla.

The remains of the *Nuestra Señora de La Regla* are believed to located at a site known locally as "Corrigan's Wreck," named after the local landowner Hugh Corrigan, who found numerous coins along the beach in the 1960s. Wreckage starts approximately 1,500 feet offshore on the third reef line, where the main concentration of ballast and three cannon are found. Inshore and on the first reef in 10 feet of water, divers can follow a trail of 19 cannon heading northwest almost into the beach. The Spanish worked the combined fleet wrecks from 1715 through 1719, and salvage master Don Joseph Clemente Fernandez reported the recovery of over 80 percent of the almost 6.4 million pesos of treasure carried by the fleet, including more than 900 chests of silver from the *Regla* in the remainder of 1715 alone. While modern salvors dived the site intermittently in the 1960s and 1970s, it wasn't until after 1980 when work at "Corrigan's" started in earnest. Since then, thousands of silver coins, numerous gold bars and disks, pistols, rapiers, silver cups and plates, buttons, and numerous other fascinating artifacts have been discovered at this site.

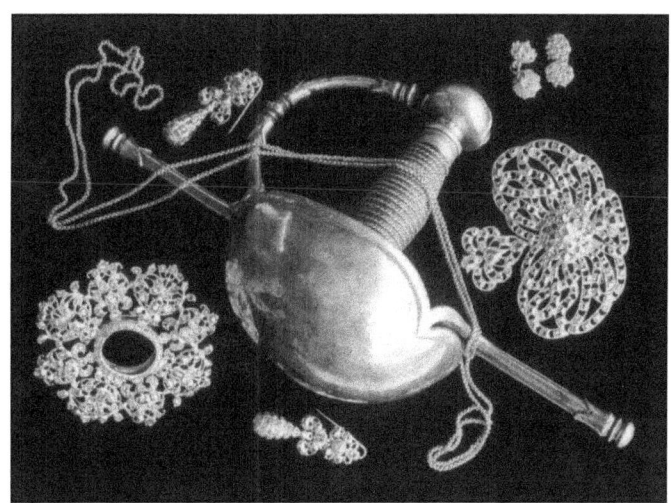

Various artifacts recovered from 1715 wrecks (Robert Weller Collection).

NUESTRA SEÑORA DE LAS NIEVES

The *Nuestra Señora de Las Nieves* was one of five ships of the *Nueva España* fleet, commanded by Captain-General Don Juan Esteban de Ubilla, which joined six other vessels from *Los Galeones* upon their departure from Havana, Cuba on July 24, 1715. The 192-ton *Nieves* was a patache, a small vessel used as a tender to the fleet, which conveyed orders, sailors, or supplies amongst the various vessels. Like the majority of the combined fleet, the *Nuestra Señora de Las Nieves* was dashed to pieces during the late-July hurricane and it is believed the wreck of the *patache* rests south of Fort Pierce Inlet. A 1964 site plan of the wreck illustrated a large cluster of material, including cannon, cannon balls and bar shot, ceramic material, deadeyes, navigational equipment;

Gold prayer book frame recovered from the *Nieves* and an Immaculate Conception brooch recovered from the *Carmen y San Antonio* (Robert Weller Collection).

numerous gold and silver disks and coins were found immediately inshore of a ballast pile located approximately 300 feet off Frederick Douglass Memorial Beach in 15 feet of water. It should also be noted that material has been found over a very large area stretching both northward and offshore. The *Nieves* officially carried no treasure on her manifest, though over the years, several thousand gold and silver coins, worked jewelry, and other valuable items well in excess of what was reported have been recovered from this site, which quickly became known as the "Gold Wreck" (also known as the "Colored Beach Wreck").

NUESTRA SEÑORA DE LAS OLAS

According to the St. Augustine Lighthouse Archaeological Maritime Program, the *Nuestra Señora de las Olas*, or "Our Lady of the Waves," was a Spanish merchant vessel that entered St. Augustine for repairs in 1593. While attempting to leave, the vessel was lost on the St. Augustine Bar.

NUESTRA SEÑORA DEL CARMEN

According to October 1778 correspondence to Lord George Germain, Secretary of State for Florida, the sloop *Nuestra Señora del Carmen* was captured off Charleston, South Carolina, by the H.M.S. *Carysfort* earlier that year. The prize was brought into St. Augustine with its Spanish master and crew, as well as several shipwrecked French sailors. Just inside the harbor, the *Carmen* grounded on a sandbar. The pilot jettisoned her cargo of salt, but the sloop failed to float free. Locals liberated a quantity of sugar and rum before she broke up in a nor'easter[167].

NUESTRA SEÑORA DEL CARMEN Y SAN ANTONIO

Captain-General Echeverz y Zubiza selected the largest of the *Galeones flota* vessels as his *capitana* (flagship), the *Nuestra Señora del Carmen y San Antonio*, to bring up the rear of the convoy. A formidable vessel, she was formerly the H.M.S. *Hampton Court*, a third-rate, 70-gun ship of the line, 150.5 feet long, 39.8 feet wide, and 1,030 tons burden, built by John Shish at Deptford Dockyard in 1678; rebuilt at Blackwall in 1701, whereupon she was 1,073 tons burden. The *Hampton Court* was captured in May 1707 by a French fleet led by René Duguay-Trouin and Chevalier de Forbin off Beachy Head on the south coast of England, eventually being acquired by the Spanish in 1712. In early 1715, Echeverz proceeded from Portobello to Havana to await the arrival of the *Nueva España flota* in June 1715. Upon their eventual departure from Havana on their fateful voyage in late July 1715, the registered treasure on the manifest was listed as follows: 79,967 pesos in gold bars and doubloons; 309 *castellanos* of gold dust; 1,175 pesos of *plata doble*; three gold chains; 7,766 pounds of cocoa; 33,600 pounds of Brazilwood; dry goods and hides. By July 30, Captain-General Echeverz realized their predicament. The crew lowered the sails and battened down the hatches for the impending bad weather. Early in the evening, the *Nuestra Señora del Carmen y San Antonio* lost her bowsprit from the pounding seas. Soon thereafter, she lost her topmasts and sails. As the vessel lost ground to the growling storm, Echeverz ordered the anchors dropped in an attempt to avoid being dashed to pieces on the threatening reef. With the ship filling with water, the captain ordered the vessel lightened, and cargo and armament were thrown overboard to prevent their sinking. The *capitana* avoided the outer reef only to crash hard into the second reef approximately 900 feet offshore, roll onto her starboard side, and sink in 20 feet of water. The next day, much of the *Nuestra Señora del Carmen y San Antonio* remained above water, marking her resting spot. Survivors salvaged what they could and made a camp on the beach adjacent to the wreck. As the wreck of the *Carmen* was easily visible, the majority of her documented cargo was recovered.

Onion bottle found on one of the 1715 shipwrecks (Mel Fisher Center, Inc., Sebastian, Florida).

The wreck of the *Nuestra Señora del Carmen y San Antonio* was salvaged throughout the 1960s and work continues to this day. Her location offshore the Riomar Country Club golf course in Vero Beach has earned the wreck the local name, the "Riomar Wreck." Nineteen cannon still can be found on the site, as well as two large anchors. Access to the site can be found by traveling 2.7 miles south of State Route 60 and then turn left on Rio Mar Drive. Just off the northernmost part of the golf course, the wreck can be found 900 feet offshore in approximately 15 feet of water. The first reef, a *sabellariid* worm rock reef, is found very close to shore. The *sabellariid* reef is composed of *Phragmatopoma lapidosa*, a tube-building polychaete worm. Divers should be aware of the numerous camouflaged holes on the seabed, and take care to minimize impact to the reef.

NUESTRA SEÑORA DEL POPULO

The 14-gun *Nuestra Señora del Populo*, also known as *El Pinque* ("The Pink" - a type of small dispatch vessel), was one of over 20 vessels of the *Nueva España* fleet that departed Cuba on July 13, 1733, on a return voyage to Spain. Unfortunately for the *Populo* and the rest of the fleet, an early-season hurricane interrupted their journey. On July 15, *Nuestra Señora del Populo*, loaded with tobacco and lumber, grounded on a reef at "La Cabeza de los Martires," or the head of the Martires, which is loosely considered the delineation of the Florida Keys' reef tract. According to a newspaper report, the *Populo* was "an unwieldy fly-boat, and would not answer her helm." The northern-most wreck of the 1733 fleet, *Nuestra Señora del Populo* was found sunk up to its poop deck and abandoned on August 2 off Elliott Key. The survivors of the *Populo*, along with the crew from the nearby *Dolores*, which was a small *aviso* (advice ship), were rescued by the 60-gun galleon *El Senor San Joseph* (*El Africa*), one of the few 1733 fleet ships to survive the storm, which returned them to Spain with news of the disaster. While the *Populo* was a total loss, the *Dolores* was later refloated.

The wreck of *Nuestra Señora del Populo* is located in 29 feet of water within the boundaries of Biscayne National Park, and consists of a moderately large ballast pile with some exposed timbers near a coral and sand patch. Hundreds of cannon balls were found throughout the site, as well as several of her cannon, including one small bronze specimen.

NUESTRA SEÑORA DEL ROSARIO Y SAN CRISTOBAL

According to Marx (1987), the Spanish *nao Nuestra Señora del Rosario y San Cristobal* was traveling alone from Cuba to Spain in 1711 when it wrecked on the coast of Florida at approximate latitude 30° 20' north, which would be near present-day Atlantic Beach, south of Mayport.

NUESTRA SEÑORA DEL ROSARIO Y SAN FRANCISCO XAVIER

Captain-General Echeverz's *almiranta*, the *Nuestra Señora del Rosario y San Francisco Xavier*, formerly an English vessel, was 101 feet in length, 28 feet in breadth, 310 tons in burden, and armed with 40 cannon, which was captained by Pedro Echeverz, Captain-General Echeverz's eldest son. Upon her departure from Havana on July 24, 1715, in the combined *Nueva España* and *Los Galeones* fleet, she carried numerous gold coins and bars, as well as silver coins, ceramic jugs, Brazilwood, cocoa, vanilla, tortoise shells, and cured hides. Like the remainder of the *flota*, the pounding surf that rolled over the reef dashed the *Rosario* to pieces. The sinking was so violent that no one survived the incident.

While the final resting spot of the *Nuestra Señora del Rosario y San Francisco Xavier* has yet to be positively identified, it is believed a site known as the "Sandy Point Wreck" north of Fort Pierce Inlet may mark at least a portion of the wreck. The *Rosario* first struck the reef line approximately 3,000 feet off the beach, rupturing her hull. As it tumbled over the reef, the vessel purged itself of ballast stone and cannon; the last cannon were found 700 feet from the beach near a sandy 12-foot deep depression. Over the years, most of the 41 cannon found at this site have been recovered; interestingly, the manifest of the *almiranta* only indicated 40 cannon onboard, which casts an element of doubt on the wreck's identity. While some treasure has been found in the area, it is possible the bulk of the *Rosario*'s cargo has yet to be located. It should also be noted that wreckage from the 119-foot long yacht *Genesee*, which grounded on a sandbar on November 3, 1925, can be found in the vicinity.

Gold escudo recovered from a 1715 shipwreck (Robert Weller Collection).

OCEAN

According to Coe (1936), the *Ocean* successfully navigated the treacherous Mosquito Inlet but then grounded on a sandbar directly west of the inlet around the time of the steamer *Narragansett's* loss (i.e., 1850s). However, I have been unable to find any additional information on this vessel or particulars on the wrecking event.

OCEAN EDGE WRECK

The "Ocean Edge Wreck" is a site in approximately 5 feet of water off Palm Beach Shores consisting of a mass of rigging, including several dead eyes. A large anchor with intact wooden stock was also found just inshore of the rigging mass, but due to looting concerns, it was moved to the U.S. Coast Guard dock at Jupiter Inlet. It is unclear if the "Ocean Edge Wreck" actually marks the final resting spot of a complete vessel hidden underneath the sand, or if it's isolated to the exposed rigging that may have been cut free from a ship during a storm.

Freighter *Ocean Freeze* dockside (Hans Rosenkranz).

OCEAN FREEZE

The *Ocean Freeze* (IMO number 5153785) was launched from the Bremerhaven, Germany shipyard of *Schiffbaugesellschaft Schichau-Unterweser A.G.* as the *Holstenau* on June 19, 1962. The 1,214-ton refrigerated freighter, or reefer, was 270.2 feet in length and 39.5 feet in breadth. In 1977, the vessel was sold to Fedros, Limited of Georgetown, Cayman Islands, and renamed *Ocean Freeze*. Towards the end of her career, the *Ocean Freeze* was owned by a Vietnamese company that went bankrupt. In June 1997, the aging freighter was purchased at auction by attorney and developer Manny Alonso-Poch, who was also part-owner of Sloppy Joe's restaurant in Coconut Grove. Over time, the lawyer managed to ignore U.S. Coast Guard citations, numerous fines and docking fees, only to somehow manage to get a bill sponsored by State Representative Bruno Barreiro (R-Miami Beach) before the legislature that would pay him $165,000 in exchange for the freighter's donation to Miami-Dade County's artificial reef program. Governor Chiles, though, spotted the allocation and vetoed the bill. With pressure mounting, the attorney finally donated the vessel to the Atlantic

Sinking of the *Ocean Freeze*, just prior to her turning turtle (Miami-Dade County Department of Environmental Resources Management).

Gamefish Foundation, who subsequently sank it as an artificial reef on July 28, 1998. The *Ocean Freeze* was renamed the *Scott Mason Chait* by Fish and Game Unlimited of Homestead, a fishing club that put up $10,000 toward the deployment. Chait was an avid fisherman and employee of the Miami Dolphins football team, who died on May 17, 1997, at age 23, after a long battle with cystic fibrosis.

When I first dived the *Ocean Freeze* in 2000, I found the wreck completely inverted and pointing northward. This orientation provides few opportunities for a grapnel hook to purchase the wreck. The rudder, turned hard to port, is the highest portion of the wreck, with the sand bottom found at 256 feet. A row of open portholes with the intact glass swing plates can be found along the stern superstructure of the ship. Other artifacts can also still be found amongst the wreck, as I found one of the ship's running lights resting partially buried in the sand adjacent to the bridge. The wreck rests on her stern superstructure, which suspends the cargo hold and the remaining length of the ship high off the bottom. This support provides between 15 to 20 feet of clearance under the wreck, creating a unique swim-through for visiting divers, with miscellaneous wreckage spilled out from the interior and down to the sand below. Under the hull amidst swarms of baitfish, several doors to the forepeak remain open. This is indeed a great dive, though it will be a shame when the superstructure eventually collapses under the weight of the wreck.

OCEAN PEARL

The schooner *Ocean Pearl*, official number 18990, was built in May 1866 at Newburyport, Massachusetts. The vessel registered a length of 89 feet, a beam of 25 feet, and a displacement of 125 tons. In September 1878, the *Ocean Pearl*, Captain Fitzgerald, was en route from San Blas for Baltimore, Maryland, when she "was totally wrecked 30 miles north of Cape Canaveral" in a hurricane[168].

OCEAN PRIDE

According to the May 12, 1936, issue of the *Sarasota Herald*, the 38-foot long shrimp trawler *Ocean Pride* was ripped apart by an explosion from the vessel's stove, sinking the vessel in 12 feet of water at Fernandina. Two men were badly burned in the explosion, but survived the ordeal.

OCEAN VENUS

In late 1940, desperate for new tonnage to offset losses, British representatives took ship plans to America to try to persuade the American government to let Britain place orders for 60 new ships. The United States agreed, however, no space existed in shipyards to allow them to be built, so it was decided to build two new emergency shipyards in Richmond, California, and South Portland, Maine, to meet the British need. The basic hull model for the vessels was based on the *Dorington Court*, a British steamer built by Joseph L. Thompson and Sons of Sunderland, which had a raked stem, cruiser stern, single screw, and balanced rudder. The main propulsion unit was a triple expansion, reciprocating steam engine whose design dated back to 1896. Because Britain had no domestic oil at the time, the vessel was to be powered by coal-fired scotch or fire-tube boilers. The plans specified a length of 441 feet, a beam of 57 feet, and a deadweight tonnage of 10,428 tons.

Ocean Vigor, sistership of the *Ocean Venus* (Mark Mondano Collection).

As an aside, the U.S. Maritime Commission made a number of alterations to the British "Ocean" design for use in the United States Merchant Fleet. Alterations were made to conform to American manufacturing and shipbuilding standards; some to accommodate the scarcity of certain materials, and some to meet the need to build as rapidly and affordably as possible. The resulting design was designated EC2-S-C1, originally referred to as "emergency ships" (E for emergency; C for cargo; 2 indicating size or capacity by the index of appropriate waterline length, 400 to 450 feet; S for steam propulsion; and C1 for the particular design). When the *Patrick Henry*, the first of these ships, was launched on September 27, 1941, President Franklin D. Roosevelt delivered a speech that boldly stated that these ships would bring liberty to Europe. It was fitting that the first vessel was named after the patriot Patrick Henry, whose speech on March 23, 1775, ended with, "I know not what course others may take; but as for me, give me liberty or give me death!" From that point forward, these cargo ships would be known as "Liberty ships."

The keel for the first West Coast vessel, the *Ocean Vanguard*, was laid down on April 14, 1941. The keel for the first East Coast vessel, the *Ocean Liberty*, was laid just over a month later, on May 24, 1941. The *Ocean Venus* was the twelfth keel laid down at yard number one of Permanente Metals Corporation in Richmond, California. After launching, a three-inch deck gun was mounted to the stern. The freighter loaded lumber, lead, and foodstuffs into her cargo hold prior to her delivery voyage to John Morrison and Sons in England. Her maiden trans-Atlantic cruise would soon carry her along a U-boat infested Florida coast.

Captain John Parkes was wisely steaming the *Ocean Venus* blacked out as he passed along the Florida east coast late on the evening of May 2, 1942. The bright moonlit night betrayed the position of his vessel, however, and *Kapitänleutnant* Reinhard Suhren quickly spotted the oncoming vessel after surfacing off Cape Canaveral. While the moonlight helped Suhren find a target, it also forced him to submerge to get into a firing position, lest the *U-564* be spotted by the lookouts on the *Ocean Venus*. After several hours of maneuvering, Suhren fired a single torpedo from a position just offshore of the freighter. The torpedo slammed into the starboard side of the ship and into the engine room, quickly disabling the *Ocean Venus*. Unable to steer his vessel, which was now quickly settling into the sea, Captain Parkes gave the command to abandon ship at approximately 2:30 a.m. on May 3.

As the crew took to the lifeboats, the *U-564* surfaced near the crippled freighter. Unbeknownst to *Kapitänleutnant* Suhren, a Canadian Naval gunner named Sid Webber remained at his post. Webber proceeded to fire 15 rounds at *U-564* before she was able to submerge once again. Webber then joined the rest of the surviving crew and moved away from the *Ocean Venus* in lifeboats. Approximately 20 minutes later, Suhren fired the *coup de grace*, a second torpedo that struck the sinking vessel amidships. The 42 survivors rowed to Cape Canaveral, while five men in the engine room perished in the initial explosion.

The partially submerged hulk of *Ocean Venus* (Mark Mondano Collection).

The wreck of the *Ocean Venus* lies just east of Port Canaveral in approximately 80 feet of water. Following the war, she was wire-dragged and demolished with explosives as a hazard to navigation. Furthermore, Captain Stefanich salvaged approximately 4,000 tons of lead ingots from the wreck in the 1940s. This work helps to explain its local name, the "Lead Wreck." Due to these efforts, the wreck today is extensively broken down and spread out. The wreck is oriented with the high stern section, resting on its starboard side, to the north, and the bow, which barely protrudes from the sand and is difficult to recognize, located to the south. Amidships, the freighter's three boilers rest over on the starboard side of the wreck, with the toppled engine located just aft; divers can easily follow shaft alley from the engine to the stern. The remainder of the wreck predominantly consists of scattered bulkheads and hull plates, which provide a tremendous amount of habitat for marine species. On one memorable visit, my dive buddy and I were joined by a large manta ray as we explored the wreck. Divers searching for artifacts have been fortunate on the *Ocean Venus*, though a great deal of effort and luck is generally needed. The majority of the hull plates are found flattened on the perimeter of the wreck, and several of these are still adorned with rows of portholes. Occasionally a random lead ingot can still be found amidst the wreckage.

Photograph of the steamer *Ocklawaha*, 1870 (Alfred H. Robson Collection).

OCKLAWAHA

The 69.9-ton inline sternwheel steamer *Ocklawaha*, official number 19109, was built in 1867 for Hubbard L. Hart for his ferry line operating on the narrow and winding Ocklawaha River in Northeast Florida. On August 31, 1877, the *Ocklawaha* reportedly caught fire while moored on the St. Johns at Palatka, becoming a total loss. It is possible she was rebuilt and put back into service, as the *Ocklawaha* later operated for the Lucas Line, which consolidated with the Hart Line around 1895. The steamer *Ocklawaha* would again catch fire and burn at Palatka on January 3, 1904.

OH KIM SOON

The *Oh Kim Soon* was built in 1891 at a shipyard in Prout's Cove, Digby, Nova Scotia. The barkentine, built from Nova Scotia spruce, was 142 feet in length, 36.5 feet in breadth, and displaced 336 tons. The *Oh Kim Soon* was traveling in ballast for Fernandina from Las Palmas in the Canary Islands when she grounded just off Lantana Beach on January 30, 1897, following a winter storm. The master of the bark, Captain Lloyd Morton, said she struck the outer reef at 9:00 p.m. With her back broken and the hull full of water, the wreck was sold at auction where she lay for $206 to Captain Smith of the schooner *Julia Frances*[169]. Unfortunately for divers, after the *Oh Kim Soon* was stripped of her rigging and fittings, locals set her afire. What is left of her hull is now totally entombed in the sand just offshore of the beach, directly under the breaking surf.

The wrecked barkentine *Oh Kim Soon* (Marine Archaeological Research and Conservation).

OHIO

The 175-ton American ship *Ohio*, Captain A. Hall, built in 1799, wrecked on January 15, 1808, near Cape Florida while sailing from Jamaica to New York. Her crew and most of her cargo was saved.

OHIOAN

Built in February 1920, the freighter *Ohioan* slid down the ways of the G.M. Standifer Construction Company of Vancouver, Washington, as the *Pawlet*. The freighter, official number 219551, was 401.4 feet in length and 53.2 feet in breadth. Displacing 6,078 tons, she was powered by a 2,800-horsepower triple expansion engine produced by the Hooven, Owens, and Rentschler Company. The single-screw vessel would soon undergo an identity crisis, as her name was changed from *Pawlet* to *Golden Wall*, then to *Willsolo*. The *Willsolo* was later bought by the American-Hawaiian Steamship Company and renamed the *Ohioan* to replace a freighter of the same name that sunk off California a few years earlier. That *Ohioan* struck the rocks off Point Lobos near San Francisco, California, on October 7, 1936. She remained there for nearly two years until she broke into three pieces and sank in deep water following an especially brutal storm.

On May 8, 1942, the *Ohioan* was attacked by the *U-564* approximately 10 miles off Boynton Beach while carrying a cargo of manganese ore, licorice root, and wool. Just after noon, a single torpedo collided with the starboard hull of the number four cargo hold. The freighter immediately began sinking by the stern and disappeared within two minutes of the attack. While 20 survivors managed to clamber onto several float-free rafts, 17 crewmembers went to a watery grave with the *Ohioan*. Many of those who perished drowned after being pulled under by the suction of the rapidly sinking ship. The *Ohioan* reportedly rests in approximately 600 feet of water directly off the Boynton Beach Inlet. Known by commercial fishermen, she has yet to be visited by divers for obvious reasons.

OJUS

The St. Augustine vessel *Ojus* stranded approximately 500 yards north of the Ponce Inlet Bar on December 21, 1936. The 22-ton *Ojus* was built in 1929.

O.L. BODENHAMER

The "Liberty" ship *O.L. Bodenhamer*, named after U.S. Army Major (ret.), former National Commander of the American Legion, and Arkansas businessman O.L. Bodenhamer, was built as hull number 2800 by Delta Shipbuilding Company in New Orleans for the U.S. Army Transportation Service. The EC2-S-C1 type freighter (E for emergency; C for cargo; 2 indicating size or capacity by the index of appropriate waterline length, 400 to 450 feet; S for steam propulsion; and C1 for the particular design) was laid down on June 20, 1944, launched on August 2, and completed later that month, which was representative of just how fast these vessels could be produced in World War II. The *Bodenhamer* was 441.5 feet long, 56.7 feet wide, and displaced 7,176 tons. After a brief service in World War II, the freighter was laid up at Mobile, Alabama. Eventually deemed obsolete, the superstructure of the *O.L. Bodenhamer* was razed and she was scuttled in 380 feet of water off Miami on May 14, 1976. Due to the extensive scrapping of the vessel, she now resembles a giant canoe on the bottom; the *Bodenhamer* offers little aside from her depth to attract the interest of technical divers.

OLGA

As reported in the *Sixty-First Annual List of Merchant Vessels of the United States*, the freight vessel *Olga* stranded at "North Jupiter Light" on January 5, 1929. The 42-ton *Olga* was built in 1903 at Biloxi, Mississippi, and was 60 feet long and 18.2 feet wide.

OLIVE BRANCH

The schooner *Olive Branch* was reported lost off Cape Florida on February 27, 1836. This was likely the Key West wrecking schooner *Olive Branch*, Captain W. Greene, which was registered in 1835.

OLYMPIA

The 8-ton gas steamer *Olympia*, official number 155348, built in 1899, burned on the St. Lucie River on March 24, 1918.

ONTARIO

As reported in *The Edinburgh Advertiser* on July 3, 1812, the *Ontario*, Captain Mix, from Liverpool, struck on the bar at Amelia Island on April 29, 1812, during a "violent gale of wind, and received so much damage, that it was supposed she would be condemned."

ORCA

On December 5, 1928, while en route from Jacksonville to Miami, the yacht *Orca* (also reported as both the *Ocora* and *Oroca* in newspaper accounts) burned following an explosion nine miles off Melbourne; three perished in the accident. Edward Satinover was rescued by a fishing smack after floating on a keg throughout the night, while Leslie Royal pulled himself ashore at Melbourne, exhausted after 24 hours in the water. According to Royal, the engine backfired around 7:00 p.m., casting a spark into some oil-covered bilge water. The resulting fire quickly spread to the fuel tanks and a series of explosions soon followed. Apparently, the yacht was involved in smuggling liquor, as after the accident, the two survivors were arraigned in federal court at Jacksonville for violating prohibition laws. The wooden-hulled *Orca*, official number 215314, was built in 1917 at Neponset, Massachusetts, and was 46.6 feet long, 10.3 feet wide, displaced 15 gross tons, and was equipped with a 450-horsepower engine. The wreck of the *Orca* has not been positively identified.

OREGON (1846)

The Maine schooner *Oregon*, wrecked on October 12, 1846, "to the northward of Mosquito Inlet" while en route from Darien, Georgia to New York; the crew was saved[170]. While the reported wrecking location would indicate the incident occurred in Florida, due to the documented route, it is possible the loss of the *Oregon* may have actually occurred farther north.

OREGON (1904)

The steamer *Oregon*, official number 155341, was built at Daytona in 1899. She was 60 feet in length, 11 feet in beam, and 21 tons in burden. As documented in the 1905 *Annual Report of the Supervising Inspector-General, U.S. Steamboat-Inspection Service to the Secretary of Commerce and Labor*, on July 29, 1904, "At 3:30 a.m., while steamer *Oregon* was lying in the Halifax River, Florida, near the mouth of Tomoka River, Florida, she was totally destroyed by fire; cause unknown. Amount of damage not stated."

The attractive passenger freighter *Oriental Warrior* as the *Hamburg* (William T. Hultgren).

ORE WRECK

Almost due east of Pacific Reef Light, the "Ore Wreck" is found in a 27-foot deep sand pocket surrounded by seagrass meadows. The site is represented by a 20-foot long pile of iron ballast, which gives the wreck its name[171]. Perhaps this is the final resting spot of the ship *Telumah*, which wrecked in the vicinity on November 18, 1845; the *Telumah* was reported to have a cargo of iron and crates.

ORIENTAL WARRIOR

The *Oriental Warrior* was a 537-foot long passenger freighter that caught fire following an engine room explosion 45 miles off Daytona Beach on May 25, 1972. The 9,008-ton ship was originally launched as the *Hamburg* at the Vegesack, Germany shipyard of *Bremer Vulkan A.G.* on December 17, 1953, and she sailed for the Hamburg-American Line on the Far East route. In 1967 she was sold to Malaysia Overseas Line, Limited, and renamed the *Oriental Warrior*. In 1972, she traded hands again, sailing for United Overseas Export Line, Incorporated. At the time of the fire, there were 100 people on the ship, all of whom were rescued by a passing ship. The captain and three crewmen remained aboard to fight the inferno, but they too fled when the flames began to approach the ship's fuel tanks. The *Oriental Warrior* was eventually towed back to Jacksonville in hopes of salvaging the ship. She continued to smolder, however, and eventually sank at her berth on the St. Johns River on May 29, 1972. The burned-out *Oriental Warrior* remained on the St. Johns River for several months, during which time a significant amount of money was spent to raise the abandoned ship and extract several thousand gallons of fuel remaining in her tanks. The *Oriental Warrior* was eventually towed 100 miles out to sea and sunk in over 2,000 feet of water on October 1, 1972.

ORION

The tugboat *Orion* was launched in 1927 as the *Trinidad* by the Panama Railroad Company at their Balboa shipyard in the Panama Canal Zone. Named after one of the rivers dammed to help create the Panama Canal, the *Trinidad* registered a length of 126 feet, a beam of 28 feet, and a displacement of 355 tons. After almost four decades guiding ships through the canal, the *Trinidad* was sold to Orion Towing Company, Incorporated of Bartow in December 1966 and renamed *Orion*. Eventually abandoned along the Miami River, she was acquired for use as an artificial reef. On December 22, 1981, the *Orion* was sunk in 95 feet of water off Key Biscayne. In August 1992, Hurricane Andrew impacted the wreck, ripping off the wheelhouse and depositing it off the starboard side of the hull. Even with the damage from the hurricane, the *Orion* remains a pleasant dive with significant relief. The tug rests in close proximity to some coral hardbottom habitat, and marine life is typically abundant.

The tug *Orion* (Miami-Dade County Department of Environmental Resources Management).

ORITHYIA

Named after the Greek goddess of cold mountain winds, the schooner yacht *Orithyia*, official number 155205, was built in 1890 at Glenwood, New York, for William M.

Walker. The vessel was 54 feet long, 16.5 feet wide, and 38 tons burden. On December 11, 1901, the *Orithyia* stranded on the St. Johns River Bar.

ORRIE V. DRISKO

The schooner *Orrie V. Drisko*, official number 19393, was built in November 1873 at Columbia Falls, Maine. The schooner documented a length of 119.5 feet, a beam of 30 feet wide, and a displacement of 321 tons. On December 22, 1891, the *Orrie V. Drisko*, Captain Burton, was lost off Cape Canaveral.

OSCAR

On October 30, 1814, *Bell's Weekly Messenger* reported, "The *Oscar*, – –-, bound to Liverpool, is burnt at Amelia Island."

OSCEOLA (1895)

On June 2, 1895, the steamer *Osceola* burned on the Ocklawaha River near Eureka[172]. While the fire resulted in the total loss of the steamer, which was valued at $4,000, there was no loss of life. The origin of the fire was undetermined.

OSCEOLA (1910+)

In 1910, Captain Clay Johnson built the freight steamer *Osceola* at Kissimmee. She was 87 tons gross, 74.6 feet long and 21.1 feet wide. According to Mueller (1966), the *Osceola* sank in the Palm Beach Canal at Fort Worth (Lake Worth) when Captain Johnson ran her into a dock, though no date was cited.

OSCEOLA (1921)

The gasoline yacht *Osceola* caught fire from a backfiring engine on the afternoon of January 24, 1921, while returning through Government Cut at Miami. The anglers that chartered the boat were able to abandon the burning vessel and wade ashore, while Captain Jones was taken off later by the *Brothers*. The burning *Osceola* drifted out of Government Cut and eventually was pushed to the south of the cut by the vessel *Brothers*, where she sank against the jetties[173]. Most likely the yacht *Osceola*, official number 209450, which was built at Jacksonville in 1911, and was 43.5 feet long, 9 feet wide, and 9 tons gross burden.

OSCEOLA (1941)

The steamboat *Osceola*, a triple-decked "floating palace," was built in 1913 at Jacksonville and became the pride of the Clyde-Mallory Line on the St. Johns River. Assigned official number 211513, the enclosed sternwheel passenger steamer was 180 feet in length, 40 feet in beam, and 474 gross tons. The steamer had cabin accommodations for 100 first-class passengers, as well as room for 25 to 50 more deck passengers, who boarded for the journey upriver as far south as Sanford. On the return journey, the *Osceola* would add citrus fruit and iced-down fish as cargo for the Jacksonville markets. The Clyde-Mallory Line retired the *Osceola* in 1929, whereupon she was employed by the Chase Fertilizer Company as a freighter. Finally, around 1935, the steamer outlived its usefulness and was put out of service. Several years later, the owners of the *Osceola* planned to have the upper decks razed and the vessel converted into a barge. In December 1941, during work to remove some of the steamer's machinery, the hull was breached and the vessel sank beneath the St. Johns River along a Jacksonville pier at the foot of Newman Street. Abandoned, the steel hull settled into the mud and was largely forgotten. On July 2, 1963, the *Jacksonville Journal* indicated pending city expansion plans would likely require the wrecked *Osceola* be removed.

OSEOLA

As reported in Volume 19 of *The Sailor's Magazine and Naval Journal*, the "Schooner *Oseola*, Lynmire, of Philadelphia, from Fall River for Florida, was lost September 6, 1846, on Mosquito Bar, on her return bound to New York."

OSIRIS

The yacht *Osiris*, official number 208932, was built in 1911 at Port Jefferson, New York. She was 109.5 feet long, 19.7 feet wide, and displaced 137 tons. On February 12, 1921, the *Osiris* burned off Miami.

The yacht *Osiris* burns near Miami.

OSPREY

The 40-foot shrimp boat *Osprey* ran aground on a sandbar in Ponce de Leon Inlet on December 18, 1955, and sank after it was towed off by a U.S. Coast Guard cutter. Captain David H. Carter and a crewman were taken off the stranded craft by the shrimper *Mako* before it sank. The *Osprey* was coming in from a day's shrimping when it lunged up on the sandbar at the entrance to the inlet at 5:30 p.m. A line was gotten aboard the grounded trawler, and when it was towed off, it started to sink, however, the cutter kept it afloat by towing it through the inlet. According to an article in the *Daytona Beach Morning Journal*, "The *Osprey* settled in about seven feet of water with only its superstructure showing."

185

OSPREY WRECK

Following the passage of a storm in August 2003, police officer Scott Hayes noticed several timbers protruding from the sand at Huguenot Park Lagoon, adjacent to Fort George Inlet. Only a small portion of the vessel was exposed, which appeared to be constructed of large timbers and iron and copper fasteners. Based on the location, it is likely this vessel was abandoned in the late nineteenth or early twentieth century.

OSTWIND

The *Ostwind*, German for "East Wind," was built along with her sister ship, *Nordwind*, in 1939. The German government ordered the construction of the yachts following a poor showing in the 1936 Olympic races. Designed by noted naval architect Heinrich Gruber, the 70-ton vessel was 86 feet in overall length, 17 feet in beam, and had a sail area of 3,076 square feet. She was constructed of mahogany planking over steel framing, with a teak, mahogany, rosewood, and walnut finish throughout the interior. Seized by the U.S. Navy towards the end of the war, she was transported across the Atlantic on the U.S.S. *Mercury* (AK-42/AKS-20). Renamed the *East Wind*, she was reconditioned at the Brooklyn Navy Yard, New York, as the U.S. Naval Academy in Annapolis, Maryland, intended to use her as a training vessel for midshipmen.

The U.S. Navy quickly realized the cost to maintain the yawl would be too high, so she was put up for auction. In 1951, the *East Wind* was sold again, purchased by John Lyman of Miami. After living on the vessel for several years, the retired U.S. Navy commander was forced to put her up for sale for $90,000 in 1966. Horace Glass eventually bought the boat and brought her to Jacksonville. Over the years, the *East Wind* suffered from neglect. In 1984, Charles Sanderson purchased the decaying yacht for $1, with plans of bringing her to Plymouth, Massachusetts, to be used as a military museum. The planned museum created uproar amongst the local community, and the *East Wind* remained at Jacksonville. Abandoned, the yacht soon became an albatross around the neck of the Jacksonville shipyard's owner. Vandals stripped the *East Wind* on numerous occasions, while the American Nazi Party wanted to buy her in order to preserve the vessel. The Miami Jewish community acquired the former *Ostwind*, and its hull was rolled off a barge and sunk on June 4, 1989.

The German yacht was resurrected, however, when it was learned the *East Wind* was sunk in 20 feet of water on a coral reef. She was eventually raised, carried offshore, and re-sunk in deep water. Due to the influence of Hurricane Andrew, the exact location of the former *Ostwind* is unknown. As the hull was in poor shape when originally deployed, it is likely there is little left of the German yacht, and certainly nothing worth diving.

Close-up view of the yacht *Ostwind* (Miami-Dade County Department of Environmental Resources Management).

It should be pointed out that much of the history attributed to the *Ostwind* in regard to Adolf Hitler and the Nazi Party appears to be complete fabrication. There is no documentation supporting the assertions that Admiral Karl Dönitz used the yacht as his command vessel, or that *Ostwind* hosted Adolf Hitler and his mistress, Eva Braun. It would appear the vessel's association with Adolf Hitler was simply a publicity or marketing stunt, which was apparently quite successful.

OTAC NIKO

The Austrian bark *Otac Niko* was built in November 1870 as the *Isaac* at Bremerhaven, Germany. She was 170.9 feet long, 34.4 feet wide, and 915 tons burden. On October 9, 1894, *The New York Times* reported:

> The *Seneca* of the Ward Line, which arrived at Havana Oct. 3 from New York, reports that on the morning of Oct. 2, when about thirty miles off the Florida coast, and about sixty five miles north of Jupiter Light, she sighted an abandoned bark; bore down to her, and sent the chief officer with a boat's crew to board her. She had evidently been hastily abandoned, as a little white dog was found to be the sole survivor of the wreck. The bark was lumber laden; her masts were sprung, bulwarks amidships carried away, and portions of her sails hung from the yards in shreds. The vessel's crew had apparently been picked up the day previous. The chief officer set fire to the

The remains of the yacht *Ostwind* prior to her initial deployment (Miami-Dade County Department of Environmental Resources Management).

wreck, it being a dangerous obstruction to navigation. The burning vessel presented a thrilling sight. The bark proved to be the *Otac Niko*, bound for a European port.

OUTCAST

On January 14, 1970, the 64-ton vessel *Outcast*, built in 1958, stranded off Fort George Inlet at the southern end of Little Talbot Island near Mayport.

OUTLINE WRECK

This particular wreck presents a dilemma. Meylach (1971) documented a wreck he called the "Outline Wreck" that plots out inshore of Long Reef, however, there is another site of the same name found inshore of Ajax Reef. Having explored this latter unidentified wreck site, I am not positive this is Meylach's wreck. The depth and general description is similar in that the site is largely buried with some protruding structure surrounded by seagrass meadows. Perhaps Meylach's published ranges were simply inaccurate. Regardless, I have included an estimated position based on Meylach's bearings to be as comprehensive in scope as possible.

OYSTER BOY

The tug *Oyster Boy*, official number 19051, was built in 1861 at New Brunswick, New Jersey, and was 74.6 feet long, 18.4 feet wide, and displaced 54.3 tons gross. The *Oyster Boy* apparently burned and sank twice, the first time on May 24, 1876, and the second and final time on November 2, 1888, at the mouth of Trout Creek on the St. Johns River near Jacksonville; her sunken hull remained adjacent to the *Seth Low* for numerous years[174].

A variety of tropical fish species inside the cargo hold of an artificial reef off Miami (Matthew W. Hoelscher).

PACIFIC

According to Volume 9 of *The Sailor's Magazine and Naval Journal*, "The ship *Pacific*, from New York to Mobile, was wrecked on Dec. 30th (1836), a short distance from Cape Florida." Other reports stated the loss of the *Pacific* occurred previous to December 23, 1836, and the crew and a part of the cargo were saved. Similar to other early wrecking events, the name of the reef where the vessel was lost was later named after the vessel.

PACIFIC REEF WRECK

A wreck site consisting of a large ballast pile approximately 300 feet off Pacific Reef Light rests in a sand patch surrounded by coral ledges in 15 feet of water[175]. Her identity is unknown, and like many other wrecks in the vicinity, salvors have worked this wreck repeatedly. According to Gene Shinn, there was a pile of ballast and brass pins protruding from scattered wooden beams visible on the wreck site when dived in the 1950s and 60s.

PALADIN

The 74-ton *Paladin*, built in 1928, burned on the Intracoastal Waterway southwest of Mayport on July 20, 1951.

PALATKA

The *Palatka* was a steamer built in 1923 at the town for which it was named; she was 63.5 feet long, 22.1 feet wide, and 73 tons burden. On December 3, 1926, the *Palatka* capsized on the St. Johns River at Picolata Landing.

PALO ALTO

On December 17, 1853, *The New York Times* reported, "The brig *Palo Alto*, of Charleston, bound from Matanzas for Boston, with molasses, was sunk on December 4 between Cape Florida and Gun Key, Bahamas, by the French bark *Nevstine*. The brig was insured in the Charleston Insurance and Trust Company for $5,000."

PANAMA

The brig *Panama*, Captain Grumley, stranded on the St. Johns Bar during a squall on the night of August 2, 1850, en route from Jacksonville for Saybrook, Connecticut, with a cargo of lumber[176].

PAN DALLAS

The U.S. Coast Guard reported the fishing vessel *Pan Dallas* sank 15 nautical miles southeast of Matanzas Inlet in 1980, at approximate latitude 29° 36.7' north and longitude 80° 57.3' west.

PAN MASSACHUSETTS

The *Pan Massachusetts* was one of many merchant vessels built during the waning days of World War I. Laid down as the *War Cape*, hull number 167 at the Alameda, California shipyard of the Bethlehem Shipbuilding Corporation, she boasted a registered length of 440 feet, a beam of 56 feet, and displaced 7,588 tons. As wartime hostilities concluded before her completion, she was ultimately launched as the *Triumph*, official number 217457, in January 1919 for the U.S. Shipping Board.

In April 1929, the *Triumph* spent time in the U.S. Navy Yard at Charlestown, Massachusetts, to be lengthened for the U.S. Maritime Commission. The work on the vessel added approximately 16 feet, bringing her total length to 456.1 feet. In 1938, the vessel again traded hands. Purchased by National Bulk Carriers, Incorporated of New York, the vessel was converted to serve as a tanker in December 1938 by Welding Engineers, Incorporated of Little Creek, Virginia. This conversion moved her new 5,000-horsepower steam turbine engine, produced by Allis Chalmers Manufacturing Company, aft to make room for the tanker holds amidships. This conversion and modernization also bumped up her registered displacement to 8,201 tons. Upon completion of this work, she was renamed *Pan Massachusetts*.

On February 19, 1942, the *Pan Massachusetts* was steaming north off Cape Canaveral, bound from Texas to New York with a cargo of gasoline, kerosene, and fuel oil. She had just passed the British freighter *Elizabeth Massey*, which was falling off her starboard quarter, and now was settled in for the final stretch of her journey. Captain Robert E. Christy and a crew of 37 men would soon learn that the war was closer to home than ever imagined. At 1:44 p.m., two torpedoes from the *U-128* struck the tanker in rapid succession on her port side amidships. It was also reported that the submarine followed up the torpedo attack with three or four shells from its deck gun. The attack transformed the *Pan Massachusetts* into a mass of flames, as the cargo of 50,000 barrels of gasoline and 50,000 barrels of diesel oil and kerosene were ignited. The 52-year old captain described the horrific scene, stating, "I was in my room when the torpedoes came. Instantly the doorway was framed with fire. There was no gasoline explosion, for our tanks were full and full tanks do not explode. I tried to get out of a porthole but it was too small. I got some heavy towels, wet them and wound them around my head, face and hands. I threw open my door and made my way forward[177]."

A crewmember in the engine room related how he was awakened "by a loud thud." Before he could get to his feet to investigate, "another thud came." He went on to describe his dramatic escape from the now burning *Pan Massachusetts*:

> Immediately the ship was enveloped in flames – everywhere I could see. I tried to open the porthole but the side of the ship was burning also. Desperately I threw on what clothes I could and made my way to the deck. Men were shouting all around me. Flames were shooting high into the air and the sea was burning all around. The lifeboats and rafts were in flames. We ran about, looking for a place to jump. When a patch would clear for a moment, somebody would jump. I picked my spot and jumped. Flames reared up around me

The tanker *Pan Massachusetts* at sea (Mark Mondano Collection).

but I managed to fight my way to open water. One by one the others followed – all that got away – about half of us. As we swam away we could see the ship burning like hell behind us. First she buckled amidships, but the bow and stern stayed up a long time[178].

Strong winds helped to push the flaming ocean away from the starboard side of the tanker so many of the crew could jump overboard, though Captain Christy and several of the officers found themselves trapped on the bow. They managed to secure a mooring line to the deck, however, and slid down it to the ocean below. There, they swam clear from the ship as she burned violently. Safely away from the inferno that raged out of control on the *Pan Massachusetts*, the survivors found themselves floating in the Atlantic amidst a cold rain and 10- to 15-foot seas.

Fortunately, the *Elizabeth Massey*, which was less than five miles away at the time of the attack, approached the scene in order to rescue the survivors. Ignoring the danger to themselves and their ship, the crew of the *Massey* broke radio silence to report the explosive destruction of the *Pan Mass*, as well as a subsequent but unsuccessful torpedo attack on their own ship at 1:51 p.m., then proceeded at full speed to the burning tanker in order to deploy lifeboats and rescue any survivors. The lifeboat struggled through the flaming ocean, soon to be joined by the U.S.C.G.C. *Forward*. The *Forward* took the lifeboat in tow and moved about the debris from the *Pan Mass*, picking up survivors and charred corpses. Captain Christy and the majority of the crew were picked up within two hours. However, Third Officer H.L. Dodge was missed by the rescue boats and continued to drift away from the scene. Without a life vest, he found his clothes to be dragging him under so he stripped out of them and treaded water stark naked. After watching the boats turn away, he gave up hope of being saved until two Navy planes passed overhead, spotted him, and directed the rescuers to his position, whereupon he was rescued after a three-hour ordeal. At the conclusion of search and rescue efforts, recovered bodies were placed aboard the *Forward*, while the survivors boarded the *Massey* and were landed in Jacksonville on February 20, many with extensive burns. Faces were seared and bandaged, appearing as though they had been "through a furnace[179]." During subsequent interviews, the survivors gave high praise to their rescuers. Radio Officer Robert Welsh stated, "They had guts. They saw us torpedoed and shelled, but came right up to the rescue[180]." Captain Christy concurred, stating, "We went through three hours of hell out there and twenty fine men are dead in the sea, but I saw some real heroes on a rescue ship. I'm going back to the sea, as quickly as I can, out of respect for those who died and those who risked death to save us[181]."

The *Pan Massachusetts* was reported to have sunk in 240 feet of water just off Cape Canaveral, though many attempts to locate the hulk over the years have been unsuccessful. On June 16, 2001, an A.U.E. dive team investigated a wreck known locally as the "Copper Wreck" and became the first individuals to visit the elusive tanker since her sinking in 1942. The "Copper Wreck" was found resting in 296 feet of water, but only consisted of the forward 300-foot long portion of a tanker that is most likely the *Pan Massachusetts*. Apparently, the hull snapped in half due to structural fatigue from the torpedo damage and subsequent fire, as described by several of the survivors. It appears that the attack severed the tanker just forward of the boilers and engine, as a dramatic fracture is found just aft of one of the cargo tanks. Near this break in the hull, debris extends out into the sand and off the portside. Gaping holes on the port side attest to the efficacy of the German torpedoes. This section of the *Pan Mass* is almost perfectly inverted, with the obtuse bow rising vertically from the bottom. The massive anchors can still be found tight in their hawse pipes. Amberjack flourish in abundance on the wreck, which tend to follow divers around the hull during their visit. The dive can be challenging due to the depth as well as the general conditions found in this area. During the summer months, the Gulf Stream is encountered closer to shore and can be running directly over this site in excess of three knots. Furthermore, upwelling events, which bring cold, nutrient-rich water onto the Continental Shelf, frequently wash over the deep wrecks off Cape Canaveral during the summer. These events can present counter-currents, very cold water (48° F) on the bottom, and low visibility. For divers who have the requisite skills and experience, the *Pan Massachusetts* is a remarkable dive, representing the first of many wartime casualties off the coast of Florida.

PAPA'S WRECK

On June 15, 1955, the coaster *Henny T.* (IMO number 5147724) was launched by *Scheepswerf Gebr. Muller* at Yard 97 in Foxhol, Netherlands. The new freighter was 493 tons gross burden, 169.2 feet long, and 27.9 feet wide. In 1975, the coaster was sold, renamed *Macvac A.*, and was reflagged in the Caribbean county of St. Vincent. She changed names again in 1988, when she sailed as *Ebbtide*. Her career quickly ended later that year, however, when the U.S. Customs Service discovered an illicit cargo of marijuana hidden on board the vessel. The freighter was sold at auction and prepared for use as an artificial reef. The coaster was renamed *Papa's Wreck* by John Yates in memory of his grandfather, Muncy Yates. On May 14, 1989, the former *Ebbtide* was scuttled in 260 feet of water off Hillsboro Inlet during the Pompano Beach Fishing Rodeo. The *Papa's Wreck* sits upright and intact in just over 270 feet of water.

Papa's Wreck, formerly the coaster *Henny T.* (Broward County Artificial Reef Program).

PARAISO III

The *Paraiso III* was a 115-foot long freighter sunk off Miami in March 2000 as an artificial reef. Little else is known about this vessel's construction or service history, though it appears she was originally built as an offshore supply vessel. The *Paraiso III* now rests in 75 feet of water between the *Rio Miami* and *Princess Britney*.

PASADENA

This three-masted centerboard schooner was originally built as the *Erastus Wiman* in February 1880 at Bath, Maine, and renamed *Pasadena* in 1897. The schooner, official number 135427, was 148.6 feet in length, 36.3 feet in breadth, 596 tons gross burden, and built with a double deck. As the *Erastus Wiman*, the schooner collided with and sank the schooner *P.H. Wheaton* in Long Island Sound on October 26, 1881, though a subsequent hearing found the *Wheaton* at fault in the accident. On the evening of November 22, 1905, en route from New York for Crandall on the St. Marys River, the *Pasadena* parted her chains during a storm and was thrown on the Fernandina jetties, becoming a total wreck.

PATHFINDER

According to the *Ocala Star-Banner*, January 22, 1962, "Three Fort Lauderdale residents were rescued Sunday when their 47-foot yacht *Pathfinder* ran aground, broke up, and sank off Little Talbot Island in Nassau Sound. They were Howard Nickerson, vice president of the Port Everglades Towing Co., Mrs. Nickerson and Douglas Grant. They sent a distress call picked up by the Coast Guard, and the Navy sent a helicopter to pluck them from the beach. The yacht was valued at about $15,000."

PATRICIA (1926)

The 73-ton motor vessel *Patricia*, built in 1922, foundered off Fort Lauderdale on August 18, 1926.

PATRICIA (1990)

On June 29, 1990, the 65-foot long tug *Patricia* was scuttled as an artificial reef off Miami. Resting in just over 50 feet of water, the tug is part of the "Miami Wreck Trek," which also consists of the shrimper *Miss Karline*, which can be found approximately 100 feet away to the south following a rebar stake trail. Though not confirmed, the *Patricia* may possibly have been the tug *North Harbor*, official number 210681, which was built in 1912 by Great Lakes Towing Company in Cleveland, Ohio. The *North Harbor* was 68.6 feet long, 17 feet wide, and originally displaced 73 tons gross. In 1966, the tug was renamed *Patricia* while owned by Bay State Tow Boat Company, Incorporated of Everett, Massachusetts. Records indicate this tug was abandoned in 1975.

PATRICIA M.

The 62-foot long shrimp trawler *Patricia M.* was built as hull number 1179 by the Diesel Engine Sales Company of St, Augustine in 1964. On June 26, 1970, the *Patricia M.* stranded north of Ponte Vedra.

PATRIOT

On August 27, 1862, the U.S.S. *South Carolina* destroyed the abandoned schooner *Patriot*, which was aground south of Mosquito Inlet. According to the *Official Records of the Union and Confederate Navies in the War of the Rebellion*:

> After some days of rather hazy weather, it cleared off somewhat today, when was observed from aloft the mastheads of a schooner some 12 or 15 miles to the southward, apparently ashore on the beach. Did not know but she might be one of the pilot boats which was to be sent between the visits of the supply steamer, and which had got ashore in the late dark nights. Got underway immediately and went down to her. She proved to be the centerboard schooner *Patriot*, of Nassau, New Providence, upon the beach and bilged. She had landed her cargo, been stripped of her sails, and was deserted. Some few bags of salt and a few barrels of salt mackerel were still upon the beach. A piece of letter addressed to a Mr. Clark was found, dated Nassau, August 12,

which spoke about some shipments of calico. After taking from her a few articles which had been left in the way of rigging and blocks, I cut away the masts and otherwise rendered her perfectly useless, and then returned to my station off Mosquito Inlet.

PAUL

The bark *Paul* was built in May 1892 at Nordby, Denmark. Owned by S. Abrahamsen, the vessel registered a length of 130.8 feet, a beam of 26.2 feet, and a displacement of 399 tons. On September 6, 1900, en route from Cuba to New York with a cargo of cedar and wine, the *Paul* went ashore below the Gilbert's Bar House of Refuge[182].

PAUL G. MAINS

Named after Jacksonville Offshore Sport Fishing Club member and *Florida Times-Union* columnist Paul Mains, the 83-foot long, 18-foot wide tug *Paul G. Mains* was sunk off Duval County to serve as an artificial reef. The tug now rests in approximately 75 feet of water, though the wheelhouse rises to within 50 feet of the surface. Numerous other materials were also deployed in the vicinity of this tug, including two barges, an old pogey boat, tons of concrete culvert pipe, and numerous old car bodies.

PAUL MARIE

On March 24, 1983, the 68-foot long fishing vessel *Paul Marie* capsized in stormy weather off Cape Canaveral, claiming two lives[183].

PEARL

On May 13, 1821, *Bell's Weekly Messenger* reported the *Pearl*, Captain Johnson, en route from Havana for Gibraltar, was lost near Cape Florida on March 8. Captain Johnson and four of the crew were brought into Charleston, South Carolina.

PECONIC

Like the other sites I had visited, the presence of the "Razor Wreck" was fairly well known to divers and fishermen, yet, the wreck was still unidentified. Compiling information on the site was difficult, as the vast majority of divers who visit these unknown shipwrecks are spearfishermen who are primarily interested in the associated marine life the wreck hosts and not the wreck itself. With the help of Captain Ronny Surrency of Jacksonville, I learned that the shipwreck was that of a large steamer and that there was an abundance of coal in and around the site. Prior to my planned dives with Captain Surrency, I searched my files for prospective candidates that fit some of the attributes I knew about the "Razor Wreck." One vessel in particular caught my attention: the steamer *Peconic*.

The steamer *Peconic* was built by the Liverpool shipyard of Royden and Sons in October 1881. She was 277 feet in length, 34.5 feet in breadth, and displaced 1,795 gross tons. An iron-screw steamer with two decks, she was brigantine-rigged and originally equipped with a 197-horsepower compound engine and one single-ended boiler; a donkey boiler was added to the vessel in 1894. She initially sailed under the British flag for the Mediterranean and New York Steamship Company, managed by the Phelps Brothers and Company, on a route that carried her between New York and various Mediterranean ports. During one such cruise in November 1898, she fortuitously rescued 18 seamen from the sinking bark *Johanna* in the vast and frigid mid-Atlantic.

In stark contrast to her heroic rescue of the *Johanna's* crew, four years later the *Peconic* was responsible for running down and colliding into the Italian royal mail steamer *Liguria* in New York harbor. Following an erratic and reckless course change in broad daylight on a sultry August afternoon in 1902, the bow of the *Peconic* sliced into the inbound *Liguria*, opening up the Italian steamer's hull to the waterline. As water poured into the hull of the Italian liner, she quickly took a heavy list to port, and it appeared the *Liguria* was moments away from capsizing. Fortunately, the *Liguria's* quick-thinking captain directed the 1,100 terrified passengers to move over to her starboard side, which resulted in the ship rolling back to starboard to a degree that it raised the gash in the hull above the water's surface, preventing further flooding. Though heavily damaged, both steamers were able to limp to their respective docks with no loss of life.

The *Peconic* was later sold to the firm of J.W. Elwell and Company of New York, and was originally engaged in the fruit trade from Central America to New Orleans. Due to a change in quarantine regulations that prohibited the importation of bananas, she began transporting coal from Philadelphia to New Orleans. In this capacity, she completed two successful voyages before her final, tragic excursion.

Late on the evening of August 27, 1905, the steamer *Peconic* was struggling to make its way southward along the Georgia coast. Bound from Philadelphia to New Orleans with a cargo of 1,500 tons of coal, she was in the midst of a fierce gale that she

> **TWENTY OF CREW LOST WITH STEAMER PECONIC**
>
> Go Down During a Gale Off the Florida Coast.
>
> **ONLY TWO SAILORS ESCAPE**
>
> Great Wave Struck the Vessel as She Was Turning and Caused the Cargo to Shift.

encountered earlier in the day. Just after midnight on August 28, the officer of the deck gave the order to put further out to sea, as he feared they were approaching perilously close to the beach. As the steamer was in the process of turning to port, an immense wave rolling in from the northeast struck the vessel. The unfortunate timing of the blow caused a shift in the cargo of coal, and the *Peconic* heeled over and almost immediately sank. The sinking was so swift that only two of her crew survived; twenty souls went down with the ship.

The survivors, Bagellini Humberti and Antonio Clark, had been in the bridge at the time of the accident. As soon as the ship began to careen, they rushed for one of the small lifeboats and managed to sever the lines just as the tumultuous Atlantic threatened to pull them under. Quickly thrown out on the waves, they watched in horror as a number of the awakened crew crowded into another lifeboat, only to be caught in the trough of a large wave, thrown against the ventilators, and wedged fast. Through the bleak darkness of the storm, the men's pitiful cries for help could be heard as the ship was consumed by the angry ocean. The two frightened survivors managed to keep their small boat afloat through the evening, and managed to safely land at Amelia Island approximately 11 hours later.

One of the articles in my files noted that the *Peconic* went down approximately 20 miles northeast of Fernandina Beach. Furthermore, knowing that the survivors landed at Amelia Island only 11 hours after their escape from the sinking *Peconic* revealed additional supporting information on the general location of the lost steamer; even with a stout northeast wind, a waterlogged lifeboat can travel but so far in 11 hours. Regardless of the value of the archival information, I knew that a visit to the wreck site was required to determine if the "Razor Wreck" was indeed the steamship *Peconic*. In May 2005, I was finally able to test my theory and explore the "Razor Wreck." The site is approximately 40 miles offshore, close to the Georgia-Florida border. I rolled off the boat into the cool emerald green water and pulled myself down the anchor line through a massive school of Atlantic spadefish. The wreck soon appeared below, resting on a sandy seafloor in 70 feet of water.

Swimming forward, it was obvious the wreck was resting hard over on her starboard side. Little of the vessel remained aside from various beams and a few scattered hull plates, punctuated by bollards and the anchor windlass towards the bow. The extreme bow, generally pointing eastward (which was the direction the *Peconic* was turning when it was struck by the fatal wave), terminated in a low, skeletal framework and a single large anchor in the sand. It appeared as if the majority of the vessel had been consumed by the sand and the Atlantic itself, not surprising for a wreck that might be almost 100 years old. Heading aft, I passed back over the massive single-ended boiler and noticed a smaller boiler in the sand pointed slightly upwards. I continued my journey aft over the fallen compound engine and along shaft alley, which terminated at an elegant, almost delicate, screw. The remainder of the stern rested on its starboard side, with disarticulated pieces of structure spilled out into the sand. Moving out into the debris field, I noticed a vast field of coal strewn across the seabed. It stretched for several hundred feet and was accented by small bits of miscellaneous debris. While the site possessed numerous diagnostic features consistent with the steamer *Peconic*, and the location and disposition of the wreck matched the historical record, it was my recovery of a decorative brass cover off a bollard that positively identified the "Razor Wreck" as the lost *Peconic*. The wreck of the *Peconic*, while technically resting off the Georgia coast, is close enough to the Florida border to warrant her inclusion in this work.

Richie Kohler with a chamber pot embossed with the shipping line logo recovered from the wreck of the steamer *Peconic* (Richie Kohler).

PEE DEE (1838)

The schooner *Pee Dee*, from Indian Key for Boston, encountered a storm on November 2, 1837, off Cape Florida. Her mainmast was carried away and she soon sprung a leak, so the captain ran the vessel ashore on Key Biscayne; while the cargo was saved, the vessel was a total loss[184].

PEE DEE (1858)

The 138-ton sidewheel (also cited as a screw steamer) steamer *Pee Dee* was built in 1845 at Charleston, South Carolina, and prior to her loss, she was employed in forwarding stores and troops to Florida. It was just one of these voyages when the *Pee Dee*, Captain Mansfield, was lost on the St. Augustine Bar on January 27, 1858, en route from Charleston to Indian River. No lives were lost, but the steamer, valued at $25,000, was deemed a total loss.

PEERLESS

The shrimp boat *Peerless*, owned by Ramos Brothers Shrimp Company, sank on the afternoon of February 7, 1939, after a collision with the shrimper *Queen Mary* around 4:30 a.m. that morning approximately one mile offshore and about three miles north of Ponce de Leon Inlet[185]. While a U.S. Coast Guard boat held the *Peerless* in tow for an extended period in hopes of saving the vessel, it was finally forced to cut it loose when it was clear the trawler was headed to the bottom.

The *Pee Wee Vreeland*, still wearing the name *Sherida Express* on her bow, is towed offshore to be sunk (Broward County Artificial Reef Program).

PEE WEE VREELAND

The artificial reef known as the *Pee Wee Vreeland*, named in memory of Fort Lauderdale fishing charter captain Harold "Pee Wee" Vreeland, started her life as the 136-foot long freighter *Neila Express* in 1957. She was later sold to Golden Shipping and renamed *Sherida Express*. On May 19, 1997, a boarding team from the U.S.C.G.C. *Maui* found one kilogram of cocaine hidden in the engine room of the freighter while she was moored off Miami. This would not be the only instance of narcotics smuggling by the *Sherida Express*, as a search of the vessel upon arrival at Miami from Haiti the following year revealed over 102 pounds of cocaine concealed within the freighter. After owners failed to pay the $819,000 penalty for the offense, the *Sherida Express* was confiscated and later sold at auction. On April 27, 1999, the stripped *Sherida Express* was scuttled off Port Everglades. I explored the freighter less than a year later, which rests in approximately 290 feet of water. The bottom slopes off significantly in this area, and the stern of the vessel, which rests to the west, is approximately 20 feet shallower than the bow. The dive was unremarkable aside from the fact that we were fortunate to have visibility exceeding 100 feet, and the entire vessel was visible from above as we descended down our shot line. The *Pee Wee Vreeland* was still free of growth at the time of our dive, and the only fish observed was a solitary angelfish. Over the years, the wreck has been transformed into a thriving, albeit small, deep-water reef.

PEGGY JOE

The *Peggy Joe* was a 69-foot long scallop trawler that capsized off Port Canaveral on the morning of January 7, 1985. The three-man crew was rescued by a passing trawler after attempts failed to stop leaks in the hull from flooding the *Peggy Joe*. The broken-down remains of the *Peggy Joe* rest in approximately 50 feet of water 10 miles east of Port Canaveral.

PETER

As reported in *The New York Times* on March 19, 1863, the "Gunboat *Gem of the Sea* captured sloop *Peter*, of Savannah for Nassau, on November 10 while trying to run the blockade at Indian River Inlet. She had a cargo of salt. Being old and leaky she was destroyed."

PETER B. MCALLISTER

The tug *Peter B. McAllister*, official number 239970, was built in 1940 by Equitable Equipment Company as hull number 108 at Madisonville, Louisiana. The tug, 75.9 feet long, 23 feet wide, and 138 gross tons, was eventually named *B.T. DeBardeleben*, then *Lilian*, and finally *Peter B. McAllister*. On August 29, 1973, while trying to haul off the grounded *Delaware Getty* in San Juan Harbor, Puerto Rico, the *Peter B. McAllister* capsized and sunk. She was apparently raised, repaired, and put back into service. The tug *McAllister* was ultimately sunk as an artificial reef on May 16, 1998, off Broward County. The wreck rests upright with her bow pointing south in 70 feet of water.

The tug *Peter B. McAllister* (Broward County Artificial Reef Program).

PETRUS

Volume 20 of the *Naval Journal* reported the "French brig *Petrus*, from Havana for Havre, went ashore on the 27th April (1848), and fell to pieces." Other sources state the brig wrecked near Cape Florida.

PHOEBUS

In 1802, the American schooner Phoebus, Captain Dominique, sailing from Norfolk, was reported as lost on the St. Augustine Bar[186].

PHOENIX

The 24-ton schooner *Phoenix*, Captain Baird, from Jacksonville bound for Lemon City with lumber, wrecked on October 11, 1895, north of Jupiter Inlet. According to the official report from the U.S. Life-Saving Service, the Phoenix was "Water-logged and stranded in easterly gale 9 ½ miles north of station; driven high upon the beach, so that crew escaped without assistance. Surfman found her deserted and sea breaking over her. Could do nothing except save some of the lightest cargo. Went to her again next day and met master. After consultation it was decided that nothing could be done to save the craft. On the 19th made another trip to wreck and found she had been stripped and abandoned."

PILITA

The September 30, 1851, loss of the *Pilita* was reported in Volume 24 of *The Sailor's Magazine and Naval Journal*. The dispatch stated, "Spanish brig *Pilita*, Ascorra, from Havana for Bilboa, went ashore on the reef off Cape Florida, night 30th ult., and stove a hole in her bottom. The captain and crew abandoned her, with eight feet water in her hold, and returned to Havana in the steamer *Ohio*." Other sources cite the wrecking of the brig on May 2, 1851, on Carysfort Reef. Regardless, records indicate the *Pilita* was a 161-ton brig built in Bilboa in 1847.

PILOT BOY

The sidewheel steamer *Pilot Boy*, which operated for the Jacksonville-Crescent City Line but had been out of service for some time, sank at Palatka in 1923 just north of the Wilson Cypress Company plant.

PIMELLOUS

Little is known about the history of the *Pimellous*. Numerous spelling variations appear in records (e.g., *Pimelious*, *Pimellis*, etc.), though none have been found to reference a former vessel. When sunk in 135 feet of water off Miami Beach on May 11, 1971, the approximately 120-foot long vessel, perhaps a converted barge, consisted of a flat, featureless hull, with a large crane truck parked on the stern deck. Since its deployment, the wooden decking of the vessel has been consumed, leaving just the steel support beams in place. The crane truck can be found resting in the sand off the wreck, though the cab of the truck has long since rusted away.

PINTA

According to Coe (1936), the *Pinta* was a schooner from Central America carrying 125,000 coconuts, which wrecked approximately four miles south of Mosquito Inlet during a hurricane in early September 1878.

PIONEER (1877)

The 44-ton paddlewheel steamer *Pioneer*, official number 20496, built in 1874 at Jacksonville, burned in April 1877 at Indian River.

PIONEER (1926)

The tug *Pioneer*, owned by Phoenix Utility Company, was blown ashore on Biscayne Boulevard during the September 1926 Great Miami Hurricane[187]. The ultimate fate of the tug is unknown.

The freighter *Pioneer I* being towed out for scuttling (Miami-Dade County Department of Environmental Resources Management).

PIONEER I

In October 1983, the 195-foot long *Pioneer I* was sunk in 220 feet of water offshore the wreck of the *Blue Fire* near Fowey Rocks to serve as an artificial reef. The scuttled freighter was also sent to the bottom with 26 steel tanks, which have now settled on the sand around the vessel. Little is known of the vessel's construction or service history.

Explosive scuttling charges detonated onboard *Pioneer I* (Miami-Dade County Department of Environmental Resources Management).

PIUTE

The 79-ton vessel *Piute*, built in 1925, stranded at Mosquito Inlet on January 27, 1927.

PIZARRO

In 1809 the *Pizarro*, carrying rice and naval stores from New York for Amelia Island, went ashore within the St. Marys Bar. The ship drifted onto Cumberland Island's south end shore, where it bilged.

POLAR

According to the U.S. Coast Guard, the 242-ton cargo vessel *Polar* reportedly sank on September 21, 1944 at approximate latitude 25° 43' north, longitude 80° 07' west (approximately two nautical miles east of the northern point of Key Biscayne).

POMONA

Built in August 1866 at Richmond, Maine, the *Pomona* was a 421-ton brig 125 feet long and 30 feet wide. The *Pomona*, Captain Brown, went ashore twenty-five miles south of Cape Canaveral on August 17, 1871, while en route from Galveston, Texas, for New York. The wrecking schooner *Resolute* saved 180 bales of cotton.

PONCE DE LEON INLET WRECK

Approximately one and a half miles south of Ponce de Leon Inlet, a wreck site consisting of an anchor and iron cannon was found in close proximity to the beach. To date, the wreck has yet to be identified.

PORT ROYAL

The sidewheel steamer *Port Royal*, official number 19900, built in 1861 at Staten Island, New York, was 96 feet in length, 23 feet in beam, and 189 tons gross burden. The steamer, while operating on the St. Johns River for the Jacksonville-Green Cove Springs Line, sank at Green Cove Springs. She was raised and towed to Jacksonville for repairs. While undergoing repairs, she caught fire and burned on October 31, 1887[188].

POTRERO DEL LLANO

The *Potrero del Llano* was formerly a 7,500-ton Italian tanker named the *Lucifero* that was seized along with all other Axis vessels in Mexican waters in April 1941. Built originally as the *F.A. Tamplin* in 1912 at Newcastle, England by the Palmer Company Limited, she was 364 feet in length and 47.5 feet in breadth. She was originally owned by the F.A. Tamplin Steamship Company. During her active service, she traded hands several times, resulting in numerous name changes. Her original name, *F.A. Tamplin*, was switched to *Arminco*, which then changed to *Lucifero*. After her seizure, she was again renamed and put into service under the Mexican flag, sailing for *Petroleos Mexicanos S.A.*

At 11:55 p.m. on Wednesday, May 13, 1942, the Mexican tanker, en route from Tampico to New York, was torpedoed by *Kapitänleutnant* Reinhard Suhren of the *U-564*. Quartermaster Eduardo Sibaja y Ramirez confirmed that the neutral tanker was steaming northward fully illuminated, with four spotlights directed at the large Mexican flags painted on either side of the ship. At the time of the attack, Sibaja was on his way to the bridge to relieve helmsman Jose Magana who had awakened him moments earlier. After being roused from sleep, Magana informed him that a submarine, which had been visible for the past half hour, was following the ship. Eduardo Sibaja was making his way forward when there was a blinding flash; the bridge was decimated in front of his eyes. Sibaja and several others recalled seeing the conning tower of a submarine moving away swiftly as they prepared to abandon the ship.

The tanker was immediately transformed into a floating inferno. Thousands of individuals lined the beaches of Miami to watch the blazing vessel drift northward. For hours they sat mesmerized by the massive flames shooting skyward and the climbing pillar of smoke before the *Potrero del Llano* sank. Out of a crew of 35, only 22 survived the attack, though one of the survivors died a few hours later from the injuries incurred during the attack. The burning tanker eventually sunk in deep water somewhere off South Florida.

On the basis of reports from the *U-564*, the German government maintained that the vessel had been in violation of international law by traveling in a war zone without lights and not having its national flag properly lighted. Based on reports from the survivors, however, the vessel was properly illuminated. Furthermore, the *U-564* had apparently stalked the vessel for half an hour before firing, which should have been enough time to verify the identity of the target. Regardless, the Mexican government

Port side profile view of the tanker *Potrero del Llano*, illustrating the prominent neutral markings (© The Mariners' Museum, Newport News, Virginia).

The *Potrero del Llano* burns off Miami (Alfred H. Robson Collection).

was outraged, compounded by the sinking of yet another Mexican tanker, the *Faja de Oro*, on Wednesday, May 20.

The sinking led to a break in relations between the two countries. The formerly isolationist country of Mexico now found itself pushing for war. There were daily demonstrations against German businesses and citizens in Mexico. President Manuel Avilo Camacho notified German residents along the coast that they would most likely be interned. On May 28, 1942, President Camacho addressed the Mexican Congress in an extraordinary session, stating:

> I have come before you to comply with one of the gravest duties which the Head of a Nation has ever had to shoulder, that of presenting to the National Legislature the necessity of resorting to the very last of the resources which a free people can dispose of to defend their destinies. As I already informed the nation during the night of the 13th of the current month, a submarine pertaining to the Nazi Fascist powers torpedoed and sunk in the Atlantic, a Mexican oil tanker, the *Potrero del Llano*. Nothing stopped the aggressors. Neither the neutrality of the country to whom the ship belonged nor the circumstance that it carried signals which could be readily observed indicating the nationality of the ship, nor the precaution taken that the ship had all the lights on in order that the colors of our flag, plainly displayed on the side of our ship, could be clearly observed, nor were there taken into consideration international and humanitarian rights of the duty to allow the crew of the ship an opportunity to save themselves. Of 35 of the crew, all Mexican, only 22 were able to reach Miami, Florida, and one of them died a few hours later, a victim of the injuries suffered during the attack. Including these, 14 lives were swept away by the attack of the totalitarian powers. Fourteen young brave men gave up their lives, and before their deaths the nation bowed its head in mourning[189].

Shortly thereafter, the Mexican senate unanimously voted to declare war on Germany. President Camacho announced this declaration of a "state of war" between Mexico and the Axis Powers during a June 1 radio broadcast.

The final resting place of the Mexican tanker *Potrero del Llano* has yet to be identified. One report stated that she drifted and finally sank off Jupiter. However, that observation may have been associated with the attack on the tanker *Lubrafol*, which occurred just four days earlier. The *Potrero del Llano* most likely rests in deep water somewhere off Miami. Captain Wayne Conn knows of two large wrecks in deep water, 735 feet and 910 feet respectively, one of which may be the *Potrero del Llano*.

POWERFUL

The former Moran Towing Corporation tug *Powerful* was sunk off Jacksonville as an artificial reef on March 8, 1992. The wreck rests upright and intact, though listing slightly to port, in 85 feet of water, with her wheelhouse encountered at a depth of 65 feet. The tug *Powerful*, official number 205637, was built in 1908 at Port Richmond, New York, for the Lehigh Valley Railroad, and was 89.4 feet long, 24.1 feet wide, and 176 tons gross burden.

PRIMA DONNA

The bark *Prima Donna*, 114.3 feet in length, 27.7 feet in beam, and 395 tons burden, was built in 1854 at Pictou, Nova Scotia. On August 16, 1861, en route from Havana to New York, the British bark wrecked on the Florida coast during a hurricane. William Smith, John Angus, and Charles McClenahan survived the event, and after much effort, reached the small settlement at Miami. After a short duration, they arranged for the fishing smack *Colonel Long* to carry them, along with a sole survivor of the wrecked bark *Sir Walter Raleigh*, to Charleston, South Carolina. While still off the Florida coast, the *Colonel Long* was intercepted by the U.S.S. *Jamestown*, which escorted the vessel to New York. The wrecked British sailors were then imprisoned at Fort Lafayette as suspected pirates.

PRINCE GEORGE

The November 11, 1769, issue of *Lloyd's List* reported the loss of the British ship *Prince George* as she was coming into St. Augustine at the end of a journey from London.

PRINCESS

The steamer *Princess*, official number 150212, built in 1881 at Jacksonville, was 53 feet long, 10.6 feet wide, and 11.4 tons burden. During a hurricane on September 26, 1894, the Palatka-Crescent City Line steamer *Princess* was sunk between Palatka and Picolata; she was valued at $12,000.

PRINCESS ANNE

Launched by Sun Shipbuilding and Drydock Company from their Chester, Pennsylvania shipyard on May 18, 1936, the auto ferry *Princess Anne* was originally 246 feet long, 59 feet wide, and displaced 1,587 tons. Designed by Raymond Loewy, the undisputed master of streamline style, for the Virginia Ferry Corporation of Wilmington, Delaware, the art deco-inspired *Princess Anne* resembled the look of a miniature ocean liner. In early

Illustration from a period postcard of the *Princess Anne* as originally built.

1954, the *Princess Anne* was cut in half and lengthened to 335.5 feet overall, which increased her displacement to 2,366 tons gross. The ferry served on the Chesapeake Bay until 1964, when she was sold to the Delaware River and Bay Authority, renamed the *New Jersey*, and put to work running between Cape May, New Jersey, and Lewes, Delaware. In 1974, the ferry was renamed *Greenport* after her sale to Mascony Transport and Ferry Service. As the *Greenport*, the ferry was employed on a run between Fire Island, New York, and Block Island, Rhode Island. In the early 1980s, the aging vessel was purchased by investors with plans of converting her into an offshore casino ship. Due to financial and legal problems, however, they abandoned their plans and deserted the *Greenport* at a shipyard in Newport, Rhode Island. The neglected ferry later sunk in a storm at her berth, but was subsequently patched and raised by Resolve Marine Group. The derelict was eventually sold for use as an artificial reef and towed to Palm Beach County, where she was again named *Princess Anne*.

Preparation of the *Princess Anne* for reefing (Florida Fish and Wildlife Conservation Commission Artificial Reef Program).

In a joint exercise between Resolve Marine Group, American Oceanics, and a U.S. Navy explosive ordnance disposal team from Jacksonville, the *Princess Anne* was scuttled on May 23, 1993. Unfortunately, due to inclement weather, the former ferry settled outside of her intended position, and came to rest on some coral hardbottom

Underwater images of the *Princess Anne*: above, the remains of the superstructure; below, the exposed engine.

habitat. For several months, the ferry sat upright and intact in approximately 100 feet of water. The vessel significantly collapsed during a December 1993 storm, which was likely aided by the extensive scrapping of the ship's infrastructure prior to sinking. The wreck has also been impacted by several hurricanes, which relegated the once streamlined ferry into a disarticulated pile of debris. The superstructure has been torn loose from the lower hull, and deposited on the inshore side of the wreck. While the *Princess Anne* has suffered from the elements over the years, the wreck still presents a fantastic dive with abundant vertical relief. It is not uncommon for divers to observe dense schools of tropical fish, as well as sharks, rays, and sea turtles around the wreck of the former ferry *Princess Anne*.

PRINCESS BRITNEY

The 298-ton general cargo vessel *Princess Britney* was launched on July 10, 1956, as the *Heinz Helmut* by *Nobiskrug Werft* of Rendsburg, Germany. Originally owned by Captain Behrens, the 165-foot long German freighter would change hands several times over the next five decades: in 1965, after being sold to Martin von Rönn, she

Sinking of the *Princess Britney* (Miami-Dade County Department of Environmental Resources Management).

sailed as the *Elbstrand* (also *Elbestrand*); renamed *Claudia* in 1973 after being purchased by Giromar Shipping Company, Limited of Cyprus; she traveled to Denmark later that same year after being bought by Eva Sörensen and then sailed as *Ellen Peter*; she was renamed *Lorelei* by Harry Jacobsen when he acquired the freighter in 1975; after a long run, the coaster was bought by Leyenda Shipping, Incorporated of Belize in 1998 and renamed *Leyenda*; and finally, in 2001, the vessel was named *Princess Britney* after her sale to Salvador Shipping and Trading. However, the *Princess Britney* sailed for but a year before being seized by the U.S. Customs Service after agents discovered more than 156 pounds of cocaine hidden underneath the deck in the freighter's engine room during "Operation Riverwalk." The forfeited vessel was subsequently cleaned and sunk in 80 feet of water off Key Biscayne on April 29, 2003. Divers will find the *Princess Britney* upright and intact, and in close proximity to several other artificial reefs, such as the *South Seas*, which rests approximately 250 feet to the southwest.

Steve Muslin swims past the wheelhouse of the *Princess Britney*.

PRINCESS MARY

The schooner *Princess Mary*, en route from Tobago to Savannah with a cargo of rum and molasses, ran aground on March 10, 1775, on a bank near Cumberland Island. While the schooner proved to be a total loss, most of the cargo was saved.

PRINS VALDEMAR

The saga of the bark *Prins Valdemar* is perhaps one of the most unusual tales in the annals of Florida maritime history. At one time, she was the bane of Miami, only to later become a colorful landmark and a familiar sight to millions of tourists, which served the city well. Originally built in January 1892 in Helsingør,

The *Prins Valdemar* entering Miami harbor (Florida State Archives).

Denmark, she was named for a Danish prince who became a beloved figure to his country by refusing the throne to Bulgaria in 1885. The steel-hulled bark, official number 213604, was 226.1 feet in length, 37.3 feet in breadth, and displaced 1,361 tons. After several routine years at sea, the history of the bark took an unusual series of turns. During the Mexican Revolution, the *Prins Valdemar* was captured running guns and summarily seized by the Mexican government. She was eventually sold to George W. McNear of San Francisco and used to carry lumber between Australia and California. In July 1916, flying under the American flag, the *Prins Valdemar* was captured by a German warship while on her way from Philadelphia to Sweden carrying a cargo of oil. The German Navy successfully utilized the ship as a blockade runner on several trips until she was chased into the neutral port of Copenhagen by a British torpedo boat. Bought by an American syndicate following the war, she sailed between the U.S. and Nicaragua carrying coconuts and other cargo. Eventually, she was put into service hauling lumber to Miami in 1925 during the area's building boom. As the largest sailing vessel ever to enter Miami Harbor, her size attracted the attention of some developers, and she was purchased with the intention of converting the bark into a floating hotel to relieve local housing congestion. During her conversion, the *Prins Valdemar* came to grief on January 10, 1926. At the time, the bark was resting precariously along the edge of a sandbar where it had run aground the day before. The receding tide combined with strong winds eroded the bark's balance, and the *Prins Valdemar* suddenly careened over on her starboard side, ultimately coming to

The *Prins Valdemar*, capsized in Miami harbor (Florida State Archives).

rest half aground and half submerged across the shipping channel. Eighty men narrowly escaped drowning during the incident, and several workers playing poker on the lower deck had a close call when they were forced to slide through a porthole as water swirled in around them.

The task of refloating the vessel took 42 days, during which time over 50 vessels carrying millions of dollars of needed building supplies were unable to enter the port to offload their cargo. The delay caused by the sinking of the *Prins Valdemar* resulted in the end of the Miami building boom. After its salvage, the steel bark was hauled ashore to a spot at Bayfront Park, berthed in a bed of concrete, and over the years was employed as an aquarium, restaurant, and a civic center. Over time, the landlocked ship started to show her age. In 1952, the city of Miami finally had the *Prins Valdemar* demolished and hauled away. The last remaining vestige of the *Prins Valdemar*, its anchor, is on display in front of the Miami Yacht Club.

The "wreck" of the *Prins Valdemar* serving as the Miami Aquarium, 1940 (Alice L. Luckhardt).

PROP WRECK

The unidentified wreck known as the "Prop Wreck" rests in 120 feet of water approximately 50 nautical miles northeast of Mayport. The site appears to be the final resting spot of a wooden-hulled steamer powered by a compound engine and long, railroad-type boilers, which was carrying railroad iron as cargo. Evidence indicates the vessel apparently burned prior to sinking, as melted brass fixtures and shattered ceramics can be found throughout the site. The wreck is named after the large square iron prop found exposed on one end of the site. To date, the vessel's identity has not been determined.

Underwater image of the large iron screw on the "Prop Wreck."

PROTECTOR

The ship *Protector* was originally built as the *Mazeppa* in 1854 at Richmond, Maine, by H. Springer. She was 162.7 feet in length, 32.8 feet in beam, and displaced 799 tons. Around 1867, the vessel was sold to Kuhler and Company, renamed *Protector*, and homeported in Stavanger, Norway. On February 12, 1877, while en route from Pensacola to Norway with a cargo of rosin, the *Protector*, Captain Falch, struck at Hillsboro; she was reported a total loss on February 18. According to the records of the U.S. Life-Saving Service, the ship wrecked 11 miles north of the Fort Lauderdale Life-Saving Station, though the crew of 20 was saved.

Known locally as the "Deerfield Beach Wreck," the site lies approximately 1,500 feet to the north of the Deerfield Beach Pier and 500 feet offshore. Over the years, a keel with a large bronze gudgeon pin was found, as well as several dead-eyes, spikes, and other assorted artifacts. Her windlass, anchor chain, and ballast lie approximately 50 feet inshore of the first reef, with the main portion of the wreck just to the north, though most, if not all, of the wreck is typically buried by sand from local beach nourishment projects. Observant divers may still spot random brass sheathing nails within the cracks of the adjacent patch reef.

PROTEUS

The freighter *Proteus* was built in 1957 by *Erste Donau D.G. Schiffswerft* at their shipyard on the Danube River in Korneuburg. The general cargo vessel was 217.5 feet in length, 33.2 feet in beam, and 993 tons gross burden. In 1971, the *Proteus* was sold to Florida Panama Lines, Incorporated of Panama, but the vessel retained its original name. The freighter apparently did not operate long for

Starboard view of the freighter *Proteus*, 1957 (Dick Sloan).

her new owners, as reports indicated she was eventually abandoned on the Miami River in 1973. During the mid 1980s, Miami began to clean up the Miami River waterfront and worked to remove the numerous derelict vessels that had been rotting along its shoreline for decades. After the owners failed to move their vessel, the superstructure of the *Proteus* was razed, and she was towed offshore and sunk as an artificial reef on January 24, 1985. The wreck now rests in approximately 70 feet of water. While originally resting upright and intact, Hurricane Andrew significantly impacted the *Proteus* in August 1992. The former freighter was twisted and ripped into two pieces, with her bow section now resting on her side and the stern partially buried in the sand.

The stripped-down *Proteus* just prior to its sinking (Miami-Dade County Department of Environmental Resources Management).

View of the running gear on the *Proteus* before Hurricane Andrew (Miami-Dade County Department of Environmental Resources Management).

PROVIDENCIA

The loss of the *Providencia* has long been associated with the history of Palm Beach. As the lore goes, the 150-ton Spanish brigantine, built at Barcelona in 1855, was on a voyage with a cargo of 20,000 coconuts when the vessel was blown ashore on the Florida coast near Jupiter on January 9, 1878. Washed along the coast, the coconuts took root, and soon thousands of palm trees appeared along the Florida coast. I won't speculate on the veracity of this account, though a January 12, 1878, dispatch in *The New York Times* indicated the *Providencia* did strand at Jupiter Inlet while on a voyage from Mexico to Barcelona, but while carrying a cargo of logwood; the crew was taken to Key West by the steamer *Morgan City*, arriving on January 11. Singer (1998) states that hides and coconuts were also included in the *Providencia's* cargo along with the aforementioned logwood.

PROVIDENZA R.

A December 15, 1901, dispatch in *The Atlanta Constitution* reported:

> The Italian bark *Providenza R.*, of which Queirolo is master, reported ashore off Amelia Island light last night, will be a total wreck, the vessel being now full of water and laying so high up the beach as to make it next to impossible for her to be saved. Her master was seen today and made a statement that he lost his bearing on account of a defective chart. This vessel is a bark of 896 gross tons with a crew of fourteen men. She left the Barbadoes some ten days ago, making a remarkably fast trip to this port.

The *Providenza R.*, built by G.B. Magnano in August 1876 at Savona, Italy, was 181.7 feet long and 34.4 feet wide.

PUNTA LUNA

The hermaphrodite brig *Punta Luna* was built in 1846 at Wolgast, Germany, as the *Johannes*. When launched, the vessel was 105 feet in length, 26.8 feet in breadth, and displaced 333 tons. In 1863, the brig was rebuilt, following which she registered a length of 112 feet, a beam of 27.3 feet, and a burden of 258 tons. In October 1881, en route from New York for Fernandina, the *Punta Luna* reportedly stranded on the north breakers of Pelican Shoals just short of its destination. Those seeking to find the *Punta Luna* should be aware of details in the *Annual Report of the Chief of Engineers, United States Army, to the Secretary of War for the Year 1905*, which stated, "The removal of the wrecks of the *City of Austin, Franconia,* and *Puntalunos* [sic] in Cumberland Sound, Georgia and Florida, was completed. This work was done under emergency contract of August 8, 1903, at a total cost of $7,213.85."

QUEEN (1818)

The 308-ton British ship *Queen*, Captain Flott, of and for London, from Jamaica, was wrecked on August 9, 1818, on the coast of Florida (also cited as on the Florida Reef on August 7); while the second mate died of fatigue, all other hands left the wreck safely and were received on board the sloop *Young Man*[190].

QUEEN (1891)

On September 14, 1891, the 15-ton schooner *Queen*, en route from Melbourne for Abaco, Bahamas, laden with a cargo of lumber, wrecked eight miles south of the Orange Grove Life-Saving Station (present-day Delray Beach).

R.B. TRUEMAN

According to Singer (1998), the 78-ton gas vessel *R.B. Trueman*, which was built in 1918, burned at Jacksonville on June 18, 1924. I have not been able to uncover any additional information on a vessel by this name.

R.W. JOHNSON

On January 15, 1886, the schooner *R.W. Johnson* stranded on the north beach of Mosquito Inlet, claiming two of the seven crewmen. The schooner, which was built in 1868, was carrying a cargo of bricks in support of the ongoing work at the Mosquito Inlet Lighthouse, now known as the Ponce de Leon Inlet Light Station. The *R.W. Johnson* was but one of several vessels lost during the work on the lighthouse. On January 28, 1886, the *Halifax Herald* reported that "out of eight or ten schooners employed in the lighthouse (Ponce de Leon Inlet Light Station) work, five have been wrecked, viz: *Godfrey*, *Augusta Wilson*, *Ajax*, *Freewind*, and the *Johnson*; the *Mary Brown*, now lying at the lighthouse dock, is crippled. We have been assured that nearly all of them received the injuries resulting in wrecks on the inlet bar or in the river. Six men have also been drowned."

RAFBORN

According to Singer (1998), the ship *Rafborn* stranded at the same place as the schooner *Mattie Richmond* (20 miles south of Jupiter Inlet) in February 1870. I have been unable to find any additional information on this vessel or wrecking event. It is possible the date or name of the vessel is erroneous, as the same original source utilized by Singer incorrectly documented two other losses attributed to this timeframe and location (brig *Moreno* and schooner *Minerva*).

RATICAN

While generally identified as a 72-foot long sailboat sunk as an artificial reef on June 3, 1991, the site of the *Ratican* also consists of a 55-foot long steel hulled vessel and concrete culverts resting in 90 feet of water off Jupiter Inlet. Due to poor record keeping, I have been unable to find any additional information on the sailboat's history.

RATTLER

A Miami harbor tug, the *Rattler* was condemned after a fire sometime after the 1920s Miami building boom[191]. She was towed up the Miami River and abandoned to rot.

RATTLESNAKE

British loyalist Josiah Smith's diary stated the galley *Rattlesnake*, two victualers (i.e., provision ships), and six private vessels were lost on St. Augustine Bar at the end of December 1782. The vessels were part of a fleet evacuating loyalists from Charleston, South Carolina, to St. Augustine[192]. According to Schoepf (1911), following the surrender of Charleston, "no less than 16 vessels bearing refugees and their effects, went to pieces" on the St. Augustine Bar, resulting in the loss of many lives. Schoepf went on to say, "A great quantity of dismal remains of vessels protrude on all sides from the sand and water."

RAVENSWOOD

The sidewheel steamer *Ravenswood*, official number 21855, was built in 1867 at New York. The vessel registered a length of 137.2 feet, a breadth of 29.8 feet, and a displacement of 430 tons. The *Ravenswood* operated on the St. Johns River as a ferry between Jacksonville and South Jacksonville. On January 18, 1895, the ferry burned at her wharf at Jacksonville. The *Ravenswood* was deemed a total loss and was insured for $5,000.

RAYCHEL

A frequent visitor to Miami, the *Raychel* was a 164-foot long Honduran freighter that carried general cargo from South Florida to ports in the Caribbean and Central America. On October 18, 1990, the *Raychel* cleared Government Cut and was preparing to turn southbound at the seaward end of the shipping channel for the Turks and Caicos Islands. On this trip, she was burdened with a cargo of cinder blocks, lumber, eight vehicles, and eight cargo containers. Captain Ray Minor had just taken over the helm from the harbor pilot, who departed the ship near channel marker number two. With winds blowing approximately 20 miles an hour, the pilot boat pulled away from the lee side of the freighter and was 300 feet away when the

The *Raychel* resting on the bottom after her accidental sinking (Miami-Dade County Department of Environmental Resources Management).

freighter's cargo apparently shifted. The *Raychel* quickly took on a list and began to capsize as the crew of nine hastily abandoned ship in a life raft and boat. While the crew escaped unharmed, the *Raychel* settled on her side in 43 feet of water.

A lighted buoy was placed on the wreck as the shipping company consulted with salvors. In the interim, local sport divers converged on the wreck and found the sandy bottom littered with the cargo of the vessel, including bicycles, PVC pipe, cinder blocks, lumber, automobiles, and crates of liquor and juice. Notably, numerous crates of Jack Daniels bourbon were liberated from the site by opportunistic divers. The *Raychel* remained at the end of the shipping channel for several months until salvage crews recovered what they could from the vessel before her planned scuttling in deep water. The freighter was then raised in several large sections and taken via barge to her final resting spot. The sections of the wreck were sunk in approximately 185 feet of water at the Pflueger Artificial Reef Site in July 1991, and now provide an interesting destination for technical divers.

REALITY

The 40-foot sailboat *Reality* sank approximately 10 miles off Stuart on January 22, 1980[193]. The recently-purchased boat was being sailed south from Maryland when the accident occurred. The owner and two friends climbed aboard a small rubber life raft, and drifted slowly north for five days without food or water until their eventual rescue approximately 95 miles off Jacksonville by the tanker *Exxon Lexington*.

REBECCA

According to the *Bell's Weekly Messenger* of December 15, 1816, "The *Rebecca*, from Cadiz and Havannah to Savannah; and the *Catharine Osmond*, Vicary, from Havannah to Salem, are wrecked at Florida. Part of their cargoes saved, and carried to Nassau."

REBECCA LEIGH

The 72-foot long shrimp boat *Rebecca Leigh* washed ashore and broke up on a sandbar at New Smyrna Beach on February 12, 1991. The fishing vessel's two crewmen jumped overboard and swam 150 feet to shore in five to eight foot surf. The *Rebecca Leigh* was en route from Brunswick, Georgia to Port Canaveral with the trawler *Billy B* when the wreck occurred. The shrimpers anchored offshore overnight, but the captain of the *Rebecca Leigh* awoke at 4:30 a.m. to find the anchor line parted and the vessel stranded on the sandbar. The *Billy B* attempted to haul the grounded trawler off the sandbar, but abandoned that effort after the 23-year old *Rebecca Leigh* started to tear apart. The shrimper, worth about $30,000, was a total loss. Debris from the wreck washed up along a mile-long stretch of New Smyrna Beach.

REBEL

On July 16, 1985, the Broward County Sheriff's Office Bomb and Arson Unit detonated four explosive charges that sent the freighter *Rebel* 110 feet to the bottom off Fort Lauderdale. The keel for the coastal freighter was originally laid down in 1940 as the *Cornelis* (IMO number 5080067) by C. Appelo's Scheepswerven at Zwartsluis, Netherlands. Due to the pending occupation of German forces in World War II, the vessel was dismantled and sunk near the yard before completion; the *Cornelis* was finally rebuilt in 1947. The coaster was 135.4 feet long, 23.6 feet wide, and displaced 288 tons. After four decades sailing throughout Europe for several owners, the *Cornelis* was sold to *Inversionista Nova Aborai S.A.* of Panama in 1981 and renamed *Island Transporter*. The following year, the freighter was renamed *Sta Andrea* after her sale to *Cachontun S.A.* In 1984, the coaster was seized by the U.S. Coast Guard for smuggling narcotics and docked on the Miami River. After sitting idle for 10 months, the *Sta Andrea* was purchased at federal auction on June 12, 1985, for $17,500 by an anonymous Fort Lauderdale resident. The individual then donated the vessel, which was renamed *Rebel*, to Broward County for use as an artificial reef. Like the majority of coasters sunk as artificial reefs off Florida, the forward portion of the wreck, consisting of the cargo holds, has collapsed outward in the sand and the bow is found resting on its port side. The stern superstructure of the *Rebel* is still upright and intact, rising over 20 feet off the bottom.

RED BRICK WRECK

Off the northern end of Long Reef, in the vicinity of the *Lugano*, rests the unidentified wreck of a nineteenth century schooner. The site earned its name from the copious amounts of red brick found amidships. Resting in only 10 feet of water, this wreck is known for its abundant and unique supply of artifacts found about its perimeter when first visited by divers in the 1960s. Elaborate china and pottery remains were scattered on the south end of the vessel, as well as a cache of opium bottles. Silverware and lead shot were also present, though no artifacts that would aid in the identification of the wreck have been recovered.

RED WING

The steamer *Red Wing*, en route from Jacksonville to St. Augustine, wrecked while crossing the St. Augustine Bar on March 9, 1887. The *Red Wing* was owned by Captain Smith and Terry and Company of Moultrie. This vessel may be the St. Johns River tug *Red Wing* that Davis (1925) reported as lost near Jacksonville, though he did not include any specific details on the vessel or its wrecking.

REFORMATION

On August 23, 1696, the barkentine *Reformation* departed Port Royal, Jamaica, for Philadelphia in a convoy of several merchant vessels escorted by the frigate H.M.S. *Hampshire*. The convoy eventually fell apart during the journey, and the *Reformation* found herself sailing alone off

Florida when it encountered a violent storm on September 23-24, which grounded the vessel north of Jupiter Inlet. The storm also claimed the *Burroughs* and *Nantwich*, which were part of the same convoy. One of the passengers onboard the vessel was Jonathan Dickinson, a Quaker merchant, who documented the wrecking and subsequent hardships in a widely-published journal. Dickinson described the situation following the grounding just after 1:00 a.m., stating, "The wind was violent and it was very dark, that our mariners could see no land; the seas broke over us that we were in a quarter of an hour floating in the cabin; we endeavored to get a candle lighted, which in time was accomplished…. The seas continued breaking over us and no land to be seen; we concluded to keep in the vessel as long as she would hold together."

Fortunately, everyone on board the *Reformation* survived the stranding. At daybreak, they abandoned the wrecked vessel and began landing supplies and provisions on the beach. The shipwrecked party was soon discovered by the local Jaega Indians from the village of Jobe (i.e., Hobe) near Jupiter Inlet. After a tense confrontation, due to the Indians' hatred of the English, one of the crewmen apparently convinced the Jaega the castaways were Spanish. Though still suspicious, the Indians spared their lives, and the survivors were taken approximately five miles south to their village at Jobe; the wreck of the *Reformation* was burned to its waterline. On September 28, Dickinson's group began their epic struggle north to St. Augustine, after which they continued on to Charleston and finally to Philadelphia via ship, arriving on April 1, 1697.

RELIANCE (1878)

The *Titusville Herald*, September 7, 1878, reported the tragic loss of the steamer *Reliance*. En route from Jacksonville to Savannah, the boiler of the steamer exploded two miles out from St. Marys, Georgia, on September 6. The first and second engineers, as well as the second mate and cook, were killed or drowned in the incident. Several of the crew members were also injured by scalding steam that was released in the rupture, but fortunately none of the passengers were hurt. The article stated that, "The upper works were blown to atoms" as a result of the explosion.

RELIANCE (1985)

The 63-foot long tugboat *Reliance* was sunk in 70 feet of water approximately 10 nautical miles east of Mayport to function as an artificial reef in 1985. This wreck may possibly be the tug *Reliance*, official number 271881, which was 63.9 feet long, 22.1 feet wide, and was built in 1956 at Houma, Louisiana.

RELIEF #5

Singer (1998) states the 87-ton barge *Relief #5* foundered off Miami on September 18, 1926, during a hurricane.

The *Renegade* sailing as the coaster *Capri* (Jelle Bijlsma).

RENEGADE

On September 12, 1951, *Scheepswerf Gebr. Coops* launched the coastal freighter *Capri* (IMO number 5419921) from its shipyard at Hoogezand, Netherlands. The coaster registered a length of 141.3 feet, a beam of 22.8 feet, and a displacement of 295 tons gross. In 1963, she was sold to Swedish owners and renamed *Falken*; she reverted to her original name *Capri* in 1966; operated as the *Karl Johan* for her new Danish owner beginning in 1971; after her sale to Colombian owners in 1977, she was known as the *Santa M.*; and, finally, she sailed as the *Sanka M.* starting in 1980. Some sources state the U.S. Coast Guard seized the Colombian freighter *Sanka M.* in 1981 off Key West after drugs were found onboard, though ultimately the vessel was abandoned on the Miami River where she sat idle for two years. The Coast Guard levied a total of $17,500 in fines against the vessel's owner to prompt the derelict's removal from the riverfront. Ben Moskoff, artificial reef coordinator for Miami-Dade County, worked out a deal where the Coast Guard would drop the fines upon the owner's transfer of the vessel to the county to serve as an artificial reef. After the fines were dropped, however, the owner reneged on his deal with Miami-Dade County, and he approached Broward County in an attempt to get more money for his rusting freighter. Angler Tom O'Connell donated $16,000 he won in the Pompano Beach Fishing Rodeo to have the freighter moved, cleaned, and inspected, whereupon he renamed the *Sanka M.* after his fishing boat, *Renegade*. On June 10, 1985, the *Renegade* was sunk in 195 feet of water off Hillsboro Inlet, approximately 800 feet north of the *Lowrance*.

Sinking of the *Renegade* (Broward County Artificial Reef Program).

REPUBLIC

The *Republic* was a 392-foot long tanker, built in 1920 by the Bethlehem Shipbuilding Corporation in Wilmington, Delaware. Her christened name was the *Weweantic*, which was later changed to *Liberty Minquas*. Owned by the Petroleum Navigation Company of Houston, Texas, the 5,287-ton tanker was on her way to Texas when she was torpedoed by the *U-504* at 11:00 p.m. on February 22, 1942, three miles east of Jupiter Inlet. Captain Alfred H. Anderson, with 36 years of experience at sea, stated that two torpedoes struck the portside of the *Republic* in quick succession, "as quick as you can say one, two[194]." In another interview, he described his reaction to the attack, "It was a terrible shock to me, but as soon as I gathered my wits, I wanted to protect my men. We got ready to leave the ship immediately as it was taking water fast and we left within ten minutes[195]."

The attack destroyed the radio room of the tanker, with one torpedo striking just amidships under the bridge. Fortunately, the radio operator John S. Lake had just left the radio room to get a cup of coffee. Had he been sitting at his post at the time of the explosions, he would have been killed instantly. Unfortunately, five men in the engine room perished in the initial explosions. The *Republic* developed a sharp list as the *U-504* surfaced nearby, observing the survivors pull away from the vessel. Third Mate Charles F. Felder detailed its activities, saying, "We'd been in the boats about ten minutes when the sub came around the ship's stern, with its conning tower awash. It just stood there and watched us for ten or fifteen minutes. It was too dark to see whether anybody came on its deck. I think it was watching to see if we signaled anyone[196]."

The U.S.C.G.C. *Vigilant* was patrolling off Melbourne when a flare was spotted by a lookout. She changed course and found the burning tanker an hour later. The cutter pulled alongside the *Republic* at 8:00 a.m. to find an overturned lifeboat alongside the blazing tanker. A survivor was observed swimming nearby, and the *Vigilant* maneuvered to rescue the panicked man. With the cutter only 50 feet away from the man, the *Republic* exploded, showering the *Vigilant* with flaming oil. The unfortunate crewmember was enveloped in flames. Undaunted, the Coast Guard cutter remained on station and rescued two other crewmen, who she later transferred to the U.S.S. *Biddle*, which was attracted by the flames and billowing smoke. Two lifeboats filled with oil-coated survivors landed successfully at Hobe Sound Beach and were cared for by local residents.

The exposed bow of the sunken tanker *Republic* (Florida State Archives).

The stern of the *Republic* came to rest on the bottom, though the bow of the tanker protruded from the water for approximately three months. The day after the sinking, two men from Jupiter rowed out to the wreck to investigate. Leonard Smith described the scene, recounting, "She wallowed in the waves, lying on her side. Water hissed through her hatches with a fearsome sound. Clothing and wreckage of all sorts drifted back and forth and the ship groaned as she moved. We found a small wire-haired terrier that had been left aboard when the crew abandoned ship the night before. He was glad to see us[197]." The wreck was eventually demolished as a hazard to navigation, but divers may still find her remains in approximately 50 feet of water. The only recognizable portion of the wreck remaining is a large boiler that towers off the bottom. Resting on a sandy bottom, her twisted hull plates and miscellaneous wreckage provide beneficial habitat to numerous marine species.

REVENGE

The French brig *Revenge*, bound from Campeche to France with a load of cochineal and logwood, wrecked near Cape Florida in September 1825. Jacob Housman of the wrecking schooner *William Henry* found the vessel abandoned on a reef off Elliott Key, three miles from Caesar's Creek. On September 7, 1825, he removed "eight

The tanker *Republic* at sea (Mark Mondano Collection).

ceroons of cochineal, two boxes of sugar, and a quantity of logwood unknown, but supposed to be twelve tons, and a parcel of sails and rigging[198]." Instead of carrying the salvaged cargo to Key West, which was the standard protocol of the day, Housman sailed for St. Augustine, arriving on September 27. There he libeled the salvaged property under the territorial law of July 4, 1823, which provided for adjudication of salvage by a five-man jury. Without the authorization of the vessel's captain or owner, the jury granted a staggering salvage award of 95 percent. Due to protests filed by the French consul, however, the award was later reduced to 66 percent. The actions of Jacob Housman raised the ire of shipping agents and other Florida Keys' wreckers, which resulted in Housman largely becoming an outcast.

REX BEAR

Launched on April 4, 1956, at the Elmshorn, Germany shipyard of Kremer Sohn, the *Rex Bear* started her troubled life as the *Ortrud Müller*. The German coastal freighter registered a length of 202.6 feet, a beam of 34.5 feet, and a displacement of 884 tons. In 1965 she was sold to a Norwegian owner and renamed *Simon*, and in 1975 her name was changed again to *Ramsland*. Reportedly, she also plied the waters under the name *God is Good* and *Rex*, before her final name change to *Rex Bear*. In 1990, she cruised into the port of Miami from Haiti, and squatted along the Miami River for over seven years while she slowly rusted under the blazing Florida sun. After efforts from local and state agencies failed to motivate representatives for the Costa Rican company that owned the derelict vessel to move the *Rex Bear*, which at many times had been illegally moored at various berths, endangered local shipping traffic, and spilled oil into the river, the U.S. Coast Guard began levying steep fines to illicit the desired response. Following a long saga played out in local newspapers and in courtrooms, the derelict vessel was ultimately donated to a local sportfishing group for use as an artificial reef. On June 16, 1998, the *Rex Bear* was sunk as an artificial reef four and a half miles south of Government Cut in memory of a local fishing tackle supplier named Augie Ferrigno. The *Rex Bear* now sits upright and intact in 240 feet of water off Miami.

The derelict *Rex Bear* moored on Miami River (Miami-Dade County Department of Environmental Resources Management).

RHEA

The wooden-hulled shrimp trawler *Rhea*, built in 1953 by Diesel Engine Sales Company at St. Augustine, foundered five miles off False Cape, north of Cape Canaveral, on January 3, 1966.

RICHMOND (1920)

The schooner *Richmond*, official number 218901, was built in 1919 at Richmond, Maine. She registered a length of 228.3 feet, a breadth of 41.9 feet, and a displacement of 1,719 tons gross. On January 5, 1920, the *Richmond* reportedly stranded at Jacksonville.

The schooner *Richmond*, prior to her grounding at New River Inlet in 1926 (Broward County Historical Commission).

RICHMOND (1926)

On September 18, 1926, the Great Miami Hurricane swept across South Florida, laying the region to waste. The three-masted schooner *Richmond*, recently purchased by R.G. Mills, was beached by the storm on the north side of the New River Inlet (Port Everglades). The vessel was deemed beyond repair, and summarily stripped and abandoned. On the evening of August 22, 1927, newspapers reported a fire destroyed the wrecked schooner *Richmond*, which was embedded in sand where she originally stranded. The remains of the schooner were eventually buried and forgotten. During excavation for the Point of Americas condominium in the late 1960s, however, portions of the schooner's lower hull were unearthed. Reportedly, initial residents of the condominium were given a desk pen mounted to a *Richmond* hull plank. Over 100 feet of anchor chain was also unearthed, which was destined to be utilized as a decoration in the garden area of the complex. It is unclear how much of the *Richmond* remains buried under the condominium, or if the majority of the wreck was removed during construction. The three-masted schooner *Richmond*, official number 206175, was built in 1909 at Sharptown, Maryland, and was 135.3 feet long, 26.5 feet wide, and 288 tons gross burden.

RIDGEWOOD

On May 9, 1888, the schooner *Ridgewood* burned to the water's edge on the St. Johns River below Jacksonville. At the time, the vessel was loaded with 40,000 feet of lumber, which was also lost in the fire; the cause of the fire was unknown. The *Annual Report of the Chief of Engineers, United States Army, to the Secretary of War for the Year 1905* reported on the wreck of the *Ridgewood*, stating "On March 27, 1905, an allotment of $4,300 was made from the indefinite appropriation made by Section 20 of the River and Harbor Act of March 3, 1899, for removal of wrecks of the schooner *Ridgewood* and the steam ferryboat *Commodore Barney* from the St. Johns River, the former near McGuire's Mill and the latter at Jacksonville."

RING WRECK

According to Meylach (1971), this site was named after a five-foot iron ring that is surrounded by coral encrusted ballast rock, iron pins, and scattered wreckage. This unidentified wreck resides in a 15-foot deep depression on Ajax Reef. In July 1956, Craig Hamilton found 18 cannon of Swedish origin at this site. The cannon, dated 1778 and 1779, were reportedly cast at foundries in Ehrendal and Överum, Sweden.

While pure speculation, perhaps this site is related to the sinking of a vessel observed by the H.M.S. *Kangaroo* in March 1821, which was documented in a March 17 dispatch from Nassau printed in *The Edinburgh Advertiser* on June 15, 1821:

> His Majesty's surveying brig *Kangaroo* was driven in from surveying the Florida Reef, where they had experienced the most dreadful weather for this last fortnight. On the morning of the 8th a large Danish ship was driven over the Florida Reef, and anchored inside; on the weather moderating, a boat was sent from the *Kangaroo* to her assistance; the Captain of the ship, however, refused any assistance which the boarding officer offered, and even refused Mr. Demayne's advice, and the offer of the pilot to anchor her in safety; the consequence of which was the loss, as it is supposed, of all the crew. Soon after the *Kangaroo's* boat returned, the gale increased to a severe storm, and in the evening a signal gun was observed from the ship, but no assistance whatever could be rendered during the night. On the following morning the ship was observed totally underwater, the masts gone, with the sea making a breach over her. In this situation great credit is due to Mr. Barnard, Master's Mate of the *Kangaroo*, and Mr. Sims, the pilot, who volunteered to go to the wreck, a distance of three miles, to save any of the crew that might be on the wreck, which they reached after going through a very heavy surf; but we are sorry to say, not one of the crew was found, and it is supposed they had all perished.

The tug *Rio Miami* as the *Brant* (Francis Palmer image, Dave Boone Collection).

RIO MIAMI

The *Rio Miami* was originally a tug built as the *Brant* for the Curtis Bay Towing Corporation. In March 1971, the tug was sold to Moran Towing and renamed *Barbara Moran*. The vessel initially worked in Moran's New York fleet, and later served with the company's Puerto Rico and Jacksonville operations. The *Barbara Moran* was eventually tied up at Jacksonville with a broken crank shaft, which prompted Moran to donate the tug for use as an artificial reef. Renamed *Rio Miami*, the vessel was scuttled in 65 feet of water off Key Biscayne on November 28, 1989. The tug is upright and intact, but listing approximately 45 degrees to her starboard side. Rebar stakes lead off the bow of the *Rio Miami* to the wreck of the nearby *Paraiso III*.

RIO YUNA

The reefer *Rio Yuna* (IMO number 5275105) was originally destined to be built as the *Mebsuta N.*, but for unknown reasons, was actually launched as the *Perregaux* on November 23, 1953, by *T. van Duijvendijk Scheepswerf N.V.* in Lekkerkerk, Netherlands. The freighter was 228.9 feet long, 33.1 feet wide, and 499 tons gross burden. In 1972, the vessel was sold to the Dominican Republic firm of *A. Martinez y Cia.* and renamed *Rio Yuna*. After sailing for two more decades, the refrigerated freighter *Rio Yuna* was laid up in 1993 and ultimately sunk as an artificial reef

The *Rio Yuna* at right, trailed by the tugs *Alexandra McAllister* and *Thomas H.* (Florida Fish and Wildlife Conservation Commission Artificial Reef Program).

on July 29, 1995, along with the tugs *Alexandra McAllister* and *Thomas H*. Resting in 83 feet of water off New Smyrna Beach, the wreck has been broken up a bit by storms since its scuttling.

RIVERSMITH

According to Volume 40 of *Hunt's The Merchants' Magazine and Commercial Review*, the ship *Riversmith*, Captain Davis, was totally lost on Pacific Reef on February 8, 1858, during a voyage from Liverpool for New Orleans. Vessel and cargo valued at $44,000; materials saved.

ROBALISS

On March 10, 1926, the *Sarasota Herald* reported the 60-foot long yacht *Robalish* [sic] had caught fire, burned, and sank several miles southeast of Cape Florida on March 9. Captain James Hawkins and nine passengers and crew safely reached shore just south of Cape Florida.

ROBERT AND SAMUEL

The *Daily Post* of December 11, 1725, stated the *Robert and Samuel*, Captain Austin, bound from Jamaica for London, was lost near Cape Florida.

ROBERT BRUCE

According to *The Sailor's Magazine and Naval Journal*, Volume 12, the "Brig *Robert Bruce*, of Baltimore, a regular trader between St. Augustine and Indian River, was lost at the latter place on January 6, 1839."

ROBERT EDMISTER

The 95-foot long Cape Class cutter WPB-95304 was built at the Coast Guard shipyard at Curtis Bay, Maryland, and commissioned into the U.S. Coast Guard on June 8, 1953. The Cape Class cutters were primarily a result of intensifying Cold War tensions and a need for shallow-draft anti-submarine vessels following World War II. As such, WPB-95304 was armed with both depth-charge racks and mousetrap launchers (rocket-propelled anti-submarine weapons), as well as standard mounted machine guns. In 1964, WPB-95304 was named U.S.C.G.C. *Cape Gull*. Her first two decades of service found the *Cape Gull* conducting law enforcement and search and rescue duties out of New York. After a major refit in 1977-1978, she was stationed at Miami and focused her attention on stemming the flood of illegal drugs being smuggled into the country. After close to another 10 years of service, the *Cape Gull* was decommissioned from the U.S. Coast Guard on May 15, 1988. The obsolete cutter was sold at auction to Dale Scutti in 1989, who planned to use the vessel as an artificial reef in memory of his friend, Fort Lauderdale real estate broker Robert Edmister, who passed away that year. On December 11, 1989, the *Robert Edmister* was scuttled in 70 feet of water off Fort Lauderdale. The wreck's aluminum superstructure has suffered over the years, with significant damage resulting from Hurricane Andrew in 1992. While portions of the wreck have collapsed, the *Edmister* still offers a pleasant excursion for novice divers.

The *Robert Edmister* as the U.S.C.G.C. *Cape Gull* (U.S. Coast Guard).

The wrecks of the *Wendy Rossheim* (*Our House III*) and *Paul L. Sherman* (*Salvager III*) rest a couple hundred feet away from the *Robert Edmister*, and can all be seen in a single dive.

ROBERT MORRIS

The July 26, 1853, issue of *The New York Times* published a July 24 dispatch from the steamship *Isabel* that stated, "The bark *Robert Morris*, from Cienfuegos, 11 days, bound to Philadelphia, ran ashore on the 22d, on Pelican Shoals – all hands were sick. The vessel was ashore when the *Isabel* left, with wreckers working hard alongside." Other reports stated the vessel ultimately bilged, so the *Robert Morris* was likely stripped and abandoned where she stranded off Fernandina.

ROBERTS

The *Roberts* sunk off Ambersand Beach just south of Sebastian Inlet during a hurricane in 1810 (possibly the October 1810 storm that also claimed the Spanish brig *African*, the Spanish ship *Union*, the ship *Caroline*, and the schooner *Triton*). Also known as the "Broken Anchor Wreck," the site was identified in after the bell of the *Roberts* was found by diver John Brandon (also cited as Carl Lazzeri). Wreckage of the *Roberts* is concentrated in a fairly compact area from just beyond the shoreline out to a depth of approximately 15 feet, and when originally found, divers uncovered five or six cast iron cannons, sheathing, well-preserved dead eyes, and keel timbers. An anchor and chain can also be found directly offshore of the main site, which was likely lost in an attempt to prevent the ship from grounding.

RODEO 25

On June 19, 1956, the *Rodeo 25* was launched as the *Nore* (IMO number 5225909) by Scheepsbouw Unie N.V. at Groningen, Netherlands. The new coaster was 214.7 feet long, 32.5 feet wide, displaced 495 tons gross, and was powered by a Klöckner Humboldt Deutz diesel engine. In 1969 the freighter was sold to William Coe and Company, Limited of Bridgetown, England, and renamed *Booker*

Rodeo 25 as *Windward Trader* (Broward County Artificial Reef Program).

Trojan. She was renamed *Caricom Adventurer* upon her sale to St. Godric's Shipping Company, Limited of Limassol, Cyprus in 1976. Later that same year, she was acquired by Carigulf Lines of Panama and operated as *Carigulf Venture*. Finally, in 1986, the freighter sailed as *Windward Trader* for Windward Shipping Corporation of Honduras. In 1990, the Honduran owners of the *Windward Trader* faced financial problems, forcing the sale of the freighter to the Pompano Beach Fishing Rodeo, which subsequently renamed her *Rodeo 25* in recognition of the Rodeo's 25th anniversary. The vessel was cleaned and sunk as an artificial reef in 130 feet of water off Fort Lauderdale on May 12, 1990, approximately 500 feet south of the tug *Mary St. Phillip* (*Mariner II*). Since her scuttling, the *Rodeo 25* has been impacted by numerous storms. The wreck lists significantly to starboard with her bow almost over on her side, and the hull forward of her stern superstructure is collapsing. Colorfully decorated with the invasive orange cup coral, the *Rodeo 25* typically hosts abundant marine life and offers an enjoyable diving experience.

View of the stern superstructure of the *Rodeo 25*.

ROLLING ON

On the morning of July 17, 2001, the shrimp trawler *Rolling On* grounded in the surf north of Vilano Beach near the St. Augustine Inlet. While newspaper reports state the fuel was removed from the vessel over fears the trawler would break up in the surf, it is unclear if the vessel became a total loss or was pulled off the beach.

RONALD B. JOHNSON

The *Ronald B. Johnson* was originally launched as the *Otto* on March 28, 1955, by *Scheepswerf Gebr. Van der Werf* at Deest, Netherlands for the Otto Shipping Company, Limited. The freighter was 226 feet long, 36.7 feet wide, and displaced 1,291 tons. For more information on this wreck, please refer to the entry for the *Corey N Chris*.

ROSA EPPINGER

The schooner *Rosa Eppinger* was built in May 1874 at Port Jefferson, New York. Owned by J.M. Bayles and Son, she was 135.7 feet long, 32.4 feet in beam, and 293 tons burden. A September 7, 1880, dispatch reported the loss of the schooner *Rosa Eppinger* approximately 16 miles north of Cape Canaveral during a storm en route from Cedar Keys to New York; first mate (also listed as the *Eppinger's* master) Joseph Bayles was lost in the wrecking.

ROSALIE

The *Rosalie* was a small steam launch built in September 1884 at Kissimmee, initially to serve as a dredge tender for the Disston Company. The sternwheel steamer was 41 feet long, 13 feet wide, and displaced approximately 15 tons. On June 25, 1893, while working for the Atlantic and Gulf Canal and Okeechobee Construction Company, the *Rosalie* sprang a leak and sank. She was abandoned in a canal near Lake Flirt, and her remains were visible for many years.

ROSALYN B. HUDGINS

In 1987, the freighter *Rosalyn B. Hudgins* was scuttled in 100 feet of water at the Harm's Ledge artificial reef site off Duval County by the Jacksonville Offshore Sport Fishing Club. This vessel may have originally been the freighter *Thuban*, official number 215823, which was built in 1917 by the Texas Steamship Company at Bath, Maine. Built for Texaco, the vessel was 96.5 feet long, 23 feet wide, and displaced 226 tons. Shortly after launching, the freighter was renamed *Texaco No. 125*, then *El Caribe* in 1936, *Elizabeth City* in 1941, and finally *Rosalyn B. Hudgins* in 1951. Additional documentation cited the *Rosalyn B. Hudgins* was converted into a fishing vessel with a reported length of 132.5 feet and a displacement of 276 tons, and was based out of Welaka.

ROSANDA

The *Rosanda* was a small yacht owned by Captain Nesbitt, which was blown ashore on Municipal Dock Four during the Great Miami Hurricane of September 18, 1926[199].

ROSE

On April 4, 1912, the *Rose*, official number 206492, a 19-ton gas screw vessel built in 1908, burned near Mandarin Point on the St. Johns River.

ROSEADA

Captain Clay Johnson built the *Roseada*, named after his daughters Albina Rose and Ada Roberts, in 1893 using

Photograph of the small steamer *Roseada* (Alfred H. Robson Collection).

the engines and boiler of the steamer *Cincinnati*. The craft was 57 feet in length and 14.7 feet in beam. In the early 1920s, the small steamer was used around Lake Okeechobee by the Kissimmee Island Cattle Company. The *Roseada* was damaged during the Great Miami Hurricane of September 18, 1926, and later abandoned at Kissimmee in 1928[200].

ROSEADALE TURO

Singer (1998) cites the total loss of the 612-ton Spanish bark *Roseadale Turo*, en route from St. Marys, Georgia, to Malaga, Spain, on May 21, 1876, on Pelican Shoals near Fernandina. However, I have been unable to find any information of a vessel by this name in *Lloyd's Register*, or of an 1876 wrecking event on Pelican Shoals.

ROSE MAHONEY

The five-masted schooner *Rose Mahoney*, official number 216507, was built in 1918 at Benicia, California, for Andrew J. Mahoney at a cost of $300,000. The 2,051-ton schooner had a length of 260.7 feet, a beam of 48.3 feet, and a depth of hold of 22.4 feet. In 1925, the schooner arrived at Miami with a cargo of three million feet of lumber to support the ongoing building boom, after which she sat idle off Bayfront Park. On September 18, 1926, the *Rose Mahoney* grounded on Bayfront Drive near the Peninsular and Oriental Steam Navigation Company docks during the Great Miami Hurricane. The *Rose Mahoney* became a tourist attraction, and a July 1928 newspaper report stated the stranded schooner, with its keel broken and listing slightly to port, hosted the annual convention for the Benevolent and Protective Order of Elks. The vessel was eventually scrapped in late 1928.

Towing the *Rossmerry* offshore for deployment as an artificial reef (Miami-Dade County Department of Environmental Resources Management).

ROSSMERRY

On October 21, 1985, approximately 300 pounds of explosives sent the 190-foot long, 25-foot wide freighter *Rossmerry* to the bottom off North Miami Beach. The wreck now rests in 240 feet of water. Little is known about the vessel's construction and service history.

ROXANNA

A map produced in 1851 by a hydrographic party under the command of Lieutenant John Rogers of the U.S. Navy entitled "Reconnaissance of Mosquito Inlet, Coast of Florida," charted the wreck of the *Roxanna*, as well as the steamer *Narragansett*. While I have been unable to find any particulars on the wrecking event, which apparently occurred just north of the inlet, this may be the 241-ton ship *Roxanna*, built at Maine in 1823. Documentation in the 1833 edition of *Lloyd's Register* indicates the ship was sheathed in copper, had a 14 foot draft when loaded, constructed of a single deck with beams, and her master was G. Miller; the vessel disappears from documentation after 1833.

ROYAL DESIRE

According to the *Bell's Weekly Messenger* of August 5, 1821, "The *Royal Desire*, Feuardant [sic], from Havannah [sic] to Havre, was lost early in June, near the Florida Coast. Crew saved, and arrived at Charleston 14th June." The *Royal Desire*, Captain J. Fuirdent, was a 177-ton brig built in 1814.

The *RSB-1* at Port Everglades (Broward County Artificial Reef Program).

RSB-1

The *RSB-1*, originally christened the *Leo Wood, Jr.* (IMO number 6701761) was built in 1965 by Bishop Marine Service at Port Aransas, Texas, for the oil industry, serving as an offshore crew and materials transport vessel. The 195-ton vessel had a 150 foot length and a 36 foot beam, and was later named the *A.B. Wood II*. In 1971, the U.S. Navy contracted with Tracor, Incorporated, who purchased the vessel and modified her equipment for the military's use. The *A.B. Wood II* gained fame in 1973 when she helped rescue two crew members from the *Johnson Sea Link* submersible, which had become entangled in the wreckage of the destroyer U.S.S. *Fred T. Berry*. As a result of this feat, and in recognition of her ability, she was added to the Supervisor of Salvage list of assets for the rescue of downed submersibles. She operated with a contract crew for the U.S. Navy until 1976, when they purchased the ship. Renamed the *Range Support Boat #1* (*RSB-1*), she operated with a civilian crew by the Naval Surface Warfare Center, Fort Lauderdale Detachment, in support of its underwater test and evaluation range. The *RSB-1* operated offshore of South Florida and near Andros Island, Bahamas, in support of underwater mine testing and development. The *RSB-1* reached the end of her useful career in 1992. She was donated to the Broward County Artificial Reef Program in September 1993. On April 23, 1994, explosives tore through the 160 foot long vessel and sent her to the bottom in three minutes. Dedicated to U.S. Navy veteran and Broward County Sheriff James Torgerson, the *RSB-1* now rests upright and intact in 115 feet of water.

The Norwegian ship *Ruby* aground off Quarantine Station, Fernandina (Florida State Archives).

Diver swimming around the port side of the *RSB-1's* bridge.

RUBY (1752)

In December 1752, the vessel *Sally* arrived in New York with a crewman from the ship *Ruby*, Captain Edwards, en route from Jamaica for Philadelphia, who reported "that his ship, by the violence of the wind, was drove ashore upon the coasts of Florida, the second of November, and bilged; that the next day they were boarded by two canoes full of Indians, who stript [sic] them, and used them very ill. That while the Indians were drinking in the cabin, the captain and his people made their escapes in the long boat. They then sail'd along shore till they got to Savannah Inlet in Georgia, and from thence to Charles Town, South Carolina[201]."

RUBY (1907A)

On January 15, 1907, the Norwegian ship *Ruby* stranded on a shoal off Fernandina. As a result of the damage sustained from the grounding and subsequent salvage, the wrecked vessel was later condemned and sold at auction. On April 11, 1907, the *Ruby* was sold back to its former master. The *Ruby* was built in 1878 at Church Point, Nova Scotia by J.D. Raymond, and was 208.8 feet long, 39.6 feet wide, and 1,418 tons burden.

RUBY (1907B)

The 17-ton steamer *Ruby* was built in 1880 at St. Simons Island, Georgia. On August 24, 1907, sometime between 10:00 and 11:00 p.m., the steamer caught fire while lying at the Davis Dock in Jacksonville and became a total loss. According to the *Annual Report of the Chief of Engineers, United States Army, to the Secretary of War for the Year 1908*, "The wreck of the steamer *Ruby* from the St. Johns River, Florida, near the westerly limits of the city of Jacksonville, was removed by Government snag and dredge boat *Florida*, December 27 to 30, 1907. A second wreck below the railroad bridge was reported a day or two after the *Ruby* was removed, and examination showed it to be a dangerous obstruction. This was likewise removed by the *Florida* January 3 to 6, 1908. The total cost of this work, including incidentals, was $400. The boiler removed from the wreck of the steamer *Ruby* was sold at auction for $50.50."

RUBY LEE

The 60-foot long excursion boat *Ruby Lee* sank at the mouth of the St. Johns River on July 4, 1941. Captain Elton Baitary stated the vessel "apparently sprang a starboard plank" shortly after the party left the pier at Mayport[202]. The 79-ton *Ruby Lee*, built in 1924, sank approximately 800 feet from shore in about 30 feet of water near the south jetty. The 47 passengers and 6 crewmen safely reached shore after spending more than an hour in the water. Due to her sinking location, the wreck of the *Ruby Lee* was likely removed as a hazard to navigation.

RUBY W

The 16-ton gas vessel *Ruby W*, official number 209197, burned at Orangedale on August 4, 1912.

RUSS

The 60-foot converted submarine chaser *Russ*, owned by Duval County Sheriff W.H. Dowling and used by him in chasing rumrunners off the Florida coast, sank 10 miles off Mayport on March 27, 1924, after an explosion ripped through the engine room. Sheriff Dowling and members of the crew left the *Russ* in a dory, which capsized soon after they had started shoreward. For two hours the survivors were tossed about by the waves until rescued by the pilot boat *Meta*, which had put out to sea when the explosion was heard. Three members of the crew were burned, one seriously, though all reached shore safely. Newspaper articles stated the *Russ* was built for the Russian government in 1917 and was purchased by Sheriff Dowling after the war when the vessel had been taken over by the government.

RUXTON #2

On December 28, 1960, the 97-ton vessel *Ruxton #2*, built in 1934, reportedly foundered approximately six miles east of Port Everglades.

RYE GALLEY

The August 18, 1774, edition of the *London Evening Post* printed, "The ship *Rye Galley*, Robert Hunter, master, from Honduras, with mahogany and logwood for Glasgow, was wrecked near Cape Florida on the 20th of last month, the vessel and cargo entirely lost. The master and part of the crew were taken up by a New England schooner bound for Nantucket; the mate and six others got to Savannah in Georgia, in the ship's long boat."

Exploring the wreck of the *Rodeo 25*.

S. & W. WELSH

On August 28, 1871, *The New York Herald* reported the 382-ton brig *S. & W. Welsh*, built in Wilmington, Delaware in March 1867, wrecked 15 miles south of Cape Canaveral while en route from Cienfuegos, Cuba, to Philadelphia. Her cargo of sugar was washed ashore, and Captain J.R. Watson was drowned.

S.E. VINSON

On November 3, 1849, a fire broke out in the hold of the schooner *S.E. Vinson* while sailing from St. Marks for New York[203]. When the flames where initially observed, the vessel was approximately 90 miles southeast of St. Marys, Georgia. The schooner was able to reach Amelia Island by the evening of November 4, at which time the fire was bursting out at every seam; the vessel and cargo were a total loss.

S.S. LUCAS

According to *The Sailor's Magazine and Naval Journal*, Volume 25, the schooner *S.S. Lucas*, from Charleston, South Carolina for Havana, Cuba, with the U.S. mail, wrecked on September 12, 1852, approximately 21 miles south of St. Augustine.

S.S. MILLS

The August 26, 1837, issue of the *Connecticut Courant* included an August 9 dispatch relating the loss of the schooner *S.S. Mills*, which foundered in seven fathoms of water just north of the Florida-Georgia border off Jekyll Island during a gale on August 6. The 90-ton schooner was en route from St. Augustine to Charleston, South Carolina, and of the 15 souls on board, only one survived the sinking.

SAGINAW

According to *The Monthly Nautical Magazine and Quarterly Review*, Volume 1, the brig *Saginaw*, of Gouldsboro, went ashore at the Nassau River on December 14, 1854, and afterwards was condemned.

SAINTE ANNE D'AURAY

The 110-foot long former French trawler *Sainte Anne d'Auray* (abbreviated as *Ste. Anne d'Auray*) was sunk in 70 feet of water off Miami on March 28, 1986. The wreck of the *Tarpoon* rests approximately 1,200 feet to the north.

SAINT GEORGE

The August 11, 1841, edition of the *London Nonconformist* reported the destruction of the ship *Saint George*, which claimed 17 lives. The article stated, "Intelligence of the loss of this splendid ship, the property of Messrs. Fletcher and Sons, was received by the underwriters at Lloyd's on Tuesday. The calamity happened on the night of Thursday, the 17th of June last, on the Florida shores, and all on board, excepting two seamen and the cabin boy, perished. From the statement of the survivors which has been received, it appears that the *Saint George* was on her voyage to New Orleans, having left London on the 29th of April last. The ship and cargo are valued at 12,000£." This may possibly be the 665-ton ship *Saint George*, Captain Weakner, built in 1836 at New Brunswick, Canada.

SALLY (1773)

The vessel *Sally*, Captain Mathews, bound from Lisbon, Portugal to South Carolina, was lost February 22, 1773, in a snow storm near St. Augustine, and all the crew except the mate perished in the wrecking event.

SALLY (1779)

On a voyage from Jamaica for England in 1779, the *Sally*, Captain Hatton, was reportedly lost on the East Coast of Florida[204].

SALLY (1804)

The sloop *Sally*, Captain Burlbutt, en route from New York to St. Augustine, wrecked around November 1, 1804, on the Florida coast south of Indian River Inlet. On the same day, the British cartel ship *L'Athenaise*, from Jamaica to France with 200 French prisoners on board, was driven on shore; and but for the circumstance of the *Sally* being laden with provisions, the whole of the people on board the cartel likely would have perished, as there were no inhabitants within some hundred miles of them[205].

SALLY BROWN

The brig *Sally Brown*, official number 23236, was built in November 1865 at Newburyport, Massachusetts, by John T. Fillmore. Owned by J.S. Emery and Company, she registered a length of 127 feet, a beam of 29.5 feet, and a displacement of 426 tons. In September 1878, while on a voyage from Pensacola for Brazil, the *Sally Brown* encountered a hurricane, eventually resulting in the crew abandoning their ship when the steamer *Carondelet* arrived to assist the distressed vessel. On September 11, the abandoned brig was reportedly sighted at latitude 29° 40' north, longitude 80° 40' west (approximately 35 nautical miles southeast of St. Augustine), dismasted and waterlogged, with the "sea making a clean breast over her."

SALUDA

On July 29, 1836, *The Charleston Courier* reported the schooner *Saluda* beached nine miles north of the Mosquito Inlet Bar during a storm. She was later sold where she lay for five dollars.

SALVAGER III

The *Salvager III* was originally built as a shrimp trawler by Capell Boat Works at Freeport Texas. Reportedly, she was 55.5 feet long, 19 feet wide, and displaced 65 tons gross. The trawler was later converted into a treasure salvage vessel. After she outlived her usefulness, the vessel, renamed the *Paul L. Sherman*, was sunk in 70 feet of water as an artificial reef 200 feet north of the *Robert Edmister* on August 18, 1991.

SALVOR II

The 53-ton scow *Salvor II*, official number 167906, built at Miami in 1920, reportedly foundered 26 miles off Port Everglades on September 27, 1931.

SAMA

The Petrovski Shipbuilding Company of Reval (present-day Tallinn), Estonia launched the four-masted auxiliary schooner *Harjumaa* in 1922. The new schooner was 167 feet long and 28.5 feet wide. In 1927, the vessel was purchased by N. Geraci and Company, which removed the rigging and converted her to a 567-ton motor vessel named *Louis Geraci*. The Standard Fruit Company acquired the freighter in 1932, and she was renamed *Sama*. In 1938, the vessel was laid up for a short period before being sold to the Bahama Shipping Company, Limited of Bluefields, Nicaragua in 1939. On May 3, 1942, the *Sama* was en route from Baracoa, Cuba to Jacksonville with a cargo of bananas when *U-506*, *Kapitänleutnant* Erich Würdemann, torpedoed the freighter as approximate latitude 25° 4' north, longitude 79° 45' west (approximately 20 nautical miles east of Fort Lauderdale); her crew of 14 survived the attack. It is unclear how far north the vessel drifted before ultimately sinking.

SAMAY

The 56-ton vessel *Samay*, built in 1926, reportedly burned at Miami Beach on October 21, 1961.

SAMSON

The 313-ton sidewheel tug *Samson* (also appears as *Sampson*) was built in 1856 at Savannah, Georgia. In 1861, she was purchased by the Confederate States of America, whereupon she was armed as a gunboat with a 32-pounder smoothbore gun and a 12-pounder gun. After being damaged during an engagement at Fort Pulaski, Georgia in January 1862, the C.S.S. *Samson* served as a receiving ship at Savannah for the next two years. In early December 1864, the *Samson* was considerably damaged during an expedition to destroy a railroad bridge over the Savannah River, after which she was later taken up the river to Augusta, where she remained until the end of the war. *The Sailor's Magazine and Naval Journal*, Volume 42, reported the wrecking of the tug *Samson* off Indian River, Florida, in October 1870. Other sources cite the loss of the vessel in February 1870 approximately 13 miles south of Indian River Inlet.

SAMUEL BOLTON

The *Samuel Bolton* was originally built as a centerboard schooner in Milton, Delaware in 1854. The 150-ton schooner wrecked near St. Augustine on November 13, 1857, while on a voyage from Boston to Jacksonville[206]. While the crew and most of the cargo was saved, the vessel, valued at $7,000, was a total loss.

SAMUEL FAUNCE

The 87-ton tug *Samuel Faunce*, official number 215909, was built in 1912 at South Shields, England, as the *Romano*, and was 81.5 feet long and 17.6 feet wide. On January 29, 1920, the *Samuel Faunce* disappeared during a storm off the Florida coast while en route from Wilmington, North Carolina, to Key West; no trace of the vessel or its crew was ever found.

SAMUEL OTIS

On January 4, 1859, *The New York Times* reported the brig *Samuel Otis* struck heavily on the Fernandina Bar while entering the inlet, sprung a leak, and was run ashore on Amelia Island to prevent its sinking. A subsequent survey determined the vessel would be a total loss. The 257-ton *Samuel Otis* was built in Belfast, Maine, in 1855, and valued at $8,000.

SAN CAYETANO

On July 21, 1739, the 24-gun, fifth-rate frigate *San Cayetano*, Captain Don Lorenzo Villafranca, appeared off St. Augustine in distress. The bow of the frigate, which was captured by the Spanish as a war prize in 1734, was stoved in and the *San Cayetano* was taking on water. Assistance from St. Augustine unloaded the vessel of her crew, supplies, and armament, however, the *San Cayetano* ultimately sank off St. Augustine.

SAN IGNACIO

According to Marx (1979), the 300-ton, 22-gun *San Ignacio* wrecked on the Florida coast along with the 340-ton *Santa Maria de la Limpia Concepción* during a storm in 1571. The few survivors eventually reached St. Augustine.

SAN MARTIN

The *San Martin* was a small, 300-ton galleon, 70.8 feet in length along the keel and 26.5 feet in breadth, which was built at Vizcaya, Spain around 1614[207]. In 1618, the *San Martin* departed the Honduran port of Trujillo with a cargo of valuable indigo dye and other cargo, eventually joining the *Tierra Firme flota* at Havana in September in preparation for the return voyage to Spain. On October 10, 1618, word reached the garrison at St. Augustine that two Spanish vessels wrecked near Fort Pierce Inlet. The governor dispatched assistance, which discovered 53 survivors of the *San Martin*; it is unknown if there were any survivors of the other vessel, believed to be a small *nao*. The wreck of the *San Martin* was discovered by Kip Wagner in the 1960s, and became known as the "Green Cabin Wreck." Initially believed to be part of the 1715 fleet, analyses of recovered artifacts revealed that the "Green Cabin Wreck" actually was lost almost 100 years earlier. Aside from coins that were dated no later than 1618, four bronze cannon were also recovered, one of which was dated 1594. In 1992, diver Mike Mayer recovered a rare astrolabe from the *San Martin* wreckage scatter, which was dated 1593. In contrast to the widely dispersed wreckage of the 1715 vessels, a section of the *San Martin* representing approximately half of the lower hull structure remains intact under the sand. Six iron cannon still remain at the site, which rests in a depression in the reef line approximately 700 feet off the beach. Approximately 1,000 feet south of the *San Martin* is "Corrigan's Wreck," believed to be the *Nuestra Señora de La Regla*. The two sites are actually intermixed, complicating interpretation of artifacts recovered in this vicinity. Additionally, the *Spring of Whitby* and *Roberts* are located just to the north of the *San Martin*, both of which add to the "shipwreck soup" found along this area of the Florida coast.

SAN MIGUEL

The 180-ton *nao San Miguel* was 83 feet in length, 22.5 feet in beam, and was armed with 22 cannon. Owned by Captain-General Don Antonio de Echeverz y Zubiza and sailing with the combined *Los Galeones* and *Nueva España* fleet, the *San Miguel* and her crew of 62 disappeared off the Florida coast early on the morning of July 31, 1715, during the brunt of a massive hurricane. While there is a theory the *San Miguel* eventually wrecked north of Cape Canaveral, to date, no trace of the vessel has been discovered.

SAN MIGUEL DE ARCHANGEL

On July 12, 1987, Palm Beach County lifeguard Peter Leo swam over an area off Jupiter where local surfers Ralph Rossini and Bob Riggs observed a dark object on the bottom. Diving down to determine what it was, he found himself "...staring face-to-face with an old object – a cannon[208]." Traces of a wreck, covered for eons by the shifting sands, were found just south of the Jupiter Inlet jetty off the public beach. Investigating the site, Peter and his friends recovered over 1,200 silver coins, several gold coins, and an 80-pound silver bar that had a mint date of 1652. While not positively confirmed, all evidence pointed to the conclusion that the fortunate lifeguard had found the wreck of the *San Miguel de Archangel*.

The *San Miguel de Archangel* was a fast, small, but well-armed ship known as an *aviso*. As an alternative to large, heavily armed *flotas*, the Spanish throne employed these unescorted ships to outrun the marauding Royal Navy. Ten days after arriving from Cartagena in December 1659, Captain Juan de Ortalaca quietly sailed out of Havana harbor and past the fortress of El Morro. Along with 120 passengers, the ship was loaded to the gunwales with treasure desperately needed by the Spanish throne, its colonial empire teetering on the brink of ruin. By dawn on the following morning, the *aviso* was sailing smoothly through the Florida Straits. In the early evening, the winds began to freshen – the first ominous signs of a tropical storm building to the east. The *Archangel* was prepared for the storm, as lanterns were lit, hatches battened down, and the sails reefed. With the vessel well south of Cape Canaveral and too far from Havana, Captain Ortalaca was forced to ride the storm out at sea. The full force of the gale crashed down on the vessel late at night, as the crew were confronted with screaming winds and crashing whitewater that swept across the deck. Soon, the ominous sound of rolling surf was heard above the clamor of the storm. The *San Miguel de Archangel* was headed towards the beach.

The *aviso* quickly became grounded on a sandbar just off the beach. Shortly thereafter, a boat was launched in a foolish attempt to reach the beach. Instantly it was shattered against the hull of the *Archangel*, its five passengers drowned. The massive seas pounded the hull of the ship without reprieve. Seams parted, and timbers buckled. Dramatically, a large section of the foredeck was torn loose along with 60 terrified passengers and carried away from the ship. Moments later, it was slammed against a rock ledge, throwing its cannon, deck planking, and passengers into the surf. By dawn of December 8, the *San Miguel de Archangel* was decimated. Only 34 passengers and crew survived the event.

The wreck, lying near the Jupiter Inlet, is buried under almost 20 feet of sand in places. Dredging operations in the inlet deposited much of this sand over the wreck. Salvage work was conducted for several years, though the main portion of the wreck could not be found. In 1995, however, a dredge working on the public beach nourishment project began to pick up large quantities of ballast stones approximately 3,000 feet off the beach, revealing a large portion of the wreck. Over the years, numerous artifacts have been recovered from the wreck, including over 10,000 silver coins, 100 gold coins, silverware, navigational tools, cannon balls, and several cannon.

SAN NICOLÁS

According to Marx (1987), the 200-ton *nao San Nicolás*, Captain Juan Christoval, en route from Colombia to Spain, wrecked near Fort Pierce in 1551.

SAN RAPHAEL

The *San Raphael* (also appears as *San Rapael* and *San Rafael*) was a vessel sunk in 280 feet of water off Miami in 1980 by Pflueger Marine Taxidermy. As this reefing was conducted before Miami-Dade County had established a formal artificial reef program, specific information on this vessel is apparently unavailable, and it is unclear if *San Raphael* was the actual name of the vessel when in service.

SANIBEL

The 44-ton gas yacht *Sanibel*, official number 116386, built in 1890 at Brooklyn, burned at Miami in March 1919.

SANTA ANNA

According to the May 14, 1815, issue of *Bell's Weekly Messenger*, "The *Santa Anna*, – —-, from Bermuda, was lost 7th March, off Amelia Island."

SANTA CLAUSE

The small freighter *Santa Clause* was built in 1922 at Daytona and was 58.6 feet long, 18 feet wide, and displaced 78 tons. On March 30, 1927, the *Santa Clause* reportedly burned at St. Augustine.

SANTA MARIA

The *Santa Maria*, Captain Wicks, from St. Augustine to Havana, Cuba, was reported lost on the St. Augustine Bar in the July 15, 1790, issue of the *British Evening Post*.

SANTA MARIA DE LA LIMPIA CONCEPCIÓN

According to Marx (1979), the 340-ton *Santa Maria de la Limpia Concepción* wrecked on the Florida coast along with the 300-ton, 22-gun *San Ignacio* during a storm in 1571.

SANTA RITA

The *Santa Rita* was an approximately 200-foot long freighter scuttled in 245 feet of water approximately one mile offshore of the *Almirante* to serve as an artificial reef on July 16, 1976. The *Santa Rita* had been a derelict on the Miami River for several years until money donated by Auto Marine Salvage owner Palto Cox allowed the vessel to be stripped and deployed off Elliott Key.

The *Santa Rita* sinking stern first off Elliott Key (George Detrio).

SANTA ROZA

On October 30, 1814, *Bell's Weekly Messenger* reported, "The *Santa Roza*, — —-, from Liverpool, is lost on Amelia Island Bar." This wreck is most likely the 202-ton brig *Santa Roza* of Boston, Massachusetts, built in 1806 and which reportedly sailed between Cork, England, and Amelia Island.

SANTÍSIMA TRINIDAD

The *Santísima Trinidad*, part of a fleet of vessels sailing back to Spain in 1626, was lost off the central east coast of Florida. She reportedly sank so slowly that the passengers and crew could be saved by other vessels. Also lost in the same storm event was the 480-ton galleon, *El Espiritu Santo el Mayor*.

SANTO CRISTO DE MARACAIBO

The September 1705 wrecking of the frigate *Santo Cristo de Maracaibo* was documented in a January 1706 letter from Governor José de Zúñiga y la Cerda to Spain, stating:

> The ship named the *Santo Cristo de Maracaibo*, having been the first to finish discharging its cargo (at St. Augustine), did not appear to want to wait for its companion and departed to continue its voyage. At a short distance, a storm hit it from the east and it was lost on this coast eight leagues to the south of this Presidio. At the same time, three bands of enemies invaded. Your Excellency sees how I have found myself with the enemies and the supplies (offloaded from the *Maracaibo*) outside and with a storm. If they would have arrived twenty days earlier, the discharge could have been made in good weather and with the same, they could have continued their voyage. They complained greatly about the delays and the long demurrage that Don Antonio de Landeche made them make in Panzacola [sic], Apalachee, and Havana. Here they had none because they were only delayed eleven days on the discharge and some more which was because of the storms.

SANTO CRISTO DE SAN ROMAN

As the combined *Nueva España* and *Los Galeones* fleet left Havana harbor on the morning of July 24, 1715, the *San Roman*, owned by Don Juan de Eguilaz, brought up the rear to guard the fleet as Captain-General Don Juan Esteban de Ubilla's *almiranta*. Aboard the *almiranta* was Admiral Don Francisco Salmon, who served as second in command of the *flota*. The 450-ton galleon was heavily armed, boasting 54 cannon. The holds of the *Santo Cristo de San Roman* contained the second largest amount of treasure within the combined 1715 fleet. Her manifest included 2,687,416 pesos in silver and gold; 53 chests of worked silver; 14 chests of Chinese porcelain; 728 leather bags of cochineal; 1,702 leather bags and chests of indigo; 139 sheets of copper; 682 tanned leather hides; 26 chests of pottery; 48 chests of vanilla beans; balsam; liquid amber; chocolate; oaxaca; cochineal; Brazilwood; and sarsaparilla. As the wind and waves increased on July 29, the fleet became separated in the darkness. Every ship fought to remain afloat.

Spanish galleon (Florida State Archives).

According to correspondence from Admiral Salmon after the disaster, the growing hurricane broke the *San Romans's* mainmast and shattered the rudder and tiller, and the bow of the *almiranta* was stoved in. Salmon dropped anchor in 60 feet of water in an attempt to keep the vessel off the beach, but both cables quickly parted under the massive strain and he soon found himself cast up on the reef in 20 feet of water. The massive seas lifted the doomed *San Roman* up and then smashed her back down onto the unmerciful reef, splitting the ship into three sections. As the vessel fell apart, cannon were scattered across the second reef line and over a 200-foot area. The bulk of the galleon sunk, while the bow and stern washed up on the beach, which fortunately resulted in most onboard the *San Roman* surviving, including Admiral Salmon; however, the wrecking of the *almiranta* still claimed 82 lives. After assessing the full extent of the damage from the storm, Salmon dispatched a launch to Cuba to notify the governor of the disaster. The *Santo Cristo de San Roman* is believed to be a wreck south of Sebastian Inlet locally known as the "Cabin Wreck," which was named after salvor Kip Wagner's cabin that was located on the beach opposite the site. The wreck site covers a large area in a swath with a slight southward bias as one runs from west to east: five cannon from the former galleon can be found amidst the first reef line approximately 150 feet offshore and just north of the McLarty Treasure Museum in Vero Beach; two anchors can be found just south of the museum again on the first reef line in shallow water; a cluster of 11 cannon can be found on the second reef line approximately 300 feet offshore and slightly south of the anchors; near the third reef line and directly offshore of the cannon cluster – approximately 1,500 feet from the beach – several more cannon, as well as ballast stone and a portion of the ship's keel can be found spread out at a depth of 22-25 feet of water; fanning out offshore from here in deeper water rest numerous kedge anchors used in the futile attempt to prevent the *San Roman's* wrecking. Due to the proximity of Sebastian Inlet, visibility can be poor in this area.

SANTO ROSARIO

About 4:30 a.m. on July 23, 1984, the 70-foot-long trawler *Santo Rosario* capsized and sank while approximately 35 nautical miles east of New Smyrna Beach fishing for calico scallops. Three crewmembers were rescued by the nearby trawler *Captain Ed*, but a fourth crewmember sleeping below deck went down with the vessel and drowned. The sinking of the *Santo Rosario* was facilitated by the operating procedures in the fishery. Typically, shrimp trawlers would store their catch below deck in the hold. When operating in the calico scallop fishery, however, the catch would be stowed on deck in massive piles due to the unloading protocol of the seafood processor at Port Canaveral. This practice would dramatically affect a vessel's stability by dangerously raising the vessel's center of gravity. At the time of her loss, the *Santo Rosario* had a pile of scallops eight feet high on her deck. A sudden shift to port when loading the port net caused the pile of scallops to slide, exacerbating the vessel's list and ultimately causing the trawler to capsize and sink in 150 feet of water.

SARAH

The November 12, 1824, edition of *The Edinburgh Advertiser* stated, "Accounts have been received at Savannah of the loss of the British brig *Sarah*, Rowe, on the beach near St. Augustine. The crew had perished."

SARAH JANE (1854)

The schooner *Sarah Jane*, of Bristol, Rhode Island, en route from Boston, Massachusetts, for Jacksonville, drifted ashore south of St. Johns Light and proved a total loss in April 1854[209].

SARAH JANE (1981)

In September 1981, the 65-foot long wooden-hulled shrimp trawler *Sarah Jane* (also cited as *Sara Jane*) was sunk in 95 feet of water to become Miami-Dade County's first official artificial reef. The wreck of the *Sarah Jane* rests approximately 300 feet east of the *D.E.M.A. Trader*.

SARAH MARY

The British sloop *Sarah Mary* was captured off Mosquito Inlet on June 26, 1864, with a cargo of nine bales of cotton; the vessel, being unseaworthy, was subsequently sunk after her cargo was unloaded[210].

SARAH R. THOMAS

The 197-ton schooner *Sarah R. Thomas*, official number 22567, was built in October 1865 at Haddam, Connecticut. On July 12, 1878, the *Thomas*, Captain J. Cole, was en route from New York for Jacksonville when she stranded during a storm approximately a half-mile south of the St. Johns River Bar; some of the cargo was saved.

SATISFACTION

The 30-ton vessel *Satisfaction*, built in 1924, reportedly foundered at Fort Pierce on April 27, 1926.

SAURWALT'S WRECK

In 1966, William C. Saurwalt discovered a shipwreck site just south of the Volusia-Brevard County line. Resting in shallow water close to the surf zone, divers uncovered silver coins, iron spikes and fittings, ballast rocks, brass and copper sheet fragments, a small brass padlock with a keyhole cover stamped "U.S.," an anchor, five cannon, a telescope, and other assorted wreckage. The latest date on any of the coins found in this area was 1821. Saurwalt recovered one of the cannon, which was a small one-pounder with the wooden carriage still attached. The British Broad Arrow was found on top of the barrel, indicating it was once British Royal Navy property.

SAVANNAH (1924)

According to a January 7, 1934, article in *The Miami News*, the *Savannah* was a two-masted schooner, which caught fire at sea and was towed into Miami Harbor in 1924. Due to the damage sustained in the fire, however, she was deemed unworthy of repair. The schooner later sunk in Biscayne Bay opposite the docks of the Peninsular and Oriental Steam Navigation Company, and only its ribs remained visible sticking out of the mud in 1934.

SAVANNAH (1964)

The 26-ton fishing vessel *Savannah*, built in 1942, stranded one mile north of Sebastian Inlet on October 23, 1964.

SAXONY

The ship *Saxony*, Captain Chase, from Boston, Massachusetts for Matanzas, Cuba with a cargo of pine, went ashore above Cape Florida (also reported as near Hillsboro Inlet) on April 8, 1854. As documented in *The Sailor's Magazine and Naval Journal*, Volume 26, Captain Chase "reported having calm weather in the Gulf, and not being able to stem the eastern set, ran in and anchored close under the land. Very soon after a breeze springing up from off the land, set sail and weighed anchor. Before way was got on the ship, the under current and ground swell caught her and bore her directly on the beach." The salvage of the *Saxony* brought wreckers $1,952.

SCALLOP KING

The *Scallop King* is the wreck of a broken down trawler resting in approximately 110 feet of water 19 nautical miles east of Port Canaveral. Little else is known about this wreck.

SCARLETT O'HARA

The *Scarlett O'Hara* was a 53-foot long, mahogany-hulled luxury motor yacht valued at $50,000, which was owned by millionaire tobacco heir Richard J. Reynolds. On February 24, 1955, while on a leisurely cruise from Nassau, Bahamas, a blast ripped through the yacht approximately five miles off Government Cut. According to Reynolds, "We had the lights of Miami well in view when wham…I found myself on the deck. The blast knocked me off my feet[211]." Captain Arthur T. Kyle, the cruiser's skipper, was pushing himself up from the deck when Reynolds spotted smoke coming from the hatch to the engines and ordered everyone over the side. After quickly grabbing a few items, Captain Kyle and Mr. and Mrs. Reynolds pushed away from the sinking vessel in the yacht's dinghy and headed towards the glow of Miami Beach. While the dinghy overturned in the crashing surf, all three made it ashore unhurt. Reynolds notified the U.S. Coast Guard of the incident, and the yacht was found several hours later with only its bow above water. While reports indicated an attempt would be made to tow in the drifting hulk of the burned yacht, it is unclear if this was successfully accomplished or if the *Scarlett O'Hara* sank offshore.

SCHOONER BALLAST WRECK

Resting in shallow water within Biscayne National Park, the "Schooner Ballast Wreck" is an unidentified sailing vessel dominated by an encrusted ballast pile. This is a fairly large wreck site, and the ballast pile rises to within six feet of the surface. The ballast mound is in two distinct sections: a 75-foot long main pile and a secondary, smaller pile connected by an exposed portion of keel. It appears the vessel was constructed with square, iron spikes. Little else is known about this wreck.

SCOTCHIE

The 35-ton *Scotchie*, built in 1949, foundered off Fort Lauderdale in March 1969.

SCOTT AND GREG

At 5:15 a.m. on December 2, 1991, the shrimp trawler *Joyce and Rose* rammed and sank the 73-foot long fellow shrimp trawler *Scott and Greg* off St. Johns County[212]. The collision ripped 10 to 12 feet of planking from the stern and port side of the wooden-hulled *Scott and Greg*, which sank in 45 feet of water 20 minutes after the incident. The fiberglass *Joyce and Rose* was practically undamaged.

SEA BIRD

The 81-ton vessel *Sea Bird*, built in 1918, reportedly foundered near the entrance to Port Canaveral on May 22, 1927.

SEABOARD

According to the 1899 *Annual Report of the Supervising Inspector-General, U.S. Steamboat-Inspection Service to the Secretary of Commerce and Labor*, on August 23, 1898, the towing steamer *Seaboard*, while lying at her dock at Pilot Town (Mayport), caught fire and was totally destroyed. There was no loss of life associated with the mysterious fire; the steamer was valued at $6,000, but was only insured for $3,000.

SEA BOY

The 31-ton *Sea Boy*, built in 1949, stranded near the Ponce de Leon Inlet jetties on December 9, 1969. It is unclear if the vessel was successfully salvaged, or if she broke apart to become a total loss.

SEA BREEZE

On January 17, 1948, the 32-ton *Sea Breeze*, built in 1944, reportedly foundered off False Cape, north of Cape Canaveral.

SEA EAGLE

The *Sea Eagle* was built in 1953 by the Diesel Engine Sales Company (DESCO Marine, Incorporated). The standard DESCO wooden-hulled shrimp trawler was 67 feet in length and approximately 99 tons gross displacement. The *Sea Eagle* stranded just east of the St. Augustine jetties on November 11, 1968.

Concrete culverts resting adjacent to the inverted hull of the *Sea Emperor*.

SEA EMPEROR

The *Sea Emperor* was a 171-foot long, 43-foot wide barge sunk as an artificial reef on October 3, 1991, as mitigation for reef damage caused by the Great Lakes Dock and Dredge Company in 1988. The barge was loaded with approximately 1,500 tons of concrete culverts and deployed in 70 feet of water off Boca Inlet. During the sinking, the barge flipped, spilling the concrete culverts off into the sand. The barge turtled and came to rest next to the pile, producing a more interesting reef site to explore. Divers can follow a line of rubble from the *Sea Emperor* to the wreck of the freighter *United Caribbean*, which was scuttled nearby.

A resident moray eel looms out from the wreck of the *Sea Emperor*.

SEA FARER

The 67-foot long fishing vessel *Sea Farer*, built in 1952, went down a half-mile offshore False Cape, near Cape Canaveral, on October 21, 1952. Another vessel, the *John Wayne*, saw the *Sea Farer* up-end and sink amid the whitecaps, though a search of the area for the three crewmen (also reported as seven men onboard) proved fruitless.

SEA FLOWER

The Rhode Island brigantine *Sea Flower*, Captain John Bristow, wrecked near Cape Florida on July 10, 1751, during its return trip from the Bay of Honduras[213]. Captain Bristow and his crew took to their long boat and reached Charleston, South Carolina 21 days later.

SEAFLOWER

The July 13, 1769, issue of the *Virginia Gazette* included a June 23 dispatch from Philadelphia, which stated, "By Capt. Kemp we also learn that the sloop *Seaflower*, Capt. Whipton, from the Bay of Honduras for this port, was drove ashore the 8th of May, on Cape Florida, where the vessel is lost; but all her sails, rigging, and part of her cargo, and people, were saved, who were brought off by some wreckers and carried to Providence."

SEAFOOD WRECK

This unidentified wreck, also known as the "Centerboard Schooner Wreck," rests in the turbid water off St. Augustine Inlet. Preliminary investigation revealed the wooden hull structure was largely buried under the sediment, and the approximate 90-foot long site was dominated by two large piles comprised of cylindrical cut stone. Other features found at the site include a capstan, a large pile of anchor chain, and iron pipes. A second nearby site to the east, the "Iron Box Site," may represent another portion of this wreck.

SEA INSPECTOR

The *Sea Inspector*, official number 506228, was a harbor tug built for the U.S. Navy in 1942 at Chicago, Illinois. She was 61.5 feet in length, 17.1 feet in beam, and 48 tons gross burden. In April 1998, she was sunk in 70 feet of water to serve as an artificial reef along with the *Sun Mariner* and *Marsha T.*, just north of the Palm Beach County line.

SEA MIST II

The *Sea Mist II* (IMO number 6515722), built by the shipyard of *A.B. Ekensbergs Varv* at Stockholm, Sweden in 1965 as the *Don Carlos*, was a 265.4-foot long, 44.3-foot wide general cargo RO-RO ("Roll On – Roll Off") vessel. The 2,353-ton freighter was sold in 1973 to Nils Hugo Sand of Oslo, Norway and renamed *Nopal Sand*; in 1977 she was acquired by *Empresa Azucarera Montelimar S.A.*, which was a sugar company controlled by Nicaraguan dictator Anastasio Somoza, and renamed *Carla*; later, the vessel was sold to Trafford Holdings, Limited of the Cayman Islands and operated as the *Aracely* in 1980; after her sale to Caribbean Tankers, Incorporated of Panama in 1988, she sailed as the *Aries Navigator*; in 1990, she traded hands to Liquid Cargo, Incorporated of Belize, whereupon she was renamed *Rosemere*; the freighter was named *Bayside* after her purchase by Bayside Marine, Incorporated in 1992; and, finally, the American company C.P. Cargo and Shipping bought the well-used vessel in 1995, and renamed her *Sea Mist II*. Unfortunately, due to financial issues, the *Sea Mist II* did not operate long for her new

Sea Mist II sailing as the *Don Carlos* (Hans-Wilhelm Delfs).

owners. The neglected vessel, rusting along the Miami River, was finally impounded by the U.S. Coast Guard due to safety and pollution violations. At a cost of $75,000, Schurger Salvage and Diving, Incorporated acquired, cleaned, and ultimately scuttled the freighter off Jupiter on May 25, 2001. The *Sea Mist II* now rests upright and intact in 215 feet of water oriented with her bow facing southward, though portions of the large vessel rise almost 90 feet off the bottom.

SEARCHER

A May 17, 1989, *Miami Herald* article detailed the strange fate of the 50-foot trawler *Searcher*. The vessel, riddled with bullet holes and circling aimlessly six miles off Boynton Beach, had apparently been stolen from Delray Harbor Marina the evening before. It was thought the thieves opted to scuttle the vessel, dousing it with gas and shooting at it from a distance. Thirty minutes after stumbling across the derelict, smoke began to pour out of the trawler, which sunk in 1,200 feet of water shortly thereafter.

SEA SCAMP

The *Sea Scamp* was a charter vessel owned by Captain Sites, which wrecked near the *Rose Mahoney* at the south end of the Municipal Docks during the Great Miami Hurricane of September 18, 1926[214].

The coastal freighter *Sea Taxi* as the *Hoheburg* (T. Diedrich).

SEA TAXI

The freighter *Sea Taxi* (IMO number 6522969) was launched on August 22, 1965, as the *Hoheburg* at the Neuenfelde, Germany yard of *J.J. Sietas Schiffswerft*. The new 682-ton coaster was 200.1 feet long and 32.8 feet wide. In 1976, the freighter was sold to Max Claussen of Rendsburg, Germany, and renamed *Marianne C.*; she was renamed *Wilmar* after her acquisition by the Wilmar Shipping Company, Limited, of Belize in 1993; in 1997 she sailed as the *Black Sea*; the following year she was bought by Ocean Cargo Shipping Company and renamed *Ocean Breeze I*; and, finally, in 2004, the freighter operated as *Sea Taxi*. On June 22, 2006, while 12 miles northeast of Miami, the *Sea Taxi* notified the U.S. Coast Guard that the engine room was taking on water and the vessel was in need of assistance. The U.S.C.G.C. *Sitkinak* responded and took the vessel in tow, leading her safely into the port of Miami. Following this incident, it would appear the *Sea Taxi* was abandoned, and the vessel was later acquired for use as an artificial reef. On December 30, 2009, the coaster was scuttled in 115 feet of water off Miami. At the time of this writing, the *Sea Taxi* is upright and intact, however, coastal freighters have not fared well as artificial reef material in shallow water off South Florida, as their hulls typically collapse after the passing of any significant storm.

SEBASTOPOL

The ship *Sebastopol* was built in 1855 at Bath, Maine, and was 138 feet in length, 28 feet in beam, and 498 tons burden. On October 4, 1866, the *Sebastopol*, Captain Savin, bound from Sagua, Cuba to New York, was abandoned after becoming waterlogged and in a sinking state following an encounter with a hurricane; the ship reportedly first encountered the storm on October 1 while approximately 24 nautical miles east of Palm Beach. The captain and crew were saved by the steamship *Mississippi*.

SELMA S.

The 17-ton vessel *Selma S.*, official number 208494, which was built in 1911, burned at Sanford on November 21, 1912.

The *Semarca* just prior to sinking (Volusia County Artificial Reef Program).

SEMARCA

The 76-foot long offshore supply vessel known as the *Semarca* was owned by Tidewater Marine Service, C.A. of Venezuela (SEAMARCA) when it reportedly foundered during an oil-pipeline project on Lake Maracaibo, Venezuela. Resolve Marine Group raised the vessel and transported it back to Florida, where it was eventually scuttled in 80 feet of water off Ponce Inlet in February 1994.

SEMINOLE (1855)

The 319-ton sidewheel steamer *Seminole*, built in 1854 by D.P. Landershire at Savannah, Georgia, was 152.5 feet long and 26 feet wide. Reportedly, former President Millard Fillmore toured the Savannah area on the new steamer when he visited the city in April 1854. Around 11:00 p.m. on December 20, 1855, a fire was discovered proceeding from the fore hatch of the steamer *Seminole*, Captain Shaw, while she was lying at her wharf in Jacksonville[215]. The alarm was immediately sounded and every effort was made to stop the progress of the flames, but without success. To prevent the fire from spreading, the *Seminole* was cast loose from her wharf, and she drifted ashore opposite Jacksonville, where she burned to the water's edge. The vessel, valued at $50,000, carried no insurance and was deemed a total loss.

SEMINOLE (1896)

On April 3, 1896, the schooner *Seminole*, destined for Miami with a cargo of building materials for the new home of *The Miami Metropolis* newspaper, was lost in a squall off the Florida coast, resulting in two deaths. Axel Johnson, the sole survivor, floated ashore four miles south of Fort Pierce on wreckage from the lost schooner. According to the official Life-Saving report, the vessel sank approximately 50 miles south of the Indian River Inlet Life-Saving Station and 4 miles offshore. Johnson and the other two crewmen had clung to the cabin top, but after a short struggle his shipmates were washed off and drowned. He was brought to the northward by the current and swept ashore at 10:00 p.m. on April 6. When he reached the Life-Saving Station, he had been without food and water for over four days. His limbs and body were terribly swollen and bruised, and his face was reportedly burned to a blister. Wreckage from the *Seminole's* cabin was found to the south of the Indian River Inlet Life-Saving Station on April 8. This wreck likely occurred to the St. Augustine schooner *Seminole*, official number 116080, built in 1885 at New Berlin, Florida, which documented a length of 65.6 feet, a breadth of 18.2 feet, and a displacement of 37.7 tons.

SEMINOLE (1935)

On June 24, 1935, an explosion erupted from the engine room of the 130-foot long yacht *Seminole*, which was moored at the Pilkington Yacht Basin (later known as Broward Marine) at Fort Lauderdale. The resulting fire spread quickly, eventually destroying all 70 "palatial" yachts at the marina and causing damage worth an estimated $2,000,000. Other notable yachts destroyed in the blaze included the *Rosecliff II* and the *Tropic*.

SENRAB

The 23-ton vessel *Senrab*, official number 203249, which was built in 1908, burned on the St. Johns River at Phoenix Park near Jacksonville on October 30, 1912.

SERVICE

On March 10, 1929, the fishing vessel *Service* foundered at Flagler Beach. The *Service*, official number 215803, was built in 1917 and registered a length of 59.2 feet, a beam of 14.6 feet, and a displacement of 33 tons gross.

SETH LOW

The sidewheel steamer tug *Seth Low*, official number 22800, originally operated for the New York Harbor Company fleet. She was built in 1861 at Keyport, New Jersey, and was 126.6 feet in length, 23.6 feet in breadth, and displaced 236 tons gross. At the outset of the Civil War, the *Seth Low* was chartered by the U.S War Department, which ultimately associated the tug with one of the most famous vessels in naval history, the U.S.S. *Monitor*. In 1862, the *Seth Low* was assigned to tow the ironclad from the Brooklyn Naval Shipyard in New York to Hampton Roads, Virginia. On March 9, 1862, the day after their arrival, the epic battle between the U.S.S. *Monitor* and the C.S.S. *Virginia* occurred, forever changing modern naval warfare and warship construction. After the war, the *Seth Low* returned to New York to resume her towing duties, as well as operating as a charter fishing vessel in New York Harbor. By the 1880s, the sidewheel tug had migrated south to Florida. On November 2, 1888, the *Seth Low* caught fire and burned while alongside her dock at Jacksonville. She was eventually cut free and burned to the water's edge at the mouth of Trout Creek; her remains and those of the *Oyster Boy* reportedly lie side by side[216].

SEVRE

The French brig *Sevre* (also cited as the *Sabre*), en route from Tampico, Mexico to Le Havre, France, stranded and went to pieces 16 miles north of Life-Saving Station No. 1 (also cited as 60 miles south of Cape Canaveral) in the September 1878 hurricane. Of the 10 souls on board, only one was lost in the wrecking. The survivors were found on the beach by a local man, who guided them to Titusville.

SHAMROCK

Available information indicates the freighter *Shamrock* was one of 965 landing craft utility (LCU) vessels built during World War II. The LCUs built during World War II were originally constructed as landing craft tank vessels (LCTs), and the Mk. 6 LCTs were eventually redesignated LCUs in April 1956. These general-purpose amphibious vessels had a length of 119 feet, a beam of 32 feet, and a displacement of 284 tons. By 1974, all LCUs (former Mk. 6 LCTs) were stricken, sold, or transferred under military aid programs. One of these LCUs was purchased and converted as a general cargo vessel, and renamed *Shamrock*. On June 2, 1978, U.S. Customs Service agents discovered 3,168 pounds of marijuana sealed in drums aboard the

Shamrock, which was subsequently seized. The U.S. government sought a motion for summary judgment and forfeiture of the vessel due to violation of numerous narcotic smuggling laws, which was ultimately granted by U.S. District Court on October 21, 1981. Following an appeal, the judgment was reversed and remanded in February 1983 due to a failure to prove either the owner or the captain of the vessel was privy to the illegal activity. While the vessel was released, the *Shamrock* did not operate long before her engine failed and she was tied up along the Miami River. After sitting idle for almost a year, her owner, Florida Marine Construction Company, agreed to sell the *Shamrock* to Miami-Dade County for $6,000, which included towing and cleaning of the former LCU. With the help of 200 pounds of dynamite and 30 tons of concrete blocks, the *Shamrock* was scuttled to serve as an artificial reef on June 28, 1985. The *Shamrock* came to rest upside down in approximately 45 feet of water off Miami Beach and is a good site for novice divers, with abundant marine life.

SHARK

On September 8, 2010, the derelict tug *Shark* was scuttled with the *Catharina Uhrweder* in 255 feet of water off Miami. The *Shark*, official number 261761, was built as the tug *Messenger* in 1951 by Lester F. Alexander and Company at New Orleans, and was 81.7 feet long, 25 feet wide, and displaced 149 gross tons. She later operated as the *Patricia Hoey*, *New Hampshire*, and *Sea Tractor* before finally named *Shark*. The tug, along with the 70.7-foot long sail-assisted cruiser *Catharina* (built in 1896 as the tug *Sandslån I*), was abandoned on the Intracoastal Waterway near Dania Beach around 2008.

SHA SHA BOEKANIER

The coaster *Sha Sha Boekanier* (IMO number 5294412) was originally built in 1962 as the *Richard Rahmann* at the Neuenfelde, Germany shipyard of shipbuilder *J.J Sietas Schiffswerft*. Documentation indicates the cargo vessel was 184.8 feet long, 31 feet wide, and 678 tons gross burden. In 1982, Richard Rahmann and Sons sold the freighter to *F. Wadepuhl Kommanditgesellschaft* of Ritterhude, Germany,

The listing stern of the *Sha Sha Boekanier*.

who renamed her *Richard I*; later that same year, she was acquired by a Panamanian company and operated as *Richard II*; in 1985 the cargo vessel returned to a string of German owners beginning with Friedrich K.H. Pahmeier, who renamed her *Wega III*; and finally, in 1997, the Honduran company Cory

***Sha Sha Boekanier* as *Wega III* (Hans Rosenkranz).**

Transport purchased the coaster, which then sailed as *Sha Sha Boekanier*. In April 2001, during an anti-narcotics sweep of vessels moored in the Miami River, U.S. Customs Service agents discovered approximately 100 pounds of cocaine hidden in the engine room of the *Boekanier*, which was summarily seized and forfeited by her owners.

On February 17, 2002, the *Sha Sha Boekanier* became the first and southern-most of four vessels sunk in 90 feet of water off Palm Beach at the Governor's River Walk Reef. The 2004-2005 hurricane seasons significantly modified the *Sha Sha Boekanier*, flattening the cargo hold area and separating the bow and stern of the freighter, the latter of which rests adjacent to the bow of the *St. Jacques*. The Governor's River Walk Reef is a fantastically exciting dive, typically known for clear water and abundant and large marine life encounters, though bathed by strong currents. Experienced divers, however, can easily hide in the lee of the structure and use the northward-moving current to jump from wreck to wreck, following large rubble corridors in between the freighters *Sha Sha Boekanier* and *Gilbert Sea*.

SHERI LYN

Launched on January 9, 1952, at the Lekkerkerk, Netherlands shipyard of *T. van Duijvendijk's Scheepswerf N.V.*, the *Sheri Lyn* (IMO number 5236575) originally sailed as the *Mirach-N* for the Greek Holland Shipping Company, Limited of Piraeus. The coastal freighter was 229 feet long, 32.3 feet wide and displaced 498 tons gross. In 1977, the vessel was sold to a Panamanian company and sailed as *Silver Fox*; she oddly reverted back to her original name *Mirach-N* in 1979; and the following year she was acquired by a shipping company in the Cayman Islands and renamed *Sheri Lyn*. In 1986, the State of Florida began imposing fines on the neglected freighter, as it sat rusting as a derelict along the Miami River. She was eventually purchased, cleaned, and sunk as an artificial reef off Miami on June 18, 1987. Resting in approximately 100 feet of

The freighter *Sheri Lyn* as the *Mirach-N* (Wim den Dulk).

water, the freighter was significantly impacted by Hurricane Andrew's storm surge, which ripped the vessel in half and separated the two sections by approximately 100 feet. The wreck of the *Sheri Lyn* rests close between, but slightly offshore of the *Paraiso III* and *Rio Miami*.

SHIRIN

On August 11, 1922, an explosion decimated the converted yacht *Shirin* three miles off Miami Beach. An hour after the *Shirin* departed Miami for Nassau an explosion ignited the 2,000 gallons of gasoline onboard the yacht, which burned violently. According to Captain Hatch of the charter fishing boat *Gypsy Queen*, which was in the vicinity of the yacht and rushed to rescue any potential survivors, "The water for half an acre around the boat was ablaze with burning oil and gas and the boat was just going down when we neared her[217]." The British yacht *Shirin* was 125 feet in length and 20 feet in breadth, and was equipped with a 150-horsepower Winton gasoline engine. Six persons lost their lives in the explosion and sinking.

SHOWBOAT WRECK

The "Showboat Wreck" is the purported remains of an Indian River steamboat that was likely abandoned at the end of her career, and now rests near the western shore of the Intracoastal Waterway adjacent to the North Beach Causeway Drive Bridge in Fort Pierce.

SHUTTLE

The screw steamer *Shuttle*, official number 202897, was built in 1906 at Bristol, Rhode Island. She registered a length of 87.8 feet, a breadth of 10.5 feet, and a displacement of 33 tons gross. Owned by Frank Spadaro, the *Shuttle* reportedly burned at Miami in April 1923.

SIDEWHEEL STEAMER WRECK

The "Sidewheel Steamer Wreck" is an unidentified wreck resting in 10 feet of water less than a mile down (south) the beach from the wreck of the *Cosme Calzada* off Hutchinson Island. The wreck, a composite or wood-hulled sidewheel steel steamship, is largely complete, with the boiler, propulsion machinery, and rigging spread just to the north of the hull and additional structure. The bow is positioned to the south, based on the location of the windlass and a small anchor. The main anchors and chain can be found directly offshore of this wreckage, and were likely deployed in a failed effort to prevent the vessel's loss.

SILVER QUEEN

On June 18, 1968, the *Press-Telegram* reported the unusual sinking of the 45-foot long *Silver Queen* off Miami. The vessel, which was carrying drums of gasoline and fuel oil, was supposedly headed to the Bahamas when it sank June 16, approximately 8 to 12 miles southeast of Fowey Rocks just two hours after departure. Three Haitian men escaped the sinking vessel and were eventually picked up in a rubber raft just off Miami Beach. The loss of the vessel inherited an air of mystery after it was learned the Haitian Ambassador to the United States, Arthur Bonhomme, earlier reported a 45-foot boat called the *Silver King* had departed Miami June 15 with 14 Haitians and presumably carrying arms that were destined to support the ongoing unrest in Haiti. It is unclear if the *Silver Queen* actually carried guns as asserted by the Haitian ambassador.

SIMMONS

The two-masted schooner *Simmons*, official number 116350, was built in Cambridge, Maryland in 1890, and was 76.5 feet long, 23 feet wide, and 62 tons gross burden. In early January 1926, the *Simmons* departed Norfolk, Virginia, bound for Fort Lauderdale with a cargo of lime, cement, and a deck-load of lumber. On January 29, the tanker *W.W. Mills* rescued Captain Alex Kohler and four crewmen from the battered and rapidly-sinking *Simmons* off Hollywood. The schooner went down shortly after the last of its crew scrambled over the rail and into the lifeboat. Harold Rosenberg, who was in command of the rescue party from the *Mills*, described the scene:

> A mile below Hillsboro Lighthouse on the Florida coast about 12:30 on January 29 we sighted the two masted schooner *Simmons* flying her ensign upside down. She signaled for a tow and after four unsuccessful attempts were made to get a line aboard the fifth try, an eight-inch hawser was gotten to the schooner. The *Mills* was flying light and heavy seas were running, piled up by a northeast gale that was blowing furiously toward the coast. With the tow the *Mills* was hard to manage because she was riding high on the churning sea. After an hour and 30 minutes the men on the schooner signaled their vessel was sinking and asked to be taken off. The tow line was snubbed up and the starboard lifeboat lowered from the after davits. When the ship's crew was called to man the lifeboat all hands

volunteered for service in the hazardous undertaking and some of the men had to be ordered from the boat before it could be lowered.

As the lifeboat touched the water it was nearly capsized and barely escaped being smashed against the side of the ship. Pulling to the schooner we found the sails about half up causing the vessel to cut and sheave. The booms had swung over the lee side, making it impossible to draw under the lee of the schooner with the lifeboat, and the dory hanging over the stern made an attempt to take the crew off from that part of the schooner dangerous and difficult, nevertheless it was from the stern that the rescue had to be effected. The five men were gotten off the schooner into the lifeboat and we started pulling back to the *Mills* against seas and gale. The *Mills* was being blown to the beach and dangerously close to reefs, and the breakers could be plainly seen rolling in shore.

As we left the *Simmons*, the sails were lashing, cargo shifting and the waves were washing over the deck. In effecting the rescue, Captain W.H. Maxwell was forced to take extreme chances with his ship. In order to keep from losing sight of our lifeboat the vessel had to be practically stopped and riding light and high as she was, there was momentary danger of her being blown and carried aground. The *Mills* was drawing 20 feet and H. Mathis, third mate, using the lead line was getting four and one-half fathoms. When the boat crew finally drew alongside with the survivors they had to clamor up the side of the ship and abandon the lifeboat to avoid further delay when each moment brought further danger of the tanker grounding. The survivors and boat crew gained the decks without a scratch, and the *Mills* put out to sea with her propeller kicking up sand[218].

Based on the above information, it would appear the *Simmons* likely sunk in fairly shallow water. Regardless, the wreck of the *Simmons* has not been positively located, possibly due to a subsequent salvage effort.

SIMPSON CREEK WRECK

The "Simpson Creek Wreck" is an unidentified wreck, reportedly a four-masted schooner, resting at the mouth of Simpson Creek behind Little Talbot Island in Duval County. The majority of the vessel was apparently stripped at the time of the wrecking or abandonment, and all that remains today is a portion of the ship's timbers.

Sir Scott as the *Lago Isoba* (T. Diedrich).

SIR SCOTT

In April 1958, the freighter *Lago Isoba* (IMO number 5202134) was completed at Bilbao by *Compañia Euskalduna* for the Spanish firm of Lakes Shipping. The new general cargo vessel was 250.4 feet long, 37.3 feet wide, and displaced 1,556 gross tons. In 1976, she was sold to *Naviera Alvargonzález* and renamed *Labrador*, though the same year she was passed on to the Panamanian company *Naviera Peninsular*, who operated the vessel as *Azuero Dos*. The freighter moved on again in 1978 to Greek interests and sailed as *Atlantis III*, skipping on to the name *Atlantis V* in 1980. That same year, she was bought by her final owners, who renamed the freighter *Sir Scott*. In 1984, the Cayman Islands owner stripped the freighter of its engine parts and other saleable items, and abandoned the vessel along the Miami River. Fish and Game Unlimited of Homestead purchased the vessel for $10,000 and donated it to Miami-Dade County for use as an artificial reef. On March 3, 1985, the freighter *Sir Scott* was sent to the bottom following the detonation of several hundred pounds of dynamite. Due to a frozen rudder that hindered its towing, the Sir Scott was actually scuttled five miles north of its intended destination. The *Sir Scott* now rests upright and intact in approximately 220 feet of water south of Fowey Rocks, three miles east of the Ragged Keys.

SIR WALTER RALEIGH

The 477-ton bark *Sir Walter Raleigh*, Captain T. Rae, was built in 1852 at Sunderland, England. On August 18, 1861 (also reported as August 15), while returning to Liverpool from Jamaica with a cargo of rum and pimentos, the British bark wrecked on Pacific Reef (another source stated the bark was lost at "Carew Creek, Cape Florida," which likely refers to Caesar's Creek). One of the crew, a man known as Perry, was picked up at sea off the coast of Florida after being seven days on a raft. Perry eventually arrived at Miami and stayed there under the care of W.A. Johnston until August 30. After recuperating, Perry joined three other British shipwrecked sailors from the bark *Prima Donna* on the fishing smack *Colonel Long*, which was to take them to Charleston, South Carolina. However, the vessel was soon seized by the U.S.S. *Jamestown* and carried into New York, where the British sailors were imprisoned at Fort Lafayette as pirates (i.e., suspected Confederate sympathizers).

The Japanese-built freighter *Skyecliffe* (Palm Beach County Artificial Reef Program).

SKYECLIFFE

Unlike the numerous, small, post-war European coastal freighters used as artificial reefs off Florida, the *Skyecliffe* was constructed in 1961 as the *Erimo Maru* at the Osaka, Japan shipyard of Namura Shipbuilding Company, Limited, and was 317.5 feet in length, 45.6 feet in width, and displaced 2,639 tons. In 1977, she was sold and renamed *Sea Venture*, and again traded hands in 1983 and sailed as *Skyecliffe*. In 1991, the freighter was purchased for use as an artificial reef after experiencing issues while at New Orleans, whereupon she was towed to Fort Lauderdale, cleaned, and ultimately sunk off Boynton Beach on November 2, 1991. The *Skyecliffe* became the largest, and at a cost of $148,500, the most expensive Palm Beach County artificial reef project.

Diver exploring the *Skyecliffe*.

The wreck of the *Skyecliffe* sits upright and intact in 200 feet of water, though her massive stern superstructure rises almost 70 feet from the bottom. The wreck rests generally inline with the typically strong Gulf Stream Current, though with the abundant amount of relief the vessel offers, divers can comfortably explore the wreck with ease. The cavernous engine room is located aft of the stern superstructure, and a large deck access hatch allows access into the interior. Small deck houses can be found amidships and near the bow, which provide divers shelter when moving forward and against a strong current. When the current is not roaring over the wreck, abundant marine life including snapper, jacks, mahi mahi, and grouper cloud around the structure. Because of this, the *Skyecliffe* is popular with fishermen, who have inadvertently decorated the shipwreck with abundant amounts of monofilament line.

SKYLARK II

On June 22, 1968, the 65-foot long, 49-ton yacht *Skylark* burned and sank approximately one and a half miles (also reported as five miles) off Palm Beach[219]. The U.S. Coast Guard responded to the fire, and attempted to save the vessel by applying chemical foam to extinguish the blaze, though their efforts were unsuccessful. The lone occupant of the vessel, owner Joseph B. Conversano, a test pilot for the National Aeronautics and Space Administration, escaped unhurt. The *Skylark* was valued at $100,000.

SNOW WHITE II

The abandoned shrimper *Snow White II*, out of Daytona Beach, grounded near Ponce Inlet on February 2, 1949. The body of the mate washed ashore several days later, but the captain was never found.

SOCIAL

The 21-ton fishing vessel *Social*, 42.4 feet in length and 13.5 feet in breadth, was built in 1922 at Fernandina. On July 29, 1928, the *Social* caught fire and burned at Fernandina.

SOLDIER KEY WRECK

Resting in only three feet of water amidst seagrass beds off the northern end of Soldier Key is the mostly buried remains of a small, unidentified wreck. A brief survey conducted in 1976 found fragments of black rum bottle glass and round ballast stones typical of those seen on eighteenth century wrecks. Archaeologist George Fischer observed no space between the frames, which he stated was typical of British naval architecture of this period. He also noted the wreck looked similar to the 1733 shipwreck *San José de las Animas*, which was originally a 327-ton merchant ship built in England.

SOLI DEO GLORIA

On October 15, 1891, the Assistant Health Officer and Port Physician at Fernandina reported the German bark *Soli Deo Gloria* ashore on the north end of Amelia Island with a crew suspected of being infected with yellow fever[220]. The bark had departed Kingston, Jamaica on September 19 with 11 men, 3 of which were lost as sea from what the captain called "sunstroke." The bark became a total wreck and was bought at public sale by the Nassau County Board of Health, which then torched the *Soli Deo Gloria*. Built in 1863 at Danzig (present-day Gdańsk, Poland), the *Soli Deo Gloria* was 125.3 feet long, 28.7 feet wide, and 426 tons burden.

SONORA

The auxiliary schooner *Sonora* sank 20 miles east of Fort Pierce on June 23, 1945, after catching fire from a defective exhaust. The ship's crew of 25, naval armed guard of six, and a dog were rescued by a U.S. Coast Guard cutter after drifting for over four hours. The diesel-powered *Sonora* was bound from Freeport, Texas to Boston, Massachusetts with a cargo of sulfur. The second assistant engineer, Lt. John Burgess, described the cause of the vessel's loss, stating, "Both starboard and port side engines of the diesel powered Panamanian craft were in top form. I had just mounted to the catwalk when I heard, even above the deafening roar of the engines, a crack, a sizzle, and then it started. Flames shot out from the port side and reached way across the engine room floor. I ran down the ladder again, burning one arm. The fire had hit the generator and out all the lights out[221]." Everyone on board evacuated the ship into two boats and two rafts and drifted north along with their burning vessel before being sighted by an aircraft, which relayed their position to rescue vessels. The three-masted *Sonora* was cited as being 250 tons in displacement and 240 feet in length.

SOUTH SEAS

In 1926, *Friedrich Krupp Germaniawerft* of Kiel, Germany, launched the palatial yacht *Firenze*, built for Norman Woolworth, the five-and-dime store heir. The *Firenze* was 170 feet in length, 27.1 feet in breadth, and displaced 700 tons. In 1930, M. Robert Guggenheim purchased the elegant vessel from Woolworth, which would soon become his prized possession. Guggenheim used the yacht extensively, and upkeep of the *Firenze*, its interior adorned with fine woods and antique French furniture, reportedly cost upwards of $250,000 per year. In 1938, Guggenheim married his fourth wife aboard the *Firenze* at Miami Beach. In early 1942, Guggenheim sold his prized yacht to the U.S. Navy for $225,000, which commissioned the vessel as the U.S.S. *Girasol* (PY-27). After her shakedown cruise, the *Girasol* was dispatched to the Pacific Theater, where she patrolled from 1943 until the war's end. Decommissioned in January 1946, the *ex-Girasol* was transferred to the Maritime Commission in July 1947.

Ben Benjamin, president of South Seas, Incorporated, eventually purchased the war surplus patrol vessel and renamed her *South Seas*. After a decade of use, the former yacht *South Seas* was retired from service in 1958 and tied up at a Miami shipyard while its owner contemplated its future. On March 13, 1961, the yacht caught fire and burned. During the battle to extinguish the inferno, so much water was pumped into the vessel that she heeled over dramatically to starboard, threatening to capsize. The following year, the *South Seas* was salvaged and converted into a restaurant and cocktail lounge adjacent to the well-known Miami restaurant, Tony's Fish Market. In 1975, the *South Seas* sank into the mud in North Bay and remained abandoned until a real estate developer bought the land in 1978 with plans to build a condominium and marina complex. Following pressure from local and state officials, who demanded the developer remove the sunken vessel, plans were drafted to sink the vessel four miles off Key Biscayne to serve as an artificial reef. Unfortunately, the *South Seas* would not go quietly. On September 23, 1982, as the *South Seas* was being towed through Biscayne Bay, the vessel grounded on a sandbar, flooded, and promptly settled in 11 feet of water. The rusting derelict was eventually salvaged and returned to her berth, where workers were forced to scrap much of the vessel prior to

The yacht *South Seas* towed from her berth at Miami (Miami-Dade County Department of Environmental Resources Management).

reefing. Following extensive work, the salvage team abandoned their ultimate plans of cutting the vessel into several large sections, and again tried to tow the lightened *South Seas* offshore on February 11, 1983. Yet again, the rusting yacht grounded on a sandbar and refused to move. At high tide the following day, however, the *South Seas* was finally pulled loose and towed offshore. In a final act of defiance, the *South Seas* drifted loose from its attending tow after the tug fouled its prop in a line. The once-palatial yacht sank on its own in 75 feet of water, which was shallower than the planned 100-foot depth and outside of the permitted artificial reef site boundaries. Over the years, portions of the *South Seas* have collapsed and scattered across the seafloor, a process likely aided by Hurricane Andrew in 1992. The shallow wreck site presents a good destination for beginner divers, while more experienced divers can practice their navigational skills by traversing the approximate 250-foot distance north to the wreck of the freighter *Princess Britney*.

SOUTH WIND II

The *South Wind II* was a 26-ton, 46-foot long yacht built in 1953. On August 12, 1967, the yacht foundered in a storm 25 miles off Palm Beach; the six passengers onboard were rescued.

SPARKLING SEA

Built in 1854 at Bristol, Maine, the ship *Sparkling Sea* was 168.8 feet long, 34.3 feet wide, and 893 tons burden. Constructed with two decks, the sheathed oak hull of the vessel was held together with both copper and iron fasteners. On the morning of January 9, 1863, the *Sparkling Sea*, Captain Walsh, wrecked on the north point of Ajax Reef en route from New York via Fort Monroe, Virginia, to New Orleans. A January 20 dispatch from Key West included in the February 1, 1863, edition of *The New York Times* described the fate of the vessel:

> The United States transport ship *Sparkling Sea*, with the Twenty-fifth New York Battery, for the Banks Expedition, reported ashore on Ajax Reef in my last letter, has since become a complete wreck, and probably all the horses, eighty in number, have been lost. The steamer *Swan*, which was sent out from here for her relief, was unable to reach the wreck, owing to the heavy sea, and for some days

was compelled to seek a harbor at Indian Key, and has since returned to this port. The latest information from the wreck is by the wrecking schooner *Coquette*, which left here on Tuesday last, at which time the horses were still alive and the sea making a constant breach over the wreck. The entire crew had abandoned her, and with the ship's boats had gone to Indian Key, leaving the horses to perish, either for want of food or water, or to be ultimately drowned.... Wreckers will save the materials of the ship, provided the heavy norther, which has now been blowing for the last ten days, has not washed everything away.

On May 18, 1864, seven members of the *Sparkling Sea's* crew were convicted of revolt and mutiny in the wake of the ship's wrecking. Reportedly, the men refused to render further service after the vessel grounded on Ajax Reef, claiming that their voyage was up. It was Captain Walsh's opinion that "he would have saved his ship from total wreck had these men fully discharged their duty." The wreck of the *Sparkling Sea*, which should rest near the northern end of Ajax Reef, has yet to be positively identified.

SPRAY

The *Spray* was a sidewheel steamer built in Kissimmee in 1882, which was owned by Arch Bass and Captain W.J. Brack, the latter operating it. At only 40 feet in length (also reported as 47 feet) and 10 feet in beam, the small steamer apparently could not carry enough cargo to be profitable, so she was eventually beached at Kissimmee, where she later burned in 1893.

SPRING OF WHITBY

The *Spring*, better known as the *Spring of Whitby*, was built in 1800 by the prominent Whitby shipyard along the Thames River in England, which also produced Lieutenant James Cook's round-the-world vessel, H.M.S. *Endeavor*. The *Spring* was 110 feet in length, 29 feet in beam, had a single deck with beams, and displaced 379 tons. Later, her displacement was increased to 395 tons. She was armed with four four-pounder cannon and four six-pounders. Upon its outfitting, the vessel was leased by the English government as a transport. *Lloyd's Register* mentions that the vessel received new topsides, a new deck, and underwent good repairs in 1814, was repaired again in 1817, and had "some repairs" in 1819. Details of her demise are scant, though she was reported lost with Captain Skelton in command during a voyage to England in 1824 or 1825.

The wreck was discovered by salvors in 1965. Identification of the wreck came with the recovery of her bell, inscribed "SPRING OF WHITBY 1801." The site is intermingled with the wreck of the *Roberts*, lost in 1810, both of which are under permit to a salvage company. The remains of the *Spring of Whitby* can be found 200 feet off the beach, adjacent to State Beach Marker number five, in approximately 18 feet of water. Four cannon can be observed just past the first reef, while two large anchors can be found seaward of the second reef. The wreck itself can be found in a depression in the reef and consists of some ballast and assorted timbers.

SPY

According to *The New York Times*, December 29, 1866, the schooner *Spy*, "Captain Perkins, soon after leaving Jacksonville, Florida, for Havana, sprung a leak, and afterward struck on the north shoal of St. Augustine Bar, where she became a total wreck. The schooner had on board a cargo of lumber, which would probably be lost with the vessel." The 155-ton schooner *Spy* was built in 1837 at May's Landing, New Jersey.

STAIRS WRECK

Found just south of the "Schooner Ballast Wreck," the "Stairs Wreck" is an unidentified wreck resting along the northern edge of a rocky shoal and just inside some large coral formations adjacent to deeper water. In this area, bronze spikes have been found, as well as a large section of iron that resembles three stair treads, hence the name[222]. Egg-rock ballast, as well as glass and pottery fragments, have been found scattered around the site.

ST. ANN

In June 1765, the H.M.S. *Speedwell*, Captain Robert Fanshaw, returned to Charleston, South Carolina with 16 crew and passengers of the French ship *St. Ann*, Captain Roisiliac [sic], which wrecked on the Florida coast on June 5, 1765, en route from the Mississippi to Cape Francois with a cargo of lumber[223].

The abandoned steamers *St. Augustine* and *St. Sebastian* rot on the Loxahatchee River (Florida State Archives).

ST. AUGUSTINE

Built shortly after her sistership *St. Sebastian*, the sternwheel steamer *St. Augustine*, official number 116308, was launched in 1890 at Wilmington, Delaware. Slightly shorter than her sistership, the passenger steamer *St. Augustine* was 110 feet in length, 24 feet in beam, and 131.6 tons gross burden. Operating initially for the Indian River Steamboat Company, the *St. Augustine* was later sold to the Indian River and Bay Biscayne Inland Navigation Company in 1897. With the inland steamboat industry waning, the *St. Augustine* was eventually towed up the Loxahatchee River and abandoned next to her sistership,

St. Sebastian, around 1901. The derelicts were steadily picked apart, with stateroom windows and doors being utilized by resourceful homesteaders in the area.

ST. AUGUSTINE WRECK

As the name would imply, the "St. Augustine Wreck" is an unidentified wreck in approximately 1,200 feet of water 70 nautical miles off St. Augustine. Seahawk Deep Ocean Technology investigated the site during several visits from 1989 through 1991. Using the Harbor Branch Oceanographic Institution's submersible *Johnson Sea Link*, numerous artifacts were recovered, including at least five cannon, several copper cooking pots, Spanish silver coins dated between 1712 and 1714, and various other items. Exposed structural hull members indicated the vessel was small for the era, potentially between 50 and 75 tons, which may have been a Spanish *aviso* or *patache*. While no positive identification was made, perhaps the vessel is one of the missing 1715 fleet vessels, which include the former French frigate *El Ciervo*, the *Nuestra Señora de Concepción*, and the *nao San Miguel*.

ST. HENRY'S EXPRESS

The *St. Henry's Express* is an approximately 120-foot long vessel sunk in 115 feet of water off Miami to serve as an artificial reef in February 1997. While there is perhaps 20 feet of relief, the vessel has little growth on it and, overall, does not have much appeal for the average diver. The *St. Henry's Express* rests in between the 160-foot long offshore supply vessel *Tortuga*, which is found approximately 300 to the south, and the 75-foot long *Betek Ar Pen*, which rests just over 150 feet to the north.

The disarticulated bow of the *St. Jacques*.

ST. JACQUES

The *St. Jacques* is one of four seized freighters sunk at the Governor's River Walk Reef off Palm Beach. Originally upright and intact when scuttled on March 15, 2002, the *St. Jacques* was significantly modified by the active 2004 hurricane season. The storm surge pummeled the freighter against the mostly bare limestone pavement, which separated the bow and stern from the collapsed cargo holds. Both sections now list at abstract angles, presenting a surreal dive experience. The *St. Jacques*, resting in approximately 90 feet of water, is located between the freighter *Sha Sha Boekanier* to the south and a concrete rubble pile to the north; the rubble pile trails off north towards the freighter *Gilbert Sea*. Divers wishing to visit the third freighter, *Thozina*, before heading last to the *Gilbert Sea* should swim slightly to the east and past concrete road barriers and an anchor with chain resting in the sand, whereupon the stern of the *Thozina* will eventually come into view. The site typically hosts abundant marine life, and it's not uncommon to observe sea turtles, sharks, and goliath grouper in and around the wrecks of the Governor's River Walk Reef.

The *St. Jacques* (IMO number 5190032) was launched in 1955 as the *Klaus Block* at the Neuenfelde, Germany yard of *J.J Sietas Schiffswerft*. A rather standard European coastal freighter, or coaster, the *Klaus Block* was 157.8 feet long, 27.6 feet wide, and 424 tons gross burden. In 1963, owner Heinrich Block sold the coaster to *Gebrüder Frommann* of Hamburg, who renamed their new vessel *Süderelv*; Willy Hagenah purchased the freighter in 1969, after which she sailed as *Tilla Doloris*; the vessel reportedly sunk, but was later raised, repaired, and sold to Medusa Shipping of Cyprus in 1978, who renamed her *Doloris*; two years later she operated as *Leticia* for Gama Navigation of Panama; in 1982, the well-traveled freighter was renamed *Terence* after her sale to Pelham Dale and Partners, Limited of England; similar to one of her earlier names, the freighter cruised as *Tilla Doris* when sold in 1990; next, Honduran company Island Transport bought the coaster in 1993 and renamed her *Deborah Jean*; and, finally, in 1997 the vessel operated first as *Mirage I* and then as *St. Jacques* for Belizean owners. While she was employed on a rather standard route between Haiti and Miami, the *St. Jacques* was twice found attempting to smuggle cocaine into the United States.

The coaster *St. Jacques* as the *Terence* (Derek Sands).

Following the second offense in July 2001, the freighter was forfeited and designated for use as an artificial reef in order to prevent her return to the narcotics trafficking industry.

The flattened forward cargo holds and amidships of the *St. Jacques*.

Diver cruises past the stern of the freighter *St. Jacques*.

ST. JOHNS

The steamer *St. Johns* was built sometime around 1853, and was used on routes between Savannah, Darien, and St. Marys, Georgia, as well as Jacksonville, Palatka, and St. Augustine. In 1856, the *St. Johns* burned at her wharf on the St. Johns River at Jacksonville in 1856. The hull of the *St. Johns* was reportedly raised and rebuilt as the *Helen Getty*.

ST. JUDEA

The *St. Judea* was a Spanish vessel of the Canary Islands, approximately 350 tons burden and armed with 22 guns. In June 1748, the H.M.S. *Fowey*, Captain Francis William Drake, was patrolling northwest of Cuba when it captured the *St. Judea*, which was sailing from Caracas, Venezuela, to Havana with a cargo of approximately 9,000 bushels of cocoa, hides, and approximately 57,000 dollars. The *Fowey* then sailed for Virginia, escorting *St. Judea* as a war prize. On June 27, 1748, the *Fowey* grounded on a reef off Cape Florida. While attempting to float the British frigate free, the *St. Judea* also ran afoul of the reef. Both vessels briefly broke loose and were refloated only to be cast up on the reef again on June 28. According to a September 22, 1748, article in the *General Evening Post*, "The ship and brigantine got off again, but his Majesty's Ship *Fowey* and the prize were both lost, it not being possible to get them off again. We destroy'd all we could of the wreck, her guns, etc. A snow from New York took us all up, and brought us safe to this place (Charleston) the 3d instant." The remains of the *St. Judea* should rest somewhere in shallow water within Biscayne National Park and in close proximity to the *Fowey*, which is located in Legare Anchorage.

ST. MARY (1770)

The *St. Mary*, Captain Carr, from Jamaica for London, was reported as totally lost on Cape Florida in 1770[224].

ST. MARY (1864)

Built in 1862 at Wilmington, Delaware, the *St. Mary* (also cited as *St. Marys*) was a 121-ton (later 378 tons) iron-hulled steamer owned by E.G. Dyke of Savannah. In December 1863, the *St. Mary* anchored in McGirts Creek off the St. Johns River two miles from Camp Finnegan (near Jacksonville), and for almost two months waited for an opportunity to run the blockade. With the approach of Union troops in the area on the evening of February 9, 1864, however, Confederate forces burned the cargo of 278 bales of cotton and the steamer was scuttled near McGirts Creek water to prevent her capture. After the war, the *St. Mary* was raised, rebuilt, and renamed *Nick King*. In April 1870, General Robert E. Lee was a noteworthy passenger when he boarded the *Nick King* in Savannah for a journey to Jacksonville and Palatka. On January 24, 1873, the *Nick King*, en route to Florida, struck a snag and sunk near Darien, Georgia.

ST. PAUL

The British three-masted barkentine *St. Paul* was built by T.A. Mosher at Avondale, Nova Scotia in 1890. The vessel documented a length of 147.1 feet, a beam of 33 feet, and a displacement of 472 tons. In 1914, the barkentine was sold and registered in the United States. Two years later, on November 8, 1916, the *St. Paul* was battered in a storm and stranded off Jensen Beach, approximately four miles north of the Gilbert's Bar Life-Saving Station, eventually becoming a total loss. At the time of her wrecking, the *St.*

Paul, Captain Marcial, was en route from New Jersey for Matanzas, Cuba, with a cargo of sulphate ammonia.

The steamer *St. Sebastian* at Rockledge (Florida State Archives).

ST. SEBASTIAN

The steamer *St. Sebastian* (spelled *St. Sebastin* in shipping registers), official number 116304, was built in 1889 at Wilmington, Delaware. The steel-hulled sternwheel steamboat was 130 feet long, 24 feet wide, and displaced 219.4 tons gross. Operating initially for the Indian River Steamboat Company, the *St. Sebastian* was later sold to the Indian River and Bay Biscayne Inland Navigation Company in 1897. The following year, the steamboat was employed under contract with the U.S. government to transport soldiers, armament, and supplies to Key West in support of the Spanish-American War. The passenger ferry *St. Sebastian* ended her short career at Fernandina, and was eventually towed up the Loxahatchee River and abandoned next to her sistership, *St. Augustine*, around 1901. The derelicts were steadily picked apart, with stateroom windows and doors being utilized by resourceful homesteaders in the area.

STAR

According to Davis (1925), the 236-ton Jacksonville-Crescent City Line steamer *Star*, built in 1861, burned on Crescent Lake; date unknown.

STAR TREK

The *Star Trek* was originally built during World War II as one of 558 amphibious vessels known as a Landing Ship, Medium (LSM). Similar to the *Lakeland* (formerly LSM-373), the *Star Trek* was 203.5 feet in length, 34.5 feet in beam, and displaced 520 tons when empty. Unfortunately, the particulars of this vessel are currently unknown, aside from the fact she was converted after the war for commercial freight service. On July 27, 1982, the former LSM was scuttled in 210 feet of water off Miami to serve as an artificial reef. The wreck is resting on her side, and it appears the influence of Hurricane Andrew in 1992 rolled the freighter over, significantly damaging her superstructure, though the vessel rolled back onto her side as the storm moved inland.

The former landing ship *Star Trek* (Miami-Dade County Department of Environmental Resources Management).

STARLIGHT

Built in 1866 at Portland, Maine, the sidewheel steamer *Starlight*, official number 22154, was 131.1 feet in length, 25.3 feet in breadth, and 261 gross tons in displacement. On May 11, 1878, the *Starlight* burned at Sanford; no lives lost. On May 2, 1905, an allotment of $800 was made for the removal of the wrecked steamer *Starlight* from Lake Monroe near Sanford; work was completed on May 15 by the dredge and snag boat *Florida*[225].

STARRY BANNER

On November 14, 1890, the *Winnipeg Free Press* documented the wrecking steamer *Starry Banner* was "lost in the bay at St. Augustine." The article stated the steamer was en route from Baltimore to Key West when she struck a bank and sank in ten minutes in shoal water; the vessel was reported as a total loss. Other sources indicate the *Starry Banner* lost power between the inner and outer bars off St. Augustine, and broke apart in the breakers. She reportedly settled near the schooner *Virginia Lee Hickman*, which wrecked in the same place in 1888. The captain and crew of six men took to the rigging, where they remained for several hours until rescued by a life-saving crew. The *Starry Banner*, official number 115149, was built at Bath, Maine in 1873, and was 60.6 feet long, 16.2 feet wide, and displaced 39.5 tons.

STELLA

Also known locally as the "Paddlewheeler Wreck," the *Stella* was a sidewheel tug that ran aground on February 16, 1911. The *Stella*, official number 115505, was built at a Brooklyn, New York shipyard for Stanley H. Miner in 1876. The wooden-hulled tug, 54 feet in length and 17 feet in beam, displaced 36.91 gross tons. At the time of her 1911 wrecking, Captain F.L. Foote was steaming the tug, then owned by the Central American Growers and Transportation Company, towards Nicaragua after having departed New York in early February. As she slowly made her way along the Florida coast, a strong nor'easter pummeled the aging tug. Barely able to keep her bow into the waves and taking on water, Captain Foote dropped anchor in an attempt to ride out the storm. During the night, her anchor line parted, and the *Stella* struggled to stay afloat. By morning, with the storm subsiding, the crew of the tug attempted to cross a bar and enter what they thought was Indian River Inlet. Unfortunately, what they thought was the inlet was simply a marshy area flooded during high tide. They soon ran aground on a bar and were hopelessly stranded. Pounding waves pushed them farther towards shore and shook her plates loose. While the vessel was quickly on her way to being a total loss, the entire crew was safely rescued by a passing fishing boat.

The *Stella* can be found 300 feet off the beach, approximately three miles north of Fort Pierce Inlet. Today, the tug's large boiler, rising within close proximity of the surface, dominates the site. Just offshore of the boiler, divers can observe the flattened-out remains of the paddlewheels. Much of the remainder of the vessel is sanded in, though some ribs and assorted wreckage extend 30 feet from the boiler. Residing in 15 feet of water, the wreck generally has good visibility, especially after calm weather or periods of gentle west winds. Numerous tropical species utilize the habitat that the ship's structure provides, and lobsters can sometimes be spotted hidden amongst the wreck.

STONEFREE

The *Stonefree* was a 57-foot Buddy Davis sportfisherman built by Davis Boat Works in 1980. Owner Felix Carcano reportedly purchased the sportfisherman for $400,000 in 2000 and had just poured another $700,000 into its restoration prior to the 2002 Miami International Boat Show. On the evening of April 11, 2002, en route from Miami to New York, the vessel began taking on water in heavy seas as they approached Cape Canaveral. Carcano realized the boat was sinking and managed to get a cell phone call off to his wife providing his position before he and a friend were forced to abandon ship as the *Stonefree* sank approximately four miles off Cocoa Beach. Fortunately, the two were rescued from the cold water about an hour later by the passing sailboat *Talia*. The following day, portions of the Buddy Davis sportfisherman washed ashore only to be pulverized by the surf.

STORM WRECK

The "Storm Wreck" is a suspected eighteenth century shipwreck located in 20 feet of water off St. Augustine Inlet near the wreck of the *Industry*. Discovered in August 2009, the site is just beginning to reveal its secrets. Artifacts uncovered around the site's buried ballast pile include a cast iron cauldron, thousands of lead shot, glass shards, and other assorted concreted iron objects. While the site has yet to be indentified, the wreck could be one of several vessels reportedly lost on the St. Augustine Bar around December 1782, including the galley *Rattlesnake*.

SUB WRECK

While this site definitely possesses an intriguing name, leading many to believe it may be a sunken German U-boat, the "Sub Wreck" actually consists of a former N.A.S.A. camera observation stand sunk offshore Cape Canaveral. It mainly consists of concrete slabs and steel beams with approximately 30 feet of relief in 90 feet of water. While definitely not a shipwreck, I have included this site due to the confusion commonly experienced because of the provocative name. This site is also different than the N.A.S.A. material deployed at "Space Reef," also known as "Hummingbird Reef" or "Ed's Wreck," which rests approximately 15 miles east of Cape Canaveral in 120 feet of water. The "Space Reef" project, deployed on August 23, 1989, was a 180-foot long barge carrying 120 tons of obsolete launch structures, including: a 60-ton umbilical tower off Launch Pad 36A, a structure that helped launch more than 75 space flights, including the Atlas-Centaur series that boosted the Surveyor system to the moon; a 40-ton missile access stand from Launch Pad 29, which supported test launches of Polaris and Poseidon missiles; and a 10-ton space shuttle support stand from Launch Pad 36A.

Sucre just prior to its sinking (Broward County Artificial Reef Program).

SUCRE

Originally launched as the *Louise* on April 2, 1957, at the Bremerhaven, Germany shipyard *Schiffbaugesellschaft Unterweser A.G.*, the *Sucre* (IMO number 5212892) was a general cargo freighter 237 feet long, 35 feet wide, and 1,041 tons displacement. In 1980, the vessel was sold and renamed *Chiloe III*; she sailed as *Kenco I* upon her sale to new owners in 1988; and finally, the freighter was acquired by her Honduran owners in 1991, who renamed her *Sucre*. In 1994, the U.S. Coast Guard seized the *Sucre* after finding

Diver over the amidships crane on the wreck of the *Sucre*.

300 pounds of cocaine onboard. The freighter was eventually put out of service and acquired for use as an artificial reef. Renamed the "Johnny Morris Offshore Angler Reef" after the president of Bass Pro Shops, the *Sucre* was scuttled off Broward County on April 27, 1996. The freighter rests upright and intact in approximately 215 feet of water, with the main deck encountered at 190 feet. The forward portion of the vessel consists of two large vacant holds, each with its own cargo crane on deck that affords an interesting photo opportunity, while the aft superstructure and engine room allows for some interesting exploration. The forward bridge bulkheads have collapsed, which has produced an odd vacant area surrounded on each side by the intact bridge wings. With the bow pointing southward, on a day with good visibility, it almost appears as if the *Sucre* is steaming along the bottom to some unknown destination.

Joe Citelli ascending above the stern of the former freighter *Sucre*.

SUMIDA

On September 18, 1926, the *Sumida* reportedly foundered during the Great Miami Hurricane. Built in 1908 at New York, the yacht *Sumida*, official number 205116, was 59.8 feet long, 11 feet wide, and 22 tons burden.

SUN MARINER

The *Sun Mariner*, official number 295852, was a 51.3-foot long tug built in Morgan City, Louisiana in 1964. In April 1998, she was sunk in 70 feet of water, along with the *Marsha T.* and the *Sea Inspector*, just north of the Palm Beach County line.

SUNRISE WRECK

In 1956, Charles and John Noyes stumbled upon a wreck while collecting tropical fish off Fort Lauderdale. After noticing some odd debris, it wasn't long before they discovered a few Spanish silver coins by fanning the sand. The brothers worked the small site, which was confined to an approximately 20-foot long area, periodically over the next several years. The site consisted of numerous encrusted and concreted objects, which were carefully extracted in hopes of identifying the lost vessel. Several artifacts were recovered, including a brass sextant inscribed "W. Hogg, London," a silver or pewter spoon with the inscription "P. Barnes & Co., London," and dozens more Spanish silver coins ranging in date from 1774 through 1839. Based upon a Cuban 1841 over-stamp struck on several of the coins, the wreck is believed to have occurred sometime after January 1841.

SUPPLY

The *Supply*, Captain Fisher, was totally lost during a heavy gale on the Florida coast on January 26, 1821, at approximate latitude 26° 20' north (near present-day Boca Raton Inlet), while sailing from Jamaica to the "Cape de Verds"; the crew was saved[226].

SUSAN

While Marx (1987) states the *Susan*, Captain Beard, was lost at Amelia Island in 1810, I have been unable to find any reference to a vessel or captain of this name being lost in the cited timeframe off Florida.

SVANEN

The bark *Svanen* ("Swan") was built in April 1878 by Martin Eldrup at Tvedestrand, Norway for the Thorvildsen Brothers. The Norwegian bark was 129.8 feet long, 30.5 feet wide, and displaced 452 tons. On March 23, 1890, the *Svanen* was lost while trying to enter Fernandina Harbor from St. Augustine with a cargo of lumber. The bark was caught in a current that carried her some distance to the southward, and she finally wrecked on the bar. A pilot boat rescued Captain Meikelsen, his two daughters, and the crew.

SWAMP WRECK

South of Walton Rocks Beach Road, and in between A1A and the beach, intrepid explorers may find the camouflaged remains of a shipwreck amidst a small mangrove swamp. The wreck is largely buried, though wooden timbers and iron spikes poke out from underneath the mud and brush.

SWAN

The Whitehall Evening Post of May 27, 1749, reported, "The *Swan*, Capt. Finch, for Antigua from Cardiaz [sic] (reported port of origin was also cited as Carolina), was in her passage lost on the Florida coast."

SWORDFISH (1921)

On April 29, 1921, the yacht *Swordfish* reportedly burned near Amelia Island. Built in 1901 at Nyak, New York as the *Rancocus*, the 151-ton *Swordfish*, official number 111369, was 116.8 feet long and 17.7 feet wide.

SWORDFISH (1992)

The *Swordfish* was an approximately 70-foot long former crewboat used by Mel Fisher during the salvage of the *Nuestra Señora de Atocha* and *Santa Margarita*, which was scuttled as an artificial reef in 80 feet of water off Boynton Beach on April 30, 1992. She was deployed just southwest of the *Budweiser Bar*, though the vessel has reportedly largely been demolished over the years.

SYLPH

The sidewheel steamer *Sylph* was built by Bishop and Simonson in 1844 at New York, and was 290 tons gross, 154 feet long, and 24.6 feet wide. On March 31, 1868, the steamer burned at Julington Creek off the St. Johns River near Fruit Cove.

SYLVINA EXPRESS II

Launched from the Flensburg, Germany shipyard of *Flensburger Schiffbau-Gesellschaft* in 1966, the *Sylvina Express* (IMO number 6608880) was a coastal freighter 196.8 feet in length, 34.2 feet in beam, and 299 tons gross displacement. During her career she changed names and owners several times: in 1973 she was sold to Nico Kähler of Kiel, Germany, and renamed *Tiger*; acquired by Danish owners P.R. Korsör, P. Jorgensen and Company in 1985, the freighter sailed as *Anna Nova*; in 1990, the vessel was sold to *Rederiet Cito I.S.* and renamed *Cito*; purchased in 1994, the freighter was renamed *Dimar B.* by her new Panamanian owners, Interocean Shipping International; later, she was acquired by owners A. Valburn of Belize and finally sailed as *Sylvina Express II*. The *Sylvina Express II* was later seized after an anonymous tip led U.S. Customs Service agents to search the masts of the freighter after it arrived in the Miami River from Cap-Haïtien, Haiti in November 1999, which led to the discovery of 832 pounds of cocaine in plastic-wrapped bricks. In 2000, the freighter was offered at auction, and ultimately was scuttled as an artificial reef off Palm Beach on July 18, 2003. In addition to the freighter, an approximately 30-foot long dissected portion of another vessel was placed on deck of the *Sylvina Express II*. The coastal freighter now sits upright and intact in approximately 280 feet of water, with portions rising over 40 feet from the bottom.

Derelict shrimper scuttled in 425 feet of water off Miami around 1985 (Miami-Dade County Department of Environmental Resources Management).

Deployment of the *Sylvina Express II* (Palm Beach County Artificial Reef Program).

T.S.O. PARADISE

The 123-ton yacht *T.S.O. (This Side Of) Paradise* was built in 1982 at the Baldwinsville Boat Yard in New York. She was 82 feet long and 20 feet in beam, and was powered by twin 130 horsepower Iveco-Ford diesel engines. After sailing up and down the East Coast entertaining clients for a New York corporation, she was anchored in Lake Worth Lagoon in 1993 where she later sunk at her mooring. The *T.S.O. Paradise* was raised, cleaned, and eventually scuttled in 60 feet of water just outside Lake Worth Inlet on July 22, 1997.

T.S.O. Paradise (Palm Beach County Artificial Reef Program).

TACOMA

In 1968, American Marine Corporation of New Orleans constructed the *Cheramie BoTruc No. 16* (IMO number 7108679) for L & M BoTruc Rental, Incorporated. The new offshore supply vessel was 166 feet in length and 36 feet in beam, which displaced 434 tons. She was later purchased by Veronica M., Incorporated, and renamed *Veronica M.*; in 1989, Premium Alaska Fishing Corporation acquired the *Veronica M.* with the intent of converting the supply vessel into a brine-chilled, fish-carrying freighter; ultimately, she sailed as the *Tacoma* following her purchase in 1997 by Caribbean Exploration Shipping, Limited for use on their inter-island freight routes. In January 2001, U.S. Customs Service agents discovered 614 pounds of cocaine hidden in a false compartment beneath the *Tacoma's* fuel tank adjacent to the cargo hold. The former offshore supply vessel was sunk on October 18, 2001, joining the *Brandy Wine*, *Etoile De Mer*, and *Miguana* at U.S. Customs Reef off Key Biscayne. The *Tacoma* rests upright and intact in approximately 130 feet of water, with the top of the bridge rising to within 80 feet of the surface. The wreck of the *Etoile De Mer* rests approximately 500 feet to the southeast of the *Tacoma*.

TAMARCO

The four-masted schooner *Tamarco* was built in 1903 at Bath, Maine as the *Hope Sherwood*, official number 96661, and was 172.8 feet long, 36.6 feet wide, and 686 tons burden. On September 21, 1929, the schooner, laden with 450,000 feet of lumber from the Putnam Lumber Company of Jacksonville, was sailing for French Martinique when she encountered a strong gale soon after clearing the St. Johns Bar. With the *Tamarco* waterlogged and the crew fearing she would break up, Captain Connolly beached the vessel near Flagler Beach. Once the vessel grounded close to shore, the crew took to small boats for the beach; one crew member drowned in the struggle through the surf. The schooner settled considerably in the soft sand off the beach, though later reports stated the *Tamarco* became a total wreck.

TAMINEND

On June 10, 1867, the sidewheel steamer *Taminend*, Captain Springer, struck on the St. Johns Bar as she was returning to Jacksonville from St. Augustine. She reportedly went to pieces, though no lives were lost. The *Taminend* was launched in 1850 from a New York shipyard as the *Miantonomi*, which was 143 feet long, 24 feet wide, and displaced 245 tons gross. In 1853, she underwent a rebuild that increased her length to 170 feet and her displacement to 255 tons. Following the rebuild, she was placed on the Salem route on the Delaware River for a few seasons before returning to New York, where she was renamed *Taminend*. The steamer apparently migrated south as she fell out of favor in the north due to her extremely slow speed.

TARPOON

As a memorial to Mike Kevorkian, owner of the Tarpoon Skin Diving Center in Miami, the 150-foot long former Haitian grain freighter *Medor Herode* was scuttled in 70 feet of water on May 10, 1988. The freighter was significantly impacted by Hurricane Andrew in 1992. The *Tarpoon* was moved several hundred feet against the base of a reef, which ultimately broke the freighter into several large pieces. Due to wreck's proximity to the reef, the scattered debris is typically enveloped in schools of grunts, glassy sweepers, and snappers.

TE AMO

The *Te Amo* was a 78.5-foot long, 97-ton auxiliary diesel ketch built in 1925 by J.W. Upham in Brixham, England as the commercial fishing trawler *Terpsichore*. She operated as a fishing vessel for several years, and in December 1930

The converted freighter *Tacoma* (Florida Fish and Wildlife Conservation Commission Artificial Reef Program).

was renamed *Mannequin* following an overhaul. In 1946, novelist A.E.W. Mason purchased the *Mannequin* and converted her to a yacht, which he named *Muriel Stephens*. The yacht was eventually sailed to Vancouver, British Columbia, where she resided for some time before being purchased by Carlton Rogers and moved south to California. During the 1960s, the yacht was repaired and refurbished at considerable cost. The sailboat eventually migrated to St. Thomas, U.S. Virgin Islands in the 1970s, where she sailed as the charter yacht *Te Amo*. On May 16, 1985, the yacht *Te Amo* ended her long journey when she was sunk in approximately 200 feet of water off Fort Lauderdale.

TELUMAH

The ship *Telumah*, Captain Borland, wrecked approximately five miles north of Caesar's Creek on November 8, 1845, during a voyage from Liverpool to Havana. According to the first officer, she rested "with the Cape Florida light house bearing N by W, 20 miles distant." He continued to describe the ship's final moments:

> On the morning of the 18th, turned to and threw overboard some of her cargo in hopes to lighten her, but to no use; at noon commenced discharging ship on board the wreckers. Three or four hours after, ship struck, she thumped very hard, and knocked her keel off. Up to this time the ship has 8 1/2 feet water in her hold. Some of the cargo is more or less damaged, in consequence of being wet. Cargo consists of iron and crates. Most of the cargo will be saved if the weather continues fine, but the ship cannot be saved as she has bilged.

A November 26 dispatch from Key West stated, "all the dry goods, ale and porter, and nearly all the crates of this ship, saved dry – some 300 tons iron will be saved by diving, as there are seven feet water in the hold of the ship – the materials of the ship will be saved, but she will be lost. Her position on the chart is 18 miles from Cape Florida lighthouse[227]." Based on the reported position of the wreck, roughly 18 miles south of Cape Florida and 5 miles off Caesar's Creek, the final resting spot of the *Telumah* may reside near Pacific Reef at a site known as the "Ore Wreck." The presence of iron ballast at the "Ore Wreck" supports this theory, but in the absence of more definitive evidence, the wreck will likely never be conclusively identified.

THALES

The stranding of the *Thales* on January 9, 1859, was reported in *The New York Times* of February 1, 1859, which detailed:

> By the arrival of the U.S. Revenue Cutter *J. Appleton*, Captain W.B. Randolph, from Miami, we learn the following particulars of the total loss on Hillsboro Bar, of the American bark *Thales*, Captain Marsh:
>
> The bark *Thales*, from New Orleans, with an assorted cargo of provisions, bound on a trading voyage to the coast of Africa, went ashore the night of the 9th, sixty miles north of Cape Florida and twelve miles above Jupiter's Inlet, on or near Hillsboro Inlet. A heavy easterly swell soon drove her high on the beach, where, with her keel out of the water, and her still some feet below the surface, and the cargo wet, Captain Marsh abandoned her and set out, with passengers and crew, in his long boat for Key West. Arriving at Miami, they boarded the cutter and were brought to this city by Lieutenant Randolph. At Miami the news of the accident was communicated to the mail boat, and was dispatched to the wreck. Captain Files, the master, reports that he reached the vessel at an early hour on the 17th. The Indians had been the "first boarders," a large number being on board and on the beach, here was burning a camp fire, but on the approach of the mail schooner, they left the vessel and retreated to the bush. Captain Files went on board and found the cabin ransacked and everything of value removed, but the cargo had not been broached. He at once proceeded to remove the hatches and get out the cargo. He was soon joined by the schr. *Gibson*, of this place, and the two vessels loaded with the entire cargo and materials of the vessel, except some lumber, left the wreck the 19th for Key West.

The 224-ton bark *Thales* was built in 1848 at Edgecomb, Maine, and at the time of her loss was owned by J. Rodewald and Company of New Orleans. Based on its intended voyage, it is likely the *Thales* was involved in the trans-Atlantic slave trade. In 1985, divers looking for the wreck of the *Gil Blas* off Fort Lauderdale found portions of another wreck under nine feet of sand that potentially may be the *Thales*.

THAMES

The wooden-hulled freight steamer *Thames* was originally launched as the *Yuma* from a Philadelphia shipyard in 1889 for the Clyde Steamship Company. The *Yuma*, official number 27635, was 160.5 feet long (between parallels), 23 feet in beam, 447 tons gross, and 369 tons net. The wooden-hulled freighter was eventually sold to the Miami Steamship Company, and migrated south around 1912. On October 25, 1921, the *Thames* sank off the Florida coast during a gale while steaming south from Jacksonville to Miami. According to *The New York Times* of October 25, 1921, "The freight steamer *Thames*, plying between Jacksonville and Miami, sank today about fourteen miles north of Jupiter, but Capt. E. J. Wuhl and his crew of fifteen men reached shore in lifeboats at Gomez." Other articles stated the freighter sank 18 miles north of Jupiter Light. Additional details on the *Thames* were included in an October 25, 1921, article in *The Miami News*, which stated, "The sinking today is not the first such disaster to befall the *Thames*. A little over a year ago she sunk in the Miami Channel with a full cargo aboard. It was believed at the time that she struck some submerged object which put a hole in her hull. Her owners were successful in raising the craft and following extensive repairs she was put back on the Miami-Jacksonville run." As the *Thames* was headed south to Miami, it is conceivable the vessel was favoring the coast to avoid the northward push of the Gulf Stream. Therefore, it's possible the wreck rests in diveable depths somewhere between St. Lucie and Jupiter Inlets.

THEODORE S. PARKER

Built in 1848 at Brown's Point, New Jersey, the oak-hulled schooner *Theodore S. Parker*, official number 24316, was 58 feet in length, 20.8 feet in breadth, and displaced a mere 34 tons. On February 9, 1886, the *Parker* stranded on Mosquito Bar while sailing from New York to New Smyrna with a cargo of furniture, bricks, and salt; only a small portion of the cargo was saved.

Photograph of the four-masted schooner *Theoline*.

THEOLINE

On September 13, 1905, the four-masted schooner *Theoline* was launched by George A. Gilchrist from his Belfast, Maine shipyard. The new schooner, official number 202471, was 185 feet long, 38.4 feet wide, displaced 981 tons gross, and was engaged in the coasting trade for the McQuestion Brothers of Boston. The *Theoline*, Captain Cummins, went ashore on the morning of May 2, 1914, near Nassau Inlet while en route from Boston to Jacksonville. The tug *Biscayne* worked for several days to pull the schooner off the sand bar and into a nearby channel; however, those efforts appear to have been futile, as the wreck of the *Theoline* was referenced in a November 1914 article reporting the loss of the *Alert* in the same area.

THETIS

According to the *British Evening-Post* of October 12, 1790, "The ship *Thetis*, of Bristol, Captain Moore, lost on reef, three leagues distance from Cape Florida in early August 1790." It was reported the *Thetis* was later set on fire after a portion of her cargo was removed.

THIRD AVENUE WRECK

The suspected remains of a mid-eighteenth century British shipwreck rests buried on the beach close to the Third Avenue East Beach Access Ramp in New Smyrna Beach. The site consists of the forward section of a vessel believed to be utilized in the lumber trade. In 2005, an individual advertised portions of the wreck, which included brass and iron fasteners, for sale on eBay, which is a blatant violation of Florida state law.

THISTLE

The wrecking sloop *Thistle* was lost during the salvage of the *Ajax*, in November 1836. Details of her loss were included in Admiralty records, which reported:

> About 3 o'clock on the afternoon of Monday, November 14, 1836, Richard Roberts, master of the schooner *Splendid*, discovered a ship ashore on the eastern part of Carysfort Reef. On boarding her an hour later, he found that she was the *Ajax*, Captain Charles A. Heim, from New York to Mobile with an assorted cargo. Captain Heim at first refused assistance, but about 7 o'clock he called for help. Roberts brought the *Splendid* alongside and transshipped cargo until midnight. The violence of the wind and waves, which parted the schooner's "fasts and chains," then made him haul off, but he anchored and promised to remain to relieve the passengers and crew, if need be. In about half an hour his anchor broke, and he stood off and on in the Gulf, having first sent a boat to the master, telling him to raise a light if he needed help.
>
> During the afternoon, the schooners *Caroline* and *Fair American* and the sloop *Thistle* had arrived. Their masters, John Wood, Latham Brightman, and Daniel Post, had consorted "ton for ton and man for man" to save goods from the *Ajax*. Their combined crews, 24 men, worked all night and "broke out of the lower hold by diving, damaged goods sufficient to load the *Thistle* by 8 o'clock the next morning." When the *Thistle* dropped off from the wreck, "she struck on the stock of an anchor carried out from the…(*Ajax*) – beat a hole in her bottom sunk and was totally lost with nearly all her lading, the weather

preventing the other vessels rendering any effectual assistance, and even compelling them to seek shelter in Caesar's Creek[228]."

It is believed the *Ajax* was lost on the reef that now bears her name off Elliott Key, and it is likely the wreck of the *Thistle* may rest in close proximity to this area.

THOMAS B. CATOR

The two-masted schooner *Thomas B. Cator*, official number 145347, was built in 1883 at Taylors Island, Maryland, and was 69.2 feet long, 23.6 feet in beam, and 46 tons gross burden. On May 12, 1920, the *Cator*, Captain A.B. Swaine, departed Jacksonville with her partner ship *Emma M. Robinson*, en route for Central America loaded with a cargo of lumber, gasoline, and oil. Unfortunately, soon after departing, the schooners encountered a gale. The *Thomas B. Cator* battled the storm for two days, losing all her sails and main anchor, and her 75-horsepower auxiliary engine was disabled. The crew finally beached their schooner near Fort Pierce on May 16 in hopes of saving their lives and cargo. On May 21, the schooner was reported to be in good condition, while the *Robinson* was going to pieces. It is unclear if the *Thomas B. Cator* was ultimately salvaged or broken apart by the surf, but the vessel does disappear from documentation following this incident.

Image of the tug *Thomas H*. (Volusia County Artificial Reef Program).

THOMAS H.

The tug *Thomas H.* was scuttled as an artificial reef in 80 feet of water off Ponce Inlet on July 29, 1995. The tug sits upright on the bottom approximately 1,000 feet west of the *Rio Yuna*, and its surfaces are encrusted with a thin layer of sponges and other organisms, which attracts significant numbers of finfish. This vessel is believed to be the tug *Thomas H.*, official number 244068, built in 1943 by Ira S. Bushey and Sons at Brooklyn, New York, and was 81.1 feet long and 24 feet wide.

THOZINA

On December 15, 2002, the *Thozina* became the fourth vessel deployed at the Governor's River Walk Reef off Palm Beach. The 174-foot long freighter was scuttled in 90 feet of water just to the east of, but in between, the *Sha Sha Boekanier* and the *Gilbert Sea*, and a large pile of rubble was

The stern of the freighter *Thozina*.

added just off the starboard bow of the wreck. All of the freighters sunk at this site have been significantly impacted by past hurricanes, which have collapsed the cargo holds and ripped apart the bow and stern sections. Nevertheless, the *Thozina*, along with the other freighters at the Governor's River Walk Reef, provide a phenomenal diving experience. Divers can typically explore all four wrecks as they are carried north by the Gulf Stream, as well as observe the large resident marine life that frequent the area, which include Goliath grouper, sea turtles, rays, and sharks.

The 425-ton German coaster was originally launched by *J.J Sietas Schiffswerft* on September 18, 1957, as the *Lisa Eichmann* for J. Eichmann of Hamburg, Germany. The freighter was sold in 1961 and was renamed *Nereus*; starting in 1987, the vessel sailed through the Caribbean for Cavalier Lines, who named her *Cavalier Star*; traded to the related shipping company Arawak Lines in 1993, the freighter served as *Arawak Star*; Star Brothers Shipping Company S.A. of Honduras purchased the vessel in 1995, who again named the coaster *Cavalier Star*; in 1998, the coaster was sold to Everline S.A. of Belize and renamed *Sea Queen*; sold in 2000 to Panamanian owners, the vessel was finally named *Thozina*. In July 2002, Palm Beach County acquired the *Thozina* from the U.S. Customs Service, which had seized the coastal freighter earlier that year with concealed narcotics onboard.

Thozina as the *Nereus* (Chas Betts).

THRACIAN

Captain Morrill of the brig *Export*, which wrecked on Ledbury Reef, mentioned that about an hour before they grounded on September 7, 1838, another ship went to pieces in close proximity to them. According to *The Hagerstown Mail*, October 19, 1838, "All hands left the ship, and are probably lost. She went to pieces, and I think it was the ship *Thracian* (also cited as *Thracien*), of Plymouth, her cargo was railroad iron, machinery and dry goods." The newspaper later mentioned, "The ship mentioned as *Thracian* is possibly incorrect. According to the commander of the U.S. Revenue Schooner *Madison*, the ship was in all probability a Boston packet for New Orleans. She had onboard a locomotive, marked "Camden," care of Hyde and Comstock, a carriage, domestics, nails, and brass sheets, and tire iron for wheels."

THREE FRIENDS

Designed and built by Napoleon Bonaparte Broward, the tug *Three Friends* would find itself the focal point of a Federal court case that would, in turn, have important ramifications on Spanish-American relations. The hull of the *Three Friends*, official number 145703, was crafted out of a combination of oak and pine, a process which lasted over a year due to lack of funds. Finally launched for Broward's Jacksonville Forwarding Company in February 1895, the tug measured 112 feet in length and 24 feet in beam. Displacing 157 gross tons, she was powered by a large triple expansion steam engine that produced 525 horsepower. Outfitting of the *Three Friends* lasted until May 1896, whereupon the workhorse found itself ready for duty. The tug was destined to be a filibuster. Cuba was in the midst of a revolution, and there was money to be made by smuggling arms, ammunition, and supplies to the revolutionaries who were trying to rid Cuba of Spanish rule. The rewards to both the ship and her crew were great, however, the risk was even greater. Several of the crewmembers from the *Virginius*, captured during a filibustering run by the Spanish Navy, were executed in Havana before diplomatic negotiations allowed for the release of the remaining prisoners. Because of this incident, the United States, who recognized the Spanish government in Cuba, agreed to help patrol Florida waters in an effort to curb filibustering activity.

Regardless of the risks, the *Three Friends* made several filibustering trips from Jacksonville to Cuba during 1896. Her luck ran out during an arms run in November. While the fast tug outran the pursuing Spanish warships, she was intercepted by the U.S.S. *Newark* on November 7 and escorted back to Jacksonville. Upon her arrival, she was seized by the collector of customs for the district of St. Johns, as forfeited to the United States under Section 5283 of the Revised Statutes (i.e., definition of a filibusterer). On November 12, she was found libel on behalf of the United States District Court for the Southern District of Florida. The libel alleged that the vessel was "furnished, fitted out, and armed with intent that she should be employed in the service of a certain people, to wit, certain people then engaged in armed resistance to the government of the King of Spain, in the Island of Cuba, to cruise and commit hostilities against the subjects, citizens, and property of the King of Spain in the Island of Cuba, with whom the United States are and were at that date at peace[229]." On March 1, 1897, however, Chief Justice Fuller, in rendering the court's decision in *United States v. The Three Friends et al.*, stated that the libel was insufficient under Section 5283 of the Revised Statues. He noted that the libel employed the word "people" in an "individual and personal sense, and not as an organized and recognized political power in any way corresponding to a state, prince, colony, or district[230]." Furthermore, in his assessment of the *Three Friends* intention, he stated that it if "they should be so subject, they would have the benefit of the necessity of proving piratical acts, rather than intentions[231]." Therefore, with this opinion, the court dismissed the libel and, in turn, legalized the act of filibustering.

The tug's days as a filibusterer came to an end, however, with the sinking of the U.S.S. *Maine* in Havana harbor and the declaration of war with Spain in April 1898. The *Three Friends* continued her runs to and from Cuba during the Spanish-American War as a dispatch boat for the *New York Herald*. Due to her respectable speed, she was employed to carry news of the war to Key West where it would then be telegraphed to New York for publication. As a side note, in 1904, Napoleon Bonaparte Broward was elected Governor of Florida, largely due to the reputation he built as a filibusterer with his tug the *Three Friends*. He was later elected to the U.S. Senate but passed away before taking office.

After the war, the tug *Three Friends* stayed in the Florida Keys to work as a salvage tug, towing disabled ships and salvaging cargoes from wrecked vessels. She participated in several wrecking

The filibustering tug *Three Friends* (Florida State Archives).

operations, including the salvage of the steamer *Alicia* in 1905. The tug eventually returned to Jacksonville and served as a harbor tug along the St. Johns River. She was a common appearance along the river, and in 1931 was given the privilege of serving as the escort vessel to greet the U.S.S. *Constitution* during her visit to Jacksonville. She continued to work through World War II, but suffered from lack of attention. During a storm in 1950, her wooden hull gave way and the *Three Friends* sunk at her moorings. While her triple expansion engine was salvaged, the remainder of the vessel was forgotten, and she slowly slipped beneath the surface of the St. Johns River. It is believed one of the hulks resting off the property of Crowley Marine Services in East Jacksonville may be Broward's tug *Three Friends*.

THREE SISTERS

On October 13, 1870, the British brig *Three Sisters*, en route from Nova Scotia for Cuba with a cargo of white pine, struck on the Florida Reef near Cape Florida. Numerous locals from the township of Biscayne apparently rowed out to the wreck and removed papers and 120,000 feet of lumber, which became the subject of an Admiralty court case. Testimony from individuals stated they went out to the vessel, which "had drifted ashore near the beach in front of Key Biscayne Bay." Further, they went out to her repeatedly, eventually finding her bilged and abandoned, "and that from appearances she had been abandoned for several days." Over time, they rafted the lumber out of the wreck and floated it to the Miami River. As they did not have boats to carry the lumber to Key West, which would have incurred "unnecessary expense," they felt obligated to salvage it locally. On January 2, 1873, the case was finally settled, whereupon the all proceeds went to the ship owners and licensed wreckers, and petitions for salvage filed by the locals were dismissed on account of misconduct and fraud. The vessel involved may be the brig *Three Sisters* built in 1854 at Newfoundland, Canada, which was 83 feet in length, 22 feet in beam, and displaced 191 tons.

TIFTON

The *Tifton* was a four-masted schooner built in 1905 at the Mystic, Connecticut shipyard of M.B. McDonald. Displacing 594 tons, the sailing vessel was 173 feet in length, 36.2 feet in breadth, and 13.8 feet in draft. She was constructed with a single deck and an elliptical stern. Homeported in Providence, Rhode Island, she was owned by the John S. Emery Company. On January 29, 1926, the *Tifton* was en route from Boston to Miami with a load of lumber when she became swamped and

Schooner *Tifton* (© The Mariners' Museum, Newport News, Virginia).

rolled over in a gale. The steamer *America* rescued the captain and three crewmen, while the remainder sought refuge in lifeboats. Unfortunately, two drowned in the stormy Atlantic. After salvaging the majority of her cargo, the vessel was abandoned. A January 31, 1926, article in *The New York Times* reported the sinking position as 12 miles southeast of West Palm Beach.

TIGER

The *Tiger* was a 50-ton bark owned by British merchant Sir John Hawkins, father of the English slave trade. On October 18, 1564, the *Tiger* sailed from Plymouth, England on a trading voyage to the West Indies and South America. During his return trip to England, Hawkings visited Ribault's settlement at Fort Caroline near present-day Jacksonville on August 3, 1565. Fort Caroline was established in June 1564, and over the next 14 months, the French settlers struggled to survive. Sympathetic to the Huguenots' plight, Hawkins provided them with provisions. Hawkins also learned from René Goulaine de Laudonnière, Ribault's lieutenant at the outpost, of the French plans to abandon Florida. Upon seeing the state of disrepair the French ships were in, however, Hawkins offered to lend or sell the bark *Tiger* to Laudonnière. Fearing a mutiny, Laudonnière accepted the proposal and purchased the bark for 700 crowns (other sources state Hawkins traded the *Tiger* in exchange for four cannon from Fort Caroline). As preparations were being made to evacuate Fort Caroline, Jean Ribault arrived with reinforcements on August 28. The *Tiger* was reportedly later scuttled when the Spanish overran Fort Caroline and Laudonnière escaped with the remaining French survivors to the *Perle* and *Levière*, which sailed back to France in late September 1565.

TIGER RED

The wreck of the *Tiger Red* is located approximately 17 nautical miles east of Port Canaveral in 85 feet of water, and reportedly consists of a disposed tug boat sunk in 1988.

TITAN

The approximately 70-foot long tug *Titan* was scuttled on July 11, 1989, approximately six nautical miles off St. Lucie Inlet in 80 feet of water. The tug was donated to Martin County by an anonymous individual, and the history of the vessel is likewise relatively unknown. The wreck of the *Titan* rests upright and faces west, and is just inshore of a natural reef line known as the "Six Mile Reef." Divers can splash just south of the wreck, drifting northward with the prevailing current, until the wreck of the *Titan* is observed in the sand a short distance away from the reef. This allows divers to explore both natural reef as well as a small shipwreck on a single dive. Unfortunately, the 2004 hurricanes did impact the tugboat, ripping off the *Titan's* wheelhouse structure and depositing it in the sand approximately 40 feet away from the hull.

TOCOI WRECK

The "Tocoi Wreck" is an unidentified wooden-hulled vessel, approximately 200 feet in length, resting largely buried in a silty bottom off Lane Landing, south of Magnolia Point on the St. Johns River. Exposed portions of the wreck exhibit signs of burning, which may have led to the vessel's loss. While there is evidence of steam machinery, it is unclear if the vessel was a river steamer or a barge. Due to the shallow depth, it is likely any valuable machinery was salvaged after the vessel's sinking or abandonment.

TOMADOR

The 78-ton charter yacht *Tomador*, built in 1959, reportedly burned off Fort Lauderdale in May 1978.

TONY

According to *Lloyd's List* of November 4, 1783, the *Tony*, Captain Welsh, bound from Charleston, South Carolina for St. Augustine, was lost on the St. Augustine Bar.

The *Tortuga* about to make her film debut (Miami-Dade County Department of Environmental Resources Management).

TORTUGA

On April 25, 1995, 40 pounds of dynamite were detonated onboard the 165-foot long offshore supply vessel *Tortuga* for the climax of the movie "Fair Game." The former Hollywood prop ultimately sank in approximately 110 feet of water off Miami. The history of this vessel is unclear, though records indicate the freighter may have formerly been named the *Champion* or *Francia Express*. The wreck now rests a short distance north of the *Atlas Barge*, and both can typically be explored on the same dive.

TRACOR DRY DOCK

The *Tracor Dry Dock* was originally built in 1944 at Eureka, California by the Chicago Bridge and Iron Company for the U.S. Navy. Tracor Marine, Incorporated eventually acquired the non-propelled floating dry dock, which was 288 feet long, 64 feet wide, and 1,200 tons displacement. On June 22, 1982, the obsolete dry dock was scuttled in 225 feet of water off Port Everglades. The wreck

Sinking of the *Tracor Dry Dock* (Broward County Artificial Reef Program).

sits upright, and rises over 40 feet from the bottom. Significant material can be found to the north of the wreck, including several Chris Craft hull molds, two 100-foot barges from Powell Brothers, Incorporated, which were sunk in May 1982, and two 43-foot long barges from Grady Marine Construction, Incorporated, which were sunk in March 2000. In fact, one of the Grady barges landed on top of the dry dock with one end in the sand, which formed an interesting swim-through similar to the one offered by the wrecks of the *Corey N Chris* and *Ronald B. Johnson*.

TRACY

In late 1997, the former 132-foot long offshore supply vessel *Tracy* was seized by the U.S. Customs Service in connection with an investigation into a drug smuggling operation. The *Tracy* was owned by Savil Dessaint, who also owned the *Vanderpool Express* (*Zion Train*), which was the freighter where five murder victims were found in July 1997. Following a long investigation into the Dessaint drug ring, detectives learned they were expecting a shipment of drugs into the Miami River aboard the freighter *Tracy*. On December 17, 1997, U.S. Customs Service agents searched the vessel and found over 125 pounds of cocaine hidden on board. During the inspection of the ship, police realized the crew of the *Tracy* had tipped off Savil Dessaint. However, law enforcement officers were able to stop Dessaint as he was fleeing his house carrying over 65 pounds of cocaine in two duffel bags. The *Tracy* was confiscated and later sold at auction. On March 2, 1999, the *Tracy* was scuttled in 70 feet of water off Broward County to serve as an artificial reef. She was renamed the *Ken Vitale*, in memory of a local dive instructor who

In lieu of explosives, the *Tracy* is scuttled via flooding (Broward County Artificial Reef Program).

suffered a fatal heart attack while diving with students off Pompano Beach in November 1998. The wreck rests upright and is located amongst a cluster of several other vessels, including the tug *Jay Scutti* and the freighter *Merci Jesus*.

Underwater view of the *Tracy's* bow.

TRINITÉ

On September 10, 1565, Jean Ribault, aboard his 32-gun flagship *Trinité* (Trinity), departed Fort Caroline (present-day Jacksonville) and sailed south towards St. Augustine to pursue the Spanish fleet led by Pedro Menéndez de Avilés, which had launched an ineffective attack on the French approximately one week earlier. Joining Ribault and the *Trinité* was the 29-gun vice-flagship *Émérillion*, Captain Nicolas d'Ornano; the 10-gun hired Dieppe transport *Perle* (Pearl), Captain Jacques Ribault (Jean Ribault's son); the 10-gun hired Dieppe transport *Levière*, Captain Vivien Maillard; the 10-gun hired Dieppe transport *Émérillion*, Captain Vincent Collas; the auxiliary *Épaule de Mouton* (Shoulder of Mutton), Captain Machonville; a privateer ship from La Rochelle, Captain Jean Du Boys; the transport *Truite* (Trout); and two small Spanish prize ships seized off Haiti. Unfortunately, the French fleet encountered a hurricane on September 12, which pushed the vessels well south of St. Augustine and eventually cast most of Ribault's fleet up on the beach. The flagship *Trinité* grounded on a sandbar north of Cape Canaveral, while the auxiliary *Épaule de Mouton*, transport *Truite*, and vice-flagship *Émérillion* reportedly wrecked within two miles of each other near (likely north of) Mosquito Inlet.

Several hundred soldiers and sailors from the three vessels wrecked near Mosquito Inlet made it ashore and headed north towards Fort Caroline, however, they encountered Menéndez and a patrol of Spanish troops at Matanzas Inlet, just south of St. Augustine. The French eventually surrendered, whereupon Menéndez had any of the survivors not professing to be a Catholic immediately killed. Approximately two weeks later, Jean Ribault and other survivors from the *Trinité* arrived at Matanzas Inlet to find Menéndez waiting. Upon their surrender the following day, Jean Ribault and 133 others were killed, while only 16 lives were spared. Matanzas, Spanish for "slaughters," bears mute testimony to the massacre of the survivors from Jean Ribault's ill-fated fleet.

Meanwhile, Menéndez had also dispatched a force north from the garrison at St. Augustine to attack the under-manned Fort Caroline. Using the cover of the hurricane, the Spaniards overwhelmed the fort, resulting in the expulsion of the French from Florida. Several of the Huguenots eluded the invading soldiers and worked their way to the mouth of the St. Johns River where they were picked up by the *Perle* and *Levière*, which survived the storm. On September 25, with less than 70 crew and survivors, which included Ribault's son and Ribault's lieutenant at Fort Caroline, René Goulaine de Laudonnière, the remaining French vessels sailed back to France. Laudonnière's vessel *Falcon*, which sailed from Havre de Grace, France, on April 22, 1564, and M. John Hawkins's 50-ton bark *Tiger*, which sailed from Plymouth, England, on October 18, 1564, and later sold to Laudonnière, were both scuttled near Fort Caroline prior to *Perle* and *Levière* sailing back to France.

During the construction of Launch Complex 39B at Kennedy Space Center in the early 1960s, numerous artifacts were uncovered near the beach. Hinges, spikes, cannons, and ship timbers were apparently observed opposite of the launch pad. The unearthed artifacts were potentially associated with the wrecking of the *Trinité*, and a subsequent fort built by the French survivors. According to a December 5, 1565, letter from Menéndez to the King of Spain, Indians told Menéndez that, "70 or 80 French were together building a fort on the Cape of Canefield [Canaveral] and a bark in order to go to France and ask aid...[and that] they had much artillery and municions [sic] which they had taken from the *nao capitana* of Juan Ribao [sic], which was lost there....[232]" Additional reference to the suspected shipwreck site and fort was provided by Captain Clinton P. Honeywell, the keeper at Canaveral Light from 1891 through 1930. Approximately 10 miles north of the lighthouse, Honeywell discovered earthworks that he took to be the remains of ramparts of fortification. Unfortunately, the site was reportedly destroyed during the construction of a road or rail right-of-way associated with the N.A.S.A. launch complex.

TRIO BRAVO

The *Trio Bravo*, official number 127257, was originally built in 1898 as the *Cumberland* by the Columbia Iron Works and Drydock Company in Baltimore, Maryland for the Consolidated Coal Company. The tug was 135 feet long, 27 feet wide, and 377 gross tons. In 1920, the *Cumberland* was sold to the U.S. Army Corps of Engineers and plied the waters of the Great Lakes. The Roen Steamship Company later acquired the tug in 1950 and renamed her *John Roen V*. The large tug remained largely on the Great Lakes until her sale to Trio Shipping Company of Honduras in 1980, after which she sailed to Florida as the *Trio Bravo*. On January 21, 1981, the *Trio Bravo* sank at her dock in Port Everglades, and remained

Trio Bravo as the *Cumberland* (Historical Collections of the Great Lakes, Bowling Green State University).

submerged until March 14. The eight-decade old tug was offered at auction in August 1981 and was later prepared for disposal as an artificial reef. On December 16, 1983, explosive charges breached the hull of the tugboat *Trio Bravo*, sending her to the bottom of the Atlantic in 145 feet of water off Fort Lauderdale. She now sits upright and intact, though her superstructure was significantly impacted from the explosions. This has also opened up access to the vessel's interior, and divers can easily swim down into the engine room to observe the large boilers resting in her belly, as well as other adjacent compartments. The exterior of the former tug has been transformed into a colorful shipwreck by gorgonians and other invertebrate species, though on the few visits I have made to the wreck, I have not noticed an abundance of fish.

Divers over the collapsed superstructure of the tug *Trio Bravo*.

TRITON

According to *The Lady's Miscellany and Weekly Visitor*, Volume 12 (1811), the Philadelphia schooner *Triton*, John Hand, junior master, was wrecked on October 19, 1810, at approximate latitude 27° 23′ north, while sailing from Havana for Richmond with a cargo of sugar. The vessel, cargo, and one man were lost. It was reported the *Triton* wrecked in the same general area as the Spanish brig *African*, the Spanish ship *Union*, and the ship *Caroline*. The reported location would place the wrecks of these vessels in between Fort Pierce and St. Lucie Inlets.

TRIUMFANTE

The Spanish brig *Triumfante* (incorrectly cited as *Tennfaute*) wrecked 60 to 70 miles north of Cape Florida off Boca Raton during a storm in November 1838. According to an April 20, 1839, report from Lieutenant Commander John T. McLaughlin of the U.S. schooner *Wave*, "Saved the crew and passengers, forty in number, with their personal effects, of the Spanish brig *Triumfante*, ashore sixty miles north of Cape Florida. Took from her sixty muskets, fifteen hundred pounds of lead, two hundred and eighty bales of cotton and moveables appertaining to her equipment, transported them to Key West, and burnt the vessel[233]." The *Triumfante* was lost in the same storm as the steamer *Wilmington*.

TRIUNFO

The 201-ton, oak-hulled brig *Triunfo* was built at Laurea, Spain in October 1878. In November 1883, the brig was en route from Cuba to Georgia when she wrecked north of Delray Beach. According to the U.S. Life Saving Station report, dated November 4, 1883:

> On this date the superintendent of the Seventh District, east coast of Florida, received information that a vessel had stranded, nine miles north of the Orange Grove House of Refuge. Proceeding as rapidly as possible to the scene of the disaster, he found upon his arrival at Lake Worth the master and crew (six men) of the brig *Triunfo*, of Barcelona, Spain, from Gibara, Cuba, bound to Savannah, Georgia. The vessel had sprung a leak two days after leaving port, and, the pumps failing to keep her free, she was run on the beach on November 2, and the crew landed safely. The keeper of the Orange Grove Station was informed of the disaster by messenger on the 5th, and upon his arrival arrangements were made for saving as much as possible of the sails, rigging, and general outfit.... The brig became a total loss, and the crew left for Key West on the 8th of November.

TROJAN

The St. Johns River tug *Trojan*, official number 145858, was built in 1900 at Palatka. The 60-ton screw steamer was 70 feet long and 18 feet wide. On March 2, 1903, the *Trojan* burned at Green Cove Springs, upriver of Jacksonville.

TROPIC ACE

On November 22, 1972, the 115-foot long Bahamian container vessel *Tropic Ace*, Captain Haysmer Haylock, sank approximately 25 miles off Fort Lauderdale. Four hours after the 85-ton vessel departed Fort Lauderdale she was on the bottom; Engineer Harold Diaz stated, "I ran down to the engine room and water was rushing over the floor. I don't know what happened. Maybe we hit something on the bottom[234]." The seven-man crew abandoned ship and were picked up by the tanker *Texaco Mississippi* after drifting 26 hours in their lifeboat.

TRUITE

The French transport *Truite* (Trout) was part of Jean Ribault's fleet that returned to Fort Caroline near present-day Jacksonville on August 28, 1565. On September 12, after an earlier skirmish with a Spanish armada, Ribault's fleet pursued the warships and prepared to overtake them near St. Augustine when an intense hurricane struck Florida. The storm pushed Ribault's fleet out to sea, allowing the Spaniards to escape. The *Truite* eventually wrecked north of Mosquito Inlet (Ponce Inlet) within 2 miles of fellow French vessels, the auxiliary *Épaule de Mouton* and vice-flagship *Émérillion*, and north (some sources cite 15 miles north) of Ribault's flagship *Trinité*, which grounded north of Cape Canaveral.

TWILIGHT

The Jacksonville-Middleburg Line steamer *Twilight* sank in Black Creek (likely near Middleburg) on July 31, 1887; engineer Grant Connor drowned in the sinking. Available information indicates the *Twilight* was eventually raised and rebuilt in 1890 may have later operated as a tug on the St. Johns River[235].

TWO BROTHERS

According to the *Daily Journal* of March 23, 1728, "The sloop *Two Brothers*, Jacob Kerslead, from New York for South Carolina, which was bringing hither, was lost on the coast of Florida."

TWO GEORGES

On March 25, 1964, a huge, freak wave capsized the 65-foot charter boat *Two Georges* as it returned from a day of sport fishing, pitching 20 persons into the Boynton Beach Inlet only a short distance from shore. Five were killed, four were hospitalized. The survivors, ranging from teenagers to elderly couples, struggled to shore or were rescued by other vessels coming into the inlet. The wave apparently formed on a sandbar, gathering speed and size before it struck the boat, which whipped her around 90 degrees and flipped her over on her port side; the captain of the *Two Georges* estimated the wave was 18 feet high. One survivor, Jerry Hopkins of New Carlisle, Ohio, said no one on the boat was wearing a life preserver. He stated, "I was under water for what seemed like forever and finally came up gasping, for breath. I heard men screaming. I heard one man yelling for his wife. She had been with him a few seconds before it happened[236]." The *Two Georges* sank as it was being towed in after the accident.

TWO PIRATES

Early on the morning of November 25, 2003, the 64-foot long trawler *Two Pirates* stranded on Ormond Beach during a gale. The crew had anchored the vessel approximately a half-mile offshore the night before, but awoke to find the boat drifting and dangerously close to the breakers around 3:00 a.m. Efforts were made to float the grounded vessel off the beach, but were unsuccessful. With the wood and fiberglass shrimper firmly embedded on the beach, Associated Marine Salvage, Incorporated, dismantled the wrecked trawler two weeks after its stranding. Reportedly, the sailboat *Obsession* and Bertram sportfisherman *Pac Man* also wrecked on the beach during the same storm.

TYRE

The *Tyre* was reported to have burned at Jacksonville on July 28, 1911. The 13-ton gas screw vessel *Tyre*, official number 145910, was built in 1901.

U.S. NAVY CONSOLIDATED PBY-5 CATALINA #08181

On March 16, 1943, a U.S. Navy Catalina flying boat attempted a landing at sea off Jacksonville Beach to rescue the pilot of a fighter aircraft who had crashed and was floating on the surface. Due to a reported lack of experience, the pilot performed a poor landing, which resulted in damage to the hull of the aircraft. The Catalina filled with water and an attempted take off only exacerbated the situation, causing the aircraft to sink. U.S. Navy PBY-5 Catalina #08181 reportedly sank in 85 feet of water with four depth bombs attached.

U.S. NAVY GUNBOAT NO. 2

The following is an extract from the *Charleston Courier*, Monday October 21, 1811:

> The U.S. *Gunboat No. 2* (schooner rigged) under the command of Mr. Lippincott, of the Navy, sailed from this port on the 29th ult. bound for St. Marys. On Friday morning, 4th inst., they made Cumberland Island, but being unable to procure a pilot, they, at night, stood off, weather very bad and a high sea. On Saturday morning, the wind increasing to a heavy gale from the N.N.E., the vessel was hove to under a trey sail, with her head to the eastward; about 11 a.m. the gale increasing, took in the trey sail, and in about five minutes after a heavy sea broke onboard, which hove the boat on her beam ends - they immediately attempted to cut away the mast, but that part of the crew which was below, in their alarm, forced open the hatches, which had been secured in the early gales and the gunboat instantly filled and went down. Several of the crew attempted to save themselves from instant death by clinging to the floating sweeps, spars, etc., but one only of their numbers escaped to tell the mournful tale; all the rest, after struggling awhile in the waves, shared the fate of those who went down with the vessel. The man saved is named John Tier, and what is very remarkable, he was one of the men saved from the wreck of *Gunboat No. 157*, lost on Charleston Bar on the 17th of May last. This man was picked up the next day, after having been 29 hours upon an oar, by Capt. Gould, of the schr. *Dolly*, of Rhode Island, and landed at Amelia Island.

Reportedly, Cumberland Island was strewn with bodies and wreckage from the loss of *Gunboat No. 2*; 25 seamen, as well as 10 officers and passengers, perished in this wrecking event.

U.S. NAVY GUNBOAT NO. 164

Gunboat No. 164 was known as a Jeffersonian gunboat, which were generally built from 1805-1812 for a fledgling navy that could not afford the construction of numerous large blue-water warships. These small ships were typically about 50 feet long and 18 feet wide, with a shallow draft for use on the rivers and in the harbors of the United States. A Jeffersonian gunboat was usually armed with two to three guns: 18- to 24-pound swivel-mounted guns or 32-pounders on traversing carriages. As each of these guns could weigh as much as 7,000 pounds, these shallow-draft vessels would not fare well in heavy seas. At the outset of the War of 1812, the U.S. Navy had only 7 frigates, 4 schooners, 4 ketches, and 170 gunboats opposing the mighty British Royal Navy.

Gunboat No. 164 was built in Beaufort, South Carolina by F. Saltus in 1810. She was armed with one 32-pounder and two 12-pounders, and was assigned to St. Marys, Georgia, in September 1811. On September 9, 1813, a massive hurricane swept through Northeast Florida and Georgia, resulting in significant destruction to property and shipping; in some ports, not a single vessel was spared. In a letter dated September 11, 1813, Commodore Campbell informs the Secretary of the Navy of the destruction at St. Marys:

> We had yesterday morning and night preceding one of the most severe gales I have ever witnessed. It commenced about 6 P.M. at N.N.E. and veered to N by W, when it blew with the greatest force, and continued until about 1 A.M. at which time the tide, which had risen to an uncommon height, ceased to flow, and for about one hour we were favored with a calm. About 2 o'clock the gale recommenced at S.W. and blew until day break with equal, indeed, I think, increased violence. Here the destruction commenced; every vessel in harbor drove on shore or sunk at their moorings. *Gun vessel No. 164*, J.R. Grayson, commander, that had just returned from conveying troops to Beaufort, upset at anchor, and of 26 souls on board at the time she went down, only six were saved. Mr. Grayson and two men reached the marsh on the Florida side, and with great difficulty supported themselves through the night and until about 11 o'clock the next day, when they were discovered and taken off[237].

Several other gunboats were sunk or driven onto the marsh, but most were successfully raised or refloated. After an initial salvage attempt in November 1813, *Gunboat No. 164*, as well as *Gunboat No. 161*, were abandoned in the St. Marys River; they were both cited to be resting in approximately 24 feet of water. *Gunboat No. 161* was built in Charleston, South Carolina by J. March in 1810. She was armed with a single 32-pounder and two 18-pounder guns.

U.S. NAVY MARTIN PBM-5 MARINER #59225

U.S. Navy Mariner #59225 was dispatched from Naval Air Station Banana River (present-day Patrick Air Force Base) on the evening of December 5, 1945, to search for five missing TBM Avengers known as Flight 19. Approximately 30 minutes after taking off, the tanker *Gaines Mill* reported observing a mid-air explosion north of Cape Canaveral. The tanker passed through a big pool of oil about 30 minutes later, yet no debris or bodies were ever recovered. At the time of the explosion, the *Gaines Mill* recorded its position at the time of the explosion as latitude 28° 59' north, longitude 80° 25' west. Over the years, extensive surveys have been conducted in this area with negative results.

Archival image of the U.S.C.G.C. *Lotus* (U.S. Coast Guard).

U.S.C.G.C. LOTUS

The Fabricated Shipbuilding Corporation and Coddington Engineering Company of Milwaukee, Wisconsin built the U.S. Army Speedwell Class mine planter *Colonel Albert Todd* at a cost of $540,000 in 1918. The new vessel was 172 feet in length, 32 feet in beam, and displaced 1,130 tons. In 1924, the vessel was transferred to the U.S. Light House Service, converted to a lighthouse tender, and commissioned as the *Lotus*. The conversion included the installation of a turtleback forecastle, a forward steel main deck, a modified wheelhouse, and a new refrigerating plant. The *Lotus* eventually assumed buoy tender duties upon the consolidation of the U.S. Light House Service with the U.S. Coast Guard in 1939. The *Lotus* was based out of Boston until 1941, when she transferred to Chelsea, Massachusetts. During World War II, the tender laid buoys and anti-submarine nets to assist convoys rallying at Newfoundland, and later conducted standard work in the Caribbean. The *Lotus* (WAGL-229) completed her career off Virginia, whereupon she was decommissioned and sold in late 1946. After a period of service with private owners, the *Lotus* was abandoned on the Miami River. On February 12, 1971, Miami-Dade County, in an effort to remove some of the derelict vessels along the Miami River, loaded the rusting *Lotus* with explosives and had it blown up at sea approximately two miles offshore. The wreck of the *Lotus* now rests upright and intact in 230 feet of water.

U.S.C.G.C. MOCCASIN

The *Moccasin*, official number 221403, was built in 1921 at Lybeck near Jacksonville as the *Liberator* for the Lybeck Ocean Harvester Company of Delaware. The *Liberator* was 102.5 feet in length, 47.8 feet in beam, and 626 tons gross displacement. Some reports state the wooden-hulled fishing vessel, renamed *Moccasin*, was later seized for violating state law by rigging an electrical apparatus to illegally shock fish, facilitating their capture. In August 1924, the U.S. Coast Guard acquired the vessel from Gibbs Gas Engineering Company to be used as their mobile floating headquarters at Fort Lauderdale to help with Prohibition enforcement activities. On September 18, 1926, the cutter *Moccasin* was wrecked during the Great Miami Hurricane, and later set on fire during the July 4, 1927, celebration. On August 22, 1927, *The Miami News* reported the burned wreck of the *Moccasin*, which still remained in the New River Sound, was cut apart and towed offshore to be sunk in the Gulf Stream.

U.S.C.G.C. SPIKE

On April 13, 1966, the Anvil Class inland construction tender *Spike* was commissioned into the U.S. Coast Guard. Built by Dorchester Shipbuilding Corporation at Dorchester, New Jersey, the vessel was 76.1 feet long, 22.4 feet wide, and displaced 129 tons. Assigned to Mayport, the pushboat U.S.C.G.C. *Spike* (WLIC-75308) operated with an 84-foot long barge equipped with a crane and diesel pile-driving and jetting equipment used for the construction, repair, and maintenance of fixed aids to navigation. In June 1985 a survey report indicated the *Spike* was inactive due to numerous mechanical issues. Because of these and other issues, U.S.C.G.C *Spike* was decommissioned on May 30, 1986. After decommissioning, the *Spike* was transferred for use as a dormitory by Safe Harbor Haven, Incorporated (presently known as Safe Harbor Boys Home) at Blount Island near Jacksonville. Eventually, the obsolete vessel was designated for use as an artificial reef. On July 17, 2009, the *Spike* was towed approximately 26 miles offshore to the Harm's Ledge artificial reef area and sunk in 110 feet of water where she now sits upright and intact.

Scuttling of U.S.C.G.C. *Spike* (U.S. Coast Guard).

U.S.S. COLUMBINE

The U.S.S. *Columbine* was originally named the *A.H. Schultz*, a sidewheel steamer built in 1850 and outfitted for tug duty in New York Harbor. The stout wooden-hulled tug was 117 feet long and 20.6 feet in beam. At the outset of the Civil War, the *Schultz* was purchased at a cost of $25,800 from Peter Schultz by Captain Drayton and the U.S. Naval Department on December 12, 1862, and renamed the U.S.S. *Columbine*. Intended to join the blockade of southern ports, the vessel was outfitted with two 20-pounder Parrott rifles by Howe and Copeland of New York. After a stint off South Carolina, the *Columbine* found herself in Jacksonville during May 1864 transporting supplies and patrolling the St. Johns River. The Union army had recently increased patrols along the St. Johns in order to suppress the activity of Captain John J. Dickson. Dickson and his small detachment of men that formed Company H were very successful in their harassment of Union forces along the river. On March 27, 1863, Dickson ambushed the large transport *Mary Benton* (also cited as the *Ben de Ford*) as it unloaded at Teasdale and Reid's Wharf, resulting in numerous Union fatalities including the commanding officer, Lieutenant Colonel Liberty Billings. Dickson's small force only suffered one minor injury. In March 1864, the *Columbine* participated in a raid on Confederate sugar refineries that resulted in the capture of two Confederate steamers.

On May 23, 1864, Captain Dickson, now commanding the Confederate Second Florida Cavalry, learned of the approach of the 132-ton Union tug from scouts along the banks of the St. Johns. Having disabled the large gunboat *Ottawa* just the day before, Dickson now prepared a warm welcome for the *Columbine* by placing two 12-pounder artillery pieces and 16 sharpshooters in the woods along the east bank of the river. Patiently waiting and well camouflaged, the Confederates allowed the tug to approach within 200 feet of their position before initiating their ambush. Taken by surprise, the *Columbine* was quickly disabled by artillery shots into her engine room. With the loss of her steam power, the tug drifted into a nearby sandbar approximately 300 feet from the bank off Horse Landing, where the remainder of Dickson's force lay in waiting. The Confederate snipers proceeded to spray the vessel with accurate fire, killing and wounding the majority of her crew. After the fierce 45-minute battle, Acting Ensign Francis W. Sanborn reluctantly surrendered to the Confederate troops. While the Confederates suffered no casualties, over 148 men onboard the *Columbine* were killed or wounded in the melee, many of whom drowned while attempting to swim across the St. Johns River. After taking the survivors as prisoners and stripping the tug of rifles and ammunition, Captain Dickson and his troops burned the *Columbine* to her waterline in order to prevent it from being salvaged by nearby Union ships. While the incident had no practical effect on the war, it did represent one of the few instances in which a Union warship was destroyed by land-based forces during the Civil War in Florida. During the spring of 1864, the Confederates managed to sink four other Union ships in the St. Johns River with the use of a new weapon – the floating torpedo – or mine.

According to the *Annual Report of the Chief of Engineers, United States Army, to the Secretary of War for the Year 1888*, the U.S.S. *Columbine* "grounded in 5 feet of water and was burned. After the war the boiler, machinery, and hull were removed. The examination showed many fragments remaining, supposed to be portions of her upper works. These lie 200 feet from the nearest bank, with about 3 1/2 feet of water over them, and are directly in the track taken by small steamers."

Until recently, the Florida Division of Historical Resources, Bureau of Archaeological Research, claimed the "the remains of *Columbine* were rediscovered and identified by sport divers in 1971. Sport divers subsequently removed many artifacts. The site was severely impacted, and few of the artifacts removed illegally are now in public museum collections. Most have long since disintegrated due to lack of conservation." It should be pointed out that the basis for this claim was not from an archaeological investigation, but merely a reckless assumption based on articles published in *Skin Diver* magazine. The articles, written by Howard B. Tower, Jr., detailed how Tower and fellow divers found scattered munitions, bottles, and other assorted artifacts in shallow water off Rodeheaver Boy's Ranch at Horse Landing in late October 1971. Unfortunately, the present-day location of Horse Landing is approximately three-quarters of a mile downriver from the historical location of Horse Landing, now known as Possum Bluff, and where the *Columbine* was sunk. Fortunately, William Rivers sorted through the conflicting information and uncovered an 1864 map that revealed the true location of Horse Landing and the historical sinking position of the U.S.S. *Columbine*.

Attack on the U.S.S. *Columbine* (Florida State Archives).

U.S.S. GENERAL HUNTER

On April 16, 1864, the 470-ton steamer U.S.S. *General Hunter* struck a torpedo (mine) near Mandarin Point on the St. Johns River. An April 17 report by Commander Balch stated, "I regret to inform you that the steamer *General Hunter* was sunk by a torpedo yesterday at 9 a.m., whilst on her way from Picolata to this place. The *Norwich* was convoying the *Cosmopolitan* and *General Hunter*, the two leading vessels having safely passed, and drawing from 3 to 4 feet more water, when the explosion took place, and by which the *Hunter* was sunk in five minutes, with the loss of a quartermaster of the *Hunter*." Historical accounts state the explosion occurred abreast the wreck of the *Maple Leaf*, possibly as close as 100 feet. The salvage firm of Johnson and Higgins, established in January 1854, was contracted to salvage the wreck of the U.S.S. *General Hunter* in October 1864. The salvors reportedly raised the vessel from the St. Johns River and delivered it to the U.S. Army in Jacksonville on June 22, 1865.

U.S.S. MINDANAO

The keel of the *Mindanao* was originally laid down on April 11, 1943, as the Liberty ship *Elbert Hubbard* by Bethlehem-Fairfield Shipyards, Incorporated of Baltimore, Maryland for the U.S. Maritime Commission. During construction, however, the vessel was converted to the Luzon Class internal combustion engine repair ship U.S.S. *Mindanao* (ARG-3), which was commissioned into the U.S. Navy on November 6, 1943. The *Mindanao* was 441.5 feet in length, 59.9 feet in breadth, and 4,023 tons in displacement. Following her shakedown, the vessel immediately steamed for the Pacific Theater, where she supported the advance of U.S forces. On the morning of November 10, 1944, the U.S.S. *Mindanao* was moored at Seeadler Harbor in Manus, Admiralty Islands, approximately 1,000 feet from the ammunition ship U.S.S. *Mount Hood*. At approximately 9:00 a.m., the *Hood*, fully laden with munitions for the pending invasion of the Philippines, erupted in a cataclysmic explosion. The U.S.S. *Mount Hood* was obliterated by the blast, which gouged a 30-foot deep crater in the seafloor; her entire crew, aside from 18 men on shore leave, perished in the disaster. The *Mindanao* also suffered in the blast: the hull and superstructure were riddled with shrapnel, which killed or wounded approximately 180 of her crew. The U.S.S. *Mindanao* fortunately stayed afloat and was eventually repaired and put back in service towards the end of December 1944. After supporting action in the Solomons, as well as the Okinawa campaign, the *Mindanao* was decommissioned on May 17, 1947 and was later transferred to the U.S. Maritime Administration, which laid her up at the National Defense Reserve Fleet at Beaumont, Texas. On March 12, 1980, Florida acquired the surplus vessel for use as an artificial reef. After her superstructure was removed at a Brunswick, Georgia shipyard, on November 11, 1980, the U.S.S. *Mindanao* was sunk in 85 feet of water approximately 12 nautical miles northeast of Ponce Inlet. The wreck has been slightly impacted by storms over the years, but is largely intact with the main deck encountered at a depth of 60 feet.

U.S.S. MONTAUK

On August 21, 1918, the U.S.S. *Montauk* (SP-392) wrecked off Cumberland Island, approximately 20 miles from Fernandina, during a gale. The patrol vessel encountered the storm on August 19, and battled the elements for over 12 hours until her engines gave out and she was forced to drop anchor. Unfortunately, her anchor chains eventually parted under the strain and she was driven ashore. While 17 crewmen survived the sinking, 7 sailors were lost in the breakers trying to reach the beach. The *Montauk* began to break up soon after grounding, ultimately becoming a complete loss. Originally a trawler built in 1880 at Kennebunk, Maine, the *Montauk* was acquired by the U.S. Navy in 1917 and converted into a patrol vessel. The former fishing vessel was 121 feet long, 19 feet wide, and displaced 161 tons.

U.S.S. MULIPHEN

The keel of the U.S.S. *Muliphen* (AKA-61) was laid down on May 13, 1944, by the Federal Shipbuilding and Drydock Company at Kearny, New Jersey. Commissioned into the U.S. Navy on October 23, 1944, the Andromeda Class attack cargo vessel was 459.2 feet long, 63 feet wide, and displaced 7,360 tons. During World War II, the "Mighty Mule" notably supported the invasion of Okinawa and participated in the landings at Iwo Jima, where she lost 11 of her landing craft. Following the war, the *Muliphen* was assigned to the Naval Transportation Service for a four-year service in the South Pacific, as well as into the cold waters off Alaska. In 1950, the U.S.S. *Muliphen* transferred to Norfolk to join the Atlantic Amphibious Force, and was eventually redesignated as the amphibious cargo ship LKA-61 in 1969. After an almost

Port side profile view of the U.S.S. *Mindanao* (Naval Historical Center).

26-year career, which, at the time, included the longest continuous active-duty period of any vessel in the U.S. Navy, the *Muliphen* was decommissioned on August 28, 1970. On November 2, 1988, the U.S.S. *Muliphen* was towed to Fort Pierce for preparations prior to her deployment as an artificial reef. At a cost of $118,000, the vessel was cleaned, towed 16 nautical miles offshore almost equidistant between the Fort Pierce and St. Lucie Inlets, and scuttled on January 20, 1989.

The wreck of the U.S.S. *Muliphen* is simply massive. While the vessel is largely upright and intact, the 2004 Hurricane Season fractured the hull of the vessel in two, which has resulted in the extreme bow and stern settling almost 20 feet deeper, and collapsed one of the cargo boom support towers, which used to rise to within 90 feet of the surface. Due to a starboard list, the main deck of the 460-foot long wreck is now encountered at a depth of 145 feet on her port side and about 160 feet on the starboard side. Divers will find a maximum depth of approximately 170 feet around the seafloor around the hull, though depths exceeding 200 feet can be reached in the considerable trench formed when the massive ship collapsed the limestone bottom upon its sinking. The vessel is oriented with her bow pointing eastward, which makes for an easy target for divers to drift into with the generally northward-moving current. Abundant gag grouper swarm about the wreck, as well as healthy populations of sheepshead, snapper, and spadefish. Numerous cargo holds allow exploration into the interior, and her superstructure produces extensive penetration potential. The wreck of the *Muliphen* is definitely an impressive and enjoyable dive when conditions are favorable.

Sub chaser *PC-1174* (National Archives).

U.S.S. PC-1174

The wreck of the PC-461 Class submarine chaser U.S.S. *PC-1174* is part of "The Corridor" off North Palm Beach, which also includes the wrecks of the *Amaryllis*, *Mizpah*, and an 80-foot long barge, which are linked by large piles of rock rubble and concrete pilings. Resting in 90 feet of water, the broken-up remains of the *PC-1174* can be observed nestled against the hull of the larger *Mizpah*. The construction contract for *PC-1174* was originally assigned to Defoe Shipbuilding Company of Bay City, Michigan, but was ultimately transferred to Leathem D. Smith Shipbuilding and Drydock Company at Sturgeon Bay, Wisconsin. The keel of the subchaser was laid down on May 13, 1943, and the vessel was eventually commissioned into the U.S. Navy on November 5, 1943. With a length of 173.7 feet, a beam of 23 feet, and a displacement of 295 tons, the *PC-1174* was initially assigned to the Gulf of Mexico Sea Frontier where she served as a convoy escort, and later participated in a convoy into the Mediterranean following a major overhaul. Following the end of hostilities, the subchaser was converted to tow targets for aircraft bombing and strafing exercises off the Virginia coast. On January 1, 1947, *PC-1174* was decommissioned and laid up in the Atlantic Reserve Fleet at Green Cove Springs. Oddly, while the vessel remained in reserve status, she was renamed U.S.S. *Fredonia* on February 15, 1956. The mothballed and surplus *Fredonia* was eventually purchased by the Palm Beach Sailfish Club, which planned to sink the vessel off Lake Worth Inlet to become one of Palm Beach County's first artificial reefs. On April 9, 1968, one day after the scuttling of the *Mizpah*, the U.S.S. *PC-1174* was sunk off Palm Beach.

U.S.S. RANKIN

Launched on December 22, 1944, from the Wilmington, North Carolina yard of the North Carolina Shipbuilding Company, the Tolland Class attack cargo ship U.S.S. *Rankin* (AKA-103) was 459.1 feet in length, 63 feet in beam, and 8,635 tons in displacement. After a shakedown cruise, the *Rankin* joined the Pacific Fleet in April 1945 and participated in the Okinawa invasion in June 1945. Later, while in Seattle, Washington undergoing repairs, Japan offered their unconditional surrender, which ended Rankin's wartime service. After a brief period in the Pacific Reserve Fleet, the *Rankin* was reactivated and assigned to the Atlantic Fleet, where she assisted with amphibious assault training operations and participated in landing of U.S. Marines at Beirut in 1958. On January 1, 1969, U.S.S. *Rankin* was reclassified as an amphibious cargo ship (LKA-103). Following an extended second career as a transport and training support vessel, the *Rankin* was decommissioned on May 11, 1971, and later transferred to the U.S. Maritime Administration.

On July 24, 1988, the U.S.S. *Rankin* was sunk as an artificial reef approximately seven miles east of St. Lucie Inlet and 13 nautical miles south of the similar U.S.S. *Muliphen*. The wreck initially came to rest on her starboard side in 125 feet of water, with her port side rising to within 70 feet of the surface. In 2004, Hurricanes Frances and Jeanne significantly impacted the former attack cargo

U.S.S. *Rankin* (Naval Historical Center).

247

vessel, breaking the vessel in half and devastating the forward section of the wreck; the stern section remains largely intact and unaffected. While Mother Nature's hand significantly compromised the integrity of the *Rankin*, the modifications have apparently appealed to many fish species – surveys of the wreck have found more species and greater abundance of fish since the passing of the 2004 storms. Due to her closer proximity to shore, visibility on the U.S.S. *Rankin* is generally lower than on the U.S.S. *Muliphen*, which is sited in deeper offshore waters.

ULTRA FREEZE

The refrigerated freighter *Ultra Freeze* was built in 1959 as the *Herbert Horn* at the Hamburg, Germany shipyard of *J.J Sietas Schiffswerft* for Heinrich C. Horn, the same original owner of the *Mimi Horn* (*Miller Lite*). In 1965, the vessel was sold to the Hamburg South American Line; United Trans-Caribbean Navigation, Incorporated of Panama acquired the reefer in 1968 and renamed her *Mary B.*; the freighter was renamed *Ultra Freeze* in 1970 following her sale to new owners; she traded hands one last time to *Carpentaria S.A.* of Panama in 1983. Following her sale to *Carpentaria S.A.*, a survey in Guayaquil, Ecuador found the *Ultra Freeze* to be in dramatically poor condition. The owners ignored the findings though, and had the freighter loaded with a cargo of 200 tons of shrimp and set sail for Miami in September 1983. En route, the *Ultra Freeze* was forced to dock at Panama for repairs, which delayed the vessel for several months even though the repairs were apparently never completed. The reefer was finally towed into Miami on December 16, 1983 with a cargo of badly decomposing shrimp, representing a loss of over $1.5 million worth of product. Numerous lawsuits were filed against *Carpentaria S.A.* claiming negligence, and the *Ultra Freeze* was eventually abandoned on the Miami River. Over the next several months, the rusting derelict was vandalized and stripped by locals. At a cost of almost $80,000, the Ultra Freeze was cleaned and sunk as an artificial reef on July 6, 1984. The *Ultra Freeze*, now resting in approximately 120 feet, is a large and impressive wreck. In 1992, Hurricane Andrew ripped the starboard side of the hull open, bent the hull 90 degrees at amidships, and stripped the pilothouse from the hull. There is extensive penetration possible, but divers should have the requisite experience before exploring the interior due to fallen electrical cables and general deterioration. Unfortunately, the *Ultra Freeze* rests in an area that apparently is subject to chronically turbid visibility.

UMTATA

Named after a city in the Eastern Cape province of South Africa, the *Umtata* was launched on August 30, 1935, at the Newcastle shipyard of Swan, Hunter, and Wigham Richardson, Limited. The passenger/cargo vessel documented a length (between parallels) of 451.3 feet, a beam of 61.3 feet, and a displacement of 8,137 tons. Upon completion, the *Umtata* was employed on the Natal Direct Line for owners Bullard, King, and Company, Limited of London. At the outset of World War II, the *Umtata* was

The passenger freighter *Umtata*.

pressed into service for the British Admiralty, and on the evening of March 9, 1942, the large steamer was moored to refuel in the Caribbean port of Castries Harbor, St. Lucia. Loaded in her cargo holds were 2,000 tons of tungsten ore, an important raw material for weapons production. However, even ships anchored in a naturally protective port were not safe during World War II. In a bold move, *Kapitänleutnant* Albrecht Achilles guided the German submarine *U-161* into the shallow harbor entrance at 11:45 p.m. and fired a single torpedo at the *Umtata*, as well as one at the Canadian steamer *Lady Nelson*, which was also moored alongside the wharf. The torpedo hit amidships, crippling the engine room. Reportedly, 24 people were killed in the attack on the *Umtata*, which burned and eventually settled to the bottom next to the *Lady Nelson*. Due to the precious nature of the *Umtata's* tungsten cargo, however, the vessel was quickly raised, and its hull was repaired with concrete.

The tug *Edmond J. Moran* was dispatched to St. Lucia along with a U.S. Navy escort to tow the disabled *Umtata* and its cargo to the United States. After stopping off at San Juan, Puerto Rico, the trio of ships continued north for Florida on June 19, 1942, arriving at Key West around July 5. The following day, the *Moran* towed the *Umtata* north with three U.S. Navy escort ships. Ignoring the presence of the enemy warships, *Kapitänleutnant* Helmut Möhlmann and the *U-571* moved into position as the convoy approached Miami and fired a torpedo at the Umtata at 2:00 a.m. on July 7. James A. Jolly was radio officer onboard the *Edmond J. Moran*, and he related the evening's events thusly, "As we passed Miami there were many lights on shore. For a submarine, this was ideal, for at night we and the *Umtata* made a silhouette target. Even though we had a Navy escort, the German submarine waited until the escort, in its circle around us, was on our land side. The submarine then torpedoed the *Umtata*. It was the middle of the night. The captain ordered the tow line to be cut so that the sinking *Umtata* would not drag the tug down with it." War records indicate the attack occurred at approximate latitude 25° 35' north, longitude 80° 02' west (approximately four nautical miles east of Fowey Rocks Light), however, Jolly indicates the convoy was likely farther north and offshore Miami. Regardless, Jolly recalled that all 92 of the *Umtata's* crew were picked up by the *Moran* and convoy escorts by 6:00 a.m. and taken into Miami while the *Umtata* sank beneath the Atlantic.

The final resting spot of the *Umtata* has yet to be documented. James Jolly indicated the torpedoed freighter was sinking rapidly due to the heavy cargo of tungsten ore. Perhaps the *Umtata* is one of the large deepwater wrecks known to rest off Miami; Captain Wayne Conn knows of two such wrecks: one in 735 feet of water and the other in 910 feet of water. Another remote possibility is that the *Umtata* drifted north in the Gulf Stream and potentially came to rest in 290 feet of water off Sebastian at a site locally known as the "Fuggedaboudit Wreck." While this scenario may perhaps be unlikely given the testimony of James Jolly, one of the dominant attributes of the "Fuggedaboudit Wreck" is the presence of some type of ore cargo in the holds of the unidentified freighter. Hopefully, future exploration of the "Fuggedaboudit Wreck" will yield some useful information.

UNCLE SAM

According to Singer (1998), the 26-ton vessel *Uncle Sam*, which was built in 1940, stranded one mile south of Ponce de Leon Inlet on February 27, 1948.

UNION

Volume 12 (1811) of *The Lady's Miscellany and Weekly Visitor*, stated the Spanish ship *Union*, Captain Domingo Antonio Lordau, went ashore on October 25, 1810, at approximate latitude 27° 23' north. She was sailing from Havana for London with a cargo of logwood when she was blown ashore in the same gale and in the same area as the Spanish brig *African* and the ship *Caroline*. The captain, mate, second mate, and two men were drowned in the wrecking; the remainder of the crew, 15 in number, were rescued by the schooner *Liberty*. The reported location would place the wrecks of these vessels in between Fort Pierce and St. Lucie Inlets.

UNION EXPRESS

The *Union Express* (IMO number 5315242) was built in 1959 as the coastal freighter *Scheldeborg* by *Scheepswerf Friesland N.V.* at Lemmer, Netherlands. The coaster was 159.2 feet long, 26.1 feet wide, and 394 tons burden. In 1969, the vessel was purchased by S. de Jong of the Netherlands, who renamed her *Adine* (also appears as *Adina*); sold to a Panamanian company in 1982, the freighter sailed as *El Masare*; and in 1988, the coaster began

The fractured bow of the *Union Express*.

The stern of the coaster *Union Express*.

operating as the *Union Express* for Honduran owners. The vessel did not operate long for her new owners, however, as the *Union Express* was escorted into Miami and impounded in 1990 after the U.S. Coast Guard found drugs hidden onboard the freighter. The Dutch coaster was eventually acquired for use as an artificial reef and ultimately sunk on April 25, 1992. Officially known as the Mariner Outboards Reef, or simply, the *Mariner I*, the freighter rests on her side in 110 feet of water. Several months after the *Union Express* was scuttled, Hurricane Andrew swept across South Florida, breaking the freighter into two sections and flattening her amidships and forward cargo holds. The bow rests on her port side and is dug into the sand bottom, while the larger and more interesting stern lies hard over on her starboard side. The *Mariner II Barge* can be found approximately 400 feet offshore and slightly north of the *Union Express*.

Another view of the stern superstructure of the *Union Express*.

UNITED CARIBBEAN

Undoubtedly, the one vessel with the most notorious history sunk in the Florida artificial reef program is that of the *United Caribbean*. The *United Caribbean* was a 150-foot long freighter sunk August 22, 2000, off Boca Raton in approximately 70 feet of water. This freighter originally made news in 1993 as the *Golden Venture*. In early 1992, Lee Peng Fei and Cheng Chui Ping coordinated a smuggling operation for Chinese nationals wishing to enter the United States. The cost for each would-be immigrant was between $15,000 and $30,000. The original plan called for the Chinese passengers to travel on a ship called the *Nadj II* from Thailand to the United States, but that ship was forced to moor off the coast of Kenya while its 300 passengers were stranded on board with inadequate food and supplies for five months. Mr. Lee then orchestrated the purchase and refitting of a second ship (which was owned by a New York Chinese organized crime ring), the Panamanian-flagged *Golden Venture*, which arrived from Singapore to pick up the stranded passengers off the coast of Kenya.

Though the *Golden Venture* was a cargo ship not licensed to carry passengers, it was already carrying between 90 and 100 Chinese nationals when it arrived in Africa, whereupon approximately 200 of the *Nadj II's* passengers joined them to continue their voyage to the United States on the *Golden Venture*. Once aboard, the passengers were confined to a 20 by 40 foot cargo hold that had only one ladder leading to the deck. The hold was split into two levels by rows of wooden boards stretching from one side of the ship to the other. Water and food were severely rationed, and there was no water for personal hygiene. The ship had only one toilet, the use of which was restricted to the crew, the smugglers, and the few women passengers on board. It had no life preservers and only two lifeboats, which in turn were adequate to carry only the (unusually small) crew of 14. Passengers who questioned the arrangements were beaten.

The 298 passengers spent between three and six months (depending whether they had boarded in Asia or in Kenya) on the ship as it made its way to the United States. Lee, who was then in New York, had hoped initially that he could arrange for small boats to rendezvous with the *Golden Venture* in the Atlantic to pick up the passengers and transport them to shore. When this plan fell through, he instructed the *Golden Venture* to approach the New York harbor. Mr. Lee Peng Fei ordered Kin Sin Lee (whom he had hired to travel on the *Golden Venture* and oversee its day-to-day operations) via ship-to-shore radio to ground the ship at full speed in the dead of night off the coast of Rockaway Point in Queens. Mr. Lee also told Kin Sin Lee to tell the passengers that those who could swim should jump off the ship and swim ashore when the boat was grounded, while the others should wait for someone to pick them up. No other arrangements were made for disembarking the passengers. Beginning about midnight on June 6, 1993, the crew began its efforts to ground the ship. After twice beginning to speed for the shore and then realizing that the location was unsuitable, the ship finally picked a spot on the ocean side of Rockaway Point, and at about 3:00 a.m. ran the ship aground. The passengers' only warning that the ship was being grounded had been given some 12 hours earlier, when they were told to brace themselves. Chaos ensued. Some passengers jumped into the rough water, which was below 60° F, and 10 of them drowned or died of hypothermia.

Stern of the *United Caribbean*, still upright, after the first round of storms.

Stern superstructure of *United Caribbean* in 2008, now listing hard to port.

The *United Caribbean* as *Golden Venture* grounded off Rockaway Beach, New York (U.S. Coast Guard).

Survivors were arrested and detained by the Immigration and Naturalization Service as they applied for asylum. The abrupt and tragic ending of the Chinese immigrants' four-month journey set off an unprecedented crackdown on illegal immigration in the United States. Of the surviving passengers aboard the *Golden Venture* apprehended by authorities, 155 were ordered deported. At least 99 of those have returned to China, and others have been sent to Latin America; fewer than 40 people have been granted asylum, with a couple others receiving artist's visas that allow them to remain permanently in the

United States. Many others spent several years in jail awaiting a decision on their future. In February 1997, President Clinton released the last 53 *Golden Venture* detainees, though ultimately only two of these immigrants were allowed to remain in the United States.

The freighter changed hands and names, eventually becoming the *United Caribbean* only to wind up as a rusting hulk on the Miami River after failing to make a profitable venture running goods between Florida and Haiti. The vessel was eventually abandoned by the owner and subsequently purchased for use as an artificial reef. The *United Caribbean* is in close proximity to the barge *Sea Emperor*, and there is a trail of large quarried rock between the two sites.

UNKNOWN ENGLISH BRIG

On August 10, 1756, the *London Evening Post* reported, "Capt. Morris, of the *Enterprise*, who is arrived in the river from Jamaica, saw on the 5th of July last on the Florida shore, in lat. 25° 30' (near the northern point of Elliott Key) a new brig seemingly English built, loaded with logwood and pimento, who had a double horse-head, was lute-sterned, and had a woman painted blue on it. No other papers were found except some letters, dated about 1750 or 51, directed to Andrew Young, Esq., at Kirkwall. There were no boats on board."

UNKNOWN ENGLISH MAN OF WAR

According to the *Post Boy* of September 24, 1720, "The pacquet boat lately arrived from the Havana brought, among other news, advice of the loss of an English man of war and several merchant ships, by hurrican [*sic*], upon the coast of Florida."

UNKNOWN ENGLISH VESSEL

In a May 16, 1777, letter, the Spanish ship *Bayona* reported that on her voyage to Cadiz she encountered a large unidentified English vessel off the coast of Florida in great distress, which foundered soon after its master, Captain Stephen Williams, and crew evacuated her[238]. Due to the speed of the English vessel's sinking, the *Bayona* could not save anything from the ship.

UNKNOWN FRENCH SHIPS

According to the *Daily Advertiser* of April 10, 1778, "A captain of a ship arrived from the West Indies, gives an account that three large French merchant ships, bound from Bourdeaux to Martinico [*sic*] with valuable cargoes, had foundered in a hard gale of wind on the coast of Florida, and that the major part of the crews were drowned."

UNKNOWN FRENCH SNOW

On February 6, 1753, the *London Evening Post* reported, "There is advice from New York, that the crew, in number thirty-seven, of a French snow, that was forced on the Florida shore in the storm on the 4th of last November (1752), were killed by the Indians."

UNKNOWN PIRATE SLOOP

The May 10, 1725, issue of the *Daily Post* stated, "There is advice by a letter from Jamaica of the 2d of March last, that Sprigg the pyrate [*sic*] has been again at the Bay of Honduras, and taken 16 sail, of whom he destroy'd one; that his consort Shipton, who commanded a sloop of 12 guns and 70 men, was cast away on the coast of Florida, where the Indians took them all, except Shipton and 12 more, who escaped in a canoe; 'Tis said the Indians eat 16 of them, and the rest were carry'd to Havana." The mentioned vessel is possibly the Boston sloop *Ebenezer*, Captain Kent, which was captured by the pirate Shipton on December 23, 1724, off the Bay of Honduras, along with the ship *John and Mary*.

UNKNOWN PRIVATEER BRIG

A June 27, 1817, dispatch included in The Times of July 31, 1817, reported:

> By the British schooner *Henry and Robert*, Tedder, five days from Nassau, we are informed, that a short time before she sailed, a privateer brig, under the Carthaginian flag, was wrecked upon Cape Florida. The crew, with about 140,000 dollars in specie, were saved by the Providence wreckers, and brought to Nassau. The government ordered them to be arrested as pirates, when a part of the privateer's men seized upon a small wrecky vessel (the *Venus*), put the specie on board her, and affected their escape. The remainder, about 18 or 20 in number, were committed to gaol [*sic*], and their trial was going on when the *Henry* sailed.

UNKNOWN PRIVATEER SNOW

On July 11, 1745, the *Virginia Gazette* published a June 27 report via Philadelphia: "We hear, via Rhode Island, that a privateer snow, Capt. Mackey, belonging to Jamaica, being much shattered in her rigging by an engagement with a French ship of superior force, in which he lost several of his men, was afterwards cast away and lost on the coast of Florida. Her men were saved by a Rhode Island privateer, and lately brought in there."

UNKNOWN SCHOONER

An American schooner from Ogeechee, Georgia was thought to have foundered in a November 1779 storm off Tybee, Georgia, but it was later learned that she had been driven ashore on the coast of Florida "between the Musquitos [*sic*] and St. Augustine" and the survivors were made prisoners[239].

UNKNOWN SHIPWRECK (1769)

Bernard Romans' 1775 map of East Florida notes a shipwreck just above Mount Tucker (present-day Turtle Mound) dated 1769.

UNKNOWN SHIPWRECK (1775)

Bernard Romans' 1775 map of East Florida notes a shipwreck approximately two nautical miles south of False Cape and five nautical miles north of Cape Canaveral; unlike the other wreck noted on the map near Mount Tucker, there is no date associated with this wreck.

UNKNOWN SHRIMP TRAWLER (2002)

A 75-foot long shrimp trawler caught fire, burned, and exploded approximately nine miles off Amelia Island on June 25, 2002[240]. The fire apparently started in the engine room around 10:00 p.m., and could not be contained, forcing the three persons on board to abandon ship in a raft. The U.S. Coast Guard rescued the trio, but the unidentified shrimp trawler was destroyed.

UNKNOWN SHRIMP TRAWLER (2003)

On the evening of October 23, 2003, an 80-foot long wooden-hulled shrimp trawler caught fire approximately 20 miles off Cape Canaveral[241]. The three fishermen on board the unidentified vessel were picked up by a Good Samaritan sailing nearby. The trawler continued to burn into the night and likely sank.

UNKNOWN SNOW

A December 12, 1768 dispatch from Charleston, South Carolina, included in the *British Evening Post* of January 28, 1769, reported, "A snow belonging to New York, Roach, master, from Pensacola with 160 officers and soldiers, is wrecked on the bar of St. Augustine; all the people on board were saved, but the baggage, etc. lost."

UNKNOWN SPANISH MEN OF WAR

On October 3, 1733, the *London Miscellany* published an extract of a letter from South Carolina dated July 21, which detailed the potential loss of several vessels in the vicinity of present-day Fort Pierce. The extract stated:

> About four days since Capt. Gazon arrived here from the island of Providence, and brings an account, that on the 3d of this month there happened a violent storm or hurricane at the said island, which lasted 12 hours, and drove ashore all the vessels in that harbour, but Capt. Smith's; that the said vessels all got off again, excepting two which are lost; and yesterday arrived Capt. Davis from St. Augustine, who reports, that 5 or 6 large masts were found on shore in the Gulph of Florida, in Lat. 27 1/2, with several pieces of vessels, and a cow but newly dead, which they supposed at St. Augustine to be the wreck of two Spanish Men of War bound from La Vera Cruz to Cadiz.

It is unknown if the observed wreckage originated from the 1733 *Nueva España* fleet, which wrecked along the Upper Florida Keys in July 1733, or if these were unique wrecks, separate from the Spanish vessels lost farther south.

UNKNOWN SPANISH SCHOONER (1766)

According to the *Public Advertiser* of August 14, 1766, "A Spanish schooner of 90 tons was stranded the first of June last on the bar of St. Augustin [sic], but the crew and silver were safely landed and as the misfortune happened from the desire of the Spaniards to trade with the English, the merchants had agreed to indemnify the owners for the loss of the vessel."

UNKNOWN SPANISH SCHOONER (1837)

The April 29, 1837, issue of *The Plaindealer* reported the grisly discovery of an unknown Spanish schooner, estimated to be about 100 tons burden, wrecked near Cape Florida Light on April 4 by Captain H. Benners of the wrecking schooner *United States*. The vessel was found dismasted and full of water, carrying 30 boxes of cochineal and numerous hides. In the ship's hold, Captain Benners also found the body of a man with a gash across his head, as well as four disarticulated feet, two hands, and one lower human jaw. A small tin box containing a gold watch, chain and seal, some gold ore, coins, and a hand press embossed with the name "LUCIANO FORNARI" was found remaining on board; Luciano Fornari was an Italian vocalist who had been performing in Mexico City months prior to this event, and it was feared he was a passenger on the schooner. No evidence of the vessel's name was discovered, and it was believed the ill-fated vessel and all those on board were the victim of pirates.

UNKNOWN SPANISH SHIP AND SNOW

A September 5, 1771, dispatch from Philadelphia included in the September 26, 1771 issue of the *Virginia Gazette* documented the loss of a Spanish ship and a snow (similar to a brig), which were sailing in a fleet of 13 vessels returning to Cadiz, Spain, from Vera Cruz, Mexico, with Spanish troops stationed at Caracas, Venezuela, along with their pay. On August 5th or 9th, the ship and snow ran on shore on Cape Florida (also cited as Bahama Bank), where they were lost. Another snow took the approximately 80 crew and passengers and "as much species, etc. as possible, with which they were proceeding on their voyage...."

Unidentified tug sunk in 412 feet of water off Miami in the 1980s (Miami-Dade County Department of Environmental Resources Management).

UNKNOWN SPANISH SHIP OF WAR

On September 6, 1770, the *Virginia Gazette* included details on the loss of a large Spanish ship of war on the Florida coast. The July 18 dispatch from Charleston stated, "About six weeks ago a Spanish ship of war of 74 guns, having on board General O'Reily, sundry other officers, and a large quantity of money, from the Havannah, for Old Spain, was cast away on the Martyrs, near Cape Florida. The general, with the other officers, and the crew, got to Cuba, but the assistance of some Bahamians, and the ship's boat. The ship and cargo, except the money, it is said, are entirely lost."

URCA DE LIMA

Sailing with the combined Spanish *flota* from Havana on July 24, 1715, the *Urca de Lima* was named after her owner, Don Miguel de Lima y Melo. *Urcas* were a type of cargo frigate constructed with a flat bottom so as to be able to sail in shallow coastal waters. Also known as the *Refuerzo*, she was heavily laden with cargo, including silver coins, worked silver, balsam, hides, chocolate, vanilla, and incense. The July 30-31 hurricane that decimated the other vessels of the fleet did not ravage the *Urca de Lima*. The crew was ordered to cut the masts away to avoid being capsized in the howling wind; they then managed to drop anchor just offshore of the beach in 15 feet of water and away from the dangerous reefs. When dawn broke on the morning of July 31, the *Urca de Lima* was still afloat. On October 15, 1715, Don Miguel de Lima y Melo wrote to the Viceroy of Mexico from Havana, stating:

> All of the ships, with the exception of mine, broke to pieces. My ship stayed intact for 30 days after this disaster until we recovered part of the cargo and then burned the ship. All of the cargos of the other ships were all lost, less a few leather bags off my ship, but this was little because by the day following the disaster the hold of my ship was completely full of water with over a codo and a half (33.9 inches) over the main hatchway. This was caused because we were unable to cut the rigging on the leeward side of the ship to dislodge the foremast. By the movements of the sea, caused by the mast still being erect, the bottom part of the ship opened and if this hadn't happened I would have been able to recover all of the cargo on my ship. However, for the first eleven hours following the ship wrecking, the ship was strong as it had been before the disaster which is the ultimate proof of its great strength.... On my own ship we lost only 30 seamen and marines, which were carried away by waves while in the waist of the ship before it finally ran aground on the coast.

The final resting place of the *Urca de Lima*, rediscovered in 1928, can be found 600 feet offshore Pepper Park north of Fort Pierce Inlet. Early salvors named the site the "Wedge Wreck" after the wedges of silver bullion that were initially found from the wreck. In 1987, the *Urca de Lima* became the first Florida Underwater Archaeological Preserve. There are two buoys just north of the park entrance that mark the wreck, which is found in between the second and third reef line in 10 to 15 feet of water. The first buoy marks a 15-foot long anchor, while the second buoy, found 100 feet farther offshore, marks several cannon, a ballast pile, and portions of the ship's timbers and keel, which are covered by light amounts of sand and coral encrustation. Due to its proximity to shore and its shallow depth, it is prudent to dive this wreck after periods of calm weather.

UTILITY

On February 21, 1932, the screw steamer *Utility* burned on the St. Johns River. The *Utility* was originally built as the *Alice Howard*, official number 107464, in 1899 at Peaks Island, Maine, and was 73.1 feet in length, 19.6 feet in beam, and 77 tons burden.

Two examples of small boats scuttled in deep water off Miami in the 1980s (Miami-Dade County Department of Environmental Resources Management).

V-1764

On the evening of September 7, 1925, a U.S. Coast Guard cutter sighted the *V-1764* approximately 12 miles off Bear Cut near Miami, and signaled the craft to prepare for an examination before entering Biscayne Bay. The V-boat, a likely rum runner, headed for the open sea, which prompted the cutter to fire a warning shot and pursue the *V-1764*. Suddenly, the *V-1764* burst into flames, forcing the occupants, Perry Stanton and Harry Smith, to jump overboard. The V-boat burned to the water's edge and sank, at a reported loss of $20,000. Stanton maintained the boat caught fire after the engine backfired. Due to a lack of evidence of bootlegging, no charges were filed against the two men.

VAHDAH

Singer (1998) states the 52-ton *Vahadah* [sic], built in 1921, reportedly foundered off Palm Beach in 1948. The 80-foot long yacht *Vahdah* was owned by New York millionaire Howland Spencer; the yacht was later sold to friend Commodore John M. Rutherford; in 1946, the *Vahdah* was purchased by E. Pardee Johnston of Toronto, who berthed the yacht at Palm Beach. As the *Vahdah* still appears in vessel registers into the 1950s, it is unclear if the yacht was actually lost in 1948.

VALCOUR

The charter yacht *Valcour* reportedly sank at her berth at Miami's Pier One, at the foot of Sixth Street, during the Great Miami Hurricane in September 1926[242].

VALKYRIE

According to Singer (1998), the 58-ton *Valkyrie*, built in 1915, stranded at Medicis Creek north of St. Augustine on November 3, 1947.

VALMASEDA

The apparent loss of the *Valmaseda* was reported in *The Atlanta Constitution* on August 8, 1910, which detailed:

> Pounding on the rocks and fast filling with water, the Spanish tramp steamer *Valmesada* [sic], which foundered Friday (August 5) near Fowey Rocks Light, will be a total loss according to reports brought here by the revenue cutter *Forward*, which returned today from the scene of the wreck. The local wreckers have abandoned the ship, but the crew is standing by to strip her. The accident was caused by the steering gear of the steamer failing to operate properly, the *Valmesada* [sic] drifting helplessly on the treacherous reef. The *Valmesada's* [sic] cargo consists of 4,000 tons of coal and she was bound from Cardiff for Vera Cruz.

While the above information appears fairly conclusive, an October 16, 1910 article in the *Galveston Daily News* casts doubt on the fate of the Spanish steamer, which posted, "Six members of the crew of the Spanish steamer *Valmaseda* were rescued from a perilous position in a small boat in the outer harbor today by custom house launches." Thus far, I have been unsuccessful in finding any additional information on the *Valmaseda*, which apparently was named after a city near Bilbao, Spain.

VAN

The *Van* was launched in December 1887 as the *Manteo* by the Pusey and Jones Company at their Wilmington, Delaware shipyard. The iron-hulled screw steamer was 190 feet long, 26 feet wide, and 719 tons gross burden. A 1921 weather summary reported the supposed loss of the steamer *Van* during a hurricane that swept across Florida on October 25, 1921. The report stated, "One coast steamer, the *Vann* [sic], plying between Jacksonville and Miami, foundered off the Jupiter coast about 10 am of the 25th. The value of the vessel and cargo was about $120,000." Information included in an annual report of the Bureau of Light Houses, however, indicated the vessel may not have foundered. It documented, "The captain of the steamer *Vann* [sic], of the Jacksonville and Miami Line, came ashore at Cape Canaveral Light Station and used station telephone to report to his Jacksonville office that his vessel was in distress and requested that a tug be sent." Subsequent newspaper articles and vessel documentation confirm that the *Van* weathered the storm and did not sink off Florida in October 1921.

VARUNA

Following the construction of the steamer *Varuna* in 1864 and its acquisition by the firm of Livingston, Fox, and Company for use on their line between New York and Savannah, *The New York Times* published a detailed description of the vessel on August 25, 1865, which stated:

> She is 195 feet 6 inches long on deck, 33 feet breadth of beam, 20 feet depth of hold, has two decks, draws, when cargo and passenger laden, 13 feet of water, and is 1,008 tons burden, old measurement. White oak and chestnut were used in the building of her frame, and they are square fastened in a masterly manner, especial care having been taken with this portion of the work; the floors are molded fourteen inches, sided eight inches, and her frames are spaced twenty-six inches from centre to centre. The bottom blank is of oak, knees are under each deck, the keelsons are of oak, and the water ways of white pine and scarphed. Her rig is that of a brig. From two vertical direct acting engines, having cylinders thirty-six inches in diameter, and a stroke of piston three feet, power is developed, and steam is generated from one tubular boiler, without blowers. The propeller is thirteen feet in diameter, and of cast iron. She is also fitted with pumps, anchors, and all

else in her every department that a vessel of her class on such a sea route, desires and demands. The cabin accommodations and mess-houses of the *Varuna* are on deck, and arranged with much neatness and comfort. The galley is well furnished, and of ample dimensions. The hull of this vessel was built by Chas. H. Mallory, Mystic, Conn., and her machinery was constructed by C.H. Delamater, New York.

On October 15, 1870, the *Varuna*, Captain Joseph T. Spencer, departed New York for Galveston with 36 passengers. Off the coast of Florida, the steamship encountered a fierce hurricane. The *Varuna's* quartermaster, William Wallace, gave the following account:

> We left New York on Saturday night at 7 o'clock, and had fine weather up to the morning of October 20, when the wind sprung up from the south. At noon there was a moderate gale, but as the sun went down it was blowing a perfect hurricane. All went well until 8 o'clock, when the wind shifted suddenly to the southwest, when the ship became unmanageable, and having to beat to port the sea commenced rushing on board on the lee side of the ship, staving in the bulwarks and cabin doors. We tried to get her off before the wind, and put on all the steam we could, but it was no use. I was at the wheel and we brought her up to the wind again and tried to fix the cabin door, but sea was rushing on board to such a degree that the men could not work. By this time the sea had stove in the engine house and was rushing at the rate of twenty tons per minute, and the ship listing over more, she was fast filling. I lashed the wheel after I felt the engine stop and went aft to get some water, as I was very thirsty, and then managed to get on the hurricane deck, when I found the two life boats were gone from the ship and then men were getting the other boat ready. I was still so thirsty that I came back to the captain's room and got a drink there and opened the weather cabin door to see how the passengers were behaving, but did not see a soul as they were all in their state rooms unable to come out on account of the ship lying beam ends on. I then came out on the hurricane deck and got into the after boat with six others. It was lying on the deck waiting for the ship to go down, she then being nearly on her beam ends. The captain, mates and engineer, ten in all, were in a boat and in less than five minutes the boats were afloat, but in such a heavy sea that I was afraid we would get foul of the ships rigging while the vessel was sinking. The other boat asked us if we were all right, and after this the steamer got foul of their boat and took her down with the ship. The boats were Ingersoll's metallic life boats, and I think the captain's boat got clear, and came up again, as a boat bottom up was seen two hours after, but no person was in it. After the ship's masthead was out of sight we thought ourselves all right, as the ship was clear of us, but we counted we without the best, for a heavy sea capsized the boat, but all managed after great exertions to right her, and get on again. The ship again went down at two in the afternoon, and at midnight the weather was moderate and all was still[243].

Wallace's lifeboat reportedly drifted at sea for 60 hours before it finally beached in view of the light house at Jupiter Inlet. Tragically, two of the men aboard the lifeboat, fireman Samuel McCormick and seaman James Flynn, lost their lives in the breakers trying to reach shore. In all, only the lifeboat holding Wallace, the second mate, and three other sailors, survived the sinking; Captain Spencer, the remainder of the crew, and all 36 passengers reportedly perished. While most reports cite the *Varuna* foundered approximately 30 miles off Jupiter Inlet, based on the fact the single lifeboat washed ashore at the inlet after being adrift for 60 hours, the catastrophe likely occurred well to the south of Jupiter. It is also unclear exactly how long the steamer may have drifted north before ultimately plunging to the bottom.

VASCO DE GAMA

The *Daytona Beach Morning Journal* of December 13, 1951, reported the shrimp trawler *Vasco de Gama* caught fire and burned to her waterline in the Intracoastal Waterway near New Smyrna on December 12, 1951. The shrimper had departed Fernandina earlier, where she was recently overhauled, when the fire broke out in the engine room.

VELASCO

According to Volume 26 of *The Sailor's Magazine and Naval Journal*, the "Schooner *Velasco*, of Bucksport, Farnham, from Nassau, East Florida, for Rockland, was totally lost, August 2, 1853, on Nassau Bar."

VENICE

The 65-foot long wooden-hulled Haitian freighter *Venice* caught fire on the evening of December 19, 1997, off Fort Lauderdale[244]. At dawn the following day, the still-burning vessel broke free of its anchor and drifted south, eventually grounding just north of Port Everglades. The charred hulk of the *Venice* reportedly went to pieces soon thereafter.

VENUS (1818)

On February 27, 1818, *The Edinburgh Advertiser* reported, "The *Venus*, Pinder, from Jamaica to New York, is lost on the Florida coast. Crew and part of the cargo saved."

VENUS (1842)

According to *The Sailor's Magazine and Naval Journal*, Volume 15, "Schooner *Venus*, of Surrey, Maine, Johnson, from Connecticut for St. Augustine, cargo granite, went ashore on Pelican Bank, between the bar and lighthouse of St. Augustine, November 25, 1842. Will be a total wreck."

VENUS (1966)

On the evening of November 17, 1966, a faulty electrical outlet adjacent to the 83-foot long yacht *Venus*, which was moored at Broward Marine in Fort Lauderdale, steadily smoldered into a raging fire. The spawned inferno quickly engulfed the *Venus*, and flames fanned by high winds ultimately spread to 12 other vessels and resulted in over $2 million worth of damage. Also lost were the 51-foot *Big Daddy* and the 102-foot long cruiser *Heather IV*, which burned to the water's edge and sunk at her moorings. The fire was similar to a June 1935 event at the same marina, then known as Pilkington Yacht Basin, which destroyed 70 large yachts.

VICTOR

In 1864, a graceful new steamer was launched in a Mystic, Connecticut shipyard. The *Victor*, official number 25686, was adorned with three decks and two masts that were brigantine-rigged. With a 205-foot length and 36-foot beam, the steamer displaced 1,339 gross tons. The *Victor*, owned by C.H. Mallory and Company, stayed close to her place of origin, with a registered homeport of Stonington, Connecticut.

During a routine voyage, Captain Gurdon Gates steamed south from New York on October 16, 1872, bound for New Orleans. On October 18 he rounded Diamond Shoals and passed Cape Hatteras. Two days later, he encountered strong breezes from the northeast as he passed Cape Canaveral at noon. By 6:00 p.m., the *Victor* was nearing Jupiter Light and still being rolled by swells generated from the strong nor'easter. At 8:10 p.m. the shaft broke even with the stuffing box, allowing water to flood in the thru-hull fitting. Captain Gates ordered the fore and aft sails raised in order to keep the ship underway as he traveled relatively close to shore in 13 fathoms of water. In order to stem the rising water in the ship, which now reached three feet in depth, every available pump was put to work. By 9:00 p.m., the leak appeared to be under control, however, the ship was still being pushed closer to shore. Knowing that the steamer was doomed if he approached the crashing breakers, Gates dropped the port anchor when he was pushed inside 50 feet of water and let out over 400 feet of chain. She raised her head sails in order to keep her bow into the seas that now pounded the anchored ship. As night fell, massive waves breached over the stem and washed across her decks. Fortunately, H.D. Pierce, the keeper on watch at the Jupiter lighthouse, spied the lights of the steamer just offshore and prepared for an early morning rescue. By dawn, the rescuers arrived on site to observe the *Victor* lying broadside to the waves. The burden of the flooding water became unbearable for the hull of the steamer and she broke in two amidships. Dropping a lifeboat in the leeside of the crippled steamer, the crew managed to run a buoyed line into the surging waves and allowed the storm-tossed surf to carry it towards the waiting rescuers on shore. After securing the line, the crew successfully landed all passengers by 2:00 p.m. on October 21, though three lifeboats were swamped in the process. Three collies successfully swam for shore, eventually to be adopted and named "Vic," "Surf," and "Wreck" by the lighthouse keepers.

At 5:00 p.m., with conditions appearing to calm a bit, the mate, chief engineer, and boat crew set out to the wreck to throw some provisions overboard. They had to act quickly as the ship was breaking up rapidly. By dusk the storm again intensified and proceeded to smash the stranded ship to pieces. First light on the morning of October 22 revealed that the ship was all but destroyed. Portions of the wreck were cast upon the rocks with nothing visible offshore but the steam chimneys and the cylinders above water. The gale continued for almost two more days before breaking. On the afternoon of October 24, the passengers of the *Victor* were picked up by the steamer *General Meade*. The *General Meade* headed south until coming upon the northbound steamer *City of Austin* just off Key West. The crew of the *Victor* were transferred to the *City of Austin* and transported back to New York, while the *General Meade* steamed on to New Orleans with the passengers of the wrecked ship. On November 6, the Key West wrecking schooner *Competitor* found the hull of the *Victor* to be on the shore and filled with sand.

The barkentine-rigged steamer *Victor* (Mark Mondano Collection).

Nothing of significance was salvaged, and the wreck was abandoned.

The wreck of the *Victor* slowly deteriorated over time, leaving two large boilers to mark the site. Apparently, the wreck was salvaged in 1957 by two men who observed the wreck while flying along the coast. Over the course of several months, they removed large amounts of scrap metal, as well as china, silverware, and numerous personal possessions. Presently, only the encrusted boilers of the *Victor* are exposed above the sand a short distance from the beach and just south of Jupiter Inlet.

VICTORY

On May 11, 1921, the New Creek Towing Company tug *Victory*, en route from Miami to New York, burned at sea 25 miles south of Matanzas Inlet. Captain Charles R. Wiebe and the crew of seven put off in small boats and safely landed at St. Augustine, while the steam tug reportedly sank in 80 feet of water at approximate latitude 29° 27.233' north, longitude 80° 52.833'. The *Victory*, official number 217171, was built in 1918 at West New Brighton, New York, and was 115.4 feet in length, 30.8 feet in breadth, and 337 tons in burden.

VIDETTE

The yacht *Vidette*, owned by a Mr. Wright, sank between Pier Five and Six at the City Yacht Basin during the September 1926 Great Miami Hurricane. She reportedly wrecked amidst the sunken charter boats *Captain Bill*, *Inis*, *Mad Hatter*, *Adventurer*, and *Hussar*[245]. The ultimate fate of these vessels is unknown.

VIGILANT

The Edinburgh Advertiser, October 17, 1794, reported the *Vigilant*, bound from Honduras to London, and another large ship were lost off Cape Florida in a hurricane on August 28, 1794.

VIKING (1952)

Two persons swam ashore and two others were brought in by the U.S. Coast Guard when the 48-foot sloop *Viking* sank after running aground on the south side of Ponce de Leon Inlet late on May 1, 1952[246].

VIKING (1975)

On August 13, 1975, the 26-ton *Viking* reportedly foundered off Boca Raton.

VILLA FRANCA

On August 22, 1865, the English bark *Villa Franca*, Captain Anderson, reportedly wrecked at approximate latitude 29° north, longitude 80° west; three crewmen were picked up by the steamer *Vera Cruz*, while the remainder were rescued by the Norwegian bark *Turnjot*[247]. The *Villa Franca* was from Sagua, Cuba, bound to New York with a cargo of sugar and molasses at the time of her loss. One article attributes the bark to St. Stephen's, New Brunswick, which identifies the 397-ton bark *Villa Franca*, built in 1859 at Calais, Maine.

VINDICATOR

According to *The Sailor's Magazine and Naval Journal*, Volume 10, the schooner *Vindicator*, of and from New York, for Apalachicola, was reported as totally lost on the Florida coast in September 1838; the crew and passengers were saved.

VIRGIN DE LAS NIEVES

The bark *Virgin De Las Nieves* was built in 1851 at Grafton, England. Owned by Fabra Riera and Company, the vessel was 109 feet long, 22.3 feet wide, and displaced 366 tons. On October 23, 1878, en route from Havana for New York, the *Nieves* wrecked two and a half miles south of the Orange Grove House of Refuge (present-day Delray Beach).

VIRGINIA (1842)

On November 23, 1842, the *Colonial Gazette* reported, "During the last month many vessels were destroyed on the American coast.... The bark *Virginia* was abandoned off the Florida coast."

VIRGINIA (1917)

The 8-ton sloop *Virginia*, official number 206656, built in 1909, reportedly stranded at Lake George on August 16, 1917.

VIRGINIA LEE HICKMAN

The schooner *Virginia Lee Hickman* was built in January 1873 at Chester, Pennsylvania, and was 115.6 feet in length, 30.8 feet in beam, and 321 tons in displacement. On January 26, 1888, the *Virginia Lee Hickman* wrecked on the St. Augustine Bar.

VIRGINIA M.

According to the *Daytona Beach Morning Journal* of February 25, 1978, the commercial fishing vessel *Virginia M.* sank 35 miles offshore New Smyrna Beach at 6:20 a.m. on February 24, 1978. Captain Steve LaCour and four crewmen were rescued by the nearby fishing boat *Angler*. According to Captain LaCour, "It happened too fast. She went down in about three minutes."

VIXEN

On August 26, 1911, the gas screw vessel *Vixen* burned at Silver Springs. The *Vixen*, official number 81175, was originally built in 1888 at Jacksonville as the screw steamer *William T. Stockton*, and, prior to her conversion, was 49.8 feet in length, 10.4 feet in beam, and 26 tons gross displacement.

VOLUSIA

According to Davis (1925), the steamboat ferry *Volusia*, which operated for the Pioneer Line, was destroyed by a boiler explosion at her slip at the foot of Newnan Street in Jacksonville on December 2, 1882.

VULCAN

The 40-foot long vessel *Vulcan*, en route from Palm Beach to Fernandina, experienced an explosion only 15 hours from its point of origin on February 20, 1930[248]. Captain Paul Rice, seriously injured by the blast, was incapacitated. Mate Jack Grand, however, spurred by the sight of several large sharks circling their sinking vessel, was forced to man the pumps for three straight days. On February 23, the two men were rescued by the tanker *G.H. Jones*. Ten minutes after they were taken off the crippled vessel, the *Vulcan* promptly sank beneath the Atlantic. While unconfirmed, this may possibly be the freighter *Vulcan II*, official number 141792, built in 1902 at Jersey City, New Jersey, which was 41.4 feet long, 13.7 feet wide, and displaced 14 tons gross.

W.D. ANDERSON

The tanker *W.D. Anderson*, official number 221648, was built as the *Tamiahua* in June 1921 by the Moore Shipbuilding Company of Oakland, California. Owned by the Atlantic Refining Company of Philadelphia, Pennsylvania, the single-screw tanker was outfitted with a rarely employed quadruple expansion engine that produced 4,000 horsepower, which was manufactured by the Hooven, Owens, and Rentschler Company. Her three single-ended boilers were provided by the Moore Shipbuilding Company. At 500 feet in length and 71.2 feet in beam, the 10,227-ton vessel bears the distinction of being the largest World War II casualty off Florida.

Captained by Albert Benjamin Walters, the *Anderson* was bound for her homeport of Philadelphia from Atreco, Texas, with a cargo of crude oil. Around 7:00 p.m. on February 22, 1942, the tanker was 18 miles offshore and approximately 12 miles north of Jupiter Light. Most of the crew of 36 were finishing their dinner and relaxing in the cool evening. Twenty-three year-old Frank Leonard Terry had retired to the fantail and was enjoying a cup of tea with his fellow shipmates, discussing the various foreign ports they had visited. Amidst the discussion, an explosion violently jolted the tanker. Moments earlier, *Korvettenkapitän* Hans-Georg Friedrich (Fritz) Poske, onboard the *U-504*, observed the blacked-out *Anderson* steaming northward off the Florida coast. Less than 24 hours earlier, Poske had sunk the 392-foot long tanker *Republic* just south of his current position. Sighting this new target offshore of the *U-504*, Poske wanted to make sure that the enormous tanker, almost twice the rated tonnage of the *Republic*, did not escape his attack, and launched two torpedoes in quick succession. As the ensuing inferno engulfed the ship, Frank Terry leapt overboard. Almost simultaneously, the second torpedo struck the doomed tanker. Terry stated that he was in the air when the second torpedo hit. As a result of the second explosion, he was sprayed with crude oil as he fell to the water. After Terry surfaced, he looked back to see one of his shipmates perched on the fantail of the ship, preparing to jump. As the crewman began to dive, a huge mass of flames engulfed him and he was never seen again. Quickly, the surface of the Atlantic became a blazing pyre. Frank Terry related his encounter with another shipmate, stating, "I bumped into something as I swam. It was a man and I thought I could help him and towed him for maybe five minutes. Then I realized he was dead, and swam on alone. I never knew who he was[249]." With no time to pity his friends, Terry worked to escape the growing fire.

The massive explosions that marked the successful torpedo attack on the *Anderson* rocked the *U-504*. In the war journal of the *U-504*, Poske described the event: "The ship stood, in a fraction of a second, from forward to astern in flames. After 12 seconds, second (torpedo) hits in the stern; the rear part broke off[250]." Fatally wounded, the *W.D. Anderson* quickly dove for the bottom.

As the blaze around the stricken tanker grew, Frank Terry was forced, literally, to swim for his life. Stripping off much of his clothing, he dove under the surface and swam as far as his lungs would allow. Upon surfacing, he found himself safely away from immediate danger, though covered in oil, burned badly, and in shock. Looking back towards the blaze, he could no longer see his ship, though he called out in vain for the other crewmembers. Wearing only pants, the relatively warm Florida Current protected him from the brisk February air. After drifting for three hours, a commercial fishing boat from Port Salerno approached the scene and found the sole survivor drifting amongst the burning debris. As he was pulled from the water, he babbled incoherently about being attacked by sharks. He recalled being bumped several times and constantly seeing fins; in shock and fearing the worst, he expected to find his legs and arms torn from his body. The fishermen noticed the sharks, however, were only friendly dolphins that were swimming about the injured man. Years later, Frank Leonard Terry succinctly summed up the sinking: "It was my first trip to Florida. I didn't like the experience[251]."

On July 30, 1943, the *U-504* was sunk with all hands in the North Atlantic by the H.M.S. *Kite*, H.M.S. *Wild Goose*, H.M.S. *Woodpecker*, and H.M.S. *Wren*. Hans-Georg Friedrich (Fritz) Poske, however, survived the war, having been promoted and re-assigned in January 1943. After four war patrols in the *U-504*, he was credited with over 82,000 tons of sunken shipping. Fritz Poske passed away in 1984.

In the war journal of the *U-504*, *Korvettenkapitän* Poske cited the depth as 40 fathoms. However, today the *W.D. Anderson* lies on her starboard side in approximately 550

The tanker **W.D. Anderson** (Mark Mondano Collection).

feet of water, 14 miles east of St. Lucie Inlet. Why the depth discrepancy? As the U-504 attacked inshore of the tanker, Poske most likely noted the depth of water at his location, rather than that of the Anderson, which was farther offshore and in deeper water. In this offshore area, the sea bottom drops off very dramatically in a rather short distance. Regardless, due to the extreme depth and demanding conditions experienced in the vicinity of the wreck site, no exploration has been conducted to date aside from a brief visit by a remotely operated vehicle from Harbor Branch Oceanographic Institution.

W.M. GODDIN

The brig W.M. Goddin, en route from Boston for Jacksonville with a cargo of ice, went ashore on the north breakers of the St. Johns Bar on February 2, 1857[252]. I have been unable to find any construction or service history on this vessel, so it's possible the newspaper report was inaccurate; perhaps the actual name of the vessel was W.M. (or William) Goodwin, Godwin, or some other derivative.

W.T. COPPEDGE, JR.

The W.T. Coppedge, Jr., official number 216000, was originally built as the South American at a Bath, Maine shipyard in 1918. The steam tug was 97.6 feet in length, 23.2 feet in breadth, and 168 gross tons in burden. The tow vessel operated out of Port Arthur, Texas, until she was sold in the early 1960s to the Florida Towing Corporation of Jacksonville, whereupon she was renamed W.T. Coppedge, Jr.; she was likely converted to diesel around this time. In 1972, the Coppedge towed the scorched hull of the Oriental Warrior (note previous entry in this work) into Jacksonville. Moran Towing Company acquired Florida Towing in 1976, and soon thereafter the Coppedge was apparently laid up. In 1987, Moran was approached by the Jacksonville Offshore Sport Fishing Club, which sought the obsolete tug for use as an artificial reef. In June 1988 the W.T. Coppedge, Jr. was sunk in 80 feet of water approximately 23 nautical miles off Mayport. The tug sits upright and intact, and has been encrusted by a thick veneer of marine encrustation. On August 31, 1989, approximately 2,000 tons of concrete culvert material, covering a 40,000-square-foot area, was deployed just off the bow of the Coppedge.

W.W. MILLER

The 29-ton gas vessel W.W. Miller, built in 1918, reportedly foundered at Sebastian Inlet on November 23, 1933.

WACCAMAW

A May 1847 dispatch included in The Sailor's Magazine and Naval Journal, Volume 19, reported, "Schooner Waccamaw, Coates, of Charleston, has bilged in the neighborhood of Cape Florida."

WALBORG POTTER

The 44-ton steamer Walborg Potter, built in 1906, reportedly foundered off Cape Canaveral on November 9, 1926.

WALKA Q.

The Walka Q. is one of several vessels deployed as an artificial reef off Miami prior to the establishment of an official Miami-Dade County program. As a result, there is a general lack of specific data on the vessel and its deployment. Available information indicates she was a 200-foot long steel freighter sunk in 280 feet of water off Miami Beach in 1980. While I have been unable to find any information on a vessel named Walka Q., there was a freighter named Walka, which records indicate foundered in 1980, though no details on her actual loss have been found. Due to the similarities in name, dimensions, and date of sinking, the vessels are likely one in the same. The Walka was launched on June 20, 1939 as the coastal freighter Gladonia by the British firm Goole Shipbuilding and Repairing Company, Limited. She was 163 feet in length, 24.6 feet in beam, and 420 tons in displacement. On January 16, 1941, she was damaged by German bombers while on the Thames. Reportedly, this was not the only attack suffered by the coaster, as the Walka was credited with shooting down two German aircraft during World War II. In 1962 the coaster was renamed Meike; sold in 1968, she operated as the Walka; she sailed as Kimbo in 1976; and again as Walka in 1978 for her Panamanian owners, Laja Lines S.A.

Photo of the Walka as the Gladonia. This may possibly be the same vessel sunk as an artificial reef off Miami in 1980.

WANDERER

According to the Galveston Daily News of December 8, 1954, the 55-foot shrimp trawler Wanderer ran aground off Crescent Beach near Matanzas Inlet on December 6. Unable to swim, Captain Joe Roy Ferguson stayed aboard while his single crewman, Wilbur Whitfield, managed to swim ashore through the breaking surf. The battered wreck of the Wanderer was later found empty and Captain Ferguson was believed lost in the accident.

WARWICK

The wreck of the Warwick was originally a 1,028-ton ferry launched in 1923 as the Chelsea by Pusey and Jones at Wilmington, Delaware, and was 200 feet in length and 55.5 feet in beam. The Chelsea, official number 223322, was originally built for the Reading Company, who employed her for service across the Delaware River at Philadelphia, Pennsylvania. In 1939, she was sold to Electric Ferries, and in 1945 she migrated south to Hampton Roads, where she was renamed *Warwick* for the Chesapeake Ferry Company. In 1964, the Norfolk Shipbuilding and Drydock Company sold the *Warwick* to the Coppedge Towing Company of Jacksonville, who planned to use the ferry's engines in one of their tugs. The hulk of the *Warwick* was eventually towed approximately 29 nautical miles east of Mayport in 1972 and scuttled in 105 feet of water.

The ferry *Warwick* as the *Chelsea* (Pusey and Jones).

WATERLOO

The British ship *Waterloo*, Captain Kelcher, en route from Jamaica for Cork, wrecked on the east coast of Florida in October 1822; entire cargo saved and carried to Nassau[253].

WATERWICH

According to *The Edinburgh Advertiser* of August 16, 1816, the schooners *Due Bill* and *Waterwich* (also appeared as *Water Witch*), both of Savannah, wrecked near St. Augustine in the beginning of June during a storm.

WAVERLY

The schooner *Waverly*, Captain Sellers, en route from New Iberia, Louisiana, bound for New York with a cargo of sugar, grounded on a reef near Cape Florida Light on March 24, 1831. "Exertions of the libellant and crew preserved the cargo (with) extreme peril and labor," resulted in the courts awarding the salvors half of the value of the recovered cargo[254].

WEE-II

Also known locally as the "Abbadash," this wreck appears to have been a former trawler that now rests in approximately 80 feet of water just over 14 nautical miles northeast of Sebastian Inlet. According to Mondano (1991), the *Wee-II* apparently burned and sank. Not much is left of the fishing vessel now, aside from scattered rigging and machinery. Most of the structure has collapsed, and one diver has described the wreck as appearing like a giant sawhorse on the seafloor. While the wreck may not have much of an historical appeal, it can still be a productive spot for anglers and spearfishermen.

WELAKA

The sidewheel steamer *Welaka* was built by Jones and Papot in 1851 at Savannah, Georgia. She was 137 feet long, 25 feet wide, and displaced 256 tons gross. On December 3, 1857, Captain McNelty guided the steamer, laden with a cargo of cotton, from the Jacksonville docks for Savannah. Just after midnight on December 4 (also reported as December 13), the *Welaka* grounded on the breakers of the St. Johns Bar and broke in two. While the crew and approximately 100 bales of cotton were saved by the steamer *Everglade*, the *Welaka* was a total loss. This vessel should not be confused with the steamer *Welaka* built at Jacksonville in 1882, which later wrecked at Tampa on June 27, 1912.

Yacht *Wendy Rossheim* (Broward County Artificial Reef Program).

WENDY ROSSHEIM

In 1947, the yacht *Natoya* was built by Defoe Shipbuilding Company of Bay City, Michigan for Harold DuCharme of Grosse Point, Michigan. One of five Defoe Cruisemaster yachts, the *Natoya* was 118 feet long and 18.5 feet wide. In the mid to late 1960s, the vessel was sold and migrated out of the Great Lakes to Florida. Renamed *Our House III*, the yacht eventually fell on hard times and was relegated for use as an artificial reef by Broward County. Renamed in memory of Wendy Rossheim, a 21-year old Fort Lauderdale resident who died of a sudden illness in December 1991, the yacht was scuttled north of Port Everglades on January 29, 1992. The *Wendy Rossheim* rests in 70 feet of water approximately 100 feet southwest of the *Robert Edmister*.

WEST END

The *West End* was reportedly a 110-foot long vessel sunk by Pflueger Marine Taxidermy in 230 feet of water off Miami in July 1973. As this deployment occurred well before Miami-Dade County established an artificial reef program, there is little to no specific information on this vessel.

WESTERN EMPIRE

Built in April 1862 at Quebec, Canada, the ship *Western Empire* was 190 feet in length, 38 feet in beam, and 1,282 tons in displacement. First reports of the ship's loss appeared in the *Crawfordsville Star* on October 5, 1875, which reported, "The ship *Western Empire*, Captain Bertie, from Pensacola, on the 11th of September, for Grimsley, with timber, became waterlogged in a hurricane on the 18th, in latitude 28° 53′ north, longitude 87° 54′ west (approximately 60 nautical miles east of the Mississippi River Delta), and was abandoned. The captain and crew landed on St. Vincent's Island, Apalachicola Bay, Florida, in boats from the ship. In landing one of the boats capsized, and eight men were drowned. The remainder, seventeen in number, including the captain, were landed at Pensacola on the 24th of September, in a destitute condition."

Later, on October 22, 1875, The New York Times noted the "Schooner Herbert E., Mount, Brazos, Santiago, 28 ds., with hides and wool to Woodhouse & Rudd. Oct. 2, lat. 25° 14′, lon. 86° 59′ (approximately 220 miles west of the Dry Tortugas), passed the wreck of ship Western Empire." Another report in the same issue stated, "Steamship City of Vera Cruz, Deaken, from Havana, arr. 20th, reports, Oct. 17. 3 P.M., lat. 26° 50′, lon. 79° 38′ (approximately 22 miles east of North Palm Beach), stopped and boarded ship Western Empire, of London, timber-loaded, water-logged and abandoned; fore and mainmasts gone, mizzenmast standing with yards across; both anchors off the bow, hanging by the chains; poop and forecastle decks well out of water, wreck of spars alongside; sails all gone except jibs, which were in ribbons; boats all gone except one, and that badly damaged."

On November 3, 1875, approximately 30 miles north of Jupiter Inlet, the wrecking steamer B&J Baker fell in with the British ship Western Empire abandoned, derelict, and swinging at anchor. According to a November 16, 1875 article in the Janesville Gazette, "in order to enable the housing out of the boats both anchors were let go to act as a drag to bring the ship's head to the wind. The length of chain allowed was 35 fathoms." That the Western Empire drifted for over 500 miles and entirely around the peninsula of Florida without any assistance at the helm is amazing in and of itself, but the feat is even more remarkable when considering she was trailing her anchors at a depth of over 200 feet, and still managed to avoid the reefs of the Florida Keys and South Florida. Materials salvaged from the wreck were brought to Key West and sold for $666.95. It is unclear what ultimately happened to the hulk of the Western Empire.

WESTMORELAND

On November 14, 1728, the Stamford Mercury reported that "Capt. Nowell brought from Gibraltar, in his ship the Isabella, Capt. Joseph Warren, late commander of the ship Westmoreland, which left Jamaica the 7th of July last, bound for London; but was unfortunately lost soon after on the coast of Florida. The captain and his crew took to their boat, which they stored in the best manner they could; by the help of which they got to the Havanna in seven days, and from thence they were brought to Gibraltar in the Tuscany, Capt. Innes."

WHEREAWAY

According to Singer (1998), the Whereaway, built in 1918, foundered at Coyler Island off Lake Park on December 5, 1962. However, newspaper reports detailed that on October 5, 1962, the Whereaway, a 70-ton houseboat, developed a serious leak while tied at her dock at Canonsport Marina in Palm Beach, which compelled the U.S. Coast Guard to tow her to Phil Foster Park on October 6, where she was beached in order to remove the water[255]. The yacht was dewatered, repaired, and towed back to her berth later that day. Due to the similarities in date, it is uncertain if the Whereaway actually foundered on December 5, 1962. While her ultimate fate is unclear, it's perhaps worth noting that yacht registers included a Whereaway II in the mid 1960s, so perhaps the owners commissioned a replacement to be built after this incident.

View of the houseboat Whim Wham, 1910 (Alfred H. Robson Collection).

WHIM WHAM

The double stern-wheeled houseboat Whim Wham, designed by H. Gielow and built at Jacksonville in 1898 for millionaire Dr. R.V. Pierce, was 91 feet in length and 23.5 feet in beam. The houseboat was reportedly wrecked in the Great Miami Hurricane of September 1926, though there is a conflicting report stating she may have been sunk off Mexico in 1929.

The petite tug White Coast.

WHITE COAST

The *White Coast* is a 33-foot long tug scuttled in approximately 65 feet of water off Miami on May 6, 1995. The small vessel rests in very close proximity to the tug *C-One*, and both the 45-foot long tug *Lady Carmen* and the 150-foot long freighter *Conception* are also within easy swimming distance.

WICKSTROM

Named after the founder and editor of *Florida Sportsman* magazine, Karl Wickstrom, the *Wickstrom* was originally launched in October 1944 as the freight supply vessel *FS-553* at the Brunswick, Georgia shipyard of Brunswick Marine for the U.S. Army Transportation Corps. The *FS-553* was 176.8 feet long, 32.1 feet wide, and displaced 560 tons. Following her completion in January 1945, the first skipper of the *FS-553* was Captain Erle P. Halliburton, founder of Halliburton. In 1964, the cargo vessel was sold to a private company and renamed *Sonic II*; she sailed as the *Tauros* following her sale in 1966; sold twice in 1979, she operated first as the similarly named *Taurus* and then later as the *Apemagu*. The vessel eventually fell into disrepair, and was tied up on the Miami River for several years before finally being purchased by Wickstrom and the Martin County Anglers Club for use as an artificial reef in 2002.

On January 21, 2003, the *Wickstrom* was scuttled in 190 feet of water approximately nine nautical miles offshore St. Lucie Inlet. The deck of the former U.S. Army freighter rests at a depth of approximately 160 feet, while the top of the mast above the bridge rises to within 120 feet of the surface. The bow of the *Wickstrom* points south towards the *Tree Barge*, which can be found approximately 500 feet away. In addition, several artificial reef modules were deployed between the two wrecks in 2005. The Gulf Stream frequently washes over the wreck, particularly during the summer, so divers should be experienced diving with significant current. Amberjack, spadefish, and grouper frequent the site, and the deep-water ivory tree coral (*Oculina varicosa*) has also established itself on the wreck.

The schooner *Wilbert S. Bartlett*, 1925 (Alfred H. Robson Collection).

WILBERT S. BARTLETT

The four-masted schooner *Wilbert S. Bartlett*, official number 216994, was launched on September 21, 1918, from the Sawyer shipyard at Milbridge, Maine. She was 183.1 feet long, 37.5 feet wide, and 741 tons gross burden. On December 19, 1925, en route from New York to Miami, the *Bartlett* stranded near Jensen Beach during a storm.

WILBUR

On the morning of June 23, 1931, the dredge *Wilbur* burned and sunk at Boca Raton Inlet following an explosion from an oil cooking stove in the galley[256]. The dredge, owned by Holloway Dredging Company, had been working to deepen and widen the channel at the inlet. The *Wilbur* was deemed a total loss following the sinking.

WILLIAM (1778)

On a voyage from Jamaica to Bristol, England in 1778, the *William*, Captain Thomas, was reportedly lost on the Florida coast[257].

WILLIAM (1816)

The August 16, 1816, issue of *The Edinburgh Advertiser* stated the brig *William*, Captain Kennedy, from Charleston, South Carolina, to St. Marys, Georgia, wrecked near St. Augustine in early June, along with the ship *Huron*, and schooners *Due Bill* and *Water Witch* [sic].

WILLIAM AND ELIZABETH

On October 7, 1790, Captain Skaise of the brig *Phoebe* reported the wrecking of the *Thetis*, Moore, of Bristol, and brig *Albion*, Birkett, of Whitehaven, and the ships *Apollo*, Craig, and the *William and Elizabeth*, Archdeacon, on the Florida shore[258]. As another source reported the loss of the *Thetis* on a reef three leagues from Cape Florida in early August 1790, it is assumed the *William and Elizabeth* was lost in the same area and around the same time.

WILLIAM BARNETT

The *William Barnett*, a steamer that began operating on the St. Johns River in 1857, suffered a boiler explosion that killed her captain and a number of passengers in 1858[259].

WILLIAM RATHBONE

On October 17, 1870, Captain Doane and three crewmen from the wreck of the bark *William Rathbone* were rescued by the steamer *Mississippi* eleven miles north of Hillsboro Inlet[260]. Captain Doane was found walking the beach barefooted, badly injured from exposure to the sun and seawater, in search of assistance. The *Rathbone* left New York on September 19 bound for New Orleans with an assorted cargo, and went ashore on October 11. The cargo of general merchandise was strewn along the beach for a considerable distance. When picked up by a launch from the steamer, Captain Doane reported he found a plank marked "*Mariposa* leaking" on the beach; a life preserver from the *Mariposa* was also found. The bark *William Rathbone* was built in 1849 by George Greenman and Company at Mystic, Connecticut, and was 158.7 feet long, 32.3 feet wide, and displaced 1,117 tons gross.

WILLIAM R. KNIGHTON

The schooner *William R. Knighton*, official number 80213, was built in August 1871 at Stony Brook, New York, and was 96.2 feet long, 26.3 feet wide, and 158 tons burden. According to Singer (1998), the schooner *W.R. Knighton* stranded 1 1/2 miles from Cape Florida Light during a storm on October 18, 1876. Volume 55 of *The Sailors' Magazine and Seamen's Friend*, however, states the Knighton wrecked in March 1883 during a voyage from Port Limon, Costa Rica for New York. It should also be pointed out that the *W.R. Knighton* remains in documentation until 1883. Therefore, it is likely the schooner was salvaged or refloated following her 1876 stranding; it is unclear exactly where the *William R. Knighton* was ultimately lost.

WILLIAM RUSSELL

The schooner *William Russell*, official number 204547, was built in 1907 at Pocomoke City, Maryland, and was 81.4 feet long, 23.4 feet wide, and 63 tons gross burden. On December 2, 1925, *The Morning News Review* reported, "The four-masted schooner *William Russell*, bound from Norfolk to Fort Lauderdale, wrecked off Fort Lauderdale. The vessel's cargo of lumber and building supplies were strewn along the coast for several miles. Captain Bert Yhalkee and his crew of four men made their way ashore in safety when the schooner grounded on a reef. The vessel, the captain said, was a total loss."

WILLIAM W. CONVERSE

The *William W. Converse* was a three-masted schooner built in December 1886 at New Haven, Connecticut by H.H. Hanscom, and was 168.8 feet in length, 37.8 feet in breadth, and 746 gross tons in displacement. On October 18, 1910, the schooner stranded at Halifax River Beach during a hurricane. According to a dispatch from St. Augustine included in the *Galveston Daily News* of October 21, 1910:

> Harrowing tales of suffering and hardship were brought here today by the five survivors off the three-masted schooner *William W. Converse* of Philadelphia, who were rescued by a launch from the life saving station. Captain E. J. Miller and two of the crew were drowned when the vessel went to pieces in the hurricane Tuesday afternoon forty miles below this city. The two men were Chas. Anderson, mate, and Frank Hayes, a seaman. Anderson succeeded in reaching the surf near the shore when a portion of the wreck struck him causing his death. Fred Miller, the 18-year-old son of the captain, together with three seamen and the negro steward, reached the shore, on bits of wreckage after fighting through a mile of pounding surf all of the survivors are in a pitiable condition. The *Converse* was bound for St. Francis, Cuba, when she ran into the hurricane while off Savannah. She was loaded with coal.

WILLIE

On August 8, 1918, the 11-ton gas steamer *Willie*, official number 205570, built in 1908, burned at Six Mile Creek near St. Augustine.

WILMINGTON

The wrecking of the steamer *Wilmington* was reported in a December 1, 1838 dispatch from Acting Lieutenant E.T. Shubrick of the U.S. sloop *Panther* published in the *Army and Navy Chronicle* (Volume 8), which detailed, "On Sunday, the 24th of November, a boat came alongside, informing that the steamer *Wilmington* was ashore to the north of Cape Florida. The *Panther* was instantly under weigh, and about fifty miles north above the cape, I had the satisfaction of rescuing the rest of her crew, sixteen in number. These, with two boats, I brought to Key Biscayne." The 229-ton *Wilmington* was built in 1829 at Philadelphia, Pennsylvania for owner William Dougal's New York Line, and was homeported in Wilmington, Delaware. In mid-1836, the steamer began running goods between Wilmington, Delaware and Fayetteville, North Carolina. The *Wilmington* wrecked in the same storm as the Spanish brig *Triumfante*, which was reported 60 miles north of Cape Florida.

WILTON

The schooner *Wilton*, owned by the Florida Land and Lumber Company, was carrying machinery and provisions for the Port Orange settlement when she ran into a severe storm off Mosquito Inlet sometime between 1866 and 1868. In an attempt to keep her from going on shore, the sailors put out anchors and cables, but the cables parted, and the *Wilton* eventually grounded on the beach four miles south of the inlet. The passengers and crew made it to shore safely, but the vessel was a total loss. Passenger J.M. Hawks sailed aboard the *Wilton* from Jacksonville to New Smyrna and described the wrecking:

> The voyage was pleasant and prosperous until we arrived the next day at Mosquito Inlet too late to go in over the bar. Captain Miner Hawks, with the life-boat and a crew of four colored men, came out to help pilot us in. Through the night we sailed off shore and on, to be ready to go in the morning; but when morning came we were away south of Turtle Mound, and a gale was blowing from the northeast, constantly crowding us on shore. All day long we tried to beat up to the inlet, but in vain. It was nearly sunset when, finding we made no headway, we cast anchor, intending to lay to till the wind should lull. At first the anchors dragged and then parted, first one, then another cable. Captain Garvin then had

the choice of two courses to pursue: he could run the vessel ashore, in which there was not likely to be much danger to life; or he could put out to sea, in attempting which there was danger of drifting on Canaveral reefs before we could get far enough out to clear them, as the mainsail was torn and disabled. We concluded to run ashore, and lose vessel and cargo if we must, and save our lives. The vessel's bow was headed straight for the shore toward the breakers; we struck the outer sand-bar, and quickly lightened the vessel by throwing off some heavy deckload; the schooner careened, slid over the ridge and in deeper water, righted again, and then sped on for the mad, wild breakers, for the tide was high. However great the hope of landing safely, there was no certainty about it, and enough of danger to make those few moments of thrilling suspense. Near the breakers the vessel struck again, careened over on her side, and the next wave drove her so high up on the beach that in wading ashore the water was scarcely waist deep, though on the *Wilton* was of six feet draught. We were on the beach about four miles south of the inlet. Considerable of the cargo was saved, but almost ruined by being soaked in salt water and mixed with sand. But life was saved. How good the solid ground felt to the feet! How dear every tree and plant seemed![261]

WINDSOR

On June 25, 1811, *The Edinburgh Advertiser* reported the British vessel *Windsor*, Captain Low in command, was lost on the Amelia Island Bar while trying to enter the port from Savannah. Also mentioned in the same article was the June 9 grounding of the *Lady Provost* on Amelia Bar (the *Lady Provost* was later refloated); therefore, it's likely the *Windsor* was wrecked in the same timeframe.

WONDER

According to Singer (1998), the 25-ton vessel *Wonder*, built in 1929, burned at Fort Pierce on November 22, 1930.

WOODSIDE

Volume 25 of *The Sailor's Magazine and Naval Journal* reported, the "Ship *Woodside*, Hodges, of New York, from Mobile for Rochefort, France, cargo spars, ran ashore on Florida Reef, near the Fowey Rocks, December 30, 1852, and soon after bilged."

X-FACTOR WRECK

Approximately two and a half miles north of the Port St. Lucie Nuclear Power Plant and just under a half mile offshore, rests the partially sanded over remains of an unidentified sidewheel steamer in 35 feet of water. Bronze and iron fasteners, a deadeye, grey granite split ballast, and encrusted wreckage, were apparently observed at the site.

YALE

On August 3, 1910, the 14-ton gas steamer *Yale*, official number 206460, built in 1903, burned at Welaka.

YANKEE GIRL II

According to Singer (1998), the 30-ton vessel *Yankee Girl II*, built in 1928, foundered off Miami on November 28, 1959.

YOUNG RACER

Small boats from the barque U.S.S. *Roebuck* chased the blockade-running British sloop, *Young Racer*, and forced her aground 15 miles north of Jupiter Inlet on January 14, 1864; the sloop, which was carrying a cargo of salt, was destroyed by her crew[262].

YTM-460

The tug *Locust Point* was launched at Brooklyn, New York, by Ira S. Bushey and Sons on February 17, 1931. Originally built for the Erie Railroad Company, with the entrance of the United States into World War II, the tug was turned over to the U.S. Maritime Commission and renamed *YTM-460*, but was manned by a civilian crew. On the evening of December 19, 1946, while under tow of the tug *Hudson* from Charleston, South Carolina, to Mobile, Alabama, both vessels wrecked on the north jetty of the St. Marys River.

The stranded steamer *Zeeburg* (Florida State Archives).

ZEEBURG

The Dutch steamer *Zeeburg* was launched August 2, 1899, by builder R. Thompson, and was 325 feet in length, 48.5 feet in beam, and 3,039 tons burden. On September 26, 1909, en route from Rotterdam to Jacksonville, the Burg Line steamer *Zeeburg* ran aground on the south jetty of the St. Johns River Bar. The sea, which was running high, washed over the bridge and pounded the hull unmercifully on the rocks. On September 27, with 16 feet of water in her hold, Captain Von Rossen decided to abandon the wreck. The vessel eventually became a total wreck, though most of the valuable portions of the cargo, consisting of general merchandise and fertilizer, were salvaged. According to the *Annual Report of the Chief of Engineers, United States Army, to the Secretary of War for the Year 1912*, work to remove the wreck as a navigational hazard began on February 6, 1912. The vessel took bottom and drifted onto the south jetty at a point about 1,300 feet from the outer end of the jetty. The stern rested on the jetty, and the bow, pointing about northward, rested on the sand bottom in six to eight feet of water at low tide. The wreck of the *Zeeburg* was broken up with dynamite and removed piece by piece.

ZETA NO. 2

The yacht *Zeta No. 2* reportedly stranded at St. Augustine Inlet on January 20, 1906. The gasoline-powered yacht, official number 201147, was built in 1904 at Parkersburg, West Virginia, and was 62.5 feet long, 15 feet wide, and 17 tons gross burden.

ZION

The bark *Zion* was originally built out of oak and pine as the three-masted schooner *Robert Dixon* by A. Hall at Damariscotta, Maine, in October 1873. According to insurance documentation in 1900, the *Zion* was 194.9 feet in length, 38.7 feet in breadth, and displaced 1,366 tons. In researching this vessel, I came across an article unrelated to its ultimate demise, but nonetheless worthy of inclusion. The November 21, 1898, article in *The Newark Daily Advocate* reported:

> The German bark *Zion*, which arrived at Philadelphia recently from Fowey, England, brought a rather peculiar cargo. It consisted of 1,800 casks of china, clay, but in addition there were put on 300 casks of arsenic. This part of the cargo had a remarkable effect on the crew. The fact that arsenic as well as strychnine helps the formation of adipose tissue when taken into the immune system in minute particles is well known, and both drugs have become favorite tonics for convalescents. On board the *Zion* the men slept very near the large array of barrels containing the drug. They were stored in the hold near the forecastle and partially exposed to the rays of the sun which streamed in through the open hatch. When only about a week out from port one of the crew mentioned to his mates that a peculiar and indescribable odor was coming from the casks containing the drug. It was not long after their attention

had been called to it that they all noticed the same thing, and strange to say, noticed it all the more forcibly a week later. Several of the German men became aware of the fact that they were filling out their clothes to a much greater extent than when they shipped. Many others, as days went by, became abnormally stout in vast contrast to the former slim appearance which many of them presented before the land was left. One man gained it is said 23 pounds. Others were affected to a less extent, but the aggregate weight put on by the entire crew was little less than 400 pounds. Several of the sailors were said to be scarcely recognizable by their former shipmates and associates when contrasted with the old days. The entire sudden taking on of avoirdupois is attributed to vapor which generated by the action of the sun on the casks, was inhaled by the seamen as they slept and acted in precisely the same manner which it does when given as a tonic in a prescription. Capt. Hemmes or the officers who slept aft in the vessel, entirely removed from the arsenic, did not show any effect of the inhalation.

In early October 1904, Captain Adrian Hemmes, Jr., guided his ship out of Pensacola Pass, bound for Liverpool with a cargo of lumber. On October 17, the *Zion* grounded on a reef five miles north of the Fort Lauderdale House of Refuge in the midst of a brutal hurricane. The following day, the captain and crew launched a small boat, but it was smashed against the hull of the *Zion*. The crew ultimately reached shore safely paddling on loose planks. Over the next few days, the crew was able to return to their ship to recover personal belongings as well as the stranded ship's dog. While the wreck of the *Zion* was salvaged over the following weeks, the hull was eventually battered to pieces over the winter.

The *Zion Train* as *Plancius*, 1981 (Alan Geddes).

ZION TRAIN

The freighter *Zion Train* (IMO number 5258456) was launched by G.J. van der Werff from their Westerbroek, Netherlands shipyard on October 27, 1961. Completed on December 27, 1961, as the *Novel* for owners Arend Brouwer and Frederik Galenkamp of Delfzijl, the coaster was 164.2 feet long, 26.3 feet wide, and displaced 400 gross tons. The Dutch cargo ship changed owners and names numerous times during her career: on September 3, 1974, the vessel was sold to H. Haveman of Hoogeveen, Netherlands, who renamed the vessel *Plancius*; she sailed as *Argo T.* following her sale on May 27, 1988, to *Argo T. Scheepvaartonderneming N.V.*; in 1993, the freighter was acquired by Monique Shipping Corporation of Belize, who renamed her *Monique*; two years later she operated as *Ines I* for Belizean owners; and Benjamin Darvil, Incorporated of Belize purchased the coaster in July 1996, whereupon she was renamed *Vanderpool Express*. While Benjamin Darvil was the registered owner, it is believed the vessel was actually controlled by Savil and Yolene Dessaint, who used the freighter to help smuggle almost 900 pounds of cocaine a month into South Florida from Haiti. The drug ring eventually collapsed following an investigation into the murders of the captain and four crew members on the *Vanderpool Express* while moored along the Miami River on July 14, 1997. The freighter was sold in August 1997 to Honduran owners, who named the vessel *Fidele Express*. Unfortunately, on October 13, 1997, the *Fidele Express* grounded on Miami Beach after her anchor broke loose during a storm. The vessel was eventually refloated and towed up the Miami River for repairs, which totaled more than $100,000. Her owners balked at the bill, however, and abandoned the vessel, which was later seized by U.S. Marshals and subsequently sold to a local salvage firm. In 2000, she was sold and registered as the *Zion Train* by her new owners, *Association Industriale Haitien* of San Lorenzo, Honduras.

The rusting freighter *Zion Train* was ultimately purchased and cleaned by Palm Beach County at a cost of $25,000. On June 2, 2002, the former Dutch coaster was scuttled in 90 feet of water off Jupiter. Originally resting upright and intact, Hurricane Frances ravaged the freighter in 2005, breaking it in half and moving the bow well over a mile south from its initial position. The bow now rests hard over on her port side, while the stern section, firmly embedded in the limestone bottom, lists to starboard. The stern section and collapsed cargo holds are located just south of the 55-foot long, upside-down barge *Miss Jenny* and the 146-foot long tanker *Esso Bonaire III*. This trio of wrecks is known to attract significant numbers of Goliath grouper during their annual spawning season in late August through September.

ENDNOTES

1. *London Evening Post*, June 4, 1763.
2. *General Evening Post*, December 9, 1790.
3. *The Nebraska State Journal*, September 29, 1940.
4. Gilpin, 1941:31.
5. Dean, 1992:160.
6. Ellms, 1841:324-329.
7. *Fort Lauderdale Daily News and Evening Sentinel*, May 12, 1942.
8. *New York Municipal Gazette*, March 15, 1847.
9. *The New York Times*, March 3, 1885.
10. *Florida Times-Union*, March 10, 1885.
11. *New York Spectator*, December 16, 1834.
12. *Chicago Daily Tribune*, June 5, 1961.
13. *Syracuse Herald Journal*, September 24, 1941.
14. Ibid.
15. Ibid.
16. *Sarasota Herald*, November 5, 1935.
17. *Lloyd's List*, March 12, 1878.
18. Davis, 1925:369.
19. Singer, 1998.
20. *The Miami News*, September 25, 1926.
21. *The Miami News*, September 25, 1926.
22. Hawks, 1887.
23. Siebert, 1943.
24. *Boston Daily Globe*, February 25, 1892.
25. *London Chronicle*, April 3, 1788.
26. Marx, 1987:227
27. *London Evening Post*, July 22, 1738.
28. *Annual Report of the Operations of the United States Life-Saving Service for the Fiscal Year Ending June 30, 1892*.
29. *The Miami News*, September 25, 1926.
30. Meylach, 1971.
31. Meylach, 1971.
32. Davis, 1925:369.
33. *Daytona Beach Morning Journal*, November 27, 1962.
34. Singer, 1998:165.
35. *Orlando Sentinel*, April 19 and 30, 1985.
36. *Orlando Sentinel*, February 7, 1987.
37. *Miami Herald*, March 20, 1984.
38. Davis, 1925:369.
39. *The New York Times*, February 24, 1942.
40. *The Racine Advocate*, April 27, 1882.
41. *New York Herald*, September 5, 1880.
42. *New York Herald*, September 5, 1880.
43. Ibid.
44. Ibid.
45. Ibid.
46. Ibid.
47. Ibid.
48. *The New York Times*, September 5, 1880.
49. *New York Herald*, September 7, 1880.
50. Ibid.
51. Mueller, 1966:70-71.
52. Davis, 1925:369.
53. *Scribner's Magazine*, June 1897.
54. Davis, 1925:369.
55. *Mitchell's Maritime Register and Shipping Gazette Weekly Summary*, June 1900.
56. Ibid.
57. Ibid.
58. *Mitchell's Maritime Register and Shipping Gazette Weekly Summary*, July 1900.
59. Harrison, 1903:507.
60. *The Sailor's Magazine and Naval Journal*, Volume 19.
61. Singer, 1998:187.
62. Mueller, 1986:412.
63. *Miami Herald*, November 12, 1930.
64. *The New York Times*, January 5, 1858.
65. Lochhead, 1954:74.
66. *The Miami News*, September 25, 1926.
67. *The Palm Beach Post*, April 11, 1923.
68. *Mitchell's Maritime Register and Shipping Gazette Weekly Summary*, January 1892.
69. *The Miami News*, September 25, 1926.
70. *The New York Times*, April 14, 1890.
71. Ibid.
72. Davis, 1925:369.
73. *The Titusville Herald*, December 15, 1930.
74. Ibid.
75. *The New York Times*, January 16, 1867.
76. *The Miami News*, September 25, 1926.
77. *The Miami News*, January 7, 1934.
78. *Galveston Daily News*, September 5, 1880.
79. *The Miami News*, January 7, 1934.
80. Singer, 1998:205.
81. *The New York Times*, July 30, 1890.
82. Ibid.
83. Ibid.
84. *Bell's Weekly Messenger*, December 15, 1816.
85. Pennington, 1930.
86. Davis, 1925:369.
87. Correspondence from U.S. Ship *Concord*, Records of the West Indies Squadron, July 7, 1836.
88. U.S. Navy Historical Center, Correspondence from U.S. Revenue Cutter *Washington*, August 17, 1836.
89. *The Washington Post*, October 18, 1907.
90. *The Marion Daily Star*, October 4, 1898.
91. *Galveston Daily News*, May 10, 1892.
92. Singer, 1998:203.
93. *Palm Beach Post*, October 22, 1943.
94. *Syracuse Herald Journal*, Sunday, October, 24, 1943.
95. George Fischer e-mail correspondence, April 22, 2002.
96. United States District Court for the Southern District of Florida, Judgement on Civil Action File No. 79-4627-Civ-CA, July 28, 1983.
97. *Federal Register*, 55 FR 50116, December 4, 1990.
98. Smith and Webber, 1932.
99. *General Evening Post*, November 7, 1751.
100. Davis, 1925:365,369.
101. Report of the Secretary of War; Being Part of the Message and Documents Communicated to the Two Houses of Congress at the Beginning of the Second Session of the Forty-Sixth Congress, 1879: Volume IV.
102. Singer, 1998:195.
103. Singer, 1998:163.
104. Ibid:154.
105. *The Sailor's Magazine and Naval Journal*, Volume 15.

[106] *The Edinburgh Advertiser*, October 13, 1813.
[107] *The New York Herald*, August 28, 1871.
[108] *The News Journal*, April 4, 1989.
[109] *Miami Daily News*, January 24, 1928.
[110] *Charleston Courier*, June 28, 1816.
[111] *The New York Times*, December 28, 1865.
[112] *London Evening Post*, January 29, 1767.
[113] *The Atlanta Constitution*, April 11, 1895.
[114] *The New York Times*, October 2, 1920.
[115] *Providence Journal*, July 24, 1985.
[116] United States Congressional Serial Set, National Archives.
[117] Ibid.
[118] Ibid.
[119] Report of the Secretary of War; Being Part of the Message and Documents Communicated to the Two Houses of Congress at the Beginning of the Second Session of the Forty-Sixth Congress, 1879.
[120] *General Evening Post*, May 21, 1748.
[121] *The Edinburgh Advertiser*, July 8, 1817.
[122] *Daytona Beach News-Journal*, December 13, 1997.
[123] Singer, 1998:190.
[124] *The Miami News*, January 7, 1934.
[125] *Kriegstagebuch U-123*, January 20, 1942.
[126] Singer, 1998:188.
[127] *City Gazette and Daily Advertiser*, October 10, 1797.
[128] *City Gazette and Daily Advertiser*, November 7, 1797.
[129] *Galveston Daily News*, October 18, 1878.
[130] *New York Herald*, September 5, 1871.
[131] *Sun Sentinel*, October 4, 1986.
[132] *The New York Times*, February 17, 1890.
[133] *The Sailor's Magazine and Seamen's Friend*, Volume 40.
[134] *Charleston Courier*, July 22, 1836.
[135] *The Sailor's Magazine and Naval Journal*, Volume 27.
[136] *Miami Herald*, January 1, 1966.
[137] *St. Petersburg Times*, December 29, 1965.
[138] *The Sailor's Magazine and Naval Journal*, Volume 15.
[139] *The Sailor's Magazine and Naval Journal*, Volume 17.
[140] *The Miami News*, July 11, 1927.
[141] *Annual List of Merchant Vessels of the United States*, 1953.
[142] *New York Herald*, October 22, 1870.
[143] *The Times*, April 1, 1851.
[144] Singer, 1998:175.
[145] *Lloyd's List*, July 13, 1779.
[146] *New Lloyd's Evening Post*, July 18, 1783.
[147] *The New York Times*, October 28, 1853.
[148] *Daily Kennebec Journal*, May 12, 1903.
[149] *Frank Leslie's Illustrated Newspaper*, April 6, 1861.
[150] *Florida Times-Union*, February 16, 1905.
[151] *The Washington Post*, March 8, 1915.
[152] Annual Report of the Supervising Inspector-General, U.S. Steamboat-Inspection Service to the Secretary of Commerce and Labor, 1899.
[153] *The Sailor's Magazine and Naval Journal*, Volume 26.
[154] *The Washington Post*, October 20, 1904.
[155] Annual Report of the Supervising Inspector-General, U.S. Steamboat-Inspection Service to the Secretary of Commerce and Labor, 1897.
[156] *The New York Herald*, November 4, 1870.
[157] *The Miami News*, December 16, 1949.
[158] Singer, 1998:204.
[159] *Daytona Beach Sunday News-Journal*, February 5, 1959.
[160] *New York Times*, December 26, 1937.
[161] *The New York Times*, October 9, 1855.
[162] *The Miami News*, September 25, 1926.
[163] *Sarasota Herald-Tribune*, October 30, 1963.
[164] *Los Angeles Times*, November 28, 1932.
[165] *The New York Times*, January 24, 1866.
[166] *Sarasota Herald*, February 16, 1930.
[167] Siebert, 1943.
[168] Report of the Secretary of War; Being Part of the Message and Documents Communicated to the Two Houses of Congress at the Beginning of the Second Session of the Forty-Sixth Congress, 1879.
[169] *Florida Times-Union*, February 7, 1897.
[170] *The Sailor's Magazine and Naval Journal*, Volume 19.
[171] Meylach, 1971.
[172] Annual Report of the Supervising Inspector-General, U.S. Steamboat-Inspection Service to the Secretary of Commerce and Labor, 1896.
[173] *The Miami News*, January 26, 1921.
[174] Davis, 1925:370.
[175] Meylach, 1971.
[176] *The Sailor's Magazine and Naval Journal*, Volume 23.
[177] *The New York Times*, February 21, 1942.
[178] *Fort Lauderdale News and Evening Sentinel*, February 21, 1942.
[179] Ibid.
[180] *The New York Times*, February 21, 1942.
[181] *The New York Times*, February 22, 1942.
[182] *Florida Times-Union*, September 9, 1900.
[183] *Lakeland Ledger*, March 25, 1983.
[184] *The Sailor's Magazine and Naval Journal*, Volume 10.
[185] *Daytona Beach Morning Journal*, February 8, 1939.
[186] Marx, 1987:224.
[187] *The Miami News*, September 25, 1926.
[188] Davis, 1925:370
[189] *Mexico News*, Department of State for Foreign Affairs, Year II, No. 17, June 5, 1942.
[190] *The Edinburgh Advertiser*, October 13, 1818.
[191] *The Miami News*, January 7, 1934.
[192] Smith and Webber, 1932.
[193] *Boca Raton News*, January 28, 1980.
[194] *The New York Times*, February 24, 1942.
[195] *Fort Lauderdale Daily News and Evening Sentinel*, February 24, 1942.
[196] *The New York Times*, February 24, 1942.
[197] Dubois, 1975:22.
[198] *East Florida Herald*, October 4, 1825.
[199] *The Miami News*, September 25, 1926.
[200] Mueller, 1966:85.
[201] *London Evening Post*, February 6, 1753.
[202] *The Evening Independent*, July 4, 1941.
[203] *The Sailor's Magazine and Naval Journal*, Volume 22.
[204] *St. James's Chronicle*, July 8, 1779.
[205] *The Times*, February 28, 1805.
[206] *Philadelphia Press*, November 26, 1857.
[207] Moore and Muir, 1987.
[208] *Soundings*, August 2000.
[209] *New York Daily Times*, April 15, 1854.

[210] *The New York Times*, July 23, 1864.
[211] *St. Petersburg Times*, February 25, 1955.
[212] *Ocala Star-Banner*, December 4, 1991.
[213] *British Gazetteer*, November 23, 1751.
[214] *The Miami News*, September 25, 1926.
[215] *Weekly Wisconsin*, January 9, 1856.
[216] Davis, 1925:370.
[217] *The Miami News*, August 12, 1922.
[218] *The Port Arthur News*, Wednesday, February 3, 1926.
[219] *Pacific Stars and Stripes*, June 30, 1968.
[220] *Third Annual Report of the State Board of Health of Florida*, May 2, 1892.
[221] *The Palm Beach Post*, June 29, 1945.
[222] Meylach, 1971.
[223] *Gazetteer and New Daily Advertiser*, August 30, 1765.
[224] *General Evening Post*, September 13, 1770.
[225] *Annual Report of the Chief of Engineers, United States Army, to the Secretary of War for the Year 1905.*
[226] *Bell's Weekly Messenger*, March 25, 1821.
[227] Lochhead, 1954:261-262.
[228] *Housman v. Ship Ajax*, Florida Supreme Court File No. 0865.
[229] United States District Court for the Southern District of Florida, 166 U.S. 1, March 1, 1897.
[230] Ibid.
[231] Ibid.
[232] *Archivo General de Indias*, 54-1-31, f.143.
[233] *Army and Navy Chronicle*, Volume 8, Number 19.
[234] *The Palm Beach Post*, November 25, 1972.
[235] Davis, 1925:370.
[236] *Lowell Sun*, March 26, 1964.
[237] *Adams Centinel*, Wednesday, October 13, 1813.
[238] *Gazetteer and New Daily Advertiser*, June 11, 1777.
[239] *The Gazette of the State of South-Carolina*, November 24 and December 1, 1779.
[240] *The Florida Times Union*, June 29, 2002.
[241] *Daytona Beach News Journal*, October 24, 2003.
[242] *The Miami News*, September 25, 1926.
[243] *Titusville Herald*, November 7, 1870.
[244] *Fort Lauderdale Sun Sentinel*, December 21, 1997.
[245] *The Miami News*, September 25, 1926.
[246] *Panama City News Herald*, May 2, 1952.
[247] *The New York Times*, August 27, 1865.
[248] *The Evening Independent*, February 24, 1930.
[249] *Fort Lauderdale Daily News and Evening Sentinel*, February 28, 1942.
[250] *Kriegstagebuch* U-504, February 22, 1942.
[251] *Palm Beach Post*, February 16, 1992.
[252] *New York Daily Times*, February 12, 1857.
[253] Marx, 1987:433.
[254] Diddle, 1947:45.
[255] *Palm Beach Post Times*, October 7, 1962.
[256] *The Palm Beach Post*, June 24, 1931.
[257] *St. James's Chronicle*, December 8, 1778.
[258] *General Evening Post*, December 9, 1790.
[259] Davis, 1925:358.
[260] *The New York Times*, October 22, 1870.
[261] Hawks, 1887.
[262] *The New York Times*, February 21, 1864.

BIBLIOGRAPHY

Admiralty Final Record Books of the U.S. District Court for the Southern District of Florida, Key West, 1829-1911. National Archives.

Berman, Bruce D. 1972. Encyclopedia of American Shipwrecks. The Mariners Press, Boston, Massachusetts.

Clowes, William Laird. 1900. The Royal Navy: A History from the Earliest Times to the Present, Volume 5. Sampson Low, Marston and Company, London, England.

Coe, Charles H. 1936. Shipwrecks on the Florida Coast. New Smyrna Beach Observer, New Smyrna, Florida.

Crane, Stephen. 1897. The Open Boat. A Tale to be After the Fact. Being the Experience of Four Men Sunk from the Steamer Commodore. Scribner's Magazine, June.

Davis, T. Frederick. 1925. History of Jacksonville, Florida, and Vicinity, 1513 to 1924. The Florida Historical Society, St. Augustine, Florida.

Diddle, Albert W. 1947. The Adjudication of Shipwrecking Claims at Key West in 1831. Tequesta, Volume 1, Number 6, University of Miami, Coral Gables, Florida

Dodd, Dorothy. 1944. The Wrecking Business on the Florida Reef 1822-1860. The Florida Historical Quarterly, Volume 22, Number 4, pp. 171-199. The Florida Historical Society, St. Augustine, Florida.

DuBois, Bessie Wilson. 1975. Shipwrecks in the Vicinity of Jupiter Light. Self-published, Jupiter, Florida.

Ellms, Charles. 1841. The Tragedy of the Seas; or, Sorrow on the Ocean, Lake, and River, from Shipwreck, Plague, Fire, and Famine. Carey and Hart, Philadelphia, Pennsylvania.

Flannery, Jim. 2000. Silver and Gold: Florida Lifeguard Discovers Shipwreck, Treasure, Court Battles and Greed. Soundings, August.

Gage, Thomas. 1763-1775. The Gage Papers, Communications Pertaining to East and West Florida. On file at the P.K. Yonge Library, Gainesville, Florida.

Gannon, Michael. 1991. Operation Drumbeat. Harper Perennial, New York. 528 pp.

Gilpin, Vincent. 1941. Bradish W. Johnson, Master Wrecker, 1846-1914. Tequesta, Number 1, University of Miami, Coral Gables, Florida.

Goldberg, Mark H. 1993. Going Bananas: 100 Years of American Fruit Ships in the Caribbean. North American Maritime Books, Kings Point, New York.

Hawks, John Milton. 1887. The East Coast of Florida: A Descriptive Narrative. Lewis and Winship, Lynn, Massachusetts. 137 pp.

Helmers, Terry. 2001. Miami Maritime History Database. Miami, Florida.

Hepper, David J. 1994. British Warship Losses in the Age of Sail, 1650-1859. Jean Boudriot Publishers, East Sussex, England.

Hopwood, Fred A. 1998. The Golden Era of Steamboating on the Indian River, 1877-1900. Florida Historical Society Press, Cocoa, Florida.

Lochhead, John L. 1954. Disasters to American Vessels, Sail and Steam, 1841-1846. Mariners Museum, Newport News, Virginia.

Marx, Robert F. 1979. Spanish Treasure in Florida Waters, A Billion Dollar Graveyard. Mariners Press, Boston, Massachusetts.

Marx, Robert F. 1987. Shipwrecks in the Americas. Dover Publications, Incorporated, New York.

Meylach, Martin. 1971. Diving to a Flash of Gold. Florida Classics Library, Port Salerno, Florida.

Mondano, Mark R. 1991. Diver's Guide to Shipwrecks: Cape Canaveral to Jupiter Light. Sandman Productions, Roseland, Florida.

Moore, David D. and Bill Muir. 1987. The Archaeology of the San Martin: Preliminary Study of the 1618 Honduran Almiranta. Seafarers, Volume 1, pp. 188-194. The Atlantic Alliance for Maritime Heritage Conservation. Key West, Florida.

Morrison, John H. 1903. History of American Steam Navigation. W.F. Sametz and Company, New York.

Mueller, Edward A. 1966. Kissimmee Steamboating. Tequesta, Number 26, pp. 53-87. University of Miami, Coral Gables, Florida.

Mueller, Edward A. 1986. Steamboat Activity in Florida during the Second Seminole Indian War. The Florida Historical Quarterly, Volume 64, Number 4, pp. 407-431.

Munroe, Ralph Middleton and Vincent Gilpin. 1930. The Commodore's Story. Ives Washburn, New York.

Pennington, Edgar L. 1930. East Florida in the American Revolution, 1775-1778. The Florida Historical Quarterly, Volume 9, Number 1, p 46.

Schoepf, Johann D. 1911. Travels in the Confederation, 1783-1784. Translated and Edited by Alfred J. Morrison. William J. Campbell, Philadelphia.

Siebert, Wilbur H. 1943. The Port of St. Augustine During the British Regime, Part II. The Florida Historical Quarterly, Volume 25, Number 1.

Singer, Steven D. 1998. Shipwrecks of Florida. Pineapple Press, Incorporated, Sarasota, Florida.

Smith, Josiah and Mabel L. Webber. 1932. Josiah Smith's Diary, 1780-1781. The South Carolina Historical and Genealogical Magazine, Volume 33.

Smith, Roger C. 1996. Treasure Ships of the Spanish Main: The Iberian-American Maritime Empires. In: Bass, George F., ed. Ships and Shipwrecks of the Americas. Thames and Hudson, New York, New York.

The Monthly Nautical Magazine and Quarterly Review. Oliver W. Griffiths, New York.

The Federal Reporter. Cases Argued and Determined in the Circuit Courts of Appeals and Circuit and District Courts of the United States. West Publishing Company, St. Paul, Minnesota.

The Sailor's Magazine and Naval Journal. American Seamen's Friend Society, New York.

United States Department of Commerce. Annual Report of the Supervising Inspector-General, U.S. Steamboat-Inspection Service to the Secretary of Commerce and Labor. Government Printing Office, Washington, D.C.

United States Department of Commerce. Annual List of Merchant Vessels of the United States. Government Printing Office, Washington, D.C.

United States Department of Commerce and Labor. Reports of the Department of Commerce and Labor 1904-1912. Government Printing Office, Washington, D.C.

United States Naval War Records Office. 1894-1922. Official Records of the Union and Confederate Navies in the War of the Rebellion. Volumes 1-27, Government Printing Office, Washington, D.C.

Report of the Secretary of War; Being Part of the Message and Documents Communicated to the Two Houses of Congress at the Beginning of the Second Session of the Forty-Sixth Congress. 1879. Volume IV. Government Printing Office, Washington, D.C.

United States War Office. Annual Report of the Chief of Engineers, United States Army, to the Secretary of War. Government Printing Office, Washington, D.C.

Wagner, Kip. 1965. Drowned Galleons Yield Spanish Gold. National Geographic, January.

Weller, Robert and Ernie Richards. 1995. Shipwrecks Near Wabasso Beach. En Rada Publications, West Palm Beach, Florida.

INDEX

A.W. THOMPSON: 1
ABACO SANDS: 1
ABBADASH: 261
ABBIE S. OAKS: 1
ABBY: 1
ADA BAILEY: 1
ADA J. SIMONTON: 1, 47
ADA TOWER: 2
ADAMELIA: 2
ADELINE: 2
ADMIRAL SAULTZEMAN: 2
ADONIS: 2
ADVENTURER: 257
AFRICAN: 2, 37, 90, 113, 207, 241
AGENORA: 2
AGNES: 2
AGRO TRADER: 2
AJAX (1836): 3, 235
AJAX (1886): 3, 22, 87, 93, 201
ALABAMA: 3, 40, 67
ALADDIN LAMP WRECK: 4
ALBATROSS: 4
ALBINA: 4
ALBINIA: 4
ALBION (1787): 4
ALBION (1790): 4, 263
ALDERLY: 9
ALECIA: 4
ALERT: 4, 138, 235
ALEXANDER: 5
ALEXANDER JONES: 5
ALEXANDER NICKELS: 5
ALEXANDRA MCALLISTER: 5, 206, 207
ALEXANDRO: 5
ALFRED: 4, 5
ALICE C. PRICE: 5
ALICE HOLBROOK: 6
ALICE TEBB: 6
ALICIA: 6, 22, 145
ALLIGATOR: 8
ALMA H.: 8
ALMIRANTE: 8, 215
ALNA: 4, 9, 40, 67
ALONZO: 10
ALPHA: 10, 119
ALTOMARY: 11
ALVARADO: 11
ALYCE B.: 12
AMANDA WINANTS: 12
AMARYLLIS: 12, 165, 247
AMAZON (1925): i
AMAZONE: 13
AMBROSINE: 14
AMELIA: 14
AMERICA (1846): 14
AMERICA (1885): 14
AMERICAN COIN: 15
AMERICAN EAGLE: 15
AMIABLE ANTOINETTE: 15
AMIABLE GERTRUDE: 15
AMOS BIRDSALL: 15
ANCHOR WRECK: 35
ANCIENT MARINER: 15, 25
ANDE: 16
ANDRO: 17
ANGLIN PIER WRECK: 18
ANN: 18
ANNA (1810): 18
ANNA (1986): 18
ANNA A. TYNG: 18
ANNA BELL HYER: 18
ANNA F.: 18
ANNIE B.: 18
ANNIE C.: 18
ANNIE WOOD: 18
ANTELOPE: 18
ANTILLES STAR: 18, 156
ANTONIO: 19
APOLLO: 4, 19, 263
ARAUCANA: 19
ARAWAK: 19
ARCADIA: 19
ARGOSY: 19
ARIDA: 19
ARIZONA SWORD: 20
ARMSMEAR: 20
ARRATOON APCAR: 20
ARROW: 22
ARTIBONITE: 22
ASHLEY: 22
ASK ME: 22
ATHENE: 22
ATHLETE: 22
ATLAS: 22, 106
ATLAS BARGE: 239
AUGUSTA WILSON: 3, 22, 87, 93, 201
AUTO WRECK: 22
AVIS: 22
B.H. LAKE: 119
BABY DARLING: 23
BABY RUTH: 23
BALLARD PINES WRECK: 23
BARBARA ANN: 23
BAREFOOT MAILMAN WRECK: 23
BEAR WRECK: 23, 56
BELCHER BARGE: 24, 25
BELIEZE: 24
BELL WRECK: 123
BELLE OF TEXAS: 24
BELLONA: 24
BELZONA ONE: 24, 25
BELZONA THREE: 25
BELZONA TWO: 24, 25
BENT ANCHOR WRECK: 23
BERNICE: 25
BEROSA: 25
BERRY PATCH (1987): 16, 25

BERRY PATCH (1988): 26, 65
BERTHA RITTER: 26
BESSIE B.: 26, 78
BETEK AR PEN: 26, 227
BETSEY (1752): 26
BETSEY (1787): 26
BETSEY (1812): 26
BETTY'S HOPE: 27
BEVERLY M.: 27
BIG AL: 27
BIG DADDY: 256
BIG LADY: 27
BIJOU: 27
BILL BOYD: 27
BILL NYE: 27
BIRD ISLAND WRECK: 27
BISCAYNE (1897A): 28
BISCAYNE (1897B): 28
BISCAYNE (1974): 28, 162
BLACK GOLD: 28
BLOCKADE RUNNER WRECK: 28
BLOOMER: 28
BLUE CHINA WRECK: 28
BLUE FIRE: 29, 194
BOBBY'S BOYS: 29
BONNE ADELLE: 30
BONNIE BIRD: 30
BORNEO: 30
BOSTON EXPRESS: 30
BOTTLE WRECK: 30, 32
BOW WOW: 30
BOXCAR WRECK: 30
BRANDY WINE: 30, 79, 161, 233
BRASS TELESCOPE WRECK: 23
BRECONSHIRE: 31
BREWSTER: 32
BRICK WRECK: 32
BRICKYARD WRECK: 32
BRITANNIA: 32
BROKEN ANCHOR WRECK: 207
BRUCE MUELLER: 55
BUDWEISER BAR: 32, 37, 40, 232
BULK TRADER: 32
BURROUGHS: 33, 203
CABANO: 34
CABIN WRECK: 216
CADILLAC: 34
CAICOS EXPRESS: 34
CAIRN: 34
CALICO: 34
CALICO JACK: 34
CALLIOPE: 34
CAMUSI: 35
CANADIAN WRECK: 35
CANNON PILE WRECK: 35, 39
CANNON WRECK: 151
CAPE CHARLES: 35
CAPTAIN BARTLETT: 35
CAPTAIN BILL: 257
CAPTAIN DAN: 35

CAPTAIN EARL: 36
CAPTAIN FURNIE: 36
CAPTAIN GREGORY: 36
CAPTAIN HARRY: 37
CAPTAIN STEVEN: 37
CAPTAIN TAP: 37
CAPTAIN TERRY: 37
CAPTAIN TOM S. BACKMAN: 37
CAPTAIN TONY: 32, 37
CAPTAIN'S TJK: 37
CAROLINE (1810): 2, 37, 241, 249
CAROLINE (1838): 37
CAROLINE (1939): 38
CAROLINE EDDY: 38, 47
CARRIE WALKER: ii
CASA BLANCA: 38
CASEY AND CANDICE: 39
CASHIER: 39
CAST IRON BALLAST WRECK: 35, 39
CASTOR: 32, 39
CATHARINA UHRWEDER: 221, 285
CATHARINE OSMOND: 40, 202
CATHERINE G.: 40
CATHERINE THOMAS: 40
CAUTION: 3, 40, 67
CELEBRATION II: 40
CENTERBOARD SCHOONER WRECK: 218
CERES: 40
CHAIN WRECK: 123
CHARLEE GIRL: 40
CHARLES CROOKER: 40, 125
CHARLES DAVIS: 41
CHARLEY'S CRAB: 41, 129
CHARLIE'S WRECK: 167
CHARMING NELLY: 41
CHARMING SALLY: 41
CHATHAM (1852): 41
CHATHAM (1910): 41
CHICHEMO: 42
CHIMAERA: 42
CHIMALUS: 42
CHLORINE BARGE: 42
CHRISTMAS TREE: 42
CHUCK-A-LUCK II: 16, 26
CINDY LEE: 42
CINNABAR: 42
CITIES SERVICE EMPIRE: 43
CITY OF AUSTIN: 45, 85, 86, 200, 256
CITY OF BRUNSWICK: 45
CITY OF GEORGETOWN: 45
CITY OF SANFORD: 45, 147
CITY OF VERA CRUZ: 46, 82, 141, 174
CLARA B.: 48
CLAUDINA: 49
CLEOPATRA: 49
CLUB ROYALE: 49
C-NOTE: 16, 25, 49
COAL WRECK: 49
COLONIST: 49
COLORED BEACH WRECK: 178

COMET: 49
COMMODORE: 49
COMMODORE BARNEY: 51, 206
COMPTON'S WRECK: 52
C-ONE: 52, 131
CONCEPTION: 52, 131
CONCRETE BARGE: 53
CONISCLIFFE: 53
CONMAR: 53
COPENHAGEN: 53, 116
COPPER WRECK: 189
COQUIMBO: 54
COREY N CHRIS: 54, 208, 239
CORINNE: 55
CORKY C.: 55
CORKY M.: 55
CORNWALL: 55
CORONA: 55
CORRIGAN'S WRECK: 177, 214
CORSAIR: 55
COSME CALZADA: 56, 222
COSMOPOLITE: 150
COSSACK: 106
COTOPAXI: 23, 56
COURIER DE TAMPICO: 4, 40, 56, 67
COURIER DE VERA CRUZ: 4, 40, 56, 67
COYLET: 57
CRAZY JIM: 57
CRICKET: 57
CROWN (1738): 58
CROWN (1857): 58, 83
CRUIZER PRIVATEER: 58, 174
CRUZ DEL SUR: 58
CUMBERLAND: 58
CUSHNOC: 59
CYNOSURE: 59
CYRUS BUTLER: 59
D & D II: 60
DAISY FARLIN: 60
DALLAS NEAL: 60
DAMOCLES: 60
DANIEL WEBSTER: 2, 60
DANTOR: 61
DAVID CLARK: i
DAVID KEMPS: 61
DAVID NICKELS: 61
DAVID T.: 61
DAVIS-HOLDEN WRECK: 61
DAYLIGHT: 62
DEAL: 62
DEEP FREEZE: 62
DEEP TUG: 62
DEEPWATER II: 62
DEERFIELD BEACH WRECK: 199
DEFIANCE: 62
DEFIANT: 63
DEL NORTE: 63
DELAWARE: 63
DELIVERANCE: 63
DELPHINE: 63

DELRAY WRECK: 111
DELTA: 63, 76
D.E.M.A. TRADER: 63, 216
DENNIS: 63
DESTINO A: 64
DEWITT CLINTON: 64
DIAMONDFIELD: 64
DIANA: 64
DICKEY BOY: 64
DIDO: 64
DIE VERNON: 65
DIXIE CRYSTAL: 65
DOC DEMILLY: 26, 65, 107
DOLPHIN (1747): 66
DOLPHIN (1748): 66
DOLPHIN (1836): 66
DONAL G. MCALLISTER: 66, 163
DONALD RAY: 66
DORA ELLEN: 71
DORIS: 67
DOROTHY: 67
DOVE: 67
DOVER: 67
DRAGON: 67
DREAD: 3, 40, 67
DRIFTWOOD: 67
DUE BILL: 68, 261
DUNHAM WHEELER: 68
DUTCH WRECK: 133
E.S. RUDDEROW: 69
EARL GALLEY: 69
EAST FLORIDA MERCHANT: 69
EBEN-EZER II: 69
ECHO (1844A): 69
ECHO (1844B): 69
ECHO (1858): 69
ED'S WRECK: 230
EDITHANNA: 69
EDITH DAWSON: 70
EDITH L. ALLEN: 70
EDMUND AND GEORGE: 19
EDWARD: 70
EIDSVAG: 70
EIGHT CANNON WRECK: 71
ELAINE: 71
EL AVISO CONSULADO: 71
EL CIERVO: 71, 227
EL ESPIRITU SANTO EL MAYOR: 71, 215
ELIM: 71
ELIZA: 72
ELIZA MALLORY: 72, 125, 154, 176
ELIZABETH: 72
ELIZABETH ELLEN: 72
ELIZABETH FREEMAN: 73
ELIZABETH MASSEY: ii, 73, 188
ELIZABETH PERRY: 73
ELLA: 73
ELVIRA GASPAR: 73
EMELINE: 73
ÉMÉRILLION: 73, 240, 242

EMILY B.: 73
EMILY SEARS: 74
EMMA: 74
EMMA KNOWLTON: 74
EMMA M. ROBINSON: 74, 236
EMMA WHITE: 74
EMMI BOGGS: 163
EMPECINADA: 74
ENDURANCE: 74
ENGLISH CHINA WRECK: 74
ENTERPRISE (1854): 74
ENTERPRISE (1871): 74
ÉPAULE DE MOUTON: 73, 74, 240, 242
ERICA OF EXUMA: 75
ERL KING: 75
ESCORT (1839): 75
ESCORT (1894+): 75
ESCORT (1926): 75
ESJOO: 75
ESMERALDA: 76, 168
ESPARTA: 77, 128
ESPERANCIA: 78
ESPÍRUTU SANTO: iii
ESSO BONAIRE III: 78, 121, 267
ETHEL (1890): 78
ETHEL (1895): 79
ETHEL (1918): 79
ETOILE DE MER: 30, 79, 161, 233
EULALIA: 79
EUNICE M.: 79
EUPHEMIA: 79
EUREKA II: 79
EVADNE: 80
EVANGELINE: 80
EVEN TIDE: 80
EVERGLADE: 80, 261
EXPORT: 80, 237
F.A. KILBURN: 81
F.C. BENNETT: 81
FAIR WEATHER: 81
FALCON: 81, 240
FAME: 81
FANNIE DUGAN: 81
FANNIE KIMMEY: 81
FANNIE S: 81
FANNY: 81
FANNY FERN: 82
FANNY SPRAGUE: 82
FATHOM II: 82
FAVORITE: 82
FEARLESS: 82
FELISA: 82
FERZIEHM: 82
FIDES: 82
FIRE BOAT: 174
FIVE BROTHERS: 83
FLEETWOOD III: 83
FLORDI GUADIANA: 83
FLORIDA (1825): 83
FLORIDA (1857): 83

FLORIDA (1904): 83
FLORIDA LEAGUE OF ANGLERS MINESWEEPER: 83
FLY: 84
FLYING CLOUD: 84
FORMENTO: 84
FORTITUDE: 84
FORTUNA II: 84
FORTUNE (1772): 85
FORTUNE (1782): 85
FOR YOUR EYES ONLY: 85
FOXFIRE: 85
FRANCES: 85
FRANCIS (1843): 85
FRANCIS (1921): 85
FRANCIS (1962): 85
FRANCIS V. SYLVIA: 85
FRANCONIA: 45, 85, 200
FRANK: 86
FRANK E. STONE: 86
FRANKLIN: 86
FRANKLIN BAKER 2ND: 86
FRED W. HOYT: 86
FREEDOM EXPRESS: 86
FREE SPIRIT ENTERPRISE: 87
FREEWIND: 3, 22, 87, 93, 201
FREIGHT CONSOLIDATOR: 87
FROLIC (1816): 87
FROLIC (1910): 87
FUGGEDABOUDIT WRECK: 87, 249
G.B. FRATE: 88
GEJA: 88
GENERAL BURNSIDE: 88
GENERAL JACKSON: 88
GENERAL PIKE: 106
GENERAL WHITNEY: 88
GENE'S CANNON WRECK: 89
GENESEE: 89, 179
GENEVA: 89
GEORGE (1778): 89, 99
GEORGE (1810): 90, 102
GEORGE AND MARY: 90
GEORGE C. COLLINS: 90
GEORGE HARRIS: 90
GEORGEA: 90
GEORGE'S WRECK: 90
GEORGES VALENTINE: 90
GEORGIE: 91
GERTRUDE: 91
GHOST: 91
GHOST TUG: 91
GIL BLAS: 91, 234
GILBERT SEA: 92, 221, 227, 236
GINGER: 93
GIOVANNI: 93
GLAD TIDINGS: 93
GLADIATOR: 93
GLADYS: 93
GLANDENA: 93
GLOBE: 93
GODFREY: 3, 22, 87, 93, 111, 201

GOLD WRECK: 178
GOLDEN LION: 93
GRACE: 94
GRACE DEERING: 94
GRACIE D. BUCHANAN: 4, 27, 94, 138
GRACIE J.: 94
GRADCO PIONEER: 94
GRANADA: 94
GRAND TURK: 94
GREEN CABIN WRECK: 213
GROUPER: 94
GULFAMERICA: 94, 128
GULFLAND: 95
GULFSPRITE: 97
GUY HARVEY: 97
GYPSY GIRL: 97
H.B. PLANT: 98
H.G. BERRY: 98
H.M.S. AMARANTHE: 23, 98
H.M.S. BERMUDA: 98
H.M.S. FOWEY: 20, 98, 228
H.M.S. OTTER: 90, 99
H.M.S. WOLF: 99, 101
H.M.S. ZENOBIA: 100
HALCYON: 100
HALF MOON: 100
HALL OF FAME WRECK: 101
HALLANDALE BEACH WRECK: 101
HALLIE K.: 101
HALSEY: 101
HAMBRO: 125
HANNAH: 102
HANOVER: 90, 102
HAPPY DELIVERY: 102
HAPPY RETURN: 102
HAROLDINE: 100, 102
HAROLD J. MCCARTY: 103
HARRIET A. WEED: 103, 149
HARRINGTON: 103
HARRIOT: 103
HARRY LEE: 104
HARRY T. HAYWARD: 104
HATTIE: 104
HATTIE ROSS: 104
HAV PARKER III: 25
HAYNE: 104
HAZARD: 104
HEATHER BARKER: 104, 118
HEATHER IV: 256
HEAVY MOON: 104
HEIDELBERG: 125
HELEN C.: 104
HELEN T.: 104
HELMA: 104
HENRY BARGER: 104
HENRY NIN: 104
HERALD: 105
HERCULES: 105
HERMITAGE: 105
HESS MARINER: 105

HESTER: 105
HETTY: 105
HIAWATHA (1919A): 105
HIAWATHA (1919B): 106
HILDA: 106
HIRAM AND WILLIAM: 106
HOPE (1791): 106
HOPE (1796): 106
HOPE FOR PEACE: 106
HORATIO: 106
HOTLINE: 106
HOWLAND: 106
HOWLET: 106
HUBBARD: 74
HUDSON: 106, 266
HUGH DE PAYENS: 107
HUGO'S APRIL FOOL: 26, 65, 107
HUNTRESS: 107
HUPALONG: 107
HURON: 107
HUSSAR: 257
HUSTLER: 108
HYDRO ATLANTIC: 108
I. HOWLAND: 110
ICAROS: 110
IDA E. LATHAM: 110
ILO: 110
IMAGINATION: 110
IMOR: 110
INCHULVA: 110
INDIAN RIVER: 111
INDUSTRY (1764): 111
INDUSTRY (1766): 112
INDUSTRY (1837): 112
INGRID: 112
INIS: 257
INTREPID: 112
IRON BALLAST WRECK: 113
IRON BOX SITE: 218
ISAAC COLLINS: 113
ISABELLA: 113
ISABELLA S.: 113
ISIS (1882): 113
ISIS (1920): 113
ISLAND CITY: 114
ISLANDER: 114
J.E. STEVENS: 115
J.H. LANE: 115
J.W. PHILBRICK: 115
JACK PILAFIAN: 115
JACKIE B.: 115
JACKIE FAYE: 115
JACKSONVILLE DRY DOCK: 115
JACQUELINE A.: 116
JADE BEACH WRECK: 116
JALI: 116
JAMES: 116
JAMES BOATWRIGHT: 116
JAMES JUDGE: 118, 156, 157
JANE: 118

JANE M. HARWOOD: 118
JANE ROSS: 118
JANET: 118
JARLINGTON: 104, 118
JAXSHIPCO NO. 4: 118
JAY DORMAN: 10, 118
JAY SCUTTI: 119, 158, 240
JEFFERSON: 119
JEFFERSON DAVIS: 11, 119
JEMINS: 120
JENNIE HIGHT: 120
JENNIFER: 121
JENNY G.: 121
JEREMIAH LEAMING: 121
JESSIE A. BISHOP: 27, 121, 138
JESSIE B. SMITH: 121
JESULA II: 121
JESUS MARIA: 121
JIM ATRIA: 121
JOAN AND URSULA: 122
JOHN H. TINGUE: 122
JOHN HOWARD: 122
JOHN MCLEAN: 122
JOHN R. WILDER: 123
JOHN WAYNE: 123, 218
JOHN WESLEY: 123, 188
JOLLY TAR: 123
JOSEPH AND JANE: 123
JOSEPH B. THOMAS: 123
JOSEPH CROWELL: 124
JOSEPH MEIGS: 124
JOSEPHINE: 124
JOSEPHINE H. II: 124
JOYCE MOORE: 124
JULIAN: 124
JULIET: 125
JUNO BEACH WRECK: 125
JUPITER: 125
JUPITER STAR: 125
K-119: 126
KEMAH: 126
KEN M.: 126
KEN VITALE: 119, 239
KENNEDY: 126
KESSIE PRICE: 76, 126
KESTREL: 126
KING FISH: 127
KINGFISHER: 127
KINSDALE: 127
KNOCKOUT: 127
KONA: 127
KORIMU: 127
KORSHOLM: 128
KOSSUTH: 129
KRINGELINE: 129
L. MCNEILL: 130
L-SILHOUETTE: 130
L.T. KNIGHT: 142
LA BARBARA: 130
LA CONCEPCION: 52

LA ESCLAVITUD: 130
LA MAGDALENA: ii
LA NATIVITÉ: 78, 131
LADY BANNERMAN: 131
LADY BEATRICE: 131
LADY CARMEN: 52, 131, 263
LADY CLARA: 131
LADY FREI: 131
LADY K: 131
LADY M. JOHNSON: 132
LADY NICOLE: 132
LADY OF THE LAKE: 132
LADY PROVOST: ii, 265
LADY SARA II: 132
LAERTES: 132
LAKELAND: 133, 229
LANDRAS: 134
L'ATHENAISE: 23, 134, 212
LAVINIA: 135
LEAD WRECK: 182
LEDBURY: 135
LEJOK: 135
LENA M. CORBETT: 135
LEONIE: 135
LEON RODDY: 136
LESLIE: 95, 128, 136
LET HER B: 137
LET'S GO: 137
LEV LOU: 137
LIBERTY: 137
LIBERTY WRECK: 68
LILLIAN L.: 137
LILLIE: 137
LINA: i
LINDA: 137
LINDA JO: 138
LITTLE STEVIE: 138
LITTLE TALBOT ISLAND WRECK: 138
LIVELY: 138
LIZZIE B. WILLEY: 138
LIZZIE BAKER: 138
LIZZIE E. DENNISON: 138
LIZZIE HEYER: 138
LIZZIE L. SMITH: 138
LOANDO: 139
LODONA: 139
LOFTHUS: 140
LOLLIE BOY: 141
LONG ISLAND EXPRESS: 141
LONG REACH: 47, 141
LOUISE: 141
LOWRANCE: 141
LOYAL SCRANTON: 142
LUBRAFOL: 142, 196
LUCY: 144
LUELLA: 144
LUGANO: 22, 144, 202
LUMBER WRECK: 145
LYNN: 145
LYON: 145

MACHOTE: 146
MAD HATTER: 257
MADAKET: 146
MADAWASKA: 146
MAGGIE II: 146
MAGGIE JONES: 146
MAGGIE MAE: 146
MAGIC CITY: 146
MAGNOLIA (1882): 147
MAGNOLIA (1928): 147
MAJO: 62, 147
MAJOR WILLIAM BARNETT: 147
MANDALAY: 74, 147
MANFRED: 148
MANNACAMP: 146
MAPLE LEAF: 148, 246
MARANA: 149
MARBERON: 150
MARCELLY: 150
MARGARET ANN: 150
MARGARET THOMAS: 150
MARGARETHA: 150
MARGUERITE: 150
MARIA (1796): 150
MARIA (1811): 150
MARIA BECKFORD: 151
MARIA M. KLOTS: 151
MARIE: 151
MARIE CONCETTI: 151
MARIE GILBERT: 49, 151
MARIGALERA: 151
MARINER I: 249
MARINER II BARGE: 155, 249
MARINER II TUG: 155, 208
MARION (1950): 151
MARION (1998): 151
MARIPOSA: 151, 263
MARS: 152
MARSHA T.: 152, 218, 231
MARTHA (1753): 152
MARTHA (1868): 152
MARTHA (1870): 152
MARTHA BRAE: 22, 152
MARTHA T. THOMAS: 152
MARY (1766): 152
MARY (1778): 153
MARY (1783): 153
MARY A. HOLT: 153
MARY AND JANE: 154
MARY ANN: 153
MARY B.: 153
MARY BELLE: 153
MARY BROWN: 3, 22, 87, 93, 201
MARY C.: 154
MARY COE: 125, 154
MARY F. CARSON: 154
MARY F. GODFREY: 154
MARY KINGSLAND: 154
MARY L.: 164
MARY LINDA: 154

MARY ST. PHILLIP: 155, 208
MARY STAR OF THE SEA: 154
MARYBOB TWO: 153
MARYLAND: 155
MASCOTTE: 155
MASSA E. GUECCO: 156
MATANZAS: 156
MATTIE RICHMOND: 156, 201
MATTIE S.: 156
MAURICE R. SHAW, JR.: 156
MAWAGRA II: 156
MAXINE D.: 156
MAY BELLE: 156
MAY LI: 156
MAYPORT: 157
MECHANIC: 157
MELBA: 157
MELDA: 157
MELROSE (1853): 157
MELROSE (1904): 157
MERCEDES I: 157
MERCEDES II: 158
MERCI JESUS: 119, 158, 159, 240
MERCI RABBI: 159
MERMAID: 159
MERRAGANZET: 106
MERRIMACK: 159
MERSEY: 159
MESSENGER: 160
METAMORA: 160
MIAMI LCI: 161
MICHELLE: 161
MIGUANA: 30, 31, 79, 161 233
MILITARY WRECK: 138
MILLER BROTHERS: 161
MILLER LITE: 161
MILLIE: 162
MINERVA (1777): 162
MINERVA (1811): 162
MINERVA (1870): 156, 162, 201
MINERVA (1920): 162
MINNIE: 159, 162
MINNIE LOUISE: 162
MIRACLE EXPRESS: 28, 162
MIRAMAR: 162
MISERY: 163
MISS CHARLESTON: 163
MISS CINDY II: 163
MISS DANIA BEACH: 163
MISS EILEEN: 163
MISS FERNANDINA: 163
MISS FLAGLER: 163
MISS GLENDA II: 163
MISS HARRIET ANN: 164
MISS ILSE: 164
MISS JENNY: 121, 267
MISS JO: 164
MISS KARLINE: 164
MISS LIBBY: 164
MISS LINDA: 164

MISS LOURDIES: 164
MISS LUCY: 164
MISS LULA: 164
MISS MARYLN LOUISE: 164
MISS SHIRLEY: 165
MISSISSIPPI (1871): iii
MISSISSIPPI (1874): iii
MIZPAH: 13, 165, 247
MOANA II: 165
MOHAWK: 166
MOHICAN: 166
MOLLIE S. LOOK: 166
MOLLY: 166
MONAHAN: 167
MONOMOY: 167
MONTAGUE: 167
MONTAGUE DOYLE: 167
MOONSHOT: 119
MORENO: 156, 167, 201
MORGAN'S WRECK: 167
MORRIS RUSSEL: 167
MUNTZ METAL WRECK: 167
MUSCOGEE: 167
MUTUAL SAFETY: 167
MY BOYS: 167
MYSTERY J.: 167
MYSTIC: 168
MYSTIC ISLE: 76, 168
NANCY LEE: 170
NANCY MORAN: 170
NANON: 170
NANTWICH: 33, 170, 203
NARRAGANSETT: 2, 170, 180, 209
NARWAL: 171
NASSAUVIAN: 171
NATHAN CLEAVES: 171
NATHAN F. COBB: 171
NATHAN HANAU: 172
NAVIGATOR: 172
NAYA: 172
NELLIE F. BURGESS: 172
NELLIE N.: 172
NELLY: 172
NELSON: 173
NEPENTHE: 173
NEPTUNE (1802): 173
NEPTUNE (1816): 173
NEPTUNE (1822): 173
NERO: 173
NERVINA: 173
NETTIE LANGDON: 173
NEVA: 173
NEW BALION: 174
NEW JERSEY: 174
NEW REPUBLIC: 47, 174
NEW RIVER: 174
NEW YORK CENTRAL NO. 3: 174
NICHOLAS ADOLPH: 174
NICHOLAS AND SARAH: 174
NICK COMOGLIO: 159

NICK KING: 228
NINA FAY: 174
NO NAME WRECK (BREVARD): 175
NO NAME WRECK (ST. LUCIE): 175
NOAH SMITH: 174
NOBLE BOUNTY: 175
NORINA: 175
NORNA: 175
NORTH: 125, 175
NORTH EASTER: 176
NORTH STAR: 176
NORTHWESTERN: ii
NOULA EXPRESS: 176
NUESTRA SEÑORA DE CONCEPCIÓN: 176, 227
NUESTRA SEÑORA DE LA POPA: 176
NUESTRA SEÑORA DE LA REGLA, SAN DIMAS Y SAN FRANCISCO SAN XAVIER: 177, 214
NUESTRA SEÑORA DE LAS NIEVES: 177
NUESTRA SEÑORA DE LAS OLAS: 178
NUESTRA SEÑORA DEL CARMEN: 178
NUESTRA SEÑORA DEL CARMEN Y SAN ANTONIO: 121, 178
NUESTRA SEÑORA DEL POPULO: 71, 179
NUESTRA SEÑORA DEL ROSARIO Y SAN CRISTOBAL: 179
NUESTRA SEÑORA DEL ROSARIO Y SAN FRANCISCO XAVIER: 179
O.L. BODENHAMER: 183
OBSESSION: 242
OCEAN: 180
OCEAN EDGE WRECK: 180
OCEAN FREEZE: 180
OCEAN PEARL: 180
OCEAN PRIDE: 181
OCEAN VENUS: 181
OCKLAWAHA: 182
OH KIM SOON: 140, 182
OHIO: 182
OHIOAN: 87, 182
OJUS: 183
OLD SILVER WRECK: 23
OLGA: 183
OLIVE BRANCH: 183
OLNEY: 9
OLYMPIA: 183
ONTARIO: 183
ORCA: 183
ORE WRECK: 184, 234
OREGON (1846): 183
OREGON (1904): 183
ORIENTAL WARRIOR: 184, 260
ORION: 184
ORITHYIA: 184
ORRIE V. DRISKO: 185
OSCAR: 185
OSCEOLA (1895): 185
OSCEOLA (1910+): 185
OSCEOLA (1921): 185
OSCEOLA (1941): 185
OSEOLA: 185

OSIRIS: 185
OSPREY: 185
OSPREY WRECK: 186
OSTWIND: 186
OTAC NIKO: 186
OUTCAST: 187
OUTLINE WRECK: 187
OYSTER BOY: 187, 220
PAC MAN: 242
PACIFIC: 188
PACIFIC REEF WRECK: 188
PADDLEWHEELER WRECK: 229
PALADIN: 188
PALATKA: 188
PALO ALTO: 188
PAN DALLAS: 188
PAN MASSACHUSETTS: ii, 188
PANAMA: 188
PAPA'S WRECK: 190
PARAISO III: 190,
PASADENA: 190
PATHFINDER: 190
PATRICIA (1926): 190
PATRICIA (1990): 76, 164, 190
PATRICIA M.: 190
PATRIOT: 190
PAUL: 191
PAUL G. MAINS: 191
PAUL MARIE: 191
PEARL: 191
PECONIC: 191
PEE DEE (1838): 192
PEE DEE (1858): 193
PEE WEE VREELAND: 193
PEERLESS: 193
PEGGY JOE: 193
PETER: 193
PETER B. MCALLISTER: 193
PETRUS: 193
PHOEBUS: 194
PHOENIX: 194
PILITA: 194
PILLAR DOLLAR WRECK: 89
PILOT BOY: 194
PIMELLOUS: 194
PINTA: 194
PIONEER (1877): 194
PIONEER (1926): 194
PIONEER I: 194
PIUTE: 194
PIZARRO: 194
POLAR: 195
POMONA: 195
PONCE DE LEON INLET WRECK: 195
PONTE VEDRA WRECK: 107
PORT ROYAL: 195
POTRERO DEL LLANO: 195
POWERFUL: 196
PRIDE (HARBOUR TOWNE): 119
PRIMA DONNA: 196, 223

PRINCE GEORGE: 196
PRINCESS: 196
PRINCESS ANNE: 197
PRINCESS BRITNEY: 190, 197, 225
PRINCESS MARY: 198
PRINS VALDEMAR: 198
PROP WRECK: 199
PROTECTOR: 199
PROTEUS: 199
PROVIDENCIA: 200
PROVIDENZA R.: 200
PUNTA LUNA: 200
QUALMANN TUGS: 10, 119
QUEEN (1818): 201
QUEEN (1891): 201
R.B. TRUEMAN: 201
R.W. JOHNSON: 3, 22, 87, 93, 201
RAFBORN: 201
RATICAN: 201
RATTLER: 201
RATTLESNAKE: 201, 230
RAVENSWOOD: 201
RAYCHEL: 201
RAZOR WRECK: 191
REALITY: 202
REBECCA: 40, 202
REBECCA LEIGH: 202
REBEL: 84, 202
RED BRICK WRECK: 202
RED WING (1887): 202
RED WING (1891): ii
REFORMATION: 33, 170, 202
RELIANCE (1878): 203
RELIANCE (1985): 203
RELIEF #5: 203
RENEGADE: 142, 203
REPUBLIC: 96, 97, 204, 259
REVENGE: 204
REX BEAR: 205
RHEA: 205
RICHMOND (1920): 205
RICHMOND (1926): 205
RIDGEWOOD: 51, 205
RING WRECK: 206
RIO MIAMI: 63, 190, 206, 222
RIO YUNA: 5, 206, 236
RIOMAR WRECK: 121, 179
RIVERSMITH: 207
ROBALISS: 207
ROBERT AND SAMUEL: 207
ROBERT BRUCE: 207
ROBERT EDMISTER: 207, 213, 261
ROBERT MORRIS: 207
ROBERTS: 207, 214, 226
ROCKLEDGE: iv
RODEO 25: 155, 207
ROLLING ON: 208
RONALD B. JOHNSON: 54, 208, 239
ROSA EPPINGER: 47, 208
ROSALIE: 208

ROSALYN B. HUDGINS: 208
ROSANDA: 208
ROSE: 208
ROSEADA: 208
ROSE MAHONEY: 76, 209
ROSEADALE TURO: 209
ROSECLIFF II: 220
ROSSMERRY: 209
ROXANNA: 171, 209
ROYAL DESIRE: 209
RSB-1: 209
RUBY (1752): 210
RUBY (1907A): 210
RUBY (1907B): 210
RUBY LEE: 210
RUBY W: 210
RUSS: 210
RUXTON #2: 211
RYE GALLEY: 211
S. & W. WELSH: 98, 212
S.E. VINSON: 212
S.S. LUCAS: 212
S.S. MILLS: 212
SAGINAW: 212
SAINT GEORGE: 212
SAINTE ANNE D'AURAY: 212
SALLY (1773): 212
SALLY (1779): 212
SALLY (1804): 212
SALLY BROWN: 212
SALUDA: 212
SALVAGER III: 207, 212
SALVOR II: 213
SAMA: 213
SAMAY: 213
SAMSON: 213
SAMUEL BOLTON: 213
SAMUEL FAUNCE: 213
SAMUEL OTIS: 213
SAN CAYETANO: 213
SAN ESTEBAN: iii
SAN IGNACIO: 213, 215
SAN JOSÉ DE LAS ANIMAS: 224
SAN MARTIN: 213
SAN MIGUEL: 214, 227
SAN MIGUEL DE ARCHANGEL: 214
SAN NICOLÁS: 214
SAN RAPHAEL: 214
SANDY POINT WRECK: 89, 179
SANIBEL: 214
SANTA ANNA: 214
SANTA CLAUSE: 214
SANTA MARIA: 215
SANTA MARIA DE LA LIMPIA CONCEPCIÓN: 213, 215
SANTA MARÍA DE YCIAR: iii
SANTA MARIA DEL CAMINO: iii
SANTA RITA: 215
SANTA ROZA: 215
SANTÍSIMA TRINIDAD: 71, 215
SANTO CRISTO DE MARACAIBO: 215
SANTO CRISTO DE SAN ROMAN: 215
SANTO ROSARIO: 216
SARAH: 216
SARAH JANE (1854): 216
SARAH JANE (1981): 63, 216
SARAH MARY: 216
SARAH R. THOMAS: 216
SATISFACTION: 216
SAURWALT'S WRECK: 216
SAVANNAH (1924): 217
SAVANNAH (1964): 217
SAXONY: 217
SCALLOP KING: 217
SCARLETT O'HARA: 217
SCHOONER BALLAST WRECK: 217, 226
SCHURGER'S BARGE: 25
SCOTCHIE: 217
SCOTT AND GREG: 217
SEA BIRD: 217
SEA BOY: 217
SEA BREEZE: 217
SEA EAGLE: 217
SEA EMPEROR: 176, 218, 251
SEA FARER: 123, 218
SEA FLOWER: 218
SEA INSPECTOR: 152, 218, 231
SEA MIST II: 218
SEA SCAMP: 219
SEA TAXI: 219
SEABOARD: 217
SEAFLOWER: 218
SEAFOOD WRECK: 218
SEARCHER: 219
SEBASTOPOL: 219
SELMA S.: 219
SEMARCA: 219
SEMINOLE (1855): 220
SEMINOLE (1896): 220
SEMINOLE (1935): 220
SENRAB: 220
SERVICE: 220
SETH LOW: 187, 220
SEVRE: 220
SHAMROCK: 220
SHARK: 221, 285
SHA SHA BOEKANIER: 92, 221, 227, 236
SHERI LYN: 221
SHIRIN: 222
SHOWBOAT WRECK: 222
SHUTTLE: 222
SIDEWHEEL STEAMER WRECK: 222
SILVER QUEEN: 222
SIMMONS: 222
SIMPSON CREEK WRECK: 223
SIR SCOTT: 223
SIR WALTER RALEIGH: 196, 223
SKYECLIFFE: 224
SKYLARK II: 224
SNOW WHITE II: 224
SOCIAL: 224

SOLDIER KEY WRECK: 224
SOLI DEO GLORIA: 224
SONORA: 224
SOUTH SEAS: 198, 225
SOUTH WIND II: 225
SPANISH HOUSE WRECK: 113
SPARKLING SEA: 225
SPRAY: 49, 226
SPRING OF WHITBY: 214, 226
SPY: 226
ST. ANN: 226
ST. AUGUSTINE: 226, 229
ST. AUGUSTINE WRECK: 227
ST. HENRY'S EXPRESS: 26, 227
ST. JACQUES: 92, 221, 227
ST. JOHNS: 228
ST. JUDEA: 98, 228
ST. LUCIE: 76
ST. MARY (1770): 228
ST. MARY (1864): 228
ST. PAUL: 228
ST. SEBASTIAN: 226, 229
STAIRS WRECK: 226
STAR: 229
STAR TREK: 229
STARLIGHT: 229
STARRY BANNER: 229
STELLA: 175, 229
STONEFREE: 230
STORM WRECK: 230
SUB WRECK: 230
SUCRE: 230
SUMIDA: 231
SUMMERFIELD: 163
SUN MARINER: 152, 218, 231
SUNRISE WRECK: 231
SUPPLY: 231
SUSAN: 231
SVANEN: 231
SWAMP WRECK: 231
SWAN: 231
SWORDFISH (1921): 231
SWORDFISH (1992): 32, 232
SYLPH: 232
SYLVINA EXPRESS II: 232
T.S.O. PARADISE: 233
TACOMA: 30, 79, 161, 233
TAMARCO: 233
TAMINEND: 233
TARPOON: 212, 233
TE AMO: 233
TELUMAH: 184, 234
THALES: 92, 234
THAMES: 234
THEODORE S. PARKER: 235
THEOLINE: 27, 138, 235
THETIS: 1, 4, 235, 263
THIRD AVENUE WRECK: 235
THISTLE: 3, 235
THOMAS B. CATOR: 236

THOMAS H.: 5, 206, 207, 236
THOZINA: 92, 227, 236
THRACIAN: 237
THREE FRIENDS: i, 6, 28, 50, 74, 237
THREE SISTERS: 238
TIFTON: 238
TIGER: 81, 238, 240
TIGER RED: 238
TITAN: 238
TOCOI WRECK: 239
TOMADOR: 239
TONY: 239
TORTUGA: 227, 239
TRACOR DRY DOCK: 239
TRACY: 119, 158, 159, 239
TRANSFER NO. 8: i
TREE BARGE: 263
TRINITÉ: 73, 75, 240, 242
TRIO BRAVO: 240
TRITON: 2, 37, 90, 113, 207, 241
TRIUMFANTE: 241, 264
TRIUNFO: 241
TROJAN: 241
TROPIC: 220
TROPIC ACE: 241
TRUITE: 73, 74, 240, 242
TUBE WRECK: 112
TWILIGHT: 242
TWO BROTHERS: 242
TWO GEORGES: 242
TWO PIRATES: 242
TYRE: 242
U.S. NAVY CONSOLIDATED PBY-5 CATALINA #08181: 243
U.S. NAVY GUNBOAT NO. 161: 243
U.S. NAVY GUNBOAT NO. 164: 243
U.S. NAVY GUNBOAT NO. 2: 243
U.S. NAVY MARTIN PBM-5 MARINER #59225: 244
U.S.C.G.C. LOTUS: 244
U.S.C.G.C. MOCCASIN: 244
U.S.C.G.C. SPIKE: 244
U.S.S. COLUMBINE: 174, 245
U.S.S. FREDONIA: 247
U.S.S. GENERAL HUNTER: 149, 245
U.S.S. MINDANAO: 5, 246
U.S.S. MONTAUK: 246
U.S.S. MULIPHEN: 62, 246
U.S.S. OWENS: 71
U.S.S. PC-1174: 13, 165, 247
U.S.S. RANKIN: 247
U.S.S. YP-429: 73
ULTRA FREEZE: 248
UMTATA: 87, 248
UNCLE SAM: 249
UNION: 2, 37, 90, 113, 207, 241, 249
UNION EXPRESS: 155, 249
UNITED CARIBBEAN: 176, 218, 249
UNKNOWN ENGLISH BRIG: 251
UNKNOWN ENGLISH MAN OF WAR: 251
UNKNOWN ENGLISH VESSEL: 251

UNKNOWN FRENCH SHIPS: 251
UNKNOWN FRENCH SNOW: 251
UNKNOWN PIRATE SLOOP: 251
UNKNOWN PRIVATEER BRIG: 251
UNKNOWN PRIVATEER SNOW: 251
UNKNOWN SCHOONER: 251
UNKNOWN SHIPWRECK (1769): 251
UNKNOWN SHIPWRECK (1775): 252
UNKNOWN SHRIMP TRAWLER (2002): 252
UNKNOWN SHRIMP TRAWLER (2003): 252
UNKNOWN SNOW: 252
UNKNOWN SPANISH MEN OF WAR: 252
UNKNOWN SPANISH SCHOONER (1766): 252
UNKNOWN SPANISH SCHOONER (1837): 252
UNKNOWN SPANISH SHIP AND SNOW: 252
UNKNOWN SPANISH SHIP OF WAR: 253
URCA DE LIMA: 175, 253
UTILITY: 253
V-1764: 254
VAHDAH: 254
VALCOUR: 254
VALKYRIE: 254
VALMASEDA: 254
VAMAR: i
VAN: 254
VARUNA: 254
VASCO DE GAMA: 255
VELASCO: 138, 255
VENICE: 255
VENUS (1818): 256
VENUS (1842): 256
VENUS (1966): 256
VICTOR: 256
VICTORIOSA: 89
VICTORY: 257
VIDETTE: 257
VIGILANT: 257
VIKING (1952): 257
VIKING (1975): 257
VILLA FRANCA: 257
VINDICATOR: 257
VIRGIN DE LAS NIEVES: 257
VIRGINIA (1842): 257
VIRGINIA (1917): 257
VIRGINIA LEE HICKMAN: 229, 257
VIRGINIA M.: 257
VIXEN: 257
VOLUSIA: 257
VULCAN: 258
W.D. ANDERSON: 259
W.M. GODDIN: 260
W.T. COPPEDGE, JR.: 260
W.W. MILLER: 260
WACCAMAW: 260
WALBORG POTTER: 260
WALKA Q.: 260
WALTER: i
WANDERER: 15, 260
WARWICK: 260
WATERLOO: 261

WATERWICH: 68, 261
WAVERLY: 261
WEDGE WRECK: 253
WEE-II: 261
WELAKA: 138, 261
WENDY ROSSHEIM: 207, 261
WEST END: 261
WESTERN EMPIRE: 261
WESTMORELAND: 262
WHEREAWAY: 262
WHIM WHAM: 262
WHITE COAST: 52, 131, 262, 263
WICKSTROM: 263
WILBERT S. BARTLETT: 263
WILBUR: 263
WILLIAM (1778): 263
WILLIAM (1816): 263
WILLIAM AND ELIZABETH: 4, 263
WILLIAM BARNETT: 263
WILLIAM R. KNIGHTON: 264
WILLIAM RATHBONE: 151, 263
WILLIAM RUSSELL: 264
WILLIAM W. CONVERSE: 264
WILLIE: 264
WILMINGTON: 241, 264
WILTON: 264
WINDSOR: 265
WONDER: 265
WOODSIDE: 265
X-FACTOR WRECK: 266
YALE: 266
YANKEE GIRL II: 266
YELLOW BRICK ROAD: 89
YOUNG RACER: 266
YTM-460: 266
ZANGA AND FAIRLEY: 106
ZEEBURG: 266
ZETA NO. 2: 266
ZION: 157, 266
ZION TRAIN: 121, 239, 267

ATLANTIC COAST SHIPWRECK COORDINATES

The following section includes coordinates for shipwrecks along the Atlantic coast of Florida grouped by county (ordered alphabetically) and in descending latitude. Due to the focus of the book, I have excluded coordinates for artificial reef sites consisting of pre-fabricated modules, concrete rubble, tanks, etc.

With over 1,000 coordinates included originating from numerous sources, I have obviously been unable to personally confirm each and every site for accuracy. However, over the years I have spent considerable time and energy improving this database and eradicating bogus coordinates. When available, I have confirmed position accuracy by utilizing geo-referenced multi-beam sonar data provided by coastal counties. In other situations, I have sought out secondary confirmation from local sources. Additionally, I have evaluated plotted positions with cited depths for deployed artificial reefs in a GIS format, and excluded those entries that are obviously incorrect. Nonetheless, some erroneous information may still exist.

When known, the manner in which the geographical information was acquired is included to help users determine accuracy of the data. While LORAN has been deactivated and is no longer a viable navigational tool, I have included LORAN coordinates as there are some programs that can convert LORAN into latitude/longitude, though the reliability of these conversions can be somewhat questionable based on a variety of parameters. Additionally, I have also included coded source information for each shipwreck entry. Users can also evaluate entries based on the origin to help determine accuracy. Over time, trends from a particular source may either bolster one's confidence in other numbers from that same source. On the other hand, a source with a bad record of accuracy may dissuade one from utilizing this information in the absence of a secondary set of coordinates when planning an excursion far offshore.

It should be noted that coordinates for numerous sites have been excluded from this section. Due to state law, I am prevented from including coordinates for sites listed in the Florida Master Site File inventory maintained by the Florida Division of Historical Resources. Additionally, at the request of individuals who provided unique position data on sites they desired to remain confidential, I have redacted that information from the following section.

The *Deep Freeze* plunges stern-first for the bottom (George Detrio).

The *Catharina Uhrweder*, built as the Swedish tug *Sandslån I* in 1896, is scuttled in 250 feet of water off Miami on September 8, 2010 (Miami-Dade County Department of Environmental Resources Management).

The tug *Shark* sinks in 255 feet of water off Miami on September 8, 2010 (Miami-Dade County Department of Environmental Resources Management).

LOCALE	WRECK NAME	TD1	TD2	LATITUDE	LONGITUDE	TYPE	SOURCE
BREVARD	WRECK			2828.483	8022.205	LORAN	18
BREVARD	WRECK	43933.0	61954.0	2827.804	8023.704	LORAN	32
BREVARD	WRECK	43855.6	61858.0	2827.800	8008.684		39
BREVARD	WRECK	43855.6	61858.0	2827.767	8008.753	LORAN	20
BREVARD	BARGE	43884.9	61896.6	2827.730	8014.772	LORAN	20
BREVARD	WRECK	43841.1	61841.2	2827.613	8005.965		39
BREVARD	WRECK	43841.1	61841.2	2827.581	8006.035	LORAN	20
BREVARD	WRECK (28')	43957.5	61987.2	2827.414	8028.662	LORAN	20
BREVARD	18 FOOT LONG BOAT			2827.373	8043.271		2
BREVARD	WRECK	43850.0	61860.0	2827.142	8008.807	LORAN	20
BREVARD	WRECK (MISSLE)	43850.0	61860.6	2827.102	8008.885	LORAN	20
BREVARD	WRECK	43839.0	61846.0	2827.091	8006.589	LORAN	32
BREVARD	SANDWITCH	43898.6	61923.2	2827.054	8018.640	LORAN	20
BREVARD	LOIS DUBOIS BARGE	43835.9	61842.0	2827.034	8005.531		10
BREVARD	WRECK	43850.0	61862.0	2827.010	8009.066	LORAN	20
BREVARD	DEFIANCE			2826.879	8021.409	GPS	1
BREVARD	WRECK	43838.6	61851.9	2826.699	8007.265		39
BREVARD	WRECK	43955.0	61994.0	2826.670	8029.433	LORAN	20
BREVARD	WRECK	43838.6	61851.9	2826.668	8007.335	LORAN	20
BREVARD	HUMMINGBIRD REEF			2825.922	8014.309	GPS	32
BREVARD	WRECK	43908.7	61961.8	2825.108	8023.879	LORAN	20
BREVARD	BIGHT WRECK	43974.2	62035.0	2825.070	8035.151	LORAN	20
BREVARD	BARGE (130')	43847.7	61890.7	2824.882	8012.700	LORAN	20
BREVARD	WRECK	43919.7	61977.7	2824.863	8026.255	LORAN	32
BREVARD	WRECK (88')	43870.0	61922.0	2824.648	8017.508	LORAN	20
BREVARD	SAILBOAT	43871.9	61924.8	2824.614	8017.932	LORAN	20
BREVARD	WRECK			2824.580	8035.220	LORAN	18
BREVARD	BARGE			2824.451	8041.614		2
BREVARD	DAMOCLES			2824.420	8016.999	GPS	1
BREVARD	TUG AND BARGE	43840.0	61892.0	2824.119	8012.597	LORAN	20
BREVARD	TUG AND BARGE	43838.0	61892.0	2823.944	8012.526	LORAN	20
BREVARD	TUG AND BARGE	43836.0	61890.0	2823.905	8012.196	LORAN	20
BREVARD	MARYLAND			2823.862	8013.230	GPS	1
BREVARD	BARGE	43840.8	61896.6	2823.875	8013.222	LORAN	20
BREVARD	BARGE	43840.8	61896.8	2823.861	8013.247	LORAN	20
BREVARD	MOHICAN			2823.841	8032.123	GPS	1
BREVARD	CITIES SERVICE EMPIRE			2823.799	8002.808	GPS	1
BREVARD	CITIES SERVICE EMPIRE			2823.743	8002.814	GPS	1
BREVARD	WRECK	43840.0	61900.0	2823.605	8013.565		39
BREVARD	OCEAN VENUS			2823.371	8017.716	GPS	1
BREVARD	DELROSE	43889.9	61977.8	2822.270	8025.300	LORAN	20
BREVARD	DELROSE	43889.7	61977.7	2822.260	8025.280	LORAN	20
BREVARD	B-52 BOMBER	43822.1	61896.6	2822.229	8012.562		30
BREVARD	ED'S BARGE	43833.2	61915.0	2821.926	8015.340		30
BREVARD	TIGER RED	43842.0	61926.0	2821.913	8016.667		10
BREVARD	R.J.P. WRECK	43834.6	61929.0	2821.071	8017.207	LORAN	20
BREVARD	CHEVIE	43834.5	61928.9	2821.069	8017.190	LORAN	20
BREVARD	R.J.P. WRECK	43834.5	61929.0	2821.062	8017.203	LORAN	20
BREVARD	WRECK	43757.5	61834.2	2820.607	8001.972	LORAN	20
BREVARD	WRECK			2820.390	8024.636	LORAN	18
BREVARD	WRECK	43919.5	62034.9	2820.327	8033.466	LORAN	20

LOCALE	WRECK NAME	TD1	TD2	LATITUDE	LONGITUDE	TYPE	SOURCE
BREVARD	WRECK			2847.320	8000.250	GPS	21
BREVARD	WRECK			2847.060	8000.090		39
BREVARD	SAILBOAT	44157.4	61986.6	2844.915	8035.126		30
BREVARD	WRECK	44058.2	61885.7	2843.695	8019.613	LORAN	20
BREVARD	CITY OF VERA CRUZ			2843.130	8023.103	GPS	1
BREVARD	PADDLEBOAT	44062.1	61900.6	2842.981	8021.567	LORAN	32
BREVARD	FREE SPIRIT ENTERPRISE			2839.429	8023.171	GPS	18
BREVARD	WRECK	43949.0	61815.8	2838.799	8006.897	LORAN	32
BREVARD	WRECK	43948.5	61816.0	2838.768	8006.823		39
BREVARD	SEA CAT			2838.764	8048.861		2
BREVARD	WRECK	43948.5	61816.0	2838.741	8006.903	LORAN	32
BREVARD	WRECK	43948.5	61816.0	2838.737	8006.897	LORAN	20
BREVARD	WRECK			2837.780	8020.530		39
BREVARD	WRECK	43961.0	61848.3	2837.742	8011.358		39
BREVARD	H.S. WRECK	43961.0	61848.3	2837.709	8011.425	LORAN	20
BREVARD	H.S.H. WRECK	44005.9	61907.8	2837.530	8020.442	LORAN	20
BREVARD	AIRPLANE			2837.496	8000.591	GPS	18
BREVARD	H.S.H. WRECK	44006.9	61909.6	2837.489	8020.699	LORAN	20
BREVARD	AIRPLANE			2837.269	8000.649	GPS	18
BREVARD	WRECK			2837.164	8048.176		2
BREVARD	AIRPLANE			2836.763	8001.129	GPS	18
BREVARD	AIRPLANE			2836.598	8001.164	GPS	18
BREVARD	AIRPLANE (MAIN SECTION)			2836.555	8000.569	GPS	18
BREVARD	WRECK	43976.0	61885.5	2836.484	8016.617	LORAN	20
BREVARD	WRECK	43974.4	61883.6	2836.476	8016.323	LORAN	20
BREVARD	DC-3	43900.6	61784.4	2836.473	8000.997	LORAN	20
BREVARD	AIRPLANE			2836.339	8001.120	GPS	18
BREVARD	LESLIE			2836.226	8016.356	GPS	1
BREVARD	WRECK			2836.080	8018.850		39
BREVARD	DICKEY BOY			2836.010	8018.860		39
BREVARD	DICKEY BOY	43983.2	61901.5	2835.978	8018.856		30
BREVARD	TRIPLE NICKEL	43947.9	61857.1	2835.961	8012.041	LORAN	20
BREVARD	WRECK	43918.1	61819.7	2835.801	8006.198	LORAN	32
BREVARD	MISS LOUISE	44015.0	61960.0	2834.495	8027.178	LORAN	20
BREVARD	MISS LOUISE	44015.2	61960.3	2834.489	8027.221	LORAN	20
BREVARD	MISS LOUISE	44015.2	61960.3	2834.478	8027.217		30
BREVARD	WRECK			2834.078	8018.915	LORAN	18
BREVARD	H.B. WRECK	44014.9	61992.1	2832.029	8031.122	LORAN	20
BREVARD	H.B. WRECK	44014.7	61992.1	2832.011	8031.115	LORAN	20
BREVARD	H.B. WRECK	44014.7	61992.1	2832.000	8031.111		30
BREVARD	DEEP WRECK	43883.7	61836.5	2831.655	8007.027	LORAN	20
BREVARD	DEEP WRECK	43883.7	61836.5	2831.644	8007.022		30
BREVARD	F.S.F.A. SAILBOAT S			2830.392	8012.998	DGPS	10
BREVARD	F.S.F.A. SAILBOAT			2830.334	8013.103	DGPS	10
BREVARD	GALLATEA	43900.8	61879.9	2830.298	8013.128	LORAN	10
BREVARD	21 FATHOM WRECK	43889.5	61865.2	2830.273	8010.921	LORAN	20
BREVARD	F.S.F.A. SAILBOAT C			2830.067	8013.198	GPS	10
BREVARD	SAILBOAT	43895.0	61877.7	2829.939	8012.639	LORAN	10
BREVARD	CAPE WRECK			2829.710	8032.481		4
BREVARD	WRECK	43859.7	61840.0	2829.304	8006.575	LORAN	20
BREVARD	LAERTES			2828.695	8022.017	GPS	1

LOCALE	WRECK NAME	TD1	TD2	LATITUDE	LONGITUDE	TYPE	SOURCE
BREVARD	WRECK	43806.0	61905.0	2820.263	8013.110	LORAN	32
BREVARD	WRECK	43806.0	61905.0	2820.260	8013.101	LORAN	20
BREVARD	SUFFIX I			2820.050	8012.167	GPS	10
BREVARD	PAN MASSACHUSSETTS			2819.952	8000.028	GPS	1
BREVARD	WRECK	43800.0	61905.0	2819.736	8012.893	LORAN	20
BREVARD	SCALLOP KING	43811.5	61923.9	2819.413	8015.758		30
BREVARD	SHELBY LEE			2819.117	8012.017	GPS	10
BREVARD	LADY HELEN			2818.786	8008.865	GPS	18
BREVARD	LADY HELEN	43770.9	61881.7	2818.760	8008.790	LORAN	32
BREVARD	MOBY DICK	43867.4	62000.0	2818.614	8027.025		10
BREVARD	WRECK (71')	43827.9	61955.2	2818.593	8020.380	LORAN	20
BREVARD	CALICO JACK	43881.5	62016.0	2818.563	8029.902	LORAN	20
BREVARD	BREVARD REEF 1	43866.3	62000.0	2818.519	8026.991		10
BREVARD	WRECK	43762.0	61875.0	2818.419	8007.582	LORAN	32
BREVARD	WRECK	43710.0	61805.9	2818.050	7956.306	LORAN	32
BREVARD	WRECK	43750.4	61877.4	2817.242	8007.495	LORAN	20
BREVARD	WRECK	43750.4	61877.5	2817.237	8007.501	LORAN	32
BREVARD	SHRIMPER			2817.069	7959.936		27
BREVARD	WRECK	43748.0	61882.8	2816.680	8008.124	LORAN	32
BREVARD	WRECK	43846.5	62003.0	2816.567	8027.150	LORAN	20
BREVARD	JOYCE MOORE	43806.7	61975.6	2815.229	8022.343		39
BREVARD	WRECK	43725.0	61884.0	2814.842	8006.939	LORAN	20
BREVARD	WRECK	43725.0	61884.0	2814.584	8007.471	LORAN	32
BREVARD	WRECK	43725.0	61884.0	2814.583	8007.478	LORAN	20
BREVARD	WRECK	43816.3	62000.0	2814.196	8025.819	LORAN	32
BREVARD	WRECK	43779.2	61969.0	2813.361	8020.602	LORAN	20
BREVARD	GALLEON WRECK	43711.5	61885.6	2813.294	8007.218	LORAN	20
BREVARD	GALLEON WRECK	43711.5	61885.6	2813.283	8007.216		30
BREVARD	WRECK	43812.1	62011.5	2812.928	8027.182	LORAN	32
BREVARD	WRECK	43792.7	61995.0	2812.549	8024.435	LORAN	20
BREVARD	WRECK			2812.470	8029.200		39
BREVARD	WRECK			2812.350	8028.650		39
BREVARD	DUNHAM WHEELER			2812.261	8019.430	GPS	1
BREVARD	CAPT. DENNIS	43815.7	62024.1	2812.227	8028.931	LORAN	20
BREVARD	KORSHOLM			2812.205	8029.032	GPS	1
BREVARD	KORSHOLM			2812.176	8029.025	GPS	1
BREVARD	DRAGON LADY	43811.7	62020.5	2812.173	8028.342	LORAN	20
BREVARD	DRAGON LADY	43811.7	62020.5	2812.162	8028.339		30
BREVARD	WRECK			2811.896	8029.386	LORAN	18
BREVARD	WRECK	43811.7	62025.5	2811.770	8028.988	LORAN	32
BREVARD	SCALLOP BOAT			2810.500	8032.610		39
BREVARD	UNKNOWN WRECK			2810.188	8028.954	GPS	1
BREVARD	SHIRLEY JOHN	43795.1	62028.3	2810.110	8028.855	LORAN	20
BREVARD	SHIRLEY JOHN			2810.099	8027.852	GPS	18
BREVARD	WRECK	43701.2	61924.0	2809.836	8012.048	LORAN	32
BREVARD	NOAH SMITH			2809.792	8012.236	DGPS	1
BREVARD	UNKNOWN WRECK			2809.694	8025.919	GPS	1
BREVARD	NAVY CORSAIR FG-1			2808.477	8014.577	GPS	1
BREVARD	UNKNOWN WRECK	43696.7	61938.2	2808.462	8013.817	LORAN	32
BREVARD	UNKNOWN WRECK	43693.5	61937.2	2808.282	8013.501	LORAN	18
BREVARD	UNKNOWN WRECK	43693.5	61937.2	2808.255	8013.576	LORAN	32

LOCALE	WRECK NAME	TD1	TD2	LATITUDE	LONGITUDE	TYPE	SOURCE
BREVARD	WRECK	43758.3	62016.0	2807.935	8026.128	LORAN	32
BREVARD	MICHELLE			2807.540	8029.644	GPS	32
BREVARD	LEDGE OR WRECK			2807.366	8002.711		32
BREVARD	LEDGE OR WRECK			2807.338	8002.740		32
BREVARD	WRECK	43633.9	61872.6	2807.286	8002.662	LORAN	32
BREVARD	WRECK	43633.9	61872.6	2807.282	8002.680	LORAN	20
BREVARD	LEDGE OR WRECK			2807.280	8002.678		32
BREVARD	WRECK	43652.5	61898.9	2807.266	8006.961	LORAN	32
BREVARD	BARBARA ANN			2805.610	8008.397	GPS	1
BREVARD	BARBARA ANN			2805.604	8008.398	GPS	1
BREVARD	WRECK	43616.4	61881.4	2805.200	8003.264	LORAN	32
BREVARD	WRECK	43616.4	61881.4	2805.194	8003.283	LORAN	32
BREVARD	LINDA JO	43598.8	61884.5	2803.460	8003.067	GPS	1
BREVARD	WEE-II			2803.113	8016.331	DGPS	32
BREVARD	D.N. WRECK	43712.8	62035.4	2802.445	8027.336	LORAN	20
BREVARD	WRECK	43700.8	62024.8	2802.284	8025.567	LORAN	20
BREVARD	WRECK	43705.7	62041.0	2801.369	8027.873	LORAN	20
BREVARD	WRECK	43705.0	62042.0	2801.225	8027.985	LORAN	20
BREVARD	AIRPLANE	43566.0	61906.0	2759.264	8004.917		39
BREVARD	WRECK	43661.0	62029.0	2758.529	8024.950	LORAN	20
BREVARD	WRECK			2757.072	8029.707		4
BREVARD	FUGGEDABOUDIT WRECK			2756.180	7958.160	GPS	1
BREVARD	BARGE	43509.2	61872.6	2756.180	7958.206	LORAN	20
BREVARD	FUGGEDABOUDIT WRECK			2756.148	7958.188	GPS	1
BROWARD	ANCIENT MARINER			2618.122	8003.729	GPS	1
BROWARD	C-NOTE			2618.101	8003.694	GPS	1
BROWARD	BERRY PATCH			2618.091	8003.688	GPS	1
BROWARD	CHUCK-A-LUCK II			2618.085	8003.708	GPS	1
BROWARD	QUALMANN BARGE			2617.977	8003.710	DGPS	5
BROWARD	SUCRE	14274.6	62090.5	2614.383	8003.411	DGPS	10
BROWARD	MILLER LITE			2614.180	8003.652	GPS	1
BROWARD	RODEO SITE -BUDDY MERRITT	14275.5	62089.8	2614.150	8003.360	GPS	10
BROWARD	PAPA'S WRECK	14274.8	62092.6	2614.102	8003.383	GPS	10
BROWARD	MARINER II BARGE			2614.089	8003.803	GPS	1
BROWARD	UNION EXPRESS			2614.077	8003.869	GPS	1
BROWARD	DEWITT CLINTON	14276.2	62096.3	2614.056	8003.666	DGPS	10
BROWARD	MARINER II TUG			2613.951	8003.812	GPS	1
BROWARD	RONALD B. JOHNSON	14274.3	62093.3	2613.880	8003.445	GPS	10
BROWARD	MERRITT BOAT MOLD			2613.872	8004.021	GPS	1
BROWARD	QUALMANN TUGS			2613.865	8004.024	GPS	1
BROWARD	COREY N CHRIS	14274.2	62093.4	2613.863	8003.432	DGPS	10
BROWARD	RODEO 25			2613.863	8003.832	GPS	1
BROWARD	RONALD B. JOHNSON			2613.863	8003.432	GPS	1
BROWARD	ALPHA	14275.5	62111.7	2613.857	8004.027	GPS	10
BROWARD	RODEO 25			2613.854	8003.827	GPS	1
BROWARD	JAY DORMAN			2613.846	8004.027	GPS	1
BROWARD	DEEP F/V			2613.740	7957.851	GPS	6
BROWARD	JIM TORGERSON/RSB-1			2613.639	8003.901	GPS	1
BROWARD	RODEO SITE -BUDDY MERRITT			2613.620	8002.280	GPS	5
BROWARD	RENEGADE	14273.4	62094.6	2613.360	8003.620	GPS	10
BROWARD	LOWRANCE			2613.221	8003.610	GPS	1

LOCALE	WRECK NAME	TD1	TD2	LATITUDE	LONGITUDE	TYPE	SOURCE
BROWARD	LOWRANCE	14272.8	62096.4	2613.202	8003.640	GPS	10
BROWARD	CAPTAIN DAN			2613.130	8003.974	GPS	1
BROWARD	IMOR	14272.6	62096.3	2613.048	8003.760	GPS	10
BROWARD	GUY HARVEY			2612.669	8003.942	GPS	1
BROWARD	CAICOS EXPRESS	14272.6	62096.4	2612.502	8003.663	GPS	10
BROWARD	COPENHAGEN			2612.349	8005.108	GPS	39
BROWARD	COPENHAGEN BOW			2611.988	8004.977	GPS	26
BROWARD	CUMBERLAND			2611.418	8005.531	GPS	17
BROWARD	BUD KROHN			2610.912	8003.058	GPS	33
BROWARD	CUMBERLAND			2610.731	8005.671		39
BROWARD	REBEL			2610.269	8004.328	GPS	1
BROWARD	F.L.A. MINESWEEPER	14269.3	62097.3	2610.250	8002.790	GPS	5
BROWARD	PETER B. MCALLISTER			2610.185	8004.707	GPS	1
BROWARD	F.L.A. MINESWEEPER	14269.2	62097.5	2610.150	8003.360	GPS	10
BROWARD	BRUCE MUELLER	14266.4	62105.0	2610.116	8004.706	DGPS	5
BROWARD	CORKY M	14268.3	62107.1	2610.085	8004.709	DGPS	10
BROWARD	JIM ATRIA	14266.5	62103.5	2609.870	8004.225	GPS	10
BROWARD	MERCI JESUS			2609.621	8004.747	GPS	1
BROWARD	KEN VITALE/TRACY			2609.571	8004.767	GPS	1
BROWARD	HARBOUR TOWNE			2609.524	8004.745	GPS	1
BROWARD	JAY SCUTTI			2609.515	8004.773	GPS	1
BROWARD	MERCEDES	14265.2	62105.2	2609.370	8004.513	GPS	10
BROWARD	WRECK			2609.254	8004.789	GPS	1
BROWARD	ROBERT EDMISTER			2609.226	8004.815	GPS	1
BROWARD	WENDY ROSSHEIM			2609.212	8004.809	GPS	1
BROWARD	WENDY ROSSHEIM	14265.9	62094.6	2609.209	8004.839	GPS	1
BROWARD	SALVAGER III			2609.197	8004.831	GPS	1
BROWARD	BILL BOYD	14265.8	62102.4	2609.088	8003.842	GPS	10
BROWARD	DEEP SAILBOAT			2608.800	8001.105	GPS	6
BROWARD	TRIO BRAVO	14264.6	62105.0	2608.722	8004.289	GPS	1
BROWARD	BULK TRADER			2608.610	8003.835	DGPS	10
BROWARD	DNR BARGES	14263.7	62108.7	2608.557	8004.637	GPS	10
BROWARD	OLD QUALMAN BARGE	14264.8	62104.6	2608.550	8004.024	LORAN	10
BROWARD	BARGE			2608.541	8004.852	GPS	1
BROWARD	BARGE			2608.516	8004.891	GPS	1
BROWARD	MATTS BARGE			2608.431	8004.825	GPS	1
BROWARD	BARGE			2608.398	8004.875	GPS	1
BROWARD	OSBORNE			2608.320	8004.830	GPS	5
BROWARD	PEE WEE VREELAND			2608.227	8003.976	GPS	1
BROWARD	WAYNES BARGE			2608.101	8004.852	GPS	1
BROWARD	HOUSEBOAT	14263.7	62107.0	2608.094	8004.381	LORAN	10
BROWARD	MOONSHOT	14263.8	62106.4	2608.059	8004.249	LORAN	10
BROWARD	HOG HEAVEN BARGE			2608.051	8004.871	GPS	1
BROWARD	SPAGHETTI BARGE	14263.7	62106.7	2608.049	8004.310		39
BROWARD	SPAGHETTI BARGE	14263.7	62106.7	2608.040	8004.305	LORAN	10
BROWARD	POWELL BARGE	14264.7	62120.1	2607.888	8003.445	GPS	10
BROWARD	MONOMOY	14263.2	62107.5	2607.814	8004.403	LORAN	10
BROWARD	64-FATHOM AIRPLANE			2607.110	8003.840	GPS	5
BROWARD	HALL OF FAME WRECK			2606.989	8006.226	GPS	1
BROWARD	64-FATHOM AIRPLANE			2606.940	8003.870	GPS	5
BROWARD	MARRIOTT REEF DC-4	14261.4	62109.8	2606.897	8004.610	LORAN	10

LOCALE	WRECK NAME	TD1	TD2	LATITUDE	LONGITUDE	TYPE	SOURCE
BROWARD	JOES NIGHTMARE BARGE			2606.802	8004.225	DGPS	5
BROWARD	TRACOR DRYDOCK	14261.2	62107.4	2606.765	8004.233	GPS	10
BROWARD	GRADY BARGES			2606.764	8004.228	DGPS	10
BROWARD	CANAL BARGE			2606.717	8005.850	GPS	17
BROWARD	SHRIMPER WRECKAGE			2605.900	8006.149		38
BROWARD	WRECK			2605.579	8005.423		2
BROWARD	56-FATHOM AIRPLANE			2605.140	8004.120	GPS	5
BROWARD	JOES NIGHTMARE BARGE	14263.3	62096.2	2604.225	8004.225	DGPS	10
BROWARD	WRECK			2602.107	8005.493	GPS	1
BROWARD	R.E. ROYDHOUSE			2600.853	8004.171	GPS	5
BROWARD	CAPTAIN DEDE	14251.1	62124.7	2600.757	8005.591	DGPS	10
BROWARD	CURRY REEF BARGE	43098.9	62123.0	2600.648	8005.606	DGPS	10
BROWARD	GRADY HOPPER BARGE			2600.615	8005.644	DGPS	10
BROWARD	SITE E - EMMI BOGGS BARGE	14263.0	62115.1	2600.606	8005.617	DGPS	10
BROWARD	MISS DANIA BEACH			2600.605	8005.502	GPS	10
BROWARD	MICHELLINE			2600.601	8005.599	DGPS	5
BROWARD	DANTOR			2600.596	8004.990		39
BROWARD	SUMMERFIELD			2600.577	8005.585	DGPS	5
BROWARD	DONAL G. MCALLISTER	14251.1	43100.9	2600.548	8005.565	DGPS	10
BROWARD	SITE E - CURRY REEF	14251.1	62093.4	2600.486	8005.606	DGPS	10
BROWARD	SITE E - HOLLYWOOD	14250.9	62124.9	2600.459	8005.623		10
BROWARD	EBEN-EZER II			2600.398	8005.589		39
BROWARD	TENNECO TOWERS SHALLOW 2			2558.937	8005.131	GPS	1
BROWARD	TENNECO TOWERS SHALLOW 1			2558.936	8005.201	GPS	1
BROWARD	MIDDLE TENNECO			2558.936	8005.126		8
BROWARD	WEST TENNECO			2558.933	8005.197		8
BROWARD	TENNECO TOWERS DEEP			2558.901	8004.808	GPS	19
BROWARD	DEEP TENNECO			2558.901	8004.799		8
DADE	CRUZ DEL SUR			2558.167	8004.637	GPS	39
DADE	MIAMI BEACH SEAWALL BARGE			2556.939	8007.713	GPS	8
DADE	SIX AT SEA			2556.915	8007.782	DGPS	10
DADE	SHARK			2554.476	8004.587	GPS	8
DADE	NARWAL			2554.638	8005.045	GPS	19
DADE	CONCEPTION	14293.0	62129.4	2554.562	8005.397	GPS	10
DADE	MERCI RABBI			2554.545	8004.848	GPS	19
DADE	PLANE			2554.543	8005.476	GPS	19
DADE	LADY CARMEN			2554.533	8005.437	GPS	10
DADE	WHITE COAST TUG	14239.0	62129.4	2554.523	8005.406	GPS	10
DADE	C-ONE	14239.0	62129.4	2554.523	8005.406	GPS	10
DADE	LADY CARMEN			2554.520	8005.441		8
DADE	TIMOTHY ALLEN REED BARGE			2554.504	8005.428	GPS	10
DADE	ROSSMERRY			2554.253	8004.623	GPS	8
DADE	HAULOVER CRANE WRECK			2553.755	8005.235	GPS	19
DADE	ANDRO			2553.611	8005.127	GPS	19
DADE	O.L. BODENHAMER			2553.497	8004.028		39
DADE	BARGE			2553.412	8005.079		8
DADE	WOOD BOAT	14239.5	62124.7	2553.353	8003.879	LORAN	10
DADE	O.L. BODENHAMER	14239.4	43104.5	2553.351	8003.956	LORAN	10
DADE	CRANE BOOM	14236.1	62133.0	2552.436	8005.358	LORAN	10
DADE	LOTUS			2550.957	8004.647	GPS	25
DADE	MINESWEEPER	14233.7	43110.7	2550.367	8004.511	LORAN	10

LOCALE	WRECK NAME	TD1	TD2	LATITUDE	LONGITUDE	TYPE	SOURCE
DADE	PIMELIOUS			2550.158	8004.924	GPS	19
DADE	SAN RAPHAEL	14233.2	43110.5	2549.865	8004.241	LORAN	10
DADE	SAN RAPHAEL			2549.812	8004.084	LORAN	8
DADE	WALKA Q	14233.1	43110.3	2549.711	8004.117	LORAN	10
DADE	WALKA Q			2549.566	8004.900	LORAN	8
DADE	WEST END	14232.4	43111.3	2549.425	8004.291	LORAN	10
DADE	GIMROCK 402 BARGE			2549.360	8005.063	DGPS	10
DADE	ST. HENRY'S EXPRESS			2549.354	8005.104	GPS	19
DADE	GIMROCK 402 BARGE			2549.353	8005.057	DGPS	8
DADE	BETEK AR PEN	14232.8	62137.0	2549.353	8005.113	GPS	10
DADE	SOUTH POINTE BARGE			2549.322	8005.100		39
DADE	WRECK	14232.8	62137.0	2549.322	8005.097		39
DADE	ST. HENRY'S EXPRESS			2549.321	8005.099		10
DADE	DEEP FREEZE			2549.311	8004.960	GPS	19
DADE	DEEP FREEZE	14238.0	62134.4	2549.303	8004.952	GPS	10
DADE	PIMELIOUS	14232.3	43112.4	2549.301	8004.948	GPS	10
DADE	TORTUGA			2549.273	8005.106	GPS	19
DADE	TORTUGA	14589.5	61568.6	2549.254	8005.086	GPS	10
DADE	ATLAS RECYCLING BARGE	14232.7	43115.5	2549.225	8005.065	DGPS	10
DADE	RAYCHEL			2549.212	8004.763	GPS	10
DADE	PASCAGOULA			2549.120	8004.897	DGPS	10
DADE	PASCAGOULA			2549.120	8004.897	GPS	19
DADE	LCI	14231.7	43112.0	2549.040	8004.335	LORAN	10
DADE	JUPITER STAR			2548.975	8004.890	GPS	25
DADE	MET BARGE			2548.840	8009.830	GPS	8
DADE	POLICE BARGE			2548.838	8005.545	GPS	19
DADE	JOHN C. KOPPIN BARGE	14229.3	62137.5	2548.820	8005.470	GPS	10
DADE	PATRICIA TUG			2548.815	8005.361	GPS	19
DADE	MISS KARLINE			2548.771	8005.345	GPS	8
DADE	BILLY'S BARGE			2548.767	8005.419	GPS	8
DADE	ANTENNA TOWERS			2548.749	8005.385	GPS	19
DADE	MATTHEW LAWRANCE REEF			2548.720	8005.409	GPS	19
DADE	LARSEN BARGE			2548.702	8005.452	GPS	10
DADE	LARSEN BARGE			2548.692	8005.436	GPS	8
DADE	WRECK #7			2548.680	8005.402		39
DADE	MATTHEW LAWRANCE REEF	14229.1	62137.0	2548.660	8005.390	GPS	10
DADE	WRECK	14229.1	62137.0	2548.660	8005.390		39
DADE	SHAMROCK			2548.572	8005.457	GPS	19
DADE	AFRICAN QUEEN	14229.3	62137.5	2548.313	8005.187	LORAN	10
DADE	OSTWIND	14230.7	62132.2	2548.301	8004.070	LORAN	10
DADE	LEON'S BARGE	14229.3	62136.9	2548.193	8005.028	LORAN	10
DADE	LANDS END AND MARY ANN I	14229.0	62137.4	2548.068	8005.100	LORAN	10
DADE	HOPPER BARGE	14229.5	43113.5	2547.690	8004.211	LORAN	10
DADE	ESJOO			2546.641	8004.319	LORAN	8
DADE	CAR REEF			2546.506	8005.933	GPS	19
DADE	CAPTAIN HARRY			2543.803	8005.098	GPS	39
DADE	CAPTAIN HARRY			2543.624	8004.987	GPS	10
DADE	SHRIMPER			2543.538	8010.448		2
DADE	HALF MOON	14217.3	62156.2	2543.500	8008.050	LORAN	10
DADE	ARIDA			2542.831	8005.170	GPS	19
DADE	SPIRT OF HEMINGWAY			2542.572	8004.520	DGPS	10

LOCALE	WRECK NAME	TD1	TD2	LATITUDE	LONGITUDE	TYPE	SOURCE
DADE	MARY STAR OF THE SEA			2542.548	8004.509	GPS	10
DADE	REX BEAR	14222.0	43123.9	2542.482	8004.633	DGPS	10
DADE	GIMROCK BARGES			2542.437	8004.870	GPS	10
DADE	GIMROCK 504 BARGE			2542.420	8004.500	DGPS	10
DADE	ESMERALDA			2542.415	8004.806	GPS	1
DADE	PROTEUS			2542.354	8005.258	GPS	19
DADE	SEA TAXI			2542.346	8005.148	GPS	8
DADE	MYSTIC ISLE			2542.346	8004.786	GPS	8
DADE	MARY STAR OF THE SEA			2542.345	8004.705	GPS	10
DADE	BISCAYNE	14217.7	62145.0	2542.263	8005.302	GPS	10
DADE	BISCAYNE			2542.260	8005.300	GPS	19
DADE	MIRACLES EXPRESS			2542.239	8005.291	GPS	8
DADE	SARAH JANE			2542.220	8005.162	GPS	19
DADE	DEMA TRADER			2542.218	8005.215	GPS	19
DADE	JACK PILAFIAN TUG			2542.196	8004.970		39
DADE	RIO MIAMI	14218.4	62144.6	2542.166	8005.232	GPS	10
DADE	RIO MIAMI			2542.158	8005.229	GPS	19
DADE	MIAMI RIVER BARGE			2542.146	8005.102	GPS	8
DADE	SHERI-LYN			2542.143	8005.171	GPS	19
DADE	SHERI-LYN (STERN SECTION)			2542.139	8005.163	GPS	8
DADE	SHERI-LYN			2542.130	8005.190		39
DADE	SHERI-LYN (BOW SECTION)			2542.122	8005.184	GPS	8
DADE	PARAISO III			2542.092	8005.238	GPS	10
DADE	LAKELAND			2542.074	8004.993	GPS	19
DADE	FLAMINGO REEF			2542.052	8005.905	GPS	19
DADE	PRINCESS BRITNEY			2542.029	8005.210	GPS	19
DADE	JOE'S WRECK			2542.026	8005.264	GPS	19
DADE	TACOMA			2542.019	8005.068	GPS	19
DADE	TACOMA			2542.010	8005.067	DGPS	10
DADE	STAR TREK	14219.0	62142.2	2542.002	8004.653	GPS	10
DADE	BRANDYWINE			2541.990	8004.952	DGPS	10
DADE	BELZONA BARGE			2541.990	8005.555	GPS	19
DADE	SOUTH SEAS			2541.990	8005.224	GPS	19
DADE	ETOILE DE MER			2541.970	8004.990	DGPS	10
DADE	MIGUANA			2541.963	8004.962	DGPS	10
DADE	STAR TREK			2541.959	8004.667	GPS	19
DADE	CUSTOMS REEF			2541.950	8004.971	GPS	19
DADE	SPIRIT OF MIAMI			2541.935	8005.217	GPS	19
DADE	JOHN MAYDEK REEF			2541.921	8005.272	GPS	19
DADE	DAVEY HURST			2541.903	8004.428		39
DADE	SPIRT OF MIAMI	14218.1	62144.6	2541.880	8005.220	GPS	10
DADE	ULTRA QUIZ HOUSEBOAT			2541.869	8005.200	GPS	8
DADE	ULTRA QUIZ HOUSEBOAT			2541.868	8005.209		39
DADE	LADY FREI			2541.841	8005.294	GPS	8
DADE	SCHURGER'S BARGE			2541.822	8005.220	GPS	19
DADE	HAV PARKER III BARGE	14220.1	43126.5	2541.820	8005.233	DGPS	10
DADE	BELCHER BARGE	14217.8	62142.2	2541.810	8005.280	GPS	10
DADE	BELZONA TWO	14217.8	62145.1	2541.758	8005.260	GPS	10
DADE	BELZONA THREE	14217.8	62145.1	2541.750	8005.240	GPS	10
DADE	BELZONA ONE	14217.8	62144.9	2541.750	8005.220	GPS	10
DADE	ORION			2541.484	8005.161	GPS	19

LOCALE	WRECK NAME	TD1	TD2	LATITUDE	LONGITUDE	TYPE	SOURCE
DADE	ORION	14217.4	62145.0	2541.460	8005.180	GPS	10
DADE	WATSON ISLAND BARGE			2541.454	8004.938	DGPS	8
DADE	MISS LUCY			2541.333	8004.573	DGPS	10
DADE	BIG LOU	14217.9	62145.2	2541.287	8004.920	LORAN	10
DADE	ADAMELIA			2540.500	8006.500	GPS	2
DADE	TRAWLER			2539.728	8008.820	GPS	39
DADE	RIPPLES			2539.636	8006.558	GPS	19
DADE	CHANNEL SCHOONER BARGE			2539.281	8009.851	GPS	2
DADE	BARGE			2539.266	8010.655		2
DADE	WRECK			2538.890	8009.580		39
DADE	FUEL BARGE			2538.842	8009.772		2
DADE	WRECK			2538.816	8010.651		2
DADE	DREDGING BARGE			2538.800	8010.740		2
DADE	BARGE			2538.783	8010.464	GPS	2
DADE	WRECK			2538.768	8010.483		2
DADE	WRECK			2538.754	8010.473		2
DADE	WRECKAGE			2538.191	8008.337		2
DADE	ULTRA FREEZE			2537.751	8005.218	GPS	19
DADE	MOBY ONE			2537.392	8005.364	GPS	8
DADE	TARPOON	14212.3	43133.8	2537.316	8005.460	GPS	10
DADE	TARPOON			2537.292	8005.462	GPS	19
DADE	HOPPER BARGE			2537.088	8005.573	GPS	19
DADE	ST. ANNE D'AURAY			2537.071	8005.446	GPS	19
DADE	SIX CANNON PATCH	14207.4	43136.8	2536.098	8006.341	LORAN	39
DADE	ARRATOON APCAR			2535.503	8005.744	GPS	26
DADE	ARRATOON APCAR			2535.498	8005.728		39
DADE	WRECK			2535.404	8009.733		2
DADE	CABIN CRUISER			2535.371	8009.693		2
DADE	WRECK			2535.280	8009.926		2
DADE	WRECK			2535.268	8009.886		2
DADE	BOILER			2535.229	8009.659		2
DADE	RAILROAD BARGE			2535.204	8005.172	GPS	19
DADE	WRECK			2534.798	8017.555		2
DADE	JOSEPH B. THOMAS	14204.7	62156.2	2534.717	8005.495	LORAN	14
DADE	JOSEPH B. THOMAS	14204.7	62156.2	2534.412	8005.537	LORAN	14
DADE	PIONEER ONE			2534.032	8005.028	GPS	19
DADE	BOTTLE WRECK			2534.011	8006.137		24
DADE	BLUEFIRE			2533.994	8005.434	GPS	19
DADE	BLUE FIRE	14204.6	62155.5	2533.976	8005.438	GPS	10
DADE	JOSEPH B. THOMAS	14204.7	62156.2	2533.623	8005.270	LORAN	14
DADE	GEORGE'S WRECK			2532.349	8007.133		24
DADE	WOODEN WRECK			2531.813	8015.588		2
DADE	SIR SCOTT			2531.796	8005.218	GPS	19
DADE	BARGE			2531.551	8017.950		2
DADE	BARGE			2531.528	8017.963	GPS	2
DADE	SIR SCOTT			2530.780	8005.219	GPS	11
DADE	TRESPASSER			2530.423	8015.537	GPS	2
DADE	HMS FOWEY			2529.331	8007.585		39
DADE	CEMENT BARGE			2528.302	8010.398		24
DADE	BRASS WRECK 2	14191.1	43153.4	2527.605	8007.910	LORAN	39
DADE	RED BRICK WRECK			2526.841	8007.295	DGPS	11

LOCALE	WRECK NAME	TD1	TD2	LATITUDE	LONGITUDE	TYPE	SOURCE
DADE	LUGANO			2526.646	8007.168	DGPS	11
DADE	MANDALAY			2526.538	8007.297	DGPS	11
DADE	BOXCAR WRECK	14186.3	43161.5	2526.137	8009.654	LORAN	39
DADE	WRECK			2525.702	8011.402		39
DADE	BOXCAR WRECK			2525.548	8009.102		24
DADE	ERL KING			2525.489	8007.462	DGPS	11
DADE	OUTLINE WRECK			2525.452	8008.100		24
DADE	SANTA RITA			2525.417	8006.692	GPS	39
DADE	SANTA RITA			2525.348	8006.493	GPS	39
DADE	ALMIRANTE			2524.986	8007.071	GPS	25
DADE	ALMIRANTE			2524.969	8007.083	DGPS	11
DADE	ALMIRANTE			2524.949	8007.054	GPS	19
DADE	WRECK			2524.808	8009.650		23
DADE	BELCHER BARGE SOUTH			2524.796	8007.144	GPS	19
DADE	BELCHER BARGE			2524.779	8007.172	DGPS	11
DADE	ALICIA			2524.734	8007.647	DGPS	11
DADE	TODD'S WRECK			2524.700	8010.640		39
DADE	STAIRS WRECK	14182.4	43166.2	2524.357	8010.346	LORAN	39
DADE	ALADDIN LAMP WRECK			2524.001	8009.586		24
DADE	SCHOONER BALLAST WRECK			2523.934	8009.633	DGPS	11
DADE	BLOCKADE RUNNER			2523.821	8008.241		24
DADE	OUTLINE WRECK			2523.695	8009.177		1
DADE	STAIRS WRECK			2523.662	8009.715		24
DADE	RING WRECK			2523.434	8008.530	DGPS	11
DADE	OCEAN FREEZE			2523.079	8007.061	GPS	1
DADE	OCEAN FREEZE			2523.072	8007.071	GPS	1
DADE	SCHOONER	14179.5	43168.9	2522.778	8010.551	LORAN	39
DADE	MORGAN'S WRECK			2522.650	8008.700		24
DADE	SCHOONER	14177.1	43173.8	2522.343	8011.767	LORAN	39
DADE	PACIFIC REEF WRECK			2522.318	8008.431		24
DADE	ORE WRECK			2522.181	8009.905		24
DADE	BERRY PATCH			2522.133	8007.813	GPS	1
DADE	F-4 PHANTOMS			2522.121	8008.114	DGPS	11
DADE	DOC DEMILLY			2522.064	8007.848	GPS	1
DADE	HUGO'S APRIL FOOL			2522.026	8007.821	GPS	1
DADE	NUESTRA SENORA DEL POPULO			2521.833	8009.676	DGPS	11
DADE	UNCORROBORATED WRECK			2521.450	8008.598		24
DADE	SCHOONER			2521.252	8011.298		24
DADE	EL AVISO CONSULADO			2521.120	8009.130	DGPS	11
DUVAL	SHARK BARGE			3035.364	8108.845		2
DUVAL	SHARK BARGE			3035.352	8108.857	GPS	21
DUVAL	HADDOCK'S HIDEAWAY BARGE	45252.5	61881.7	3034.518	8107.916	GPS	10
DUVAL	HADDOCK'S HIDEAWAY BARGE	45252.5	61881.7	3034.513	8107.879	LORAN	39
DUVAL	HADDOCK'S HIDEAWAY BARGE			3034.486	8107.891	GPS	2
DUVAL	HADDOCK'S HIDEAWAY BARGE			3034.475	8107.896	GPS	21
DUVAL	LOST BARGE			3033.063	8058.021	GPS	21
DUVAL	BARGE			3032.999	8107.382	GPS	2
DUVAL	BARGE	45210.2	61852.6	3032.510	8103.540	LORAN	10
DUVAL	RABBIT'S LAIR WRECK			3032.085	8109.693		39
DUVAL	BARGE	45247.8	61906.9	3032.060	8109.710	LORAN	10
DUVAL	AIRPLANE			3031.963	8023.156	GPS	21

LOCALE	WRECK NAME	TD1	TD2	LATITUDE	LONGITUDE	TYPE	SOURCE
DUVAL	WOOD WRECK	45247.6	61916.2	3031.310	8110.460	LORAN	10
DUVAL	TUG	45247.8	61916.5	3031.277	8110.242		39
DUVAL	WRECK			3030.928	8112.498	GPS	2
DUVAL	BARGE			3030.677	8056.384	GPS	34
DUVAL	BARGE	45151.4	61800.0	3030.670	8056.382	GPS	10
DUVAL	BARGE			3030.661	8056.395	GPS	21
DUVAL	TUG			3029.594	8057.598		39
DUVAL	TUG			3029.549	8057.631	GPS	21
DUVAL	TUG	45151.5	61815.1	3029.538	8057.378		39
DUVAL	TUG	45151.5	61815.1	3029.537	8057.595	GPS	10
DUVAL	WRECK			3029.258	8057.188	GPS	21
DUVAL	NORTH WRECK	45249.6	61948.6	3028.940	8113.200	LORAN	10
DUVAL	MONAHAN TUG			3028.642	8104.935	GPS	21
DUVAL	ANNA			3027.795	8055.994	GPS	34
DUVAL	ANNA			3027.789	8056.029	GPS	21
DUVAL	BILL'S BARGE	45248.8	61962.8	3027.774	8114.287	LORAN	10
DUVAL	ANNA			3027.773	8056.015	GPS	21
DUVAL	ANNA	45128.8	61808.8	3027.708	8055.770	DGPS	10
DUVAL	BILLS BARGE			3027.708	8114.256	GPS	2
DUVAL	UNKNOWN JAX WRECK			3027.166	8119.320		4
DUVAL	WRECK			3027.162	8119.321		2
DUVAL	BARGE			3026.870	8113.458	GPS	21
DUVAL	BARGE	45237.0	61958.9	3026.870	8113.470	LORAN	10
DUVAL	EAST BARGE			3026.718	8113.272	GPS	21
DUVAL	EAST BARGE	45234.5	61958.0	3026.710	8113.270	LORAN	10
DUVAL	TUG			3026.641	8113.348	GPS	21
DUVAL	TUG	45234.6	61958.7	3026.637	8113.054	LORAN	10
DUVAL	RELIANCE	45232.7	61958.9	3026.460	8113.260	LORAN	10
DUVAL	TUG	45231.1	61959.7	3026.210	8112.979	LORAN	10
DUVAL	BUSEY'S BONANZA			3026.038	8110.453		39
DUVAL	CARPET BARGE	45210.8	61937.0	3026.020	8110.470	LORAN	10
DUVAL	WRECK	45210.8	61937.0	3025.992	8110.218		39
DUVAL	WRECK			3025.990	8110.230		39
DUVAL	WOODEN TUG	45194.6	61917.7	3025.910	8108.150	LORAN	10
DUVAL	WOODEN TUG			3025.904	8108.132	GPS	21
DUVAL	BUS STOP BARGE	45200.6	61925.7	3025.880	8109.090	LORAN	10
DUVAL	OLD GIBBS DRYDOCK	45195.5	61919.6	3025.870	8108.330	LORAN	10
DUVAL	UPSIDE-DOWN BARGE	45229.1	61962.2	3025.864	8113.353	LORAN	10
DUVAL	BUS STOP BARGE			3025.858	8109.067	GPS	21
DUVAL	UPSIDE-DOWN BARGE			3025.812	8113.373	GPS	2
DUVAL	UPSIDE DOWN BARGE			3025.809	8113.383	GPS	21
DUVAL	OLD GIBBS DRYDOCK			3025.800	8108.380	GPS	21
DUVAL	BARGE			3025.736	8113.425	GPS	2
DUVAL	MORANTZ BARGE	45198.3	61925.0	3025.710	8108.930	LORAN	10
DUVAL	BARGE			3025.695	8108.914	GPS	21
DUVAL	BARGE			3025.657	8114.429	GPS	2
DUVAL	WRECK			3025.609	8108.812	GPS	21
DUVAL	TUG			3025.359	8113.489	GPS	2
DUVAL	MAXIE'S BARGE	45218.9	61956.4	3025.312	8112.417	LORAN	10
DUVAL	MAXIE'S BARGE			3025.283	8112.452	GPS	2
DUVAL	MAXIE'S BARGE			3025.280	8112.450	GPS	21

LOCALE	WRECK NAME	TD1	TD2	LATITUDE	LONGITUDE	TYPE	SOURCE
DUVAL	AIRPLANE			3025.070	8050.970	GPS	21
DUVAL	WRECK			3024.779	8115.608	GPS	2
DUVAL	MYSTERY WRECK			3024.773	8115.601	GPS	15
DUVAL	WRECK			3024.724	8135.539		3
DUVAL	POWERFUL TUG	45093.2	61804.9	3024.600	8053.940	GPS	10
DUVAL	POWERFUL TUG			3024.584	8053.946	GPS	21
DUVAL	WARDS BANK WRECK			3024.513	8123.790		4
DUVAL	NM SITE - FISHING BOAT	45194.6	61937.2	3024.380	8109.770	LORAN	10
DUVAL	WRECK			3024.366	8109.761	GPS	21
DUVAL	BARGE	45198.6	61945.2	3024.170	8110.600	LORAN	10
DUVAL	JAX JETTY WRECK			3024.095	8122.850		4
DUVAL	CHATHAM			3024.081	8122.741		4
DUVAL	WRECK	45261.8	62027.9	3023.817	8119.978	LORAN	18
DUVAL	WRECK			3023.755	8122.493	GPS	41
DUVAL	TUG	45193.2	61944.5	3023.710	8110.280	LORAN	10
DUVAL	WRECKAGE			3023.675	8121.729	GPS	41
DUVAL	TUG			3023.670	8110.306	GPS	2
DUVAL	TUG			3023.656	8110.311	GPS	21
DUVAL	WRECK			3023.594	8138.809		3
DUVAL	TAR BARGE	45192.0	61944.8	3023.568	8110.251	LORAN	10
DUVAL	TAR BARGE			3023.525	8110.266	GPS	2
DUVAL	WRECK			3023.514	8138.689		3
DUVAL	BARGE			3023.507	8110.282	GPS	21
DUVAL	TUG	45192.1	61946.6	3023.420	8110.420	LORAN	10
DUVAL	WRECK	45262.6	62034.3	3023.380	8120.541	LORAN	18
DUVAL	NINE MILE BARGE	45192.9	61948.6	3023.358	8110.608	LORAN	10
DUVAL	JAX CHANNEL WRECK			3023.353	8120.840		4
DUVAL	NINE MILE BARGE			3023.345	8110.626	GPS	21
DUVAL	NINE MILE BARGE			3023.335	8110.616	GPS	2
DUVAL	WRECK			3023.317	8108.308	GPS	21
DUVAL	VIC'S BARGE			3023.300	8110.215	GPS	2
DUVAL	VIC'S BARGE	45191.5	61947.6	3023.298	8110.462	LORAN	10
DUVAL	BARGE	45191.7	61947.9	3023.295	8110.496	LORAN	10
DUVAL	VIC'S BARGE			3023.261	8110.515	GPS	21
DUVAL	BARGE			3023.260	8110.512	GPS	2
DUVAL	BARGE			3023.226	8109.111	GPS	21
DUVAL	BARGE			3023.175	8109.507	GPS	2
DUVAL	BARGE			3023.170	8109.522	GPS	34
DUVAL	BARGE			3023.160	8109.525	GPS	21
DUVAL	BARGE			3022.898	8127.622		3
DUVAL	PIPES WRECK			3022.811	8032.358	GPS	21
DUVAL	USCGC SPIKE			3022.531	8053.689	GPS	10
DUVAL	ROSALYN B. HUDGENS	45077.3	61814.0	3022.372	8054.008	GPS	10
DUVAL	ROSALYN B. HUDGENS			3022.368	8053.998	GPS	34
DUVAL	ROSALYN B. HUDGENS			3022.361	8053.988	GPS	2
DUVAL	ROSALYN B. HUDGENS			3022.353	8054.009	GPS	21
DUVAL	NINE MILE BARGE			3022.184	8109.055	GPS	21
DUVAL	BARGE			3022.177	8104.769	GPS	21
DUVAL	BIG WRECK			3021.870	8050.256	GPS	21
DUVAL	NORTH BARGE	45050.1	61785.2	3021.860	8050.240	LORAN	10
DUVAL	OCEAN GOING TUG #2	45050.2	61786.8	3021.850	8050.430	LORAN	10

LOCALE	WRECK NAME	TD1	TD2	LATITUDE	LONGITUDE	TYPE	SOURCE
DUVAL	TUG	45051.2	61786.8	3021.841	8050.176		39
DUVAL	BARGE #1	45050.1	61785.8	3021.820	8050.290	LORAN	10
DUVAL	TUG			3021.809	8050.392	GPS	21
DUVAL	WARWICK FERRY	45047.5	61783.7	3021.740	8049.980	LORAN	10
DUVAL	WARWICK FERRY			3021.718	8049.994	GPS	21
DUVAL	WRECK			3021.705	8050.604	GPS	2
DUVAL	TUG	45050.1	61786.8	3021.704	8050.315		39
DUVAL	OCEAN GOING TUG #1	45050.7	61788.7	3021.680	8050.562	LORAN	10
DUVAL	TUG			3021.667	8050.591	GPS	21
DUVAL	AIRPLANE WRECK	45040.1	61779.2	3021.340	8049.250	LORAN	10
DUVAL	BARGE			3020.828	8112.873		2
DUVAL	BARGE			3020.828	8112.873	GPS	2
DUVAL	BARGE	45179.2	61969.5	3020.320	8111.790	LORAN	10
DUVAL	NORTH BARGE	45174.4	61964.7	3020.250	8111.150	LORAN	10
DUVAL	BANANA BOAT			3020.201	8111.183	GPS	21
DUVAL	BANANA BOAT	45174.0	61964.9	3020.200	8111.150	LORAN	10
DUVAL	TUG			3020.169	8111.154	GPS	21
DUVAL	PAUL MAINS TUG	45170.1	61964.7	3019.848	8110.951	LORAN	39
DUVAL	BARGE			3019.816	8110.979	GPS	21
DUVAL	PAUL MAINS TUG	45170.1	61964.7	3019.804	8110.718		39
DUVAL	NAVY BARGE			3019.791	8111.128	GPS	21
DUVAL	NAVY BARGE	45170.6	61965.8	3019.790	8111.080	LORAN	10
DUVAL	SOUTH TUG	45170.0	61964.9	3019.780	8110.740	LORAN	10
DUVAL	NAVY BARGE			3019.773	8111.097	GPS	34
DUVAL	THREE FRIENDS			3019.540	8137.619		4
DUVAL	LITTLE WRECK	45073.9	61847.9	3019.495	8056.698	LORAN	10
DUVAL	LITTLE WRECK			3019.475	8056.737		2
DUVAL	LITTLE WRECK			3019.454	8056.754	GPS	21
DUVAL	WRECK	45236.0	62051.9	3019.321	8120.877	LORAN	18
DUVAL	BARGE			3019.098	8138.015		3
DUVAL	WRECK			3018.677	8137.802		2
DUVAL	NORTH TUG	45117.0	61914.3	3018.560	8104.360	LORAN	10
DUVAL	TUG			3018.547	8104.365	GPS	21
DUVAL	SOUTH TUG	45116.5	61914.7	3018.500	8104.360	LORAN	10
DUVAL	RONNIE'S PLANE			3018.461	8048.361	GPS	21
DUVAL	CLAYTON HOLLER	45112.0	61912.5	3018.257	8103.950	LORAN	39
DUVAL	TUG	45130.7	61937.2	3018.130	8106.910	LORAN	10
DUVAL	TUG	45130.7	61937.6	3018.075	8106.691		39
DUVAL	CASA BLANCA			3017.530	8049.321	GPS	34
DUVAL	CASA BLANCA			3017.522	8049.278	GPS	2
DUVAL	CASA BLANCA			3017.507	8049.318	GPS	21
DUVAL	W.T. COPPEDGE	45065.7	61866.0	3017.361	8057.887	GPS	10
DUVAL	W.T. COPPEDGE			3017.302	8057.898	GPS	21
DUVAL	W.T. COPPEDGE			3017.301	8057.849	GPS	34
DUVAL	W.T. COPPEDGE			3017.294	8057.925	GPS	21
DUVAL	AIRCRAFT			3017.198	8113.554	GPS	2
DUVAL	WRECK	45110.1	61923.7	3017.151	8104.596		39
DUVAL	GULFAMERICA	45165.2	61998.3	3016.670	8113.630	LORAN	10
DUVAL	GULFAMERICA			3016.618	8113.648	GPS	34
DUVAL	GULFAMERICA	45164.7	61998.9	3016.567	8113.385		39
DUVAL	GULFAMERICA			3016.564	8113.862	GPS	34

LOCALE	WRECK NAME	TD1	TD2	LATITUDE	LONGITUDE	TYPE	SOURCE
DUVAL	BARGE			3016.554	8113.864	GPS	2
DUVAL	GULFAMERICA			3016.549	8113.649	GPS	21
DUVAL	BARGE			3016.509	8113.883	GPS	21
DUVAL	J.W. SITE - MTC 120 BARGE	45165.9	62000.7	3016.310	8113.560	DGPS	10
DUVAL	WRECK	45147.0	62038.0	3011.715	8116.004	LORAN	18
DUVAL	PLUMMER'S POINT WRECK			3011.369	8139.537		3
DUVAL	WRECK			3010.460	8140.194		4
DUVAL	MAPLE LEAF			3009.507	8141.012		39
DUVAL	MAPLE LEAF			3009.490	8140.787		39
DUVAL	MAPLE LEAF			3009.276	8140.848		39
FLAGLER	BARGE	44633.6	61825.4	2939.630	8035.390		30
FLAGLER	WRECK	44595.4	61780.7	2939.338	8029.264		30
FLAGLER	ARAWAK			2936.015	8053.987		40
FLAGLER	WRECK			2935.614	8110.562		4
FLAGLER	ARAWAK			2935.528	8054.313	GPS	12
FLAGLER	ARAWAK			2935.520	8054.300	GPS	31
FLAGLER	WRECK			2935.277	8053.463	GPS	21
FLAGLER	CHLORINE BARGE	44592.1	61831.4	2935.249	8034.099	LORAN	39
FLAGLER	WRECK			2934.025	8108.974		4
FLAGLER	LEDGE AIRPLANE			2930.510	8053.809	LORAN	32
FLAGLER	LEDGE AIRPLANE	44672.2	61993.4	2930.503	8053.809	LORAN	39
FLAGLER	WRECK			2930.181	8011.182	GPS	21
FLAGLER	WRECK	44435.0	61748.0	2930.181	8011.820		39
FLAGLER	FLAGLER WRECK			2929.100	8101.640		39
FLAGLER	FLAGLER WRECK	44712.0	62057.4	2929.083	8101.383		39
FLAGLER	SAILBOAT	44617.4	61982.4	2926.354	8050.677		30
FLAGLER	ALLIGATOR			2925.231	8127.918	GPS	1
GEORGIA	WRECK	45486.7	61864.4	3059.946	8118.160	LORAN	18
GEORGIA	BARGE			3058.713	8058.615	GPS	21
GEORGIA	WRECK			3058.670	8123.170	LORAN	18
GEORGIA	WRECK	45479.5	61873.2	3058.480	8118.415	LORAN	18
GEORGIA	TAMPA TUG			3058.185	8058.818	GPS	21
GEORGIA	PROP WRECK			3054.011	8036.424	GPS	1
GEORGIA	PROP WRECK			3053.996	8036.440	GPS	21
GEORGIA	PECONIC			3053.746	8052.994	GPS	1
GEORGIA	AIRPLANE			3053.109	8047.722	GPS	21
GEORGIA	ESPARTA			3050.845	8110.171		39
GEORGIA	WRECK			3049.542	8056.444		7
INDIAN RIVER	IRON BALLAST WRECK			2752.632	8027.275	GPS	32
INDIAN RIVER	IRON BALLAST WRECK			2752.630	8027.333	GPS	1
INDIAN RIVER	PINES WRECK			2751.268	8026.514	GPS	39
INDIAN RIVER	PINES WRECK			2750.818	8026.340	GPS	36
INDIAN RIVER	CABIN WRECK (FIVE CANNON)			2750.132	8026.003	GPS	1
INDIAN RIVER	CABIN WRECK (TWO ANCHORS)			2749.870	8025.867	GPS	1
INDIAN RIVER	CABIN WRECK (CANNON)			2749.829	8025.650	GPS	1
INDIAN RIVER	CABIN WRECK (BALLAST PILE)			2749.829	8025.537	GPS	1
INDIAN RIVER	CABIN WRECK (CANNON)			2749.780	8025.796	GPS	1
INDIAN RIVER	EUGEANS TUG			2748.549	8000.022	LORAN	18
INDIAN RIVER	ANCHOR WRECK			2748.379	8025.088		39
INDIAN RIVER	CANNON PILE WRECK			2748.199	8024.699		39
INDIAN RIVER	CAST IRON BALLAST WRECK			2747.702	8024.609		39

LOCALE	WRECK NAME	TD1	TD2	LATITUDE	LONGITUDE	TYPE	SOURCE
INDIAN RIVER	CANNON PILE WRECK			2747.643	8024.740		39
INDIAN RIVER	CANNON PILE WRECK			2747.620	8024.689		39
INDIAN RIVER	AIRPLANE	43433.9	61911.9	2747.236	8001.341	LORAN	20
INDIAN RIVER	AIRPLANE	43433.9	61911.9	2747.225	8001.340		30
INDIAN RIVER	ROBERTS			2747.050	8024.373	GPS	36
INDIAN RIVER	SPRING OF WHITBY			2745.947	8023.763	GPS	36
INDIAN RIVER	SAN MARTIN			2745.598	8023.470	GPS	36
INDIAN RIVER	SAN MARTIN			2745.429	8023.210	GPS	39
INDIAN RIVER	CORRIGAN'S WRECK			2744.080	8022.621		39
INDIAN RIVER	CORRIGAN'S WRECK			2744.011	8022.632		39
INDIAN RIVER	CORRIGAN'S WRECK			2743.857	8022.737	GPS	36
INDIAN RIVER	BARGE			2742.983	8022.128	GPS	16
INDIAN RIVER	TRAWLER ENGINE			2741.980	8022.040	GPS	16
INDIAN RIVER	TRAWLER TANKS			2741.630	8022.038	GPS	16
INDIAN RIVER	NAVY AVENGER			2741.490	8021.840	GPS	16
INDIAN RIVER	BRECONSHIRE			2739.147	8021.123	GPS	1
INDIAN RIVER	BRECONSHIRE			2739.135	8021.049	GPS	1
INDIAN RIVER	RIOMAR WRECK			2738.688	8020.572		39
INDIAN RIVER	RIOMAR WRECK			2738.502	8020.837	GPS	36
INDIAN RIVER	RIOMAR WRECK			2738.431	8020.921		39
INDIAN RIVER	RIOMAR WRECK			2738.250	8020.500		39
INDIAN RIVER	SANDY POINT WRECK			2735.905	8019.812	GPS	36
INDIAN RIVER	SANDY POINT WRECK			2735.599	8019.650		39
INDIAN RIVER	WRECK	43318.1	61946.4	2735.015	8002.676	LORAN	32
INDIAN RIVER	WRECK	43317.6	61946.4	2734.971	8002.660	LORAN	32
INDIAN RIVER	WRECK	43317.1	61946.9	2734.898	8002.721	LORAN	32
INDIAN RIVER	WRECK	43285.0	61943.3	2732.239	8001.123	LORAN	20
INDIAN RIVER	WRECK	43222.4	61953.3	2726.092	8000.633	LORAN	32
MARTIN	COSME CALZADA			2714.516	8011.235		39
MARTIN	COSME CALZADA			2714.412	8011.098		22
MARTIN	W.D. ANDERSON	43099.6	61943.7	2714.375	7954.638	GPS	39
MARTIN	UPSIDE-DOWN BARGE	43120.5	62010.9	2713.933	8006.160	LORAN	10
MARTIN	TENSION BARGE 13			2713.527	8000.261	DGPS	10
MARTIN	WICKSTROM REEF			2713.492	8000.318	GPS	25
MARTIN	TREE BARGE			2713.419	8000.270	DGPS	10
MARTIN	PIPE BARGE	43115.5	62013.4	2713.349	8006.413	LORAN	10
MARTIN	LANDING CRAFT	43110.7	62013.4	2712.933	8006.273	LORAN	10
MARTIN	GUARDIAN BARGE REEF	43110.2	62013.3	2712.924	8006.324	GPS	10
MARTIN	TRAFFIC BARGE	43110.3	62013.5	2712.893	8006.278	LORAN	10
MARTIN	OWL BARGE	43107.5	62012.5	2712.700	8006.087	LORAN	10
MARTIN	BIG CEMENT BARGE	43106.5	62012.7	2712.670	8006.401		39
MARTIN	BIG CEMENT BARGE	43106.5	62012.7	2712.639	8006.599		39
MARTIN	MARTIN REEF	43107.3	62013.8	2712.626	8006.533	LORAN	10
MARTIN	BARGE	43106.5	62012.7	2712.601	8006.089	LORAN	10
MARTIN	DAVID T.			2712.235	8002.875	GPS	9
MARTIN	MERCEDES II	43091.1	61993.0	2712.148	8002.373	LORAN	10
MARTIN	MERCEDES II	43091.0	61993.0	2712.140	8002.315	LORAN	10
MARTIN	INLET BARGE	43096.8	62008.9	2711.971	8005.136	LORAN	10
MARTIN	GEORGES VALENTINE			2711.930	8009.787	GPS	39
MARTIN	USS RANKIN			2711.360	8001.459	GPS	9
MARTIN	USS RANKIN			2711.333	8001.431	GPS	1

LOCALE	WRECK NAME	TD1	TD2	LATITUDE	LONGITUDE	TYPE	SOURCE
MARTIN	WRECK			2711.242	8016.142		39
MARTIN	TITAN TUG			2711.215	8002.615	GPS	9
MARTIN	WRECK	43072.8	62004.2	2710.108	8004.016		39
MARTIN	CORNER BARGE	43063.8	62000.4	2709.380	8003.290		39
MARTIN	NORTH BARGE	43063.7	62000.8	2709.350	8003.340		39
MARTIN	BARGE	43063.8	62000.4	2709.265	8002.675	LORAN	10
MARTIN	BARGE	43063.7	62000.8	2709.244	8002.740	LORAN	10
MARTIN	BARGE	43062.7	62000.3	2709.159	8002.620	LORAN	10
MARTIN	SHRIMPER	43057.8	62008.7	2708.559	8004.541		39
MARTIN	PECK BARGE	43064.3	62024.9	2708.240	8007.350		39
MARTIN	WRECK			2705.522	8017.412		39
MARTIN	WRECK			2701.129	8004.764		4
MARTIN	BARACUDA	14352.1	62027.6	2700.878	8005.188		39
MARTIN	WRECK			2700.819	8005.148		4
MARTIN	REPUBLIC			2700.758	8002.687		39
MARTIN	REPUBLIC			2700.620	8002.686		39
MARTIN	GULFLAND	14351.8	62026.0	2700.468	8004.795		39
MARTIN	WRECK			2700.385	8002.598	LORAN	18
MARTIN	GULFLAND			2700.325	8005.191		39
MARTIN	WRECK			2700.280	8005.143		4
MARTIN	MG-111 BARGE	14351.7	62010.3	2658.670	8001.490	GPS	10
MARTIN	THREE TUGS 3			2658.621	8000.963	GPS	1
MARTIN	THREE TUGS 2			2658.581	8000.971	GPS	1
MARTIN	THREE TUGS 1			2658.564	8000.981	GPS	1
NASSAU	UPSIDE DOWN WRECK			3045.684	8023.303	GPS	21
NASSAU	FERNANDINA WRECK			3045.550	8114.960		7
NASSAU	GYPSY GIRL			3043.480	8121.410		7
NASSAU	SHRIMPER			3043.298	8121.254		39
NASSAU	WRECK			3043.273	8124.744	GPS	2
NASSAU	WRECK			3042.740	8123.100	LORAN	18
NASSAU	WRECK			3042.531	8124.955		2
NASSAU	WRECK			3042.389	8124.201	GPS	2
NASSAU	DESERT WRECK PLANE			3042.086	8030.661	GPS	21
NASSAU	WRECK			3040.913	8127.640		2
NASSAU	FERRY BARGE			3040.662	8110.012	GPS	21
NASSAU	FERNANDINA BEACH WRECK			3040.211	8125.691		4
NASSAU	SAHLMAN'S GULLEY BARGE	45308.1	61874.1	3040.116	8109.560	LORAN	10
NASSAU	WHITTAKER'S TUG			3039.358	8114.110	GPS	2
NASSAU	WHITTAKER'S TUG	45326.8	61915.2	3039.338	8113.874	LORAN	10
NASSAU	WHITTAKER'S BARGE			3038.736	8112.870	GPS	2
NASSAU	WHITTAKER'S BARGE	45314.4	61907.1	3038.719	8112.641	LORAN	10
NASSAU	AIRPLANE			3037.796	8037.974	GPS	21
NASSAU	SHARK BARGE	45264.8	61886.2	3037.685	8104.718	DGPS	10
NASSAU	BARBETT WRECK			3037.180	8111.160		39
NASSAU	BARBETT WRECK			3037.145	8110.961		39
NASSAU	POGEY BOAT			3037.124	8111.171	GPS	21
NASSAU	BARBETT WRECK	45292.2	61898.9	3036.580	8110.580	LORAN	10
NASSAU	SNAPPER BARGE	45293.0	61908.4	3036.406	8111.914		39
PALM BEACH	ESSO BONAIRE III	14351.3	62006.5	2657.850	8000.480	GPS	10
PALM BEACH	MISS JENNY	14351.2	62006.4	2657.830	8000.440	DGPS	10
PALM BEACH	ZION TRAIN			2657.782	8000.440	DGPS	10

LOCALE	WRECK NAME	TD1	TD2	LATITUDE	LONGITUDE	TYPE	SOURCE
PALM BEACH	NELLIE			2657.500	8039.483	GPS	2
PALM BEACH	SEA MIST II			2657.488	7959.106	DGPS	10
PALM BEACH	RATICAN	14351.4	62006.4	2656.810	7959.627	LORAN	10
PALM BEACH	SAN MIGUEL DE ARCHANGEL			2656.508	8004.057	GPS	36
PALM BEACH	VICTOR			2655.824	8003.988	GPS	1
PALM BEACH	WRECK			2655.020	8002.990		4
PALM BEACH	CONRAD BARGE			2654.754	8003.440	GPS	10
PALM BEACH	TEGRA			2654.153	8038.903		3
PALM BEACH	MURPHY II BARGE			2648.125	8001.092	GPS	1
PALM BEACH	DONATION BARGE			2647.945	7959.465		10
PALM BEACH	KORIMU			2647.915	7959.383	GPS	1
PALM BEACH	ROYAL PARK BARGE 2			2647.772	8001.064	GPS	1
PALM BEACH	ROYAL PARK BARGE 1			2647.703	8001.104	GPS	1
PALM BEACH	PRINCESS ANNE			2647.616	8000.230	GPS	1
PALM BEACH	SYLVINA EXPRESS II			2647.600	7959.185	GPS	1
PALM BEACH	SPEARMAN'S BARGE	14334.0	62023.7	2647.590	8000.350	GPS	10
PALM BEACH	WRECK			2647.581	8000.174	GPS	1
PALM BEACH	WRECK			2647.435	7959.724	GPS	1
PALM BEACH	CLASSIC BARGE P1	14335.2	62017.4	2647.420	7959.100	LORAN	10
PALM BEACH	RESEARCH TEAM REEF BARGE	14333.1	62027.6	2647.360	8001.000	GPS	10
PALM BEACH	AMARYLLIS	14333.0	62027.5	2647.300	8000.960	GPS	10
PALM BEACH	CLASSIC BARGE P6	14334.7	62019.1	2647.300	7959.380	LORAN	10
PALM BEACH	ANDE			2647.296	7959.574	GPS	1
PALM BEACH	SPINY BARGE - NORTH			2647.220	7959.310		39
PALM BEACH	MIZPAH	14332.9	62027.6	2647.180	8000.960	GPS	10
PALM BEACH	CLASSIC BARGE			2647.174	7959.330		39
PALM BEACH	SPINY BARGE - SOUTH			2646.970	7959.470		39
PALM BEACH	BARGE			2646.969	8000.646		1
PALM BEACH	EIDSVAG	14331.1	62028.7	2646.020	8000.500	GPS	10
PALM BEACH	BARGE			2645.840	7959.740		39
PALM BEACH	T.S.O. PARADISE	14330.2	62031.9	2645.790	8001.290	DGPS	10
PALM BEACH	CROSS CURRENT BARGE	14330.5	43011.7	2645.690	8001.260	DGPS	10
PALM BEACH	GILBERT SEA (STERN)			2645.201	8000.631	GPS	1
PALM BEACH	THOZINA			2645.147	8000.577	GPS	1
PALM BEACH	ST. JACQUES (STERN)			2645.099	8000.612	GPS	1
PALM BEACH	SHA SHA BOEKANIER (STERN)			2645.066	8000.599	GPS	1
PALM BEACH	MIKE'S BARGE			2643.330	7959.950		39
PALM BEACH	OH KIM SOON			2635.037	8002.194		26
PALM BEACH	OH KIM SOON			2634.390	8002.309		26
PALM BEACH	LOFTHUS			2633.776	8002.309	GPS	39
PALM BEACH	SKYECLIFFE			2633.438	8001.054	GPS	1
PALM BEACH	BECKS			2628.878	8002.342	GPS	1
PALM BEACH	BUDWEISER BAR	14300.5	62065.0	2628.750	8002.310	GPS	10
PALM BEACH	CASTOR			2628.741	8002.236	GPS	1
PALM BEACH	SWORDFISH	14300.5	62065.0	2628.700	8002.330	GPS	10
PALM BEACH	INCHULVA (BOILERS)			2627.211	8003.367	GPS	1
PALM BEACH	GHOST TUG			2624.612	8003.490	GPS	28
PALM BEACH	LUMBER WRECK			2621.775	8003.715	GPS	39
PALM BEACH	KRINGELINE			2619.728	8002.602	GPS	1
PALM BEACH	PROTECTOR			2619.688	8004.316		4
PALM BEACH	HYDRO ATLANTIC	14286.2	62116.6	2619.500	8003.043	GPS	10

LOCALE	WRECK NAME	TD1	TD2	LATITUDE	LONGITUDE	TYPE	SOURCE
PALM BEACH	HYDRO ATLANTIC			2619.494	8003.024	GPS	1
PALM BEACH	HYDRO ATLANTIC	14284.2	62083.0	2619.490	8003.040	GPS	10
PALM BEACH	HYDRO ATLANTIC			2619.464	8003.047	GPS	1
PALM BEACH	SEA EMPEROR			2619.339	8003.551	GPS	1
PALM BEACH	NOULA EXPRESS			2619.286	8003.454	GPS	1
PALM BEACH	UNITED CARIBBEAN			2619.268	8003.539	DGPS	10
PALM BEACH	MISS LOURDIES			2619.133	8003.213	GPS	28
PUTNAM	SHIPWRECK			2938.615	8136.238		3
PUTNAM	SHIPWRECK			2938.182	8135.488		3
PUTNAM	USS COLUMBINE			2932.137	8141.859		39
ST. JOHNS	HUGH DE PAYENS			3013.659	8122.430	GPS	1
ST. JOHNS	BARGE	45079.5	61941.3	3012.881	8104.753	LORAN	10
ST. JOHNS	HESTON BARGE			3012.857	8105.018		39
ST. JOHNS	WRECK			3012.816	8105.029	GPS	2
ST. JOHNS	DEBRIS			3012.590	8104.906		2
ST. JOHNS	BUNNIE'S WEB - SAILBOAT	45127.5	62030.5	3010.440	8114.830	GPS	10
ST. JOHNS	SAILBOAT			3010.409	8114.812	GPS	21
ST. JOHNS	WRECK			3010.063	8116.792	LORAN	18
ST. JOHNS	WRECK			3008.720	8116.844	LORAN	18
ST. JOHNS	NAVY DRYDOCK	44839.4	61710.9	3007.608	8033.570	LORAN	10
ST. JOHNS	NAVY DRYDOCK			3007.087	8033.614	GPS	34
ST. JOHNS	O.S.J. SITE - DRYDOCKS	44839.4	61710.9	3007.060	8033.570	LORAN	10
ST. JOHNS	DRYDOCK (NORTH END)			3007.053	8033.614	GPS	21
ST. JOHNS	DRYDOCK (SOUTH END)			3006.976	8033.587	GPS	21
ST. JOHNS	F-4 PHANTOM			3005.813	8040.621	GPS	21
ST. JOHNS	HELICOPTER			3005.453	8029.057	GPS	21
ST. JOHNS	AIRPLANE			3005.186	8041.888	GPS	21
ST. JOHNS	PETER JR.	44710.7	61586.0	3003.658	8015.537		39
ST. JOHNS	WRECK	45054.0	62054.0	3001.443	8113.695	LORAN	18
ST. JOHNS	REGGIE'S TUG	44893.8	61872.2	3000.387	8050.873		13
ST. JOHNS	WRECK	45054.0	62068.8	3000.248	8115.029	LORAN	18
ST. JOHNS	FOUR MILE WRECK	44986.0	62091.2	2956.430	8110.450	LORAN	10
ST. JOHNS	FOUR MILE WRECK	44986.0	62091.2	2956.430	8110.450		39
ST. JOHNS	DOROTHY LOUISE BARGE			2956.318	8057.517	GPS	21
ST. JOHNS	DOROTHY LOUISE BARGE			2956.316	8057.508	GPS	13
ST. JOHNS	DOROTHY LOUISE BARGE			2956.193	8057.378	GPS	21
ST. JOHNS	SHRIMPER			2955.061	8116.370		39
ST. JOHNS	SHRIMP BOAT 3	44909.3	61965.5	2954.694	8100.157		13
ST. JOHNS	A-6 INTRUDER	44829.4	61872.2	2954.339	8048.167	DGPS	10
ST. JOHNS	A-6 INTRUDER			2954.334	8048.185	GPS	21
ST. JOHNS	A-6 INTRUDER			2954.328	8048.215	GPS	21
ST. JOHNS	A-6 INTRUDER			2954.311	8048.178	GPS	21
ST. JOHNS	A-6 INTRUDER			2954.308	8048.205	GPS	21
ST. JOHNS	A-6 INTRUDER			2954.293	8048.171	GPS	21
ST. JOHNS	A-6 INTRUDER	44827.6	61871.8	2954.186	8045.012	GPS	10
ST. JOHNS	A-6 INTRUDER			2954.186	8048.030	GPS	21
ST. JOHNS	LEON RODDY TUG	44964.4	62038.3	2954.176	8109.078		13
ST. JOHNS	WRECK			2954.162	8109.082	GPS	21
ST. JOHNS	A-6 INTRUDER			2954.162	8048.033	GPS	21
ST. JOHNS	A-6 INTRUDER			2954.141	8048.028	GPS	21
ST. JOHNS	A-6 INTRUDER			2954.135	8048.073	GPS	21

LOCALE	WRECK NAME	TD1	TD2	LATITUDE	LONGITUDE	TYPE	SOURCE
ST. JOHNS	ST. AUGUSTINE BARGE			2953.557	8058.523	GPS	21
ST. JOHNS	SHRIMPER	44903.1	61975.5	2953.375	8100.840		39
ST. JOHNS	SHRIMP BOAT			2953.325	8100.862	GPS	21
ST. JOHNS	SHRIMP BOAT 2	44903.1	61975.8	2953.222	8100.860		13
ST. JOHNS	WRECK	44965.1	62079.4	2950.918	8112.640	LORAN	18
ST. JOHNS	INNER PLANE WRECK	44873.6	61971.9	2950.870	8059.300	LORAN	10
ST. JOHNS	LST	44873.6	61972.5	2950.801	8059.389		13
ST. JOHNS	VERONICA EXPRESS	44858.8	61954.8	2950.780	8056.860	GPS	10
ST. JOHNS	VERONICA EXPRESS	44858.7	61954.9	2950.776	8057.143		13
ST. JOHNS	VERONICA EXPRESS			2950.760	8057.170	GPS	21
ST. JOHNS	VERONICA EXPRESS	44858.8	61954.9	2950.760	8057.120		39
ST. JOHNS	AIRPLANE	44656.0	61960.0	2950.343	8057.569		39
ST. JOHNS	OUTER PLANE WRECK	44858.3	61963.4	2950.070	8057.650	GPS	10
ST. JOHNS	F-4U CORSAIR	44858.3	61963.4	2950.047	8057.836		39
ST. JOHNS	JEWEL BOX WRECK			2948.451	8034.429	GPS	21
ST. JOHNS	TUG	44937.4	62082.0	2948.087	8111.863	LORAN	18
ST. JOHNS	WRECK	44937.4	62089.6	2947.469	8112.581	LORAN	18
ST. JOHNS	BEAR WRECK			2947.369	8037.435		39
ST. JOHNS	BEAR WRECK	44708.5	61814.5	2947.317	8037.167		39
ST. JOHNS	BEAR WRECK	44707.9	61814.3	2947.293	8037.455		30
ST. JOHNS	BEAR WRECK			2947.271	8037.496	GPS	21
ST. JOHNS	CRESCENT BEACH WRECK			2946.944	8115.108		4
ST. JOHNS	WRECK	44702.5	61814.5	2946.773	8036.903	LORAN	18
ST. JOHNS	FLORIDA			2946.691	8114.091	GPS	39
ST. JOHNS	ST. AUGUSTINE WRECK (PIECE)	44821.3	61962.5	2946.680	8056.396		13
ST. JOHNS	ST. AUGUSTINE WRECK	44821.4	61962.4	2946.480	8056.320	LORAN	10
ST. JOHNS	ST. AUGUSTINE WRECK	44818.9	61962.5	2946.462	8056.303		13
ST. JOHNS	ST. AUGUSTINE WRECK			2946.375	8055.968		12
ST. JOHNS	WRECK	44924.0	62090.5	2946.132	8112.179	LORAN	18
ST. JOHNS	SAILBOAT			2944.638	8046.817	GPS	21
ST. JOHNS	WRECK	44754.9	61945.3	2941.843	8052.159		30
ST. JOHNS	AIRPLANE			2941.838	8052.118	GPS	21
ST. JOHNS	WRECK	44744.3	61946.6	2940.763	8051.873		30
ST. JOHNS	MATANZAS BARGE	44783.4	61994.3	2940.689	8058.023		13
ST. LUCIE	WRECK	43285.0	61943.3	2732.240	8001.117	LORAN	32
ST. LUCIE	STELLA			2731.123	8018.407		4
ST. LUCIE	STELLA			2731.110	8018.431		39
ST. LUCIE	URCA DE LIMA (ANCHOR)			2730.313	8017.980	GPS	1
ST. LUCIE	URCA DE LIMA (CANNON)			2730.311	8017.959	GPS	1
ST. LUCIE	WRECK			2728.787	8016.731		4
ST. LUCIE	WRECK			2728.760	8016.770		39
ST. LUCIE	WRECK			2727.780	8016.307		4
ST. LUCIE	LEE'S BARGE			2726.680	8010.227	GPS	1
ST. LUCIE	FT. PIERCE BARGE 2			2726.651	8010.351	DGPS	10
ST. LUCIE	FT. PIERCE BARGE 1			2726.650	8010.300	GPS	10
ST. LUCIE	TWIN BARGES			2726.637	8010.302	GPS	1
ST. LUCIE	BARGE	43259.2	62005.2	2726.199	8009.346	LORAN	10
ST. LUCIE	WRECK			2725.725	8011.262	LORAN	18
ST. LUCIE	WRECK			2725.719	8011.227	LORAN	18
ST. LUCIE	WRECK	43214.1	61945.1	2725.311	8000.373		39
ST. LUCIE	DOUGLASS BEACH WRECK			2725.299	8016.276	GPS	39

LOCALE	WRECK NAME	TD1	TD2	LATITUDE	LONGITUDE	TYPE	SOURCE
ST. LUCIE	DOUGLASS BEACH WRECK			2725.281	8016.150		39
ST. LUCIE	DOUGLASS BEACH WRECK			2725.062	8016.090	GPS	36
ST. LUCIE	WRECK	43215.9	61968.3	2724.766	8002.692		39
ST. LUCIE	FT. PIERCE DEEP WRECK 1			2724.599	7955.194	GPS	37
ST. LUCIE	FT. PIERCE DEEP WRECK 2			2724.594	7955.170	GPS	37
ST. LUCIE	VACUME	43206.6	61957.8	2724.453	8000.718		39
ST. LUCIE	USS MULIPHEN			2724.447	8000.862	GPS	1
ST. LUCIE	KEN M.	43210.2	61963.0	2724.444	8001.283	LORAN	10
ST. LUCIE	WRECK	43218.4	61978.4	2724.433	8004.361		39
ST. LUCIE	WRECK	43209.7	61964.0	2724.416	8001.925	LORAN	32
ST. LUCIE	BIG TUG WRECK	14396.9	43204.5	2724.409	7959.406	LORAN	39
ST. LUCIE	WRECK	43204.2	61954.1	2724.393	8000.161	LORAN	32
ST. LUCIE	DEEP TUG			2724.390	8000.200		39
ST. LUCIE	STAN'S REEF TUG	43204.5	61954.2	2724.334	7959.681	LORAN	10
ST. LUCIE	TUG	43204.1	61954.2	2724.292	7959.648	LORAN	10
ST. LUCIE	WRECK			2724.160	8003.700		39
ST. LUCIE	WRECK	43200.0	61960.3	2723.720	8001.020	LORAN	32
ST. LUCIE	WRECK			2723.695	8003.646		39
ST. LUCIE	WRECK			2723.650	8003.010		39
ST. LUCIE	BEVERLY M			2723.634	8001.064		10
ST. LUCIE	BEVERLY M	43199.3	61960.7	2723.552	8000.589	LORAN	10
ST. LUCIE	AMAZONE			2723.504	8003.638	GPS	9
ST. LUCIE	WRECK			2723.351	8003.200	LORAN	18
ST. LUCIE	WRECK			2723.259	8003.218	LORAN	18
ST. LUCIE	WRECK			2720.450	8004.880		39
ST. LUCIE	WRECK			2720.395	8004.464	LORAN	18
ST. LUCIE	WRECK			2720.159	8004.433	LORAN	18
ST. LUCIE	HALSEY			2720.155	8004.574	GPS	9
VOLUSIA	AIRPLANE	44630.5	61755.0	2944.412	8028.180	LORAN	20
VOLUSIA	AIRPLANE TRES	44664.1	61998.0	2929.406	8053.966	LORAN	35
VOLUSIA	A-6 INTRUDER			2921.271	8021.448	GPS	21
VOLUSIA	A-6 INTRUDER	44400.0	61785.0	2921.250	8021.740	GPS	10
VOLUSIA	DEFIANT TUG			2921.232	8021.447	GPS	21
VOLUSIA	SITE #9 AIRPLANES			2921.230	8021.382	LORAN	32
VOLUSIA	LONG JOHN	44433.6	61830.7	2921.026	8027.346		39
VOLUSIA	BOAT	44393.0	61794.7	2919.926	8022.114	LORAN	20
VOLUSIA	WRECK	44393.0	61794.7	2919.909	8021.799	LORAN	18
VOLUSIA	MAXINE D.	44521.6	61960.2	2919.390	8044.840	GPS	10
VOLUSIA	ANTILLES STAR			2919.198	8044.770	DGPS	10
VOLUSIA	BARGE	44517.7	61958.4	2919.179	8044.530	GPS	10
VOLUSIA	AIRPLANE UNO	44521.8	62008.6	2915.638	8049.996	LORAN	35
VOLUSIA	WRECK	44521.9	62008.8	2915.625	8050.024		30
VOLUSIA	AIRPLANE DOS	44525.9	62014.4	2915.550	8050.755	LORAN	35
VOLUSIA	AIRPLANE DOS	44525.4	62014.2	2915.521	8050.717	LORAN	35
VOLUSIA	WRECK	44525.3	62014.2	2915.507	8050.717		30
VOLUSIA	AIRPLANE DOS	44525.2	62014.2	2915.503	8050.710	LORAN	35
VOLUSIA	AIRPLANE DOS	44522.3	62014.2	2915.241	8050.609	LORAN	35
VOLUSIA	AIRPLANE DOS	44522.0	62014.2	2915.214	8050.599	LORAN	35
VOLUSIA	DEEP WRECK	44280.5	61733.5	2913.929	8010.647		30
VOLUSIA	WRECK	44280.5	61733.5	2913.929	8010.647		39
VOLUSIA	GINGER	44328.8	61801.0	2913.687	8020.211		30

LOCALE	WRECK NAME	TD1	TD2	LATITUDE	LONGITUDE	TYPE	SOURCE
VOLUSIA	COMMODORE	44281.1	61736.5	2912.220	8046.438		39
VOLUSIA	USS MINDANAO	44458.0	61982.0	2912.000	8044.860	GPS	10
VOLUSIA	THOMAS H.	44455.9	61982.6	2911.730	8044.930	GPS	10
VOLUSIA	RIO YUNA	44455.0	61982.0	2911.710	8044.740	GPS	10
VOLUSIA	ALEXANDRA MCALLISTER	44454.3	61982.3	2911.628	8044.804	DGPS	10
VOLUSIA	DAYTONA WRECK	44461.7	61989.3	2911.592	8045.679	LORAN	39
VOLUSIA	ATLAS	44453.8	61984.6	2911.370	8045.030	GPS	10
VOLUSIA	BARGE	44411.3	61959.4	2909.534	8040.423	LORAN	10
VOLUSIA	BARGE	44409.1	61959.0	2909.368	8040.300	LORAN	10
VOLUSIA	SEMARCA	44407.2	61959.3	2909.200	8040.520	GPS	10
VOLUSIA	ARGOIL	44394.7	61972.1	2907.110	8041.590	GPS	10
VOLUSIA	WRECK	44226.1	61793.5	2904.975	8014.809	LORAN	18
VOLUSIA	F/V GHOST			2904.825	8052.957		3
VOLUSIA	PONCE INLET WRECK #6			2904.771	8054.545		4
VOLUSIA	PONCE INLET WRECK #5			2904.622	8054.247		4
VOLUSIA	WRECK	44448.0	62063.9	2904.578	8053.137	LORAN	18
VOLUSIA	PONCE INLET WRECK #4			2904.428	8054.572		4
VOLUSIA	PONCE INLET WRECK #1			2904.227	8053.281		4
VOLUSIA	WRECK	44441.1	62062.7	2904.057	8052.780	LORAN	18
VOLUSIA	PONCE INLET WRECK #2			2903.948	8053.136		4
VOLUSIA	PONCE INLET WRECK #3			2903.901	8052.593		4
VOLUSIA	MISS DEBBIE	44211.3	61793.8	2903.648	8014.591	LORAN	20
VOLUSIA	MISS DEBBIE	44211.3	61793.8	2903.636	8014.619		30
VOLUSIA	BARGE	44339.8	61984.1	2901.260	8041.030	GPS	10
VOLUSIA	MOUND WRECK			2900.477	8017.340	LORAN	32
VOLUSIA	SANTO ROSARIO	44187.0	61812.2	2900.226	8015.781	LORAN	32
VOLUSIA	SANTO ROSARIO	44187.0	61812.7	2900.185	8015.805	LORAN	20
VOLUSIA	SANTO ROSARIO			2900.173	8015.832		30
VOLUSIA	SANTO ROSARIO			2900.168	8015.779	GPS	21
VOLUSIA	SNOWY GROUPER WRECK	44132.2	61746.0	2859.728	8005.771	LORAN	32
VOLUSIA	SNOWY GROUPER WRECK			2859.713	8005.744	GPS	1
VOLUSIA	SNOWY GROUPER WRECK			2859.701	8005.755	GPS	32
VOLUSIA	SNOWY GROUPER WRECK			2859.686	8005.823	GPS	32
VOLUSIA	SNOWY GROUPER WRECK	44132.2	61746.8	2859.676	8005.866	LORAN	32
VOLUSIA	WRECK			2859.599	8015.455	LORAN	32
VOLUSIA	TUG	44180.0	61812.0	2859.582	8015.095		39
VOLUSIA	TUG			2859.562	8015.119	GPS	18
VOLUSIA	LUBRAFOL			2858.864	8011.333	GPS	1
VOLUSIA	WRECK			2857.909	8011.955	GPS	21
VOLUSIA	BARGE	44130.0	61800.1	2855.951	8012.060	LORAN	20
VOLUSIA	NAVY FM-1 WILDCAT			2854.427	8023.160	GPS	1
VOLUSIA	NAVY FM-1 WILDCAT			2854.423	8023.153	GPS	1
VOLUSIA	NAVY FM-1 WILDCAT			2854.418	8023.158	GPS	1
VOLUSIA	FOXFIRE (VERY SMALL)			2852.812	8022.515	GPS	1
VOLUSIA	WRECK	44097.2	61805.9	2852.643	8011.479	LORAN	32
VOLUSIA	FANNIE DUGAN			2852.102	8117.276	GPS	29
VOLUSIA	MOSQUITO WRECK			2851.995	8045.705		4
VOLUSIA	WRECK	44108.0	61836.2	2851.551	8015.523	LORAN	32
VOLUSIA	CRANE WRECK			2850.843	8025.465	GPS	21
VOLUSIA	MADAKET			2850.812	8025.802	GPS	1

ABOUT THE AUTHOR

Michael C. Barnette is an accomplished diver, author, and photographer. In 1995, he founded the Association of Underwater Explorers, a coalition of divers dedicated to the research, exploration, documentation, and preservation of submerged cultural resources. Barnette has been actively researching and exploring shipwrecks for almost 20 years, resulting in the identification of more than 30 shipwrecks. He has dived on numerous historic shipwrecks, including the ironclad U.S.S. *Monitor*, the liner *Andrea Doria*, the battleship U.S.S. *Virginia*, and the H.M.H.S. *Britannic*, sister ship of the fabled R.M.S. *Titanic*. In 2009, he was elected as a fellow to The Explorers Club. Barnette is a marine biologist employed by the National Oceanic and Atmospheric Administration.

OTHER BOOKS BY THE AUTHOR

Barnette, Michael C. 2003. Shipwrecks of the Sunshine State: Florida's Submerged History. Association of Underwater Explorers, Tampa, Florida. 195 pp.

Barnette, Michael C. 2008. Images of America: Florida's Shipwrecks. Arcadia Publishing, Charleston, South Carolina. 128 pp.

www.ingramcontent.com/pod-product-compliance
Lightning Source LLC
Chambersburg PA
CBHW081209230426
43666CB00015B/2691